INTERNATIONAL HANDBOOK OF PRACTICE-BASED PERFORMANCE MANAGEMENT

To our children—
Thomas, Peter, and Alexander
Katherine and David
Laura, Claudia, and Robert
Ivy

INTERNATIONAL HANDBOOK OF PRACTICE-BASED PERFORMANCE MANAGEMENT

EDITED BY

PATRIA DE LANCER JULNES
Utah State University

FRANCES STOKES BERRY
Florida State University

MARIA P. ARISTIGUETA
University of Delaware

KAIFENG YANG
Florida State University

SAGE Publications

Los Angeles • London • New Delhi • Singapore

For information:

Sage Publications, Inc.
2455 Teller Road
Thousand Oaks,
California 91320
E-mail: order@sagepub.com

Sage Publications India Pvt. Ltd.
B 1/I 1 Mohan Cooperative Industrial Area
Mathura Road, New Delhi 110 044
India

Sage Publications Ltd.
1 Oliver's Yard
55 City Road
London EC1Y 1SP
United Kingdom

Sage Publications Asia-Pacific Pte. Ltd.
33 Pekin Street #02–01
Far East Square
Singapore 048763

Printed in the United States of America

Library of Congress Cataloging-in-Publication Data

International handbook of practice-based performance management/Patria de Lancer Julnes . . . [et al.].
        p. cm.
Includes bibliographical references and index.
ISBN 978-1-4129-4012-2 (cloth)

    1. Government productivity. 2. Administrative agencies—Management.
3. Administrative agencies—Auditing. 4. Nonprofit organizations—Management.
5. Organizational effectiveness. 6. Total quality management.
7. Performance—Measurement. I. Julnes, Patria de Lancer.

JF1525.P67I68 2008
352.3'75—dc22   2007008883

Printed on acid-free paper

07   08   09   10   11   10   9   8   7   6   5   4   3   2   1

Acquiring Editors:	Lisa Cuevas-Shaw and Vicki Knight
Associate Editor:	Sean Connelly
Production Editor:	Sarah K. Quesenberry
Copy Editor:	Carla Freeman
Typesetter:	C&M Digitals (P) Ltd.
Proofreader:	Penny Sippel
Indexer:	Wendy Allex
Marketing Manager:	Stephanie Adams

Contents

PART V. QUALITY AND PERFORMANCE IN PUBLIC AND NONPROFIT ORGANIZATIONS

PART VI. PULLING IT ALL TOGETHER

Prologue

Patria de Lancer Julnes

Frances Stokes Berry

Maria P. Aristigueta

Kaifeng Yang

"The Public Service is a public trust," offered Florida Governor Reubin O'Donovan Askew in his inaugural address in January 1971. This sentiment, reflecting the ideals of public service in a democracy, underlies the modern performance measurement movement. Considerable efforts have been made in advancing this movement. For example, in the 1970s and 1980s, financial auditing was widely used at all levels of government (as it still continues to be) to ensure that money was not stolen or grossly misused. In the late 1980s and throughout the 1990s, the private sector management techniques of total quality management (TQM), customer service, and measurement of processes and activities diffused widely across all levels of the public sector. Governments around the world were also adopting market-based ideologies (often combining democratic reforms with open economies). Countries with many government-owned assets, such as Great Britain, divested themselves and turned to the private sector to help restart sluggish economies, transform sluggish government sectors with competition and management reforms, and, in general, reduce the size of government to the private sector.

This is the historical context of the "New Public Management," which has evolved from the 1980s to the present into a broad series of often radical innovations known as "performance management systems." Implementation of measurement systems, however, has revealed challenges and complications in their use. Recent approaches have acknowledged these limitations and developed new practice-based strategies for effective ongoing measurement of program activities and use in guiding management. It is our goal for this handbook to serve as the vehicle for dissemination of these cutting-edge strategies.

With this goal in mind, we have invited nationally and internationally known scholars and practitioners to contribute chapters that range from introductions, to different aspects of performance management, to case studies describing experiences of government entities around the world, to hands-on application of techniques for improving government's use of performance data. Thus, the information should be useful to students, academics, and practitioners interested in developing and sustaining performance management systems.

After the prefatory grounding provided in Part I, "State of the Art," chapters in the following four parts of the handbook are organized as follows:

1. Introduction to the section

2. Theoretical discussions and cases

3. Skill building

Within each part, there is an introductory chapter that discusses the latest theories and major debates surrounding a particular aspect of performance management. This introduction identifies the major themes that will be discussed in the subsequent chapters and relates them to existing theory and practice. This introductory chapter of each part is followed by three theoretical discussion and/or case study chapters. Each chapter provides background information on performance measurement and management in the particular state, region, or country the chapter focuses on, describing and analyzing the experiences and providing some lessons learned. These chapters also include questions intended to elicit further discussion in a classroom setting. Third, concluding each part, readers will find a skill-building chapter that provides explicit "how-to" guidance, focusing on one or several aspects of the themes of the section. The guidance is provided through discussion of techniques, methods, and/or exemplary practice.

The handbook ends with the concluding Part VI, "Pulling It All Together," which summarizes and analyzes the major themes that emerge in this volume. To prepare us for confronting these themes, we now offer some definitions of terms that will be used throughout the handbook. This is followed by a brief description of the 23 chapters included in this handbook.

_____ What Is Performance Management?

As succinctly put by Harry P. Hatry in Chapter 1 in this volume, using performance information "transforms performance _measurement_ into performance _management_" (p. 1). Joe Wholey (1999) goes further in his definition by stating that performance-based management or managing for results is "the purposeful use of resources and information to achieve and demonstrate measurable progress toward agency and program goals" (p. 288).

As can be concluded from the definitions provided above, an essential component of performance management is performance measurement, the regular and careful monitoring of program implementation and outcomes (de Lancer Julnes, 2006). Such careful monitoring requires that organizations develop performance measurement systems that can provide numerical data and narratives for analysis to assess progress toward organizational goals and objectives (Wholey, 1999). Thus, a performance measurement system should include the following types of indicators or measures of performance:

- _Inputs_ are the funds (budget amounts), number of staff, and other resources that are used in government agencies.
- _Outputs_ are the specific activities or immediate results of the program services that are funded by the inputs. So, for example, the outputs of a training program on accounting spreadsheets would be the number of people trained during the session, while the outputs for a transportation program would be the number of miles of road paved.
- _Outcomes_ are the consequences of outputs and are often more complex to measure.
  - ○ _Intermediate outcome:_ an outcome, to include quality measures, that is expected to lead to a desired end but is not an end in itself. An example of intermediate outcomes would be teachers improving the curricula used in their classrooms after completing a curriculum improvement workshop.
  - ○ _End outcome:_ the end result that is sought, such as the number of students mastering a subject.
- _Efficiency measures_ indicate the ratio of output-to-input or outcome-to-input. This is also call "unit-cost ratio."
- _Explanatory information_ provides the context for readers to interpret data. This is especially important when outcomes are poor or better than expected.

The information provided by these indicators can then be used by managers for budget formulation, resource allocation, employee motivation, accountability to stakeholders and the public, reporting, program evaluation and control, improving the quality of programs, and enhancing citizens' trust.

The different uses of performance measurement are discussed and illustrated throughout this book. Furthermore, some chapters focus on a critical aspect of performance management: having a high-quality performance measurement system.

Chapter Content Descriptions

Part I. State of the Art

Part I serves as an introduction to the handbook, providing the context for the theoretical and practical discussions that will be presented in the chapters ahead. The three chapters included here relate the historical and theoretical background of performance management in the public and nonprofit sectors. They also discuss the future direction of performance management and the areas in which there needs to be more research in order to support practice.

An assessment of current trends around the world leads Harry P. Hatry to predict in his chapter, "Emerging Developments in Performance Measurement: An International Perspective," that the public sector accountability for results and for using information to improve services is here to stay. However, Hatry also notes that, for a number of reasons, certain performance measurement efforts will not continue at the current pace. After providing an overview of current performance measurement efforts at different levels of government, across sectors, and in disadvantaged countries, Hatry reviews recently emerged technical developments that have greatly improved the quality of performance data and highlights what is still missing in this arena. After pointing out an almost exclusive use of performance information for accountability, he discusses emerging ways to encourage effective use of performance information by decision makers.

Kathryn Newcomer notes in her introductory chapter to this volume, "Assessing Performance in Nonprofit Service Agencies," that, increasingly, nonprofit agencies are asking questions about the results of their programs. Newcomer explores the factors that have contributed to these demands, including those as varied as local governments and private foundations. She also explains that even though there is evidence that service providers are measuring output and, to a limited extent outcomes, in order to meet demands for programmatic performance information, this has not gone unopposed. The measuring of performance has created tensions for executives and managers of social services because of the choices they must make when designing and implementing performance measurement systems. Newcomer discusses this tension and also provides some insight into the less-tractable and still-evolving challenges facing nonprofit service providers.

In the chapter "Performance: A New Public Management Perspective," Owen E. Hughes provides us with a theoretical and cross-national discussion about transition from traditional public administration to managerial models like "New Public Management" (NPM). Central to this discussion is the idea that improving performance is fundamental for most managerial reforms. While traditional models of public administration reform sought to improve performance, for a number of reasons they fell short of this goal. One of those reasons addressed by Hughes is the inherent difficulty of measuring performance in the public sector. Nonetheless, Hughes argues that it is necessary for governments to measure performance in order to show that public purposes are being served. To make this point, Hughes discusses the NPM perspective in the context of performance management. He also explores the purposes of performance management, the need for performance measurement, and the criticisms often raised about performance indicators. The chapter also provides an overview of the different management reforms that have become part of the NPM.

Part II. Using Performance Information to Improve Program Performance and Accountability

To introduce Part II, Patria de Lancer Julnes deals with the thorny question about the potential contribution of performance information. In her chapter, "Can Performance Measurement Support Program Performance Improvement and Accountability?", de Lancer Julnes provides a discussion about the major debates surrounding the claims of the contributions of performance measurement to decision making and accountability. She develops her arguments on the basis of the notion that performance measurement may have a less direct, but nonetheless important, impact than proponents of the tool might hope. She also discusses an apparent accountability paradox-accountability efforts may actually hinder performance improvement, the limitations of performance measurement, and ways to overcome those limitations. Examples of state and local government performance measurement systems in the United States are provided at the end of the chapter.

In their chapter, Monica Brezzi, Laura Raimondo, and Francesca Utili discuss "Using Performance Measurement and Competition to Make Administrations Accountable: The Italian Case," an innovative program designed to elicit competitive and cooperative behaviors in order to encourage performance improvement and accountability in six southern regions of Italy. The program is called the "6% performance reserve system" and was part of a development program, cofinanced by the European Union, that Italy started in 1999 to help increase territorial competitiveness and attract capital to the southern regions. It distributed €2.6 billion (6% of the total amount of a large development program for southern regions financed by the European Union) to administrations in those regions, based on their performance results on 12 indicators. Using agency theory, Brezzi, Raimondo, and Utili provide insight into why the "6% performance reserve system" worked and about the challenges encountered during the implementation of such a highly complex program.

The chapter "Recognizing Credible Performance Reports: The Role of the Government Auditor in Canada," by Barry Leighton, deals with three poignant questions about the quality and truthfulness of performance reports: Was the intended audience satisfied with the quality of the performance information presented? Did people get the right information? Was the information balanced, understandable, and credible? In this context, Leighton discusses how certain events have led to what he calls an "audit society," increasingly demanding independent assurance of the fairness and reliability of performance reports. Leighton presents Canada's attempt to address these demands through the Office of the Auditor General's "model for good performance reporting." Using a logic model approach, the model's criteria focus on the accomplishments of the department or agency and the quality and use of performance information. Leighton concludes that despite some weaknesses, the model seems to work and provides useful lessons for those interested in instituting similar performance information audit models.

In their chapter, "Advancing Performance Measurement and Management for Accountability: King County's Collaborative, Incremental Approach," Cheryle Broom and Edward T. Jennings, Jr. use the theory of incremental decision making to describe and explain the efforts of King County, in Washington State, to implement a performance management system. That King County has made only baby steps toward developing and implementing their system does not surprise the authors. It is not unusual for organizations with competing interests to use this approach. Broom and Jennings explain that such strategy has allowed the county to build a "foundation for a viable countywide performance measurement program transparent to King County's citizens. The county has been able to build on experience; policymakers appear to have embraced the concept; and there appears to be buy-in from other participants.

Based on the notion that governments need good analysis, David N. Ammons presents in his chapter, "Analyzing Performance Data," a number of relatively easy-to-use techniques for analyzing performance data. Ammons argues that applying these techniques can greatly improve the usefulness of performance information for management decision making. The impetus for this chapter is Ammons's own observation that managers tend to focus on reporting data for accountability purposes and miss the chance to develop information that can help them improve service delivery. To help decrease this gap, Ammons discusses a variety of techniques "suitable to addressing common governmental problems." Thus, for example, Ammons illustrates how to use ratios and performance standards and benchmarks to answer staffing questions. He also shows how a simple adjustment for inflation can make an analysis of revenues and expenses more useful and accurate from one year to the next.

Part III. Informing and Involving
Citizens and Other Stakeholders

In Chapter 9 of this handbook, "Making Performance Measurement Relevant: Informing and Involving Stakeholders in Performance Measurement," Kaifeng Yang discusses the rationale, importance, practice, and challenges of informing and involving citizens in performance measurement. He argues that since government agencies often have multiple, competing, and changing expectations, their performance measurement has to be understood in relation to an open and dynamic process of coalition building and policy making in which stakeholders must be involved. Yang challenges public managers to take advantage of the accountability pressure and emphasize performance management from the wider perspective of democracy, governance, and citizenship as part of an integrated effort to solve public problems.

In his chapter, "Citizen-Involved Performance Measurement: The Case of Online Procedures Enhancement for Civil Applications in Seoul," Seungbeom Choi demonstrates the effects and success factors of the OPEN system, an award-winning reform program developed by the Seoul Metropolitan Government, in South Korea. OPEN is an Internet-based system that posts online the details of the status of 26 civil applications in areas such as transportation, urban planning, and construction. Both government and citizens can use the system to monitor the performance of the civil servants processing the applications. Citizens can also obtain additional information and communicate with civil servants via the system. Initial evidence shows that the OPEN system has increased transparency, reduced corruption, enhanced productivity, and improved citizen trust in government. Choi further attributes the success to factors such as strong leadership, creative use of information technology, decentralization, citizen participation, and effective strategic management.

Education performance and accountability is an important policy area, and whether and how stakeholders can be involved in this area is of great significance. In "Performance Measurement and Educational Accountability: The U.S. Case," Katherine E. Ryan briefly reviews education performance measurement and critically analyzes the standards, assessments, and accountability requirements of standards-based education reform as manifested by the No Child Left Behind Act of 2001 (NCLB). In particular, she examines the potential role of stakeholders, such as states, school districts, public officials, educators, parents, students, and citizens, in determining standards, assessments, and accountability. Acknowledging that these stakeholders have had limited participation in discussions about education performance measurement, Ryan proposes that values inquiry and public engagement can be employed to facilitate stakeholder and citizen action to improve school accountability.

Both performance measurement and stakeholder participation are activities that may be lengthy, costly, and technically demanding. In integrating the two types of activities, one faces even more barriers and hindrances. However, in "Experience With Trained Observers in Transition and Developing Countries: Citizen Engagement in Monitoring Results," Katharine Mark shows that simple techniques such as trained-observer rating can be used to achieve the integration even when resources are limited. Laypeople, especially stakeholders such as community residents, can be trained to use well-designed ordinal rating scales to evaluate a specific public service area and make recommendations. With cases from traditional and developing countries, Mark illustrates the principles, processes, methods, and positive effects of using trained-observer rating in local governments. She demonstrates that this technique can produce rapid results, facilitate community improvement, and result in strengthened and durable collaboration between civil society and government.

Starting from the observation that traditional bureaucratic institutions and performance measurement are not friendly to citizen participation, Marc Holzer and Kathryn Kloby, in "Helping Government Measure Up: Models of Citizen-Driven Government Performance Measurement Initiatives," offer an in-depth review of citizen-driven models of performance measurement and argue that institutions and mechanisms outside of government can be designed to align administrative policies with citizen preferences. They review five best practices from projects sponsored by the Alfred P. Sloan Foundation's Performance Assessment of Municipal Government program. The five cases show that citizens and nonprofits can work with local governments or alone to identify performance aspects they value most, help collect performance data, monitor government performance, and push for performance improvement. Holzer and Kloby also identify four challenges of citizen-driven performance measurement: how to ensure transparency and cooperation from government agencies, how to maintain the integrity of such efforts, how to improve the marketability of such initiatives, and how to make them sustainable by creating win-win partnerships.

Part IV. Performance Budgeting

The introductory chapter to Part IV, titled "Performance Budgeting Internationally: Assessing Its Merits," is written by Frances Stokes Berry. She introduces a short history of the development of performance budgets, summarizes the studies that assess the use of performance data in decision making and management, and addresses the issues that must be resolved to increase the effectiveness and use of performance budget information. This sets the stage for in-depth case studies of how performance budgeting is carried out in states and countries around the world.

Developing a standard framework of budgetary reforms that incorporate performance measures is the starting point for "Performance-Based Budgeting in Latin and South America: Analyzing Recent Reforms in the Budgetary Systems of Brazil, Chile, Colombia, and Mexico," written by David Arellano-Gault and Edgar E. Ramírez de la Cruz. After the presentation of commonalities, the authors provide short case studies of budgetary reforms in the four countries. While all four countries share similar forms of government and similar economic and social problems, the budgeting systems function very differently and allow for some distinct comparisons and lessons to be drawn. They also demonstrate that the political economy of the countries can greatly impact the success or failure of a management reform like budgeting. Budgeting reform is often considered a technical reform, but, in fact, it influences important decisions about whether programs receive more government funding, how allocation decisions will be made, and what the role is of the central budget agency to the program agencies. All of these issues raise conflict and keep a "technical" management system like budgeting from being implemented smoothly and fully.

The state of Florida was an early adopter of performance-based budgeting among the states (in 1994) and was viewed as an exemplar of a central budgeting system with widespread agency discretion over the development of performance measures and targets. Martha Wellman and Gary VanLandingham, in "Performance-Based Budgeting in Florida: Great Expectations, More Limited Reality," provide an insider's view of the experience. Their chapter provides a rich discussion of the key issues addressed in implementing a major systemwide reform and links deficiencies in the process back to the scholarly literature on budgeting—demonstrating that some of the key frustrations continue under Florida's performance-based budgeting. The authors conclude that much useful information for managers, citizens, and policymakers is generated under this new system but that full usage is still in its infancy; one can view the glass as "half full" or "half empty," and they believe the evidence points most accurately to the glass being half full.

Two countries that have the best international reputations in the last two decades for comprehensive and workable performance management systems are New Zealand and Australia. John Halligan, in "Performance Management and Budgeting in Australia and New Zealand," provides a comparative discussion of how these two systems developed across three generations of change and the choices made in each country to make their systems distinctive and different from each other. These countries have tackled some of the perennial questions of public administration: Can policy development and implementation be separated? How can transparency and accountability best be achieved? What is the role of incentives and sanctions on managers' performances? What should the relative roles of central agencies and program agencies be vis-à-vis performance implementation and decision making? Halligan concludes that parliamentary systems of government may provide the most conducive environment to the adoption of comprehensive performance management systems but that even in a supportive environment, performance data are used at best sporadically for resource allocation.

To conclude Part IV, Carl Moravitz writes a lively skill-building chapter, "Performance-Based Budgeting: Integrating Objectives and Metrics With People and Resources," on the U.S. federal government's budgeting system. He gives many examples from current studies of how performance budgeting is working (or not) at the federal level and how its integration into broader management systems of strategic planning, human resource management, and information technology systems can improve organizational performance. Drawing on his many years working in federal agencies and advising them on system improvement, Moravitz provides a seasoned view of the best and the still-to-be-developed operations of performance-based budgeting in a large national government.

Part V. Quality and Performance in Public and Nonprofit Organizations

Maria P. Aristigueta introduces this part of the handbook with her chapter, "The Integration of Quality and Performance." In this chapter, Aristigueta explores the theoretical disconnect in the quality and performance movements. She defines *quality* and the requirements of performance management and explores the changing definitions of the movements that have occurred in order to allow for the integration of quality and performance. Through a number of examples, Aristigueta illustrates the integration of performance and quality movements in the United States. Trends such as the use of the balance scorecard and quality award programs (e.g., Baldrige Award, Delaware Quality Award) as well as quality and performance initiatives at the state and local levels are explored. Software available for quality initiatives is also mentioned as a step to successful implementation of quality and performance initiatives.

In his chapter, "Quality and Performance Management: Toward a Better Integration?", Wouter Van Dooren argues that quality management and performance management are disconnected and need to be integrated. His discussion includes the next steps in the development of quality models and performance management. In particular, Van Dooren asks how performance management and quality management should adapt in order to deal with supraorganizational realities, such as multiorganizational collaborative networks within and across policy sectors. The rephrasing of performance management and quality management is complicated by an increasing awareness of the need for collaboration in networks. Performance measurement, performance management, and quality management have to adapt to new organizational realities.

In "Performance Information of High Quality: How to Develop a Legitimate, Functional, and Sound Performance Measurement System," Miekatrien Sterck and Geert Bouckaert discuss the availability of high-quality performance information as a crucial condition for success of performance and quality management. They argue that a systems approach is necessary, as the quality of a performance measurement system is more than the technical quality of the indicators. Besides producing valid and reliable information, a performance measurement system should be legitimate and functional. It has to be supported by the employees of an organization and has to contribute to the goals of the organization. Quality of information has to be a point of interest throughout the measurement process. Control measures have to be taken and an ex post and independent audit of the performance measurement system may be necessary. Auditing performance information may provide incentives to further improve the performance measurement system, but the benefits should outweigh the costs, and organizations have to determine the acceptable level of data quality.

In the "how-to chapter" in this part of the handbook, "Applying the Common Assessment Framework in Europe," Nick Thijs and Patrick Staes explain the quality management movement and its rise in Europe. This brief historical and contextual overview is useful in providing context to the Common Assessment Framework (CAF), a quality management tool specially designed by and for public sector organizations of the European Union. Thijs and Staes examine a shift in thinking about quality from a focus on inspection and control, output, and assurance to a focus on the processes, to reach a final state where quality management is seen as organizational management. Performance management from this point of view becomes organizational performance management and quality, a necessary component to a well-functioning public sector organization. The last part of this chapter focuses in detail on the CAF in practice and the application of the CAF as a European quality tool. On the basis of experiences with the implementation of the CAF, practical remarks and recommendations are formulated.

Part VI. Pulling It All Together

Performance management can be viewed from the perspective of three levels, write John M. Kamensky and Jay Fountain in "Creating and Sustaining a Results-Oriented Performance Management Framework." Those levels are the microlevel (individual agencies), the mesolevel (across policy areas and agencies and jurisdictions), and the macrolevel (across national levels). Each level offers a different set of uses of performance measures and performance systems that require performance measurement in contracts and through intergovernmental or international grants. The authors go on to offer detailed and step-by-step advice on how to use and implement a performance management system in the micro- and mesolevels.

For those managers who are given the tasks of getting their employees to contribute to and use a performance measurement system, they offer proven steps and best practices to make the performance management effort a success.

References

de Lancer Julnes, P. (2006). Performance measurement: An effective tool for government accountability? The debate goes on. *Evaluation, 12,* 219–235.

Wholey, J. (1999). Performance-based management: Responding to the challenges. *Public Productivity and Management Review, 22,* 288–307.

Acknowledgments

We are deeply indebted to our board of advisors: Allen Lomax, U.S. Government Accountability Office; Vache Gabrielyan, American University of Armenia; Gerasimos (Jerry) Gianakis, Suffolk University; George Julnes, Utah State University; Martha Marshall, Management Consultant; Byron Price, Rutgers University; and Shawn (XiaoHu) Wang, University of Central Florida. They all did a commendable job providing a multitude of timely, insightful, challenging, and positive comments and recommendations on early drafts of the chapters included in this handbook.

Many thanks also to all the authors and coauthors for their excellent contributions to this handbook. But we are especially grateful to John Kamensky and Jay Fountain. They had the monumental task of reading every single one of the chapters in order to come up with a concluding chapter of their own that synthesizes diverse ideas and provides practical guidance for advancing the practice of performance-based management. They also provided useful feedback to several authors on the early drafts of their chapters.

The unique features of our handbook, integrating theory and practice from an international perspective, are possible because many of the chapters were originally presentations made at the International Symposium on Practice-Based Performance Management held during the annual meeting of the American Society for Public Administration (ASPA) in April 2005. The symposium was cosponsored by ASPA's Center for Accountability and Performance (CAP) and the IBM Center for the Business of Government, with the goal of doing what is accomplished too rarely: bringing together the foremost experts in a field and integrating their wisdom with applied skill-building workshops.

Finally, we wish to thank Lisa Cuevas, at Sage Publications, for believing in our book.

PART I

State of the Art

1

Emerging Developments in Performance Measurement

An International Perspective

Harry P. Hatry

The performance measurement world has been expanding in recent years at an incredible pace. This movement has been greatly affected in the United States by the congressional bipartisan Government Performance and Results Act of 1993 (GPRA) and the major impetus by the federal Office of Management and Budget (OMB) toward performance measurement and the idea that results are critical. On the international front, the World Bank and most other major multilateral and bilateral donors have been making major efforts in recent years to encourage a results orientation and performance measurement in the disadvantaged countries they are helping.

Will this continue? Is this just a passing fancy? Realistically, we can expect in future years some cutback of effort and interest. This will occur either because the use of performance measurement has been well established and accepted as a normal part of government (a good reason) or because the actual implementation has not produced sufficiently useful information and is believed to cost too much for its benefits (an unfortunate reason).

Nevertheless, it is likely that the basic principle that public service agencies should be accountable for results and for using performance information to improve services will remain an important feature of public administration and the public policy arena.

Throughout this chapter, *performance measurement* is defined primarily as measurement that relates to the measurement of outcomes, as distinct from outputs. This chapter first discusses the current scope of performance measurement activity—to provide the setting in which to discuss emerging developments. Then, emerging technical developments in performance measurement are identified. Finally, the chapter addresses a major current limitation of the performance measurement movement: the lack of use of the outcome information to help agencies improve their services. The use of this information transforms performance *measurement* into performance *management*.

Scope of Current Activity, Some History, and Trends

The current activity in, and literature on, performance measurement is extensive and growing. It is difficult for anyone to keep up with everything that is going on. The following are some of the most important efforts of which this author is aware.

Local Government

Government-wide, regular outcome measurement was first undertaken at the local government level. (Though some agencies at state and federal levels have been collecting and reporting outcome data for many years, such as crime rates, numbers of traffic accidents and fatalities, and infant mortality rates.) A small number of local governments in the United States have, since the early 1970s, measured outcomes on a regular basis. This may be because the results of their services are often immediately observable to their constituents and because of the close proximity of local officials to the public, with resulting public pressure for outcomes, such as clean streets, low crime levels, passable streets, and service timeliness. State and federal governments, on the other hand, do much of their work through other levels of government, and their work (such as the operation of prisons and state parks) is not as directly apparent to citizens.

In the 1970s, many local governments began attempting to add a focus on outcomes and service quality information, including Charlotte (North Carolina), Dayton (Ohio), Metro Nashville Davidson County (Tennessee), New York City, Phoenix (Arizona), and St. Petersburg (Florida). In recent years, many more have begun regularly reporting service outcomes.

State Governments

State governments were the next level of government in the United States to move into regular performance measurement. An early milestone was its introduction by the state of Texas in the early 1990s, with the support of Governor

Ann Richardson and the state legislature. This effort had considerable influence on other states and on the federal government's later efforts. The process survived changes in the administration, including both Democratic and Republican governments. Texas even includes outcome indicators in its annual Appropriations Act.

Currently, over 30 states have some form of legislation requiring performance measurement and reporting to the legislature.[1] Today, you can look at the Web sites of many state governments and their agencies and find a collection of performance indicators being reported, usually a mixture of output and outcome indicators (though some of these Web sites lack reasonably current data).

Federal Government

The GPRA of 1993 was unanimously passed by both houses of Congress. Probably very few legislators really knew exactly what they were passing, but it evidently sounded good to them. GPRA requires annual plans from each agency for each major federal program. These plans are required to contain both outcome and output indicators. Each agency is required to report within six months after each fiscal year on the values for each performance indicator. Full implementation did not occur until fiscal year 1999 and even then had many holes.

The version implemented by the current administration contains "Performance and Accountability Reports," required from each major agency, and the PART (Program Assessment Rating Tool) process. Under PART, each federal major program is examined—both on results achieved and on its design, planning, and management. The findings of the PART have been used, along with other considerations, as part of the OMB federal budget review process. This clear linkage to the budget appears to have escalated the focus on outcome measurement within federal agencies.

A number of federal agencies have for many years collected and reported national outcome data on a regular, sometimes annual basis, such as outcome data on health, education, and the economy. However, some of this reporting has been done primarily as a statistics-gathering effort, rather than being used for managing federal programs.

In some areas, such as mental health and education, the U.S. federal government has been sponsoring in-depth program evaluations for many years, beginning in the late 1970s and into the current time. The linkage of outcome measurement and program evaluation has been somewhat controversial. Some evaluators believe these are antagonistic to each other, with outcome measurement absorbing funds and attention that should be used for more in-depth evaluations. Others believe that these are complementary activities. The information from regular, ongoing outcome measurement can often be used by program evaluators and should be a source for developing annual program evaluation agendas. Program evaluation findings from completed evaluation reports are supposed to be included in annual performance reports. The findings can override the regularly tracked outcome data because the evaluation data are likely to be based on considerably more in-depth, and more comprehensive, work.

Many program evaluations over the years, particularly after-the-fact evaluations, have resembled outcome measurement. The information obtained is based on tracking available outcome data, but with in-depth fieldwork to get at the reasons for outcomes changes. These studies may also involve collection of additional outcome data, sometimes data that a comprehensive outcome measurement system might have routinely collected.

Private Charitable Foundations

Private charitable foundations have become increasingly involved with both in-depth program evaluations and in encouraging their grantees to use and report the outcomes accomplished. Foundations such as Annie E. Casey, Hewlett, Kellogg, Packard, and Alfred P. Sloan have at various times pressed hard for outcome measurement in some form. Foundation involvement has been in the form of supporting development of grantee outcome measurement processes, encouraging or requiring grantees to undertake and/or report outcome information to the foundation, and the foundation's own evaluations of its grantees or the foundation's own outcomes.

Private Nonprofit Service Providers

Private nonprofit organizations delivering "public" services have increasingly come under pressure from both government and foundations to undertake regular outcome measurement. Since the late 1990s, United Way of America has led a push, along with a number of "leading-edge" local United Way organizations, including those in Milwaukee, Minneapolis, New Orleans, San Antonio, and Toronto, to encourage local United Way organizations and their grantees to seek outcome information—both in proposals and, subsequently, to show what outcomes were achieved. Thus far, local United Way organizations have been reluctant to use the outcome information to affect their funding decisions, but this appears to be increasingly occurring.

Recently, United Way groups (and other community groups) have begun to focus on "community impacts." Instead of providing funding only to a wide number of diverse nonprofit organizations that provide a wide array of services, some local United Way organizations are using at least a portion of their discretionary funds (which they receive from contributions) to concentrate on specific community-wide problems. This enables the United Way to apply more significant levels of funding to tackle these problems and thereby have a considerably greater chance of affecting community-wide outcomes. For example, United Way of Tucson and Southern Arizona chose to focus initially on issues such as increasing children's readiness to enter school, helping seniors remain independent, and after-school safety.

See Kathryn Newcomer's chapter (Chapter 2) on nonprofit agencies for a more detailed discussion of the activities of private nonprofit providers and foundations.

International Donors

Over the last decade, international donor organizations have been giving increasing attention to the results they are achieving through their support of disadvantaged countries—and to encouraging those governments to track their own service outcomes. The focus has been on reducing poverty, improving health, and improving the standards of living in those countries.

This effort has included most of the major donor organizations, such as World Bank, Inter-American Development Bank, Asian Development Bank, and African Development Bank (multilateral donors), and Canada, Germany, United Kingdom, and United States (bilateral donors). This has been a major effort. Some donors, such as World Bank and Inter-American Development Bank, have required proposals to identify objectives, provide indicators of outcomes expected, and, subsequently, report information on what results have been accomplished. Often, these efforts have yielded primarily what most professionals would call information on outputs and processes. However, there is little question that linkage to outcomes has become an important concern. The Millennium Development Goals (MDGs) for improving the quality of life in disadvantaged countries, signed by most members of the United Nations, include about 50 indicators. A majority of these are directed at outcomes. International long-range targets have been identified for each indicator. While the MDGs have focused on national level measurements, increasingly, these are being adapted to local governments as well.

Disadvantaged Countries

Encouraged by the donors, a number of disadvantaged countries have begun implementing outcome measurement efforts on their own. At the national government level, countries such as Brazil, Colombia, Mexico, and Uganda have made good progress.

A number of performance measurement efforts have also occurred at the local government level, particularly because of the current thrust of these countries to decentralize and give local governments more responsibility for delivering services. In countries such as Albania, Georgia, Indonesia, India, and Pakistan, a number of local governments have experimented with basic performance measurement, with support from international aid organizations. To what extent these efforts will be sustained is yet to be seen.

National "Professional" Interest Groups

In the United States, an important development has been the interest of national professional interest groups in encouraging and helping their affiliate local members to introduce outcome measurement. United Way of America was one of the first. In addition, outcome measurement support has been undertaken by organizations such as the International City/County Management Association (ICMA), which currently provides annual data comparisons on a number of service outcome and output indicators with data provided by over 100 city and county governments that voluntarily participate in this effort; American Red Cross; Big Brothers of America; Boys and Girls Clubs of America; Commission on Accreditation of Rehabilitation Facilities (CARF); and Volunteers of America.

Legislative Bodies

For the most part, legislatures have made little use of the outcome data provided by the executive branch, at least not on a systematic, regular basis. While many legislatures at state and national levels in the United States and in other countries have passed legislature requiring performance measurement, its use by these legislatures appears to be small. Recently, the National Conference of State Legislatures and National League of Cities have led efforts to encourage legislators to greater use of outcome information in their budget review and policy-making roles and in their communication with citizens (an effort labeled "legislating for results"). More focus on legislatures is also emerging in the efforts of some international donors.

Emerging Technical Developments

Successful implementation and usefulness of outcome information require data of reasonable coverage and quality. If credible outcome information were already readily available, many more public officials both in the executive and legislative branches at all levels of government would probably make more use of it. This section discusses some "technical" elements that have recently been emerging and some additional ones that need to be addressed.

Computer Technology

A major element that has occurred over the past decade is the availability of inexpensive, high-powered computers, including small, handheld, portable computers. This makes feasible many vital elements that can make performance measurements more feasible, faster, and really useful. Three of these key elements are as follows:

1. Extensive amounts of data can be processed and reports made available very soon after the data become available. Timeliness of the outcome data is a basic element of data usability.

2. Programs are now able to tabulate and analyze a variety of outcome indicator breakouts, such as by customer demographic and service characteristics.

3. The capability exists to produce very physically attractive reports.

In this author's view, these advantages, especially the first two, have too seldom been sufficiently used. Some of this technology is being made available to developing countries, usually through donor support.

Surveys of Citizens, Customers, and Clients

Surveys of citizens, customers, and clients have in recent years become one of the major, and increasingly common, tools for outcome measurement. Initially, the focus has been on sample surveys of the total population of the jurisdiction. Such surveys are needed for obtaining data on the whole population and on identifying the extent to which various segments of the population are using or not using specific government services, and why. However, usually such surveys cannot obtain at low cost detailed information from service customers on specific services, nor can they, because of sample size limitations, provide data on many geographical subareas of a jurisdiction.

User surveys, which survey the particular customers of specific services, are becoming more common. In the United States, for example, police departments, fire departments, social service departments, mental health agencies, public transport agencies, and others have surveyed their own customers, those who received service during a recent specified time period. These surveys seek more detailed information as to clients' experiences and perceptions of the quality of the service they received and the outcomes of that service.

The employment of user surveys is still quite limited but has extraordinary promise in the field of outcome monitoring. Their use has been limited by perceptions such as their perceived cost and the belief that the process is beyond the capacity of the agency or is not the job of the agency. User surveys are usually sponsored, and often administered, by the agency itself and at low cost. While the survey procedures are generally less technically proficient than multiservice household surveys (which are usually administered by a professional survey organization), these internal surveys have usually appeared to be reasonably objective and accurate. They obtain timely and specific in-depth information on the particular service for immediate use by the program's management.

Follow-Up of Customers After Services Are Completed

Special measurement problems arise for programs in which outcome information is needed after the customers have completed the service, rather than at the time of the customer's last visit. In this case, a major obstacle in obtaining valid data is the lack of follow-up information on former customers after some minimum time has elapsed, such as 6, 9, or 12 months later.

This is particularly true for human service agencies, whose objective is not only to provide immediate help but also to improve their customers' condition for a substantial period of time. For outcome monitoring, such follow-up efforts should probably not go beyond 12 months. After 12 months, tracking can become very difficult and probably falls into the scope of in-depth program evaluations. For example, programs that seek to prevent health or other problems, such as those that seek to reduce dangerous alcohol, drug, or sexual behavior, are intended to have long-term effects on clients. Unless some tracking is done of what happens after clients leave the program, it is difficult to assess success in achieving these objectives.

Fortunately, many such programs initially have good contact information on their customers and reasonably good relations with them. Mailing questionnaires to former customers is a potentially low-cost approach, including allowing for multiple mailings, if most former clients are literate and have addresses. Use of the mail can be inexpensive, and if multiple mailings and other techniques are used to encourage responses, an organization should be able to achieve response rates of about 50%. For some situations, in-person interviewing might be appropriate, such as when it is appropriate to obtain information at one of the organization's facilities or, for developing countries, when in-person interviewing is considerably more feasible than interviewing by mail or telephone.

Even the smallest nonprofit organizations should be able to do follow-ups of their customers. These organizations normally have the trust of those customers as well as having contact information.

Mail surveys have been gaining respectability, particularly since the wide use of telephone-answering devices and cell phones have substantially lowered response rates for telephone surveys. Response rates of about 50% are increasingly accepted by survey professionals as adequate. This acceptance has been helped by studies that have found responses to survey questions by those who responded to the first or second mailing (when completion rates were quite low) to be very similar to the responses from those who responded to later mailings. However, it is not known to what extent and under what conditions this occurs.

For developing countries, *in-person surveys* are usually the current choice because of limited mail and telephone applicability and the low cost of interviewers.

Hopefully, more service agencies will begin to seek information on the outcomes of their former clients.

Logic Models/Outcome Sequence Charts

Running rampant in the United States is the use of *logic models,* or *outcome sequence charts.* This is a very good tool, both for identifying which outcomes should be tracked and for training program personnel on outcome measurement. The international donor community's "log frame" is a mechanism that has been similarly used. This type of diagram identifies the sequence of products expected from inputs and resulting activities. For example, for a stop-smoking program, once the program has been designed and publicized, the progression of outcomes might be diagrammed as follows: (first) persons enroll in the program; (second) participants complete the program; (third) participants stop smoking initially; (fourth) participants stop smoking permanently; and (fifth) participants avoid later illnesses and premature death.

The process of thinking through the sequence can also help program personnel design new programs and then identify what outcome indicators should be tracked.

Related to this is the emergence in recent years of the important, and often very useful, distinction between *intermediate* and *end outcomes.* This distinction is particularly important at the higher levels of government (e.g., state and national). Higher levels often work through lower levels, which, in turn, deliver services to citizens. Getting the lower levels of government to complete certain actions, such as passing legislation, preparing plans, and establishing mechanisms locally for service delivery, are intermediate outcomes for the higher level of government.

A major service area where the distinction between intermediate and end outcomes may be seen is that of human service programs that seek to improve clients' conditions. These programs may, first, attempt to improve their clients' knowledge of what is unhealthy behavior and change individuals' attitudes toward such behavior and, then, help the clients improve their actual behavior, thus improving their long-term health prospects. Improving clients' knowledge and attitudes is an intermediate outcome. Improving clients' conditions, such as their health, is an end outcome. Improving clients' behavior usually would be considered an intermediate outcome. However, if substantial evidence exists that such behavior change almost always leads to substantial improvement in the client's condition, behavior change can be considered as a proxy end outcome.

Breaking Out Aggregate Outcome Data

A key technical element unfortunately often neglected is *breaking out aggregate outcome data into subgroups, usually demographic subgroups,* such as separating clients by age group, gender, geographical location, income group, and race/ethnicity. For program evaluators, such break outs are commonly tabulated. However, for outcome measurement, reporting disaggregated data is considerably less common, even at the program level.

Such disaggregations can greatly aid program and high-level officials in identifying those who benefit from their programs and those who do not. This permits a much more informed determination as to what actions might be needed. Such break outs also provide information on the distribution and equitableness of individual public service.

Similarly, outcome data can be broken out by *service characteristics*. For each client, information on the type and amount of service provided can be recorded and then related to the outcomes for each particular client. This would enable the program to assess which types and amounts of service have been achieving good outcomes and which have been achieving poor outcomes. This kind of break out has seldom been used in outcome measurement systems, with one exception. Agencies doing outcome measurement that have more than one service unit providing approximately the same kind of service sometimes report data for each unit. Thus, each responsible service manager has outcome data relevant to his or her own area of responsibility.

The lack of use of such break outs has been justified in past decades because of major problems in tabulating the data. Now, the advent of inexpensive and powerful computers means that the tabulation problem is minimal. The major problem is to record the data so tabulations can be made. Another problem is that break outs considerably increase the volume of data to be reported. However, this problem can be readily handled by exception reporting combined with tailoring reports to the interests of each type of report user.

Closely related to the above, and triggered in part by ready availability of quality geographical information systems (GIS), is *reporting data by small geographical areas*, especially individual neighborhoods within cities. This requires local governments to collect outcome data that can be geographically identified. Small-area outcome data are a major emerging trend.

Program Analysis for Future Choices

The focus on outcome measurement and program evaluation in recent years has had a negative effect. It has reduced the emphasis on development of processes for systematically analyzing alternative future options. Such procedures have been called by such names as *program analysis, systems analysis,* or *policy analysis*. These systematically examine future alternatives to help decision makers make choices. Few government agencies in the United States have significant numbers of staff assigned to systematically analyzing alternative programs or policy choices. Alternatives are usually considered in public decisions, but systematic analysis of these alternatives seems rare.

An exception has been the systems analysis work in the U.S. Department of Defense (DOD) for a few decades in defense planning in the United States. DOD has used tools such as large-scale computer simulations, war games, and statistical projections, including estimates of the future costs of weapon systems based on key system characteristics—though not always with great success. Such efforts in nondefense services, however, have been much less frequent.

This leads to the point that information obtained through outcome measurement and program evaluation is about the past. But public sector decisions are about the future. Public service organizations are continually making budgeting and program and policy decisions. These decisions all involve making assumptions and extrapolations about the future. The historical data from outcome measurement and program evaluation, while valuable, are far from sufficient for making projections about the future. This is particularly true when estimating the outcomes or costs of new service delivery options. It is very difficult to project into the future. People have problems estimating what will happen even one day into the future, such as fluctuations in the stock market. Much more difficult is trying to project what will happen several years into the future, in order to consider a variety of policy choices, such as when developing a budget.

A key to this process is projecting the future environment and its effects on future costs and outcomes. Many governments make population and revenue projections for at least a few years into the future to help with some decisions. Historical cost and outcome information, and information from past program evaluations, can help project future costs and outcomes, especially for programs that are expected to continue to operate the same way they have in the past. But what about new options? Progress requires consideration of new ways of delivering services in the future. What would the outcomes and costs of these new systems be?

This area of program, system, and policy analysis is wide open. Considerably more attention to, and work on, these elements is badly needed, even though the future will, inevitably, always be uncertain.

Emerging Ideas for Making
Outcome Information More Useful

Thus far, technical issues in obtaining information have been discussed. This section addresses emerging ideas for helping make that information more useful to decision makers—whether in the public or private nonprofit sectors. Some of these ideas may be obvious to many readers, but it is amazing how infrequently these are done.

Providing outcome data to officials in a timely and frequent way. This may be obvious, but outcome information is often not sufficiently timely. The focus of performance measurement in the United States, and probably throughout the world, has been on providing outcome information on an annual basis— as part of budgeting. But program managers and their staffs need more frequent information in order to make operating decisions. And, unfortunately, for some indicators, such as those based on large-scale surveys, the data do not become available for months, if not years, after the period to which they apply.

The frequency of outcome data collection and reporting depends somewhat on the individual indicator. For outcome indicators for which changes are not expected to occur frequently, annual information may be sufficient. However, the values of many outcome indicators can be affected at almost any time and should be reported more frequently. Progress reporting is common in many government agencies, commonly on a quarterly basis, though usually the reporting does not include much, if any, outcome information. More frequent outcome reporting can become a basis for "How Are We Doing?" sessions, discussed further below.

Providing disaggregated outcome data by demographic and service characteristics. This type of information, already mentioned in the technical developments discussion, can provide considerable actionable information. For example, break outs by each organizational unit delivering a service can be very useful to program managers, such as managers of various police or fire districts, offices, health facilities, schools, parks, and libraries. It is important that managers of each unit be provided with information concerning their own area of responsibility and be able to compare that information with other similar units. Such information can help program officials identify which approaches to service delivery work best, and for which types of customers. Programs can even use the outcome measurement process to conduct their own "experiments" by randomly assigning customers to different service types and amounts (making sure to record who received what) and then subsequently linking that information to the outcomes for each customer. (This process comes close to the more scholarly randomized evaluation designs.)

Providing comparisons of the latest outcome data to benchmarks. This is the first line of analysis for outcome measurement systems. Not only do officials need to obtain outcome data, but they need to be able to tell whether the data indicate their programs are doing well or badly. A number of such comparisons are being used, each of which provides valuable information. These include comparing the latest outcome data

- to the values for previous periods—the traditional approach;
- across various demographic groups—if break out data are available;
- across various service characteristics—if break out data are available;
- to targets set by the program at the beginning of the year—this is becoming common; and
- to similar programs in other communities—if comparable outcome data are available.

Requiring explanations for unexpected findings. This is emerging as an integral, explicit part of performance measurement processes. This obvious but usually neglected step is seldom included as a *formal* part of reporting performance information. Exceptions to this include the states of Texas and Louisiana, where the legislatures have required state agencies to provide an explanation whenever the latest value for an indicator differs by 5% from the target set by the agency, whether the findings are unexpectedly good or unexpectedly bad.

Inevitably, some explanations for unexpected findings will be merely defensive and vague, necessitating further pressing for concrete, meaningful explanations. This step on the whole, however, is likely to encourage program managers to look for the reasons and, when possible, to correct them.

How can such explanations be obtained? The ideal would be in-depth program evaluations, but these are usually expensive and time-consuming. They can seldom be undertaken for more than a very small percentage of an organization's programs in any given year. Explanations, however, might come from more analysis of the data, such as data disaggregations and special cross-tabulations, or from field investigations. Even if explanations are only qualitative, such as from staff feedback, they can still be helpful.

An important step in examining explanations is to distinguish factors over which the program has a reasonable degree of influence from those over which the agency has little control.

Another important advantage of formally calling for explanations for unexpected findings is that this provides program managers some assurance that their perspectives on weak results will be known. If they know they have a chance to explain what has occurred, this is likely to somewhat lessen their worries that the data will be misinterpreted and misused.

Extracting highlights and summarizing each performance report. This appears to be seldom done, whether for operations managers, for top-level department officials, or for elected officials. Executive and legislative staffs can make the lives of officials and managers much easier. These decision makers usually have little time for, or interest in, poring through pages of data. Highlighting the major findings can be very helpful to decision makers. *Highlighting* means identifying unexpected findings, whether they are particularly good or bad. This can be done by simply circling or highlighting in red particular data points on tables. It also means summarizing the major findings into brief, perhaps one- or two-page reports that contain what is expected to be of importance to users of the reports.

Making performance reports user-friendly. It is surprising how often report presentations have been badly done. Considerable technical advances are being made in report presentation. In recent years, computers enable those reporting data to use very attractive devices, including color, charts, diagrams, and the like. However, it is clear from early experience with computer-generated reporting tools that some report designers are overdoing it. Reports may provide too much information and use too many gimmicks that cloud the data, such as three-dimensional bar charts, too much color, and too much data. These can interfere with interpretation of what is being presented. "Prettiness" should not be achieved at the expense of substance and readability.

Improving the Way
Outcome Information Is Used

At present, possibly the major weakness in the outcome measurement movement is the almost exclusive focus on using the outcome information for
accountability purposes and lack of use of the information for improving the
quality and effectiveness of services. This applies to both public and private
nonprofit organizations in the United States. It seems likely this will gradually change, especially as managers become more exposed to outcome data
and become more comfortable with it.

Of course, accountability is important. It is important to be able to justify to elected officials and the public that their money is being used to
achieve the desired results. However, probably even more important in justifying the time, effort, and money spent on performance measurement is
whether the outcome information is used to make improvements and in
learning how to provide more effective services.

The previous section discussed ways to make outcome information more
useful. This section considers emerging ways to encourage decision makers
to use the information *effectively*.

Emerging Ways to Use
Performance Measurement Information

Increasingly, outcome information is being used to help operating managers and their staffs to better allocate their resources. A long-standing but
not widely known example is the use by the New York City Sanitation
Department (since the early 1970s) of regular trained-observer ratings of
the cleanliness of New York City streets. The department has used the condition ratings to generate regular reports on the percentage of streets that
are clean to various degrees in various locations. The findings are published
in the annual "Mayor's Management Report." More to the point here, the
department has used the findings on the street cleanliness outcomes as a
basis for allocating the work of its sanitation crews.

Trained-observer rating procedures have the advantage of providing
timely information that operating personnel can use to take early corrective
actions. In addition in New York, a nonprofit organization, the Fund for
the City of New York, has in recent years used handheld computer technology to undertake ratings of a variety of neighborhood conditions, including the condition of roads, streets, sidewalks, traffic signs and signals, and
other physically observable conditions.

This trend is present internationally, as well. In Albania, a combination
of school and other government personnel in a number of cities have used
trained observers to rate the condition of school buildings, identifying the condition of major building components (such as ceilings, lighting, temperature,

and bathrooms). A number of Albanian city governments have used the information to help choose how and where they should allocate their very scarce funds.

High school and college students in a number of cities in the country of Georgia have been rating street cleanliness for the city governments. The cities are using that data, along with information from citizen household surveys, to help allocate their public works resources. (For more information on trained-observer rating procedures, see Chapter 12, by Mark, in this volume.)

Agency record data and information from household and user surveys can, of course, also be used to identify problems needing attention and to help allocate resources accordingly.

Using Information in Budgeting

A common, and major, use of outcome information has been to include outcome information in the budgeting process. Unfortunately, often this has occurred only because a higher level of authority has required that such information be provided. The outcome information is used primarily as a "display piece." Much less common is the use of outcome information to help formulate program and agency budget proposals, and then justify the budget levels proposed.

A problem is the difficulty in estimating the resources required to achieve specified outcome levels. For some outcomes, usually intermediate rather than end outcomes, this can be done reasonably accurately, such as in estimating the costs required to improve response times by a certain amount. However, estimating the resources required to reduce juvenile delinquency by particular amounts or to improve citizen satisfaction with a service by, say, 5 percentage points, is considerably more difficult.

In past decades, budgeting practices such as PPBS (planning-programming-budgeting systems) and ZBB (zero-based budgeting) sought to use outcome information in this way but did not succeed. But those attempts came at times when outcome information was not as readily available as it is today.

Using Information for Motivating Personnel

When outcome information from the latest reports becomes available, the information can be used to help motivate personnel to improve services. Recently, a number of approaches have been used.

Providing recognition rewards for good or outstanding outcomes (or for making major improvements in outcomes). This is an inexpensive approach. It is likely to be applicable to every service and every governmental and nongovernmental organization. The rewards might be to individuals or, probably better, to groups or teams. This form of motivation is not used enough, but seems likely to become more prominent in the future as more organizations collect and use outcome information.

Holding "How Are We Doing?" sessions. In such sessions, a manager brings staff together soon after the latest performance report has been disseminated. At the session, the group goes over areas in which the outcomes have been good and those in which they have not been good. Group members are asked to identify reasons for "good" and "unsatisfactory" results and actions they feel might help correct problems or be used to expand the use of successful practices. In subsequent "How Are We Doing?" sessions, the group would assess whether the actions taken had improved the outcomes.

In recent years, a "Stat" movement has become a major approach for some U.S. cities. New York City and the City of Baltimore, Maryland, have led the way. New York City's Police Department started with its "CompStat" process. Periodically, precinct commanders meet at headquarters to address issues posed by senior administrators about concrete operational issues that have arisen in the field. Data on crime statistics are the centerpiece. This process has spread to a number of other New York City agencies, including the Parks and Recreation Department (ParkStat) and the Human Resources Administration (JobStat). In the City of Baltimore, the mayor himself has for several years held similar meetings, meeting with department personnel on a regular, biweekly basis to review a variety of statistics. Those statistics include not only outcome information but also related information such as output information and data on employees, such as absenteeism. Both cities have reported significant improvements in outcomes after introducing this process.

Introducing "pay for performance." This is the most famous of the motivational approaches. However, it is particularly controversial. Whenever money comes into the picture, the level of anxiety and potential for misuse seem to follow. U.S. governments at all three levels have experimented with this approach, with what appear to be quite mixed results.

A major problem here is that the final decisions on who gets money and how much have usually been based largely on the judgments of supervisors, and those judgments are not always agreeable to other staff. In Urban Institute studies many years ago, it was found that such plans could be counterproductive because of the subsequent resistance and perceptions of unfairness among employees—unless a high proportion of the staff received monetary rewards. (This has particularly been the case with school system monetary incentive plans for teachers in the United States.) In general, unions and employee associations become very concerned when pay is based to any significant extent on the judgments of supervisors, due to concerns over issues such as favoritism and poor judgment.

We are likely to see considerable pressure in the future from external groups, such as the business community, to introduce pay for performance into nonprofit organizations, both public and private. As outcome measurement improves in quality and as judgment plays less of a role in determining rewards—and if all parties accept the fact that "windfalls and pratfalls" affecting outcomes will inevitably occur—this approach may become more constructive. The question will remain, however, as to how much outcome improvement occurs due to added pay for public and private nonprofit employees.

Using Information to Help Communicate With Citizens

Transparency has become a popular issue in recent years. The typical response to the issue of transparency in the United States has been to put performance reports on agency Web sites. The U.S. federal government and its agencies, many state governments and their agencies, and many local governments currently do this. This is good. However, a major problem is that currently many citizens, particularly disadvantaged individuals, do not have ready access to computers. Some may not know of the availability of the information on Web sites. Also, keeping Web sites up-to-date requires a major effort, and often the desired information is difficult for individuals to find on the Web site or is no longer current.

An emerging trend is for government agencies to issue annual "State of the Government" reports to citizens. These are generally available in hard copy and on Web sites. In the past, most of these reports have focused on describing activities and providing input (expenditure) data, with little information on service outcomes. Increasingly, outcome information is slipping into these reports to citizens. Perhaps the most dramatic example of this is the U.S. federal budget document and its backup materials. For the first time, the publicly available "FY 2006" and "FY 2007" budget documents contained outcome information. (However, very little outcome data was included in the "FY 2008" budget document.) While many might not agree with the self-selective nature of the indicators included, at least a first step to such reporting has taken place. In addition, the OMB posts on its Web site, and in a reasonably timely way, its evaluations of each major federal program (as part of the PART process noted earlier), which can be viewed throughout the world.

A Special Note on Citizen Involvement

Many different levels of government both in the United States and around the world have been attempting to involve citizens in participating in some way in decisions about how funds are spent. The following are four stages of citizen involvement.

Determining what outcomes should be tracked. This usually occurs in the form of government-sponsored focus groups, in which small numbers of citizens gather to discuss (for perhaps a few hours) what they like, dislike, and want from a particular government service. Such sessions can be useful, but inevitably only very small numbers of individuals provide input into this process. Another approach is for public officials to hold open meetings with citizens in various parts of their jurisdictions to obtain feedback from citizens. This approach, which has been tried particularly at the local and state levels in the United States, involves more citizens. However, each person's opportunity to have a say is highly limited, and, again, the representativeness of the citizens attending these meetings is highly questionable. Nevertheless, such sessions do provide some, even though highly limited, opportunity for citizen input. In the future, many governments, especially local governments in developing countries that are decentralizing, are likely to use similar practices.

Helping to evaluate services. Citizens can be asked to provide assessments of their experiences, including the outcome and quality of individual services they received. This information is usually obtained using systematic surveys. As noted earlier, the use of such surveys has grown considerably in recent years and seems likely to expand further. Surveys are being used frequently throughout the world, as both developed and developing countries increase their interest in obtaining citizen feedback—with funding for the surveys for developing countries usually coming from donors. (Many national governments have central statistical units that at least annually undertake population surveys. These surveys provide valuable statistical information but are not focused on the types of management and public administration decisions discussed in this book.)

Most government surveys seeking citizen assessments of services use random samples of the total population in a jurisdiction. The questionnaires include questions relating to a wide variety of the public services. Recently, more attention has been given to surveys of users of particular services.

Helping to explain reasons for good or poor service outcomes. Citizens are sometimes asked to help identify reasons for poor, or good, performance, typically using focus groups. This application seems to be rare. It is likely to be used when the sponsoring agency has had some serious issue about which it otherwise has not been able to obtain adequate information. This means citizen involvement may become more frequent in the future as outcome information becomes more prevalent and findings become more controversial.

Citizens' use of outcome information. A question that has seldom been addressed is the extent to which citizens are interested in outcome information and put it to use themselves. It is often assumed that citizens have a substantial continuing interest in being kept apprised of the outcomes of government activities and for a wide variety of services. However, it may be that most individual citizens are probably interested in the quality of government services primarily when they have a problem with a service. However, as the movement toward reporting outcome data by neighborhood (noted earlier) produces such information and makes it readily available to households, this is likely to considerably increase citizen interest and activism. For example, if citizens have access to readily available data that indicate that conditions are worse in their neighborhood than in others, will residents start pressing for improvements?

What About Efficiency Indicators?

This chapter has focused on outcome indicators, not *efficiency* indicators. Efficiency indicators are here defined as the ratios of the amounts of input required to achieve specific amounts of product. The product can be expressed as the amount of output (the current common approach) or the amount of outcome achieved. The danger in using output-focused efficiency is that if incentives are attached to increasing efficiency, "improvements" in this ratio can occur at the expense of deteriorating service quality.

As outcome information becomes more common and accepted, more attention to "cost per unit of outcome" can be expected. For example, instead of the indicator "cost per client served," efficiency could be calculated as "cost per client served *whose condition had improved.*"

Final Comments

In the near future, we are likely to see increased use of such technical procedures as trained-observer ratings, surveys of service customers, and the use of disaggregations of outcome data led by GIS applications leading to the reporting of outcomes by small geographical areas.

What has been lacking, and, hopefully, will grow considerably in the future, is increased use of outcome information by service managers and elected officials for budgeting and improving services. This will be considerably encouraged by better quality, relevance, and timeliness of data resulting from "technical" advances such as those noted above. Low-cost employee motivational approaches, such as the "How Are We Doing?" process as piloted in the "Stat" movement, and use of recognition awards, also seem promising.

Finally, considerably more focus is needed on how to use outcome data to help make decisions about the future. The field of policy and program analysis has taken a back seat to evaluation and performance measurement. More attention needs to be given, both for budgeting and planning, to assessing alternative ways to better deliver services to the public.

The greatly increased attention to outcome measurement in recent years throughout the world and at all levels of government and the nonprofit sector should lead to further advances in both the technical components and the effective use of regularly collected and reported outcome information. It seems inevitable that outcome measurement will remain a constant in pubic administration.

Note

1. The National Conference of State Legislatures in 2000 examined the legislation in all states. It reported that 33 states at the end of 1999 had some form of performance-measurement-related information (Liner et al., 2001). Julia Melkers and Katherine Willoughby (2004) found the same number.

Selected Readings

Ammons, D. N. (1996). *Municipal benchmarks: Assessing local performance and establishing community standards.* Thousand Oaks, CA: Sage.

Aristigueta, M. (1998). *Managing for results in state government.* Westport, CT: Quorum Books.

de Bruijn, H. (2003). *Managing performance in the public sector.* London: Routledge.

Epstein, P., Fountain, J., Campbell, W., Patton, T., & Keaton, K. (2005, July). *Government service efforts and accomplishments performance reports: A guide to understanding.* Norwalk, CT: Governmental Accounting Standards Board.

Fink, A. (Ed.). (2003). *The survey kit.* Thousand Oaks, CA: Sage.

Forsythe, D. W. (2001). *Quicker better cheaper? Managing performance in American government.* Albany, NY: Rockefeller Institute Press.

Friedman, M. (2005). *Trying hard is not good enough: How to produce measurable improvements for customers and communities.* Victoria, Canada: Trafford.

Gormley, W. T., & Weimer, D. L. (1999). *Organizational report cards.* Cambridge, MA: Harvard University Press.

Government Performance and Results Act of 1993, Pub. L. No. 103–62 [S20] 107 Stat. 285.

Guajardo, S. A., & McDonnell, R. (2000). *An elected official's guide to performance measurement.* Chicago: Government Finance Officers Association.

Hatry, H. P. (2006). *Performance measurement: Getting results* (2nd ed.). Washington, DC: Urban Institute.

Henderson, L. J. (2003). *The Baltimore CitiStat Program: Performance and accountability.* Baltimore: IBM Endowment for the Business of Government.

Kamensky, J. M., & Morales, A. (2005). *Managing for results 2005* (IBM Center for the Business of Government). Lanham, MD: Rowman & Littlefield.

Kusek, J. Z., & Rist, R. C. (2004). *Ten steps to a results-based monitoring and evaluation system.* Washington, DC: World Bank.

Lampkin, L. M., & Hatry, H. P. (Eds.). (2004). *Series on outcome management for nonprofit organizations.* Washington, DC: Urban Institute.

Liner, B., Hatry, H. P., Vinson, E., Allen, R., Dusenbury, P., Bryant, S., et al. (2001). *Making results-based state government work.* Washington, DC: Urban Institute.

Mackay, K. (2006, January). *Evaluation capacity development: Institutionalization of monitoring and evaluation systems to improve public sector management.* Washington, DC: World Bank.

Melkers, J., & Willoughby, K. (2004, November). *Staying the course: The use of performance measurement in state governments.* Washington, DC: IBM Center for the Business of Government.

Miller, T. I., & Kobayashi, M. M. (2000). *Citizen surveys: How to do them, how to use them, what they mean* (2nd ed.). Washington, DC: International City/County Management Association (ICMA).

National Conference of State Legislatures. (2003). *Legislating for results.* Denver, CO: Author.

New York City Mayor's Office of Operations. (Annual). *Mayor's management report, City of New York.*

O'Connell, P. E. (2001). *Using performance data for accountability: The New York City Police Department's CompStat model of police management.* Washington, DC: Pricewaterhouse Coopers Endowment for the Business of Government.

Shah, A. (2005). *Public sector governance and accountability series: Public services delivery.* Washington, DC: World Bank.

United Way of America. (1996). *Measuring program outcomes: A practical approach.* Alexandria, VA: United Way of America.

Walters, J. (1998). *Measuring up: Governing's guide to performance measurement for geniuses and other public managers.* Washington, DC: Governing Books.

2 Assessing Performance in Nonprofit Service Agencies

Kathryn Newcomer

Leaders in nonprofit social service agencies across the United States are asking questions about the results of their programs. Their questions vary, and the evidence obtained to address their questions certainly also varies, but the motivation exists across the sector. Interest in nonprofit programmatic results has risen dramatically over the last three decades.

What and who have provoked this interest? Why? And what have been the intended and unintended consequences for the program managers? This chapter provides an overview of the changed and changing landscape in which nonprofit service providers operate. The origins of and demand for data from service providers on programmatic results are described, as well as the complex environment surrounding the supply of relevant data. The intriguing tensions facing executives and managers are examined, and, finally, what appear to be evolving challenges for these providers are identified.

What Is Programmatic Performance Assessment?

Assessing or measuring programmatic performance in agencies that provide social services is a growing and increasing phenomenon common in public and nonprofit providers across the United States. However, the decisions and activities involved in measuring performance typically produce tensions and some discomfort for the service providers. Why? Performance is itself a very amorphous concept, open to a multitude of operational definitions by different stakeholders (Newcomer, 1997). Programmatic assessment entails evaluation, or systematic analysis and measurement of program operations and results, and that analysis activity presents risks for the staff and board members who have invested themselves in the program. The risks of looking bad, losing public confidence and/or funding, and being forced to change are typically not welcome.

In addition, for many providers, resources to support measurement and reporting on their operations and results may compete with resources to serve their clients. Despite the uncertainties and challenges service providers face, however, the current incentives to measure performance outweigh the psychic and monetary costs of measurement. Performance measurement and reporting in public sector agencies, at all levels of the U.S. government, has increasingly become part of business as usual during the last two decades, as well. The intricate network involving public and nonprofit providers in many service areas has produced similar expectations of both governmental and nonprofit entities. An overview of the factors pushing demand for measurement within the public and nonprofit sectors over the last four decades can help explain how the current environment within which social service providers operate has evolved.

Increasing Demand for Evidence of Results

Looking back over the last four decades, it seems that demand for systematic data about social services has increased due to the noncoincidental convergence of actions by a number of institutions with stakes in the delivery of these benefits. Local governments and the federal government, foundations, the United Way of America, think tanks, and academics with interests in improving the delivery of services have all contributed to an increasing focus on programmatic measurement. Both the level and sophistication of the dialogue surrounding the merits of measuring and reporting about the operations and results of social services have notably increased since the 1970s.

As depicted in Figure 2.1, a number of noteworthy actions were undertaken by a variety of governmental and nongovernmental institutions that contributed to public dialogue about the merits of systematically measuring and reporting on the efforts of social service providers. Initial experiences with measuring performance and results of local governments started in the 1970s, in particular in California communities facing taxpayers' revolts, challenging their city governments to show them what they were getting for their money (for example, see Ammons, 1995; Osborne & Gaebler, 1992; Poister, 2003). Local governments in the United States were ahead of state governments and the federal government in experimenting with systematic measurement and reporting about public programs, reflecting a global trend toward such measurement as one part of the "New Public Management" (Kettl, 1997, 2000).

American foundations were also putting money into social services in the 1970s, and the key player was the Robert Wood Johnson Foundation, established in 1972, with a public commitment to measuring the results of its investments. When it began operating, the Robert Wood Johnson

Figure 2.1   A Timeline: Key Actions Contributing to Rising Demand for Outcome Assessment in Nonprofit Service Providers

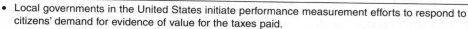

1970

- Local governments in the United States initiate performance measurement efforts to respond to citizens' demand for evidence of value for the taxes paid.
- The Robert Wood Johnson Foundation is established, with public commitment to measuring results (1972).
- Evaluation: *A Forum for Decision-Makers* is first published by the Minneapolis Medical Research Foundation (1972).
- Leading think tanks such as The Urban Institute focus attention on performance measurement for local government service providers.
- Two new journals are established that focus on evaluation and assessment in nonprofits: *Evaluation and Program Planning: An International Journal* and *Evaluation Quarterly* (later changed to *Evaluation Review*) (1978).

1980

- Many new foundations are established to support social services with espoused interest in measuring results.
- A few leading foundations (e.g., Annie E. Casey Foundation) focus attention on community-level performance measures.

1990

- Key journals in the nonprofit sector begin publishing articles about evaluation, for example, *Nonprofit and Voluntary Sector Quarterly, Nonprofit Management and Leadership,* and *Voluntas* (1990).
- There is an increasing professionalization of nonprofit management with concern with strategic planning, measurement, and accountability.
- The U.S. Congress passes the Government Performance and Results Act of 1993, which requires all agencies to provide performance measures for programs, including those operated by nonprofit grantees (1993).
- The United Way of America establishes a task force made up of leading service providers, foundations, and experts to develop a work plan training and approaches to promote outcome assessment (1994).
- The United Way of America publishes *Measuring Program Outcomes: A Practical Approach* and issues a public call encouraging all recipients of United Way funding to measure and report on outcomes (1996).
- Increased attention is given to performance measurement in the nonprofit sector by prominent organizations, for example, the Independent Sector and Grantmakers for Effective Organizations.
- Increased attention is focused on outcomes assessment in nonprofits by academic journals and think tanks such as The Urban Institute.
- Organizational score cards developed for private firms are promoted for use in the public and nonprofit sectors.

2000

- Some large foundations take the lead in drawing attention to evaluation, including measuring outcomes across clusters of providers, for example W. K. Kellogg Foundation.
- The United Way (and other organizations) increasingly survey service providers about outcomes assessment.
- The Urban Institute, among others, provides practical guidance on outcomes assessment via the Internet.
- The U.S. Congress and the Office of Management and Budget focus increasingly upon measurement of program outcomes (rather than outputs) and program effectiveness by all providers of social services receiving federal funds.
- An increasing number of articles and books are written by academics and organizational consultants focusing on outcomes assessment, theories of change, and evaluation strategies for nonprofit providers.

(Continued)

(Continued)

- The United Way of America encourages use of a community-wide impact focus and requests proposals from service providers that focus upon preselected outcome indicators, for example, juvenile delinquency rates.
- There are efforts to establish sets of community indicators with Web sites in dozens of communities across the United States (for example, see http://www.communityindicators.net).
- Many foundations are suggesting that community indicators be used to assess the impact that a number of providers are having in improving the health and well-being of residents in specific neighborhoods and communities.

2007

Foundation was the second-largest foundation in the United States, and the board espoused an interest in identifying and solving policy problems, such as the availability of primary health care and the more equitable delivery of health care, and using "field trial" policy interventions to systematically track results (Hall, 2004; Nielsen, 1985, pp. 123–124). Other foundations were beginning to show interest in discussing the role of evaluation in foundations. The Urban Institute, a think tank with a long-standing interest in evaluating public and nonprofit programs, also started devoting attention to the use of performance measurement under the leadership of Harry Hatry in the 1970s.

Academic interest in evaluating nonprofit program performance was evidenced with two new journals established in 1978 that included articles on the application of evaluation methods to assess service delivery. Coverage of performance measurement in social service agencies was expanded later when articles promoting measurement appeared in journals targeted to nonprofit managers in the 1990s, for example, *Nonprofit and Voluntary Sector Quarterly* (Hall, 2004).

There was a notable increase in the number of foundations established during the 1980s and 1990s that funded social services, and many of these newer foundations answered to boards that included executives from the private sector who brought a "results-oriented" perspective. During the 1990s, a few of the foundations with the largest portfolios, such as the Atlantic Philanthropies, the Lilly Endowment, and the W. K. Kellogg Foundation, were quite public in calling for their grantees to systematically document results (Hall, 2004).

The W. K. Kellogg Foundation was a leader in devoting resources to examining how evaluation of grantees and of foundation activities could be most effectively utilized. A study funded by Kellogg in 1998, reported in *Evaluation in Foundations: The Unrealized Potential,* by Patrizi and McMullan, articulated the views shared by many in the foundation world that valid and reliable data from grantees were needed to inform foundation decision making. The Kellogg report raised the bar for grantee assessment in calling for foundations to ask questions such as the following: Are they sound institutions with the ability to get things done? Are they effective at what they do? Have they proposed strategies likely to effect desired change? Do they have the capacity to implement these strategies well? (Patrizi & McMullan, 1998).

The U.S. Congress passed the Government Performance and Results Act (GPRA) in 1993, which requires all federal agencies to submit strategic plans, performance plans, and performance reports on all federal programs to Congress. The law requires agencies to identify performance measures for all programs funded with federal funds. Since many federal programs rely on nonprofit providers, the requirement for selection of performance measures by the federal grantees imposed requirements for measurement among social service providers (for more on GPRA, see U.S. Government Accountability Office [GAO], 2004).

In fact, the "perfect storm" of converging requirements for systematic measurement and reporting about social services hit the nonprofit sector in the mid-1990s, as major foundation funders, the federal government, and the United Way of America all called for performance measurement (Light, 2002, 2004). The United Way established a task force to develop a plan, training, and approaches to promote outcome assessment in nonprofit providers receiving United Way funds, and in 1996, the organization published a guidebook on measuring program outcomes (United Way of America, 1996). The United Way has continued to promote measurement of program results and periodically surveys its constituents to document implementation of measurement processes (for example, see United Way of America, 2000).

During the late 1990s, prominent organizations in the nonprofit sector, such as the Independent Sector and Grantmakers for Effective Organizations, reinforced the call for grantees to document their accomplishments. The Robert Wood Johnson Foundation and the Aspen Institute Nonprofit Sector Research Fund funded efforts to raise awareness about performance measurement and assess evaluation practice. One of the surveys these organizations jointly funded found that as of 1998, 56% of the responding agencies reported that they measured program outcomes (Fine, Thayer, & Coghlan, 1998).

Performance measurement efforts undertaken by nonprofit social service providers increased in response to the demands imposed by their funders in the 1990s. The amount of advice offered on measurement approaches and reporting strategies by foundations, academics, and independent consultants clearly rose as well.

From the 1990s to the present, the use of program logic models to depict the theory of change targeted by a program has been promoted to service providers by a multitude of organizations (for example, see McLaughlin & Jordan, 2004; Murray, 2001; Savaya & Waysman, 2005). Logic models graphically depict inputs supporting a program, program activities, program outputs (such as the number of persons served), intended outcomes for those persons (or communities) served in the short term and long term, as well as external factors affecting the achievement of providers but outside their control. Logic models have been promoted by foundations (e.g., W. K. Kellogg) and others as a useful tool to help providers identify what to measure and to communicate to funders about programmatic performance. Figure 2.2 displays an example of a program logic model depicting the intended outcomes of a tutoring program run by George Washington University to support high school students in an inner-city school. The logic model is used to illustrate the intended theory of change underlying the use of university students to tutor at-risk high school students.

Since the 1990s, sophisticated reporting schemes have been promoted by consultants and academics to assist service providers in communicating about programmatic performance. For example, Robert Kaplan (2001), cocreator of the "balanced scorecard" tool for the profit sector, adapted this tool for conveying performance along multiple dimensions for non-profit service providers, and others have joined in developing the supply of tools to address the rising expectations from funders to see evidence of programmatic success (Moore, 2003).

Between 2001 and 2006, a good number of foundations and other non-profit organizations have offered online technical assistance to service providers that must respond to measurement and reporting requirements. Table 2.1 displays a list of some major providers of online technical assistance and tools. The increase in the number of providers of such Web-based assistance over the last decade no doubt reflects recognition of the increasing demand for service providers to step up their measurement efforts.

In fact, since about 2002, foundations have raised expectations for measurement efforts as they have called for more attention to assessing results for communities rather than simply tracking individual grantees' outcomes (for example, see Woodwell, 2005, and "Results and Performance Accountability, Implementation Guide," at http://www.raguide.org). Shifting the focus from individual providers' performance to the performance of coordinated efforts of multiple providers is increasingly happening in many large foundations. For example, the Annie E. Casey Foundation, a leader in funding community interventions to improve the quality of life of children and families, is pushing grantees and their own program officers to make a positive difference in three ways:

Impact: Changes in the condition of well-being of the children, adults, families, or communities directly served by grants, programs, agencies, or service systems

Influence: Changes in policies, regulations, systems, practice, or public opinion

Leverage: Changes in investments by other public or private funders in Casey-related strategies to improve outcomes for children and families (Personal communication, Thomas Kelly, Annie E. Casey Foundation, February 3, 2006).

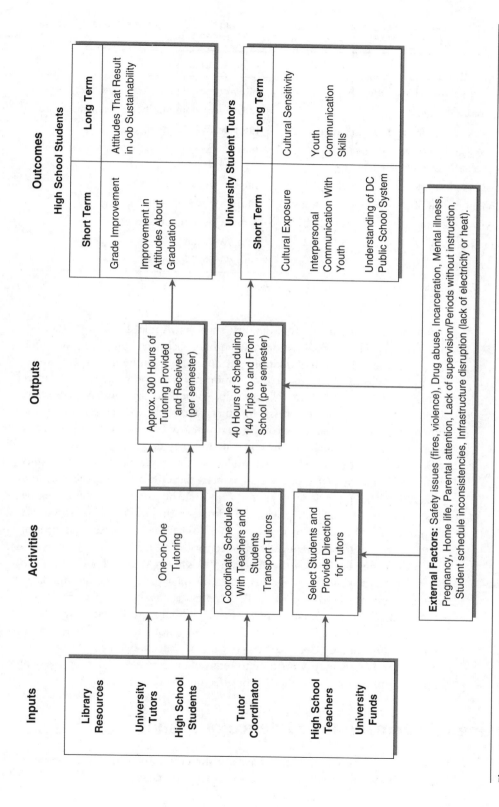

Figure 2.2 Tutoring Program Logic Model

SOURCE: Cantu, Cleveland, and Shall (2006).

Table 2.1   Sources of Evaluation Assistance for Nonprofit Service Providers Available on the Internet

Provider	Internet Address
1. Balanced Scorecard Institute	http://www.balancedscorecard.org
2. Community Builders	http://www.communitybuilders.nsw.gov.au
3. Grantmakers for Effective Organizations	http://www.geofunders.org
4. Harvard Family Research Project (The Evaluation Exchange)	http://www.gse.harvard.edu/hfrp/eval.html
5. Innovation Network	http://www.innonet.org
6. National Council of Nonprofit Associations	http://www.ncna.org
7. United Way of America	http://www.unitedway.org
8. Urban Institute	http://www.urban.org
9. W. K. Kellogg	http://www.wkkf.org

SOURCE: Urban Institute (2002).

Outcomes targeted by foundations such as Annie E. Casey, the Bill and Melinda Gates Foundation Millennium Scholars program, and the J. W. McConnell Family Foundation, in Canada, are community-level changes that are more likely to be analyzed and understood as complex systems, rather than linear cause-and-effect relationships produced by funders (Westley, Zimmerman, & Patton, in press). In other words, the expectations of some foundations for assessment of provider performance have risen along with their visions of intended changes in the communities they target for improvement.

One last source of heightened attention on assessment of the results produced by social service providers has been the Office of Management and Budget (OMB) in the federal government (see http://www.whitehouse.gov/omb/part/index.html). Starting with the administration of President George W. Bush, in 2001, OMB has instituted a process whereby each year, one fifth of federal programs are systematically assessed for their effectiveness. OMB examiners use a rating tool called the Program Assessment Rating Tool (PART) to award 1 to 100 points to programs based on their program design, management, and results. OMB's use of the PART process has resulted in a very transparent and public examination of performance data on all federally funded social service programs. While the PART scores do not automatically determine congressional funding (GAO, 2005), the threat that inadequate performance data from providers may contribute to reduced executive and/or congressional support for programs is another factor affecting the demand curve.

Meeting the Demand for Evidence of Results _____

So, foundations, governments, boards of directors, and citizens are increasingly likely to press social service providers to measure and report their performance. How are the providers responding? There is substantial survey evidence that providers are measuring what they do (outputs) and, to some extent, what difference they are making for their clients (outcomes; Fine et al., 1998; Thayer, 2006; United Way of America, 2000).

The overwhelming reality is that social service providers are capturing data to submit to funders and responding to reporting requirements in grants. Accounting for how funds are used is a requirement understood by all grantees. For more on use of performance data for accountability, see Broom and Jennings, Chapter 7, and Ammons, Chapter 8, in this volume. Using performance data to inform program improvements and organizational learning is also taking place in some quarters; for example, The Urban Institute has published a useful series of guidebooks titled *Outcome Management for Nonprofit Organizations,* which draw upon providers' experience to offer advice on how to develop an outcome management process (2003c), survey clients about outcomes (2003d), develop community-wide outcome indicators for specific services (2003a), find out what happens to former clients (2003b), analyze outcome information (2004a), and use outcome information (2004b).

Many national organizations, such as The Urban Institute, United Way of America, Harvard Family Research Project (Evaluation Exchange), and the National Council of Nonprofit Associations, are supplying encouragement and tools to nonprofit service providers to help them move beyond collecting data merely to meet funders' requirements. In fact, social service providers have reported using the performance data they collect to improve programs in a variety of ways (Hendricks, 2002; Houchin & Nicholson, 2005; Kopczynski & Pritchard, 2004; Plantz, Greenway, & Hendricks, 1997; United Way of America, 2000; Urban Institute, 2004a, 2004b). The Urban Institute found that nonprofits report using client outcome data for a variety of purposes both within their organizations as well as for external outreach, as displayed in Table 2.2. There are certainly many ways in which valid and reliable data on clients can serve nonprofits, so what might constitute a downside in performance measurement and reporting?

Tensions Arising From Evaluation for Service Providers

Collecting and reporting performance data may evoke uncertainty for managers of social service providers due to the choices they face regarding a number of basic questions, such as the following:

- Why should they measure performance?
- What should they measure?
- Who will collect and analyze the data?
- When should they measure?
- How should they measure?

Table 2.2   Basic Uses for Outcome Information

Internal Uses

1. Clarifying agency and program purposes for staff
2. Identifying where improvement is needed
3. Identifying what works and good practices
4. Informing, training, and motivating staff
5. Seeking explanations and outcomes
6. Identifying trends and making other comparisons
7. Using outcome data to help motivate clients
8. Giving more voice to clients
9. Supporting budgeting and planning
10. Facilitating in-depth studies and program evaluation
11. Informing the board of directors

External Uses

1. Increasing accountability to funders and the community
2. Providing data for marketing and fundraising
3. Attracting volunteers and clients
4. Helping other organizations

SOURCE: Urban Institute (2004b).

As displayed in Figure 2.3, program managers must address a number of issues when they design, implement, and use performance measurement systems.

There are always issues surrounding objectives and intended use for data documenting programmatic accomplishments. From the perspective of the social service providers, when grant requirements specify that grantees must report on who they served and how much improvement their services made, the message is that accountability is the objective of the measurement. Materials provided from organizations such as the United Way and The Urban Institute encourage service providers to use the data they collect to improve program operations, but the incentives provided from funders to report are likely to receive higher priority when time and resources are tight, as they usually are (Hendricks, 2002; Newcomer, 1997). Simply collecting data raises the risk that evidence of "effectiveness" may not surface. Performance data provide the ammunition that can be used by program detractors as well as supporters—and this is not lost on program managers.

So, what are the most appropriate measures? In some arenas, quantitative evidence abounds. For example, in health services, data on matters such as immunization rates, morbidity, and mortality rates have been available and used for years. In other service arenas, such as shelters for homeless women and families and community revitalization initiatives, professionally recognized standard measures may not have been established. When

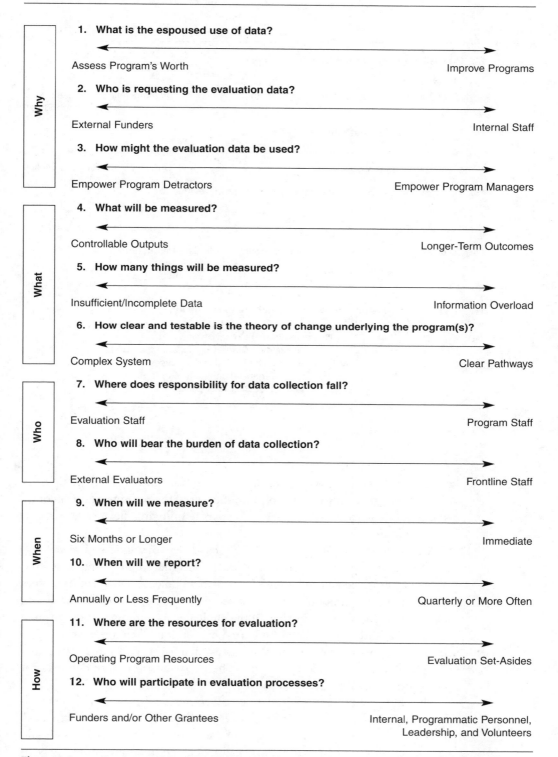

Figure 2.3   Tensions Arising From Evaluation Uncertainties for Nonprofit Service Providers

(Continued)

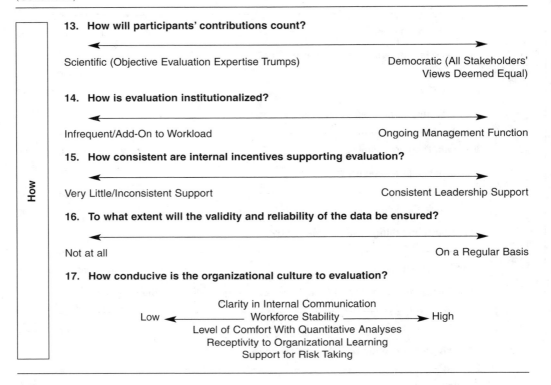

programs have clearly specified, understood, and validated theories of change, agreement on appropriate measures for outputs and outcomes is more likely to exist than in providers employing newer, less tested interventions.

A definite trend over the last decade has been for funders (and taxpayers) to ask for data on program outcomes rather than outputs. Robert Fischer (2001) deemed this move to prioritizing measurement of outcomes a "sea of change in nonprofit human services" (p. 561). The United Way's seminal guidebook in 1996 framed the challenge as outcomes (not outputs) assessment, and in June 1996, the organization launched a 3-year study to follow the experience with outcomes assessment of seven United Way agencies (United Way of America, 1996). The Urban Institute's guidebooks for nonprofits focus on outcomes as well.

The United Way (1996) has defined *outcomes* as "benefits or changes for individuals or populations during or after participating in program activities" (p. 1). The notion is that the focus of measurement for providers should be on the results of the services they provide. *Outputs* are more likely to constitute workload reporting (e.g., clients trained) and not capture achievement of service goals. Tabulation of services delivered is much more feasible for the providers than assessing results. Workload is controllable; clients typically are not. Tracking results of services entails follow-up, and this translates into more work for providers and will require more resources. Simply finding clients for programs serving quite transient populations may be severely challenging as well as time-consuming (Urban Institute, 2003b).

A quite common dilemma that agencies collecting performance data face is determining how many things to measure. Again, it depends on the sort of service provided and how far out on the outcome chain one goes, but there is rarely an obvious, "correct" set of measures (Cutt & Murray, 2000). Experience with the U.S. federal and local governments has shown that typically, service providers measure too many things and the information overload can become distracting rather than enlightening.

A common complaint voiced by nonprofits that receive funding from multiple sources is that they are required to count different things, or count similar things differently, for different funders. The burden of data collection can then constitute a challenge in itself.

Who bears the burden of data collection? Typically, nonprofit staffs collect data, and small- to medium-sized agencies usually lack separate trained evaluation staff for this purpose. It is possible that earmarked evaluation set-asides permit agencies to hire contract help or professional evaluators to bear the collection burden. However, the more common trade-offs in allocating operational funds for evaluation versus service delivery are not welcome by program managers.

Both timing and frequency of data collection activities clearly contribute to the perceptions and real monetary burden imposed by measurement. Following up with clients is time-consuming, as noted, and the degree to which the feasible measurement of outcomes is in sync with reporting requirements can produce more headaches for providers. For example, when grant-reporting requirements specify submission of measures on an annual basis and program theory indicates a longer trajectory for demonstrating effectiveness, providers face some tough choices.

Resources available for evaluation affect many choices agency managers make regarding measurement. When the funding to support performance data collection must compete with operating resources, it is likely that program assessment will suffer. Follow-up is expensive, and commitment of regular program staff to program assessment is likely to seem too costly.

Evaluation processes within nonprofits vary tremendously. For example, there has been a noticeable trend toward involving more stakeholders in program evaluation or assessment, planning, and implementation (Fine et al., 1998; Thayer, 2006). Boards, staff, volunteers, and clients are more and more likely to participate to some degree in performance assessment processes, in cooperation with professional evaluators internal or external to the agency. For more on inclusion of stakeholders, see Chapter 13 in this volume, by Holzer and Kloby. The extent to which the "voice" of the various stakeholders counts in evaluation assessment planning or oversight no doubt varies and may provide interesting power dynamics for program managers.

The manner in which regular performance assessment processes are institutionalized in agencies can provide yet more dilemmas for program managers. Routinized, virtually seamless systems for serving and tracking clients certainly make performance assessment less disruptive for program management. However, design and maintenance of systems impose requirements and require staff investment—both in time and commitment.

In the end, leadership support and organizational culture will significantly affect the receptivity to evaluation and performance assessment within service providers. Consistent leadership support throughout organizations has been repeatedly identified as a critical ingredient for useful and smooth performance measurement (Newcomer, 2002; Poister, 2003). The priority that leadership places on assessing the quality of services is yet another critical factor that can facilitate receptivity to collecting data from beneficiaries. See Chapter 19 in this volume, by Aristigueta, for more on quality assessment.

Service agencies in which the professional backgrounds of the staff make them comfortable with research and/or quantitative analyses are more receptive to performance assessment. In addition, agencies with lower turnover are also likely to provide more stability for supporting assessment systems. However, the tone set by agency leadership and reinforced in the culture will shape the way evaluation plays out.

Aspects of organizational culture that are correlated with receptivity to organizational learning, such as clarity in communication and support for risk taking, certainly are likely to increase the probability that providers will develop useful assessment strategies (Poole, Davis, Reisman, & Nelson, 2001). The assessment William Woodwell (2005) recently offered about the use of evaluation in foundations applies to the providers they fund as well.

Results. Impact. Return on Investment. These and similar words are becoming part of the lexicon in grantmaking today. Among the reasons: calls for more accountability and transparency from boards, the media, and others to show quantifiable results—and fast.

It is a climate in which evaluation has attracted increasing attention in the philanthropic community. However, among grant makers who are leading the way in evaluating their work, there is a growing sense that the purpose of evaluation is not only to track results and impact. Evaluation also can be a powerful tool for learning. . . . Viewing evaluation as a pathway to learning is the latest stage in grant makers' thinking about the role of evaluation in philanthropy. (p. 4)

Woodwell noted that organizational cultures that support collaboration, for example, foundations that encourage open dialogue between grantors and grantees about what is working successfully, are more likely to produce more effective knowledge sharing and learning.

Evolving Challenges

Meeting the demands of funders and other stakeholders for information about results means service providers must face difficult choices on how to measure performance. Routine reporting on program outputs and outcomes is the new reality for social service providers. Quandaries over resources and data collection challenges are likely to persist into the future. But what are some of the less tractable and still-evolving challenges social service providers face in performance and evaluation? The following list of issues highlights areas in which more research on the actual use of evaluation written nonprofits is needed.

How do we move beyond measuring outcomes to attributing results to programs? Measuring the net impact of an intervention requires more sophisticated research methodology than routine outcome assessment. Random experiments or the use of comparable comparison groups are typically out of the realm of the possible for many nonprofit providers. The challenge is to provide evidence of plausible attribution, so that client outcomes can be reasonably linked to programs. Linking improved client outcomes to service is easier for some services than for others, and disentangling the relative contributions of different programs to clients who receive benefits from multiple providers constitutes yet another challenge. For example, measuring the outcomes of more intangible services, such as preventative health media campaigns or policy advocacy programs, is still elusive, although innovative tools are being offered (for example, see the National Council of Nonprofit Association Toolkit, 2004). Research on cost-effective means of assessing outcomes of informational services is needed.

How do we develop feasible and useful benchmarking processes? Proponents of "scorecards" and "dashboard" tools argue that monitoring key measures can be useful for both accountability and internal management. But balancing the sets of measures to support management as well as report to funders is not easy, as there are multiple users, with different values. Benchmarking requires identifying comparable client bases, external environments, and valid and reliable data. Determining when and how benchmarking can be useful to support organizational learning remains an interesting challenge, one meriting more in-depth research on effective use of such tools.

How do we move beyond measuring programmatic outcomes to community-level indicators? Foundations, governments, and citizens are increasingly asking how well communities are served by collections of individual service providers. There is much dialogue about reframing the target of providers to community improvement. Community Builders in Australia provides guidance on the World Wide Web for nonprofit service providers to help them focus on "results accountability," which they define as "accountability by the community to the community for the well-being (results) of a population. It organizes the work of programs, agencies, communities, cities, countries, and states around the end conditions we seek for those who live in the community" (see http://www.communitybuilders.nsw.gov.au).

Some foundations, such as the Annie E. Casey Foundation, are asking grantees to focus on community impact. For example, in 1999, the Casey Foundation started a 10-year, 10-community initiative, "Making Connections," that provides funding for evaluation infrastructure to help the service providers they fund measure community-level change. They are encouraging the multiple providers in the 10 communities to collaborate in developing community-level measures. Participation of citizens and local governments as well as the set of social service providers is invited. Such extensive collaboration is no easy task. Developing and sustaining useful participation for stakeholders in program evaluation has received much attention in the professional literature (Cousins & Whitmore, 1998; deNegri, Berengere, Ilinigumugabo, Muvandi, & Lewis, 1998; Fetterman, 2001; King, 1998; and Thayer, 2006). Most observers agree that participation is necessary and valuable yet time-consuming for service providers. Case study research is needed on how stakeholders of service providers participate in evaluation endeavors and their use of evaluation findings.

How do we develop performance measurement systems that support provider and community learning? Ideally, ongoing measurement can support information needs for accountability, management, and evaluation. As Figure 2.3 illustrates, programmatic measurement processes can inform all three vital organizational functions: management, evaluation, and accountability. Yet moving beyond "counting for accountability" is hard when resources are tight, funder expectations about appropriate questions to address (e.g., impacts) are rising, and provider staff lack the skills and/or commitment to use data to learn about what works.

Foundations and other funders typically do not provide funds to train nonprofit staff in evaluation methods or in managing cultural change, and changing the perspectives of nonprofit staff about the value of an evaluative mind-set may well constitute the largest obstacle. There have been public dialogue and academic writing about the potential for "gaming," "creaming," and selective reporting when performance measurement is required of service providers by funders (for example, see Fischer, 2001; Forsythe, 2001; Kravchuk & Schack, 1996).

However, malfeasance on the part of managers or staff is far less likely to constitute a barrier than is benign neglect. Lack of confidence in the validity and reliability of data collected, lack of trust in the espoused use of the data, and lack of time and/or commitment to analyze and make sense of the data are far more formidable barriers to learning than purposeful manipulation for deceitful ends. Research would be helpful on the benefits reaped by managers in service providers as their performance measurement systems mature.

Learning how to ask and address useful questions about agency performance to improve programs is harder than it sounds. Identifying appropriate leading indicators to signal the likelihood of reaching longer-term outcomes for clients may be tricky, especially for services targeting complex problems. The potential is there for providers to better understand the complex processes through which agency actions interact with contextual factors in the community (e.g., rising unemployment, the actions or inactions of other providers) to affect the well-being of clients, their families, and neighborhoods, but it may be an unrealized potential. Empowering staff in service providers to take ownership in measurement processes and to devote the time needed for reflection on what the data can tell them continues to present a critical lever to move measurement beyond counting merely for accounting.

References

Ammons, D. N. (1995). *Accountability for performance: Measurement and monitoring in local government.* Washington, DC: International City/County Management Association.

Cantu, S., Cleveland, C., & Shall, K. (2006). *An evaluation of the Anacostia senior high school tutoring program.* Unpublished manuscript.

Cousins, J. B., & Whitmore, E. (1998). Framing participatory evaluation. *New Directions in Education, 89,* 8–23.

Cutt, J., & Murray, V. (2000). *Accountability and effectiveness evaluation in nonprofit organizations* (Routledge Studies in the Management of Voluntary and Nonprofit Organizations, Series). New York: Routledge.

deNegri, Berengere, E., Ilinigumugabo, T. A., Muvandi, I., & Lewis, G. (1998). *Empowering communities: Participatory techniques for community-based programme development, 1(2). Trainer's manual (Participant's handbook).* Baltimore: Centre for African Family Studies (CAFS), in collaboration with the Johns Hopkins University Center for Communication Programs and the Academy for Educational Development.

Fetterman, D. M. (2001). *Foundations of empowerment evaluation.* Thousand Oaks, CA: Sage.

Fine, A. F., Thayer, C. E., & Coghlan, A. (1998). *Program evaluation practice in the nonprofit sector.* Washington, DC: Innovation Network.

Fischer, R. L. (2001). The sea of change in nonprofit human services: A critical assessment of outcomes measurement. *Families in Society, 82,* 561–569.

Forsythe, D. (2001). *Quicker, better, cheaper: Managing performance in American government.* Albany, NY: Rockefeller Institute Press.

Government Performance and Results Act of 1993, Pub. L. No. 103–62 [S20] 107 Stat. 285.

Hall, P. D. (2004). A historical perspective on evaluation in foundations. In M. T. Braverman, N. A. Constantine, & J. K. Slater (Eds.), *Foundations and evaluation: Context and practices for effective philanthropy* (pp. 27–50). San Francisco: Jossey-Bass.

Hendricks, M. (2002). Outcome measurement in the nonprofit sector: Recent developments, incentives and challenges. In K. Newcomer, E. T. Jennings Jr., C. Broom, & A. Lomax (Eds.), *Meeting the challenges of performance-oriented government* (pp. 99–123). Washington, DC: American Society for Public Administration.

Houchin, S., & Nicholson, H. J. (2005). Holding ourselves accountable: Managing by outcomes in Girls Incorporated. *Nonprofit and Voluntary Sector Quarterly, 33,* 271–277.

Kaplan, R. S. (2001). Strategic performance measurement and management in non-profit organizations. *Nonprofit Management & Leadership, 11,* 353–370.

Kettl, D. F. (1997). The global revolution in public management: Driving themes, missing links. *Journal of Policy Analysis and Management, 16,* 446–462.

Kettl, D. F. (2000). *The global public management revolution: A report on the transformation of governance.* Washington, DC: Brookings Institution Press.

King, J. A. (1998). Making sense of participatory evaluation practice. In E. Whitmore (Ed.), Understanding and practicing participatory evaluation. *New Directions for Evaluation, 80,* pp. 57–68. San Francisco: Jossey-Bass.

Kopczynski, M. E., & Pritchard, K. (2004). The use of evaluation by nonprofit organizations. In J. S. Wholey, H. P. Hatry, & K. E. Newcomer (Eds.), *Handbook of practical program evaluation* (2nd ed., pp. 649–669). San Francisco: Jossey-Bass.

Kravchuk, R. S., & Schack, R. W. (1996, July). Designing effective performance measurement systems under the Government Performance and Results Act of 1993. *Public Administration Review,* pp. 348–358.

Light, P. C. (2002). *Pathways to nonprofit excellence.* Washington, DC: Brookings Institution Press.

Light, P. C. (2004). *Sustaining nonprofit performance: The case for capacity building and the evidence to support it.* Washington, DC: Brookings Institution Press.

McLaughlin, J. A., & Jordan, G. B. (2004). Using logic models. In J. S. Wholey, H. P. Hatry, & K. E. Newcomer (Eds.), *Handbook of practical program evaluation* (2nd ed., pp. 7–32). San Francisco: Jossey-Bass.

Moore, M. (2003, May). *The public value scorecard: A rejoinder and an alternative to "strategic performance measurement and management in non-profit organizations," by Robert Kaplan* (Working Paper #18). Cambridge, MA: Harvard University, Kennedy School of Government, Hauser Center for Nonprofit Organizations. Also available online at http://www.ksg.harvard.edu/hauser/PDF_XLS/workingpapers/workingpaper_18.pdf

Murray, V. (2001, Spring). The state of evaluation tools and systems for nonprofit organizations. *New Directions for Philanthropic Fundraising, 31,* 39–49.

National Council of Nonprofit Association Toolkit. (2004). *Evaluation for state associations.* Washington, DC: Author. Available online at http://www.ncna.org/_uploads/documents/live//Evaluation_Tool_Kit.pdf

Newcomer, K. (Ed.). (1997). *Using performance measurement to improve public and nonprofit programs.* San Francisco: Jossey-Bass.

Newcomer, K. (Ed.). (2002). *Meeting the challenges of performance-oriented government*. Washington, DC: American Society for Public Administration.

Nielsen, W. A. (1985). *The golden donors: A new anatomy of the great foundations.* New York: Dutton.

Osborne, D., & Gaebler, T. (1992). *Reinventing government: How the entrepreneurial spirit is transforming the public sector from schoolhouse to statehouse, city hall to the Pentagon.* Reading, MA: Addison-Wesley.

Patrizi, P., & McMullan, B. (1998). *Evaluation in foundations: The unrealized potential.* Battle Creek, MI: W. K. Kellogg Foundation Evaluation Unit.

Plantz, M. C., Greenway, M. T., & Hendricks, M. (1997). Outcome measurement: Showing results in the nonprofit sector. *New Directions for Evaluation, 75,* 15–30.

Poister, T. H. (2003). *Measuring performance in public and nonprofit organizations* (Jossey-Bass Nonprofit and Public Management Series). San Francisco: Jossey-Bass.

Poole, D. L., Davis, J. K., Reisman, J., & Nelson, J. E. (2001). Improving the quality of outcome evaluation plans. *Nonprofit Management & Leadership, 11,* 405–421.

Savaya, R., & Waysman, M. (2005). The logic model: A tool for incorporating theory in development and evaluation of programs. *Administration in Social Work, 29*(2), 85–103.

Thayer, C. (2006). *Participatory evaluation in nonprofit organizations: Rhetoric or reality?* Doctoral dissertation, The George Washington University, Washington, DC.

United Way of America. (1996). *Measuring program outcomes: A practical approach.* Fairfax, VA: Author.

United Way of America. (2000). *Agency experiences with outcome measurement: Survey findings* (Outcome Measurement Resource Network). Fairfax, VA: Author. Available at http://national.unitedway.org/files/pdf/outcomes/agencyom.pdf

The Urban Institute. (2002). *Findings from a symposium: How and why nonprofits use outcome information.* Washington, DC: Author.

The Urban Institute. (2003a). *Developing community-wide outcome indicators for specific services* (Series on Outcome Management for Nonprofit Organizations). Washington, DC: Author. Available at http://www.urban.org/UploadedPDF/310813_OutcomeIndicators.pdf

The Urban Institute. (2003b). *Finding out what happens to former clients* (Series on Outcome Management for Nonprofit Organizations). Washington, DC: Author. Available at http://www.urban.org/UploadedPDF/310815_former_clients.pdf

The Urban Institute. (2003c). *Key steps in outcome management* (Series on Outcome Management for Nonprofit Organizations). Washington, DC: Author. Available at http://www.urban.org/UploadedPDF/310776_KeySteps.pdf

The Urban Institute. (2003d). *Surveying clients about outcomes* (Series on Outcome Management for Nonprofit Organizations). Washington, DC: Author. Available at http://www.urban.org/UploadedPDF/310840_surveying_clients.pdf

The Urban Institute. (2004a). *Analyzing outcome information: Getting the most from data* (Series on Outcome Management for Nonprofit Organizations). Washington, DC: Author. Available at http://www.urban.org/UploadedPDF/311040_OutcomeInformation.pdf

The Urban Institute. (2004b). *Using outcome information: Making data pay off* (Series on Outcome Management for Nonprofit Organizations). Washington, DC: Author. Available at http://www.urban.org/UploadedPDF/311040_OutcomeIn formation.pdf

U.S. Government Accountability Office. (2004). *Results-oriented government: GPRA has established a solid foundation for achieving greater results* (GAO-04–38). Washington, DC: Author.

U.S. Government Accountability Office. (2005). *Program evaluation: OMB's PART reviews increased agencies' attention to improving evidence of program results* (GAO-06–67). Washington, DC: Author.

Westley, F., Zimmerman, B., & Patton, M. (in press). *Getting to maybe: How to change the world.* Toronto, Canada: Random House.

Woodwell, W. H. (2005). *Evaluation as a pathway to learning: Current topics in evaluation for grantmakers.* Washington, DC: Grantmakers for Effective Organizations.

3

Performance

A New Public Management Perspective

Owen E. Hughes

The period since the early 1990s has seen quite remarkable reform in the public sectors of many countries around the world (Kettl, 2000). The similarity of these reforms is a matter of some contention, as is their relative extent (Pollitt & Bouckaert, 2004). It can be argued, however, that the centerpiece of the managerial reforms has been that of performance management, broadly defined. Over this time, as the Organisation for Economic Co-operation and Development (OECD) argues, its member administrations "have become more efficient, more transparent and customer oriented, more flexible, and more focused on performance" (OECD, 2005, p. 10). These managerial reforms based on markets and focused on improving public sector performance are often referred to as "New Public Management" (NPM), a term coined by Hood (1991) that has developed widespread currency in public management, especially in countries other than the United States.

This chapter is concerned mostly with the transition from traditional public administration to managerial models, especially that of NPM, in a theoretical and cross-national sense, rather than looking at the details of any one country. Improving performance is central to NPM and other managerial reform; indeed, the transition to managerialism was driven to a large extent by concerns over the performance of traditional public administration.

It will be argued that the earlier, traditional model of public administration did aim at organizational performance, but only indirectly. Agencies and individuals were to achieve results of some kind, but it was assumed that the best way of doing this was through strict bureaucratic organization. One-best-way thinking in public administration, exemplified by scientific management (Taylor, 1911), led to the view that the bureaucracy would determine the single most rational outcome and implement it. Through organization and rationality, performance would result and, implicitly, did not need to be measured directly.

A managerial approach requires performance to be considered in a new way. Bureaucratic organization, by itself, is insufficient to ensure results. It follows that there needs to be some other way to measure performance. *Performance indicators, performance appraisal, performance management,* and other such terms have become part of the discourse of public management and the reality on the ground. The use of these ideas has attracted some criticism along the lines that performance cannot be measured adequately in government, that performance indicators are inherently flawed, and that performance appraisal of individual civil servants is unfair as public sector staff are hard to compare in terms of their competence and skill. It is often claimed that a public agency has no measure comparable to that of profit in the private sector. Surely this means that performance measurement in government is inherently problematic.

On the other hand, if a government agency is spending taxpayer money, it needs to be able to demonstrate that public purposes are, in fact, being served. It needs, therefore, to show that it is achieving whatever task it has been given. In other words, the agency, its programs, and its staff have to show that they have performed. Of course, no measurement system can work perfectly. The key point is whether or not performance measurement and performance management are better than they were before. It is argued here that agencies and individuals are inevitably judged in some way and that logical, understandable systems of performance measurement are, even with their limitations, much better than the ad hoc ways used before. Once a manager is responsible for the achievement of results, it follows that there needs to be some way of showing that the required results have in fact been achieved.

This chapter looks at performance in the transition from traditional public administration to managerial models, especially that of NPM, in a theoretical and cross-national sense. This transition was largely driven by concerns that traditional public administration did not ensure that performance would be achieved and that more direct means of measuring performance were needed.

From Administration to Management and Performance

It can be argued that there are differences in the meanings of *administration* and *management* (French & Saward, 1983; Hood, 2005). The key difference evident throughout the philology and etymology is that management is rather more active than administration: An *administrator* serves, obeys, and follows instructions; a *manager* takes charge and gets results (see Hughes, 2003). Both words derive from Latin, with administration deriving from *minor*, than *ministrare*, meaning, "to serve, and hence later, to govern." Management comes from *manus*, meaning, "to control by hand." The essential difference in meaning is between "to serve" and "to control or gain results." Management does include administration but also involves organization to achieve objectives, as well as genuine responsibility for achieving results.

The adoption of management principles within government with NPM-type reform reflects these differences. Hood (2005) argues that *public management* "remains a well-established term that has succeeded in becoming embedded into government and academic institutions" (p. 11). He also argues that "linguistic change takes place for a reason" (p. 12). It is argued here that the reason for *public management* being more widely used is simply that that it has become a better description of the work in the public sector. A public manager is required to achieve results and to take personal responsibility for doing so. *Public administration* focuses on process, procedures, service, and propriety. All these are undoubtedly worthy and should not be lost. However, the most important point in the shift from public administration to public management is that a manager is to be accountable for the achievement of results.

Performance management in the traditional model of administration was inadequate, and this applies to either the performance of individuals or the organization. Measures that did exist were only impressionistic and far from systematic. Certainly public administrators had to organize the bureau, hire staff, and train and promote them and perform all the other aspects of the personnel system, but the *controlling* of performance, in terms of meeting objectives, financial management, and personnel management, was always rather weak. And an administrator in the true sense of the word could evade responsibility by saying that the instructions were not adequate and that monitoring performance was the role of whoever issued the instructions.

Furthermore, measuring performance in a comprehensive way was often considered too difficult in the traditional administrative model. Often, government agencies had no explicit objectives as to what they were trying to achieve other than merely administer their mandates. The financial systems available in traditional administration were unable to provide information in a form to enable real monitoring of performance. Financial management was concerned only with inputs, regardless of what was produced, how well it was produced, and whether or not what was produced was valued or desired. Assessment of individual personnel performance was seen as intrusive and unfair, which is why there was resort to such unsatisfactory devices as the seniority system for promotion. All these factors have changed substantially; all are now in some way able to be measured.

It is undeniable that there are difficulties in measuring performance in the public sector when compared with the private sector, but it seemed that little effort was made during this era. Evaluation of programs or people was infrequent and inadequate, with no idea of progress toward objectives, if, indeed, there were any objectives specified. The old system "generally worked well when governments had less complex and more standardized tasks to perform—and when complying with the rules was considered more important than efficiency or effectiveness" (OECD, 2005, p. 57).

A key reason for managerial reform in government was a view in the community, or at least in the more informed parts of it, that the public sector was not performing well. The 1970s and 1980s witnessed attacks on government on the basis of size, scale, and crowding out of the private sector as well as on the bureaucratic model of administration as being inadequate for a new age that demanded results. Economic problems meant that governments reassessed their bureaucracies and demanded changes.

Reforms followed in a number of countries (Kettl, 2000). The managerial reforms included widespread privatization, much greater use of contracting, real cuts in public servant numbers, reducing employment conditions to those more common in the private sector, lateral recruitment to all levels, and financial management reforms that include program budgeting and full accrual accounting, to name but a few. The single biggest driver is that of improving performance. As an OECD (2005) paper argues,

> Over the past two decades, enhancing public sector performance has taken on a new urgency in OECD member countries as governments face mounting demands on public expenditure, calls for higher quality services and, in some countries, a public increasingly unwilling to pay higher taxes. (p. 56)

Governments wishing to cut the public sector found little opposition from a community seemingly disillusioned with bureaucratic performance. The reform movement was in large part a response to this view that more and better performance was needed. Public management reforms, especially NPM reforms, have been controversial, but it is undoubted that a major factor in the reform process was the widely held view, including from political leaders, that public services were simply not delivering the required level of performance.

The real leaders of NPM reforms, most notably in the United Kingdom, New Zealand, and Australia, have more often been elected political leaders who wish to get something done. As Rubin and Kelly (2005) argue, part of the reason for some of the reforms "is because they seem to give elected officials more policy control, more policy tools" (p. 586). Early reforms in the United Kingdom were highly ideological (Pollitt, 1990), as exemplified by the reforms of Prime Minister Thatcher in the 1980s. Later, however, the reform process seems to have been driven more pragmatically by what may deliver more service for less money. Political leaders of the Left and the

Right in different countries have followed a similar agenda of improving performance through bringing in economic principles and private sector management practices to government.

The NPM Reforms

One of the difficulties in using the term *New Public Management* is that there is no real agreement as to what it includes. There is no single key theorist and no authoritative exposition, so NPM is sometimes used as a catchall phrase for all recent economic and managerial reform in government. Hood's original 1991 description of NPM was that of a perceptive observer who had noticed and was worried about—Hood was in no sense an advocate—what appeared to be a set of reasonably consistent reforms coming from governments and put them all together under that name. The term did become widely accepted, perhaps because it filled a need.

Different views do agree, however, that the improvement of performance is a major part of NPM reform. One of the starting points of managerial reform, in 1982, was the Financial Management Initiative (FMI) in the United Kingdom that aimed at promoting "an organization and a system in which managers at all levels have clear view of their objectives; and means to assess, and wherever possible, measure, outputs or performance in relation to those objectives" (U.K. Treasury and Civil Service Committee, 1982). The FMI had implications for financial management but also for personnel and performance. Indeed, all three were to be linked together in a new management system that involved the specification of objectives for all government policies and for individual units within the bureaucracy, precise allocation of costs to activities and programs, and "the development of performance indicators and output measures which can be used to assess success in achieving objectives" (Carter, Klein, & Day, 1992, p. 5).

In 1991, the OECD claimed that most countries were following "two broad avenues" to improve production and delivery of publicly provided goods and services. One was to use markets more extensively; the other was to "raise the production performance of public organizations to improve the management of human resources including staff, development, recruitment of qualified talent and pay-for-performance . . . [and] relax administrative controls while imposing strict performance targets" (OECD, 1991, p. 11).

Hood (1991) argues there were seven main points to the NPM reform movement, including "explicit standards and measures of performance," whereby goals are required to be defined and performance targets set, and "greater emphasis on output controls," whereby resources would go to areas according to measured performance (pp. 4–5). This point is echoed in Osborne and Gaebler's (1992) 10-point plan for "entrepreneurial governments," which includes as one of the points that "they measure the performance of their agencies, focusing not on inputs but on *outcomes*" (p. 20).

In these specifications of managerial or NPM reform, there is a substantial focus on improvement of performance. Agencies are expected to develop performance indicators as a way of measuring the progress made toward achieving declared objectives. Managers need to achieve results and to demonstrate explicit measurement of such performance. Staff are to be appraised and rewarded or sanctioned accordingly. Other aspects of the NPM reform—privatization, contracting out, shrinking the size of the public sector—in many ways also focus on more and better performance.

Performance Management Purposes

There are two main purposes in measuring performance. Although Behn (2003) lists eight primary purposes for performance measurement—to *evaluate* performance, to *control* behavior, to *budget,* to *motivate* people, to *promote* an agency's competence, to *celebrate,* to *learn,* and to *improve*—he adds that "for the measurement of performance, the public manager's real purpose—indeed, the only real purpose—is to improve performance" (p. 598), and the others are means to that end. The first purpose, then, is to measure performance in order to improve performance.

The second main purpose is the need to show results to the wider community. In her 2005 Donald Stone Lecture, Ingraham argued that the demand for performance is "at its heart, about governance and accountability":

> Performance is a siren for modern government and justly so. Performance promises may be difficult to keep, but they are the right promises. It is right to expect that citizens' dollars are spent as efficiently and effectively as possible. It is important to expect that citizens see and understand the results of government programs. It is necessary that public employees and their leaders not twiddle their thumbs when public dollars are wasted on poorly planned or unrealistic public programs. Performance is, at its heart, about governance and accountability. For public organizations, and the role they play in governance, that link is essential. We must make the connection, even when it is painful to do so. (p. 391)

The public sector does need to be able to demonstrate to the wider citizenry that public money is not being wasted and that public employees are gainfully employed. One of the purposes of performance information is to build support for the important things that governments and public servants actually do.

A good manager realizes the need to build support in the wider community. Holmes and Shand (1995) regard a good managerial approach as including "a more strategic or results-oriented (efficiency, effectiveness, and service quality) approach to decision-making" in order to focus attention "on the matching of authority and responsibility as a key to improving performance" and, importantly, "greater accountability and transparency through requirements to report on results and their full costs" (p. 555). Accountability and transparency enable a positive story to be told, and this empowers agencies and managers for the future. As argued earlier, a manager is responsible for the achievement of performance, and this means that the performance needs to be visible in some way. Public managers are more often regarded as professionals who can be trusted to carry out their jobs, but this trust needs to then be verified through measures of individual and agency performance.

Performance Measurement

To show that performance has occurred, there is an obvious need to set out measures of that performance. Accountability for performance requires establishing "expectations for the outcomes that the agency will achieve, the consequences that it will create, or the impact that it will have," and as this cannot be done with rules or procedures, "we need some kind of objective, goal, or target—a clear benchmark of performance" and an "explicit measure of how well the agency has done against the expectations we have set for it" (Behn, 2001, p. 10).

Pollitt (2001) argues there are a number of general elements of the new model accepted by most commentators, one of which is "a shift towards more measurement, manifesting itself in the appearance of batteries of performance indicators and standards" (pp. 473–474). Agencies in many parts of government are expected to develop indicators to measure the progress the organization has made toward achieving declared objectives.

Government agencies do need to be able to specify objectives, that is, what they are trying to achieve. If objectives are clear, the measures of success or failure should be easy to set out. This is not easy to do. The mandates of an agency are in its legislation and regulation, but these usually provide only a partial basis for setting objectives. It is also necessary to develop reliable data and systems of collection to assist in setting objectives and concomitant measures of performance. Technology assists this process. It is no accident that the expansion in the use of performance indicators came at the same time as the expansion of the use of computers and complex databases within government.

Objectives need to be specified in terms that can be measured, but this is often difficult in practice. What is the precise objective of a health department, a hospital, or even a social welfare agency? Strategic management can assist in specifying objectives (Nutt & Backoff, 1992), but there is often ambiguity and goal displacement in government. It may be more difficult to determine objectives or to measure results in the public sector, and this may be one of the key differences between the public and private sectors. It is also difficult in much of the private sector as well, with profit not being the only objective or measure of performance. On the other hand, surely some attempt needs to be made to set objectives, as without objectives or purpose, why have a particular agency or government function at all?

Performance indicators are criticized for trying to specify the unspecifiable, given the inherent difficulties of measuring performance in the public sector. Some public servants will argue that the benefits brought by their particular organizations cannot be quantified or that empirical measurement distorts what it does by focusing only on those things that can be quantified and are able to be processed by the information system (Bellamy & Taylor, 1998). This may be a danger, but it can be overcome by setting measures directly related to the organization's overall success. Also, once objectives are set, they should not be set in concrete, but should be reasonably flexible. There is no point in rigidity, and it can even be counterproductive to persist with measures that have outlived their usefulness.

Measures need to be meaningful but parsimonious and have a direct impact on the operations of that part of the public sector being assessed. Poorly chosen performance measures may result in management focusing on achieving satisfactory results by the measures used, instead of achieving the best possible performance by the organization as a whole in a more abstract sense. An alternative is that the performance system as a whole, or the particular indicator, should be improved. A pattern seems to occur in which performance measures are initially both opposed and poorly conceived. Osborne and Gaebler (1992) argue that "this pattern—adoption of crude performance measures, followed by protest and pressure to improve the measures, followed by the development of more sophisticated measures—is common wherever performance is measured" (p. 156).

Flynn (2002) argues that much progress has been made in the development of performance management and measurement but there are still problems "caused by the fact that performance measurement is used for many different purposes" (p. 225). He states that "measures which are appropriate for external accountability may not be the right ones for improving management" and "measures which are used to expose poor performers publicly may not be the best ones for helping management to bring about improvements" (p. 225). This debate is discussed further by de Lancer Julnes, in Chapter 4 of this volume.

Carter, Klein, and Day (1992) argue similarly that different indicators can be developed for different purposes:

> Given different policy objectives, different kinds of performance indicator systems will emerge. So, for example, if the prime concern is with the efficient use of public resources, the emphasis will be on trying to devise output (and, if possible, outcome) measures: the approach of the economist. . . . If the prime concern is with accountability, then a rather different emphasis may emerge: process indicators which measure the way in which services are delivered to the public—their availability, their timeliness, may be more relevant. If the focus of attention is on managerial competence, then the stress may be on setting targets for the performance of individual units or branches. These objectives may, of course, coexist within the same branch. (p. 181)

Perhaps too much can be claimed for the use of performance indicators. Rather than being performance *measures*—perfect surrogates for profit in the private sector—they are really *indicators* of performance that are simply pointers to good or bad performance and do not try to measure it precisely. Not measuring performance is now inconceivable, but there are many better ways in which performance indicators can and should be used.

Performance indicators are undoubtedly hard to implement. There are particular problems in trying to measure all public activities in a meaningful way. Despite the difficulty, however, the attempt does need to be made. A manager without performance information would operate in a vacuum and could not be brought to account for either praise or blame. No one could point to successes or failures.

Financial Management

Financial management has been arguably the most successful of the public management reforms. These reforms have also been able to provide the data for wider performance purposes in ways not available in the traditional administrative model. The most important change in this area has been that of performance and program budgeting systems to replace the older line-item budget and accounting systems. The focus was formerly on inputs rather than outputs, or on what the agency actually does. A program budget allocates money according to specific programs of the agency, with all costs listed at program, subprogram, and even lower levels. Instead of staffing being determined by a separate, independent central agency for personnel, it becomes part of the program budget. The line-item system of budgeting was precise in a control sense, but, in practice, governments had little information on actual program delivery or performance in terms of efficiency.

NPM requires increased attention to be paid to the best use of resources. This includes cutting costs but also involves directing resources to emphasize programs that most assist the attainment of strategic objectives. Accrual accounting, as used in some more advanced countries, brings private sector practice to government accounts, providing much more information to decision makers. And governments have been able to control spending by having better information, in ways not available in traditional financial management. As Kamarck (2000) argues,

> Performance-based budgeting, the use of new accounting systems, and the general interest in accountability exhibited by some of these reform movements are part and parcel of an effort to bring the public sector's financial management more in line with commonly accepted practices in the private sector. Like civil service reform, many of the experiments in financial management reform seek to close the gap between the public and the private sector. (pp. 246–247)

The traditional budget makes no express link between allocation of money and performance. As this is its main failing, it seems an obvious enough reform to somehow link the budget with outputs and performance. The deficiencies of the line-item budget led to demands for better forms of budgeting, mainly by governments arguing that the traditional method of budgeting did not provide enough information for decision-making purposes.

Measuring Staff Performance

The performance of staff is also to be measured more systematically than before as part of overall performance management. The performance appraisal system aims to measure the performance of individual staff members, defining the key contributions expected over the year, which are then compared with actual achievement at the end of the year. This can extend to rewarding or sanctioning staff according to progress toward agreed objectives. Informal methods of appraisal are ineffective, often unfair, usually biased for and against particular social or ethnic groups, and lead to inferior organizational outcomes. There is a general aim to monitor and improve the progress of staff and agencies toward achieving objectives.

The traditional model seemed to give up on the whole idea of trying to measure staff performance. The idea of deciding who is an effective staff member and who is not may be against an egalitarian view of bureaucracy. It is also against the view that in the machine model of bureaucracy, individuals were to be mere ciphers, only implementing rules without judgment or discretion. This misplaced egalitarianism, combined with real difficulties of measuring individual performance, led to the widespread usage of seniority systems in personnel administration. In a seniority system, everyone in a given cohort is assumed to be equal and inherently better than those in next year's cohort. There may be countries and parts of the public service where seniority is still used, but no one now thinks that seniority was a good system of personnel management. It simply abandons any idea of trying to gauge who is actually the best worker.

Reforms to personnel management are aimed at better performance. They include staffing changes designed to better fit staff for their positions, to appraise their performance, and to reward them accordingly with merit pay. The emphasis on performance also leads to short-term appointments by contract and being able to terminate staff members who are not performing. There is much more lateral recruitment; indeed, recruitment to the base grade—the norm in the traditional bureaucracy—has almost vanished in some jurisdictions. It is by no means unusual for staff to be hired on contracts or to be appointed to the highest levels from outside. These changes derive from the private sector, where staffing and budgeting flexibility have long been utilized. They are buttressed by theoretical considerations from economics that organizations and individuals will not perform to their fullest unless an appropriate system of incentives is in place.

However, despite the attractions of a rigorous system of performance appraisal of staff in identifying both good and bad performers, it is difficult to design a system that provides reliable comparisons and is accepted by those involved. There have been problems of morale, and if the aim is to change the organizational culture, a new culture may be some distance away. Pollitt (1990) argues that "on the contrary, such evidence as there is points towards a widespread demoralization of those working in the public services, and a deep resentment and suspicion of the way they are being treated" (p. 178). Whether or not such demoralization continued beyond the early days of managerial reform is arguable. It may well have been difficult for staff to accept performance appraisal systems when they were first introduced. Since Pollitt wrote, however, it has become a fact of life in the private sector and the public sector that staff appraisal is here and here to stay. The positive side of the story is that employers are better able to find good performers in an era when it is hard to find and retain talented staff in public service.

Limitations of Performance Management

Performance measures are needed in order to judge the manager's achievement of results. There are limitations, though, even within an NPM view. As Holmes and Shand argue (1995), "Our contention is that performance measurement and its wider use in performance management is a worthwhile exercise as long as it is done in full knowledge of its limitations" (p. 563). There are limitations to performance management in government. Five of these are discussed here: the difficulties of implementation, operating in a political environment, comparison with the private sector, cultural change, and limitations of the NPM model itself.

The first limitation is that of implementation. Even if it is generally agreed that performance should be measured, there are obvious difficulties in getting a system in place. Flynn (2002) argues that if performance measurement is to improve performance, "all the relevant measures must be made, not just those that are easy to count," and, he adds, "managers and workers must be consulted about which measures are true reflections of their success; users of services must also be involved in choosing relevant criteria, and managers should only be held to account for those elements over which they have some control" (p. 225). It would be unfair to blame managers for lack of achievement over matters they could not influence.

Rigidity in the implementation of performance management may cause problems, as an OECD (2005) paper argues:

> The performance orientation of public management is here to stay. It is essential for successful government. Societies are now too complex to be managed only by rules for input and process and a public-spirited culture. The performance movement has increased formalized planning, reporting

and control across many governments. This has improved the information available to managers and policy makers. But experience shows that this can risk leading to a new form of bureaucratic sclerosis. More attention needs to be given to keeping performance transactions costs in check, and to making optimal use of social and internalized motivators and controls. (p. 81)

A good performance management system would be one that did not add greatly to costs, was reasonably flexible, and was meaningful. However, managing performance is not easy. It is hard to implement performance management systems: Indicators can always be disputed; appraisal can be unfair, even if not as unfair as no appraisal; and performance budgeting can submerge real information with a morass of detail. Nonetheless, performance management is the essence of management itself and is therefore worth the effort.

A second limitation is that performance must take place within a government and in a political environment, and this affects the utility of performance measurement. The public service must serve the interests of a political party in power: a party headed by politicians. This imposes limitations on how far objectives can be specified or ranked and how they might be achieved. As Zifcak (1994) argues, "a multitude of complex, value-laden and conflicting societal demands press in upon the administration generating within it an impressive but bewildering array of competing purposes incapable of easy reconciliation" (p. 190).

Performance measures are inevitably affected by the political environment: Performance data can be used as ammunition in political debate. Even if originally established to monitor agency and managerial performance, the numbers derived from performance indicators can be used to create an impression of government competence or incompetence. Perhaps this is just another part of the political game, which has become more driven by data than it was. But it can also mean some downplaying or understating of performance measures by politicians who may become less enthusiastic about their use. There is, then, a need to develop performance measures that politicians as well as public managers are quite happy to use. The political basis of the public sector does complicate the management task, but public managers have shown a great deal of adaptation to the new environment so that the complexities of managing in a political context become part of the overall managerial task.

A third limitation is how far measures in government can compare with those in the private sector. The original idea of the managerial reformers was to provide some surrogate measure for the use of profit and other measures in the private sector. Without some attempt at measuring performance, the other aspects of the managerial program will not work. It is important, however, that performance measures be developed for the specific needs of the public sector and to realize that all measures have their limitations. It is obviously easier to use indicators for programs where there are tangible outputs in a process sense; it is harder, though possible, in complex areas such as health and education and "very difficult to apply to activities such as policy advice where the service is non-tangible and outcomes are not visible" (OECD, 2005, p. 75).

It is unlikely that any one measure of performance in the public sector will be as good as that of profit in the private sector, although it is also the case that the private sector has major issues with performance management, too. In reality, private sector companies use a variety of measures other than simply profit. Accounting standards are not fixed, but are constantly being refined. And while a sustained period of financial loss can affect the standing of management, there is by no means a direct and certain form of accountability. A company can have objectives other than immediate profit, such as increasing market share. A poor result can be explained away by managers.

There is an entire industry in the private sector providing performance assessments of companies. This occurs because there is no single agreed-upon performance measure, so there are various competing ratings, rankings, and indices. Competition is probably a more effective driving force than any form of measurement. Again, this is analogous to the public sector. Public organizations are competitors for scarce budgetary resources, and governments wish to have some means for deciding which parts of their operations are using resources well.

Of course, there are difficulties in measuring performance and greater ones in the public sector, but this does not mean that no attempt should be made. The tenor of much criticism seems to suggest abandonment of performance management altogether because it is too difficult in the public sector by comparison to the private sector. One problem with this view is that in neither public nor private sector is performance perfection to be found.

A fourth limitation concerns some doubt about using performance measures to drive cultural change. In one of the earlier views of performance indicators, Pollitt (1990) argues that the main impact has been on staff morale and that the impact of change on performance has not been great despite the cost and staff cuts that have accompanied managerial change, adding that "there is as yet little evidence of fundamental cultural change in most public services" (p. 178). In addition, in something of a contrast to the OECD's normal role as one of the leaders in pushing for public management reform, a 2005 publication by that organization mentions a similar point about cultural change. It argues that governments should "be wary of over-rating the potential of performance-oriented approaches to change behavior and culture, and of underestimating the limitations of performance-based systems" (OECD, 2005, p. 11).

This warning may be apt, but it is also obvious and overdone. In the narrow sense, there might be some point in warning that the adoption by agencies of performance systems may not lead to direct and measurable cultural change. What they apparently do not consider is that such change is well accepted in the sector as a whole, at least in jurisdictions where reform has been substantial.

It has become normal for staff to expect performance appraisal. It is normal for the organization and its constituent parts to be measured in some way. Staff recruited in more recent years not only accept this, but would find it odd for such measures not to be in place. Measurement is pervasive, so pervasive that there are few public servants with memories of the old system before performance-based reforms occurred. This reflects a substantial cultural change, but there is a limitation in that any expectation of overnight change and acceptance is clearly unrealistic.

The fifth and final limitation discussed here is that of the NPM model itself. There are many strengths in NPM: Economic thinking is clearly valuable with a governmental context, and, indeed, it is unrealistic to keep it out; private management practice can be applied to government with benefits; some activities formerly within government should not have been there; and focusing on performance and efficiency is surely right and proper. That being said, there are limitations in the adoption of NPM.

NPM, at least in its earlier, more ideological incarnations, shares with the traditional model of administration a one-best-way view of the world. The bureaucracy, by its monopoly on the sources of information, would ideally make the single best decision, which would then be a precedent for the future as recorded by the files. In NPM, the one best way to act is that which is informed and predicted by economic theory. If a policy prescription could work in theory, it would be assumed to be workable in practice, but the public sector environment is more complex than that of the market sector. Economics works best where there are markets; private management practices and theories need careful translation in their application to government. This is not to say that these theories should not be used; rather, they should be used judiciously.

Another point is that, as argued earlier, NPM reforms focus on allowing the manager to manage by determining objectives and later measuring the achievement of results. To achieve objectives, a manager should be able to decide how to do just that and ideally to do so with considerable managerial flexibility. In reality, managers are still often subject to the same kinds of rule constraints as were evident in the traditional model—indeed, sometimes even more.

Despite the limitations, there are several reasons why performance measures will continue to be used. First, individual public servants may see the use of indicators and appraisals as a threat, despite the fact that they can become opportunities by pointing to good practices and good performance, both of which may be rewarded. Second, any public activity is under threat of being cut or removed altogether in the current climate, and a function or position in which measures of performance are inadequate is much more vulnerable. Third, there is little point in setting clear objectives or funding programs accordingly, unless there is some means by which progress toward objectives can be monitored.

Conclusion

Monitoring and measuring performance is without doubt a major feature of the public management reforms in general and NPM reforms in particular. Agencies are required to state their objectives, and their performance against those objectives is then to be measured. Performance indicators point to achievements. Performance budgeting allows the achievements of an agency to be measured against its budget, and accrual accounting provides much better information on the effects and effectiveness of government funding. Personnel management has moved some distance away from the unsatisfactory methods of the traditional model, whereby, in the name of equity, personnel procedures almost guaranteed mediocrity. Performance can be measured in the public sector, not perfectly, it is true, but perfection is an unattainable goal in any management system.

Comparisons or studies should not look at how well the reforms work in the abstract—how they approach perfection—but rather how well they compare with what went before them. In the traditional model of administration, financial management, personnel management, and performance management were of dubious quality; therefore, any change at all should prove to be a significant improvement. The inadequacy of performance measures in the past may have led to the suspicion that this shortcoming served to hide poor performance. Accordingly, the suspicion, if not the actuality, of poor performance has been one of the key reasons put forward for reducing the size of the public sector. In some countries, notably Australia and New Zealand, it would be inconceivable to manage now without formal systems of performance management.

Public management reforms in general and NPM reforms in particular look at results first, with no preconceived notion as to how these should occur. The focus on results has led, in turn, to the establishment of financial, performance, and personnel systems for some assessment of success in achieving goals and objectives. There are now greater imperatives to ensure that money is not wasted, which was more than likely the main reason for the managerial reform process being started in the first place.

NPM does not work in all circumstances, but, then, neither does the traditional model of bureaucracy. What is important is to be clear as to the strengths and weaknesses of both and the situations in which each may work best. The traditional model paid little attention to the monitoring and measurement of performance; the NPM model focuses on the achievement of performance above everything else. The way ahead, as is increasingly realized in countries where NPM reform has proceeded furthest, is to achieve requisite levels of performance without losing altogether some of the traditional values underlying public administration. A set of radical reforms introduced at the beginning of the NPM movement is changing to a relatively pragmatic approach to use whatever works in a given circumstance. What has not changed, and will not, is the need for public agencies and public managers to demonstrate that they are achieving results: In other words, that they are performing.

References

Behn, R. D. (2001). *Rethinking democratic accountability*. Washington, DC: Brookings Institution Press.

Behn, R. D. (2003). Why measure performance? Different purposes require different measures. *Public Administration Review, 63*, 586–606.

Bellamy, C., & Taylor, J. A. (1998). *Governing in the information age*. Buckingham, UK: Open University Press.

Carter, N., Klein, R., & Day, P. (1992). *How organisations measure success*. London & New York: Routledge.

Flynn, N. (2002). *Public sector management* (4th ed.). Harlow, UK: Pearson Education.

French, D., & Saward, H. (1983). *Dictionary of management* (2nd ed.). Aldershot, UK: Gower.

Holmes, M., & Shand, D. (1995). Management reform: Some practitioner perspectives on the past ten years. *Governance, 8*, 551–578.

Hood, C. (1991). A public management for all seasons? *Public Administration, 69(1)*, 3–19.

Hood, C. (2005). The word, the movement, the science. In E. Ferlie, L. E. Lynn, & C. Pollitt (Eds.), *The Oxford handbook of public management* (pp. 7–26). Oxford, UK: Oxford University Press.

Hughes, O. E. (2003). *Public management and administration* (3rd ed.). Basingstoke, UK: Palgrave.

Ingraham, P. W. (2005). Performance: Promises to keep and miles to go. *Public Administration Review, 65*, 390–395.

Kamarck, E. C. (2000). Globalization and public administration reform. In J. S. Nye & J. D. Donahue (Eds.), *Governance in a globalizing world* (pp. 229–252). Washington, DC: Brookings Institution Press.

Kettl, D. F. (2000). *The global public management revolution*. Washington, DC: Brookings Institution Press.

Nutt, P. C., & Backoff, R. W. (1992). *Strategic management of public and third sector organisations: A handbook for leaders*. San Francisco: Jossey-Bass.

Organisation for Economic Co-operation and Development. (1991). *Public management developments: 1991*. Paris: Author.

Organisation for Economic Co-operation and Development. (2005). *Modernising government: The way forward*. Paris: Author.

Osborne, D., & Gaebler, T. (1992). *Reinventing government: How the entrepreneurial spirit is transforming the public sector*. Reading, MA: Addison-Wesley.

Pollitt, C. (1990). *Managerialism and the public services: The Anglo-American experience*. Oxford, UK: Blackwell.

Pollitt, C. (2001). Clarifying convergence: Striking similarities and durable differences in public management reform. *Public Management Review, 3*, 471–492.

Pollitt, C., & Bouckaert, G. (2004). *Public management reform: A comparative analysis* (2nd ed.). Oxford, UK: Oxford University Press.

Rubin, I. S., & Kelly, J. (2005). Budget and accounting reforms. In E. Ferlie, L. E. Lynn, & C. Pollitt (Eds.), *The Oxford handbook of public management* (pp. 563–590). Oxford, UK: Oxford University Press.

Taylor, F. W. (1911). *Principles and methods of scientific management.* New York: Harper.

UK Treasury and Civil Service Committee. (1982). *Efficiency and effectiveness in the civil service.* London: HMSO.

Zifcak, S. (1994). *New managerialism: Administrative reform in Whitehall and Canberra.* Buckingham, UK: Open University Press.

PART II

Using Performance
Information to Improve
Program Performance
and Accountability

4

Can Performance Measurement Support Program Performance Improvement and Accountability?

Patria de Lancer Julnes

P art II in this volume deals with the use of performance measurement information for improving program performance and supporting accountability. Performance measurement, the ongoing production of information about an organization's performance with regard to services or programs, has been touted as an important component of management. The importance of performance measurement hinges on the potential for the information that it provides to be used to guide decision making regarding program management and to promote accountability. In what follows, we discuss the major debates surrounding these claims.

Specifically, we analyze the debates regarding the expectation of instrumental use of performance measurement information and its purported contributions to performance improvement and program accountability. After exploring these debates, we address the limitations of performance measurement and conclude by illustrating the central role that performance measurement appears to be playing in state and local governments in the United States. References to efforts in other countries are also made throughout the discussion.

Introduction

Some early proponents of performance measurement in the United States envisioned a management information system in which program and policy decisions would be driven by information collected on program performance. Due in part to a rapid erosion of citizens' trust, prompted by social, economic, and cultural trends, more recent proponents of performance measurement advocated an emphasis on performance information with a results orientation (Roberts, 2005). It was believed that among other things, such information could help managers make better decisions about the allocation of scarce resources and could be used for holding government accountable. This vision evoked fears in others that performance measurement would be destructive by giving the appearance of rational decision making but in reality being distorted to support political goals (Perrin, 1998). Such concerns are often valid, as performance measurement is not value-free. The act of measuring implies that resources be directed toward the goals of those activities, thereby informing allocation decisions among activities. Furthermore, managers measure what they value; so, "performance measurement becomes a value-defining exercise as well" (Kelly, 2002, p. 287).

Both the optimistic view of rational decision making and the pessimistic view of performance measurement as a political tool presume instrumental use of performance measurement. However, as Weiss's (1988) work in evaluation has shown, in the public sector, we often find a less direct but still rational use of information. Extant research on performance measurement and some of the cases presented in the subsequent chapters of this volume corroborate Weiss's claim. Performance measurement may have little direct impact on decision making and yet serves a meaningful role in "enlightening" various stakeholders. These stakeholders include managers and citizens.

Continuing with the instrumental use, in his introductory chapter to this volume, Harry P. Hatry laments that use of performance measurement information has been limited to accountability and little or no attention has been given to using the information for improving the quality and effectiveness of programs and services (David N. Ammons makes a similar point in Chapter 8 of this volume). And yet, if we go a step further and define accountability as "performance-based accountability," Hatry might be more disappointed. Accountability in this context entails holding someone responsible for something, and being accountable implies responsibility for one's actions and their consequences, suggesting a direct relationship between actions and results (Behn, 2003; Roberts, 2002). Such conception of accountability "requires the specification of outputs and outcomes in order to measure results and link them to goals that have been set, in accordance with the norms of management practice" (Roberts, 2002, p. 659).

Why would Hatry be disappointed? He would be disappointed because performance-based accountability requires that organizations (a) move beyond the adoption phase of performance measurement, the production of performance information, and (b) proceed to implementation, actual use of the information or converting the performance information into action, as suggested by de Lancer Julnes and Holzer (2001). This action could take several forms, including, but not limited to, incorporating the performance information into resource allocation decisions, strategic planning, and program monitoring and control. Current research suggests that implementing performance measurement efforts have proven difficult in public organizations.

Moreover, if accountability is defined in terms of "oversight and compliance," executed through the act of reviewing reported out performance information, the disappointment will continue. Current research shows that less than one half of organizations are inclined to report performance information to the public and its representatives. In their study, Poister and Streib (2005) found that only 48% of the cities in their study report performance measures associated with strategic plans to the city council and only 35% report to the public on a regular basis.

Nonetheless, the accounts presented in this volume, and specifically in this section of the handbook, will show that progress is being made in the direction of using performance measurement information for both program improvement and accountability. But again, the caveat is that such uses may not be as direct as proponents of the tools had hoped. Yet even if performance measurement information is used only to enlighten the dialogue, that too can be considered a contribution of performance measurement. This chapter discusses these potential contributions that performance measurement efforts can make to program improvement and accountability. This is done in the context of the major arguments that are part of the current performance-based management dialogue.

Performance Measurement and Program Improvement

The "ultimate purpose of performance measurement is to use the measurement information to make improvements—whether to expand, delete, or modify programs" (Hatry, 1996, p. ix). Performance measurement in this view is a self-correction and improvement tool. It is a tool for learning from past experience, because the data provide "the input for analysis to derive the lessons and the ideas to be tested in the future" (Halachmi, 2002, p. 6). The information developed can be used to improve management and program effectiveness. Proponents of performance measurement state that this can be done by using the information to guide budget formulation and the allocation of other resources (e.g., staff time, and equipment) to motivate employees and set program goals and objectives, as well as for planning, evaluation, and control (Wang, 2002; Wholey & Newcomer, 1997).

Thus, performance measurement may lead organizations to improve the quality of their policy making and decision making (de Bruijn, 2003). In essence, a performance measurement system requires that organizations establish clear goals, objectives, and measures or indicators. In time, these systems allow for the production of knowledge to help guide policy and decisions. While de Bruijn warns that the information is likely to have contradictions and be one-sided and unreliable, it is still useful because it "contributes to the aim of making policy as 'evidence-based' as possible" (p. 12).

However, given the political nature of organizations (de Lancer Julnes & Mixcoatl, 2006; Roberts, 2005; Wildavsky, 1961), perhaps it is unrealistic to expect that many public organizations will explicitly make decisions, especially resource allocation, based on performance information (this point is further illustrated by the theoretical discussion of incrementalism in Cheryle Broom and Edward T. Jennings, Jr.'s Chapter 7, in this volume). This, in and of itself, does not constitute failure of the performance measurement system, however. Instead, our disappointment may be a reflection of our own failure to accept what Weiss (1988) has already illustrated in evaluation research: that organizations tend to make less direct and more subtle use of evaluation information in decision making. This observation can also be seen to apply to performance measurement when we consider the following responses from two participants in a study reported by de Lancer Julnes (2006): "They [performance measures] are used to analyze what's going on in the program and to bring it to the attention of the city council," and "They are also used to explain, not necessarily for decision making" (p. 226). When performance measurement utilization is assessed only in concrete (instrumental) terms, we miss the opportunity to see the more modest contributions highlighted by the respondents. Those include using performance measures to justify budgets (read: budget decisions are made using criteria other than performance measurement information), to fulfill current mandates for transparency (read: reporting out information), and to inform debate among administrators and elected officials (read: enlightening, not necessarily leading to decisions).

The measurement of performance also provides an opportunity for citizens to be part of the dialogue and deliberation with government about the things that matter the most to them. Such deliberation makes it possible for the appropriate values to be represented and ensures that the measures that are developed and implemented are meaningful to citizens. This idea of citizen involvement is developed further in the chapters found in Part III of this book.

A related argument for performance measurement is that performance measurement information can serve as a tool for maintaining communication between citizens and government (Dusenbury, Blaine, & Vinson, 2000). Good communication is essential for (re)building citizen's trust in government. One of the characteristics of the process of measurement itself is that it provides a common language. Also, because performance measurement reduces to a few measures what organizations do, the information can be easily conveyed. Those measures can keep citizens informed about what they are getting for their tax dollars and how that is improving the quality of their lives. This communication and transparency can help to build trust.

The Accountability-Performance-Performance Measurement Relationship

From its limited beginnings as an instrument for holding public managers accountable for the performance of their programs (Roberts, 2005), performance-based accountability is now a global phenomenon permeating all levels and types of organizations. According to Benner and Witte (2004), globalization has given rise to new arrangements for collaboration between government organizations, nongovernmental organizations, and international organizations to address a variety of issues. These new arrangements require not only the reconceptualization of accountability and the processes to address accountability but also the introduction of performance-based accountability as a mechanism to assess what these new partnerships do and to what extent they "live up to their self-proclaimed goals" (Benner & Witte, 2004, p. 7).

Governments go to great lengths to promote accountability, sometimes providing cash incentives for organizations and other times charging a separate government institution to ensure accountability. Chapter 5 in this volume, by Brezzi, Raimondo, and Utili, provides an example of the former in Italy. Canada provides an example of the latter. In his keynote address at the conference on "Accountability in the 21st Century," Peter Aucoin (2004) explained how Canada pursues results-based accountability in four ways: (a) results-based reporting by government departments/agencies to parliament and the public, (b) results-based appraisal of public service management in delivering results, (c) performance-based reviews of public administration by independent agencies, and (d) results-based auditing of public management by parliamentary auditors. Barry Leighton elaborates Canada's experience in Chapter 6 of this volume.

Governments also attempt to do this using special legislation. The Government Performance and Results Act (GPRA) of 1993, discussed elsewhere in this volume, is an example of such legislative attempts. Another example is Hong Kong's Principal Officials Accountability System (POAS). In 2002, 5 years after Hong Kong became a Special Administrative Region (SAR) of the People's Republic of China, the POAS was established to respond to the calls for accountability by the people of Hong Kong, who blamed the chief executive of the Hong Kong SAR for mismanagement and poor leadership (Loh & Cullen, 2005). Among other objectives, the POAS seeks to "enhance the accountability of Principal Officials for their respective portfolios" and "to enable senior officials to appreciate the aspiration of and better respond to the community" (Loh & Cullen, 2005, p. 159).

According to Watt, Richards, and Skelcher (2002) and as poignantly illustrated by Hong Kong's POAS, the need for accountability arises because of a lack of trust on the part of the principal (accountability holder) that the agent (the one being held accountable) will act in the principal's interest. At the core of this distrust by the public (the accountability hold-ers) is a fear about whether their tax dollars are being spent by public orga-nizations in an efficient and effective manner. This concern has given rise to a movement toward accountability for results.

In the United States, while no one questions the need to be accountable, much less the need to be accountable for results, there has been much debate about what accountability means and how accountability relates to performance. Specifically, scholars (Dubnick, 2005; Greene, 1999; Halachmi, 2002; Kelly, 2005) raise questions such as the following: What is the logic of the current clamor for accountability? Are performance mea-surement and accountability compatible? Is performance measurement an appropriate tool for accountability?

To some extent, the answers to the questions above depend on the mean-ing given to accountability, and its purpose. Several meanings and purposes have been put forth; in essence, they all relate to the core idea that account-ability involves giving accounts for actions taken and being held account-able for those actions. In this context, Jonathan Koppell's (2005) typology of conceptions of accountability embodies that which citizens appear to seek from public organizations. Accountability in Koppell's typology con-sists of five dimensions and key determinations:

1. Transparency: Did the organization reveal the facts of its performance?

2. Liability: Did the organization face consequences for its performance?

3. Controllability: Did the organization do what the principal (e.g., Congress, president) desired?

4. Responsibility: Did the organization follow the rules?

5. Responsiveness: Did the organization fulfill the substantive expec-tation (demand/need)? (p. 96)

Viewed from this perspective, the contributions of performance measure-ment to accountability also become apparent. Performance measurement can contribute directly to transparency, controllability, and responsiveness and indirectly to liability. Furthermore, when it comes to the fourth dimen-sion, responsibility, performance measurement can also contribute, given that whether or not the organization followed the rules can be determined by monitoring the process.

Nonetheless, this typology does not entirely clarify the highly debated relationship between performance and accountability and would not appease critics of performance measurement. For example, Dubnick (2005) argues that there is no empirical evidence to suggest that accountability unequivo-cally leads organizations to improve their performance. Using a "social mech-anisms" approach, Dubnick develops the argument that there may be some mechanisms exogenous to the relationship between accountability and per-formance that may be responsible for the apparent link (or lack of one) between these two concepts. The mechanism, according to Dubnick, can be derived from the context in which "account giving and desired performance occur" and include expectations and trustworthiness (p. 403). He also points to an "accountability paradox" responsible for tension between accountability and performance, in which accountability emerges as a hindrance to improving performance.

Evidence for this apparent paradoxical relationship can be found in interviews reported in de Lancer Julnes (2006). The responses reported suggest that the emphasis on accountability in some circumstances can actually lead to setting up the organization for failure. For example, some respondents indicated that there was fear in their organizations as to how the information (reported performance measures) was going to be perceived. Another stated that agency managers were afraid of being held accountable for outcomes because they were setting nice goals that they feared their agency would not be able to achieve. Thus, concluded de Lancer Julnes, "Accountability is a double-edged sword": While calls for accountability may encourage the development of performance measurement systems, even when the appropriate measures have been developed, such calls can deter actually using the information in an effective manner. In fact, argues Muller-Smith (1997), accountability is a source of frustration for managers. Managers may find that their efforts are not leading to the intended results, and employees may find that the new responsibility of accountability is simply adding to their already overwhelming work responsibilities.

Similar to Dubnick's arguments, Kelly (2005) argues that the relationship between government performance and citizen satisfaction is problematic. Although we assume that there is a positive relationship between the performance of government and citizen satisfaction, we don't even know whether this relationship actually exists. Furthermore, Kelly criticizes the assertion that when organizations measure the performance of their services, they are being accountable to citizens for the outcomes of those services. Basically, measuring in and on itself does not constitute accountability.

Arie Halachmi (2002) also criticizes the interchangeable use of the words *accountability* and *performance* and, further, posits that performance measurement for accountability is inconsistent with performance measurement for enhancing performance. Halachmi argues that measurement for accountability deals with the question "Was it done right?" whereas measurement for improving performance asks "Was the right thing done?" (p. 6). Therefore, when used for accountability, performance measurement shows "alleged achievements so that consumption of resources can be meaningfully related to results" (p. 6). On the other hand, when performance measurement is used for improving performance, it is "about exploration and learning from experience" (p. 6). But this exploration and learning will also require that we ask the question "What might be 'more right'?" That is, whether we determine that the right thing was done or not, we will still want to know what can be done to improve the program. This also suggests that we need to be clear about the purposes of performance measurement and that our efforts need to be directed toward the development of systems that match the information needs to the information-gathering activities (Julnes, 2006).

Limitations of Performance Measurement

Supporters of performance measurement conclude that performance measurement is essential to good management. Accordingly, say Linder, Dawson, and Brooks (2005), "Without a clear, comprehensive way to measure results and the value they produce, performance management in itself becomes a fruitless exercise" (p. 5). But there is a catch. Performance measurement information tells us only what has happened with regard to outcomes—that we have or have not achieved our goals—not "how" or "why" it happened.

Critics of performance measurement contend that there is an inherent problem in using performance measurement information for accountability purposes. The current calls for accountability in the public sector presume that there is a direct relationship between program activities and observed results. These claims of causality or attribution, contend program evaluators, call for the more intensive methods that aren't part of performance measurement systems. Causality cannot be established by outcome data collected on a routine basis—that is, performance measurement (Scheirer & Newcomer, 2001). Yet, state Shadish, Cook, and Leviton (1990), we often find managers drawing up unwarranted conclusions of causality based on these types of data.

Because of this inability to establish causality, critics say that it is inappropriate to make decisions such as budget allocations based on performance measurement data (Perrin, 1998). Thus, critics contend, if the performance information indicates that the program outcomes are not as expected, moving resources away from the program might be the wrong decision. It is quite possible that the hoped-for outcome is a function of factors outside the control of the manager. Another possibility is that the logic underlying the program was faulty to begin with.

A second issue raised by critics is that performance measurement systems may contribute to goal displacement. *Goal displacement* refers to individuals or organizations purposely changing their behavior when they are measured, in order to improve their performance ratings (Bohte & Meier, 2000; Mark, Henry, & Julnes, 2000). The problem is that sometimes in changing their behavior, they distort the validity of the measure, forsake the organization's priorities in order to promote their own interests, and may even engage in outright cheating. A classic example of goal displacement is "teaching to the test." Here, a previously appropriate indicator of achievement becomes distorted and inappropriate.

A third major criticism, advanced by Greene (1999), is that traditional measures of performance, which are supposed to represent in a few numbers the essence of what an organization does, are not capable of properly capturing and representing program quality. Quality entails interpretation and reporting of often complex experiences and values. Thus, for example, the evaluation of the quality of a customer service experience in a welfare office is likely to be affected by the perceptions and values of the service providers as reflected by their behavior toward the customer. Moreover, the interpretation of this behavior by the service recipient, whose own behavior is shaped by his or her perceptions of reality and internalized values, also affects the evaluation of quality. How is a simple measure supposed to capture such complexity?

Overcoming Limitations

At this point, the following question may be plaguing the reader's mind: If, as the critics say, performance measurement should not be used for decision making or program accountability and it may lead to cheating and underperformance, why should I argue for establishing a performance measurement system in my organization? The contributions noted above provide reasons to persevere, and, furthermore, there are ways to overcome the limitations.

Although performance measurement tells us only what has happened, in many cases, knowing "what" is sufficient information to make a decision about a particular program or activity. Two reasons can be cited. First, measuring indicators helps to monitor progress toward a desired goal. Second, when things go well, we could assume that the program in question is working well enough. As long as outcomes are as expected, this assumption based on performance measurement information may be adequate, particularly in the case of programs that are not too complex, as will be illustrated later.

When the outcomes are not as expected, however, we might need to look elsewhere for answers. This leads to the larger point: A performance measurement system should be part of a more holistic approach to management. For example, knowing what we have not achieved does not tell us what should be done about it. Thus, good measurement also requires having the right tools that can tell us what the determinants of an outcome are, so that we know what to do about them in order to achieve the desired results. These latter points bring us to the heated debate between proponents of performance measurement for accountability and program evaluators.

For example, when it comes to attribution, there are circumstances in which patterns of changes in the outcomes monitored are often reasonable indicators of causal relationships. For goal displacement, the most problematic part is when performance measurement is used as an "accountability hammer." When used in a more reflective manner, goal displacement is less likely. This suggests that as long as there is fear, unfounded or not, that performance measurement information will be used for retribution, the accountability paradox will continue to exist. This is not to say that organizations should not be liable for poor or bad performance. Certainly, the Enrons of the world should be liable for their wrongdoing. But in the context of organizations that are not able to reach their goals, steps should be taken to help them improve the service delivery strategies and processes that are not conducive to the expected performance.

Similarly, the difficulty in capturing quality is less problematic when performance measurement is used in a thoughtful and reflective manner and in combination with other techniques that allow for development of better measures of quality. To that end, proponents of performance measurement suggest cooperation between program evaluators and program managers, policy analysts, and others who can help with various aspects of developing and implementing a robust performance measurement system (Scheirer & Newcomer, 2001; Wholey, 1996). As noted earlier, an effective performance measurement system should be based on a combination of methods. For example, suppose we have performance information that shows that a particular program or service is not performing as expected. If the service or program is not complex (e.g., garbage collection, street cleaning, city recreation services), a simple technique such as talking to citizens can help us determine "why" this is the case.

Another technique that can lead to determining the reasons for poor performance is an implementation evaluation. In these evaluations, the core question is this: Was the program implemented as it was intended to be? It might be that something is wrong with the implementation, and, once corrected, the intended results will be achieved. Take the simple example of a weight loss program. Assuming that the individual has been given the right combination of diet and exercise to follow in order to lose weight, if no weight reduction is observed, the question to ask in an implementation evaluation is this: Is the individual following the plan as suggested?

On the other hand, when the outcome information from a complex program, such as drug prevention or sex abstinence, indicates poor performance, determining the "why," the "how," the impact, and the "what now?" requires a more complex methodology. In this case, performance measurement can be made useful by combining it with program evaluation. Program evaluators' toolboxes typically include sophisticated methods for collecting, maintaining, and analyzing data. Also, program evaluators have at their disposal a number of methods and approaches to determine which of a variety of explanations is most plausible. Thus, the skills and knowledge of evaluators could prove useful for performance measurement in collecting multiple measures of a particular indicator and conducting more thorough causal analyses. Furthermore, program evaluation can be used to improve the reliability of performance measurement data. For example, a program evaluation can suggest the types of indicators that need to be developed and the types of data necessary to make the appropriate decision.

It is also important to note that performance measurement can contribute to program evaluation. In many evaluation studies, performance measurement information has served as the backbone of the study, providing low-cost data or showing where more in-depth analysis is needed.

Conclusion

This brief introduction to Part II of this volume has discussed the major debates surrounding the issue of using performance measurement information for performance improvement and accountability. Within the context of these debates, the limitations of performance measurement have been explored. It is hoped that this discussion will elicit further dialogue that can help illuminate these debates.

Limitations notwithstanding, it is clear that the potential contributions of performance measurement to performance improvement and accountability have led many public organizations in the United States to adopt performance measurement, if not fully implement it. Furthermore, the cases discussed in subsequent chapters also provide evidence of the importance attributed to performance measurement, not only in the United States but also abroad.

This chapter concludes with an Appendix that shows selected examples of performance measurement efforts at the state and local levels in the United States. The intention is not to present the most successful examples of these efforts. Rather, this is done to provide additional resources to the reader of available information on the practice of performance measurement for performance improvement and accountability.

Appendix

The state of Oregon has long set an example for performance measurement efforts. The current statewide performance measurement system in Oregon, which is part of the state's strategic plan, attempts to determine whether Oregon's government is providing quality services at a reasonable cost to taxpayers. The performance measures are used to gauge achievements and to make a broad range of policy decisions, as well as for planning and for budget-related activities (see Oregon Progress Board: http://www.oregon.gov/DAS/OPB/obm.shtml). As shown in their "2005 Benchmark Performance Report," which focuses mostly on end outcomes, the state reports on how much progress is being made toward achieving benchmarks, cases in which the situation has improved or worsened, cases in which the situation has not changed, and how the state compares to others (see http://www.oregon.gov/DAS/OPB/docs/2005report/05BPR.pdf).

In the state of Iowa, each state department develops performance plans and strategic plans. The purpose of the strategic plan is for departments to make use of the performance measurements to help identify "improvement opportunities" and to develop and implement strategies that can help them achieve better results. The departments are also able to make more informed decisions, tell what they have accomplished, and target resources more effectively (see http://www.resultsiowa.org/department_performance.html).

In the state of Louisiana, the performance measurement system is used in conjunction with the strategic planning and policy development processes to measure progress toward desired results. The state has instituted the Louisiana Performance Accountability System (LaPAS), a performance-reporting system, through which all executive branch departments and agencies submit their quarterly performance reports. The state has also instituted a performance-based rewards and penalties system. This system includes the Louisiana's Exceptional Performance and Efficiency Incentive Program (see http://www.doa.louisiana.gov/opb/pbb/pa.htm).

At the local level, there exists some empirical evidence of the contributions of performance measurement to performance-based management and accountability. For example, Poister and Streib (2005) found that performance measurement helped to explain 28% of the variation in the perceived success of strategic planning in the municipalities participating in the study. Important to this success was that performance measures associated with the strategic plans were reported on a regular basis to the public. Below are two examples at the county and city levels of what are considered successful performance measurement systems.

In Fairfax County, Virginia, performance measurement is one of the tools used to improve the county's operations and service delivery. Furthermore, in an effort to ensure accountability, the county has integrated its performance measures with the budget. The budget document allows citizens and elected officials to assess program results based on the resources being utilized (see http://www.fairfaxcounty.gov/dmb/perf_measure.htm). Over the years, the city has consistently reported improved measures of outcomes.

The 2000 Government Performance Project declared the City of Phoenix a leader in managing for results. Consistent planning and measurement of performance have led the city to achieve tremendous improvements in service delivery (see http://governing.com/gpp/2000/gp0mr.htm). Measurement and a concern for results and accountability are not new to Phoenix. In the 1970s, the city began monitoring work standards, resources used, and outputs. In the 1980s, the city transitioned to measuring productivity and customer satisfaction, making the shift in the 1990s to measure results. The city reports a very strong managing-for-results culture, one where results information is naturally used to help managers make decisions (see http://phoenix.gov/AUDITOR/index.html).

References

Aucoin, P. (2004, November). *Holding governments to account: Trends and prospects.* Paper presented at "Accountability in the 21st Century," School of Public Administration, University of Victoria, Canada. Available at http://www.web.uvic.ca/padm/future04/pdfs/aucoin_keynote.pdf

Behn, R. (2003). Rethinking accountability in education: How should who hold whom accountable for what? *International Public Management Journal, 6,* 43–73.

Benner, T., & Witte, J. M. (2004). *Everybody's business: Accountability, partnerships, and the future of global governance.* Berlin and Geneva: Global Public Policy Institute. Available at http://www.globalpublicpolicy.net/fileadmin/gppi/Everbody_s_business.pdf

Bohte, J., & Meier, K. (2000). Goal displacement: Assessing the motivation for organizational cheating. *Public Administration Review, 60,* 173–182.

de Bruijn, H. (2003). *Managing performance in the public sector.* London: Routledge

de Lancer Julnes, P. (2006). Performance measurement: An effective tool for government accountability? The debate goes on. *Evaluation: The International Journal of Theory, Research, and Practice, 12,* 219–235.

de Lancer Julnes, P., & Holzer, M. (2001). Promoting the utilization of performance measures in public organizations: An empirical study of factors affecting adoption and implementation. *Public Administration Review, 61,* 693–708.

de Lancer Julnes, P., & Mixcoatl, G. (2006). Governors as agents of change: A comparative study of performance measurement initiatives in Utah and Campeche. *Public Performance and Management Review, 29,* 405–432.

Dubnick, M. (2005). Accountability and the promise of performance: In search of the mechanisms. *Public Performance and Management Review, 28,* 376–417.

Dusenbury, P., Blaine, L., & Vinson, E. (2000). *States, citizens, and local performance management.* Washington, DC: Urban Institute.

Government Performance and Results Act of 1993, Pub. L. No. 103–62 [S20] 107 Stat. 285.

Greene, J. (1999). The inequality of performance measurements. *Evaluation, 5,* 160–172.

Halachmi, A. (2002). Who gets what, when, and how: Performance measures for accountability? For improved performance? *International Review of Public Administration, 7*(1), 1–11.

Hatry, H. (1996). Foreword. In A. Halachmi & G. Bouckaert (Eds.), *Organizational performance and measurement in the public sector* (pp. xi–xii). Westport, CT: Quorum Books.

Julnes, G. (2006, June 1–3). *Contextual approaches to using measurement to improve performance.* Paper presented at "A Performing Public Sector: The Second TransAtlantic Dialogue," Leuven, Belgium.

Kelly, J. M. (2002). If you only knew how well we are performing, you'd be highly satisfied with the quality of our service. *National Civic Review, 91,* 283–292.

Kelly, J. (2005). The dilemma of the unsatisfied customer in a market model of public administration. *Public Administration Review, 65,* 76–84.

Koppell, J. G. (2005). Pathologies of accountability: ICANN and the challenge of "Multiple Accountabilities Disorder." *Public Administration Review, 65,* 94–108.

Linder, J., Dawson, C., & Brooks, J. (2005). *The road to high performance in the public sector: Insights into statewide performance management.* Palo Alto, CA: Accenture Institute for High Performance Business. Available at http://www.oregon.gov/DAS/OPB/docs/Reports/Accenture.pdf

Loh, C., & Cullen, R. (2005). Political reform in Hong Kong: The principal officials accountability system. The first year (2002–2003). *Journal of Contemporary China, 14,* 153–176.

Mark, M., Henry, G., & Julnes, G. (2000). *Evaluation: An integrated framework for understanding, guiding, and improving policies and programs.* San Francisco: Jossey-Bass.

Muller-Smith, P. (1997). The problem with accountability. *Journal of Perianesthesia Nursing, 12,* 109–112.

Perrin, B. (1998). Effective use and misuse of performance measurement. *American Journal of Evaluation, 19,* 367–380.

Poister, T., & Streib, G. (2005). Elements of strategic planning and management in municipal government: Status after two decades. *Public Administration Review, 65,* 45–56.

Roberts, A. (2005). Issues associated with the implementation of governmentwide performance monitoring. In S. Anwar (Ed.), *Public services delivery* (pp. 1–38). Washington, DC: World Bank.

Roberts, N. C. (2002). Keeping public officials accountable through dialogue: Resolving the accountability paradox. *Public Administration Review, 62,* 658–669.

Scheirer, M., & Newcomer, K. (2001). Opportunities for program evaluators to facilitate performance-based management. *Evaluation and Program Planning, 24,* 63–71.

Shadish, W., Cook, T., & Leviton, L. (1990). *Foundations of program evaluation.* Thousand Oaks, CA: Sage.

Wang, X. (2002). Assessing performance measurement impact: A study of U.S. local government. *Public Performance and Management Review, 26,* 26–43.

Watt, P., Richards, S., & Skelcher, C. (2002). *Review of public administration in Northern Ireland, briefing paper: Accountability.* Birmingham, UK: School of Public Policy, University of Birmingham.

Weiss, C. H. (1988). Evaluation for decision: Is anybody there? Does anybody care? *Evaluation Practice, 9,* 5–20.

Wholey, J. (1996). Formative and summative evaluation: Related issues in performance measurement. *Evaluation Practice, 17,* 145–149.

Wholey, J., & Newcomer, K. (1997). Clarifying goals, reporting results. *New Directions for Evaluation, 75,* 91–98.

Wildavsky, A. (1961). Political implications of budgetary reform. *Public Administration Review, 21,* 183–190.

5 Using Performance Measurement and Competition to Make Administrations Accountable

The Italian Case

Monica Brezzi

Laura Raimondo

Francesca Utili[1]

In 1999, Italy finalized the preparation of a large investment program in six southern regions for the 2000-to-2006 period, the so-called Southern Development Program (referred to in this chapter as "the Program"), which was submitted to the European Union for financing. In 1999, the gross domestic product (GDP) per capita of these beneficiary regions (Basilicata, Campania, Calabria, Puglia, Sardinia, and Sicily) was around 12,800, more or less half the value of the GDP per capita of the rest of Italy and below 75% of the European average, while the unemployment rate was almost four times higher than in the rest of Italy, 22.8% versus 6.6%.

The Program was meant to increase the territorial competitiveness of the regions and attract increasingly mobile capital. The strategy rationale originated in the idea that southern Italy is endowed with significant natural, human, and cultural resources that are largely idle and can be better used to produce significant social and economic returns. Policies were defined for economic exploitation of idle resources and for "agglomerations" (cities, local productive systems) where social, economic, and administrative relations concentrate and are promoters of development: Investments in social capital and relational capital and provision of public services would improve the context within which firms and people work. They would reduce diseconomies negatively affecting both expectations and investment productivity of private investors and create positive supply externalities. This was expected to induce, through positive expectations for growth rates, an increase in private investments and consequently a steady increase of employment rates.

The growth, development, and social objectives of the Program were ambitious. Thus, to be successful and credible for private investors, this strategy had to be based on quantified intermediate and final objectives and on a general upgrading of public investment and capacities within public administration. Furthermore, substantial modifications in the behavior of private and public institutions had to occur in order to increase the capacity of a given territory to attract mobile resources. This capacity largely depends on the quality of services produced or promoted by public action. In the period observed, the quality of services was highly constrained by delays or lack of implementation of major reforms of the public administration and of specific sectors, such as water, solid waste, and environmental monitoring and control, information and communications technology, and services to firms.

A reform of the voting system was introduced in 2000, for the first time allowing presidents of regions to be elected directly by citizens in a majority system. Regional governments were endowed with specific and wider constitutional competencies in territorial policies, both with 2001 and 2004 constitutional reforms. The change in the voting system actually took place a few years after major reforms were enacted, providing for more autonomous administrative and political power to the regions. The decentralization process left central administrations with competencies in national strategic matters (e.g., research, security, and higher education), coordination, monitoring, and, to a certain extent, evaluation. In this framework, relations between different layers of governments can be characterized by competition and cooperation (Shannon & Kee, 1989).

The strategies and governance of the Program were influenced by the Italian institutional framework, and, at the same time, the Program anticipated the decentralization process giving regions greater responsibilities than in the past. A break with the past in the governance of large development plans was indeed introduced in the Program: Most funds and responsibilities for selecting projects were allocated to the regions in accordance with the increased competencies in territorial policies and on the assumption that regions would be able to mobilize much of the knowledge needed to enact the Program from private and public stakeholders, because of more involvement by citizens in decision making, increased participation in the political process, and easier signaling of preferences.

Complex programming and high-quality project selection required a deep and rapid modernization of each region's administrative structure. The governance of the program was thus based on a set of rules, rewards, and sanctions aimed at reaching the ambitious objectives of the Program both through (a) supporting competition and partnership between levels of government and (b) providing incentives for regions to implement the program. The structure of incentives factored into the Program was designed with the aim of encouraging economic subjects and administrations, on one hand, to perform in a cooperative way when designing the rules and, on the other, to behave in a competitive way when performing their respective functions (Barca, 2000, 2001). Within this framework, it was decided that 6% of funds allocated to the Program would be assigned to the regional administration beneficiaries of the public funding Program, on the basis of their performance results and according to a competitive model on the implementation of administrative and sector reforms. At the same time, the incentive system was expected to build upon "horizontal competition" among subcentral governments and to provide a powerful tool to organize and monitor a share of such competition within a limited period of time (see Salmon, 1987).

The issues and challenges addressed in the Program as described above can be depicted as part of a strategic situation whereby both cooperative and competitive behaviors are regulated by rules set in the agreement signed by Italy with the European Union. This chapter focuses on the 6% *performance reserve system*[2] and analyzes how the system was designed in order to properly reward regional administrations on the basis of performance benchmarks and to induce changes in the behavior of public administration. The performance mechanism can be analyzed as a principal-agent situation, whereby a binding contract can favor the search for an efficient solution. More precisely, it can be viewed as an incomplete contract, whereby the incentive scheme simulates that of a "tournament" (to be discussed later in the chapter).

This chapter discusses the characteristics of the performance mechanism in terms of competition and accountability, originated by the incentives set to obtain efficient behaviors that could produce the common public objectives established by the Program. Moreover, it describes the actions designed and implemented in the performance system in order to overcome the incompleteness of the contract or, more specifically, to reduce the partial information, to avoid the risk of opportunistic behavior, and to regulate the uncertainty.

Vignettes in the form of boxed text are included throughout the chapter to further illuminate, with examples, the challenges encountered and the solutions adopted in the mechanism set for the performance system.

The 6% Performance Reserve System

Rules and Financial Allocation Mechanism

The Program of public investments for the southern regions lasted 6 years, from 2000 to 2006, and amounted to €44 billion, cofinanced by the European Union. The administration beneficiaries of funds, and responsible for selecting projects, were six regions (endowed with almost 80% of the total resources) and six central administrations responsible for sector Programs. The Department for Development Policies of the Ministry of Economic Development acted as a coordinating and managing authority of the Program (for the remainder of this chapter referred to as the "managing authority"), with the task of setting general rules and guidelines for monitoring and evaluation.

The performance reserve mechanism amounted to €2.6 billion (6% of the overall Program), to be assigned to the administration beneficiaries of funds on the basis of their performance results achieved by September 2002, 2 years after the rules were set and the competitive mechanism was started. The performance reserve mechanism was designed to create proper incentives to pursue the following objectives, which are strictly connected with the strategy of the development Program: (a) foster institutional enhancement through the modernization process of public administration and the diffusion of institutional innovation necessary to accelerate and make effective structural funds spending, (b) promote and anticipate reforms in some of the sectors crucial to the achievement of the defined development objectives of the Program, and (c) concentrate funds on selected priorities and integrate actions to select and implement more complex and higher-quality projects. (For a complete description of the mechanism, see Anselmo, Brezzi, Raimondo, & Utili, 2006, and the Department for Development Policies and Cohesion, Ministry of Economy and Finance, n.d.; here, for simplicity, we describe only the incentive scheme applied to the regions.)

Twelve indicators were chosen to represent intermediate objectives and necessary conditions to achieve the results of improving the effectiveness of the public administration's action and the quality of public spending (see Table 5.1). A block of 10 indicators referred to different aspects of institutional enhancement and sector reforms, while the remaining indicators referred to territorial integration of projects and concentration of financial resources. Examples of indicators of institutional enhancement and sector reforms were delegation of managerial responsibilities to officials, creation of control and evaluation units within public offices, implementation of one-stop shops for enterprises (reform aimed at reducing the amount of time and papers needed for a company's startup), implementation of public employment services, development and use of information society, and implementation of urban waste and water management reforms.

Indicators had different weights corresponding to the relative importance in the performance reserve system. Weights, determined through a collective decision of the interested administrations, were distributed over a total of 60 points. Each indicator of institutional enhancement was weighted 3.5, for a total of 35 points; the indicator of integration of territorial projects was weighted 15 points; and the indicator for concentration was weighted 10 points.

Regional administrations were required to reach fixed minimum standards for the indicators of institutional enhancement, while for the indicators

Table 5.1   Criteria and Indicators for the Allocation of the 6% Reserve for Regions

Criteria	Indicator	Benchmark	Points
A. Institutional Enhancement			35
Implementation of national legislation fostering the process of public administration reform	• Delegation of managerial responsibilities to officials (legislative decree n. 29/93)	• Adoption of the decree n. 29/93 and managers' evaluation for the year 2002	3.5
	• Set up and implementation of an internal control management unit (legislative decree n. 286/99)	• Setup and proof of activity of the internal control management unit	3.5
	• Implementation of one-stop shops	• At least 80% of the regional population covered by the one-stop shops, and at least 90% of papers processed on time	3.5
	• Implementation of public employment services	• At least 50% of the regional population covered by employment offices	3.5
Design and implementation of organizational and administrative innovation to accelerate and carry out effective structural funds spending	• Setup of regional and central administration evaluation units (L. 144/99)	• Setup of the evaluation unit by April 2001, appointment of the director and experts by July 2001	3.5
	• Development of the "information society" in the public administration	• Transmission of data regarding at least 60% of total expenditures	3.5
Carrying out measures aiming at the implementation of sector reforms	• Preparation and approval of territorial and landscape programming documents	• Meet regional benchmarks of territorial landscape programming	3.5
	• Concession or management by a private/public operator of integrated water services (L. 36/94)	• Approval of the concession or management by a private/public operator of integrated water services	3.5

(Continued)

Table 5.1 (Continued)

Criteria	Indicator	Benchmark	Points
	• Implementation for urban solid waste within optimal service areas	• Choice of management mode and its implementation within optimal service areas	3.5
	• Setup and operational performance of regional environmental agencies	• Appointment of the director of the agency and approval of management rules, allocation of resources, and personnel	3.5
B. Integration			*15*
Implementation of territorial integrated projects	• Incidence of commitments of integrated territorial projects on the total amount of resources budgeted for integrated territorial projects in the operational program	• Incidence of commitments and disbursements of integrated territorial projects on the total amount of resources budgeted for integrated territorial projects in the operational program higher than the average over all the regions	15
C. Concentration			*10*
Concentration of financial resources	• Concentration of financial resources within a limited amount of measures	• Concentration of financial resources within a lower amount of measures than the average over all the regions	10
Total (A + B + C)	*Number of Indicators: 12*		*Total Score: 60*

on integration and concentration, the thresholds were based on the average performance of participants; therefore, relative performance was taken into account.

All the targets had to be achieved by September 2002, or earlier for a few intermediate steps; therefore, administrations had approximately 2 years to put into place actions to reach targets (the 6% performance reserve system was officially started in August 2000). Each target attained gave access to a portion of total reserve funds, the ratio of this choice being that each indicator, if satisfied, could positively contribute to improve the programming process and its implementation.

Each administration involved had a potential endowment equal to 6% of its program total budget; the full amount of performance reserve was gained when all the targets were achieved. Only in the case of resources not assigned in the first round (i.e., when some administrations did not succeed in achieving all the targets) would administrations get additional amounts, proportional to their performance and their budgets. Therefore, the system encompassed competition between administrations through the allocation of unassigned resources, in addition to the direct competition related to target setting on relative performance for integration and concentration indicators.

An Incomplete Contract With an Incentive Scheme

In recent years, the institutional framework and the functions of public management have been represented through certain types of agency models, whereby a principal (a single central administration) and many agents (local governments) regulate their relation through a contract. Nevertheless, it soon became apparent that functions and subsequent actions of different levels of government cannot be described through a full contract, or, as it is commonly called, a *complete contract*. The Italian performance reserve can be described as an incomplete contract, enclosing an incentive scheme between the managing authority (acting as the principal) and the six regions (the agents) that receive rewards or suffer penalties according to their performance on 12 indicators. The principal wants to define an efficient scheme of incentives that influence the agent's decisions in a way to obtain the principal's best payoff; in the Italian case, this meant designing an incentive scheme to influence the administration's actions to pursue the common public objectives of the development program. If both parties have complete information, the optimal solution, which maximizes both the principal's and the agent's utilities, can be reached (Hart, 1995; Tirole, 1999; for a detailed survey of the theory of contracts and incentive schemes, also see Nicita & Scoppa, 2005). In most real situations, however, the information available to the parts is partial and/or asymmetric; therefore, the contract is said to be incomplete, either because it cannot foresee all the contingencies or because the cost of writing them is too high. In these cases, only suboptimal solutions can be reached, such that the contract is implemented with some kind of inefficiency.

In the presence of asymmetric information, when the principal retains less information than the agents, the contract cannot describe either the agent's effort or action, but only its outcome; and therefore, the incentive scheme has to be chosen in a way that reduces the inefficiency coming from opportunistic behavior. Furthermore, the outcome of an agent depends not only on its effort but also on random components (unknown both to the principal and to the agent); therefore, there is always a trade-off between the amount of incentive given to the agent and the risk the agent is willing to take (the higher the financial prize, the more productive the agent but also the higher the risk the agent takes).

To reduce the uncertainty on the agent's behavior, the principal tries to acquire more information through monitoring during the enforcement of the contract. The monitoring function can be assigned to a third party, with the task of making the progress of the agent toward the objectives and their outcomes available to all the participants and therefore reducing the incompleteness of information.

When many agents interact with a single principal on the same set of objectives, the incentive scheme commonly used is the *tournament*. The main features of a tournament are that (a) the principal sets the rules and the prizes before the competition takes place and (b) the agents are rewarded according to their relative performance, compared with that of other agents (see Ahmad, Tandberg, & Zhang, 2002; and Salmon, 1987, for an application of tournaments to horizontal competition between subcentral governments). The main advantage of a tournament is that assigning prizes on the basis of relative performance, the effect of the random component, when it takes the form of a common shock (that is to say, it affects the agents indiscriminately), is reduced since it does not affect the relative position of the agents; in this case, the trade-off between agents' productivity and risk allocation is lowered, and the agents are willing to take a bigger risk.

Two more advantages of a tournament over other forms of incentive schemes should be mentioned: (a) In the cases when it is difficult or too costly to measure the agents' absolute performance, setting a tournament permits rewarding the agents according to their relative (among themselves) performance; and (b) the tournament is preferable when it is difficult for the principal or a third party to verify the agent's performance. On the other hand, the two more relevant disadvantages of this form of contract are that (a) there is a risk of collusion among the agents, who could agree to keep the effort low and invalidate the system, and (b) one or more agents may try to corrupt or to exercise influence over the principal.

However, the functions of public management in the Italian performance system can be framed in an agency model only to a certain extent, mainly for two reasons: first, when the principal is a public administration and has a strong interest that all agents understand and accept the contract, fully participate in the competition, and achieve at least some of the awards. Indeed, in the Italian performance system, the Department for Development Policies and Cohesion (Dipartimento per le Politiche di Sviluppo e Coesione, or DPS), acting as the principal, had an interest in all the regions meeting some minimum standards.

Second, the link between local governments' actions and their results is often affected by many uncontrolled variables, including the fact that the agents perform different tasks at the same time (which can also display competing goals), have more than one objective (Dixit, 2002), and not only react to the principal's incentive but also respond to their electorates (though, ideally, that should be the drive for good performance). Therefore, some devices are needed to strengthen the incentive mechanism and to increase its visibility.

The Italian performance system partially shares the characteristics of a tournament; at the same time, it is designed to reflect the overall scheme of the Program, that is to say, to foster cooperation between administrations in designing the rules and to spur competition when they are performing their respective functions. Therefore, the mix of competition and account-ability originated by the mechanism shows how the Italian performance mechanism is in many regards more complex than a tournament.

The following sections describe the main features of the Italian incentive scheme and discuss, with some examples, the reasons why a simple tourna-ment could not be applied. More precisely, after a discussion on how indi-cators and targets have been selected, the chapter analyzes three issues:

1. Since the principal is interested in the agents reaching some minimum standards and being committed to the objectives, some targets were set as external benchmarks identical for all the agents, with prizes indepen-dent of the others' performance. The other case, when the agents were rewarded according to their relative performance, will be described as well.

2. Due to the partial information of the contract, an independent party (technical group) was needed to define indicators and set targets cor-rectly, to monitor the process as well as the participation of the bene-ficiary regions, and to verify their performance.

3. Incentives for the agents had to be added, since the direct competition on relative performance is limited to a few indicators.

Characteristics of the
Incentive Scheme in the Italian Case

Partnership and Cooperation
in Selecting Indicators and Targets

The design of the performance mechanism required a very careful effort. First of all, it was important to collect information from subjects who had knowledge of the specific issues considered. Second, it was necessary to choose indicators and set targets that were relevant to achieve the objectives and that could lead agents toward the desired behavior. However, agents could keep private information on their characteristics from the principal and other agents. As a way to reduce the asymmetry of information and to set objectives, indicators, and targets, which were significant for all participants to the game, a participatory process was put in place. Through partnership, agents revealed their preferences, and private information was reduced.

In the design of the system, the role played by partnership was relevant at different levels. Partnership processes were adopted at various steps to contribute to the choice of indicators, to identify their exact measurable definition, and to design the competition mechanism (i.e., to agree on the rules to assign the resources). At the same time, through partnership, the knowledge needed to implement the strategy was informally spread (Anselmo & Raimondo, 2000).

The process was thorough and lasted for a significant period of time, from the second half of 1999 to April 2001, when the final document, including both a detailed description of indicators and of the rules to assign financial resources, was finally approved. Many different actors were involved. The main actor was the DPS, whose evaluation unit was in charge of a draft proposal of the performance indicators and the rules governing the process. The participatory process also included institutional partnership at the horizontal level with departments with knowledge of specific indicators (e.g., the Ministry of Labor for Public Employment Services, the Ministry of Culture for Territorial Planning) and at the vertical level with the European Commission and the regional governments.

The partnership process was started with various panels of discussion by national and regional policymakers, experts, and stakeholders, with the aim of developing a better definition of the investment strategy and policy objectives for regional governments. Afterward, a subset of goals of strategic relevance was selected, together with the time sequence of actions required to attain them. However, since rewards and sanctions were attached to the achievement of those objectives, the need of correct measurability acted as a constraint on feasible objectives.

A choice was made, on the basis of characteristics of precise measurability and availability of data for measurement, among the preliminary list of objectives and indicators of institutional enhancement initially included in the mechanism. Some indicators were defined together with other administrations who held specific responsibility and knowledge of the issues. They gave their contributions in setting targets that were measurable and reachable. In a number of cases, the administrations realized that the performance reserve mechanism was a strong tool for supporting regional administrations and other local levels of government to implement important administrative acts. It resulted in a strong commitment by those administrations

(Ministry of Labor, Ministry of Culture, Department for Innovation in Public Administration) to cooperate in fixing the targets and to directly participate in monitoring and assessing progress; this increased the overall accountability of the system.

Feasibility was also checked in horizontal partnership with other administrations with specific knowledge on the topics. At the same time, a thorough analysis was made of the situation of each region involved in the performance mechanism in relation to the fields of interest. For some indicators, simulations were made taking into account similar experiences elsewhere in the country. Some targets were either made more ambitious or lowered according to the results of the accurate information collected.

Only in a limited number of cases did regions make significant changes on the first draft prepared by the DPS. For example, they suggested increasing the weight of the "institutional enhancement" block, which in first proposals had the same weight as the two other blocks (integration of territorial projects and concentration of resources). The regional administrations had clearly understood that institution building was the real innovation of the mechanism, and thus there was an advantage in having it adequately rewarded (with financial resources) in order to obtain visible results. In this case, they were also revealing some private information by signaling their own interest in getting the results associated with the achievement of targets. DPS was also keen to obtain general agreements on all the rules of the game from the very beginning of the process. Thus, a very limited number of changes to the approved document were made afterward.

The final document, including precise definition of indicators and the rules of assignment of financial resources, was completed 15 months after the first draft was sent to regional governments. It was a learning process for all the subjects involved: Monitoring and competition mechanisms were better defined, and the "credibility" of the incentive scheme was strengthened through the agents' participation.

Setting Targets: The Use of Absolute Thresholds Versus Relative Performance to Reward the Agents

All 10 indicators relating to different aspects of institutional enhancement and sector reforms had external benchmarks, which were identical for all the regions. Many reasons were behind this choice. First of all, the risk of not having full participation in the system was taken into account when the targets were set. The mechanism was designed so as to make the administrations as accountable as possible for results. The indicators were clearly defined in advance and strongly dependent on the actions of the administrations, both at regional and local levels. In addition, the time span available was short enough to also make the political level directly accountable for results. As mentioned earlier, the new voting system was enacted in 2000 with the direct election of regional presidents, a few months before the official launch of the performance system.

Moreover, the administrative and sector reforms covered by the "institutional" block of indicators were considered necessary conditions to fully implement the strategy of the Program and reach the developmental objectives. The path to accomplish these intermediate objectives was clear and to some extent the same for all the administrations; the incentive was then given to accelerate the process toward these goals.

A third reason in favor of external benchmarks was to reduce the risk of the effects of heterogeneity of the agents or, more specifically, of the different stages the competing administrations occupied with regard to the indicators at the beginning of the performance reserve period. Rewarding the administrations only on the basis of relative ranking could have discouraged participation on the part of the administrations that were lagging behind. The heterogeneity of the agents was taken into account also in terms of time needed to reach some targets; in fact, after the conclusion of the performance reserve system and the assignment of rewards, additional time was given to the lower-performing regions to meet certain targets and receive reduced rewards (Anselmo et al., 2006).

The targets chosen for these indicators represented minimum standards, equal for all, to be attained in order to consider a modernization of the administration complete and operational. The regions therefore were measured not according to their own absolute performance, but against a common benchmark fixed in absolute terms; and therefore voters could perceive them as relative performance. More precisely, it was decided to measure only the attainment of the targets and not the absolute performance of an administration. Thus, if an administration behaved even better than the target, it did not receive an additional reward.

Nonetheless, in a few cases, fixing an external benchmark was very difficult, and the functioning of the mechanism was not completely satisfactory. Some administrations were afraid that setting absolute thresholds for all the indicators of institutional enhancement would mean that the administrations, which had very different backgrounds (or special legislation), were asked to perform different efforts and actions to meet the target. Therefore, the regional administrations asked for indicators to be customized and negotiated with each administration according to its level of progress. Of course, there was a clear advantage in measurability and comparability of results, homogeneity of evaluation, and transparency of a system with absolute benchmarks, equal to all. Nonetheless, indicators and thresholds had to be chosen very carefully in order to avoid disparities by regions.

**Vignette 1: External Targets and Inappropriate Attribution of
Responsibilities: The Example of the "One-Stop Shop"
for Enterprises**

The example of the "one-stop shop" for enterprises indicator can be seen as a case
where it would have been advisable to set the target on the basis of the relative performance of the agents, thus eliminating the effect of the common random shock.
The target of this indicator was defined on the basis of regional implementation, even
though municipalities (within regions) were actually in charge of setting up one-stop
shops. Therefore, responsibility was not appropriately attributed. The fact that the
implementation of one-stop shops was not under the direct control of the regional
administrations was acknowledged only after the indicator had already been chosen
as one of the performance indicators. Not having applied the feature of a tournament
that rewarded relative performance led the technical group to try to control and
reduce the importance of the uncertainty as to implementation common to all
regions by taking a number of specific actions. These included advertisements on
Web sites and in local papers, TV spots on local TV and on the administration's
Internet channel, meetings with the highest administrative and political representatives of the regions to help find consensus among different levels of local governments and establish the needed connection with the municipalities, and workshops
in the regions to meet with the municipalities and provide technical assistance.
Thanks to these actions, the administrations participated in the competition on this
indicator, which could therefore be measured at the deadline.

The main feature of a tournament, the performance measured on a
relative scale and prizes assigned on the basis of the ranking, was fully
adapted in the Italian performance reserve scheme for only two indicators.
The indicators were for the implementation of territorial integrated projects and the concentration of financial resources on limited objectives. The
respective targets were set on the average result of the competing administrations, and the performance was assessed on the relative ranking. Even
though relative performance applied for only these two indicators, in terms
of financial prizes, they accounted for 40% of the total potential reward
for a region.

The reason for setting these two indicators on the basis of relative
performance was that, at the time when the incentive mechanism was
designed, it was difficult to imagine how the administrations would have
pursued the principles contained in the Program on integration of projects
and concentration of resources. Especially for the integration's principle,
when the contract was written, the regional administrations seemed to
have interpreted it in many different ways. Therefore, it was difficult to
find a common external benchmark to measure the performances, and,
as a result, the threshold for achieving the target was set on the basis of

the average performance of the agents, measured as the incidence of regional expenses for integrated projects. Moreover, it was believed that the uncertainty as to the implementation of this indicator would be common to all the agents. In other words, the common shock would prevail on the individual one, and therefore, according to the theory of tournaments, it would be more appropriate to use relative performance to filter the uncertainty.

Vignette 2: Filtering the Uncertainty Through the Use of Relative Performance: The Example of Integrated Projects

A general delay in defining integrated projects took place for all the regional administrations, generally due to the difficulties encountered in activating complex projects; therefore, the amount of expenses in the regional programs for integrated projects on which to calculate the achievement of the performance's target was unexpectedly low in 2002. Having set the threshold for the integration target as the average performance of the participants, the small amount of expenses did not prevent measurement of the indicator and assigning the prizes. If an external, absolute target had been set, it probably would not have been met by any region, and therefore the indicator could not have been verified.

Figure 5.1 shows the performance of regional governments on the indicators. Overall, 62.5% of targets were reached by September 2002 (Anselmo et al., 2006). This general result derives from quite differentiated performances: One outlier (Basilicata) satisfied all 12 indicators; the other regions were strongly differentiated into two groups. The first included three regions (Campania, Puglia, and Sicily), which achieved 8 or more indicators (64% of the targets), and the second included two regions (Sardinia and Calabria), which were positioned below 30% (with 4 or less indicators achieved). The distribution of the performance of each region among indicators shows that all indicators were reached by at least one administration and half the indicators (6 out of 12) were satisfied by the four most successful administrations. Only 2 indicators turned out to be particularly difficult to reach (reforms in the "water services" and in the "waste management" sectors), and the other 2 were apparently easy ("setup of regional evaluation units" and "concentration of resources"). All targets were achieved by at least one region, and all regions achieved at least a few targets. Only 1 indicator was reached by all regions. This shows that targets and thresholds were ambitious, but achievable, and were probably set correctly in most cases.

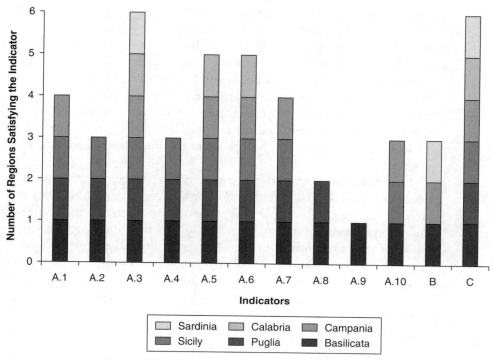

A.1 Delegation of managerial responsibilities to officials
A.2 Setup and implementation of internal control management unit
A.3 Setup of regional and central administration evaluation units
A.4 Development of information society in public administration
A.5 Implementation of one-stop shop
A.6 Implementation of public employment services
A.7 Preparation and approval of territorial and landscape programming documents
A.8 Management of integrated water services
A.9 Management of urban solid waste within optimal service areas
A.10 Setup and operational performance of regional environmental agencies
B Implementation of territorial integrated project:
C Concentration of financial resouces

Figure 5.1   Indicators Achieved by Region by September 2002

SOURCE: Anselmo et al. (2006).

Dealing With Partial Information:
The Role of the Technical Group
and Transparency of Information

With the aim of reducing the uncertainty during the implementation of the contract, monitoring and evaluation of the performance reserve were designed so as to fully share information among all actors. In addition to the principal (the managing authority) that assigned the prizes and the agents (the regions) that participated in the competition, the Italian performance's reserve included the presence of a technical group, as a "third party," with the role of verifying the contract, evaluating the actions of the agents, and measuring agents' performance. The technical group included two members of the evaluation unit of the Ministry of Economy and two members designated by the network of evaluation units of the regional administrations. While not directly involved in the implementation of the Program, the technical group was in charge of addressing problems that might arise during the implementation of the performance mechanism. Thus, the main objectives of the technical group were to reduce the risk of lack of enforcement and to regulate the uncertainty enclosed in the contract.

In addition, the technical group had an independent role that was helpful in reducing the risk of corruption or the temptation on the part of an agent to exercise influence over the principal and thus not cooperate with the system. Transparency of information and the third party's presence, as a guarantee of fairness in the evaluation, spurred the region's participation and cooperation in the performance mechanism. The methods used by the technical group to pursue these objectives were the production of monitoring reports and the widespread diffusion and public discussion of information on the performance of each region on different targets.

Monitoring Reports

Every 6 months during the period of implementation of the incentive mechanism, each region was asked to provide the technical group with a regional report describing the level of progress for each indicator. Matching this information with additional relevant information, the technical group prepared a report. After the deadline for the achievement of performance indicators (September 2002), the technical group provided the managing authority with a final report, giving all the relevant information needed to appreciate the administrations' progress and assign rewards and sanctions.

In a few cases, the assessment made by the technical group led to proposals to change specific aspects of the performance system. After the first period of implementation of the mechanism, more information was available that would have changed the terms of the contract. The technical group, being independent from both sides of the contract, could propose changes to take new information into account. For example, the deadline to declare the integrated regional projects that would run for the indicator of integration was changed due to a generalized delay in procedures independent of regional governments. Overall, changes were limited, and they did not compromise the credibility of the mechanism. Moreover, they were approved according to a formal procedure already envisaged in the rules governing the investment program.

Vignette 3: Misspecification of Targets: The Case of the "Information Society" Indicator

---

During the implementation of the performance reserve system, it became apparent that it was not clear how to measure the indicator on "Information Society," mainly because of the existence of technical alternatives to reach the target and the imperfect comparability of solutions. The technical group attempted to overcome this problem, by defining the list of technical alternatives admitted and asking a specialized office within the DPS to monitor the indicator. Nevertheless, in our opinion, the achievement of the target could not be adequately verified at the deadline of the performance system.

Transparency and Comparability of Information

To make the progress of the administrations comparable throughout the period of the performance reserve and to clarify the chain of responsibility so as to overcome possible obstacles, the decision was made to report information in the same format for each administration and also take into account any specific situation. Therefore, the evaluation was as transparent as possible, and the administrations were fully accountable for the results of their actions.

Moreover, the comparability of progress among regions prompted a *reputation effect*. It was evident that the monetary reward assigned at the end of the period according to the number of targets achieved was not the only incentive at work. During the implementation of the mechanism, the public availability and comparability of information highlighted good and bad intermediate performance and pushed regions toward good behaviors. According to Wrede (2001), comparability of relative performances of regional governments against the same benchmark in a decentralized context increases accountability of governments and restricts the discretionary power of politicians. Thus, to fully exploit this additional incentive, the DPS and the technical group promoted actions to make information accessible to social partners (representatives of major trade union and employers associations) and the public at large, who could, in turn, put pressure on the agents to reach the objectives. Hence, accountability of all the parts involved in the system was increased.

Special efforts were made to make the information available to a larger and less technical public than the one directly involved with European funds. The participation in conferences with seminars and workshops about some aspects of the performance system, the interviews, and advisory articles on specialized newspapers and Web channels are examples of these efforts. Finally, the reports were available on the Web sites of the regions and the

Ministry of Economy, the information being accessible this way to the public at large.

The involvement of administrations from very early stages and the full transparency of the process, which implied public knowledge of the rules of the mechanism and public verifiability of results, limited attempts to exercise pressure on the principal. As a result, the final allocation of resources was accepted by all the participants.

Strengthening Competition Among Regions

As discussed earlier, the 6% incentive mechanism considered relative performance and therefore direct competition among agents with respect to only two indicators ("integration of territorial projects" and "financial concentration"). Thanks to the transparency of the mechanism and the wide diffusion of monitoring information, as described before, the performances of different agents were comparable, and a mechanism of *competition by comparison* was at work. This mechanism was reinforced by the institutional system of direct election of regional governments, whereby members of the electorate can efficiently express their votes on the basis of the observed performance. In an ideal world with complete information, this mechanism would be sufficient to ensure efficient behavior by regional governments in reaching the objectives.

A number of reasons suggested the need to strengthen competition, however. First of all, the new regional electoral system had just been implemented when the performance reserve mechanism was designed, and there was no previous experience of performance-based evaluations to lead the electorate's decision. Second, information on the outcome and on the link between regional governments' actions and outcomes could be blurred because of the actions of many unrelated variables and unpredictable shocks. Therefore, it was considered appropriate to include an additional degree of competition among regions: The rewards not assigned in the first round, in the case of regions that did not succeed in reaching all the targets, were assigned to the others on the basis of their performance and their original budgets. In this respect, the reward for achieving the results for which all regions were striving, or the penalty for failing to obtain it, was increased, thus introducing more competition among agents (see Vickers, 1995, for a definition of different concepts of competition).

The assignment of the 6% resources took place in March 2003, with the approval of the proposal prepared on the basis of the final report by the technical group. As a result of the mix of competition and accountability that characterized the tournament model and the complementary activities enacted to enforce it (strengthening partnership, cooperation, and transparency), the agents received different rewards according to their performance.

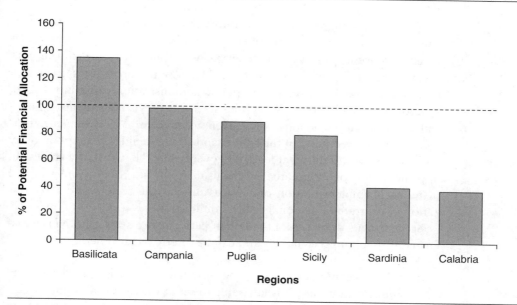

Figure 5.2   Performance of Regions as Percentage of Final Financial Assignment on Initial Potential Budget

SOURCE: Anselmo et al. (2006).

Figure 5.2 shows the final financial outcome of the system. The variability in the performance of regions on the number of indicators achieved already mentioned was strengthened by additional rewards to good performers. One region (Basilicata) received almost 140% of its initial endowment; three regions (Campania, Sicilia, and Puglia) received from 98% to 79%; and two regions (Sardinia and Calabria) received around 40% (Anselmo et al., 2006). Note that because of the mechanism of indirect competition that redistributes the resources not assigned in case of indicators not achieved, the variance of the final financial distribution was higher than the one based on the number of indicators achieved, and the best performer received more than 100%. In addition, indicators have different weights, which also influenced the final allocation.

Conclusions and Lessons Learned

The analysis of the mechanism as a principal-agent relationship was very useful to pinpoint strengths and weaknesses of the system. A competitive model was applied in the search for the most efficient behavior by regional governments in a recently decentralized system. The main objective of the system was to supplement the decentralization process with the provision of financial rewards or penalties to influence the performance of regions (sub-central governments) toward a number of selected objectives considered indispensable for the success of the development strategy.

This chapter highlighted the features that make the mechanism more complex than a simple tournament, where only relative performance is taken into account, and the actions that were put into place to deal with asymmetric and partial information. The 6% performance system is a remarkable innovation for Italian public administration (Anselmo, Brezzi, Raimondo, & Utili, 2004). With rules set at least 2 years in advance, financial rewards and sanctions were given to subcentral governments, thus increasing the credibility of the system and strengthening the accountability and cooperation of different levels of government. Thanks to the successful implementation of an incentive mechanism, significant results were achieved in terms of implementation of reforms in strategic sectors and modernization of central and regional public administration.

Some lessons drawn from the Italian performance system have been discussed throughout the chapter and can be briefly recalled here:

1. When a contract enclosing the incentive scheme is agreed upon by public institutions, it is advisable to set at least some absolute targets (as opposed to relative performance among the agents) because of the intrinsic value attached by the principal (central government) to the fact that most agents could reach some minimum thresholds.

2. The use of absolute external targets also prevented the risk of collusive behavior of agents (often highlighted as one of the disadvantages of tournaments). However, in the presence of absolute thresholds, agents do not have to compete, since financial rewards are independent. Consequently, the performance reserve system provided an additional reward achievable only if the others did not reach their targets, thus linking performance of agents and promoting peer control on outcomes.

3. In the presence of asymmetric and partial information, the active participation of agents from the very early stages of the mechanism design was necessary in order to choose the indicators and set the targets and the rules correctly. Moreover, the partnership process helped in increasing regions' accountability, since the objectives of the performance indicators were assumed as their own priorities. This helped the regions to accept the rewards or sanctions.

4. Public availability of information when the incentive scheme was active (for example, through the periodic monitoring reports) contributed to avoiding the risk of collusion among the agents and corruption of the principal. At the final deadline, regional electorates already had a lot of information on performance of the governments on which to base their judgment.

5. Besides the monetary reward, the reputation effect played an important role. During the implementation of the mechanism, the public availability and comparability of information highlighted good and bad intermediate performance and pushed regions toward good behaviors.

Comparability of relative performances of regional governments against the same benchmark in a decentralized context increases accountability of governments and restricts discretionary power of politicians.

Notes

1. The views expressed in the paper are those of the authors and do not necessarily involve the responsibility of the Ministry of Economic Development.

2. A performance reserve system with similar features was also put into place in the Program on the basis of indicators related to correct management of funds, proposed by the European Commission. For its more limited scope, the system is not the object of this paper; for a description, see Anselmo et al. (2006).

Discussion Questions

1. A contract agreed on by a central administration and one or more local administrations describes the respective responsibilities and functions in order to achieve a common objective. Nevertheless, in practice, the contract cannot foresee all the contingencies, because one or both parties lack information. Based on the case presented in the chapter, discuss what relevant information both the principal and the agents could be missing.

2. What actions should be carried out in order to increase administrations' accountability in implementing public policies? (Suggestion: Also take into account the role of public opinion.)

3. Based on the experience presented in the chapter, should competition be introduced among public administrations? If so, how much competition should be promoted? What are the risks of making public administrations compete for financial resources?

4. What is the relevance of partnership among administrations, and how can it be strengthened?

References

Ahmad, E., Tandberg, E., & Zhang, P. (2002). *On national and supranational objectives: Improving the effectiveness of targeted expenditure programs* (IMF Working Paper, WP/02/209). Washington, DC: International Monetary Fund.

Anselmo, I., Brezzi, M., Raimondo, L., & Utili, F. (2004). *Making administrations accountable: The experience of the Italian performance reserve system.* Proceedings of the Fifth European Conference, "Evaluation of the Structural Funds," Budapest, Hungary.

Anselmo, I., Brezzi, M., Raimondo, L., & Utili, F. (2006). The performance reserve mechanism in Italy. *Materiali Uval, 9*. Available at http://www.dps.tesoro.it

Anselmo, I., & Raimondo, L. (2000, September18–19). *The objective 1 Italian performance reserve: A tool to enhance the effectiveness of programmes and the quality of evaluation.* Paper presented at European Commission Conference "Evaluation for Quality," Edinburgh, Scotland.

Barca, F. (2000). *Una politica per la competitività territoriale: Spunti teorici e disegno istituzionale* [A policy for territorial competitiveness: A theoretical and institutional framework]. Paper presented at the Annual Conference of Società Italiana degli Economisti, Cagliari, Italy.

Barca, F. (2001, April 30–May 1). *Rethinking partnership in development policies: Lessons from a European experiment.* Paper presented at the "Conference for Exploring Policy Options for a New Rural America," Kansas City, MO.

Department for Development Policies and Cohesion, Ministry of Economy and Finance (n.d.). Home page. Available at http://www.dps.tesoro.it/uval_linee_premialita.asp

Dixit, A. (2002). Incentives and organizations in the public sector: An interpretative review. *Journal of Economic Resources, 37*, 696–727.

Hart, O. (1995). *Firms, contracts, and financial structure.* Oxford, UK: Oxford University Press.

Nicita, A., & Scoppa, V. (2005). *Economia dei contratti* [Contract theory]. Rome, Italy: Carocci.

Salmon, P. (1987). Decentralization as an incentive scheme. *Oxford Review of Economic Policy, 3*(2), 24–43.

Shannon, J., & Kee, J. E. (1989). The rise of competitive federalism. *Public Budgeting and Finance, 9*(4), 5–20.

Tirole, J. (1999). Incomplete contracts: Where do we stand? *Econometrica, 67*, 741–781.

Vickers, J. (1995). Concepts of competition. *Oxford Economic Papers, 47*(1), 1–23.

Wrede M. (2001). Yardstick competition to tame the Leviathan. *European Journal of Political Economy, 17*, 705–721.

6 Recognizing Credible Performance Reports

The Role of the Government Auditor in Canada

Barry Leighton[1]

Once a report on the performance of an organization is made public, a number of questions usually come to mind, the foremost being, "What difference did it make?" In other words, "Did the intended audience actually read the report, and did it provide them with key information they needed about the performance of the organization so that they could make a judgment or decision?" Too often, performance reports have sat unread, just gathering dust. But if some of the intended audience has indeed read the report, then "were they satisfied with the quality of the performance information presented? Did they get the right information for their use, and was it balanced, understandable, and credible?"

In recent years, trust in the source of performance information has been a relatively scarce commodity. In the wake of Enron and WorldCom, corruption appears to have gone mainstream in the private sector. These events have spilled over into the public sector by serving as a tipping point for public trust in all private and public institutions, giving rise to calls for more oversight. Indeed, the decline of trust in public and private institutions has, as Power (1997) observed, contributed to the trend toward the "audit society," in which assurance is sought on the credibility of all information. Consequently, accountability and transparency have become the watchwords of the day. As a result, there is a heightened demand for professions and organizations that can satisfy the escalating demand for accountability by providing independent assurance on the fairness and reliability of performance reports.

This chapter discusses the role of the government auditor in providing assurance to elected representatives and the public about the reliability and fairness of performance information reported by government departments and agencies to a legislative or representative body. The example used to illustrate this role is the auditor for the federal government of Canada when assessing the quality of annual performance reports submitted to the Parliament of Canada.

The Need for Performance Reports

For a government in a representative democracy to be held to account for its performance concerning public funds entrusted to it by taxpayers, elected representatives must have confidence in the accuracy and fairness of the information on how those funds were used.

A performance report is the main vehicle used by management for communicating to a governing body the actual results of an organization's performance against its planned results over a specified period so that it can be held to account. Commitments for planned or expected results are usually made through a public planning document, such as a business or corporate plan, and while it may be a separate document, planning and performance information is often combined into a single annual report that is both retrospective and prospective.

A good performance report provides a credible performance story about how well an organization met its planned results. It presents the appropriate type and amount of information necessary for decision making, such as about allocating or reallocating funds from programs that have been found not to work toward other programs that have been shown to work well.

A performance report does not only address external accountability. The performance information reported should also reflect a roll-up of similar, more detailed information used by managers at all levels within the organization to produce better results. Reporting performance information externally at a more aggregate level also enables the external governing body to manage its own, broader affairs in ways that will produce better results. Four categories of uses may be captured by a 2-by-2 table, with the rows distinguishing between an organization's external and internal environment, while the columns capture two types of use: accountability for results and managing for results (see Figure 6.1).

Historically, government reporting focused primarily on resource inputs (what they spent), their activities (what they did), and their outputs (what they produced). By contrast, more recent approaches to good management require managers to focus on the actual results achieved, namely, the impacts and effects of their programs. Taking such a "managing-for-results" or "results-based management" approach requires that the expected results are clearly defined, the results achieved are measured and evaluated, and adjustments are made to improve both efficiency and effectiveness.

		Performance Management (MFR)	
		Robust Accountability	Results-Driven Decisions
Performance Reporting	External	1. For example, departmental performance reports	4. For example, collective results, horizontal initiatives, whole-of-government reporting
	Internal	3. For example, performance agreements/contracts, performance pay	2. For example, business intelligence, management information systems (e.g., balanced scorecard)

Figure 6.1   Internal and External Accountability and Managing for Results

Role of the Auditor

Auditors Provide Independent Assurance

A variety of means have been developed by which some degree of confidence can be gained for reports about organizational performance and contribute to the confidence of stakeholders in the fairness and reliability of performance information. First, confidence in the credibility of performance information may be obtained from within the organization, through internal controls, such as a data quality assurance framework consisting of standards, systems, and practices. Assurance may also be given to management about this information by way of internal audits. However, those outside the organization may prefer to seek independent assurance from external sources. External checks and balances on government departments and agencies include oversight and controls, such as committees of the legislature, commissions of enquiry, codes of conduct, rules, regulations, and laws, as well as external audits.

Requirements for a credible assurance provider include being independent, objective, and unbiased by political influence or considerations. This is most possible through a self-governing profession that is formally recognized and has a rigorous methodology, professional standards, and ethics. It will have appropriate governance arrangements to provide for monitoring of member compliance with standards, as well as formal qualifications, testing for entry via certification, and exit criteria with fair procedures for exit.

This is also one of the few professions to hang up a shingle in the marketplace and offer to provide assurance on these matters. Auditors have become socially recognized authorities in the assurance-provider business, for the financial conditions of organizations as well as for their nonfinancial performance.

Who Is an Auditor?

An auditor is an independent, professional person who is suitably qualified to perform an audit. The objective of conducting an audit is to enable the auditor to provide the person or body to whom the organization is accountable with an independent, professional, and informed opinion that assesses the extent to which the information, statements, and assertions contained in a report prepared by the organization's management conform in all significant respects with some suitable, previously agreed-upon criteria. The auditor bases this opinion on, among other things, an examination of the report using evidence-gathering methods that meet generally accepted standards of the profession. In providing such an opinion, the auditor offers some level of assurance that the information contained in the organization's report is reliable and both fairly reflects and presents the financial and other conditions of the organization, such as the progress made by the organization toward its planned results.

The permanent client of government auditors—or *legislative auditors*—is the legislature of elected representatives. Through appropriate legislation, this body provides the mandate for a permanent, statutory engagement of the auditor to conduct audits. Such is the case with the Office of the Auditor General of Canada (OAG), which has the status of an Officer of Parliament. Similar arrangements have been established at the state and provincial levels, as well as at the local and municipal levels. Federal legislative auditors are known by the peculiar term of *supreme audit institutions* (SAIs), to distinguish them from auditors serving other levels of government. Along with the OAG, the U.S. Government Accountability Office (GAO), the National Audit Office of the United Kingdom (NAO), and the Australian National Audit Office (ANAO) are all supreme audit institutions. One difference between the GAO and the OAG is that the former is routinely directed by Congress to conduct specific audit work, while the latter has no formal obligation to respond to similar requests from Parliament but takes them into consideration and, in recent years, has chosen to conduct many of the audits requested. Overall, SAIs are "independent voices, backed by the application of commonly accepted auditing standards and principles" (Divorski, 2005, p. 261).

The OAG

The OAG has about 600 auditors and other employees, of which about two thirds are financial or attest auditors and the remainder are performance auditors. Both roles are essential: The first ensures that money is spent according to where Parliament authorized it to be spent, while the second role answers questions about what value was given to taxpayers for those expenditures.

Founded in 1878 as a fully independent organization, the OAG stresses being an independent audit office that serves Parliament and the well-being of Canadians, while contributing to an accountable government, to an ethical and effective public service, and to good governance. This is accomplished by "conducting independent audits and studies that provide objective information, advice, and assurance to Parliament, government, and Canadians" (OAG, 2006).

As with many other legislative audit offices, the OAG has financial auditors who attest to whether the government and its departments and agencies are keeping proper accounts and records, are presenting their financial information fairly, and are complying with relevant authorities. Performance or value-for-money auditors usually determine whether departments and agencies are being managed with due regard to economy and efficiency, whether they have established satisfactory procedures to measure and report on the effectiveness of programs, and whether they are complying with authorities. This leads to an OAG responsibility to pay attention to departmental performance reports as a "matter of significance" worthy of bringing to the attention of Parliament as its sole "client," usually through an audit report. Probably uniquely, the OAG also audits whether money has been spent with due regard to the environmental effects of those expenditures in the context of sustainable development (Auditor General Act, 1995).

Government auditors usually provide their audit reports in either of two ways. One is to deliver them directly to the legislature as their clients under an ongoing legislative mandate. Alternatively, in an "attest engagement," auditors provide an audit opinion, statement, or "attestation" to the department or agency that engaged them. The department would then include it in a report that would usually be submitted to the legislature.

Requirements for Reporting

Most governments require an accountability document of some kind that provides sufficient, appropriate information to hold a government department or agency to account, not only for funds expended on past performance but also on how well those funds were managed. At the federal level in the United States, the Government Performance and Results Act of 1993 requires all agencies to submit such an annual report. The Office of Management and Budget (OMB) provides oversight for the reporting requirements under this act.

In the Canadian federal government, this same obligation is somewhat more complex or, perhaps, more indirect in how this obligation to report is placed on the 90 or so departments and agencies. They are required to submit a performance report to Parliament every fall as Part III of the Estimates, as determined by the Treasury Board. This is the central agency empowered under the Financial Administration Act (1985) to decide the nature, form, and content of these reports. It also issues policies and guidelines as well as provides direction, advice, and other support to departments and agencies. Accordingly, the Treasury Board Secretariat (TBS) asks that a performance report outline what the department has accomplished over the past year against the commitments is made in its planning report submitted in the prior year. It also releases annual guidelines, including reporting principles, for the preparation of these reports. These guidelines also reflect the emphasis placed by the federal government on the importance of good performance reporting in *Results for Canadians* (TBS, 2000).

Parliamentary Interest in Performance Reports

Members of Parliament have also been interested in the quality of the reports they have been receiving. When reviewing the "Estimates documents"—the government's planning reports that allocate funds to departments and agencies by way of parliamentary "votes"—parliamentarians in committees have sometimes found it useful to also examine the track record of past funding in similar areas as those planned for the upcoming year. Expecting to find useful information about "what works," they have been routinely disappointed. Nonetheless, parliamentarians have, on occasion, questioned senior management of departments about the performance of their programs.

Although various attempts have been made over the years to improve the quality of information flowing to Parliament, a further step was taken in 1995 with a Parliament-led Improved Reporting to Parliament Project. This project separated a department's plans for the coming year from an account of its past performance reported against an earlier plan, a combination that seemed to be two unconnected exercises. The project also kick-started the effort to move away from reporting just program inputs and activities toward a focus on results, starting by adding outputs as the focus of reporting, followed a few years later by a prime focus on program outcomes. Similar developments in the United States, Australia, and England are described elsewhere (Divorski, 2005).

What Auditors Do About Performance Reports

An auditor can fulfill many roles that are related to performance measurement and reporting (see Divorski, 2005; also Epstein, Grifel, & Morgan, 2004). The OAG pursues some of these roles to a greater or lesser extent, including the following:

1. *Assessing the fairness and reliability performance information* included in the annual reports of three special status agencies against commitments made in their corporate plans

2. *Assessing the quality of annual performance reports* of selected departments and agencies by rating them against criteria for good-quality performance reports and indicating the level reached by each report against each of these criteria

3. *Auditing the performance reports* as one line of enquiry within a broader audit focusing on a specific department or agency program

4. *Auditing the reliability* of specific types of performance information reported (such as survey results)

5. *Auditing the use of performance information* to manage a department or agency for better results under a "managing-for-results" approach

The first of these is done on an annual basis. The remaining roles are fulfilled on an occasional basis, as determined by an analysis of significance and risk, and when placed in priority of other concerns the auditor may have with the department or agency.

The OAG mandate, however, does not extend to some of the additional roles described by Epstein et al. (2004). For example, it does not have a mandate to directly measure or assess the *actual* performance of a department or agency, such as by conducting an evaluation of a program. Instead, it audits whether departments and agencies have done this themselves.

As well, the OAG does not generally provide departments and agencies with consulting or expert advice on developing the right performance indicators, on measuring and then populating the indicators with good data, or on using the performance information to manage for better results. Nonetheless, advice is often requested on an informal basis, such as in an early stage during the assessment of the annual reports of the three special status agencies. Any informal advice offered, however, is given prior to shifting to formal audit mode, when the auditors carefully maintain their independence and objectivity. As such, any advice followed cannot be used by the organization being audited to justify any subsequent shortcomings in its final report.

Levels of Assurance

Assurance engagements usually provide either a high or moderate level of assurance. Applied to performance reporting, an auditor giving a high level of assurance provides an audit opinion using sufficient, appropriate evidence to provide reasonable but not absolute assurance that the substance of a report (e.g., about program results) is reasonable within the context as a whole. Giving absolute assurance would be unrealistic, largely because it is impossible to state that all significant risks, errors, or misstatements have been identified.

There are also inherent limitations on the nature of the internal controls an organization can place on data quality because there are usually trade-offs, such as between data accuracy and the timeliness of when these data are provided. Furthermore, data on organizational performance are usually less precise than financial data because, like most social science data, they tend to fall within a specified range of acceptable accuracy.

Finally, as in all social science, the evidence is seldom, if ever, fully appropriate or complete and "sufficient" because there could always be evidence to the contrary lurking out there yet to be gathered. Consequently, much of this available evidence is persuasive, rather than conclusive in a pass-fail way.

All of this adds up to the need for an auditor to exercise "professional judgment," which is usually based on training and experience. Based on the evidence gathered, the auditor uses professional judgment to form an overall conclusion about whether or not the information is accurate and is both fairly interpreted and presented in a performance report.

By contrast, a moderate level of assurance is more limited in scope. Auditors provide a statement (but not an audit opinion) about whether they are aware of any significant modifications that should be made to the report in order to satisfy the agreed-upon criteria for a good performance report. In other words, auditors report on whether the performance report would mislead readers. This is done by determining the plausibility of performance information reported and forming a conclusion about whether anything has come to the auditor's attention that causes him or her to believe the performance information provided does not conform, in all significant respects, to the criteria. Consequently, by stating that he or she can find nothing wrong that would suggest the performance information in the report is not accurate and fairly presented, the auditor is providing a form of "negative assurance."

Audit Standards and Criteria

While audits are conducted in compliance with procedural and methodological standards, auditors are not usually standard setters. Instead, they defer to their professional associations to fulfill this role, such as the Canadian Institute for Chartered Accountants (CICA). For public reporting standards, federal government auditors in Canada look to the Public Sector Accounting Board (PSAB) of CICA. In the United States, auditors look to the Governmental Accounting Standards Board (GASB) of the Financial Accounting Foundation, which has developed its own public reporting principles (GASB, 2003).

In developing the criteria against which a performance report is audited, auditors will also look for substantive standards. As Mayne and Wilkins (2005) note, however, the absence of generally accepted principles and criteria for assessing performance information and performance reporting has been a challenge for government auditors. While there are not yet any counterparts to the Generally Accepted Accounting Standards (GAAS), it is only a matter of time before "generally accepted public performance-reporting principles" emerge and are formally adopted by professional auditing bodies.

Most notably, around the turn of the present century, the CCAF developed a set of performance-reporting principles based on consultations with key experts and senior management from private and public sectors across Canada. Initially produced as a discussion paper, it was finalized in 2002 (CCAF, 2002). These principles have now been adapted, in one way or another, for local circumstances by government auditors in 4 of the 10 Canadian provinces. At least one of these jurisdictions has succeeded in having performance-reporting principles endorsed by the provincial legislature. At the federal level, the TBS adapted an early draft of the CCAF principles as part of its 2001 annual guidance to federal departments and agencies when preparing their annual performance reports. These TBS guidelines are updated every year, and their particular principles have been modified over time as needs change.

There have since been two other developments. First, the Canadian Council of Legislative Audit Offices (CCOLA), through its Performance Reporting and Auditing Group (PRAG), developed an audit framework for public reporting, based on these same CCAF principles (CCOLA-PRAG, 2004). Second, these CCAF performance-reporting principles were developed further by the CICA Public Sector Accounting Board (PSAB) with a Statement of Recommended Practice, or SORP (CICA-PSAB, 2006), designed to operationalize the principles for report preparers. While a SORP usually reflects current best practices, this one tends to "lead practice." In June 2006, it was approved by PSAB for release as guidance to report preparers. However, it may take at least 5, if not 10, years of monitoring practices before these principles become part of the formal standards for Canadian auditors. This ongoing development may be seen as a healthy sign of interest in improving the quality of public sector performance reporting.

Case Study: Auditing Departmental Performance Reports

Audits of Performance Reports

The OAG has been concerned about the quality of performance reporting for nearly two decades, as demonstrated by a series of audits it has conducted on the issue. For example, in 1988, auditors found clear shortcomings in departmental performance reports as a basis for accountability but also noted that these reports were still the best single source of information about departmental programs (OAG, 1988). Four years later, another audit elaborated on these shortcomings, including inconsistencies between what departments did and what they reported, as well as overall weaknesses in reporting results and effectiveness (OAG, 1992).

Another audit looked at the state of federal government reporting in 1997 by examining the 16 pilot departments and agencies in the Improved Reporting to Parliament Projects. Auditors found that while the basic reporting was sound and progress had been made, Parliament received little information it could use to identify what value Canadians were getting for their taxes (OAG, 1997). Instead, departments reported only on their activities, products, and services.

Three years later, OAG auditors once again examined the quality of departmental performance reports and concluded that progress in improving the quality of performance reporting to Parliament by federal departments and agencies was "disappointing," to say the least (OAG, 2000). While recognizing that changing the culture of government toward a results-based one is difficult and takes time, auditors found only marginal improvements in the quality of reporting.

Nonetheless, this latest round of informing Parliament about the state of reporting by the government's auditor seems to have attracted the interest of parliamentarians. In 2001, the House of Commons Standing Committee on Public Accounts (PAC) emphasized the importance of good-quality performance reporting and asked the OAG to randomly select one or two departmental performance reports each year "in order to verify, among other things, that the information contained in these reports is a fair representation of accomplishments against goals and objectives" (PAC, 2001). However, at that time, there were no formal standards on the quality of performance reports.

What Makes a Credible Performance Report?

Given the initial absence of available criteria on what makes a good performance report, a series of OAG audits and studies in the 1990s laid the groundwork for the later development of more formal criteria. In 2002, the OAG took these emerging criteria and elaborated upon them in a "model for good performance reporting" against which reports could be assessed and Parliament informed about the quality of these reports (OAG, 2002a). Until its standard setting body, the CICA, establishes public performance-reporting principles, these interim criteria have been useful for auditing federal departmental performance reports.

The OAG model for good-quality performance reporting was designed to help the preparers of performance reports produce compelling performance stories while effectively communicating good-quality performance information to parliamentarians. This model has five key criteria:

1. Organizational context and strategic outcomes are clear.

2. Performance expectations are clear and concrete.

3. Key results are reported against expectations.

4. Performance information is credible and balanced.

5. Use of performance information is demonstrated.

The first three criteria capture what has been accomplished by the department or agency, while the remaining two criteria indicate the quality and use of the performance information. They roughly follow the logical sequencing implied in a program logic model or "results chain" by focusing at the outset on the broad public purpose served, then on the specific commitments made (i.e., the planned results), then on the actual results achieved, followed by steps to improve future results based on this feedback.

More specifically, the first criterion expects that a department or agency will be crystal clear about its overall strategic direction by stating its core business in terms of the public purpose served. This should reflect its mandate and mission. Broad strategic outcomes and the priorities for the reporting period should be identified. Activities undertaken within major programs or business lines should be placed in the context of an operating environment that identifies limitations, constraints, and opportunities, as well as key partners contributing to any shared outcomes. There should also be a brief description of the major risks and challenges for the organization in fulfilling its broad, strategic outcomes.

According to the second criterion, performance reports should precisely state what benefits will be provided for taxpayers as a whole or for a specific group during the reporting period. Concrete targets for outputs and outcomes should include the amount and direction of the planned changes (i.e., increase, decrease, or no change), the time frame in which those changes will be made, and management accountabilities for the results (OAG, 2006). These commitments are carried forward from the earlier planning document covering the same period and should be presented in a way that shows how they are aligned with departmental priorities and how they contribute to government priorities. However, because some of the earlier commitments may no longer be relevant and new ones may have subsequently arisen, any changes should be accompanied by explanations.

At the core of good reporting is the third criterion, which expects that a performance report will provide an answer to the question of whether or not the department or agency achieved what it promised to do. Key results should be reported against the planned results in terms of how well the targets were met. In audit language, the variance between the planned and expected results should then be analyzed and explained. Interpretation of this variance is best done by comparing the results achieved, not just against the commitments but also against trends over the past few years, any benchmarks, and any public or private sector norms or standards. Evidence from evaluations, studies, internal audits, and other sources should be integrated into the discussion interpreting the results. The discussion should also identify how well any expected risks or challenges to meeting the targets were overcome. A good report describes the organization's contribution to the planned outcomes relative to other organizations that also contributed to the shared outcome. A good report also identifies the cost of producing the outputs that contributed to the outcomes.

The fourth criterion expects the report will contain information about the quality of the performance data, including their accuracy and whether they are fit for the use intended. This includes addressing the credibility of the data sources. As well, a good report should be balanced, in terms of describing both successes and shortcomings, in the sense that there are never any failures—only learning opportunities. Balanced reporting lends credibility to all the performance information provided.

Finally, a good performance report should demonstrate how the results information on past performance is used as feedback to help improve future results. If it does not achieve this, then it may only be part of a reporting exercise solely for external accountability. This fifth criterion expects that performance reports will show the ways in which performance information is used to help departments make strategic decisions, highlight lessons learned, and identify how weak performance will be corrected to improve future results. The report should also provide a credible discussion about the capacity of a department to produce sustainable results by continuing to perform well in the future.

As mentioned, these criteria are designed to roughly approximate a program logic model because reports that present information about results using this format are usually very successful at communicating the "theory" of the program. When populated with evidence, logic models help to communicate the full performance story. A logic model initially captures the intended impact and the key program elements that lead up to that impact. The logic of a logic model provides for a causal flow, from the financial, human, technological, and knowledge resources that form the inputs to a program, to the activities or processes carried out, to the outputs produced by those activities, and then to their impacts, in terms of short-term, medium-term, and final outcomes.

When the impacts are mainly within the control of the program, direct attribution for the outcome may be claimed. However, in practice, this is seldom the case, because there are also partners contributing to the same outcome as well as competitors working against the outcome. Usually, there are other factors that are outside the control of the organization that also positively contribute to the outcome as well as some that have an unintended, counterproductive impact on a program. Consequently, an organization can be held accountable only for those factors within its full control. It can then share the credit for planned results met—or share the blame for targets not fully met.

How the Model Works

In the OAG model, each of the five criteria also has five levels. These are labeled as *basic, fair, good, very good,* and *excellent.* The fifth level represents a performance report demonstrating excellence on that criterion or attribute of public reporting. At this highest level, a report would provide information about actual performance against planned or expected performance. An *excellent* report would enable users to assess how well the organization has met its targets and the extent to which its outputs have contributed to its outcomes. It would provide this results-oriented information in a logical sequence, by taking the "theory" of how the program is expected to work, preferably presented in a program logic model, and then populating it with actual results data. This would form the framework for a compelling "performance story" about what difference the organization makes for taxpayers and constituents.

By contrast, at the first or lowest level, a "minimalist" report would provide only some basic descriptive information, mainly about activities, without reference to how they contribute in a causal sense to the planned outcomes. Judgments about the lower levels of the model are anchored in earlier audits and reviews of performance reports, supplemented by advice from experts in the field. Anchoring the highest level is a challenge because there were no exemplary reports found through the earlier audit work. Consequently, this highest level of good reporting is a projection of what an ideal performance report would look like.

Ratings on each of the five criteria generally indicate the extent to which the performance story told by the report is a credible one (see Figure 6.2). Nonetheless, the model does not provide an overall score for a report by combining the ratings. This is because it is dangerous to construct a combined or overall score either by assuming each of the five criteria is equal in importance or, alternatively, by assuming they are not equally important and then giving them each an appropriate weighting to reflect their relative importance.

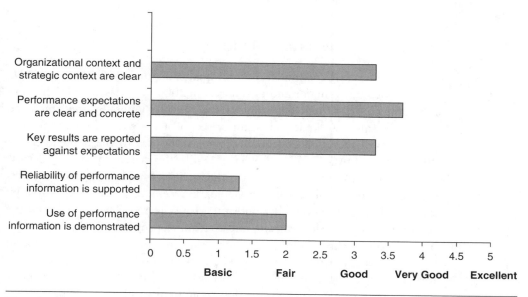

Figure 6.2   Example of a Rating of Report Quality

Example of a Rating

Strengths and Weaknesses of the Model

There are some advantages to this learning and development approach. First, it recognizes that the quality of performance reports varies widely across the federal government. Second, most reports are not ready to be audited against the fifth or highest level in the model. Consequently, this is a "pre-audit" strategy for helping report preparers improve future reports by giving them feedback. When a report is deemed to be "audit ready," in the sense that it has a good chance of receiving a good or "clean" opinion, then it would be audited against the highest level in the model on a pass-fail basis. In this sense, the model takes a learning, developmental, maturity, or formative approach. Challenges for government auditors in taking this approach have been discussed elsewhere (Boyle, 2005).

There are, however, some potential drawbacks to this approach. First, while the auditor provides feedback on how close or far away a report is from achieving a level of quality that would make it auditable on a pass-fail basis, assurance that these criteria have been fully or partially met is not provided. Second, in this pre-audit mode, the audit methodology used would at most be that associated with a moderate level of assurance, which in practice amounts to a "desk review." Third, while the fourth criterion places the burden on the reporting organization to demonstrate why the performance information is credible and can be relied upon, this model does not ask an auditor to directly test the accuracy of the data. Nonetheless, the model provides useful information for Parliament about the quality of performance reporting by federal departments and agencies.

Audits Using the Rating Model

Since publishing the model of good-quality reporting in 2002, the OAG has conducted two major audit exercises. In 2003, it assessed and then compared the reports of nine departments and agencies whose business included the public safety and national security sector. They were also examined to see how well they had coordinated their responses to the September 11, 2001, crisis (OAG, 2003). However, while the reliability of the performance information was not covered, the audit examined how fairly the performance information was interpreted and presented. These are captured by the first three criteria together with the fifth criterion. The audit found the reports to be generally wanting and that more progress would have to be made on the quality of reporting on government performance. It also found that if parliamentarians and the public looked to rely on these annual performance reports for information about the capacity of the government to respond to national emergencies, they would have to look elsewhere.

A second audit was conducted in 2005, this time of 3 departments that were among the original 16 pilot departments participating in the 1995 Improved Reporting to Parliament Project. This enabled a "longitudinal comparison" of the extent of improvements made in the quality of these reports over a 9-year period (1995–2004) compared with improvements made by the same departments over a recent 2-year period (2003–2004). A second notable aspect of the 3 departments is that they had a substantial science base to their activities, thereby raising the reasonable expectation that they would have a good capacity for measuring their performance. However, this did not appear to be the case. Instead, the audit found little improvement in quality over this period and that the earlier reports from 1995 were more clear and more understandable, largely because they focused only on program activities whereas the later ones were more complex due to their more appropriate focus on program outcomes (OAG, 2005a).

Some provincial legislative auditors in Canada have had parallel experiences (see Epstein et al., 2004). Notably, the province of Alberta has produced a highly regarded, whole-of-government annual report, *Measuring Up* (Alberta Finance, 2005). Perhaps the best example of a provincial government department or agency report comes from the province of British Columbia, where the annual report of the WorksafeBC (2006) was audited by the provincial legislative auditor and was found to meet the provincial principles for good public performance reporting.

Challenges to Good Reporting

Over the past decade or so, the OAG has suggested there are five main reasons for the limited progress in improving the quality of performance reports (OAG, 2005b). First, many of the core concepts and principles of good performance reporting are generally neither well understood nor well applied. Earlier OAG audits criticized the TBS for not showing stronger leadership in promoting better understanding and applications (e.g., Divorski, 2005; OAG, 1997). However, TBS has, over the past decade, encouraged efforts to change the focus from activities to outcomes in performance reporting. Further, a recent TBS requirement to report against a departmental program structure shows promise, as long as key program performance indicators and data become available.

Second, the environment of performance reporting is political because the importance of reporting shortcomings as well as successes has not yet been widely accepted. The lack of balance in honestly reporting and then explaining the variance between planned and actual results is not yet part of the management culture of government. Indeed, departmental performance reports, or "DPRs," are sometimes more like "deep PR" documents. Nonetheless, there is a growing recognition that such public relations reports are simply not credible or appropriate.

Third, there are neither incentives for good reporting practices nor sanctions for poor reporting in the Canadian federal government. Unlike their counterparts in the United States, House of Commons committees do not control departmental budgets, and unlike the U.S. Office of Management and Budget (OMB) in the Office of the President, there are no explicit organizational rewards for good management within the current expenditure management system. Instead, rewards are given by way of individual performance pay to senior management. Nor are there any "sports league tables" in which departments might be listed in rank order of the quality of their performance reports as a way of "naming and shaming" poor performers. Consequently, it is difficult to see why senior management would seek a better balance between good and poor performance against commitments if greater transparency meant being open to criticism without some compensating factor. On the other hand, rising above shortcomings by presenting them as challenges and opportunities for a learning organization to improve future results could be an alternative, more acceptable image to portray.

Fourth, performance reporting is unofficially considered to be a low priority, largely because of the above reasons. Senior management seldom become involved with departmental performance reporting because the type of information they provide to Parliament is seldom used internally by departments to manage results or used externally by the government to manage government-wide initiatives. Furthermore, departments have found it very challenging to establish key performance indicators for programs, to develop appropriate measures for these indicators, and to populate them with good-quality data. Accordingly, some critics have argued that the bar for the performance expectations of public administrators has been set unrealistically high (Clark & Swain, 2005). However, the Canadian federal government has set this bar itself, and the OAG is merely auditing against these high expectations. Further, the alternative to some form of evidence-based, rational, decision-making model is "political responsiveness" (Aucoin, 2005).

Fifth, despite government initiatives over the past 30 years or so that were undertaken with the objective of improving the quality of performance reports, they have not been successful, because they focused primarily on the quality of the supply side. More attention should be paid to the demand side of reporting, particularly to the information needs of parliamentary users for the express purposes of holding departments to account for specific programs, rather than generally for all of their programs. Information can be used for decision making about budgets, based on what works and why, under what circumstances, and for whom. While House committees at the federal level in Canada do not directly control budgets, they do have the power to recommend to the House a reduction in a budgetary allocation or vote. Although this may be largely a symbolic action, it does place the spotlight on the issue and forces the government of the day to make a formal response. As well, questioning of senior departmental management when making appearances before House committees might be better served if it focused on the performance of particular programs against specific planned commitments rather than focusing on overall departmental performance. Nonetheless, some observers of parliamentary behavior have noted that parliamentarians have taken little interest in the wealth of performance information provided to them in performance reports and rarely discuss them (Savoie, 2003).

Lessons Learned and Conclusion

One of the lessons learned from the Canadian experience is that a performance report fails when the information it provides does not form the basis of a dialogue between senior management and the legislature to whom they are accountable. That is, a report is inadequate when there is a lack of fit between what the elected representatives want to know and what management chooses to tell them. This is usually because management does not ask their target audience what information they need, and once the report is delivered, the elected officials do not appropriately challenge the information provided. However, often the legislators themselves do not have a clear expectation of what would constitute useful information. Accordingly, more effort needs to be done to improve the demand side of performance reporting.

Another lesson learned is that auditors gain credibility when they apply their own standards to their own performance reports. While this was done by the OAG to help improve its own reporting, it was also done independently by the TBS. Both exercises produced favorable results and suggested that the OAG reports were at least as good as any of the other reports it examined. The TBS also identified the OAG logic model of its audit program as a good practice. Overall, this demonstrated that auditors can actually practice what they preach.

A third lesson learned from this experience is that auditing a report on a department's entire performance generally holds less interest for readers than an audit of a specific program. Such a focus allows many related questions to be asked, not just about the quality of reporting but also about whether the program worked and what value was achieved for the taxpayers' money. It can lead to a better understanding of an organization's performance as well as what lies behind the information reported.

Because one department or agency is seldom responsible on its own for the outcome of a specific program, a fourth lesson learned is that it is usually necessary to identify the other organizations that also contribute to the shared outcome. Under these circumstances, there are usually several departments and agencies contributing to the same outcome under what are often called a "sectoral" or "horizontal" program. To identify the relative impact of each organization, an "attribution analysis" would be done, usually by developing a parallel logic model for each organization contributing to the shared outcome and estimating the relative weight of their respective contributions. Auditors might then audit all the key contributors, including the quality of reporting on the performance of the program by each party or by a combined performance report on the program.

A fifth lesson is that not all performance information is of the same kind. The formidable task of auditing the accuracy of performance information is made easier when different types of information are audited separately. For example, in 2005, the OAG audited the quality of surveys and the quality of reporting survey results to Parliament (OAG, 2005b). The audit found minimal to no information reported about the quality of surveys, despite the reports using survey results to buttress arguments about good performance.

Where there is a mixed level of report quality, then a further lesson is that it might be useful if auditors choose to provide a moderate level of assurance. This approach focuses on whether there are adequate systems and procedures to support good-quality data for reporting. However, it should not attempt the near impossible by going down every data rabbit hole in the quest for a high level of assurance on performance data (see also Mayne & Wilkins, 2005).

Finally, where there is slow progress in improving the quality of performance reports, then a learning and development approach may be appropriate. Later, when reports are close to the desired quality, they can be audited on a pass-fail basis, with assurance provided to the body to which the organization is accountable.

At the current pace of change, however, it might take a decade or so to overcome the five main challenges to improving the quality of performance reports in the Canadian federal government. This is because they can be addressed only by fundamentally changing the management culture of government of both the report preparers on the "supply side" and the report users on the "demand side."

Of course, the other driver to improved performance reporting is the call for greater oversight, control, and accountability in an era of skepticism and declining trust in the credibility of government institutions and organizations. The quality of performance information and the quality of the performance reports themselves is fundamental to effective accountability by government organizations to elected representatives and for the decisions and actions that result. When elected representatives and the public are provided with fair and reliable performance information through a credible regime of performance reporting, greater confidence and trust in government will follow.

Note

1. The views expressed in this paper are not necessarily those of the author's institutional affiliations.

Discussion Questions

1. What evidence would help you decide whether a performance report is good fiction or good nonfiction?

2. Is an initial learning and development approach helpful to organizations trying to improve their performance reports, or should they—and auditors—focus only on the criteria for excellent reports?

3. Are legislative auditors the best way of obtaining independent, objective assurance about the quality of performance reports?

4. If performance information is found to be inaccurate, does it matter whether the results are fairly interpreted and presented?

5. If more attention were paid to the needs of users of performance reports (i.e., the "demand side"), then would this help improve the quality of the performance reports (i.e., the "supply side")?

References

Aucoin, P. (2005). *Decision-making in government: The role of program evaluation* (Discussion paper). Ottawa, Canada: Treasury Board Secretariat. Available at http://www.tbs-sct.gc.ca/eval/tools_outils/aucoin/aucoin_e.asp

Auditor General Act, R.S., 1985, c. A-17, as amended in 1995, c. 43, s. 5. Available at http://www.oag-bvg.gc.ca/domino/other.nsf/html/bodye.html

Alberta Finance. (2005). *Measuring up: Government of Alberta 2004–05 Annual Report*. Edmonton, Canada: Author.

Boyle, R. (2005). Assessment of performance reports: A comparative perspective. In R. Schwartz & J. Mayne (Eds.), *Quality matters: Seeking confidence in evaluation, auditing, and performance reporting* (pp. 279–277). Somerset, NJ: Transaction Publishers.

CCOLA-PRAG. Canadian Council of Legislative Auditors, Performance Reporting and Auditing Group. (2004). *Audit program*. Ottawa, Canada: CCOLA Secretariat, Office of the Auditor General of Canada.

Canadian Institute for Chartered Accountants, Public Sector Accounting Board. (2006, March). *Statement of recommended practice for public performance reporting*. Toronto, Canada: Author.

CCAF. (2002). *Reporting principles: Taking public performance reporting to a new level*. Ottawa, Canada: CCAF-FCVI.

Clark, I. D., & Swain, H. (2005). Distinguishing the real from the surreal in management reform: Suggestions for beleaguered administrators in the government of Canada. *Canadian Public Administration, 48*, 453–476.

Divorski, S. (2005). How Supreme Audit Institutions help to assure the quality of performance reporting to legislatures. In R. Schwartz & J. Mayne (Eds.), *Quality matters: Seeking confidence in evaluation, auditing, and performance reporting* (pp. 261–277). Somerset, NJ: Transaction Publishers.

Epstein, P. D., Grifel, S. S., & Morgan, S. L. (2004). *Auditor roles in government performance measurement: A guide to exemplary practices at the local, state, and provincial levels.* Altamonte Springs, FL: Institute of Internal Auditors Research Foundation.

Financial Administration Act, R.S., 1985, c. F-11.

Governmental Accounting Standards Board. (2003). *Reporting performance information: Suggested criteria for effective communication.* Norwalk, CT: Author.

Government Performance and Results Act of 1993, Pub. L. No. 103–62 [S20] 107 Stat. 285.

House of Commons Standing Committee on Public Accounts. (2001). *Report 8: The Committee's report on the performance and plans and priorities of the Office of the Auditor General of Canada* (Adopted by the Committee on May 29, 2001). Ottawa, Canada: House of Commons. Available at http://www.cmte.parl.gc.ca/cmte/CommitteePublication.aspx?COM=228&Lang=1&SourceId=36785

Mayne, J., & Wilkins, P. (2005). Believe it or not? The emergence of performance information auditing. In R. Schwartz & J. Mayne (Eds.), *Quality matters: Seeking confidence in evaluation, auditing, and performance reporting* (pp. 237–259). Somerset, NJ: Transaction Publishers.

Office of the Auditor General of Canada. (1988, December). Information for Parliament: Audit of the Estimates document. *Report of the Auditor General of Canada* (chap. 5). Ottawa, Canada: Author.

Office of the Auditor General of Canada. (1992). Information for Parliament: Departmental reporting. *Report of the Auditor General of Canada* (chap. 6). Ottawa, Canada: Author.

Office of the Auditor General of Canada. (1997). Reporting performance in the expenditure management system. *Report of the Auditor General of Canada* (chap. 5). Ottawa, Canada: Author.

Office of the Auditor General of Canada. (2000, December). Reporting performance to Parliament: Progress too slow. *Report of the Auditor General of Canada* (chap. 19). Ottawa, Canada: Author.

Office of the Auditor General of Canada. (2002a, April). A model for rating departmental performance reports. *Report of the Auditor General of Canada* (chap. 6). Ottawa, Canada: Author.

Office of the Auditor General of Canada. (2002b, December). Modernizing accountability in the public service. *Report of the Auditor General of Canada* (chap. 9). Ottawa, Canada: Author.

Office of the Auditor General of Canada. (2003). Rating departmental performance reports. *2003 Status Report of the Auditor General of Canada* (chap. 9). Ottawa, Canada: Author.

Office of the Auditor General of Canada. (2005a, April). Rating selected departmental performance reports. *Report of the Auditor General of Canada* (chap. 5). Ottawa, Canada: Author.

Office of the Auditor General of Canada. (2005b, November). The quality and reporting of surveys. *Report of the Auditor General of Canada* (chap. 2). Ottawa, Canada: Author.

Office of the Auditor General of Canada. (2006). *What we do.* Available at http://www.oag-bvg.gc.ca/domino/other.nsf/html/bodye.html

Power, M. (1997). *The audit society: Rituals of verification.* Oxford, UK: Oxford University Press.

Savoie, D. J. (2003). *Breaking the bargain: Public servants, ministers, and Parliament.* Toronto, Canada: University of Toronto Press.

Treasury Board Secretariat. (2000). *Results for Canadians: A management framework for the government of Canada.* Ottawa, Canada: Author.

WorksafeBC. (2006). 2005 Annual report and 2006–2008 service plan. Available at http://www.worksafebc.com

7 Advancing Performance Measurement and Management for Accountability

King County's Collaborative, Incremental Approach

Cheryle Broom

Edward T. Jennings, Jr.

In the midst of substantial growth in population and increased demand for regional and other public services, King County government in Washington State has endeavored to establish a countywide system of performance measurement and management. Through an incremental approach engaging all three branches of government, the county has laid a foundation for a system that will increase performance and accountability. These steps follow a set of largely unfulfilled initiatives from the 1990s. This introduction describes governance in King County and those early initiatives, providing the context for an assessment of the county's current strategy for developing and fully implementing a performance management system.

King County is the largest county in Washington State. Nine full-time council members elected by district in partisan elections lead the legislative

NOTE: Opinions expressed are the authors'; they do not reflect any official position of the King County Auditor's Office. The authors wish to acknowledge the contributions of Michael Jacobson, Ron Perry, Yaeko Rojnuckarin, and Susan Baugh from the county and Chris Veit from SMG/Columbia Consulting Group, as well as others mentioned throughout this chapter.

branch.[1] An elected, partisan county executive has authority similar to the governor's at the state level (strong executive form of government). Also elected countywide are superior and district court judges, the assessor, the sheriff, and the prosecuting attorney.

The County Auditor's Office is within the legislative branch. Established by the county charter as an organization somewhat similar to the U.S. Government Accountability Office (GAO), the King County Auditor conducts performance and financial audits and other oversight reviews.

A 1991 survey by the King County Auditor (King County Auditor's Office, 1991) found that most performance indicators used by county agencies measured the volume of activities rather than performance outcomes. Moreover, the county's budget review process was oriented toward future spending and did not consistently address performance questions. Legislation enacted by the county council in 1995 required four executive departments to develop goals and performance measures under the oversight of an external committee administered by the county auditor. In early 2001, the retiring county auditor advised the council that the committee should be allowed to sunset, in part because "there was little, if any, real buy-in to the performance measures process from the executive branch" (Eklund, p. 1, 2001). Eklund suggested that "performance measures should be considered in a much larger context related to the business of county government" (p. 1).

During the same time period in which the council and county auditor were promoting an oversight effort, the county executive prepared to launch his own performance measurement initiative, which formally occurred in 1999 (the Performance Measurement Program). This program required that executive departments submit business plans (defined as strategic plans including goals and measures) with their budget requests as part of the annual budget development cycle.

A series of significant revenue declines may have delayed the executive's initiative from getting under way in earnest. In 2001, county officials projected a shortfall of $41 million in the general fund budget (8% of an approximately $490 million total current expense budget), with the deficit increasing to $53 million in 2003 and approximately $24 million the following 2 years. Measures to address the shortfall required operating expenditure reductions as well as additional revenue sources. In practice, performance measurement was not a major management and budget driver. One point of view hypothesized that due to downsizing and focus on only core services, no management or other staff resources were available with the time and expertise to fully implement a performance measurement program. No one disputed the potential value of performance measurement, at least in concept, although skeptics questioned how it would add value in this environment.

Between 1995 and 2000, county policymakers established dual mandates for the county to be more performance based. One performance measurement effort was led by a council-initiated advisory group facilitated by the county auditor and the other by the county executive's budget office.

Neither mandate resulted in a significant difference in how the county conducted its business. The externally driven need to reduce county costs appeared to be the major motivator to improve government efficiency.

The low rating King County received from *Governing Magazine*'s "Grading Governments" research was a wake-up call (Barrett, Greene, & Mariani, 2002). While Washington State scored high marks in "managing for results," King County received a less stellar grade of C overall and in "managing for results." The unacceptable ratings helped put performance management back on the agenda. Shortly after "Grading Governments" was published, the chair of the King County Council's Labor, Operations, and Technology Committee reinvigorated council discussions on how the county could improve its performance management orientation and performance results. He turned to the Auditor's Office (KCAO) for advice. Following presentations to the committee by experts in the field, a series of council motions were passed reiterating the council's intent to implement performance-based government and empowering the "countywide performance measurement work group" that continues today (Motion 11561, 2002; Motion 11739, 2003).

This chapter describes the development of King County's jurisdiction-wide performance measurement endeavors from 2002 up to 2006, emphasizing the council-directed approach led by the KCAO, while noting related initiatives of the county executive and individual agencies. We share lessons learned and preliminary conclusions on the extent to which the current approach is meeting the mandated goal of "establishing a countywide performance measurement program that provides decision makers useful performance information that can be used for budget allocation purposes and publicly reported" (Motion 12005, 2004).

Theoretical Considerations

The process of developing a performance management system in King County is consistent with incremental models of policy making, both descriptively and strategically. Scholars who study decision making often contrast *incremental* and *rationally comprehensive* (or *nonincremental*) decision making. This framing draws on the long-term debate over the advantages and disadvantages of alternative decision-making strategies, first enunciated by Charles Lindblom and subsequently addressed by scores of scholars and practitioners. The contrast between approaches is based largely on the magnitude of change, the scope of the decision, and the range of information required and incorporated in the process. From this perspective, it is viewed as a debate over cognitive limits on rationality. Typically, incremental decision making is taken to require less information and makes fewer cognitive demands than more comprehensive approaches to analysis and decision making. Thus, one basis for distinguishing between approaches is to look at the use of information and the scope of the decision.

In "The Science of Muddling Through," Lindblom (1959) identified *incrementalism* as a decision strategy that focuses on small variations in existing policy to reduce conflict and make the best use of available information. Incrementalism reduces the consequences of errors and allows opportunity for midcourse corrections to keep change on track. In "Still Muddling, Not Yet Through," Lindblom (1979) suggested that incrementalism actually has three meanings: (a) analysis limited to policy alternatives only marginally different from the status quo; (b) disjointed incrementalism, or analysis supported by a set of mutually supported strategies to simplify decision making, including fragmentation of analysis to many participants; and (c) analysis focused on a small set of thoughtfully chosen strategies that simplify complex policy problems. He argued that complete analysis is not possible, trying to do it is unproductive, and trying to be synoptic is misleading.

Critics suggest that incremental strategies are inherently conservative, fail to produce large-scale benefits, and often lead to bad policy instead of marginal improvements over time (Etzioni, 1967). Hayes (1992) argued, for example, that the Vietnam War is a good example of incremental policy, with a series of incremental decisions leading eventually to disaster for American policy.

Beyond viewing it as a strategy for decision making, many scholars suggest that incrementalism reflects political reality. In a political system of dispersed power with competing actors promoting alternative values, it can be difficult to produce any movement, much less large-scale, dramatic change. The more extensive the array of competing interests to be reconciled in the process and the more widespread the effects of a decision, the more difficult it is to produce large-scale change (Hayes, 1992; Lindblom, 1959, 1979). Before change of any type can be implemented, a sufficient group of decision makers has to agree. Reaching that agreement may require participants to modify their objectives; in administrative circles, it may simply take time as the competing priorities of different actors draw their attention elsewhere (Pressman & Wildavsky, 1973).

The challenge of building support for policy change in a world of shared power led Bryson and Crosby (1992) to consider the differences between changes in degree (small wins) and changes in kind (big wins) (pp. 228–235). As they see it, incremental and nonincremental approaches involve different (a) strategies for change, (b) risks, (c) demands on decision makers, and (d) resource commitments. Bryson and Crosby suggested,

> Because big wins are much more difficult to achieve than small wins, wise strategists should consider how a series of small wins might be organized around a strategic direction to achieve the same effect as a big win without the concomitant risks of big failure. (p. 232)

Small wins make change real and help preserve gains. They cost little and reduce risk. More broadly, they allow support for change to build and provide an opportunity to demonstrate that new approaches can work. They can be a means of building support from disparate sources. Bryson and Crosby argue that small wins can add up to changes in kind.

While incrementalism may be a strategy, it is also quite clearly the reality of most policy development. Wildavsky and his colleagues and others portrayed this reality for an earlier generation of public administration scholars (Davis, Dempster, & Wildavsky, 1966; Wildavsky, 1984). Baumgartner and Jones (1993, 2002) have led a new wave of research in recent years, demonstrating the pervasiveness of stability and incrementalism in policy. In studies of punctuated equilibria, they and others have demonstrated in a wide variety of policy settings considerable stability of policy with only very occasional bursts of substantial change. They account for stability by examining issue images and the venues of decision making. More particularly, stable political patterns are consistent with incremental development of policy. Incrementalism is likely when power is widely shared, competing interests are present, established routines are in place, and no dramatic changes occur in the economic, social, or political environments. Under such conditions, advocates of change are likely to have to take it in small steps, building support as they go. The work of Baumgartner and Jones and others identifies instances of nonincremental policy making and helps identify conditions under which it occurs or is needed (Baumgartner & Jones, 1991, 1993, 2002; Sabatier & Jenkins-Smith, 1999; Schulman, 1975).

Given competing interests in King County government, it is not surprising that the development of performance management has proceeded in a disjointed, incremental manner. We can characterize King County's incremental approach as taking baby steps; those steps are, however, moving in the desired direction of building a foundation for a viable countywide performance measurement program transparent to King County's citizens. Though the jury is still out regarding the impact of performance management on the cost-effectiveness of county services and public satisfaction or confidence with county government, leaders have laid the groundwork to achieve these purposes.

A Countywide Focus: Gradual Development

Achieving a focus on performance measurement evolved slowly for King County from the late 1990s through 2002. Elected officials concentrated attention on actions to deal with shrinking revenues; for example, they consolidated six executive agencies into two departments to achieve program reductions and administrative efficiencies. As part of its response to the fiscal crisis and subsequent consolidation of several organizations in 2001, the council passed an ordinance (Ordinance 14199, 2001) calling for the development of performance measures to gauge the effectiveness of this reorganization. By the time the consolidation was effected in 2002, immediate savings resulting from the reorganization were known; yet measures to assess long-term performance impacts were at only a nascent stage of development. Consequently, council and KCAO staff suggested an emphasis on developing measures to subsequently evaluate how well the newly structured departments delivered services and met goals. The KCAO offered to review the business/strategic plans, including performance measures, of departments (King County Auditor's Office, 2003).

The council soon moved more broadly on performance measurement, adopting two mandates unanimously in 2002. One motion encouraged the broader development and use of performance measurement throughout King County, both as a management tool and to enhance accountability to the public (Motion 11561, 2002). It also requested the executive to submit department business or strategic plans to the council during the annual budget process. Previously, the executive budget office received these plans but did not uniformly transmit them to the council with the proposed budget.[2]

A companion motion (Motion 11558, 2002) passed at the same time outlined criteria for defining performance measures, including customer service measures; that measure was called out separately to ensure attention to concerns that consolidation of functions not result in reduced customer services.

In addition, the 2003 budget ordinance adopted in November 2002 prohibited expenditure of $100,000 in the budget office's appropriation pending submittal of a work plan for implementing a performance measurement system for executive departments (Ordinance 14517, 2002). That work plan was submitted in the spring of 2003. Council staff reported that the work plan met the technical requirements but not the full intent of the council mandate. For example, the plan provided only a partial range of performance measures—most often lacking outcome and efficiency measures—and covered only five of the seven executive departments. Nor did the quality of mission and goal statements meet the requirements of the budget proviso. Nevertheless, the response reflected progress, providing evidence that executive agencies were proceeding with implementation of performance measurement.

The Council-Mandated Performance Measurement Work Group, Phase I: Training, Guidelines, and Plan Reviews

On June 30, 2003, the council approved the work program and schedule for the executive's Performance Measurement Program. The council also asked the executive to participate in an advisory performance measurement work group managed by the KCAO with participation from the executive's Office of Management and Budget, executive departments, and the council (Motion 11739, 2003). At that point, the purpose of the work group was to serve as a sounding board for the review and critique of performance measures and business plans prepared by executive departments.

The KCAO procured expertise to provide technical assistance and facilitation to the work group. The consultant conducted three training sessions for council and audit staff. By the conclusion of the third session, participants appeared to be internalizing the applicability of performance measurement theory to the practice of their work. As expected, questions were again raised about the feasibility of integrating performance measurement into the "real world" of policy making and budgeting. Council staff members who understood the dynamics of decision making in the legislative environment were particularly concerned. Nonetheless, some council staff leaders submitted cases of using a coordinated process that was essentially strategic planning without labeling it as such. One example was county policymakers agreeing on new goals and strategies in the juvenile justice arena for helping repeat-offender youth. The results were both major changes in program policy and operations and, ultimately, improvements in the outcomes for youth.

A tangible product of this first stage of the council's Phase I performance measurement undertaking was a draft strategic planning template with guidelines for each of its components.

The template would serve as the tool for reviewing agency business or strategic plans, for providing a common definition of terms for all county branches and departments, and for taking a systems approach to performance measurement and management. It would reinforce the importance of linking oversight functions (e.g., policy direction and budgeting) to departments' strategic plans.

Organizing the performance measurement advisory committee to review four county departments' business plans was the next order of business. High-level representatives from these departments, the executive's budget director and performance measurement staff person, council staff (policy director and lead performance measurement staffer), and the county auditor and deputy county auditor started meeting as a work group in early 2004. Not surprisingly, it took the work group a while to establish a common purpose and protocols, as there can be a natural tension between these parties given their roles in county government. The budget office representatives expressed reservations about how this work group's activities would be coordinated with the existing executive's performance measurement program to avoid additional burdens on time-strapped agency management or replacing the executive's program. Department managers wanted to ensure that the effort would be consistent with existing requirements and also help—not punish—agencies that became more performance based. Council staff felt that they could not speak for the nine council members on what the council would do with the information developed by the work group—except to explain what had been publicly articulated by individual members or stated in legislation, which included mandating and supporting a work group process. The KCAO, which also wanted a value-added process, encouraged

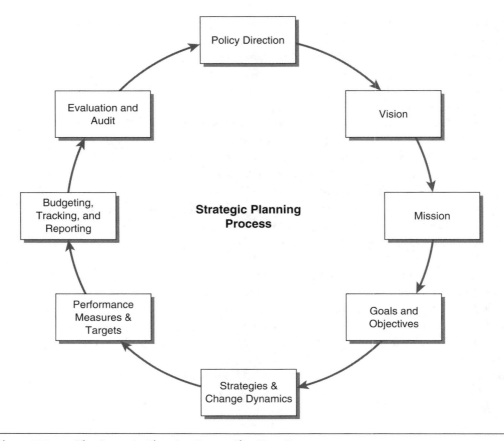

Figure 7.1   The Strategic Planning Process for King County

participants to make a good-faith effort to lead the way in determining an effective approach that would meet legislative intent and their needs.

Using the process and guidelines associated with Figure 7.1, the consultant-facilitator critiqued each plan, which the work group subsequently reviewed. Refinements to the guidelines accompanied the evaluation of a business plan. For example, the Department of Community and Human Service's plan identified the King County Framework Policies for Human Services as the department's goals. The framework provided a countywide umbrella or a structure (components and steps) for departments' business plans. This is one area where the council adopted countywide policies, thus reinforcing the work group's guidelines that policy direction should drive departmental goals.

Participants provided constructive feedback on the guidelines and received helpful input on their strategic plans in a nonthreatening atmosphere. Dialogue among the work group members became open, lifting the earlier veil of skepticism. When it was time to propose the next steps, the work group quickly achieved consensus on several recommendations.

Recommendations to Move Forward

The work group wanted to move forward with establishing a workable countywide framework. The uppermost priority was capacity building and helping departments succeed, while balancing expectations with resource availability. The group cautioned managing the details by establishing a hierarchy of measures for different audiences ranging from the lowest organizational level to the public. Members wanted to encourage the council to deal with performance issues at the policy level and not get bogged down in operational details. At the same time, they expressed the importance of clearly establishing linkages between operational measures for internal management and departmental measures that would be reported to policymakers and the public (King County Auditor's Office, 2004). Complementary to the work group's recommendations, the consultant advised reallocating resources to create a sustainable process, integrating business planning and performance management into daily management processes, and building on the collaboration established by the performance measurement work group.

In a few short months, the work group embraced the idea that a countywide approach was feasible for King County government. With this encouraging momentum, the county auditor submitted a decision package to the county council. Incorporating the work group's and consultant's perspectives, the KCAO recommended the next steps to the council:

1. Continue the work group and expand its membership to include representatives of agencies headed by separately elected county officials.

2. Empower the work group to develop a work plan to determine feasible next steps, such as developing legislation revising county code provisions on performance measurement to promote a uniform, countywide performance measurement and reporting system.

3. Establish goals for a countywide strategic performance measurement and reporting system.

Without hesitation, the council unanimously adopted a motion to continue developing a countywide system of strategic performance measurement and reporting. This motion charged the auditor to continue the work group and requested participation from the remaining county entities headed by separately elected officials (Superior Court, District Court, Prosecuting Attorney's Office, Department of Assessments, and Sheriff's Office). To foster participation, two council members (Constantine & Patterson, 2004) took the extra step of sending a special invitation letter to those officials. In a subsequent meeting of these separately elected officials, the council policy director and county auditor received strong support for the work group's purpose and commitment to participate. The county prosecuting attorney's comment summed up their response: "We want to work together on this; it just makes sense" (King County Prosecutor Norm Maleng, personal communication, April 20, 2005).

The Council-Mandated Performance Measurement Work Group, Phase II: Expanded Work Group Proposes Countywide Work Plan

The expanded work group adopted the framework created by the initial work group. A similar committee process and the guidelines reflected in Figure 7.1 were used as the group reviewed the plans of the Department of Assessments, Prosecuting Attorney's Office, Sheriff's Office, District Court, and Superior Court. As expected, these plans were more varied than those of the executive agencies because the agencies are led by separately elected officials. Some used the operational master planning process to establish agency goals and measures. For example, the District Court Operational Master Plan (OMP) contained specific strategies and action plans for objectives the court wanted to accomplish over the next few years. The OMP did not include performance measurement, though the plan recommended development of service standards. The consultant-facilitator found that the rigor used to develop the OMP should allow the district court to readily prepare its strategic plan.

After several meetings to complete plan reviews, the work group turned its full attention to "developing a work plan to determine feasible next steps to establish a countywide system of strategic performance measurement and reporting directly linked to resource allocation decision and publicly reported" (Motion 12161, 2005). Their proposed work plan consists of four phases:

1. Continuation of ongoing improvements in strategic planning and performance measurement, such as providing training and technical assistance to preparers of agency business (strategic) plans.

2. Determining and obtaining a consensus on the high-level framework for linking strategic planning, performance measurement, and budgeting to countywide priorities.

3. Detailed design of the system, including designating roles, responsibilities, an implementation schedule, and any necessary changes to the county code.

4. Implementation.

Threaded throughout the overall plan was recognition of the need for adequate resources and training, continuing a consensus-building process, and ensuring that policymakers provide direction and the citizenry is engaged. Moreover, the countywide framework embraced the systems approach illustrated in Figure 7.1. Goals and performance measures for the county would be established and used for management, policy, and budget decision making. Their success would also be tracked and evaluated so improvements could be made in the directives that drove the system as well as the outcomes.

Figure 7.2 summarizes the mission and vision of the work plan.

Mission Statement

King County will develop an effective system of countywide strategic planning, performance measurement, and management designed to enhance government accountability, service performance, and resource allocation.

Vision for the Future

The following bullets describe the preferred vision for King County strategic planning, performance measurement, and management in the future.

- There is consensus among county leadership that the strategic planning and performance measurement and management system effectively aligns collaborative efforts toward common county goals while respecting the needs of individual agencies to pursue organization goals and separately elected officials' obligation to deliver on their commitments to the citizenry.
- Building on current efforts and with input from citizens, elected leaders and policymakers develop countywide prioritized goals and align services to those goals.
- Performance measures inform and are linked to policy and resource allocation decisions.
- The county publicly reports to citizens how well it is meeting its performance goals and engages the citizenry in the countywide performance management program.
- Performance measurement is used by managers for strategic planning, program evaluation, operational improvements, and budgeting.
- Performance measures are not used in a punitive manner, but are used to support organizational learning in collaboration with the workforce.

Figure 7.2   Mission and Vision for the Work Plan for Developing a Countywide Strategic Performance Measurement and Reporting System

Consistent with an effective performance measurement and management program, the emerging work plan reflected thoughtful attention by the diverse participants to King County's unique environment. Some members of the work group expressed concern about establishing countywide priorities. How would this occur? How would they relate to the county executive's priorities as outlined in the annual budget or the council's 2006 legislative priorities or the policy prerogatives of the separately elected officials? How long would it take to reach agreement on inclusive priorities? These were valid questions that could be addressed more fully when the plan components were developed in more detail.

Corollary to these questions was the discussion of endorsement of the plan. Work group endorsement occurred by consensus after final edits were made to the plan. While there was no disagreement with the components per se, participants recognized that many details were pending that needed to be addressed a step at a time. Council staff indicated that a key next step was for the council to weigh in on how to proceed. Recognizing the necessity of increased resources for implementing the work plan would be one factor for council consideration.

Securing endorsements of separately elected officials was more sensitive. Some work group members believed that the council would be interested in whether the other elected officials endorsed the plan. Work group representatives of the independent entities could not speak for their bosses, though most were willing to encourage their endorsement. After discussing several approaches to secure the endorsements, the county auditor made the rounds and received verbal support of the mission, vision, and next steps articulated in the work plan from the separately elected officials. One sent a letter taking a strong stand, since her department was actively pursuing strategic planning and performance-oriented management changes (Rahr, 2006).

These issues and deliberations reflected the reality of dispersed power in local government. The most effective performance measurement system requires participation of the council, executive, and separately elected officials, including officials of the judiciary. Bringing them all onboard requires attention to their distinct concerns and needs. It also guarantees a slower process than if the council and county executive were to move just the executive agencies ahead.

Moving the Plan Forward: Critical Next Steps Pending

Performance measurement in King County is at a crossroads. The work group is willing to review and advise; the KCAO is prepared to continue facilitating the work group. Council staff can draft legislation to clarify strategic (business) planning requirements and update the county code. The executive's budget office can monitor compliance with business planning criteria. The KCAO can continue to evaluate performance measurement/management by agencies it audits. And departments can continue to evolve their performance management programs. These are valuable components of the county's efforts. They do not, however, constitute the integrated countywide system envisioned in the work group's proposal.

Phase II of the work plan is a critical next step: *Scope the long-term effort and resource requirements needed to meet the vision for a performance management and measurement system.* In October 2006, the council directed the auditor by motion to have the work group advise on implementation of Phases I and II. The work group has drafted a framework for a countywide performance measurement system and is considering options for implementation of the framework. During these next steps, there are other factors to consider, such as whether the momentum will continue, given other emergent priorities of, or changes in, county government. Maintaining legislative visibility of something that neither is an immediate problem in the public's eye nor requires immediate attention is always a challenge. Extensive media attention on restoring public confidence in the election process and ensuring accountability for the sheriff's internal investigations functions received prompt and proactive engagement of county policymakers. Those involved in public policy making understand that this environment can be very dynamic and demanding. A dozen council committees meet weekly or bimonthly to consider legislation and conduct legislative oversight. Performance-based government is considered by some to be principally a management tool; for elected officials to collectively support it over time is notable.

On the other hand, *public engagement* is a missing link. King County has significant public involvement with advisory boards and commissions on specific matters (e.g., the council's Citizens' Elections Oversight Committee and the executive's Independent Task Force on Elections). The work group acknowledges that citizen involvement has been limited in the performance measurement context. In that regard, a representative of the Governmental Accounting Standards Board (GASB) briefed the work group and other interested county representatives on the guidelines for service efforts and accomplishments reporting (Fountain, 2005). This included discussion of the expectation for citizen engagement and examples of models other jurisdictions are using. Recognizing that public involvement is embedded in the overall work plan, it would be desirable to start that engagement in the upcoming planning process.

Finally, the work plan addresses how the countywide performance measurement program will be integrated with related performance endeavors. This includes maintaining the prerogatives of separately elected officials while pursuing the countywide vision. Ideally, this assessment should respect the individual endeavors while identifying how they are integrated under the broader umbrella of the countywide system. These considerations reflect why a participatory, albeit stepwise, approach should keep the county on track.

Highlighted below are other major performance measurement/management endeavors in the county, which are varied but compatible with the countywide movement. Assessing that compatibility is one of the tasks specified in the work plan.

Business Plans for Budget Review. Compatibility between the countywide program and the county executive's performance measurement program should not be an issue. The work group has collaborated on guidelines published with the executive's budget instructions and has reviewed over half of the county departments' business plans. Tasked under Phase I of the work plan are preparation of business plans and use of the guidelines for all county agencies. In preparation for 2007 budget submittals, the executive's budget office is promoting relevant performance measures to indicate how goals are being met.

KingStat. In 2005, the county executive decided a management oversight program was needed similar to Baltimore's CITISTAT and New York City's ComStat (Powell, 2005). KingStat is designed to complement the broader countywide endeavor by focusing on management-level performance data collection, reporting, assessment, and resolution. KingStat builds upon the business plans, performance reporting, and customer service measures that the executive branch has instituted in many agencies over the past 4 years.

The executive's new performance management director is participating in the design and implementation of the countywide performance measurement and management work plan. Articulation of the Phase II long-term scope and responsibilities will more clearly define the director's pivotal role in maintaining connectivity between the executive's and the countywide endeavor.

"Measuring Up." This was the theme of the council's 2006 budget review process in October and November 2005, and council members indicated they wanted to continue this theme throughout 2006. One council objective called for standing committees to review the business plans of select departments using the work group's guidelines. Some council members expressed interest in having the ability to demonstrate to the public at year's end what has been accomplished. Before undertaking their review of the executive's proposed 2007 budget, the council adopted a motion establishing a set of 11 "Priorities for People" to guide their budget deliberations (Motion 12367, 2006). Subsequently, the council initiated a citizen engagement process to help establish similar priorities or goals for the 2008 budget process (Ordinance 15652, 2006). While not yet directly linked to the countywide work group's endeavors, this process is consistent with advancing to meet the mission and vision of the Countywide Strategic Planning Performance Measurement and Management System.

Auditor's Office Review of Agencies Goals and Measures. During the past 4 years, the KCAO has consistently reviewed strategic planning and performance measurement efforts relevant to performance audits on the office's annual work program. Recent reviews included the Sheriff's Office, Transit Capital Planning, and Human Services Contracts. The business plan guidelines developed by the countywide work group made up one of the criteria applied in these reviews.

Operational Master Planning (OMP). In recent years, county officials have required development of operational master plans to identify ways and means of achieving service improvements and operational efficiency. Aspects of these plans, which touch upon performance expectations as well as future program and capital needs, have some similarities to strategic plans. This partially explains the work group's recommendation to incorporate OMP definitions and expectations in the countywide performance measurement framework. It also illustrates the importance of linking major performance improvement endeavors to avoid duplication and promote effective coordination. Recent OMP developments by the Sheriff's Office and District Court acknowledge this intent.

Accountable Business Transformation (ABT). The county is replacing aging legacy mainframe systems with integrated accounting, human resources, and budget systems. A performance measurement component is contemplated but is yet to be included. Measuring the achievement of the county's priorities should be addressed in the design.

Other County Performance Measurement Programs. Some county agencies or enterprises have an established track record with performance measurement and reporting programs. For example, in 2005 and 2006, the annual performance measure report of the Department of Natural Resources and Parks received the Association of Government Accountants' Certificate of Excellence in Performance Reporting. The 10-year record of the King County benchmark report on progress in implementing countywide planning policies is another example of a sustained performance-tracking program.

One interesting feature of these two programs is their comparative tracking over several years. Trends and analysis on achievement of targets, such as net increase in new housing units and reductions in the amount of waste requiring disposal, are available for public scrutiny and policy consideration.

King County also participates in conferences and symposiums that enrich the county's ability to undertake meaningful performance measurement and management. The county was one of the sponsors of the "Driving Change and Getting Results Conference"[3] held in 2005, in Bellevue, Washington, bringing together experts in the field to explore opportunities to advance performance measurement and community indicators in the Cascadia region (Pacific Northwest and British Columbia). Three representatives from King County now serve as members of the Cascadia Progress and Performance Network Steering Committee, which is an outgrowth of that conference. In a similar vein, the county auditor cochaired the Association of Government Accountants' first performance management conference, which focused on using performance reporting to improve government operations and build public trust.

Is King County's Unique Approach Moving in the Right Direction?

We believe the incremental approach, which incorporates practices used in other jurisdictions, should prove effective in King County. Broadly, these practices include strategic planning and performance tracking by agencies, movement toward setting government priorities, relating performance to the budget process, and oversight by policymakers and the County Auditor's Office. Over the past 4 years, the council's policy director has portrayed the movement to a countywide program as one requiring baby steps, but the county is now positioned to move forward in larger increments.

We noted Lindblom's contention that there are several varieties of incrementalism: marginal changes from the status quo, fragmentation of analysis to many participants, and analysis focusing on a small set of strategies. The King County process has been built on a series of marginal adjustments to the status quo with the expectation that the performance measurement process that eventually emerges will have broad scope and deep impact. In other words, leaders expect the end result to be a nonincremental change in policy making and management. In practice, much of the development of performance measurement systems in King County has been disjointed, but the disparate elements provided a basis for the development of an integrated countywide system.

Some might ask whether the county has actually improved county services; the answer would be mixed. Realizing significant quantifiable outcomes throughout county government is probably down the road, but the county can point to impacts of individual agency performance management efforts reflected in performance targets met by departments such as Natural Resources and Parks.

Progress to date also provides greater assurance that the evolving system will make a broader difference, be sustainable, and allow for public accountability. Officials have established a framework for collaboration between all branches of government. The work group process is open and representative and provides a forum for communication that did not exist earlier. The legislative and executive branches, while retaining their respective prerogatives, have a genuine interest in undertaking an inclusive countywide program rather than pursuing dual, potentially incompatible tracks. The small-wins strategy effectively moves the county forward by building one piece on another, generating support by demonstrating the feasibility of each part of the system. The process reduces risk for decision makers and provides the opportunity to build support among diverse elected officials.

These attributes provide a powerful basis for optimism, as does the expertise that county administrators are developing in performance measurement and management. Tools and resources are more readily accessible at conferences and symposiums, where participants focus on sharing success stories and providing mentoring. Also, with an improved financial picture, the county can better afford to invest in performance measurement. Securing appropriate resources is a critical success factor highlighted in the work plan.

Evolving culture change in King County also tips the scales in favor of sustainability. After its initiation in the early 1990s, the performance movement lacked continuity, cycling through spurts of activity and relative inactivity. During the past few years, momentum built incrementally, and indications are that performance-based government will be a context for how King County does business for at least the next 3 years.[4] Nonetheless, this optimism is grounded in the county's recent accomplishments, as well as the likelihood that the work plan recommendations will be adopted and pursued to meet future challenges.

Lessons Learned to Address Key Challenges

Readers who have followed the performance-oriented government movement are well aware of potential curves in the road that could derail achievement of the vision. Proactive due diligence is required in several areas:

- *Policy-Driven Engagement:* Continued support of policy officials is imperative. While direct involvement may vary, the commitment needs to be highly visible and supported with the prerequisite authority and resources. Currently, the county appears to possess this advantage.

- *Leadership/Continuity:* Senior staff or management must ensure the program advances in fact and not just on paper. For busy public administrators, a commitment to the vision is also critical. Performance measurement and management must be integrated into the ongoing business of government. This is the intent of King County's system approach.

- *Linkages/Coordination:* King County is at a milestone. Agencies are making good progress developing or fine-tuning their strategic plans and performance measures. "Measuring Up" goals discussed by the county council for 2006 confirm the council's interest in providing accountability for measuring results. Opportunities to establish this connectivity rest in part with implementing the next steps of the countywide performance measurement plan. That plan provides a mechanism for ensuring linkages between agency goals and priorities, elected officials' goals and priorities, and pending countywide goals and priorities. Presumably, a forum like the work group will provide regular communication and consensus building.

- *Budget Usage/Relevance:* Council mandates have repeatedly stated that a primary purpose of the countywide performance measurement program is to inform the budget or allocation process. In this regard, theory and research on performance budgeting suggests not overpromising results too quickly (Joyce & Tompkins, 2002). The County Executive's budget development process requires executive departments to submit business plans, and those plans are starting to mature and be more informative. One of the "baby steps" the council took was to approach its 2006 budget review process with the theme "Measuring Up." The council's decision to review some department business plans throughout the year marked another milestone in terms of the council embarking more systematically on a performance measurement oversight role. Nonetheless, the county has a ways to go before decision makers establish a direct connection between performance measures and the allocation and management of resources.

- *Public Engagement:* The GASB and other experts in the performance-based government movement advocate engaging the citizenry in meaningful ways. Locally, the City of Bellevue, which incorporates citizen impact and feedback in its performance measurement system, has received the Certificate of Excellence in Service, Efforts, and Accomplishment reporting from the Association of Government Accountants (AGA) in 2 consecutive years (2005 and 2006). Engagement can range from the public providing feedback on government services to citizens initiating goals with performance targets (Epstein, Fountain, Campbell, Patton, & Keaton, 2005). Despite its extensive forums for citizen participation on specific program and policy issues,

King County has not yet developed a broad-based citizen engagement plan. The council has undertaken a citizen engagement process to help identify 2008 budget priorities, and the executive's annual indicators and measures report that was submitted with his proposed 2007 budget recently received recognition by AGA for its performance reporting. Moreover, the work group's proposed vision statement and the more detailed work plan call for broad-based citizen engagement.

- *Incentives and Recognition:* When the question is asked about why government is not high performing compared with the private sector, the initial response typically cites the lack of comparable and clear bottom lines for government services, plus the public-policy-making process, legal mandates, fiscal constraints, partisan politics, and expectations of stakeholders, customers, and voters. The implications of these factors for public administrators are that there may be competing incentives and disincentives to meet performance targets. If a program provides the same services at less cost, will the savings be used to enhance that program or appropriated to a needier program? If a well-managed agency does not meet its target due to external factors, will the budget office reduce that agency's budget? Will active engagement in performance measurement distract managers from other important tasks? These are simplistic examples of a complex issue surrounding performance incentives. During the work group's review of agency strategic plans, there were no repercussions for not having a plan that met the guidelines. The process was collegial and educational. Yet future reviews of the quality of plans and their achievements could impact policy, budget, and operations. The county's work plan appropriately acknowledges that incentives and recognition are features to be developed.

- *Real Change/Sustainability:* As noted, the county is moving deliberately to establish a countywide performance measurement program driven by strategic planning and county priorities. It has taken at least 5 years to get to this stage, but with consensus on and commitment to the vision, the next phases could proceed expeditiously. Moreover, the comprehensive plan proposed by the performance measurement work group incorporates critical success factors: project management of plan implementation, measuring results of the countywide effort, adapting and maintaining flexibility in the process, and sustaining engagement of county leaders.

Discussion Questions

This real-life, real-time case study raises provocative questions. We offer three here, although readers will likely identify more.

1. *How can theory be applied to practical application?* King County's performance measurement evolution may suit the incrementalist's perspective

of small steps toward large goals. Although taking a somewhat different path than the U.S. federal government, where the Government Performance and Results Act of 1993 (GPRA) mandated strategic planning and performance measurement for all agencies, the county is gradually trying to keep departments on target with strategic planning and performance measurement and broaden that effort to encompass all county agencies. Much has been written about whether GPRA and the related presidential initiatives are working. Some of the criticisms reflect a belief that the federal government tried to do too much at once and failed to build on experience. King County adapted its process on the basis of what it learned from its experience and research, recognizing that there is no blueprint for a "one-size-fits-all" perfect model. Perhaps a question is this: How are theory and academic research helping local jurisdictions stay the course as their varied approaches go through phases that do not mirror any one model? A related question is whether a different model is needed for this level of government given its mix of services and governance structure. If so, what would that model look like?

2. *What is the role of policymakers in the administration of a performance-based program?* Determined to have an operable performance measurement/management program, the council has legislated its intent, and the executive has mandated his expectations. Thus far, their respective purposes are compatible. It seems that the other elected officials have also embraced the concept, although some are still developing an understanding of what performance measurement/management means for King County and how they will use it. Continuing cooperation established through the countywide performance measurement work group process gives optimism that policymakers will continue to lead the efforts and be on the same page. Determining how the next steps will be implemented necessitates legislation that clarifies responsibilities. This is heightened by the fact that all branches of county government (courts, executive, and council) and the other separately elected officials (prosecutor, sheriff, and assessor) are participating. Not yet determined is how to agree on countywide priorities and how oversight of implementation will proceed. What would be the effect of one of the court systems or a separately elected official opting to no longer participate?

3. *Is incrementalism a deliberate model or a reaction to circumstances?* An outsider might portray the county's approach as "muddling through," questioning why the county does not establish policy directives, empower the executive to implement the goals of countywide performance measurement, and get on with it. In fact, at times, the consultant working with the KCAO and work group found the process somewhat murky and slow, even though the county staff generally remained upbeat that progress was being made. Competing priorities, such as the annual budget process and the practical logistics of scheduling a meeting involving representatives from so many county entities caused gaps between meetings. The KCAO led the meetings but had no authority to require attendance or active engagement. Inevitable

changes in membership occurred over the course of 3 years, though most key executive and legislative participants remained the same. Irrespective, a collaborative, highly functioning work group evolved from a small executive/ legislative committee that spent its first few meetings establishing common ground to a much larger one representing all branches of county government that rarely have an opportunity to come to the table for this kind of venture. Yes, a plan could have been produced faster, but would all the key players have bought into it? A quicker process does not necessarily yield more effective results.

The process in King County reflects the realities of dispersed power in local government and the sometimes competing, sometimes complementary objectives of different actors. Incrementalism has been a product of circumstances, but it has also reflected a deliberate strategy of building support and cooperation for the performance measurement system. In the end, the success of the strategy will be reflected in the uses to which the system is put.

Conclusion

King County's collaborative, incremental approach to performance measurement and management is a work in progress. Most agencies conduct strategic planning to some extent; the strategic plans are increasingly incorporated in the annual budget process; the strategic planning guidelines are used by most departments; a collaborative framework for moving forward has been developed, and elected officials have almost unanimously voiced support for instituting a countywide system. When the work group conveyed its first set of recommendations to the council in September 2004, the county auditor advised (Broom, 2004) that potential goals for pursuing a countywide strategic performance measurement and reporting system might include the following:

1. Improving the performance of county programs and accountability to the public

2. Increasing the public's satisfaction and engagement in county government

3. Providing measurable performance information for policy making, including allocation decisions

4. Articulating and achieving county priorities and maximization of limited resources

5. Demonstrating further efficiencies and cost savings

This chapter has highlighted how King County gradually laid a solid foundation to meet these goals. It recognizes that much more work is needed to have a viable countywide system. Staying the (flexible) course will occur in increments, with the occasional step backward, before movement forward is solidified. Nevertheless, many—if not most—of the participants in this undertaking have optimism that the groundwork provides a solid foundation, and perhaps even an ultimately faster track, to meet the five countywide overarching goals.

Notes

1. An initiative passed in 2005 reduced the council from 13 to 9 members effective January 2006.

2. Since 2003, however, the county executive's budget submittal has included countywide priorities or goals.

3. Cochair was Michael Jacobsen, Performance Measures Lead, Department of Natural Resources and Parks, and a member of the network's subsequent steering committee (along with the deputy county auditor and a district court staff person). In 2006, he was appointed by the county executive to the new performance management director position.

4. In the November 2005 general election, the county executive was reelected to another 4-year term, and the nine council members were selected during that same election process. All were previously serving on the council, though one had filled a vacancy in early 2005 and so was a fairly new council member.

References

Barrett, K., Greene, R., & Mariani, M. (2002, February). The government performance project: Grading the counties. *Governing Magazine,* p. 7.

Baumgartner, F. R., & Jones, B. D. (1991). Agenda dynamics and policy subsystems. *Journal of Politics, 53,* 1044–1074.

Baumgartner, F. R., & Jones, B. D. (1993). *Agendas and instability in American politics.* Chicago: University of Chicago Press.

Baumgartner, F. R., & Jones, B. D. (2002). *Policy dynamics.* Chicago: University of Chicago Press.

Broom, C. (2004, September 14). *Advancing countywide strategic performance measurement and reporting* (Memorandum to Metropolitan King County Council Labor, Operations, and Technology Committee Chair. Public document).

Bryson, J. M., & Crosby, B. C. (1992). *Leadership for the common good: Tackling public problems in a shared power world.* San Francisco: Jossey-Bass.

Constantine, D., & Patterson, J. (2004, September 9). *Advancing performance measurement efforts in King County* (Memorandum to separately elected King County officials. Public document).

Davis, O. A., Dempster, M. A., & Wildavsky, A. B. (1966). Theory of the budgetary process. *American Political Science Review, 60,* 529–547.

Eklund, D. (2001, March). *Performance measures* (Memorandum to Metropolitan King County Council Members. Public document).

Epstein, P., Fountain, J., Campbell, W., Patton, T., & Keaton, K. (2005). *Government service efforts and accomplishments performance reports: A guide to understanding.* Norwalk, CT: Governmental Accounting Standards Board.

Etzioni, A. (1967). Mixed scanning: A third approach to decision making. *Public Administration Review, 27,* 385–392.

Fountain, J. (2005, August 23). *Developing, managing with, and reporting performance information* (Briefing to King County countywide performance measurement work group and other King County representatives. Public document).

Government Performance and Results Act of 1993, Pub. L. No. 103–62 [S20] 107 Stat. 285.

Hayes, M. T. (1992). *Incrementalism and public policy.* New York: Longman.

Joyce, P. G., & Tompkins, S. (2002). *Using performance information for budgeting: Clarifying the framework and investigating recent state experience.* Washington, DC: American Society for Public Administration/Center for Accountability and Performance.

King County Auditor's Office. (1991). *County agency performance monitoring survey.* Seattle, WA: Author.

King County Auditor's Office. (2003, February). *King County Auditor's Office 2003 work program* (Work program adopted by Motion 11635).

King County Auditor's Office. (2004, June 16). *Countywide performance measurement work group meeting minutes.*

Lindblom, C. E. (1959). The science of muddling through. *Public Administration Review, 19,* 79–88.

Lindblom, C. E. (1979). Still muddling, not yet through. *Public Administration Review, 39,* 517–526.

Motion 11561. (2002, October 14). Seattle, WA: King County Council.

Motion 11558. (2002, October 14). Seattle, WA: King County Council.

Motion 11739. (2003, June 30). Seattle, WA: King County Council.

Motion 12005. (2004, September 20). Seattle, WA: King County Council.

Motion 12161. (2005, July 18). Seattle, WA: King County Council.

Motion 12367. (2006, October 9). Seattle, WA: King County Council.

Ordinance 14199. (2001, September 4). Seattle, WA: King County Council.

Ordinance 14517. (2002, November 25). Seattle, WA: King County Council.

Ordinance 15652. (2006, November 20). Seattle, WA: King County Council.

Powell, M. (2005). *CitiStat: Making a city work for its citizens.* Baltimore: Baltimore Mayor's Office.

Pressman, J. L., & Wildavsky, A. (1973). *Implementation* (3rd ed.). Berkeley: University of California Press.

Rahr, S. (2006, April 27). *Sheriff's response to performance measures work plan* (Letter from King County Sheriff to King County Auditor).

Sabatier, P. A., & Jenkins-Smith, H. C. (1999). The Advocacy Coalition Framework: An assessment. In P. A. Sabatier (Ed.), *Theories of the policy process* (chap. 6). Boulder, CO: Westview Press.

Schulman, P. R. (1975). Nonincremental policy making: Notes toward an alternative paradigm. *American Political Science Review, 69,* 1354–1370.

Wildavsky, A. B. (1984). *The politics of the budgetary process.* (4th ed.). Boston: Little, Brown.

8

Analyzing Performance Data

David N. Ammons

Many governments measure performance. Some attempt to do so comprehensively, while others focus on major departments or key functions. Some rely primarily on output measures that report how much service is being provided, while others include measures that gauge outcomes and efficiency. These measures can serve two complementary purposes, if designed and managed properly: accountability and performance improvement. Too often, government agencies focus only on the former while overlooking the value of performance measures for the latter.

Typically, governments that measure performance hope, somewhat vaguely, that these measures will provide feedback to departmental officials that will be valuable to them as they attempt to manage their programs. Most of these governments are less vague about their intentions to report at least a portion of their measures to persons beyond the program or department level—senior management, legislators, media, or the public—often in their budget documents and occasionally in separate performance reports or Web site postings. The publishing of performance data reflects the government's desire to demonstrate accountability for the delivery of suitable public services.

Public reporting on the work of government is important. However, reporting summary statistics to public officials and citizens is only the first of two fundamental uses of performance data. Analyzing performance data for the purpose of service improvement is the other. In too many instances, governments do not reap the full benefit from the performance information they collect. Too often, they miss opportunities to use this information to bring improvements in effectiveness or efficiency. Fortunately, there are some relatively easy-to-apply analytical techniques that can greatly increase the usefulness of performance data for decision making.

Chapter Objectives

The objectives of this chapter are to examine the contribution that analysis of performance data can make to government operations and to introduce several practical analytic techniques. First, we consider some instances in which the work of analysts clarified the nature of two very different problems confronting selected governments, as a preliminary step to solving those problems. We then proceed to review a series of analytic techniques suitable for addressing common governmental problems, beginning with the persistent debate over appropriate levels of staffing.

This chapter offers techniques and advice to help government decision makers reap greater benefit from their data for the following commonly encountered purposes:

- Analyzing staffing
- Using performance standards and benchmarks
- Describing data
- Analyzing demand
- Determining costs for various purposes
- Routing travel
- Adjusting for inflation to analyze revenues and expenditures
- Analyzing the costs of capital projects
- Applying useful analytical techniques for benchmarking projects

The Place of Analysis in Government Operations

Governments *need* good analysis.

In the mid-1990s, an African American motorist was beaten to death by police officers in a White neighborhood just outside Pittsburgh. Police–community relations in the Pittsburgh metropolitan area were already strained before this incident. The beating death escalated the problem to a crisis.

In a separate action, the American Civil Liberties Union filed a class action suit against the city of Pittsburgh on behalf of 52 plaintiffs alleging excessive force and verbal abuse by officers. Prompted by growing racial tension and the pressing need to find answers and solutions, the city controller in Pittsburgh conducted a performance audit to examine the nature, pattern, and disposition of complaints against officers over an 11-year period. The review of facts and figures by analysts consisted largely of the systematic sorting of tabular displays of data arranged by complainant and officer characteristics. Their analysis showed that African American complainants were as likely to object to the actions of African American officers as they were to complain about Caucasian officers. Although this finding "tend[ed] to negate a systemic racial interpretation" of community relations problems (City of Pittsburgh, 1996, p. 25), the analysts did not stop there. They proceeded to conduct what they termed a "bad-apple analysis" and discovered that while most officers had received one complaint or none, three officers generated a combined 83 complaints over the 11-year period of study. The controller urged the development of appropriate training and counseling strategies for officers in general, and for the high-complaint generators, a thorough review to answer the troubling question of "How, after 33 citizen complaints, could a police officer possibly be in a position to attract a 34th?" (City of Pittsburgh, 1996, p. 32).

Some analyses in government are prompted not by major societal issues or crises, but instead by an operational or resource issue. For example, the Property Maintenance Division of the City of Savannah assumed that code enforcement officers were working at the maximum manageable caseload level. However, systematic analysis focusing on careful time study and the computation of maximum manageable caseloads revealed that they were functioning at only 58.6% of capacity (Robinson, 1995). The analyst attributed much of the problem to unproductive time in the office and called for streamlined procedures, reduction of required paperwork, and improved supervision to reduce unproductive activities. Subsequent procedural and caseload adjustments were made, and 4 years later, code enforcement officers were operating at 74.8% (Ammons & Williams, 2004).

In these cases, analyses aided the efforts of policymakers and management officials to address problems. Too often, however, important decisions to expand, reduce, upgrade, or downgrade public services; decisions to change procedures or service delivery methods; and decisions designed to address policy issues are made without the benefit of careful analysis. Decision makers take considerable risk by relying on intuition, anecdotal evidence, or the hype from a reportedly successful implementation of a new system in another government. Careful analysis can help them more accurately assess current conditions and services, the likely costs and benefits of apparent alternatives, and the potential "fit" of a given option. Chances of a good decision are thereby increased and chances of a misstep, reduced.

Cynics sometimes scoff at the relevance of systematic analysis for government operations. They doubt the commitment of public sector managers and employees to improve government services. They doubt the ambitiousness and skills of government analysts to conduct relevant analyses. And they doubt the interest of public officials in the results of such analyses, if conducted. Politics, they say, trumps everything else. Why devote time and resources to analysis?

It is true that politics often takes priority—and *should* take priority—in a democratic governmental setting. It also is true that well-reasoned administrative recommendations, anchored on careful analysis, are sometimes rejected on the basis of politics alone in favor of seemingly less rational alternatives. But the cynics are wrong when they imply that public managers are unwilling to tackle service improvement initiatives, that government professionals are incapable of performing systematic analysis, or that thorough analysis has little chance of influencing public sector operations or major policy or service decisions. Careful analysis can inform and influence public sector decisions.

Preparation of Analysts

Much can be said about the value of advanced statistical training for analysts and the applicability of advanced analytic techniques to pressing issues facing government. In many cases, however, even less sophisticated techniques applied by careful and perceptive analysts—whether or not they have mastered advanced statistical methods—are suitable for addressing problems that confront governments and their operations. In fact, several observers note the greater tendency of governments to rely more on analysis rooted in management science techniques than analysis rooted in advanced statistical techniques (DeLorenzo, 2001; Hy & Brooks, 1984; LaPlante, 1989).

A recent study of the selection and training of analysts in the 50 largest municipal governments in the United States revealed that most major municipalities preferred analyst candidates with advanced degrees but that 80% would hire persons with only a bachelor's degree if they had the right experience (Ammons & Williams, 2004). Few cited mastery of particular analytic skills as especially important for analyst candidates. Some sought background or preparation in budget and finance, while a handful cited the value of accounting skills, computer skills, statistics, performance measurement, spreadsheets, and skill in financial calculations. Many provided training manuals to newly hired analysts; some provided in-house training; some sent analysts for training elsewhere; and several assigned new analysts to work with veteran analysts. Combinations of strategies featuring on-the-job learning were common.

The choice of analytic techniques varies widely among analyses focusing on government issues and operations. Some chosen analytic techniques are complex, but in many more cases, the applicable techniques are easy to learn and apply. Even a person with limited formal training in statistics and research methods can easily master many simple techniques and perform valuable analyses.

A variety of practical, easy-to-apply analytic techniques are introduced in this chapter. Each is a tool that provides the decision maker with a more reliable picture of reality and a better basis for examining options and predicting ramifications than the alternative practice of relying on anecdotes, intermittent observation, and intuition to form an impression of current conditions. Armed with these simple techniques, any agency can perform basic analysis of many of the most common operational issues.

Addressing Staffing Questions

Among the most common analytic challenges for administrators and budget makers are questions regarding appropriate staffing levels. Suppose, for instance, that a department head claims that his staff is stretched too thin, while budgeteers are not at all sure that this contention is correct. Can some form of analysis help?

Staffing Ratios

The chief of police argues that he needs more officers. The department, he says, is woefully short of the national average for officers per 1,000 population. "The national standard is 2 officers per 1,000 residents, and we have only 1.6 officers per 1,000."[1]

Is the analytic task here merely a matter of simple arithmetic—that is, the calculation of the number of additional officers needed to reach what the chief mistakenly proclaims to be the national standard? Or are other kinds of analysis potentially more helpful?

Population as a Proxy for Demand?

As a starting point, consider the possibility that the denominator in this staffing ratio (i.e., 1,000 population) is offered as a proxy for demand. Anyone prescribing a staffing ratio of two officers per 1,000 population (one officer per 500 population) believes that a pool of 500 persons will generate a year's worth of work for an officer. Although most of the people in this pool will behave themselves, enough of them will cause trouble or become victims of crime to generate the officer's workload. Is this a reasonable prediction? Perhaps not.

Population would be a fine proxy for service demand if we could assume that any one group of 500 persons would be pretty much like any other group of 500 persons, insofar as their need for police services is concerned. However, we know that criminal behavior is more prevalent among adolescent males and young men than among senior citizens and more prevalent in poor neighborhoods than in wealthy neighborhoods. Why, then, should we accept population as a proxy for demand, without giving any consideration to other factors known to be relevant?

Why not find a better indicator of demand for police services? Perhaps we should use a direct measure of demand rather than a proxy.

Production Ratios

Many communities report "calls for service per officer" or "officers per 1,000 calls for service." Each is a more direct measure of the activity or production of the typical officer—and the need for more or fewer officers—than is a ratio based on population and a theoretical demand for services. Comparing actual production ratios to standards or norms among respected counterparts is usually preferable to analysis tied to weak proxies. A wise analyst remains wary of weak proxies that make sweeping assumptions about service demands in other functions as well (e.g., firefighters per 1,000 population, human resource staff per 100 employees, recreation employees per 1,000 population or per 100 participants, and pupil-to-teacher ratios).

Careful analysis might reveal that the police department (or another function being analyzed) is not understaffed after all. Despite perhaps having a lower number of employees per 1,000 population (a proxy for service demand), a low-crime community might enjoy a favorable employee production ratio (a relatively low and quite manageable number of actual units of service per employee). Such a discovery would blunt the chief's call for hiring additional officers.

Availability Ratios

How much slack time do employees have? How much should they have? The answer to the latter question differs from function to function and the nature of one's responsibility. In general, slack time is something to be minimized, a sign of waste. Only a little slack—just enough to prevent burnout and ward off backlogs during sudden rushes of activity—is considered prudent in most cases. There are, however, a few exceptions, where larger doses of uncommitted time are desirable. Consider, for instance, a supervisor so consumed by daily tasks that she has no time to observe her subordinates on the job or to hear their professional or personal concerns. A little uncommitted time could allow her to be a better supervisor. Or consider the role of a police officer. How much uncommitted time is desirable for performing that role effectively?

In recent years, many communities have embraced a strategy called *community-oriented policing*. This approach departs from the more conventional pattern of merely responding to calls for help. In community-oriented policing, officers spend time getting to know the people in the neighborhoods they patrol; they build trust and cooperation; and they work with the community to solve neighborhood problems. This level of interaction and trust is difficult to achieve if officers are forced to spend all of their time responding to calls for service or performing other assigned duties. For this reason, some law enforcement agencies track "patrol availability factor," which is defined as the percentage of total time available for "undirected patrol." Patrol availability factor is calculated by subtracting from 100% the percentages of time devoted to responding to calls for service, testifying in court, completing paperwork, and performing other assigned duties. Law enforcement agencies that are most serious about implementing community-oriented policing typically have targeted their patrol availability factor at 35% to 45%.

So, how many police officers are needed in a given community? Providing a good answer requires more than simply knowing what the resident population is and applying a prescribed officer-to-population ratio. A good answer would also take into consideration the actual demand for police services and perhaps the strategy in place to combat the occurrence of crime.

Using Performance Standards and Benchmarks

Performance standards and benchmarks serve as useful gauges for a wide range of performance dimensions. Here, we consider the applicability of engineered standards and benchmarks—in this case, the employee output ratios achieved by other leading organizations—to questions of staffing.

Engineered Standards

Often associated with the work of industrial engineers and stopwatch-wielding efficiency experts, engineered standards declare the amount of time needed by a competent worker to complete a given task. Examples relevant to government workers include "flat rates" for mechanics, prescribing the amount of time in standard hours that a given repair should require for a specified make and model of vehicle (Hearst Business Communications, n.d.; Mitchell International, n.d.); custodial time standards (Building Service Contractors Association International, 1992; U.S. Department of the Navy, 1987); and landscaping time standards (U.S. Department of Defense, 1984). Some government agencies have adopted these standards or developed their own as a method not only of judging the efficiency of their employees but also of prescribing the appropriate size of the workforce, given the anticipated workload.

A municipal fleet maintenance operation, for instance, could record the maintenance or repair job, vehicle type, prescribed standard hours, actual hours, and the name of the mechanic for each service performed in the city garage. The efficiency of the team of mechanics or mechanics individually could be calculated by dividing standard hours by actual hours (i.e., producing an efficiency rating greater than 100.0, if repairs are completed in less time than prescribed by standard hours).

Although this system of evaluating employee performance appears to emphasize efficiency over quality, the latter can be factored in, too. Quality of work can be incorporated into the calculation by tracking any vehicles brought back to the garage with problems that persist even after the initial effort at repair. When such vehicles reappear at the garage, the additional rework time should be added to the original time record. In most cases, this will push the actual hours beyond the standard hours, constituting a penalty for shoddy work the first time.

Performance Marks of Others

When engineered standards are not available, some government operations rely instead on employee-to-output ratios reported by counterparts (Ammons, 2001). Usually, these ratios are far less precise than engineered standards (typically, they are expressed as outputs per full-time equivalent employee), but they nevertheless provide a rough gauge that can help an analyst judge whether the efficiency and staffing level of a given operation is at least "in the ballpark."

Focus on the Problem Rather Than the Presumed Solution

Too often, staffing debates skip right past the analysis of operating problems and the consideration of various options for solving these problems. Instead, they focus on a single, presumed solution: more resources in the form of additional staff. While additional staffing ultimately might be the best solution, it often is not the best place to begin the consideration.

Analysis That Considers Other Possible Solutions

When an agency head or program director declares the need for additional staff, he or she perhaps defends the request by noting the growth of the service population or other indications of increasing demand since the last adjustment to the size of the staff. This is not an unreasonable basis for asking for additional personnel, but a prudent analyst might wish to explore the ramifications of the presumed staff shortage before reaching a conclusion.

In some cases, a program director who is pressed to explain the problems created by a staff shortage might have difficulty citing specific evidence. Perhaps, in reality, expansion of the general population actually puts little additional demand on this service. Perhaps technological advances in this office have allowed the current staff to handle increasing workloads without much difficulty. On the other hand, if the program director cites long lines and a growing backlog, the analyst might wish to consider technological options or strategies to reduce demand peaks before moving on to consider increasing the size of the staff. The analyst might also wish to examine the manner in which the staff currently is being deployed, just to be sure that resources are being used to maximum effect.

Blackout Analysis

A superb example of analysis focusing, first, on the demand for service; second, on the deployment of current resources; and, third, on the need for additional personnel can be found in the work of the city auditor following a request for additional officers by the chief of police in Kansas City, Missouri (City of Kansas City, 1998). The analysis identified instances termed *blackouts,* when all patrol units on duty were engaged on service calls and an additional call would overload the system. The response to such calls would be delayed, as officers would have to be pulled from lower-priority calls. Analysts examining a year's data discovered 150 instances of blackout in Kansas City, usually lasting less than 3 minutes. Analysts found generally reasonable correlations between staffing patterns and calls for service by day, time, and geographical location; but analysis of instances of blackout led to a series of recommendations that included the use of nonpatrol personnel for certain traffic calls, steps to reduce false intrusion alarms, and improved practices in the assignment of compensatory time, as well as some increases in patrol staffing.

Remember the Basics and Use Them Wisely

Some of the most basic lessons in elementary statistics provide fundamental summary descriptions that give us an important glimpse at a population, all the relevant cases or incidents of a particular type, or just a sample. They tell us what is typical and how much variation exists beyond whatever is deemed typical (for additional information, see, for example, Meier, Brudney, & Bohte, 2006; O'Sullivan, Rassel, & Berner, 2003). The basic lessons about elementary descriptive statistics are simple, but sometimes administrators and even analysts in their most practical work seem to remember only one option for what is typical—the arithmetic mean—and to forget altogether about measures of dispersion.

Measures of Central Tendency

The mean (average value arithmetically), median (middle value in an ordered array of numbers), and mode (most common value) are measures of central tendency. Each identifies in its own way a value that is typical of the group. Because each has its own peculiarities, one might be a better choice in some cases and weaker in others. None is the perfect measure of central tendency; yet the arithmetic mean seems to be the default value in practice, even in cases where the median might be the better choice. A thoughtful analyst will consider the options.

Suppose the mayor asks for the average police salary. The simple and common response is to add all the salaries in the police department and divide by the number of employees. After all, that is what the "average" is. Consider, however, the possibility that in asking for the average, the mayor wanted to know the *typical* police salary. The mean will provide one version of "typical," but it will be a version distorted by the police chief's salary—an outlier in the range. The median is less influenced by extreme outliers and might be a better choice as representation of typical.

Measures of Dispersion

When we say that the fire department's mean response time to emergencies is 6.1 minutes or that its median response time is 5.8 minutes, may we assume that all response times are clustered tightly around the chosen measure of central tendency? We should not make that assumption without evidence to support it. We need a measure of dispersion.

Statisticians will call for the calculation of variance or standard deviation to gauge dispersion. The variance may be calculated by, first, finding the mean of the numbers involved, squaring the difference between each number and the mean, adding those squared values together, and dividing by the number of values in the set. This is the variance. The standard deviation is the square root of the variance. The formula for the standard deviation is as follows:

$$s = \sqrt{\frac{\sum_{i=1}^{N}\left(X_i - \bar{X}\right)^2}{N}}$$

Variance and standard deviation are not difficult to calculate, and many analytic techniques call for one or the other of these statistics as part of their formulas. However, the most common measures of dispersion reported in practical analyses are even simpler.

The simplest manner of reporting dispersion is to announce the range: the lowest value and highest value in the set. Here, the fire department would report that emergency response times ranged from 1.6 minutes to 17.2 minutes. A better choice would be to report the interquartile range (sometimes described as the "middle half" in presentations to lay audiences): the more limited span from the 25th percentile value to the 75th percentile value (see Figure 8.1). By excluding the first and fourth quartiles, the interquartile range eliminates unusual occurrences (outliers) and reports the range where half of all instances fall. Here, the fire department would report that the interquartile range of responses was from 3.9 minutes to 8.2 minutes.

An alternative way of expressing dispersion in a manner that will be understood easily by audiences of laypersons is to report the percentage of occurrences within a specified range (e.g., between 0 and 9 minutes). Here, the fire department would report that, say, 81% of all emergency response times were less than 9 minutes.

An appropriate measure of central tendency is important for conveying key information about a set of figures and so is a suitable measure of dispersion.

Plotting Job Travel to Diagnose Scheduling Problems

Many government services require some amount of travel to complete service delivery or collection routes, to get to job sites, or to conduct inspections. The careful design of efficient routes and the careful scheduling of service calls can conserve important resources. Simply plotting job travel can create a picture that will reveal inefficiencies or confirm that reasonable care is being given to work scheduling. Sometimes, completed work orders or job logs will give the analyst all the data needed to form this picture.

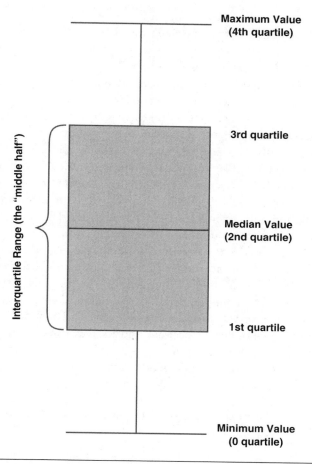

Figure 8.1   Interquartile Range, as Reflected in a Box-and-Whiskers Plot

Time in a car or pickup is necessary for conducting many jobs, but the objectives of this analysis are to avoid crisscrossing patterns across town and across the routes of other employees, to avoid backtracking, to maximize the geographic clustering of work, and to eliminate unnecessary trips. Programs seeking additional resources to improve the quality of their services can sometimes find them by pursuing greater efficiency in the use of resources they already have on hand.

Adjusting for Inflation to Analyze Revenues and Expenditures

Politicians and administrators who compare revenues from one year to another without accounting for the effects of inflation risk are understating or overstating the difference. "We are drawing more revenues from the beleaguered taxpayers of this community than ever before" might be a correct statement in raw dollars but hyperbole in terms of inflation-adjusted dollars—that is, in comparing the buying power of last year's and this year's revenues. The same is true for expenditures. A budget that increases spending by 5% in a given department might not feel like much of an increase when inflation is up by 8%. Arguably, it is a budget decrease—at least in constant dollars.

Just a few simple steps are all it takes to convert current dollars to constant dollars. The most popular price index to use for this purpose, although not the only one and not even necessarily the best one, is the Consumer Price Index (CPI), compiled by the Bureau of Labor Statistics (see Table 8.1). The CPI tracks price changes in a variety of consumer products and is frequently used as a guide for cost-of-living adjustments for wages and inflation adjustments for contract services.[2] The rate of change in the CPI from one year to another—for example, from 172.2 in 2000 to 195.3 in 2005, a rise of 13.4%—reflects inflation in consumer prices.

Although the CPI has the advantage of being more familiar to most audiences, a different inflation index compiled by the U.S. Department of Commerce's Bureau of Economic Analysis (BEA) might be a better choice as an inflation gauge for state and local governments. The index of "gross output of general government" for state and local consumption expenditure, found in the BEA's regularly updated Price Indexes for Government Consumption Expenditures and General Government Gross Output, is

Table 8.1 Average Annual Consumer Price Index for All Urban Consumers (CPI-U), 1995–2005

Year	Average Annual CPI	Change From Previous Year
2005	195.3	3.39%
2004	188.9	2.66%
2003	184.0	2.28%
2002	179.9	1.58%
2001	177.1	2.85%
2000	172.2	3.36%
1999	166.6	2.21%
1998	163.0	1.56%
1997	160.5	2.29%
1996	156.9	2.95%
1995	152.4	2.83%

SOURCE: U.S. Department of Labor, Bureau of Labor Statistics (2006).

Table 8.2   State and Local Gross Output Index (SLGOI)

State and Local Consumption Expenditures: Gross Output of General Government

Year	State and Local Gross Output Index (SLGOI)	Change From Previous Year
2005	120.748	5.13%
2004	114.860	3.88%
2003	110.575	4.37%
2002	105.942	2.83%
2001	103.026	3.03%
2000	100.000	4.45%

SOURCE: Data drawn from Table 3.10.4, "Price Indexes for Government Consumption Expenditures and General Government Gross Output," U.S. Department of Commerce, Bureau of Economic Analysis. "Gross Output of General Government (State and Local)" is Line 48 on this table. This information may be found online by visiting http://www.bea.gov and navigating to "Interactive Data Tables," then "National Income and Product Accounts, then "All NIPA Tables," and then section "3" for government. The data displayed above were drawn from http://www.bea.gov on February 27, 2006.

based specifically on the kinds of goods and services that state and local governments purchase. We refer to this index here somewhat more simply as the State and Local Gross Output Index (SLGOI).

Quarterly and annual SLGOI figures are displayed on the BEA Web site.[3] Annual SLGOIs for state and local governments from 2000 through 2005, along with instructions for finding this information online, are shown in Table 8.2.

Converting today's dollars, or current dollars, to constant dollars is a simple matter, as shown in Table 8.3. First, the analyst selects a base year, so that today's dollars may be expressed as constant dollars for that base year. If the analyst chooses 2001 as the base year, the object would be to express today's dollars in terms of their 2001 buying power—in other words, as 2001-constant dollars. Next, the analyst will multiply current dollars by the ratio of the base-year SLGOI to the current SLGOI. The resulting figure expresses current dollars in base-year constant dollars.

Demand Analysis

The object of demand analysis is to learn whether a program's demands and resources are aligned with one another. The pattern of service demands may be plotted by time of day, day of the week, geographically, or in whatever manner is determined to be relevant. Then, the pattern of resource deployment in dollars, workers, or other relevant values is plotted on the same dimensions as

Table 8.3   Using the State and Local Gross Output Index (SLGOI)

Formula for converting "current dollars" to "constant dollars" for a selected base year:

current dollar revenue or expenditure	×	$\dfrac{\text{base-year SLGOI}}{\text{current SLGOI}}$	=	current revenues or expenditures in base-year dollars

the demand pattern (for additional information on demand analysis, see, for example, Thomas, 1980). A comparison of the two graphs will reveal the degree of alignment or disparity in service demands and resource deployment. If major disparity exists, strategies should be developed to increase alignment by revising the deployment of resources, altering the pattern of demand, or both.

The demand pattern for ambulance services (see Figure 8.2) aligns reasonably well with the on-duty availability of ambulance units (i.e., resources) in Kansas City (see Figure 8.3). In many demand analysis cases, however, mismatches of demand and resource patterns are revealed, usually signaling the need to add resources or move resources from low-demand times or low-demand locations to high-demand times or locations. Ill-conceived hours of operation (for example, opening at 8 a.m. and closing at 5 p.m., when the demand for service is greatest from noon to 8 p.m.) and poor management practices (for instance, routinely scheduling lunch breaks during peak-demand periods or scheduling vacations during peak-demand months) often become apparent with demand analysis.

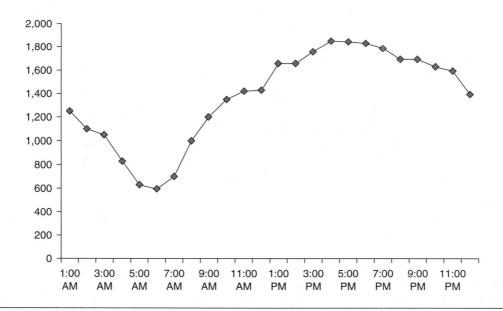

Figure 8.2   Ambulance Calls Received in Kansas City by Hour of Day

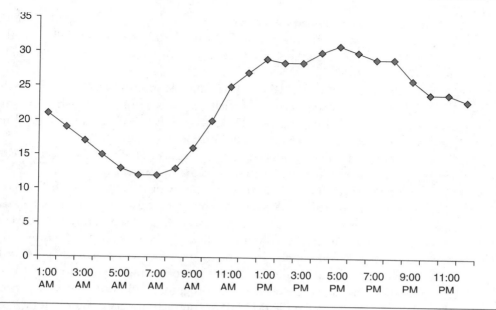

Figure 8.3 Ambulance Deployment in Kansas City by Hour of Day

Full-Cost Accounting Versus "Go-Away Costs"

Many government budgets understate the actual costs of a department or program, sometimes by a wide margin. This is not because officials are attempting to deceive anyone. Rather, it is simply because some of the costs associated with a program or department's operation have been paid in full at an earlier time or are reported in a different section of the budget. Buildings constructed decades ago but still used by the program today and vehicles purchased last year are not really "free" this year, even if the budget shows no current outlays for them, nor are the time and talents of the city manager, finance director, payroll clerk, and other "overhead services" that support the program administratively really free, even if the department's budget shows no charges for them.

Program analysts will encounter many occasions that demand the identification of the full costs of a program (e.g., Abrahams & Reavely, 1998; Brown, Myring, & Gard, 1999). Full-cost accounting will be valuable, for instance, when establishing user fees or when assessing the relative efficiency of a program compared with counterparts. In such cases, it will be important to capture all of the costs associated with the program or activity under review, meticulously dividing the costs associated with workers engaged only partially in the program or activity and including the portion of costs associated with the activity and excluding those that are not. It also requires appropriate allocations of fringe benefit costs; full accounting of all operating expenses, including a "rental" fee for building space and vehicles, even if they are owned by the department or agency; and assignment of the program's fair share of overhead costs. Worksheets are available in other publications to help the analyst identify all of these costs (see, for example, Ammons, 2002, pp. 122–136).

Although full-cost accounting is valuable in efforts to set user fees for services or to assess relative efficiency, it is a poor choice when deciding whether to contract out for a given service. Instead, "go-away costs," not full-cost accounting, should guide contracting decisions.

Full-cost accounting provides a fair statement of all of the costs associated with a program, but the decision to actually contract out the program will rarely eliminate all of these costs. In other words, only some of these costs would go away with the decision to contract for this service. Some of the costs in the full costs of the program are go-away costs, and some are not. The costs of most workers directly involved in delivering the services are go-away costs, as are most of the supply, equipment, and utility costs. But what about the overhead costs and building costs? A share of the finance director's salary, for instance, should be included in the program's full costs, but that expense will not go away with the decision to contract the service, nor will the costs associated with building space, unless a decision is made to rent out the space.

Consider an in-house program with full costs of $400,000. Suppose a contractor proposes to provide the program at an equal level of quality but at a cost of $350,000. Arguably, the contractor is the more efficient service provider, but should the government accept the bid and enter a contract for the service? The decision should be guided by consideration of go-away costs. If $35,000 of the department's $400,000 total consists of overhead and indirect costs that will not go away, the actual go-away costs are $365,000, leaving an apparent saving of $15,000 by entering the contract. But wait! If officials project a cost of $20,000 to administer and monitor the contract, the decision to enter the contract would actually cost the government $5,000, rather than saving any money at all.

Only by including go-away costs alone and excluding from consideration any costs that will remain whether the program is contracted or retained in-house will the decision be based on all the relevant information. If service quality would be equal with each option, the comparison should be between go-away costs, on one hand, and the contract fee plus contract administration costs, on the other.

Annualizing the Cost of Capital Items

Capital items last for a while; they are not consumed quickly. A wise capital investment provides benefits not just for this year, but over the whole life of the item.

Suppose we are asked to report the annual costs of a program that acquires capital equipment from time to time. We carefully tabulate expenditures for personnel, utilities, supplies, and the like, but what about those capital items?

It would be misleading to apply all of the costs for a capital item to the year in which it is purchased and assign none of the costs to other years in which the equipment is also used.

Consider a piece of equipment purchased in 2007 and having a useful life of 4 years. If the equipment costs $40,000 and that full amount is counted in the year of purchase, this organization might appear to be a high-cost service producer in 2007 and an extremely efficient service producer in 2008 through 2010 (because it is using "free" equipment the last 3 years). In fact, neither might be true. It might be a service producer with rather average expenditures when the cost of capital items is spread across their useful lives. Two of the simplest methods of spreading the costs of a capital item over its useful life are allocations based on usage rate and allocations based on straight-line depreciation (for additional information, see Kelley, 1984).

The premise for allocating costs according to usage rate is the belief that some capital items having varying levels of use from year to year deteriorate more from use than simply from the passage of time. A machine that can be expected to last through 10,000 hours of operation—whether those hours occur in 2 years' time or 10 years' time—is a good example. If the cost of such a machine is $16,500 and it is expected to have a salvage value of $1,500, it would be reasonable to assign costs for that equipment at the rate of $1.50 per hour of operation. The annual cost would be dependent on the anticipated or actual usage of the equipment per year. The formula for usage rate allocation of cost is as follows:

$$a_i = \frac{u_i}{U}(C - S)$$

where a_i = capital expense allocation for time period i,

u_i = usage units consumed during time period i,

U = total estimated usage units in the life of the asset,

C = cost of the asset, and

S = salvage value after U usage units.

Straight-line depreciation is another method of annualizing capital costs. This method requires only an estimate of the useful life of an item rather than a projection of usage in a given year. Straight-line depreciation is a suitable method if the amount of usage per year is expected to be uniform across the life of the capital item or if deterioration of the item is perhaps as much due to the passage of time as to actual usage.

The capital costs of light rolling stock—automobiles and pickups, for instance—could be annualized using either usage rate or straight-line depreciation. If we project that the useful life of a sedan is, say, 100,000 miles, we could calculate the capital cost per mile. Alternatively, we could check the records and see that sedans in a given department are driven an average of

18,000 to 22,000 miles per year and calculate the straight-line depreciation for this vehicle, using the following formula and an estimated life of 5 years:

$$a_i = \frac{C - S}{N}$$

where a_i = capital expense allocation to each time period,

C = cost of the asset,

N = total number of time periods in the item's expected life, and

S = salvage value after N periods.

Life-Cycle Costing

An item might have a lower price tag than all of its competitors, but that does not mean that it is the best buy or even the least expensive over the long run. The cost of owning and operating an item includes more than its purchase price alone.

The technique known as *life-cycle costing* provides a method of determining the total cost of owning an item, including costs associated with the item's acquisition, operation, and maintenance. It focuses not simply on the purchase price of the item, but on these other costs as well.

Life-cycle costing can be applied to many government purchases but is most often used to determine the lifetime costs of moderately expensive, energy-consuming equipment. Prime targets for applying life-cycle costing include motor vehicles, climate control systems, data-processing equipment, lighting systems, and similar items. Consider the case of a government that is about to purchase a 15-horsepower electric motor and must choose between a pair of competing units (see Table 8.4). The motor offered by Vendor A has the lower price tag and therefore seems less expensive than the motor offered by Vendor B. However, Motor A has a higher rate of energy consumption (14.40 kilowatts/hour) than Motor B (12.58 kilowatts/hour), a very important factor in this decision because the government plans to run the motor 10 hours a day, 5 days a week (i.e., 2,600 hours per year). As shown in Table 8.4, Motor A will actually cost $6,119 more than Motor B over their lifetimes, assuming equal maintenance costs.

To perform a life-cycle cost analysis, an analyst must account for acquisition cost, energy costs, lifetime maintenance costs, and the eventual salvage value of the item (see Figure 8.4). The acquisition cost of an item includes its purchase price, transportation costs, and installation fees, less any discounts and trade-in credits. The cost of electricity or other fuel to operate the item must be added in, as well as costs to keep it functioning (for additional information, see Coe, 1989).

In most cases, life-cycle cost analyses based solely on acquisition costs, maintenance costs, energy costs, and salvage value will be sufficient. For a

Table 8.4   Supplementing Purchase Price With Lifetime Energy Costs

Life-Cycle Cost	Motor From Vendor A	Motor From Vendor B
Horsepower	15	15
RPM	3,450	1,160
Bid cost	$1,956	$2,935
Duty cycle	2,600 hrs./yr.	2,600 hrs./yr.
Life	15 years	15 years
Efficiency rating	78.2%	86%
Energy consumption (kilowatts/hour)	14.40	12.58
Energy costs (kwh consumption rate × $.10/kwh × 39,000 hours)	$56,160	$49,062
Life-cycle cost (bid cost + energy cost)	$58,116	$51,997
Life-cycle cost difference ($58,116–$51,997) = $6,119		

SOURCE: Ammons (2002, p. 154).

few especially large purchases, however, several other life-cycle costs could be significant and should be incorporated into the projection: *failure costs,* including downtime, production losses, and rental costs for replacement equipment; *training costs; consumable supply costs* arising from an item's use; *storage costs* for the item or for repair parts; *secondary costs* for disposal of by-products associated with the item's use; *labor costs* for operators; and *money costs,* including interest paid if a loan was necessary to purchase the item or interest forgone on money that could have been invested elsewhere if not used for this equipment purchase.

Analytic Techniques Useful for Benchmarking Projects

The desire for excellent services and state-of-the-art operations leads some organizations to adopt a technique known as *benchmarking*. Benchmarking in the public sector can take different forms. The form adopted by many governments entails comparing performance statistics from their own operations to relevant benchmarks, often in the form of performance standards or performance targets or results achieved by leading counterparts. If the government's performance record is generally consistent with the benchmarks, the comparison offers reassurance that the operation is on track. On the other

---

The basic life-cycle cost formula is

life-cycle costs	**= acquisition cost + lifetime maintenance costs + lifetime energy costs – salvage value**

Where

acquisition costs	= purchase price + transportation cost + installation cost – trade-ins and discounts,
lifetime maintenance costs	= anticipated costs of keeping the item in operable condition,
lifetime energy costs	= energy consumption rate × cost of energy × duty cycle × life of the item, and
salvage value	= anticipated worth at the end of the item's projected life.

The components of the lifetime energy costs are

energy consumption rate	= the rate at which energy is consumed (kilowatts/hour),
cost of energy	= dollars per energy unit (cents per kwh),
duty cycle	= annual number of hours item is used (number of hours in use per day × number of days in use), and
life	= length of time until item is replaced (number of years in use based on the duty cycle).

Figure 8.4   Formula for Life-Cycle Costing

SOURCE: Adapted from League of California Cities, *A Guide to Life-Cycle Costing: A Purchasing Technique That Saves Money* (Sacramento: League of California Cities, December 1983, pp. 3–4). Adapted by permission of the League of California Cities.

hand, if substantial performance gaps become evident, the organization might be prompted to conduct further analysis leading to operating changes.

Organizations performing this kind of benchmarking sometimes turn to regression analysis to control for selected variables when identifying top performers (for a technical explanation of regression, see, for instance, Schroeder, Sjoquist, & Stephan, 1986). A regression program will calculate the relationship between two or more variables using data from multiple observations. The program will draw a regression line through the scatterplot of observations that approximates this relationship.

Suppose that an analyst is focusing on the unit cost of a given service and suspects that economies of scale come into play—that is, the cost per unit declines among governments serving larger populations. Regression analysis would confirm or refute the suspected relationship between cost and scale. If the relationship is confirmed, points on the regression line could be considered to represent the expected value of unit cost at various population levels along the line. Observations that deviate the most in a favorable direction from the line reflect the organizations that are most efficient in providing this service when controlling for population.

Some governments adopt a different form of benchmarking, patterned after the approach followed in the private sector. Corporate-style benchmarking is narrow in scope, focusing on a single key process in a given organization. It is more analytic than the other form of benchmarking in that it systematically examines the steps in a selected key process, not simply the results being achieved. Furthermore, it is prescriptive, not merely diagnostic. The purpose is to identify "best practices" among top performers and adapt those practices for the benchmarking government's own use.

Governments that are engaged in corporate-style benchmarking select a key process (e.g., emergency dispatching, the reservation process for renting civic center space, the handling of citizen complaints, the requisition process for government purchases) and identify outstanding performers of that process—that is, organizations that are achieving superior results. They attempt to persuade top performers to cooperate as benchmarking partners, sharing information on the details of their process. The basic steps in this type of benchmarking are depicted in Figure 8.5.

A slightly more detailed description of corporate-style benchmarking, developed for the application of this technique in the public sector, includes seven steps:

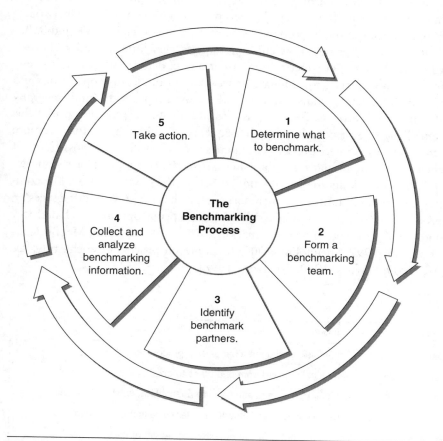

Figure 8.5 The Benchmarking Process
SOURCE: Spendolini (2000).

- Decide what to benchmark
- Study the processes in your own organization
- Identify benchmarking partners
- Gather information
- Analyze
- Implement for effect
- Monitor results and take further action as needed (Southern Growth Policies Board and Southern Consortium of University Public Service Organizations, 1997).

Each step in the benchmarking process is important, but the steps of particular relevance to this chapter are those dealing with the gathering of information about the process being studied and the analysis of that information. How can this information about the process as conducted by the government and its benchmarking partners be compiled and recorded systematically, so that important differences contributing to superior results might be revealed? Process flow charting can help.

In *process flow charting*, all the steps in a routine procedure are recorded in sequence. Each detailed step is categorized and given one of five labels: operation, transportation, inspection, delay, or storage (see Figures 8.6 and 8.7).

Rudimentary process flow charting requires very little specialized knowledge. It does require meticulous attention to detail and perceptiveness, for the analyst strives to eliminate unnecessary or duplicative operations and inspections, reduce transportation and delay components, and generally streamline the process. Each step is scrutinized: What is the purpose of this step? Why does it come here in the sequence? Could it be performed more effectively by someone else? The analyst will consider the possibility of cheaper, faster, or more reliable alternatives. In the context of corporate-style benchmarking, the process flow chart for the government will be compared with the charts of benchmarking partners to reveal differences in procedures and draw the analyst's attention to prime options for change (for additional information on benchmarking, see Keehley, Medlin, MacBride, & Longmire, 1997; Spendolini, 2000; for more on process flow charting, see Aft, 2000; Haynes, 1980; Summers, 1998).

Symbol	Name	Defnition
O	Operation	An item is acted upon, changed, or processed.
⇨	Transportation	An object is moved from one place to another.
☐	Inspection	An object is examined to be sure quantity and/or quality is satisfactory.
D	Delay	The process is interrupted as the item awaits the next step.
▽	Storage	The item is put away for an extended length of time.

Figure 8.6   Process Flow Chart Symbols

Process Chart

Present Method ☐
Proposed Method ☐

SUBJECT CHARTED _____ DATE _____

_____ CHART BY _____

_____ CHART NO. _____

DEPARTMENT _____ SHEET NO. _____ OF _____

Dist. in Feet	Time in Mins.	Chart Symbols	Process Description
		○ ⇨ ☐ D ▽	
		○ ⇨ ☐ D ▽	
		○ ⇨ ☐ D ▽	
		○ ⇨ ☐ D ▽	
		○ ⇨ ☐ D ▽	
		○ ⇨ ☐ D ▽	
		○ ⇨ ☐ D ▽	
		○ ⇨ ☐ D ▽	
		○ ⇨ ☐ D ▽	
		○ ⇨ ☐ D ▽	
		○ ⇨ ☐ D ▽	
		○ ⇨ ☐ D ▽	
		○ ⇨ ☐ D ▽	
		○ ⇨ ☐ D ▽	
		○ ⇨ ☐ D ▽	
		○ ⇨ ☐ D ▽	
		○ ⇨ ☐ D ▽	
		○ ⇨ ☐ D ▽	
		○ ⇨ ☐ D ▽	
		○ ⇨ ☐ D ▽	
		○ ⇨ ☐ D ▽	
		○ ⇨ ☐ D ▽	
		○ ⇨ ☐ D ▽	
		○ ⇨ ☐ D ▽	
			Total

Figure 8.7   Process Chart

Conclusion

Careful, systematic analysis of a perceived staff shortage, an outdated service fee that no longer recovers full costs, a volatile service demand pattern, or another operational issue or problem improves the likelihood of an accurate diagnosis and a good solution. Will recommendations based on facts and careful analysis carry every decision? Not every time—not in an environment where tradition, emotion, and politics matter, too. Still, good analysis will carry some decisions and, in other cases, can at least influence the decision process. Progressive governments count on conscientious analysts and administrators to bring the products of careful analysis to the decision table to be sure that analysis provides all the influence it can.

Notes

1. A standard of this sort is mentioned frequently in various communities during budget deliberations, but such prescribed ratios are on shaky ground. According to the International Association of Chiefs of Police, "Ready-made, universally applicable patrol staffing standards do not exist. Ratios, such as officers-per-thousand population, are totally inappropriate as a basis for staffing decisions. . . . Defining patrol staffing allocation and deployment requirements is a complex endeavor which requires consideration of an extensive series of factors and a sizable body of reliable, current data" (http://www.theiacp.org, displayed February 6, 2006). Among the factors considered relevant are number of calls for service, population density, and transience of population.

2. For CPI information online, see the U.S. Bureau of Labor Statistics Web site at http://www.bls.gov/cpi/.

3. For SLGOI information online, see the U.S. Bureau of Economic Analysis Web site at http://www.bea.gov.

References

Abrahams, M. D., & Reavely, M. N. (1998, April). Activity-based costing: Illustrations from the state of Iowa. *Government Finance Review, 14,* 15–20.

Aft, L. S. (2000). *Work measurement and methods improvement.* New York: Wiley.

Ammons, D. N. (2001). *Municipal benchmarks: Assessing local performance and establishing community standards* (2nd ed.). Thousand Oaks, CA: Sage.

Ammons, D. N. (2002). *Tools for decision making: A practical guide for local government.* Washington, DC: CQ Press.

Ammons, D. N., & Williams, W. A. (2004). Developing and applying analytic capabilities in major American cities. *Public Administration Quarterly, 27,* 392–409.

Brown, R. E., Myring, M. J., & Gard, C. G. (1999, Summer). Activity-based costing in government: Possibilities and pitfalls. *Public Budgeting and Finance, 19,* 3–21.

Building Service Contractors Association International. (1992). *Building Service Contractors Association International production rate recommendations.* Fairfax, VA: Author.

City of Kansas City. (1998, January). *Kansas City, Missouri, police department patrol deployment: Blackout analysis.* Kansas City, MO: Office of the City Auditor.

City of Pittsburgh. (1996). *Performance audit: Department of public safety office of professional standards.* Pittsburgh, PA: Office of City Controller.

Coe, C. K. (1989). *Public financial management.* Englewood Cliffs, NJ: Prentice Hall.

DeLorenzo, L. (2001). Stars aren't stupid but our methodological training is. *Journal of Public Administration Research and Theory, 11,* 139–145.

Haynes, P. (1980). Industrial engineering techniques. In G. J. Washnis (Ed.), *Productivity improvement handbook for state and local government* (pp. 204–236). New York: Wiley.

Hearst Business Communications. (n.d.). *MOTOR labor guide manual* (updated annually). Troy, MI: Author.

Hy, R. J., & Brooks, G. H. (1984, Fall). An assessment of evaluation skill needs in state evaluation agencies in the south. *Review of Public Personnel Administration, 5,* 25–33.

Keehley, P., Medlin, S., MacBride, S., & Longmire, L. (1997). *Benchmarking for best practices in the public sector.* San Francisco: Jossey-Bass.

Kelley, J. T. (1984). *Costing government services: A guide for decision making.* Washington, DC: Government Finance Officers Association.

LaPlante, J. M. (1989). Research methods education for public sector careers: The challenge of utilization. *Policy Studies Review, 8,* 845–851.

League of California Cities. (1983, December). *A guide to life-cycle costing: A purchasing technique that saves money.* Sacramento, CA: Author.

Meier, K. J., Brudney, J. L., & Bohte, J. (2006). *Applied statistics for public and nonprofit administration.* Belmont, CA: Wadsworth.

Mitchell International. (n.d.). *Mechanical labor estimating guide* (updated annually). San Diego, CA: Mitchell International.

O'Sullivan, E., Rassel, G. R., & Berner, M. (2003). *Research methods for public administrators.* New York: Addison Wesley Longman.

Robinson, C. L. K. (1995). *The effects of caseload on code enforcement case completions.* Paper submitted for Master of Science in Administration degree, Central Michigan University, Mount Pleasant, MI.

Schroeder, L. D., Sjoquist, D. L., & Stephan, P. E. (1986). *Understanding regression analysis: An introductory guide.* Newbury Park, CA: Sage.

Southern Growth Policies Board and Southern Consortium of University Public Service Organizations. (1997). Benchmarking best practices. *Results-oriented government, Module 2.* Research Triangle Park, NC: Author.

Spendolini, M. J. (2000). *The benchmarking book* (2nd ed.). New York: AMACOM.

Summers, M. R. (1998). *Analyzing operations in business: Issues, tools, and techniques.* Westport, CT: Quorum Books.

Thomas, J. S. (1980). Operations management: Planning, scheduling, and control. In G. J. Washnis (Ed.), *Productivity improvement handbook for state and local government* (pp. 171–203). New York: Wiley.

U.S. Department of Defense. (1984). *Roads, grounds, pest control, & refuse collection handbook: Engineered performance standards* (NAVFAC 0525-LP-156–0016). Washington, DC: U.S. Government Printing Office.

U.S. Department of Labor, Bureau of Labor Statistics. (2006, February 7). *Consumer Price Index table.* Available at http://www.bls.gov/cpi/home.htm#tables

U.S. Department of the Navy. (1987). *Janitorial handbook: Engineered performance standards* (NAVFAC 0525-LP-142–0061). Washington, DC: U.S. Government Printing Office.

PART III

Informing and Involving
Citizens and Other
Stakeholders

9 Making Performance Measurement Relevant

Informing and Involving Stakeholders in Performance Measurement

Kaifeng Yang

An important question in performance measurement is how to make the practice relevant to democratic governance, public management, and government performance. Otherwise, it is questionable as to why performance measurement deserves valuable public resources and managerial attention. Indeed, performance measurement could be manipulated or misused and depart from its original purposes or intentions (Kelly, 2002; Smith, 1995). Some critics fear that performance measurement may repeat past reforms, such as the Planning, Programming, and Budgeting System (PPBS), and add burdens to administrators who are already littered with data systems and reports that are rarely used for decision making (Radin, 1998). To prevent performance measurement from becoming a political gimmick or management fad, it is important to ensure that it is relevant and valuable for public organizations and their stakeholders.

A number of issues must be addressed in order to make performance measurement relevant, such as sustaining political leadership, obtaining managerial authority/flexibility, maintaining stakeholder support, tying performance to budgets, integrating performance measurement with other management reforms, and linking performance measurement with an overall effort of modernizing government. Most of these topics are discussed in other sections of this handbook. Part III focuses on a particularly important strategy for making performance measurement relevant: involving stakeholders in performance measurement and presenting the results to stakeholders in a simple, interesting, and compelling manner. Some practical strategies in this regard are described, with lessons drawn from leading-edge projects. This chapter briefly reviews the rationale, importance, practice, and challenges of linking performance measurement with stakeholder involvement.

Why Are Stakeholders Important for Performance Measurement?

Informing and involving stakeholders in performance measurement has had a long history. The New York Bureau of Municipal Research used citizen surveys before the 1930s to study government operations and compiled scorecards to report results to politicians and the public (Williams, 2003). The U.S. National Committee on Municipal Reporting (1931) emphasized performance reporting in government administration, expressing "disquiet over the failure of popular participation in the civic process that is shown by officials throughout the country, whose efforts for improvement have not been durable because of the lack of public support" (p. 9). These efforts left an important legacy that measurement should be pursued not for its own sake, but for social problem solving and democratic governance. In addition, experience with citizen surveys has long shown that citizen surveys can effectively incorporate citizen participation into performance measurement and local governance (Watson, Juster, & Johnson, 1991).

To make performance measurement relevant is to make the practice achieve the goals it is supposed to achieve. However, public organizations usually have multiple and competing values and goals, as they have multiple stakeholders with diverse interests and preferences. Any group or individual who can affect or is affected by the achievement of a public organization's objectives is a stakeholder of the organization, such as elected officials, managers, employees, private businesses, nonprofits, citizen groups, and individual citizens. The stakeholders may have different opinions about what constitutes "performance" and how it should be measured. The relevance of performance measurement and performance information is in the eye of beholder. Therefore, informing and involving stakeholders in performance measurement is necessary and fundamental for public organization management.

Informing stakeholders about government performance is consistent with the democratic spirit of transparency and informed citizenship. An important value of performance measurement is to improve democratic governance and citizen trust in government by informing the public and their representatives how well the government is performing. Without accurate and timely performance information, citizens may be hijacked by ideological prejudices or anecdotal evidences and lose their trust in democratic institutions, including the government (Berman, 1997; Goodsell, 1994). It is for this reason that the foremost purpose of the Government Performance and Results Act (GPRA) of 1993 is to "improve the confidence of the American people in the capability of the Federal Government" and to "improve congressional decision making by providing more objective information on achieving statutory objectives" (p. 1). Similarly, the Governmental Accounting Standards Board (GASB) (1987) states, "Accountability requires governments to answer to the citizenry. . . the citizenry has a 'right to know,' a right to receive openly declared facts that may lead to public debate by the citizens and their elected representatives" (p. 56).

Involving stakeholders, particularly citizens, in performance measurement is normatively desirable in and of itself. Citizen engagement is a fundamental value for participatory governance, whereby citizens are educated and enriched. Performance measurement is an important government activity, and the involvement of citizens demonstrates community empowerment and ensures democratic control of the activity. Civic engagement and community building is one of the two trends or challenges that contemporary local government professionals face in their work (Nalbandian, 2005). Admittedly, in the United States, the level of authentic citizen participation in administrative decision making is relatively low at present (King, Feltey, & Susel, 1998), and the level of social capital has declined in the past several decades (Putnam, 2000). However, as performance measurement activities at the local level relate directly to citizens' personal lives, those activities are likely to generate more participation interest among citizens.

Informing and involving stakeholders are actions that complement and reinforce each other. Informing stakeholders requires useful information to be generated from the measurement system, which, in turn, calls for stakeholder involvement in establishing goals, indicators, and targets (Ho & Coates, 2004; Yang & Holzer, 2006). Without stakeholder involvement, performance measurement may be guided by bureaucratic interests and the technocratic logic and produce numbers that external stakeholders cannot understand. In turn, when elected officials and citizens are better informed about government performance, they are more likely to participate. A common myth about citizen participation assumes that citizens do not participate because they are lazy, incompetent, apathetic, or uncommitted (Rosenbaum, 1978). Others consider that citizens are already overburdened with their personal lives and do not believe their participation will change things. However, citizens are likely to participate when "bad" performance information is presented to them in a simple, interesting, and compelling manner (Epstein, Coates, & Wray, 2006). And their participation is likely to make a difference when more citizens are energized to participate.

Informing and involving stakeholders is also necessary for the successful adoption and implementation of performance measurement. First, stakeholders' perceptions of the irrelevance of performance measurement may lead to resistance and cynicism toward the implementation of performance measurement (de Lancer Julnes, 1999; de Lancer Julnes & Holzer, 2001).

Second, stakeholder support is a major component of government capacity for performance measurement (Berman & Wang, 2000). With stakeholder support, government organizations are more likely to obtain resources and make institutional changes that are necessary for managing for results. Third, stakeholder involvement helps ensure that the performance information is of stakeholders' interest, so that they are more likely to use it for decision making. As GASB observes,

> If citizens were to be expected to use the information, it is important that the information being reported be relevant to their needs and interests. . . . This could be best accomplished by including citizens in the process of selecting what to measure and report. (Fountain, Campbell, Epstein, & Robinson, 2002, p. 12)

Informing and involving external stakeholders helps improve public management in general, particularly when public organizations are increasingly working in a network-based governing system. External stakeholders may have perspectives regarding government operations that are different from those of public managers. Their involvement in performance measurement may stimulate managers' interest in pressing community problems, expand managers' horizon in alternative choices, and encourage strategic innovations. External stakeholders, particularly citizens, are usually not policy experts, and their knowledge may not be professional or comprehensive; however, their knowledge is a valuable addition to professional expertise, which is especially important in performance measurement because government activities are difficult to quantify and assess. It is worth noting that an emphasis on external stakeholder involvement does not exclude the fact that performance measures should be tied to what management is doing and help management do their work better.

Are Stakeholders Informed and Involved?

Informing and involving citizens is usually included in performance measurement projects, at least in principle or as an "espoused theory." In the United States, the GPRA mandated federal agencies to develop strategic plans that include performance targets, requiring that "when developing a strategic plan, the agency shall consult with the Congress, and shall solicit and consider the views and suggestions of those entities potentially affected by or interested in such a plan" (p. 2). GASB, influential in state and local governments, specifies that performance reports should include a discussion of the involvement of citizens, elected officials, management, and employees in the process of establishing goals and objectives (Fountain, Campbell, Patton, Epstein, & Cohn, 2003).

In the United Kingdom, stakeholding is the core concept for New Labour's program in office (Prabhakar, 2004). For example, the United Kingdom Local

Government Act of 1999 mandated the Best Value (BV) initiative to secure continuous improvement in economy, efficiency, and effectiveness. It requires local governments to consult the following parties:

> (a) representatives of persons liable to pay any tax, precept or levy to or in respect of the authority, (b) representatives of persons liable to pay non-domestic rates in respect of any area within which the authority carries out functions, (c) representatives of persons who use or are likely to use services provided by the authority, and (d) representatives of persons appearing to the authority to have an interest in any area within which the authority carries out functions.

The Service First program in the United Kingdom requires that public and private organizations involved in public service delivery carry out consumer and user surveys (United Kingdom Cabinet Office, 1998). Stakeholder participation is considered one of nine principles of the Service First, the starting point for service and organizational reviews, and part of best practice in developing and implementing policy and legislation. The white paper *Modernising Government* highlights the role of stakeholder consultation in United Kingdom government reform, stating,

> The Government needs to ensure that bodies are clearly focused on the results that matter to people, that they monitor and report their progress in achieving these results and that they do not allow bureaucratic boundaries to get in the way of sensible co-operation. (United Kingdom Cabinet Office, 1999, p. 35)

Informing and involving stakeholders, however, is not a "theory-in-use" in many performance measurement projects. In the United States, while managing for results has been widely adopted, much remains to be done to better inform and involve stakeholders. At the federal level, the GPRA process in 1997[1] was an internal top-down process, with little stakeholder consultation taking place (Franklin, 2001). This situation largely continued in 2000 (Franklin & Long, 2003). At the state level, few states statutorily require citizen participation in strategic planning or performance measurement (Snell & Grooters, 2000), and state legislatures, interest groups, and individual citizens are much less involved in setting performance goals than are governors, budget offices, and state agencies (Moynihan, 2003). At the local level, motivation for using performance measures has more to do with management than with accountability (Wang, 2002). A study found that only 12% of respondents consider citizens' boards to be the intended audiences of performance measures (Poister & Streib, 1999). Local governments are only somewhat effective in using performance measurement for external communication (Melkers & Willoughby, 2005), and only a limited number of local governments frequently used citizen involvement in measuring performance (12% to 13%) or evaluating program achievement (16% to 28%) (Yang & Callahan, 2005).

This is true in the United Kingdom as well (Boyne, Gould-Williams, Law, & Walker, 2002; Prabhakar, 2004). Most observers conclude that stakeholding in the United Kingdom had a "short shelf-life" under New Labour (Heffernan, 2001). It "does not function as an overall organizing project in the way that was once suggested" (Prabhakar, 2004, p. 568). Based on a study of 127 BV pilot services in Wales, Boyne et al. (2002) found that performance reporting does not provide appropriate information that could be used to improve external accountability. It remains unclear whether and how organizations use performance information to engage in dialogue with stakeholders.

Nevertheless, there are success stories in implementing the principle of informing and involving stakeholders (Epstein et al., 2006; Ho & Coates, 2004; Holzer & Kloby, 2005). For example, nine Iowa cities experimented with an idea called "Citizen-Initiated Performance Measurement" (CIPA), as illustrated in Figure 9.1. The goal of CIPA is "to shift the power of information back to citizens by engaging them in the design and use of performance measurement, so that performance measures reflect the concerns and priorities of citizens and can be used by policymakers in decision-making" (Ho & Coates, 2004, p. 31). CIPA had positive results on departmental practices, administrative procedures, performance measures, and staff attitudes

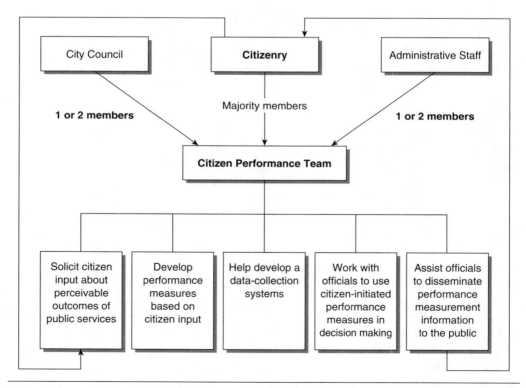

Figure 9.1   Citizen-Initiated Performance Measurement in Iowa

SOURCE: Iowa CIPA Project (2005).

(Ho & Coates, 2004). More examples are available in Chapter 13 of this volume, by Holzer and Kloby.

Issues and Challenges

At least three issues are related to the implementation of stakeholder-centered performance measurement: technical/conceptual, organizational, and institutional.

Technical

The technical dimension refers to how performance management may be integrated with stakeholder communication and involvement, addressing analytical techniques. As illustrated in Figure 9.2, four dimensions must be taken into account when linking stakeholder participation with performance measurement: (a) Various stakeholders: Different types of stakeholders may play different roles in performance management; (b) Performance management processes: Performance management has a number of steps, such as identifying goals, setting targets, and reporting results; (c) Participation objectives: Public agencies may involve or inform stakeholders for different purposes, such as educating stakeholders and legitimizing performance measures; and (d) Participation mechanisms: Stakeholder communication and participation can be achieved though various channels or mechanisms. Taken as a whole, the framework indicates that public organizations, depending on their unique circumstances, may involve different stakeholders in different performance management steps via different mechanisms and for different purposes.

Public managers have to ask themselves exactly why they need stakeholder involvement in performance management, and then make appropriate plans. At the beginning stage, a comprehensive stakeholder analysis is necessary (Bryson, 2004):

- Identify all potential stakeholders.
- List the criteria each stakeholder would use to evaluate the organization's performance.
- Decide how well each stakeholder thinks the organization is doing from the stakeholder's point of view.
- Specify how each stakeholder influences the organization.
- Specify to what extent each stakeholder is interested in the organization.
- Decide what the organization needs from each stakeholder.
- Compare the stakeholders' importance to the organization based on their power, legitimacy, and attention-getting capacity.
- Identify what can be done quickly to satisfy each stakeholder.
- Identify long-term issues with each stakeholder.

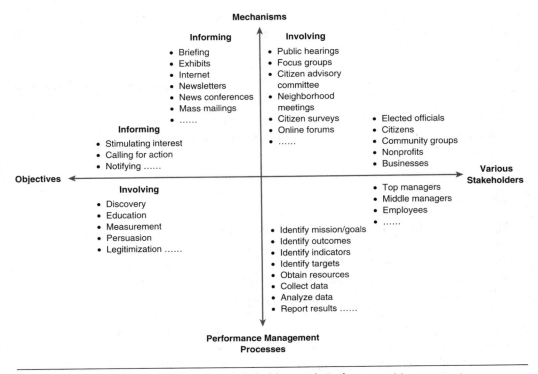

Figure 9.2   A Framework Integrating Stakeholders With Performance Measurement

To evaluate alternative plans for linking stakeholders with performance measurement, the following best-practice criteria on citizen engagement may be considered (Creighton, 2005):

- Representativeness: whether the participants are representative of the population
- Independence: whether the participation process is unbiased
- Early involvement: whether the participants are involved as early on as possible
- Influence: whether the participation results have genuine impact on policy
- Transparency: whether the process is transparent
- Resource accessibility: whether the participants have resources to fulfill their roles
- Task definition: whether the nature and scope of the participation are clearly defined
- Structured decision making: whether the participation uses appropriate mechanisms
- Cost-effectiveness: whether the process is cost-effective

Organizational

The organizational dimension is concerned with how public managers can mobilize organizational resources to implement stakeholder-centered performance management. First, perhaps the most important factor is sustained leadership—both political and administrative (Berman & Wang, 2000; McDavid & Hawthorn, 2006; Melkers & Willoughby, 2001). Second, another factor is the lack of resources. Both performance measurement and stakeholder participation require resources, but elected officials may be reluctant to allocate such resources because performance measurement is often adopted to reduce cost in the first place. Third, also at issue is lack of training. Many government managers are not used to using performance information for forward-looking purposes. They are familiar with workloads and inputs, but not with outputs and outcomes. They also lack skills in working with citizens, such as conducting stakeholder analysis, choosing appropriate participation mechanisms, designing feasible participation processes, coordinating participation efforts, listening to citizens, facilitating deliberations, and bridging conflicting interests. Training also helps reduce fear and resistance toward stakeholder-centered performance management. In addition, stakeholders themselves need to be educated; they need to understand government operations and their roles in performance measurement (Ho & Coates, 2004).

Fourth, organizational culture is an important concern. Performance measurement involves adopting new organizational values and norms (de Lancer Julnes & Holzer, 2001; Melkers & Willoughby, 2001) and so does stakeholder participation (King et al., 1998). Without a culture that emphasizes transparency, trust, results, honesty, and change, performance information could be distorted and misused. As Adams (1993) commented,

> Managers can easily distort information flows to prevent proper feedback either by manipulating budget targets to make them relatively easy to achieve, or by manipulating data relating to actual performance in order to giver the appearance of satisfactory short-term performance. (p. 48)

Similarly, stakeholder participation requires a culture that is transparent, open to innovation, flexible, and ready to learn.

Finally, also challenging is to obtain and sustain stakeholder interest and participation. Stakeholders, especially citizens, often do not have enough time to work on performance management matters. When they do participate, they want to see immediate impact, though visible results from performance measurement may take months or years to appear (Ho & Coates, 2004). This is true not only in American experience but also in other countries. For example, according to a survey of chief executive officials of local governments in England, "lack of public interest" is ranked the foremost obstacle to public participation (Lowndes, Pratchett, & Stoker, 2001). The lack of public interest makes it more difficult to obtain representativeness of stakeholder participation. Public officials often find the same handful of citizens participating, and they are likely to be community activists and White, with higher levels of income and education. While disadvantaged groups need to participate and make their voices heard, they are less likely to have the resources and skills to do so.

Institutional

Both performance management and citizen participation require institutional changes to be made in traditional bureaucratic systems. Managing for results demands that public managers have the authority and flexibility to overcome red tape and implement innovations, but federal and state experiences show that many public managers are not granted enough authority (Moynihan, 2006; U.S. General Accountability Office, 2004). Citizen participation also requires that administrative systems and procedures be changed to make information sharing and citizen involvement possible, but those changes are difficult to make (King et al., 1998).

Franklin and Long (2003) observed that there are structural and process constraints that impede external consultation in the GPRA implementation. The structural factors include lack of interest and commitment from Congress, different expectations among various congressional committees, and independency among federal programs. The process factors include lack of continuing interest on the part of interest groups and the difficult-to-resolve diverse inputs from external groups. The fragmentary nature of the American political system and its political culture, characterized by distrust, add to the difficulty in sharing and reporting performance information (Radin, 2000). Although these observations are based on federal experience, they are also applicable to state and local governments. It is common to all levels of government that performance is subjective and stakeholders may have conflicting expectations. Moreover, performance measurement efforts often depend on a high-level champion within the government, but this is constrained by the rapid turnover that is characteristic of many high-level government positions.

Nevertheless, although radical institutional changes rarely happen overnight, incremental adjustments are possible, and public managers can always make a difference by strategically mobilizing stakeholders, shaping environments, and influencing policy making (Moore, 1995). As Kettl (2005) commented, "The reform process works more like a ratchet than a pendulum, with government's capacity increased one step at a time" (p. 84). Evidence does show that governments, particularly local governments, can use stakeholder participation to achieve relevant performance measurement (Epstein et al., 2006; Ho & Coates, 2004; Holzer & Kloby, 2005).

Opportunities and Prospects

To deal with the technical, organizational, and institutional challenges of informing and involving stakeholders is not easy in a political environment characterized by distrust, conflicting interests, and budget deficits. A strategic leader must identify the opportunities faced by communities and organizations and take advantage of the opportunities to increase stakeholder-centered performance management.

First, public managers must take advantage of the unceasing accountability pressure and emphasize the value of performance management not only from the perspective of sound management but also from the wider perspective of democracy and citizenship. Improving democratic accountability is perhaps the best justification for requesting political support and financial resources. This is true not only for government but also for other public organizations, such as public schools, as reflected in Chapter 11 of this volume, by Katherine Ryan. In particular, public organizations may place performance measurement in an overall strategic pursuit of community problem solving, linking performance measurement with stakeholder participation by community efforts aiming to tackle pressing issues. The effective community governance model, proposed by Epstein et al. (2006), is illustrative in this regard (see Figure 9.3).

In Figure 9.3, Area 1 is defined as *community problem solving*, referring to aligning citizen engagement and getting things done. Area 2 is labeled

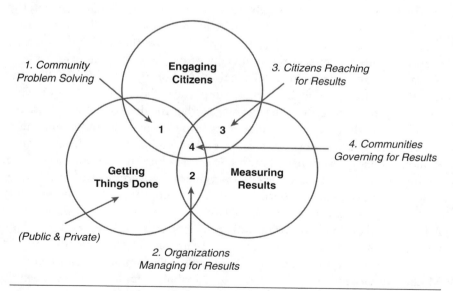

Figure 9.3   The Effective Community Governance Model

SOURCE: The model, used with permission, is explained in the book *Results That Matter* by Paul Epstein, Paul Coates, and Lyle Wray, published by Jossey-Bass, an imprint of John Wiley & Sons, 2006, and on the Web site www.resultsthatmatter.net.

organizations managing for results, indicating alignment between measuring performance and getting things done. Area 3 is labeled *citizens reaching for results,* requiring alignment between citizen engagement and performance measurement. Area 4 stands for *communities governing for results,* which aligns all three core skills. In Chapter 12 of this handbook, Katharine Mark demonstrates that many communities have used a simple technique, trained-observer rating, to involve citizens in evaluating issues such as the cleanliness of streets. Performance measurement becomes a civic engagement process that educates citizens, raises their awareness, stimulates their participation, and eventually helps solve the problem.

Second, public managers must recognize that public organizations increasingly work in network settings in collaboration with private and nonprofit sectors. The performance of governance as a whole is what matters to citizens, and measuring the performance cannot and should not be conducted by government alone. Government can partner with businesses, foundations, nonprofit organizations, and community groups to measure not only the quality of government services but also the overall quality of life. Through partnerships, performance management costs can be shared. Public managers may support and take advantage of extant community activities, including those initiated by citizen groups to measure quality of life and community health. For example, the "healthy community movement," attempting to improve public health by working on a broad range of factors that influence the quality of life, has spread to over 7,000 communities worldwide and 1,200 communities in the United States (Kesler, 2000). It adopts an approach of collaborative community governance, whereby collaboration is organized among citizens and people from business, government, and other sectors of society who recognize that their interconnection can be used to impact the well-being of the entire community.

Another example is the National Neighborhood Indicators Project (NNIP) (see http://www.2.urban.org/nnip/), a collaborative effort by The Urban Institute and its local partners to further the development and use of neighborhood-level information systems in policy making and community building. It seeks to develop measures of changing social, physical, and economic conditions of neighborhoods, helping local institutions develop a comprehensive set of indicators so that citizens, government officials, and civic leaders can plan appropriate strategies to improve their communities.

Public managers may seek help from foundations. For example, the Alfred P. Sloan Foundation has advocated for citizen-driven performance measurement and sponsored a series of projects to promote its spread and institutionalization. One of its programs, "Performance Assessment of Municipal Governments," focuses on "making municipal governments more responsive to their citizens" and emphasizes "public involvement to ensure that what is measured and reported is what matters to citizens and that the data are not corrupted by the natural tendency of officeholders and government professionals to report favorable outcomes" (Alfred P. Sloan Foundation, 2007). A similar idea has been presented by the experts from

The Urban Institute. Liner et al. (2001) recommended establishing performance partnerships among state agencies, local government agencies, private businesses, nongovernmental organizations, citizen groups, and individual citizens to help identify missions, specify indicators, set targets, and assign responsibilities. They suggested the use of citizen charters, regular measurement of citizen/customer satisfaction with state services, inclusion of customer outcomes when determining incentive awards, and marketing performance reports at service delivery points.

Third, public managers must leverage the role of technology. The Connecticut Policy and Economic Council (CPEC), a nonpartisan not-for-profit organization, initiated a City Scan project in Hartford, Connecticut. The organization wanted to provide a way for Hartford residents to identify and prioritize problems, such as potholes and drug paraphernalia in parks, in order to pressure the city to take action. Armed with handheld computers, custom-designed software, and digital cameras, a group of high school students conducted a sophisticated, high-tech summer survey of Hartford's parks. They documented conditions and provided the city with a first-of-its-kind resource for municipal government.

An emerging trend is to use the Internet to facilitate stakeholder-centered performance measurement. Performance indicators and results can be posted online, allowing stakeholders access 24 hours a day, 7 days a week. E-mails and Web sites can be used by stakeholders to send complaints and feedback. Online forums allow stakeholders to deliberate on performance-related matters and design solutions. Tools such as online surveys, online polling, online voting, and digital town hall meetings can help identify stakeholders' preferences. The Internet enables stakeholders to participate in performance measurement and problem solving with great convenience and at low lost. In Chapter 10 of this volume, Seungbeom Choi describes how the Korean government has used the Internet to facilitate citizen participation in performance management.

Technology also helps present performance results in a more compelling and interesting manner. As stakeholders have different needs in performance information, managers must prepare different versions of performance reports to match those needs and increase the attractiveness of the reports. Managers can use software packages such as Microsoft Excel, PowerPoint, and geographic information systems (GIS) to produce visual displays. The Fund for the City of New York (FCNY) (see http://www.fcny.org) has extensively used GIS and maps to communicate results, both in hard copy and on the Internet. With GIS, performance information is broken down and compared across communities, boroughs, and streets.

Finally, public managers may join professional networks to seek advice, disseminate information, and advocate for the practice. For example, the International City/County Management Association (ICMA) advocates for citizen participation and performance measurement. It publishes textbooks and reports in areas such as conducting citizen surveys and using citizen participation in the budgeting process. It provides training and opportunities for local mangers to meet and learn from one another. The National Center for Public Productivity at Rutgers University offers an online certification program focusing on the central idea of citizen-driven performance measurement. The program links the central idea with management topics such as performance measurement, strategic management, e-government, and citizen surveys. Workshops in this area are regularly offered at the annual meetings of the American Society for Public Administration (ASPA).

Note

1. GPRA (1993) required agencies to prepare strategic and performance plans by September 30, 1997. So, 1997 was the first year when all federal agencies implemented GPRA. The implementation process was coordinated by the federal Office of Management and Budget (OMB) and evaluated by the U.S. General Accountability Office (GAO).

References

Adams, D. (1993). Using performance indicators for effective public sector management. *Management Accounting, 71*, 48–52.

Alfred P. Sloan Foundation. (2007). *Making municipal governments more responsive to their citizens.* Available at http://www.sloan.org/programs/stndrd_performance .shtml

Creighton, J. L. (2005). *The public participation handbook.* San Francisco: Jossey-Bass.

Berman, E. (1997). Dealing with cynical citizens. *Public Administration Review, 57,* 105–112.

Berman, E., & Wang, X. (2000). Performance measurement in U.S. counties: Capacity for reform. *Public Administration Review, 60,* 409–420.

Boyne, G., Gould-Williams, J., Law, J., & Walker, R. (2002). Plans, performance information, and accountability: The case of best value. *Public Administration, 80,* 691–710.

Bryson, J. (2004). What to do when stakeholders matter. *Public Management Review, 6,* 21–53.

de Lancer Julnes, P. (1999). Lessons learned about performance measurement. *International Review of Public Administration, 4*(2), 45–55.

de Lancer Julnes, P., & Holzer, M. (2001). Promoting the utilization of performance measures in public organizations. *Public Administration Review, 61,* 693–708.

Epstein, P., Coates, P., & Wray, L. (2006). *Results that matter.* San Francisco: Jossey-Bass.

Fountain, J., Campbell, W., Epstein, P., & Robinson, B. (2002). *GASB research report: Report on the GASB citizen discussion groups on performance reporting.* Norwalk, CT: Government Accounting Standards Board.

Fountain, J., Campbell, W., Patton, T., Epstein, P., & Cohn, M. (2003). *Reporting performance information: Suggested criteria for effective communication.* Norwalk, CT: Government Accounting Standards Board.

Franklin, A. (2001). Serving the public interest? Federal experiences with participation in strategic planning. *American Review of Public Administration, 31,* 126–138.

Franklin, A., & Long, E. (2003). The challenge of changing federal management processes. *International Journal of Organization Theory and Behavior, 6,* 534–552.

Goodsell, C. (1994). *The case for bureaucracy.* Chatham, NJ: Chatham House.

Governmental Accounting Standards Board. (1987). *Concepts Statement No. 1: Objectives of financial reporting.* Stamford, CT: Author.

Government Performance and Results Act of 1993, Pub. L. No. 103–62 [S20] 107 Stat. 285. Available at http://www.sc.doe.gov/bes/archives/plans/GPRA_PL103–62_03AUG93.pdf

Heffernan, R. (2001). *New Labour and Thatcherism.* London: Palgrave.

Ho, A., & Coates, P. (2004). Citizen-initiated performance assessment: The initial Iowa experience. *Public Performance & Management Review, 27,* 29–50.

Holzer, M., & Kloby, K. (2005). Public performance measurement: An assessment of the state-of-the-art and models for citizen participation. *International Journal of Productivity and Performance Measurement, 54,* 517–532.

Iowa CIPA Project. (2005). Available at http://www.andromeda.rutgers.edu/~ncpp/cdgp/cases/iowa/detalied%20case.pdf

Kelly, J. (2002). Why we should take performance measurement on faith. *Public Performance & Management Review, 25,* 375–380.

Kesler, J. T. (2000). The Healthy Community Movement: Seven counterintuitive next steps. *National Civic Review, 89,* 271–284.

Kettl, D. (2005). *The global public management revolution* (2nd ed.). Washington, DC: Brookings Institution Press.

King, C., Feltey, K., & Susel, B. (1998). The question of participation. *Public Administration Review, 58,* 317–326.

Liner, B., Hatry, H. P., Vinson, E., Allen, R., Dusenbury, P., Bryant, S., et al. (2001). *Making results-based state government work.* Washington, DC: Urban Institute.

Lowndes, V., Pratchett, L., & Stoker, G. (2001). Trends in public participation: Part 1: Local government perspectives. *Public Administration, 79,* 205–222.

McDavid, J., & Hawthorn, L. (2006). *Program evaluation & performance measurement: An introduction to practice.* Thousand Oaks, CA: Sage.

Melkers, J., & Willoughby, K. (2001). Budgeters' views of state performance budgeting systems: Distinctions across branches. *Public Administration Review, 61,* 54–64.

Melkers, J., & Willoughby, K. (2005). Models of performance-measurement use in local governments. *Public Administration Review, 65,* 180–190.

Moore, M. (1995). *Creating public value.* Cambridge, MA: Harvard University Press.

Moynihan, D. (2003). Managing for results. In P. Beekman et al. (Eds.), *Paths to performance in state and local government: A final assessment from the Maxwell School of Citizenship and Public Affairs* (pp. 153–172). Syracuse, NY: Alan K. Campbell Public Affairs Institute.

Moynihan, D. (2006). Managing for results in state government: Evaluating a decade of reform. *Public Administration Review, 66,* 78–90.

Nalbandian, J. (2005). Professionals and the conflicting forces of administrative modernization and civic engagement. *American Review of Public Administration, 35,* 311–326.

Poister, T. H., & Streib, G. (1999). Performance measurement in municipal government: Assessing the state of the practice. *Public Administration Review, 59,* 325–335.

Prabhakar, B. (2004). Whatever happened to stakeholding? *Public Administration, 82,* 567–584.

Putnam, R. (2000). *Bowling alone.* New York: Simon & Schuster.

Radin, B. (1998). The Government Performance and Results Act (GPRA): Hydra-headed monster or flexible management tool? *Public Administration Review, 58,* 307–315.

Radin, B. (2000). The Government Performance and Results Act and the tradition of federal management reform: Square pegs in round holes? *Journal of Public Administration Research and Theory, 10,* 111–135.

Rosenbaum, W. (1978). Public involvement as reform and ritual. In S. Langton (Ed.), *Citizen participation in America* (pp. 81–96). Lexington, MA: Lexington Books.

Smith, P. (1995). On the unintended consequences of publishing performance data in the public sector. *International Journal of Public Administration, 18,* 277–310.

Snell, R., & Grooters, J. (2000). *Governing for results: Legislation in the states.* Denver, CO: National Conference of State Legislatures.

United Kingdom Cabinet Office. (1998). *Service first.* London: The Stationery Office.

United Kingdom Cabinet Office. (1999). *Modernising government.* London: The Stationery Office.

United Kingdom Local Government Act of 1999. Available at http://www.opsi.gov.uk/ACTS/acts1999/19990027.htm

U.S. General Accountability Office. (2004). *Results-oriented government* (GAO-04–594T). Washington, DC: Author

U.S. National Committee on Municipal Reporting. (1931). *Public reporting.* New York: Municipal Administration Service.

Wang, X. (2002). Assessing performance measurement impact. *Public Performance & Management Review, 26,* 26–43.

Watson, D., Juster, R., & Johnson, G. (1991). Institutionalized use of citizen surveys in the budgetary and policy-making processes. *Public Administration Review, 51,* 232–238.

Williams, D. (2003). Measuring government in the early twentieth century. *Public Administration Review, 63,* 643–659.

Yang, K., & Callahan, K. (2005). Assessing citizen involvement efforts by local governments. *Public Performance & Management Review, 29,* 191–216.

Yang, K., & Holzer, M. (2006). The performance-trust link: Implications for performance measurement. *Public Administration Review, 66,* 114–126.

10 Citizen-Involved Performance Measurement

The Case of Online Procedures Enhancement for Civil Applications in Seoul

Seungbeom Choi

As the administration-centered paradigm gives way to the citizen-involved governance perspective in recent years, growing concerns are focused on the performance measurement of public services (Callahan, 2004; Holzer & Lee, 2004). Many studies on citizen involvement and performance measurement are emphasizing citizen participation in the decision-making process and valid estimation of citizen satisfaction with services (Edwards & Thomas, 2005; Kweit & Kweit, 2004; Pollanen, 2005). Securing legitimacy through consensus building from citizen participation and gaining accurate results through proper methods from evaluation surveys are important themes in that research.

There are, however, at least two questions to be answered in the study of citizen-involved performance measurement. One is whether citizen-involved performance measurement produces desirable outcomes as expected. The other is under what conditions citizen-involved performance measurement brings outcomes. Though many local governments adopt citizen involvement and performance measurement as tools to enhance administrative accountability and efficiency, the effects of the arrangement is not clear. Citizens sometimes do not trust government efforts to improve the effectiveness of citizen involvement, because they have little chance to know the new institutional arrangements, to communicate with bureaucracy, and to collaborate with professional experts (Stich & Eagle, 2005). On the other hand, bureaucrats, who are familiar with procedure-oriented culture and have experienced government bashing, tend to have negative attitudes toward citizen participation (Yang, 2005). There also can be various impediments to the prevalence of performance measurement, such as the lack of appropriate measures, the expedient use of measures, and the vagueness of performance objectives (Pollanen, 2005). There are also various factors that influence the implementation of performance measurement: leadership, institutional arrangements, technical accessibility, organizational culture, and interest of stakeholders (Halachmi, 2005).

Especially when corruption is rampant in the delivery of public services, the simple adoption of performance measurement does not guarantee the accountability and productivity of government administration. In Korea, when a regime changes, new power holders usually try to reform administration to achieve legitimacy from the public. Nevertheless, it was hardly believed that corruption controls had brought government efficiency and effectiveness.

There is, however, a case in which much progress has been made in reducing corruption and enhancing transparency in Korean local administration. The former mayor of Seoul, Goh Kun, adopted "a systematic approach" to reduce corruption in his local administration. One of the main tools of the approach was the Online Procedures Enhancement for civil applications, which is called OPEN. OPEN is an Internet system that allows citizens to access and check as to whether their civil applications for registration, approval, or permission are being processed rightly and promptly throughout the whole handling process. By reviewing their applications, citizens can evaluate the performance of service providers as well as monitor the transparency of the process. Citizens can also communicate with the public servant in charge of the application through the Internet and be informed of the need to supplement documents. Public servants must handle the applications on time, or they will receive a warning, which can delay promotion in the future. The auditing and inspection bureau of Seoul also conducts a survey with OPEN users and various anticorruption surveys to citizens almost every year. The bureau uses the survey outcomes to improve the operation of the OPEN system and other anticorruption measures.

The OPEN system has been said to produce successful results in reducing corruption and improving service performance. It has also attracted much attention from domestic and international societies. The central government designated OPEN as an advanced innovative case in the field of public management in November 1999 and developed a similar application-handling system. Almost all local governments were strongly recommended to adopt the system thereafter. By now, every local administration has actually adopted it, though the content of the system is a little different from the original OPEN system.

Therefore, it is time to analyze the effects of the OPEN system on the corruption control in Seoul. The purpose of this chapter is to show how a performance measurement program combined with citizen involvement can enhance the transparency and productivity in the Seoul Metropolitan Government (SMG). To complete the purpose, at least three subjects are to be analyzed: the development process of the OPEN system, the features of the system, and the performance of the system.

Development of the OPEN System

A Brief History of Korean Regimes and Local Innovations

Since the Constitution of the Republic of Korea was enacted in 1948, every administration has adopted its own reform ideologies and strategies, as shown in Table 10.1. The new public management style of reform was activated quite recently in Korea, because the earlier regimes pursued economic development. The economic crisis of 1997 in particular made performance-based administrative reform possible, mainly initiated by the central government.

The current participatory government emphasized administrative reform and innovation at both central and local levels when the administration took power in 2003. The regime established an innovation implementation system, which includes the Senior Secretary to the President for Innovation at the Blue House, Headquarters for Government Innovation Within the Ministry of Government Administration and Home Affairs, Presidential Committee on Government Innovation and Decentralization, Innovation Planning Officers in central agencies, and Innovation and Decentralization Bureaus in provincial governments.

The central government induces every local government to develop its own administrative innovation strategies by giving financial incentives. Local governments are sometimes inventing new performance measurements and other times benchmarking domestic or foreign innovative programs. Therefore, many municipal and provincial innovative performance measurements in Korea are actually fueled and driven by the central government rather than initiated by local governments themselves. Many local governments superficially implement performance measurement programs compelled by the central government. The performance measurement adopted by local governments is rarely designed from the perspective of a comprehensive approach to productivity improvement (Holzer & Yang, 2004). Many of the programs are in the beginning stage of the whole process now.

The birth of the OPEN system, however, is a very exceptional case of administrative reform made by a local government. In 1999, SMG initiated some reform activities, including the OPEN system. It was designed to increase transparency and to control corruption from a comprehensive perspective. The central government and foreign countries acknowledge the effectiveness of the system. The OPEN system has been introduced to all local governments as a model case of administrative innovation.

Table 10.1   Korean Regimes and Reforms

Regime	Reform
1st–2nd Republic (1948–1962)	• The nation's priorities were to reconstruct the nation and restore order.
3rd–4th Republic (1963–1979)	• Government attempted reform for economic development. • The Administrative Reform Research Committee was established under the jurisdiction of the prime minister's office.
5th Republic (1980–1988)	• The previous committee was dismissed, and only a small research lab was operated for political and sporadic reform measures.
6th Republic (1988–1993)	• The Administrative Reform Committee was established and operated for 14 months. • Reform proposals were made through the participation of civilians, but few were actually put into practice.
Civilian Republic (1993–1998)	• The Administrative Innovation Committee was established and persisted throughout the regime. • The committee annually published white papers on reform. • The regime pursued small government and democratization.
People's Government (1998–2003)	• Reform agencies became a formal organization of the government: Planning and Budget Committee, Ministry of Planning and Budget, Government Innovation Committee, etc. • The regime simultaneously promoted democratization and market economy. • The regime performed various New Public Management reform measures due to the Asian economic crisis. • The regime aspired to become a small government and an entrepreneurial government.
Participatory Government (2003–present)	• The regime set five goals of innovation; building flexible administration system, providing high-quality public services, expanding autonomy and responsibility, expanding disclosure of public information, and encouraging people's participation.

SOURCE: Reprinted with permission of the Korea Institute of Public Administration.

The Role of the Mayor and His Staff

The OPEN system was unthinkable without the initiation of the mayor, Goh Kun. When the mayor won the election in 1998, Korea was in a situation of deep economic recession and under the control of the International Monetary Fund (IMF). Seoul also suffered from multitudes of shutdowns of business firms and factories and increasing numbers of the unemployed and homeless. The first imperative of the new central government, headed by Kim Dae Jung beginning in February 25, 1998, was the difficult task of rebuilding the economy and helping the needy. The new mayor of Seoul had the same mission, to revitalize the declining economy and to spend relief money for the jobless efficiently and effectively.

To accomplish the two goals, Mayor Goh decided to restructure the city government as soon as he took office. He reduced the size of the city organization by one fifth, shedding 10,200 employees. Many departments in the city hall were regrouped and merged, and many services were privatized and contracted out. At the same time, he poured all his efforts into making his administration accountable and responsive to the citizens.

Mayor Goh launched a reform team to re-create the city hall to be "as transparent as crystal," as he promised in the campaign.[1] The new mayor and his team analyzed the rampant problem of corruption from a "systematic approach," which is composed of four major lines of action: preventive measures (deregulation and ending the vicious circle of irregularity), punitive measures ("one strike and you're out," zero tolerance for corruption, and corruption report card to the mayor), ensuring transparency in administration (OPEN and announcement of Anti-Corruption Index[2] by each administrative district), and public-private partnerships (Integrity Pact,[3] joint inspection with citizens, and citizen ombudsman). OPEN is one of the innovative anticorruption measures created by Mayor Goh and his reform team.

After determining the 26 civil application fields, the city hall created the OPEN development team, composed of three officials in charge of analyzing the cases and nine program developers. The team members held discussions with government staff in charge of permission, approval, and inspection in order to decide which of the details would be open to the public and what method would be used for the disclosure. Simultaneously with the field analysis, the team developed a system, which involved categorizing the application fields, analyzing each field into its procedures, and designing a flow chart.

The team designed standardized data entry formats for the city staff to process the data easily. While designing the system, it was emphasized that the system should meet citizens' needs for the information they wanted. The information includes application-processing procedures, required paperwork, related documents, and search functions. The system was also designed to include information on the city department and the staff in charge, the telephone number, and when and how the filing will be processed. The city hall trained a total of 5,000 employees, handling applications in 485 city departments, to operate the system and process the data. They were given IDs and passwords.

The Birth of the OPEN System and the Wide Coverage of Services

The OPEN system, with a total of 26 civil application fields, started to serve the public on April 15, 1999. Ten months later, an additional 15 fields with potential irregularities were made public. From July 2000, 13 more fields were open to the public. An additional 16 fields in 2003 and 41 fields in 2004 were disclosed to the public. Now, the OPEN system provides a service of 111 civil application fields to citizens. The enlargement process of the fields is shown in Figure 10.1, and the number of fields in each working area is presented in Table 10.2.

The Differences in Mayors' Policies

Mayor Lee,[4] who became the incoming mayor in 2002, accepted Goh's systematic approach to anticorruption measures. He also emphasized the transparency of city administration and insisted on no wrongdoing by public employees. Lee had a career as CEO in one of the largest corporations, the Hyundai group, so he tackled corruption with a business mentality. He pursued "maximum results with minimum costs" by encouraging active citizen participation, eliminating inefficiency, and establishing a productive working culture. Anticorruption is related to only one or two of his five main directions for the operation of municipal administration: humanistic administration for the neglected neighbor, environmental revitalization and economic vitality, balanced regional development, active citizen participation, and businesslike efficient administration. As shown in Table 10.3, he abolished the Administrative Reform Bureau, which had operated in the OPEN system during Goh's administration. The Auditing and Inspection Bureau is now in charge of the operation of the OPEN system.

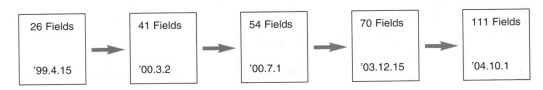

Figure 10.1   Enlargement Process of Information Disclosed to the Public

Table 10.2   Information Disclosed to the Public in 2005

Working Area	Field	Area	Field
Housing & Construction	9	Environment	10
Construction Work	7	Culture & Tourism	7
Transportation	11	Industry & Economy	9
Urban Planning	6	Welfare & Women	7
Firefighting	4	Administration	1
Administrative Committees	40	Total	111

SOURCE: Detailed information can be accessed via the Internet: http://www.open.metro.seoul.korea

Table 10.3   Budget Allocated to Anticorruption-Related Bureaus (in Millions, Korean Currency)

Bureau	2001	2002	2003	2004	2005
Auditing & Inspection Bureau	1,720	8,493	8,691	7,693	8,099
Information System Planning Bureau	36,220	38,663	39,306	39,703	37,872
Administrative Reform Bureau	563	1,009	–	–	–

SOURCE: http://www.metro.seoul.kr

Table 10.4   Budget Allocated to Anticorruption-Related Programs (in Millions, Korean Currency)

Anticorruption Program	2001	2002	2003	2004	2005
Integrity Pact & Anticorruption Index	261	210	427	229	207
OPEN System	–	300	175	–	–
Asset Registration	187	119	71	73	205

SOURCE: http://www.metro.seoul.kr

Mayor Lee also decreased the money allocated into the program, as shown in Table 10.4. No money has been allocated to the operation of the OPEN system since 2004, because it is no longer an independent anticorruption program. It became a routinized procedure for civil applications. It is clear that Lee took less interest in the OPEN system than Goh. However, he continued to budget allocations to other anticorruption activities, such as the Integrity Pact, Anti-Corruption Index, and Asset Registration. This means that Lee pays much attention to the transparency of municipal administration, though he does not give much credit to the former mayor's achievement, the OPEN system.

Features of the OPEN System

The Construct of the OPEN System and Its Transparent Data-Handling Process

To show how the OPEN system is structured and operated is very important to understanding the mechanism of the prevention of corruption. Figure 10.2 shows how an application for authorization or license is handled and processed.

A citizen who submits an application and wishes to check its status or look up the services open to the public can visit the Seoul homepage (see http://www.metro.seoul.kr) and select "OPEN System." After a citizen files

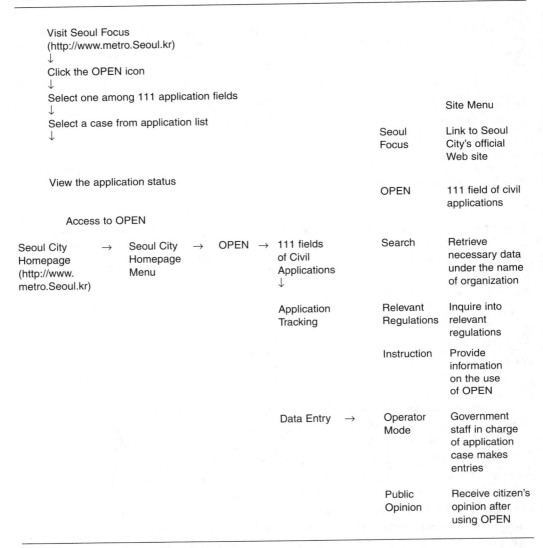

Figure 10.2   Tracking Application

an application for a needed service, the public official in charge posts the details of the received application on the OPEN site. Using any computer terminal connected to the Internet, the citizen can monitor in real time whether the application has been received, who is handling and reviewing the case, when the permit or approval is to be granted, and, if it is returned, for what reasons.

All input data must be processed on the due date for the next stage. This procedural requirement allows the applicants to check on the status of their applications and confirm the information. Daily notifications to the offices responsible for data input are made regarding delays in processing, requiring immediate input of the reasons for such delays. Each stage of processing appears with approval dates signed by officials, assistant directors, and directors, indicating the exact date and time of approval. Ongoing application procedures are automatically listed as "in process," preventing further important delays.

Information on related regulations is made available through a link between the homepage of the Ministry of Legislation and the regulation search system provided by SMG. The link with the outside information network and the provision of regulation information furnish correct information to the users.

OPEN users are asked to respond to a survey on the overall quality of management and their satisfaction with services. The survey is made for the following purposes: (a) to verify whether the disclosed information satisfied citizens' needs, (b) to verify the utility of the disclosed information, (c) to encourage citizens' active participation, (d) to motivate data management personnel to conduct honest data input, and (e) to register citizens' requests.

Finally, the Audit and Inspection Bureau checks whether there is data omission and input delay. The inspection of data input is conducted through three channels. First, an inspection via computer system is made every midnight to check all documents entered during the day. A list of documents about the input and processing delays is generated and sent to corresponding departments. Second, a manual inspection of typos, inaccuracies, and negligence that cannot be detected by computers takes place every day. Third, the Audit and Inspection Bureau officials visit data management offices on a monthly or bimonthly basis to verify false data input or intentional omission of documents.

The OPEN System as a Comprehensive Anticorruption Performance Measurement

Citizens and elected officials usually want to see an immediate improvement in efficiency and accountability of the public services. This impatience causes administrative bodies to adopt simple strategies and quick fixes, such as "cutting the fat," "private sector efficiencies," "reducing the government's appetite for resources," and so on (Holzer & Yang, 2004). However, public agencies accomplishing high performance do not make and execute performance measurement in a simple way. They integrate advanced management techniques into a "comprehensive approach," whose key concepts consist of measuring for performance, managing for quality, developing human resources, adapting technologies, and building partnership (Holzer & Yang, 2004).

The OPEN system is also a kind of comprehensive approach to productivity and accountability improvement. The system is one of the SMG's anticorruption programs, which are composed of at least four interrelated diverse and robust measures, mentioned above: preventive measures, punitive measures, increased transparency in administration, and enhanced public-private partnership.

The purpose of *preventive measures* is to eliminate potential collusion between civil servants and applicants through deregulation. There has been a long tradition of assigning jurisdiction over a specific area to one individual in Korea. Therefore, officials in the areas of building and housing, sanitation, taxation, and construction are especially prone to corruption. However, SMG abolished this tradition, and officials are now assigned their duty on a daily basis to handle applications from different areas.

Punitive measures mean that city officials are punished for any wrongdoing. SMG adopted a direct-reporting system to the mayor under the "principle of zero tolerance" for corruption. Every month, return postcards are sent to clients who have business with the city government. They are asked to report directly to the mayor about any wrongdoing by city officials.

Increased transparency in administration is to be accomplished by utilizing the Internet and expanding the scope of administrative information disclosure. Citizens can check their applications through the OPEN system on a real-time basis. The Online Bidding System is a digital bidding system that oversees the entire process online, from posting the notice of tender to finalizing the successful bidder. In addition, the Administrative Information Disclosure System upholds citizens' rights to information, guides citizen participation, and delivers transparent and open administration to citizens.

The *public-private partnership* includes the Citizen Ombudsman System and Anticorruption Citizen Inspection Group. Respected civilians with professional backgrounds in inspection supervise the city affairs and protect the rights of citizens. In alliance with citizen groups, SMG monitors suspected corrupt officials, unfair administrative procedures, and rude behavior on the part of civil servants.

The anticorruption effect of the OPEN system is supported by the other anticorruption measures included in the above-mentioned "systematic approach." In a word, the OPEN system, once combined with other measures, becomes a powerful tool to control corruption.

The OPEN System as a Citizen Evaluation Program

The OPEN system is in itself a citizen evaluation program of public services. By monitoring the handling process of civil applications, citizens can check as to whether public servants work promptly and satisfactorily. The operational staffs of the OPEN system also conducted user surveys about the system in 1999 and 2000 and reported the results of the surveys. They asked Transparency International (TI-Korea) to conduct surveys on OPEN system users in 2000 and 2001 and the Audit and Inspections Bureau to conduct surveys in 2004. The survey included items such as the following: information sources about the OPEN system, motivation to use the system, degree of transparency enhancement, factors to enhance transparency, reduction of corruption, and user satisfaction.

Citizen survey on the OPEN system is conducted almost every year. The questionnaire items of the survey are almost the same in every survey, though the conductors of surveys in Goh's administration were different from those in Lee's administration. Civilian research institutions made surveys in Goh's administration, while the Audit and Inspection Bureau currently does so.

As a monitoring device, the OPEN system can provide opportunities to report a delay of the process. The survey as a citizen evaluation program gives information about citizen satisfaction with the whole system.

Performance Improvement in City Administration

Strengthening ethical codes, strictly punishing violators, and giving pecuniary incentives such as salary increases are the most frequently adopted policies to control corruption around the world (Quah, 1999). However, it is also doubtful whether such policies can result in satisfactory outcomes (Anechiarico & Jacobs, 1996). Thus, the interesting question is whether the OPEN system as a new anticorruption measurement really has made noticeable performance. The evidence will be suggested by analyzing the motivation of citizens, the amount of access, contributions of the system, perceptions about the reduction of corruption, and public trust in administration.

Motivation of Citizens to Access the OPEN System

The OPEN site has a survey questionnaire, which aims to check visitors' reactions to the system. According to SMG statistics, 618 citizens responded to the survey in 1999 and 913 in 2000, though the number of respondents differs in each item of the questionnaire. Responses to these items provide precious information about how and why citizens access the OPEN system.

The analysis of the item asking where the respondent got the information about OPEN for the first time shows that people are living in an "Information Age." As shown in Table 10.5, 43.99% of the respondents attained the information through the Internet in 1999, and the number increased by 2.20 % in 2000, which means that the Internet is becoming a powerful tool for citizens to access the government and to participate in city administration. Citizen service centers are the next important information sources for OPEN users. Though "newspapers or broadcasting" and "introduction from others" are still significant information sources, their importance is lessening. The percentages of respondents using these traditional communication media went down by 2.95% and 1.96%, respectively, between 1999 and 2000. This means that the Internet is becoming a more important communication mechanism in responsive and credible government administration, while the role of traditional media is decreasing.

Table 10.5   Information Sources About OPEN

	1999		2000	
Sources	N	%	N	%
Internet	260	44.0	412	46.2
Citizen service center in administrative districts and wards	90	15.2	139	15.6
Newspaper or broadcasting	85	14.4	102	11.4
Seoul city advertisement	50	8.5	82	9.2
Introduction from others	44	7.5	49	5.5
Seoul citizen service center	9	1.5	27	3.0
Other	53	9.0	81	9.1
Total	**591**	**100.0**	**892**	**100.0**

SOURCE: http://www.metro.seoul.kr/cgi/paper204_list.cgi

The motivation for citizens to access the OPEN site sheds some light on understanding what people are truly interested in and what makes people participate in community affairs. Table 10.6 shows the purposes of citizens for entering the site. Both in 1999 and 2000, the curiosity to know about OPEN and the need for general citizen service information were the most frequently mentioned reasons to enter the site. To monitor how one's civil application is processed was only the third most common motivation during the 2 years. However, there is an important difference between the changes in respondent percentages. While the percentages of those responding to the items of curiosity and general service information decreased by 3.32 and 1.31, respectively, the percentage of those responding to the item of monitoring one's application increased by 5.63. If these trends continue in the future, the motivation to monitor the process of handling applications will be the most important reason for citizens to access OPEN. In general, then, curiosity, general information, and monitoring, which would be inconceivable to gauge without the OPEN system based on information and computer technology (ICT), are the most significant factors that contribute to the participation of citizens in city administration.

Amount of Access to the OPEN System

The OPEN system has increased active citizen participation in public administration. Citizens can easily access the local government without making telephone calls or visits. Citizens can also monitor through the Internet the whole handling process of their civil applications, anytime and anywhere.

Table 10.6   Purposes for Accessing OPEN

Purposes	1999		2000		Changes of % (1999–2000)
	N	%	N	%	
Curiosity to know about OPEN	183	31.3	248	28.0	−3.32
To obtain general citizen service information	170	29.1	246	27.8	−1.31
To monitor processing of civil applications	109	18.7	215	24.3	+5.63
Automatically linked through Internet	25	4.3	29	3.3	−1.00
Others	97	16.6	147	16.6	0
Total	**584**	**100.0**	**885**	**100.0**	

SOURCE: http://www.metro.seoul.kr/cgi/paper204_list.cgi

Easy access allows more citizens to visit the OPEN site. Table 10.7 shows the number of disclosed and reviewed civil applications in each working area between 1999 and 2004. Since the OPEN system started service to the public on April 15, 1999, a total of 1,763,241 cases of civil applications were registered on the site. The registered number of visitors to the OPEN system was 9,459,992 during the same period, which means that about 4,500 citizens per day visit the site. The visitors can be civil applicants or their neighbors who are interested in the applications. The OPEN system enhances the interest of citizens and induces their participation in city affairs. The areas of "Housing and Building" and "Construction" were the main concerns to citizens.

Contribution of the OPEN System to the Enhancement of Transparency

It is always questionable how much innovative strategies in local administration will affect performance. The OPEN survey shows that most respondents acknowledge the contribution of the OPEN system to the enhancement of transparency in SMG and are satisfied with the results OPEN has brought in the past. As discussed below, it is also clear that the results depend on the mayor's leadership.

Table 10.8 illustrates the degree to which citizens think the OPEN system has contributed to the enhancement of transparency in the city administration. Almost all respondents acknowledged the contribution, though the degree differs. About 59.69% of the respondents in 1999 and about 58.77 % in 2000 marked "contributing somewhat" on the scale. The

Table 10.7   Number of Civil Applications Disclosed to and Reviewed by the Public (1999–2004)

Working Area	Disclosed Numbers (%)	Reviewed Numbers (%)
Housing & Building	529,225 (30.0)	5,327,528 (56.3)
Construction	412,565 (23.4)	1,883,203 (19.9)
Transportation	288,169 (16.3)	526,424 (5.6)
Firefighting	132,915 (7.5)	282,893 (3.0)
Industry & Economy	92,106 (5.2)	178,930 (1.9)
Environment	82,466 (4.7)	173,515 (1.8)
Health & Welfare	82,166 (4.7)	298,725 (3.2)
Tour & Culture	58,204 (3.9)	210,884 (2.2)
Urban Planning	51,273 (2.9)	494,723 (5.2)
Administration	21,336 (1.2)	63,654 (0.7)
Committees	2,816 (0.2)	19,513 (0.1)
Total	**1,763,241 (100.0)**	**9,459,992 (100.0)**

SOURCE: http://www.metro.seoul.kr/cgi/paper204_list.cgi

Table 10.8   Contribution of OPEN to the Enhancement of Transparency, 1999–2004

Degree of Contribution	1999		2000		2004	
	N	%	N	%	N	%
Contributing very much	101	17.5	167	19.4	385	63.5
Contributing somewhat	345	59.7	506	58.8		
Contributing a little	112	19.4	159	18.5	221	36.5
Contributing not at all	20	3.5	29	3.4		
Total (1,493)	**578**	**100.0**	**861**	**100.0**	**606**	**100.0**

SOURCE: //www.metro.seoul.kr/cgi/paper204_list.cgi

number of respondents who responded "contributing very much" is almost the same as the number of people who responded "contributing a little." It is important to notice, however, that the number of the former increased by 1.93%, while the number of the latter decreased by 0.91%. The difference between these numbers indicates that more citizens were becoming aware of the positive effects of the OPEN system.

The percentage of respondents who marked on "contributing very much" and "contributing somewhat" decreased in 2004, however. This means that the level of the contribution of the OPEN system to administrative transparency decreased after Lee Myung-Bak became mayor in 2002, which shows that the mayorship has been very important to the effectiveness of the innovative system.

Respondents also answered the item regarding which factor of the OPEN system contributes most to increased transparency in the city administration. Table 10.9 shows that having the contents of civil applications be open to the public was designated to be the most important factor to the enhancement in transparency. The second was the exposure of the government staff to the public, which means that the information of the office and the official in charge and his or her e-mail address are shown in the application file on the Web site, and any citizen can see them. The Internet linkage to the ongoing procedures was the third factor, and the notification of application review date and processing status was the fourth.

Table 10.9   Factors Designated by the Respondents to Enhance Transparency, 1999–2001

Factors	1999*		2000a*		2000b**		2001**	
	N	%	N	%	N	%	N	%
Contents of civil applications open to the public	207	36.9	300	35.4	62	41.3	40	33.6
Notification of the application review date and processing status	82	14.6	133	15.7	48	32.0	35	29.4
Notification of the office and the official in charge and official's e-mail address	155	27.6	238	28.1	5	3.3	3	2.5
Internet linkage to the processing procedures	105	18.7	153	18.0	26	17.3	33	27.7
The first entry date	12	2.1	22	2.6	9	6.0	8	6.7
Total	**561**	**100.0**	**846**	**100.0**	**150**	**100.0**	**119**	**100.0**

SOURCE: http://www.metro.seoul.kr/cgi/paper204_list.cgi (1999 & 2000); **TI-Korea (2000 & 2001)

Reduction of Corruption by the OPEN System

In addition to the Internet survey on the OPEN site, city hall asked Gallup Korea to do another survey every year, which aimed to reveal how citizens submitting civil applications thought about the transparency of city administration and how much effort each working area was making to reduce corruption. The city hall calculated the Anti-Corruption Index (ACI) by adding the scores measuring citizen responses and scores measuring SMG anticorruption efforts. The ACI in Table 10.10 shows that the level of transparency gradually increased year by year in almost all service areas (the higher the score, the lower the level of corruption). In 2003, the ACI decreased in the areas of "Housing and Building" and "Construction." It is not clear whether the decrease was related to the OPEN system.

It is probable that there is a relationship between the abolishment of the Administrative Reform Bureau in Lee's administration and the decrease of the transparency level in the two areas mentioned. Citizens submit many more civil applications in housing and building and construction areas than in other areas, as was shown in Table 10. 7. This means that the more houses and buildings constructed, the less the transparency of those areas. Therefore, it may not be a coincidence that the two indexes and mayoral concerns in the OPEN system decreased simultaneously. This finding paradoxically indicates the importance of the OPEN system in reducing corruption.

Nevertheless, there are limitations to the importance of the OPEN system. Though park and taxation services are not covered by the system, their transparency indexes have increased every year. This means that there are other elements that enhance the transparency level in Seoul, perhaps other anticorruption measures such as deregulation, corruption report cards, severe punishment for every wrongdoing, citizen ombudsman system, and public-private inspection and assessment, which are conceptually based more on the behavioral and structural approaches to control corruption. It is conceivable that both the new technology and traditional anticorruption measures can combine to increase performance.

For objective evidence of the decrease of corruption, the number of behavioral types and cases submitted to disciplinary measures is examined in

Table 10.10   Anti-Corruption Index (ACI) Results (score), 1999–2003

Working Area	1999*	2000*	2001*	2002*	2003**
Housing & Building	60.8	65.9	65.3	68.3	64.9
Construction	58.7	68.3	70.2	71.9	66.6
Transportation	–	69.1	68.9	71.7	81.5
Firefighting	69.5	72.8	73.7	74.6	81.2
Environment	–	–	72.6	73.2	77.1
Sanitation	67.5	68.9	69.3	70.2	78.4
Park Services	–	67.0	74.9	72.0	88.7
Taxation	63.6	65.8	68.0	69.7	78.8

SOURCE: *http://www.seoul.go.kr/ICSFiles/afieldfile/2003/08/22/pressrelease(2002ACI).hwp;
**http://www.seoul.go.kr/ICSFiles/afieldfile/2005/09/23/3_20050923.hwp

NOTE: The higher the ACI score, the lower the level of corruption in the working area.

Table 10.11 Number of Behavioral Types Submitted to Disciplinary Measures, 1997–2003

Behavioral Type	1997	1998	1999	2000	2001	2002	2003
Bribery	39(29.5)	17(14.5)	17(13.6)	9(10.7)	13(15.5)	22(24.2)	5(6.0)
Peculation	10(7.6)	7(6.0)	1(0.1)	1(1.2)	–	–	1(1.2)
Negligence	57(43.2)	35(29.9)	32(25.6)	18(21.4)	21(25.0)	6(6.6)	11(13.1)
Unfair treatment	23(17.4)	50(42.7)	73(58.4)	52(61.9)	39(46.4)	48(52.7)	61(72.6)
Other violations of law	3(2.3)	8(6.8)	2(1.6)	4(4.8)	11(13.1)	15(16.5)	6(7.1)
Total	**132(100.0)**	**117(100.0)**	**125(100.0)**	**84(100.0)**	**84(100.0)**	**91(100.0)**	**84(100.0)**

SOURCE: SMG (1998–2004), the Annual Audit Report.

NOTE: In the rows across, the first number refers to the *number* of cases of the behavioral type submitted to disciplinary measures in the given year, and the number in parentheses, refers to the *percentage* represented by that number.

Tables 10.11 and 10.12. Table 10.11 shows that bribery and peculation, the most typical types of corruption, are generally decreasing. In addition, negligence is also reduced. It is highly probable that the other anticorruption measures, mentioned above, can contribute to the working ethos of public servants.

On the contrary, the numbers for "unfair treatment" and "other violations of law" are increasing. However, it is not clear whether these types of wrongdoings are directly related to corruption. Table 10.12 also makes it clear that the number of cases submitted to disciplinary measures is generally decreasing, except in those working areas not subjected to the OPEN system.

Public Trust in City Administration

Public trust in the government gained greater importance as social capital in the 1990s (Coleman, 1990; Putnam, 1993). Networks of civic engagement and norms of reciprocity are major ingredients of public trust, which, in turn, enhances government performance. Though not in the form of horizontal and interpersonal relationships with each other, citizens can access information about local affairs, monitor the services they receive, and share the ethos of civic engagement through the Internet. Therefore, the level of satisfaction with the OPEN service can be a precious index to measure the degree of public trust in the city administration.

In Table 10.13, each respondent to the OPEN user survey marked the 5-point-scale about users' satisfaction with the system. The percentage of respondents satisfied with the system is much higher than for those dissatisfied with it. However, it is not clear whether the level of satisfaction with the OPEN system is slowly moving up as time goes on, because the results also show fluctuation. Nevertheless, it is conceivable that the high level of satisfaction can lead to enhancing public trust in city hall.

Policy Implications

The OPEN system as a citizen-involved performance measurement to reduce corruption and to enhance efficiency in SMG is well recognized in both domestic and international societies. Several lessons can be learned from the innovative system.

It was found, once again, that leadership is always the most important contributor to government reform or innovation diffusion. The role of leaders is absolute in both the initiation of performance measurement and its continuous implementation. For example, former Prime Minister of Singapore Lee Kwan Yew had a strong will to eliminate corruption in his country and adopted effective anticorruption strategies, such as increasing salaries and improving working conditions for the civil servants (Quah, 1999). Goh Kun himself initiated several anticorruption plans to reduce

Table 10.12 Number of Cases Submitted to Disciplinary Measures in Working Areas, 1997–2003

Working Area	1997	1998	1999	2000	2001	2002	2003
Housing & Building	22(16.7)	15(12.8)	22(17.6)	10(11.9)	9(10.7)	2(2.2)	11(13.1)
Construction	25(18.9)	9(7.7)	25(20.0)	5(6.0)	7(8.3)	23(25.3)	5(6.0)
Transportation & Planning	20(15.1)	12(9.1)	2(1.6)	–	2(2.4)	2(2.2)	4(4.8)
Finance & Taxation†	26(19.7)	14(10.6)	5(4.0)	5(6.0)	4(4.8)	8(8.8)	8(9.6)
Sanitation & Environment	6(4.5)	17(12.9)	14(11.2)	13(15.5)	6(7.2)	4(4.4)	1(1.2)
General Administration	10(7.6)	7(6.0)	10(8.0)	9(10.7)	7(8.3)	16(17.6)	17(20.2)
Official Discipline†	14(10.6)	21(17.9)	20(16.0)	17(20.2)	15(17.9)	10(11.0)	5(6.0)
Firefighting	7(5.3)	11(9.4)	22(17.6)	19(22.6)	19(22.6)	7(7.7)	29(34.5)
Etc.†	2(1.5)	11(9.4)	5(4.0)	6(4.8)	15(17.9)	19(20.9)	14(16.7)
Total	**132(100.0)**	**117(100.0)**	**125(100.0)**	**84(100.0)**	**84(100.0)**	**91(100.0)**	**84(100.0)**

SOURCE: SMG (1998–2004), the Annual Audit Report.

NOTE: In the rows across, the first number refers to the *number* of cases submitted to disciplinary measures in the given year, and the number in parentheses, refers to the *percentage* represented by that number.
† Working areas not subjected to the OPEN system.

Table 10.13   OPEN User Satisfaction, 2000, 2001, 2004

OPEN User Satisfaction	2000*		2001*		2004**	
	N	%	N	%	N	%
Not at all	1	0.8	2	1.3	189	31.0
A little	4	3.3	11	7.4		
Fairly	36	30.0	64	43.0		
Considerably	69	57.5	58	38.9	417	69.0
Very much	10	8.3	14	9.4		
Total	**120**	**100.0**	**149**	**100.0**	**606**	**100.0**

SOURCE: *TI-Korea (2000 & 2001); **From an internal report of Audit & Inspection Bureau of SMG (2004).

corruption in Seoul and pushed them to be implemented against contentions to those programs. Lee Myung-Bak has also continued his predecessor's programs and strengthened them with an emphasis on efficiency and business mentality. Though the current allocations of personnel and budget to the operation of the OPEN system are not as much as those during Goh's administration, the system still shows effectiveness in the reduction of corruption and the enhancement of public participation.

The OPEN system shows the possibility that local governments can accomplish administrative reform more easily than central governments. In many governments, anticorruption policies have been initiated and implemented by the central government for a long time. Sometimes the central initiation has worked, but it has also resulted in bureaucratic problems such as overcentralization, goal displacement, rigidity, incapability, and bribery (Anechiarico & Jacobs, 1996; Crozier, 1964; Holbrook & Meier, 1993; Kim, 1994; Knott & Miller, 1987; Rohr, 1998, Quah, 1999). Korea is no exception to these problems. Many local governments, however, have recently introduced innovative and efficient strategies to reduce bureaucratic problems, including corruption (Hondeghem, 1998; Osborne & Gaebler, 1992). At the local level in Korea, mayors hold financial and personnel power, which can be threatening to local public officials. At the same time, the central government only indirectly controls local governments and their employees through regular audits and inspections, by which the central government cannot punish local public officials. Therefore, the combination of mayoral power and innovative ideas can result in more effectiveness in city administration than the central initiation by itself (Holzer & Kim, 2002; Kang, 2005).

The OPEN system shows an example of "costs less and works better." The development of ICT made it possible to build the OPEN system at a low cost. Unlike the economic incentive strategies, the system needs no more expenditures to reduce incentives for corruption apart from the initial cost of establishing Internet infrastructure and developing the software. Even this initial cost was not so high, though, because the city administration had already been computerized. Less costliness made the system more feasible. Both citizen participation and performance measurement incur expenses, but ICT may help reduce costs when bridging the two.

In the OPEN system, officials are not vulnerable to personal attacks for the way they handle civil applications. Contrary to the traditional anticorruption strategies that blame the moral degradation of officials and threaten to punish them, the new performance measurement program does not criticize bureaucracy. The OPEN system merely changes the environment and structure in which officials process civil applications. ICT and the openness of the handling process provide less chance for public officials in charge to meet their clients face-to-face and reduce opportunities for corruption. Consequently, officials will not be blamed for having unnecessary contact with their clients.

The pure effect of the OPEN system as an Internet service is not easily measurable, but it is clear that the system enables citizens to access public services through the Internet. In both Eastern and Western societies, the increasing rigidity and remoteness of public administration from the public has been a pathologic problem to be solved. When the bureaucracy is out of sight from citizens and builds its own empire by various regulations, it is destined to be corrupt. Many scholars emphasize two ultimate goals of public administration, efficiency and democracy, and suggest that the decision power of public services should be devolved to the citizens (Anechiarico & Jacobs, 1996; Ostrom, 1989). The accessibility through the Internet provides opportunities for citizens to participate in and communicate with the governing body (Bellamy & Taylor, 1998). Citizens can gather information about their cases, pay attention to other cases, and "talk to city hall" about their interests through the new media. Internet access also gives the opportunity for users to evaluate the handling process of their civil applications. The OPEN system shows the possibility of achieving efficient and democratic administration.

Finally, when it is combined with other anticorruption programs, the OPEN system as a citizen-involved performance measurement makes for high productivity in the enhancement of efficiency and accountability. The "systematic approach" or the "comprehensive approach" provides a new way for improved performance measurement.

Conclusion

In Korea, the cultural heritage of collectivism and nepotism have made it difficult to evaluate colleagues and subordinates in organizations and to trust the handling process of civil applications in public institutions. The high level of uncertainty in the evaluation of employees and the reviews of applications also led to the prevalence of corruption in the public sector. However, as described in this chapter, a mixture of factors such as leadership, ICT, decentralization, citizen participation, and effective strategies can reduce the level of corruption and improve the productivity of public services. The development of the OPEN system in Seoul provides some evidence of the possibility of accomplishing both purposes. It also indicates that innovative anticorruption performance measures can be made and diffused at the local level of government in a traditionally centralized, low-trust society.

It becomes very difficult to measure the pure effects of innovative strategies, because productive agencies tend to take comprehensive approaches to productivity enhancement. Nevertheless, the importance of systematic approaches rather than simple strategies is growing. The OPEN system as an anticorruption measure enhances performance when implemented with other measures, and further research needs to be conducted to find conditions in which performance measurement is more meaningful.

Notes

1. Goh Kun, "Measures Against Corruption (II)," January 25, 1999, press conference statement.

2. The Anti-Corruption Index (ACI) was developed in 1999 by SMG to measure the level of administrative efforts to eliminate corrupt behavior of public employees and to check the response of citizens to the efforts. The ACI was calculated on two scores: the level of integrity of each administrative unit and the survey response of those who actually submitted civil applications.

3. The Integrity Pact is one of the innovative anticorruption measures in SMG, which is made between SMG and contractors applying for construction work and public services. When signing a contract, public officials and contractors are required to make a statement that they will not commit a corrupt act, such as bribery. If contractors violate the statement, they are forbidden to bid for public works and services. Citizen ombudsmen also monitor the implementation process of selected cases of works and services.

4. Lee Myung-Bak served as mayor between 2002 and 2006. Oh Se-hoon became the new mayor of SMG on July 1, 2006.

Discussion Questions

1. Under what conditions can performance measurement provide the most productive outcomes?

2. What kind of performance measurement in the public sector can be made in the age of information and communication technology?

3. How and when can citizens trust government and, conversely, can government trust citizens?

4. Who can initiate innovative measures at the municipal or higher level of government? If so, under what conditions can municipal governments do better than the higher level of governments?

References

Anechiarico, F., & Jacobs, J. B. (1996). *The pursuit of absolute integrity: How corruption controls makes government ineffective.* Chicago: University of Chicago Press.

Bellamy, C., & Taylor, J. A. (1998). *Governing in the Information Age.* Buckingham, UK: Open University Press.

Callahan, K. (2004). Performance measurement and citizen participation. In M. Holzer & S. Lee (Eds.), *Public productivity handbook* (pp. 31–42). New York: Marcel Dekker.

Coleman, J. (1990). *Foundations of social theory.* Cambridge, MA: Harvard University Press.

Crozier, M. (1964). *Bureaucratic phenomenon.* Chicago: University of Chicago Press.

Edwards, D., & Thomas. J. C. (2005). Developing a municipal performance-measurement system: Reflections on the Atlanta Dashboard. *Public Administration Review, 65,* 369–376.

Halachmi, A. (2005). Performance measurement: Test the water before you dive in. *International Review of Administrative Sciences, 71,* 255–266.

Holbrook, T. M., & Meier, K. J. (1993). Politics, bureaucracy, and political corruption: A comparative state analysis. In H. G. Frederickson (Ed.), *Ethics and public administration* (pp. 28–51). Armonk, NY: M. E. Sharpe.

Holzer, M., & Kim, B. (Eds.). (2002). *Building good governance: Reforms in Seoul.* Seoul, Korea: NCCP and the Seoul Development Institute.

Holzer, M., & Lee, S. (2004). Mastering public productivity and performance improvement from a productive management perspective. In M. Holzer & S. Lee (Eds.), *Public productivity handbook* (pp. 1–16). New York: Marcel Dekker.

Holzer, M., & Yang, K. (2004). Performance measurement and improvement: An assessment of the state of the art. *International Review of Administrative Sciences, 70,* 15–31.

Hondeghem, A. (Ed.). (1998). *Ethics and accountability in a context of governance and new public management.* Amsterdam: IOS Press.

Hwang, H. S. (2005). Change, challenges, and chances: Public reform in Korea. In J. Kim (Ed.), *A new paradigm for public management in the 21st century.* Seoul, Korea: Korea Institute of Public Administration.

Kang, H. (2005). Administrative discretion in the transparent bureaucracy. *Public Administration Quarterly, 29,* 162–185.

Kim, Y. J. (1994). *Bureaucratic corruption: The case of Korea.* Seoul, Korea: Chomyung Press.

Knott, J. H., & Miller, G. J. (1987). *Reforming bureaucracy: The politics of institutional choice.* Englewood Cliffs, NJ: Prentice Hall.

Kweit, M. G., & Kweit, R. W. (2004). Citizen participation and citizen evaluation in disaster recovery. *American Review of Public Administration, 34,* 354–373.

Osborne, D., & Gaebler, T. (1992). *Reinventing government: How the entrepreneurial spirit is transforming the public sector.* New York: Addison-Wesley.

Ostrom, V. (1989). *The intellectual crisis in American public administration* (2nd ed.). Tuscaloosa: University of Alabama Press.

Pollanen, R. M. (2005). Performance measurement in municipalities: Empirical evidence in Canadian context. *International Journal of Public Sector Management, 18,* 4–24.

Putnam, R. D. (1993). *Making democracy work: Civic traditions in modern Italy.* Princeton, NJ: Princeton University Press.

Quah, J. S. T. (1999). Corruption in Asian Countries: Can it be minimized? *Public Administration Review, 59,* 483–494.

Rohr, J. A. (1998). *Public service, ethics, and constitutional practices.* Lawrence: University Press of Kansas.

Stich, B., & Eagle, K. (2005). Planning to include the public: Transportation policy implementation with effective citizen involvement. *Public Works Management & Policy, 9,* 319–340.

Yang, K. (2005). Public administrator's trust in citizen: A missing link in citizen involvement efforts. *Public Administration Review, 65,* 273–285.

11

Performance Measurement and Educational Accountability

The U.S. Case

Katherine E. Ryan

Educational performance measurement systems have always been an important part of educational program administration. Throughout the 1990s, the role of these systems in the international arena has shifted toward management for results and accountability, reflecting "New Public Management" (NPM; Behn, 2001).[1] The U.S. educational accountability context reflects this change, particularly since the passage of the No Child Left Behind Act of 2001 (NCLB). This legislation essentially institutionalizes the reliance on high-stakes tests (performance indicators) as a key mechanism for improving student achievement.

There is no argument here—educational accountability is a fundamental right of citizens in a democratic society serving the public interests. Efficient and appropriate resource use is and should be a cornerstone of public accountability in education. The goal of this performance-based educational accountability is noteworthy: to improve teaching and learning for all students. Educational equity is a critical public interest that is promoted by educational accountability. Performance indicators are an efficient way to identify educational inequalities by within- and across-school achievement comparisons (Rizvi, 1990).

Nevertheless, there are substantial criticisms of the NCLB performance measurement approach to educational accountability, including failure to incorporate stakeholders' and the public's views in creating educational accountability, overreliance on multiple-choice exams for measuring performance, failure to measure important learning outcomes, and lack of information about how to improve teaching and learning. These criticisms reflect significant complications and challenges in conceptualizing and implementing performance measurement systems as the signature means for holding individuals and organizations accountable within the educational arena (Lee & Wong, 2004; Linn, 2003; Raudenbush, 2004a, 2004b; Resnick & Zurawsky, 2005; Ryan, 2002b, 2005).

In this chapter, I critically examine how the NCLB performance measurement framework evolved. I begin with a brief discussion of educational performance measurement and the global marketplace. I describe and critically analyze the standards, assessments, and accountability requirements of standards-based educational reform that became the foundation of NCLB educational accountability. The role of stakeholder and citizen participation in determining the standards, assessments, and accountability is examined. After briefly summarizing NCLB accountability, I highlight major concerns with how NCLB is conceptualized and implemented. I close with suggestions about strengthening and improving U.S. educational accountability, including stakeholder and citizen participation.

Educational Accountability, Performance Measurement, and the Global Marketplace

The notion of accountability is not new (Cronbach et al., 1980). Appearing around 25 years ago in education, educational accountability is now increasingly associated with external control of education in both centralized and decentralized educational systems (Nevo, 2002). While *educational accountability* can be defined in a number of ways, it often serves an audit function. This is essentially a performance measurement system that uses indicators of productivity (gains in achievement test scores) to represent increased school productivity.

Educational Accountability and Performance Measurement

Currently, U.S. educational accountability is thought to be influenced by globalization (Burbules & Torres, 2000; Stein, 2001; Suarez-Orozco & Qin-Hilliard, 2004). Globalization is demanding more of education as markets have shifted from industrial production to one of service, with information technology receiving more attention (Stein, 2001; Teachers College Annual Report, 2004). Nations now vie for highly competitive positions within the global marketplace (Anderson, 2005). As a consequence, governments are paying increasing attention to the performance of their educational systems. Concerns about quality and the enormous resources directed to education are increasing demands for information about school performance that are being addressed with the implementation of performance measurement systems reflecting NPM practices.

This form of quantitative measurement is considered to represent both *more* and *better* education. Influential international policy units like the Organisation for Economic Co-operation and Development (OECD), International Education Association (IEA), and National Center for Educational Statistics (NCES) have aimed their respective policy efforts at developing this particular perspective. Student achievement is ranked and compared on international assessments like the Third International Mathematics Science and Math Study (TIMSS) and Programme for International Student Assessment (PISA), which are used to examine cross-curricular competencies (Stronach, 1999; Stronach, Halsall, & Hustler, 2002). These cross-country assessment comparisons are linked to economic performance in these countries in the global economy (Stronach et al., 2002).

U.S. Education and the Global Marketplace

The United States has been and continues to directly acknowledge the importance of the global marketplace and education. For instance, the current U.S. Department of Educations (2002) strategic plan explicitly ties education to the economy and democracy with the following: "Since *A Nation at Risk* . . . we have acknowledged the importance of our education system to our economy. . . . Now we acknowledge its importance . . . to the strength of our democracy itself" (p. 6). Being educated for the new economy means the labor force needs higher-level skills and knowledge to function successfully in the labor force and to compete successfully in the international arena. With this shift to a knowledge-based society comes the demand that students be educated for the new world order to remain competitive in the global economy.

One important way the United States has responded to the concerns about the global marketplace and education is to incorporate educational standards, assessment, and accountability into the U.S. educational system. In the next section, I present a brief history of how these three components were conceptualized and implemented. Further, their respective roles in the current educational accountability landscape and educational performance measurement system are outlined.

Standards-Based
Education in the United States

In fact, the publication of *A Nation at Risk* (National Commission on Excellence in Education, 1983) was the linchpin event that set the stage for educational testing and accountability in the United States. While hailing "our [United States] once unchallenged preeminence in commerce, science" (p. 1), the report attributed the erosion of this preeminence primarily to mediocrity in the school system. Taking the overarching position that the United States was losing its competitive edge in math, science, and technology, this report used information from international comparisons to make its case. Findings such as the fact that only 31% of high school graduates completed intermediate algebra, 6% took calculus, and 25% of all high school coursework completed was outside the academic course track signaled a problem with the quality of U.S. education. Further, when comparing performance of industrialized nations on international comparisons of student achievement, the United States was last seven times. Employers became increasingly concerned about the meaningfulness of high school diplomas (Resnick & Zurawsky, 2005).

The Standards-Based Educational Reform Vision

By the late 1980s and early 1990s, a U.S.-standards-based education reform effort was emerging to steer education (Linn & Miller, 2005). Essentially, standards-based education was oriented toward identifying what was important to learn, teaching it, and assessing what was learned. Initial ideas were drawn from education systems with a national curriculum (e.g., France, Germany), whereby students studied a common curriculum through fourth or eighth grade. Here, discussions about curriculum and planning, as well as public and political processes involved in this kind of initiative, address larger societal issues illuminating the role and function of school in a society (Westbury, 2003). Further discussions between and among stakeholders and the public play a critical role by bringing to light what groups, communities, and the public value in relationship to schooling and society.

Academics and representatives from the American Federation of Teachers (largest teachers union in the United States) were participants in initial discussions about how standards-based education could address the U.S. educational problems (Resnick & Zurawsky, 2005; Smith & O'Day, 1991). After the endorsement of national goals at the 1989 President's Education Summit With Governors, the standards-based education reform movement really gained wings when the bipartisan National Education Goals Panel was established. After debate and discussion, policymakers from both parties, academics, and individuals from business and other fields devised and endorsed a plan for a decentralized standards-based education that honored local educational control (Resnick & Zurawsky, 2005). Incorporating groups like educators, parents, citizens, and potential employers in setting standards was intended to explicitly acknowledge local control, a critical and enduring value in U.S. education. Essentially, the U.S. approach involved global standards and assessments but left the specifics of curriculum and instruction to local (schools and districts) discretion. Four principles were to guide the development of standards-based education (Resnick & Zurawsky, 2005):

1. Establish the content and performance standards using a public process involving educators, parents, community members, and the business community.

2. Develop assessments (performance measurement systems) directly linked to the standards so teachers align their instruction with standards and assessment.

3. Encourage schools and districts to align their instruction and professional development around the standards.

4. Develop accountability systems to determine whether students are meeting the standards.

What Really Happened

Like many visions, the reality of conceptualizing and implementing a standards-based education in the United States proved to be more challenging than expected. There have been significant concerns with the standards, the assessments, and the accountability requirements developed within the standards-based reform (Lee & Wong, 2004; Linn, 2000, 2003; Porter, 2002; Resnick & Zurawsky, 2005; Ryan, 2002a, 2002b). In particular, while the notion of using a public process involving parents, community members, and the business community was a cardinal principle in delineating standards-based education, this proved to be very difficult to do. While there are likely many reasons for this, the notion of local educational control, a historic hallmark of U.S. education, is one issue. So, states were targeted to coordinate standards and assessment development, not a nationalized curriculum.

Issues remained about how to involve parents, community members, and the business community in a public process. At the state (or federal) educational level, there was no infrastructure or capacity to include these groups. Ideas about the role of the public in this public process or how they could be included were not developed. Moving to the state or federal levels was something new for U.S. education. Below, I present some of the challenges encountered in developing and implementing these new state standards, assessments, and accountability requirements.

Standards

Standards are, in essence, a way in which society and education can envision what students should be able to know and do. However, the notion of standards proved to be confusing for nearly everyone, because it was not clear what *standards* meant and what kinds of inferences could be drawn from them (Jang & Ryan, 2003). The most common types of standards connected with the standards-based reform were content (what students should know and be able to do) and performance (level and quality of knowledge and skills) standards that focus on student learning.

Furthermore, who would write the standards became a significant issue in the early 1990s. Professional associations like the National Council of Teachers of Mathematics prepared the first set of national standards (Resnick & Zurawsky, 2005). However, states quickly became actors in this process. By 1994, the Improving America's Schools Act (the revised Elementary and Secondary Educational Act [ESEA]) institutionalized the state role in standard setting. This legislation required states to adopt standards for Title 1 (low-income, low-achieving) students that were similar to the standards that existed for other students.

Efforts were made to include teachers, school administrators, citizens, and business interests as participants in standard setting on state-level committees convened to prepare the statewide standards. However, there was limited experience at the state level in how to include these kinds of groups, so the process was not carefully articulated. As a result, only a small number of individuals from these groups participated in standards development. Further, because the process was not well-defined, the stage was set for groups that formed coalitions to gain power in determining what the standards might be. For example, in Illinois, there was a coalition between large school districts and the business community. This coalition actively lobbied for more rigorous standards and increased accountability.

The next question involved what standards should look like—whether they should be set for every grade or for grade spans (e.g., Grades 1–5) (Resnick & Zurawsky, 2005). The early efforts at standards development focused on broader, periodic standards to support local educational control. There have been concerns about how useful broader, episodic standards are for guiding teaching and learning (Resnick & Zurawsky, 2005). In addition to the general level of the standards, and so on, the quality of these state standards have been criticized (*Education Week*, 2004; Klein et al., 2005; Stotsky & Finn, 2005). In fact, there is some disagreement about what constitutes quality educational standards (Resnick & Zurawsky, 2005). Further, standards documents are presented as if there were perfect agreement among the standard setters. Moss and Schultz (2001) argue that standards documents should include issues that remain unresolved, as well as agreements, and concrete examples (vignettes, narratives of standards users) to assist teachers and administrators in understanding and implementing the standards.

In summary, the quality of educational standards is crucial to the quality of education. Standards that are too general or fail to capture what important knowledge and skills are present a significant challenge in directing teaching and learning. Further, the standards are the foundation of performance measurement systems. Efforts to involve the public in determining educational standards met with some success, but it was limited. Any problems with the standards, intended or not, are incorporated in the development and implementation of the assessments and the accountability requirements.

Assessments

The original standards-based reform included exams that students could prepare for: the development of standards-based assessments. These assessments were intended to direct teaching and learning in addition to providing information about what students know and can do (Resnick & Zurawsky, 2005). Modeled after European examination-based systems, curriculum and teaching were intended to be directly linked to the exams and aimed at helping students do well. The Advanced Placement Exams, which are connected to high school courses in the United States and offer the opportunity for students to gain college credit, are an example.

These types of exams are often composed of multiple methods, such as multiple-choice questions, essays, problem-solving tasks, and the like, that measure the achievement of educational standards. These exams can also include performance assessments, which provide a longitudinal perspective on student work by including pieces of students' work over an extended time. Importantly, these exams are intended to have a fixed frame of reference (compare students' performance to a fixed standard), not a relative one (compare students' performance to each other) for interpreting assessment performance.

While there were efforts by some states to develop this kind of state curriculum-based assessment system (e.g., Kentucky; Kifer, 2001), other states either purchased published tests or prepared a standards-based assessment based primarily on multiple-choice items. Given the kinds of expertise and expense required for developing these "curriculum" exams, it is not surprising that states were unable or unwilling to create this kind of assessment system. On the other hand, using published norm-referenced exams in place of standards-based systems created significant problems.

These tests are based on specified content, a kind of "average" curriculum, but not aligned to a specific curriculum (Resnick & Zurawsky, 2005). Instead, these tests are designed to compare students with each other (norm-referenced or relative). Test item selection is based primarily on how well the item discriminates among students, based on the statistical characteristics of the items. Obviously, this type of exam does not measure the standards. It is not possible to make judgments based on this kind of exam about whether students are learning the standards.

There were also problems with the standards-based exams that were developed in some states. These exams were primarily composed of multiple-choice items. While multiple-choice exams are efficient and do provide a snapshot of student learning, it is impossible for a single assessment method to fully represent the content and complexity of educational standards.

Other kinds of assessment methods, like essay and problem-solving items requiring students to supply a solution, are essential to adequately measure the full range of standards. Because these kinds of methods are best at assessing higher-level critical thinking, the most challenging standards are systematically not assessed or underrepresented on these exams. In addition to relying primarily on one assessment method, there are also issues concerning how well the state standards-based assessments are actually aligned with state standards. A recent study suggested that the match between state standards and tests for most states is weak (Porter, 2002).

Aligning Instruction and Accountability

Further, there were significant challenges in aligning instruction with the standards, irrespective of their quality. Teachers were being asked to make many changes all at once: Align what they teach to a set of standards, perhaps change how they teach the curriculum, and adjust the kinds of assessments used for making judgments about student performance. The quality and quantity of resources (e.g., professional development) available to support these kinds of changes were uneven. The educational accountability consequences, such as rewards, penalties, and interventions, introduced as incentives for improving achievement varied substantially from state to state. For example, Tennessee implemented a system whereby teacher salary increases were tied to improved achievement, while Illinois's system did not have such requirements.

Major Issues in the Standards-Based Reform

In short, there were significant issues with the standards and assessments developed and implemented during the standards-based reform. When considering the principles that were intended to guide the development of standards-based education, key features of these principles were left out of the development process. Clearly, there are concerns with (a) the extent to which the standards, assessments, and accountability requirements were developed as part of a public process that includes stakeholders; (b) the degree to which the assessments are aligned with the standards and instruction; and (c) the capacity for schools and districts to actually align their instruction with the standards.

There were also widespread concerns about early signs of pathology introduced by standards-based reform. Corruption of indicators, such as manipulating data (changing test scores or giving out answers to tests), primarily selecting indicators that can be easily manipulated (referrals to special education), avoiding constructs that are difficult to measure (citizenship), and avoiding measurement techniques that are difficult to implement (performance assessment and portfolios), are some illustrations of this pathology. In turn, there were concerns and some empirical evidence that the standards-based reform was actually narrowing the curriculum (Chudowsky & Behuniak, 1997; Koretz, Barron, Mitchell, & Stecher, 1996).

Finally, the "high-stakes" assessments used for consequences like grade promotion, certification, or the award of salary increases in some states also drew attention. Certainly, the consequences of high-stakes assessments impact all students, teachers, and schools. Nevertheless, while the goal of standards-based education was to improve teaching and learning for all, particular groups of schools, teachers, and students (e.g., low achievers, who are often low income) were vulnerable to being disproportionately affected when high-stakes accountability requirements were enacted.

For example, there were concerns from the beginning that instituting high school graduation tests would increase the probability that the lowest-achieving students would drop out (Heubert & Hauer, 1999; Jacobs, 2001). To date, findings about whether high-stakes consequences contribute to improved student achievement is mixed (Amrein & Berliner, 2002; Carnoy & Loeb, 2002; Clotfelter & Ladd, 1996; Jacobs, 2001). As a consequence, there is substantial controversy and debate around this issue (Lee & Wong, 2004).

NCLB and Educational Accountability

Despite the issues described in the previous section, high-stakes educational accountability was essentially "layered" on top of all this with the passage of NCLB (Resnick & Zurowsky, 2005). NCLB has defined a vital role for high-stakes, performance-measurement-based accountability in preparing students for the new economy. Essentially, NCLB holds schools accountable through auditable performance standards reflected in NPM. The NCLB performance-based accountability is built on the foundations of the "existing" standards and assessments implemented during the standards-based reform. All the standards and assessments issues and concerns identified in the previous section were "inherited" by NCLB accountability.

The U.S. Educational Accountability Model

The current U.S. educational accountability model institutionalized by NCLB requires each state to design and implement an educational accountability system to meet the NCLB legislative requirements. Reflecting its standards-based reform foundation, the state-based systems (a) include content and performance standards that focus on student learning, (b) emphasize the measurement of student achievement as a basis for school accountability, and (c) determine standards for annual yearly progress (AYP).[2] With the passage of NCLB, all districts, each school in each district, each tested grade in each school, and each student in each tested grade receives either a 4 (exceeds standards), 3 (meets standards), 2 (below standards), or 1 (academic warning) to determine whether schools have achieved AYP.

However, a key difference with NCLB educational accountability and standards-based reform is the standardized consequences or sanctions for not meeting AYP. Under NCLB, when schools and districts do not meet AYP for more than 2 years, a summative evaluative judgment of "unsuccessful" is triggered. Students then may legally enroll in another school, a policy reflecting a free-market approach to improving student learning and meant as a mechanism for reforming education. No extra resources are allocated to see whether increased resources can assist in improving a school's performance. After 5 years of not meeting AYP, the school can be closed—essentially "going out of business."

Strengths and Weaknesses of NCLB Educational Accountability

When considering the standards-based foundations of NCLB performance measurement, it is no great surprise that there are significant tensions reflected in the NCLB educational accountability landscape. Both the American Educational Research Association (AERA, 2000) and the American Evaluation Association (AEA, 2001) have prepared public statements on what they see as major concerns with NCLB high-stakes testing. On one hand, NCLB serves the public interests in important ways. This legislation focuses national attention on (a) the efficient and appropriate use of resources; (b) achievement for all, including students with greatest needs; (c) closing the achievement "gaps"; (d) challenging content for all students; and (e) providing all students with qualified teachers. These are noteworthy goals.

At the same time, there are challenges with this approach, especially a lack of balance. Those responsible (districts, teachers, parents) for educational outcomes have little say in what they should be. There are significant problems with current achievement measures, including an overreliance on multiple-choice tests. The measurements of the auditable performance standards represented by "annual yearly progress" have been widely criticized for their technical adequacy (a lack of consistency and validity) (Linn, 2003, 2007). The goals to be achieved are unrealistic given historical levels of progress. Perhaps most important, the current performance measurement system does not provide information about how to improve teaching or learning.

Improving U.S. NCLB Educational Accountability _____

Educational Accountability has the potential to improve the quality of our schools and the experiences and achievements of our children. . . . Such systems can strengthen teaching, learning, and educational governance. (American Evaluation Association, 2004)

Educational accountability in the United States stands at a crossroads. Using results from the current U.S. performance measurement system to *describe* school performance is justified (Linn, 2007). However, there are enough problems with the current performance measurement systems that using these results to *sanction* schools is questionable (Raudenbush, 2004a, 2004b). To realize the goal of improving teaching and learning for all students, there will need to be substantial changes in the U.S. educational performance measurement system as articulated by the NCLB legislation.

Are there some lessons to be learned from this critical analysis of the current U.S educational accountability and its foundations? The AEA public statement on educational accountability, above, suggests that incorporating public participation, rigorous and appropriate methods, and quality assessment would improve educational accountability systems. While there are no doubt many issues, I focus on four suggestions drawn from my earlier work on educational accountability for strengthening and improving the U.S. educational accountability (Ryan, 2002b).

Incorporate Broad, Public Participation

Who are the potential stakeholders and audiences in developing educational accountability systems? Certainly, federal and state policymakers are concerned with educational outcomes and how they impact policy. However, educators, parents, community members, and the business community are also critical participants. To date, states, school districts, public officials, educators, parents, students, and citizens have had limited participation in discussions about who, what, when, where, and how to decide what educational standards and outcomes should be (Lefkowits & Miller, 2005; Ryan, 2005). Nevertheless, these individuals and groups are held accountable for improved test scores as a key performance measurement. Incorporating their views may alter key features of NCLB educational accountability. For example, teachers, principals, and superintendents are interested in how and whether high-stakes assessments can adequately measure student learning.

Values Inquiry

Of course, it is easy to talk and write about incorporating broad participation in any public process. It is much more challenging to achieve. Values inquiry is one approach (Mark, Henry, & Julnes, 2000). In Ryan (2002b), I presented this example of how values inquiry might broaden participation in deciding what and how to measure a valued outcome, like a high school diploma.

In contrast to assuming a high-stakes assessment is the appropriate performance measurement, teachers, principals, and school superintendents could be surveyed to identify various meanings of a high school diploma, the most important aspects of the construct, and whether they regard test scores as adequate measures of what a high school diploma represents. Parents or other interested groups could also participate. While passive, this opens up a conversation about the meaning of a high school diploma, what constructs are important, and how to broaden outcomes. Focus groups and group interviews are additional values inquiry methods (Mark et al., 2000). Within the values inquiry approach, the information may be used to make decisions about what kinds of outcomes to include in the accountability system.

Public Engagement

While values inquiry is an approach to incorporate public and stakeholders views on specific issues, the notion of public engagement has recently been proposed as a means to organize citizen action to improve public education, including school accountability (Puriefoy, 2005). Public engagement is oriented toward the local level. Public engagement covers a wide range of activities for initiating and sustaining change. These include the following: (a) communicating information to raise awareness about public education issues, like school improvement and accountability; (b) involving groups in school activities to increase resources; (c) initiating collaborations among schools, groups, and the community to share resources for addressing educational issues and concerns at the local and even state level; and (d) changing local or state policy (Puriefoy, 2005).

The Public Education Network (PEN) is a national association of local education funds and individuals working to advance public school reform in low-income communities across the country (see http://www.publiceducation. org/aboutus.asp). This network is devoted to supporting efforts to involve local communities in reforming their schools. To date, public engagement has not been studied systematically. However, there are case studies in the literature describing successful school reform efforts based on public engagement strategies (Puriefoy, 2005).

Do Performance Measurement Right

The U.S. educational accountability system is similar to or even based on Wholey's approach to performance measurement (Ryan, 2002b). However, the Wholey performance measurement approach goes well beyond standardized test scores and outcomes. He has developed a highly regarded, implemented, and utilized approach that involves assessing a program's readiness for evaluation—evaluability assessment. Based on this assessment, a program is classified at a specific level of development, and prescribed evaluation activities are associated with each of these levels (e.g., establish program definition: Level 0). Essentially, a program must meet four criteria before a program can be evaluated: (a) Program goals, objectives, and side effects are well-defined; (b) the program goals and objectives are achievable given the available resources; (c) program performance information is available or can be collected at a reasonable cost; and (d) stakeholders generally agree on how the evaluation results will be used (Wholey, 1994).

Precursors to Performance Measurement

Wholey sees performance measurement as (a) the measurement of program performance, (b) the making of comparisons (actual and expected results) based on those measurements, and (c) the use of these results in program management. However, Wholey (1994) emphasizes that programs are not ready to be evaluated and that indicators cannot be selected until the program definition is clearly articulated. In the current U.S. educational landscape, the educational outcomes are specified and measured. However, whether educational programs are defined or the logic of the program is sufficiently well developed is less clear. The extent to which at least some educational programs meet Wholey's "evaluability" criteria is an issue. (According to Wholey, 1983, a *program* is "the provisions of federal funds and administrative direction to accomplish a prescribed set of objectives through the conduct of specified activities" [p. 24].)

Furthermore, Wholey (personal communication, October 6, 1998) recommends studying a small number of programs as case studies to supplement the outcomes. Such case studies can illustrate what exemplary programs look like and what they do. It is equally important to include case studies of programs with significant problems. In the context of educational accountability systems, case studies across and within states would be useful. While there are studies of accountability systems or dimensions of systems at the state level (e.g., Clotfelter & Ladd, 1996), studies investigating within-state differences (e.g., why one district is clearly successful and another fails) are absent from the literature.

Preventing Corruption of Indicators

Wholey (personal communication, October 6, 1998) also recommends prevention strategies for addressing concerns about the corruption of indicators. He suggests that triangulation is key. In this context, other standardized assessments and districtwide assessments could be used to either triangulate or provide a broader representation of student performance. In addition, he recommends doing evaluation studies to obtain a fuller picture of performance, particularly focusing on how it fits with the outcome indicators (standardized test scores). Finally, checks by outside auditors are yet another approach for addressing the potential corruption of indicators.

Nonetheless, Wholey (personal communication, October 6, 1998) emphasizes that a key prevention for corruption to indicators is the openness of the process in selecting what these indicators might be. It is clear with the current version of the educational accountability system that many of the decisions involving the technical characteristics of the system are made by the "state," with a limited public process involving stakeholders.

Broaden Performance Measurement Constructs by Mixing Methods

The content and performance standards that are the foundation for educational accountability systems emphasize high achievement, including complex understanding of subject areas and higher-order thinking (Kupermintz, Ennis, Hamilton, Talbert, & Snow, 1995; Ladd, 1996). No single assessment method can adequately represent these student outcomes. There is a clear articulation between these kinds of complex understanding (what to do to improve student performance) and assessment practices like performance assessment and portfolios. However, these measurement techniques are difficult and expensive to implement on a large-scale basis. This kind of educational evaluation is labor-intensive and time-consuming (Eisner, 2001).

Test scores have a place in the representation of student achievement. However, using multiple methods (e.g., essays, portfolios, problem-solving tasks) to assess the same student outcomes and multiple methods to measure different student outcomes provides a much broader picture of student achievement (Ryan, 2002b, 2005). Multiple methods are fairer, giving students multiple opportunities to show what they know and can do. With multiple assessment methods, teachers can disentangle what students know and can do on a test from what students know and can do in class.

Conduct Studies Identifying Intended and Unintended Consequences

The intended effect of the implementation of content and performance standards and their measurement with large-scale assessment is to increase student achievement. However, there are substantial concerns that the reductive nature of performance measurement indicators tends to shape program quality representations that are oversimplified (Stake, 2001). As a consequence, teachers may narrow their teaching and classroom assessment practices. To address these concerns, the study of unintended consequences can be considered.

Implementation theory, anchored in the notion that if program activities are conducted as planned, the desired results will be achieved, is one approach to studying the intended and unintended consequences of educational accountability. One of evaluation's analytic frameworks, implementation theory, which explicitly defines the connections between program objectives and activities, articulates how the objectives will be translated into program activities (Weiss, 1998). Developing a theory of implementation for delivering educational programs focuses on how to improve student performance: the specifics of learning, that is, instruction, curriculum, and assessments, that will be provided to students. Whether the plan is communicated and then implemented as intended, as well as the actual quality and extent of the instruction, curriculum, and assessments are as important as program theory. Including a theory of action specifies the causal links that tie program inputs to program outputs, making explicit the logical connection between program theory and program implementation (Weiss, 1998).

To date, there is a modest amount of evidence from surveys and focus groups that suggests that teachers are concerned about a number of issues related to the unintended consequences of educational accountability. These issues include narrowing of the curriculum, devoting time to test preparation instead of broader goals, spending more instructional time on the content areas tested, feeling pressure for students to do well on these tests, and students feeling more anxious about their assessment performance (Abrams, Pedulla, & Madaus, 2003; Chudowsky & Behuniak, 1997; Koretz et al., 1996; Stecher & Chun, 2001). A recent study confirmed findings about spending significantly more time on tested areas of the curriculum (Center for Educational Policy, 2006). However, there is a need for further systematic study and more evidence to adequately assess the unintended consequences and the extent of any negative impact.

The Future of U.S. Educational Accountability

NCLB educational accountability serves the public interests in a variety of important ways. These include emphasizing achievement for all, a focus on closing the achievement "gaps," and encouraging the teaching of challenging content for all students, and require qualified teachers while calling attention to efficient and appropriate resource use. At the same time, there are significant challenges to achieving these illustrious goals. Educational accountability systems need further study and improvement like those suggested in this chapter if these goals are to be met.

Notes

1. New Public Management is a set of initiatives characterized by a regulatory style that makes individuals and organizations accountable through auditable performance standards (Power, 1997). These standards are intended to improve internal performance and to make these improvements externally confirmable and public. Performance is formed by economy, efficiency, and effectiveness.

2. For instance, in Illinois, annual yearly progress is (a) the percentage of reading and math scores that meet or exceed standards, compared with the annual state targets, and (b) the participation rate of students in taking the state tests, which must meet or exceed 95%.

Discussion Questions

1. How can the U.S educational accountability model be improved? What kinds of conceptual resources from the performance measurement literature might be useful for improving educational accountability in the United States?

2. To date, U.S. educational accountability is widely criticized for relying primarily on information from standardized test scores for making judgments about school quality. What kinds of information should be collected? How will this information improve judgments about educational quality?

3. What are the issues with using the same meaning and logic for holding individuals, groups, and organizations responsible, irrespective of whether we are considering financial expenditures or student learning or health care? What might be the advantages?

4. Is the assumption tenable that students and financial resources are interchangeable units? Defend your position.

References

Abrams, L. M., Pedulla, J. J., & Madaus, G. F. (2003). Views from the classroom: Teachers' opinions of statewide testing programs. *Theory Into Practice, 42,* 18–29.

American Educational Research Association. (2000). *AERA position statement: High-stakes testing in preK–12.* Retrieved January 6, 2006, from http://www .aera.net/policyandprograms/?id=378

American Evaluation Association. (2001). *American Evaluation Association position statement on high-stakes testing in PreK–12 education.* Retrieved March 30, 2002, from http://www.eval.org/hstlinks.htm

American Evaluation Association. (2004). *Town meeting: Developing an AEA public statement on educational accountability.* Presentation at the Annual Meeting of the American Evaluation Association, Atlanta, GA.

Amrein, A. L., & Berliner, D. C. (2002). High-stakes testing, uncertainty, and student learning. *Education Policy Analysis Archives, 10*(8). Retrieved January 5, 2006, from http://epaa.asu.edu/epaa/v10n18

Anderson, J. A. (2005). *Accountability in education.* Paris: UNESCO, International Institute for Educational Planning.

Behn, R. D. (2001). *Rethinking democratic accountability.* Washington, DC: Brookings Institution Press.

Burbules, N. C., & Torres, C. A. (Eds.). (2000). *Globalization and education: Critical perspectives.* New York: Routledge.

Carnoy, M., & Loeb, S. (2002). Does external accountability affect student outcomes? *Educational Evaluation and Policy Analysis, 24,* 305–331.

Center for Educational Policy. (2006). *From the capital to the classroom: Year 4 of the No Child Left Behind Act.* Washington, DC: Center for Educational Policy.

Chudowsky, N., & Behuniak, P. (1997, March). *Establishing the consequential validity for large-scale performance assessments.* Paper presented at the National Council of Measurement in Education, Chicago.

Clotfelter, C. T., & Ladd, H. F. (1996). Recognizing and awarding success in public schools. In H. F. Ladd (Ed.), *Holding schools accountable: Performance-based reform in education* (pp. 23–63). Washington, DC: Brookings Institute.

Cronbach, L., Ambron, S. R., Dornbusch, S. M., Hess, R. D., Hornik, R. C., Phillips, D. C., et al. (1980). *Toward a reform of program evaluation: Aims, methods, and institutional arrangements.* San Francisco: Jossey-Bass.

Education Week. (2004, January 8). Quality counts 2004: Count me in, p. 1.

Eisner, E. W. (2001). What does it mean to say a school is doing well? *Phi Delta Kappan, 82,* 367–372.

Elementary and Secondary Education Act, Pub. L. 89–10, 79 Stat. 77, 20 U.S.C. ch.70 (1965).

Heubert, J. P., & Hauer, R. M. (Eds.). (1999). *High stakes: Testing for tracking, promotion, and graduation.* Washington, DC: National Academy Press.

Improving America's Schools Act, Pub. L. 103–382 (1994).

Jacobs, B. A. (2001). Getting tough? The impact of high school graduation exams. *Educational Evaluation and Policy Analysis, 23,* 99–121.

Jang, E., & Ryan, K. E. (2003). Bridging gaps among curriculum, teaching and learning, and assessment. *Journal of Curriculum Studies, 34,* 499–512.

Kifer, E. (2001). *Large-scale assessment: Dimensions, dilemmas, and policy.* Thousand Oaks, CA: Corwin Press.

Klein, D., Braams, B. J., Parker, T., Quirk, W., Schmid, W., Wilson, W. S., et al. (2005). *The state of the math standards 2005.* Washington, DC: Thomas B. Fordham Foundation.

Koretz, D. M., Barron, S., Mitchell, K. J., & Stecher, B. M. (1996). *Perceived effects of the Kentucky instruction results information district (KIRIS).* Santa Monica, CA: Rand.

Kupermintz, H., Ennis, M. M., Hamilton, L. S., Talbert, J. E., & Snow, R. E. (1995). Enhancing the validity and usefulness of large-scale assessments: I. NELS:88 mathematics achievement. *American Educational Research Journal, 32,* 525–554.

Ladd, H. F. (Ed.). (1996). *Holding schools accountable: Performance-based reform in education.* Washington, DC: Brookings Institute.

Lee, J., & Wong, K. K. (2004). The impact of accountability on racial and socioeconomic equity: Considering both school resources and achievement outcomes. *American Educational Research Journal, 41,* 797–832.

Lefkowits, L., & Miller, K. (2005, April). Fulfilling the promise of the standards movement. *MCRel Policy Brief,* 1–7.

Linn, R. L. (2000). Assessments and accountability. *Educational Researcher, 29*(2), 4–14.

Linn, R. L. (2003). Accountability: Responsibility and reasonable expectations. *Educational Researcher, 32*(7), 3–13.

Linn, R. L. (2007, January). *Educational accountability systems.* Paper presented at the Annual Conference at the Center for Research on Evaluation, Standards, and Student Testing, Los Angeles, CA.

88‌‍‍‌‍

Linn, R. L., & Miller, M. D. (2005). *Measurement and assessment in teaching.* Upper Saddle River, NJ: Pearson.

Mark, M. M., Henry, G., & Julnes, G. (2000). *Evaluation: An integrated framework for understanding, guiding, and improving policies and programs.* San Francisco: Jossey-Bass.

Moss, P. A., & Schultz, A. (2001). Educational standards, assessment, and the search for consensus. *American Educational Research Association, 38*(1), 37–70.

National Commission on Excellence in Education. (1983). *A nation at risk: The imperative for educational reform.* Washington, DC: U.S. Government Printing Office.

Nevo, D. (2002). Dialogue evaluation: Combining internal and external evaluation. In D. Nevo (Ed.), *School-based evaluation: An international perspective* (pp. 3–16). Kidlington, UK: Elsevier Science.

No Child Left Behind Act of 2001, Pub. L. No. 107th Cong., 110 Cong. Rec. 1425. 115 Stat. (2002).

Porter, A. C. (2002). Measuring the content of instruction. *Educational Researcher, 31*(7), 3–14.

Power, M. (1997). *The audit society.* New York: Oxford Press.

Puriefoy, W. (2005). *Taking responsibility: Using public engagement to reform our schools.* Washington, DC: Public Education Network.

Raudenbush, S. W. (2004a). *Schooling, statistics, and poverty: Can we measure school improvement?* The Ninth Annual William H. Angoff Memorial Lecture. Princeton, NJ: Educational Testing Service.

Raudenbush, S. W. (2004b). What are value-added models estimating and what does that imply for statistical practice? *Journal of Educational and Behavioral Statistics, 29,* 121–129.

Resnick, L., & Zurawsky, C. (2005, Spring). Standards-based reform and accountability: Getting back on course. *American Educator,* pp. 1–13.

Rizvi, F. (1990). Horizontal accountability. In J. Chapman (Ed.), *School-based decision-making and management* (pp. 299–324). Hampshire, UK: Falmer Press.

Ryan, K. E. (2002a). Assessment validation in the context of high stakes assessment. *Educational Measurement: Issues and Practices, 21*(1), 7–15.

Ryan, K. E. (2002b). Shaping educational accountability systems. *American Journal of Evaluation, 23,* 453–468.

Ryan, K. E. (2005). Making educational accountability more democratic. *American Journal of Evaluation, 26,* 443–460.

Smith, M., & O'Day, J. (1991). Systematic school reform. In S. Fuhrman & B. Malen (Eds.), *The politics of curriculum and testing* (pp. 233–267). Philadelphia: Falmer Press.

Stake, R. E. (2001). How modern democracies are shaping evaluation and the emerging challenges for evaluation. *American Journal of Evaluation, 22,* 349–354.

Stecher, B., & Chun, T. (2001). *School and classroom practices during two years of educational reform in Washington State* (CSE Tech. Rep. No. 550). Los Angeles: University of California, National Center for Research on Evaluation, Standards, and Student Testing.

Stein, J. G. (2001). *The cult of efficiency.* Toronto, Canada: House of Anansi Press.

Stotsky, S., & Finn, C. E. (2005). *The state of state English standards 2005.* Washington, DC: Thomas B. Fordham Foundation.

Stronach, I. (1999). Shouting theatre in a crowded fire: Educational effectiveness as cultural performance. *Evaluation, 5,* 173–193.

Stronach, I., Halsall, R., & Hustler, D. (2002). Future imperfect: Evaluation in dystopian times. In K. Ryan & T. Schwandt (Eds.), *Exploring evaluator role and identity* (pp. 167–192). Greenwich, CT: Information Age Publishing.

Suarez-Orozco, M., & Qin-Hilliard, D. M. (2004). *Globalization: Culture and education in the new millennium.* Berkeley: University of California Press.

Teachers College Annual Report. (2004). *New rules, old responses.* Retrieved, October 1, 2004, from http://www.tc.columbia.edu/news/article.htm?id=4741, 8/31/2004

U.S. Department of Education. (2002). *U.S. Department of Education strategic plan 2002–2007.* Retrieved November 1, 2004, from http://www.ed.gov/about/reports/strat/plan2002–2007/index.html

Weiss, C. H. (1998). *Evaluation: Methods for studying programs and policies.* Upper Saddle River, NJ: Prentice Hall.

Westbury, I. (2003). Evaluating a national curriculum reform. In P. Haug & T. A. Schwandt (Eds.), *Evaluating educational reforms: Scandinavia perspectives* (pp. 189–207). Greenwich, CT: Information Age Publishing.

Wholey, J. S. (1983). *Evaluation and effective public management.* Boston: Little, Brown.

Wholey, J. S. (1994). Assessing the feasibility and likely usefulness of evaluation. In J. Wholey, H. Hatry, & K. Newcomer, *Handbook of practical program evaluation* (pp. 15–39). San Francisco: Jossey Bass.

12 Experience With Trained Observers in Transition and Developing Countries

Citizen Engagement in Monitoring Results[1]

Katharine Mark

Performance management has the potential to provide benefits—improved services and greater transparency and accountability—that have increasingly appealed to local governments. These benefits are heightened in the context of transition and developing countries where weak public services, limited resources, and a lack of trust between government and citizens create a vicious circle of poor performance and no accountability.

The entry costs, however, can often seem high to jurisdictions considering the implementation of performance management. The focus on outcomes—the effect of services on citizens—requires a sharp shift from the traditional emphasis in the public sector on revenue and expenditure. Measurement is often perceived as a lengthy, costly, and technically demanding process; the emphasis on the citizen's perspective sometimes seems synonymous with citizen surveys, which may appear prohibitively costly and elaborate to conduct. The use of the performance data appears to be a complex and obscure process. Public officials are reluctant to subject themselves to the scrutiny that comes with reporting on performance, afraid of being blamed for problems that may not be within their control. And, finally, despite the fact that the citizen is the focus of the approach, it is not always apparent that these measurements will be understandable to citizens—or, for that matter, to elected officials or even nonspecialist staff. Trained-observer ratings may provide a way to leapfrog some of these concerns. Our international experience, in particular, has demonstrated that these ratings can be a "jumpstart" for communities, quickly manifesting the benefits of performance management by engaging citizens and quickly and inexpensively producing visible results. This chapter reviews some of that experience and in particular explores the role of citizens in these cases.

Background

In the last decades, as decentralization has gathered momentum around the world, there has been a need for tools to address the need for both better local services and the development of a new and more constructive relationship between government and citizens. Performance management has turned out to be particularly effective in meeting both these needs. Through requiring identification of specific outcomes, setting targets, and measuring progress, it provides a focused, constructive, and practical approach to improving services; through the provision of transparent outcome information, it strengthens the government-citizen relationship. This chapter reports on some efforts to introduce performance management to local governments in decentralizing countries and focuses in particular on one technique for collecting performance data, trained-observer ratings, whose characteristics—low cost, practical, and able to deliver tangible improvement in services and direct citizen engagement in the short term—have made this tool especially effective in that context.

Trained-observer ratings, a form of data collection carried out by laypeople with a modest degree of training, provide consistent and reliable ratings of conditions over time and across raters. Trained observers can rate physical conditions, such as road rideability, the state of repair of buildings, street cleanliness, and adequacy of parks, and measure a host of other outcomes, including school readiness of young children or the progress of clients with disabilities (such as their ability to perform common activities of daily living). In each case, the trained use of a systematic, well-defined scale ensures that different observers across time and in different locations would give approximately the same rating to similar conditions.

The process for carrying out trained-observer ratings is fairly simple. After a decision is made regarding the scope of the rating, a rating scale is designed. For instance, it might be decided that 20 randomly selected blocks in a city will be assessed for cleanliness, based on a 4-point scale ranging from "very dirty" to "very clean." Raters are trained (a process that can be as short as 1 or 2 days) and carry out the ratings. Provisions need to be made to ensure that ratings will be compiled and analyzed accurately and consistently. Finally, results should be reported and acted upon. As with other methods of collecting performance data, the information should be used both to report on current conditions for accountability purposes and to decide how to improve performance, for instance, through allocating additional resources to areas that are weaker or drawing examples from areas that are performing well.

Experiences

This chapter describes experiences in several transition and developing countries around the world in which trained-observer ratings have been used in local governments to monitor service outcomes.[2] The purpose of this chapter is not to assess the success of these projects, but rather to explore through them the feasibility of successfully implementing trained-observer ratings in developing and transition countries and the role volunteers can play in that effort, and to identify their possible contributions to increased engagement of citizens.

In this section, a brief summary of each case is provided, with special attention to some of the key characteristics of each experience, such as who carried out the rating, what impediments were encountered and how they were resolved, and how the results were used.

Rating Local Services in Albania

Albania was one of the first transition countries in which performance management was introduced at the local government level.[3] It typified the characteristics of many transition countries: a highly centralized political and economic structure, a history of deferred maintenance and poor local services, and weak (or nonexistent) mechanisms for communication and information flows between local governments and citizens.

Performance management was introduced in several local governments as a way of addressing these problems, starting in 1999. As an inexpensive data collection tool, trained-observer ratings were considered early in the process. By 2005, trained-observer ratings were being used in more than 10 cities in Albania, over a range of services, usually in the context of service improvement action plans that identify key service outcomes and set targets for improvement.

The first effort to use trained-observer ratings in Albania was in 1999 in the commune of Baldushku, as a tool to improve the condition of their roads and footbridges. Although ultimately short-lived, the Baldushku experience served to illustrate the ways in which the approach would be especially useful in low-income transition countries and also some of the obstacles to sustainable implementation.

Baldushku is a rural commune in central Albania, consisting of 14 villages, with an average population of 400 inhabitants. Adequate condition of both the roads and the small footbridges used to cross the many streams throughout the commune is essential to allow access to work, schools, hospitals, and markets. Commune roads were generally unpaved, and the quality of gravel, where there was any, was too thin to withstand general winter conditions. Potholes, mud, and standing water were the norm for commune roads, and footbridges were often dilapidated or nonexistent.

Trained-observer ratings seemed particularly appropriate because the commune is widely dispersed across a large area, making it hard for the commune government to obtain timely information on road conditions without great expense. The commune working group, charged with leading the effort, first established a clear range of conditions: five levels of rideability for roads, ranging from "very bad" to "very good." To depict the quality, they reviewed a large number of photographs taken of roads in the commune and selected two photos to describe each level. When reviewing the photographs and assigning levels, the working group decided that no photograph in Baldushku represented the conditions they felt should be the "ideal," their Level 1, so they selected a photograph of a higher-quality road from outside the commune (Mark & Nayyar-Stone, 2004).

The complete Baldushku rating system includes the photographs and written descriptions of each level (see box, "Road Rideability Grading System"). The grading system asks the rater to consider smoothness, bumpiness, presence and size of potholes, how conditions affect the speed at which vehicles can drive, problems with drainage, potential safety hazards, and need for repair.

Road Rideability Grading System Developed for Use in Baldushku

1. *Very good:* Appears to be smooth and has little if any standing water problem.

2. *Good:* Slightly bumpy rideability, but minimal decrease in speed required. May be characterized as having some minor bumps or minor potholes, or one large single bump or single pothole. Some minor maintenance required.

3. *Acceptable,* but in need of repair to improve general rideability (40 km/h maximum in normal conditions). Characterized by many bumps and/or potholes and may have problems during the rainy season.

4. *Bad* and in need of heavy repair (25–40 km/h maximum). Considerably bumpy rideability, potential safety hazard or cause of major jolting. Two-way traffic inhibited by large holes or other interruptions in paving/grade.

5. *Very bad* (0–25 km/h maximum) and in need of total reconstruction. Safety hazard, unrideable, disappears almost entirely under bad weather conditions.

Armed with this set of photos and a brief summary of conditions that characterize each level, the rater should be able to walk around the commune and compare what he or she is actually seeing with the photographs and choose which of the five levels depicted is closest to the actual road. In this way, different raters are likely to reach the same conclusion.

Despite these preparations, trained-observer ratings were not actually implemented in Baldushku (although the commune did make a number of improvements to their road network, including building several new footbridges with community cooperation). It became clear that the local governments would need more help with training and implementation in order to actually use the methodology.

Beginning in 2003, trained-observer ratings were more successfully introduced to a number of cities in Albania. Building on lessons learned from the Baldushku case, training on the design and the rating scale as well as rating techniques were provided to several cities fairly quickly, to give the system a better chance to be implemented. A number of cities put trained-observer ratings into action, focusing mostly on street cleanliness, solid waste collection, or road conditions, and three or four of those became effective very rapidly. A separate set of seven cities began to rate school conditions; that special case will be described in greater detail below. Once a few cities became successful, there was a multiplier effect, both because of the visibility of the positive impact and because the more successful raters became trainers and mentors for others.

In Rreshen, trained observers were used to rate road conditions (Rreshen Municipality, 2005). Rreshen is a mountainous municipality of about 16,000 people, with about half the population living in a relatively rural environment around the city. The city divides the road network into primary roads, secondary roads, and rural roads, with the rural roads making up almost 90% of the total road kilometers. A group of citizens rated the condition of both roads and sidewalks, and on the basis of those findings set targets for improvement for 2006 (see Table 12.1) based on plans to carry out major rehabilitation of the road network, to be funded by increased allocations of the locality's own revenues.

The municipality of Lezha focused on cleanliness and solid waste collection. Lezha is an old city, founded in 385 BC not far from the Adriatic Sea

Table 12.1   Percentage of Roads Receiving Ratings of 1 or 2 ("good" or "fairly good")

Road Category	2005 Baseline	2006 Target
Primary roads	23%	50%
Secondary roads	44%	60%
Rural roads	10%	40%

SOURCE: Adapted from Rreshen Municipality (2005).

(Lezha Municipality, 2005). The population of about 30,000 lives predominantly in the urban area. Cleaning and garbage collection service is provided by a private company, which sweeps the streets and collects garbage from 200 specified collection spots where residents deposit their household garbage. The Lezha working group decided to introduce trained-observer ratings in order to obtain accurate information on the cleaning situation. The raters were students, members of the Lezha Youth Parliament. Each of the students spent 3 days carrying out ratings, and the ratings were compiled by the project coordinator.

The observers rated cleanliness in the street, on the sidewalk, at the garbage collection site itself (either a bin or a concrete form), and of the area around the collection spot. Street cleanliness for five different neighborhoods varied between 2.0 and 2.5 (where 1 is "very clean" and 4 is "very dirty"), with two neighborhoods, Marleka Hill and Skenderbeg, identified as having the worst conditions. When specific spots within Skenderbeg were rated, 3 out of 5 streets rated had ratings of about 3.0 ("dirty"). In Marleka Hill, the bins and the areas around the bins were considerably worse, with the "best" rating at 3.6 (about halfway between "dirty" and "very dirty") and the worst at 4.0. Not surprisingly, cleanliness near the collection spots tracked closely with the rating for cleanliness of the respective street. Raters also made some additional observations, such as "incinerated garbage near the cemetery," "spread over 200 square meters," "debris and garbage thrown in front of a religious institution," and "very huge pile."

The volunteers collecting the ratings listed the failure of citizens to throw garbage in designated places as one of the main causes. Other factors they mentioned were an insufficient number of bins and the summer influx of vacationers on their way to the beach. They also noted an irregular distribution of bins around the city.

Based on these findings, the municipality decided to allocate funds to purchase additional bins (raising the citywide total from 52 to 200) and to organize and carry out an information and awareness campaign for citizens and businesses. To fund the improvement of the service, the city increased the fee and planned to work to increase the collections rate from 32% to at least 50% by 2006.

While these efforts are still under way, it is already clear that the city is much more informed about the level of cleanliness in the city and the nature and location of the worst problems, and it has developed a specific strategy to address those problems.

Altogether, about 13 cities in Albania have been using trained observers to rate one or more services, and the number is increasing. Saranda, a city on the Adriatic coast in the south of Albania, recently learned about trained-observer ratings, and in 2006, the city council allocated the necessary funding to institute trained-observer ratings for street cleanliness. The city's decision to fund trained-observer ratings is a strong indication that this is a well-established method of data collection and that it is perceived to be worthwhile.

Table 12.2   Albanian Cities Using Trained-Observer Ratings

City	Service Rated	Raters
Berat	Schools	City staff, teachers, parents
Bushat	Schools	City staff, teachers, parents
Elbasan	Street cleaning	Students
	Schools	City staff, teachers, parents
Fier	Street cleaning	Volunteers, NGO staff, youth
Kucove	Street cleaning	
Kukus	Roads	Teachers
Lezha	Street cleaning	Youth Parliament
	Schools	City staff, teachers, parents
Patos	Street cleaning	Volunteers
Pogradec	Schools	City staff and school parents
	Parks, beach	Staff and students
Puka	Cleaning	Youth
Rreshen	Roads/sidewalks	Citizens
	Schools	City staff, teachers, parents
Rubik	Schools	City staff, teachers, parents
Saranda	Street cleaning	
Shkoder	Roads	City staff and citizens
	Schools	City staff, teachers, parents

The use of trained-observer ratings is usually instituted quite early in the process of improving services through performance management and has become the norm for cities interested in improving their cleaning services in particular. Table 12.2 lists some of these cities, the services they rated, and who the raters were. As can be seen, the raters were drawn from a variety of sources, and in many cases, these were volunteers. About half of the trained-observer rating systems now active are rating street cleanliness, with the others rating road condition, parks, or school conditions.

Rating School Conditions in Albania

The application of the trained-observer rating method to the condition of school facilities in Albania was a special case. This task turned out to have special significance in the process of decentralization, because the maintenance of schools was one of the first centrally controlled tasks to be explicitly devolved to the local level.

One of the first cities to turn to this issue was Pogradec, a city on Lake Ohrid, in eastern Albania. The city began by forming a two-person rating team (municipal staff members) who would visit each school to rate specific characteristics—whether windows were broken, toilets were in working condition, electrical wires were exposed, or there were holes in the playground.

Pogradec was especially successful in this process, and following their initial success, the two municipal staff members who managed the rating program were asked to train raters in a number of other cities. Eventually, seven cities in all were rating school conditions by 2004. Raters included municipal staff, teachers, and parents of school children. In each school, individual classrooms, halls, stairwells, restrooms, and building exteriors were rated. Within each area, certain aspects were identified and required individual ratings. For example, in each classroom, conditions of ceiling, walls/pillars, windows, doors, balconies/porches, and overall cleanliness were to be rated. Once the ratings were completed, the findings were presented to a group of stakeholders in each city, who then discussed which problems should be considered priorities for city funding.

The ratings were highly visible and became increasingly popular. They prompted several cities to increase budget allocations for priority school maintenance and led in most instances to better school conditions. Nevertheless, the approach encountered a number of problems in the stages of data review and analysis and the reporting of results.

The initial approach was based on experience in the United States and asked raters to evaluate conditions across several different categories; for instance, they had to assess the number of problems, whether each problem was "limited" or "widespread" (according to specific definitions) and whether it was considered "hazardous." Unfortunately, this led to some confusion. On one hand, it proved difficult to keep track of so many items—a number of problems in each room, specific types of problems across each system (plumbing, electricity, construction), different characteristics, and across several schools—especially since most cities did not have access to computers and/or computer-trained staff. Further, the categories in some instances led to double counting (for instance, a problem could be both "limited" and "hazardous" and was therefore in some instances counted twice). Additional problems identified included reporting errors (for instance, reporting the average instead of noting the full range, so that the worst problems were obscured), confusion on forms, and using the rater's own experience or estimated cost instead of the actual ratings to identify priorities.

A sample spreadsheet for primary school "Qamil Guranjaku," one of six schools rated in the city of Elbasan, is shown in Table 12.3, illustrating the complexity of tracking data presented by the multiplicity of aspects to be rated: 28 aspects, ranging from caulking of windows to cracks in the ceiling, presence of vermin, and structural problems with doors, over a total

Table 12.3   Sample Rating Sheet for School in Elbasan

Building: 8-year school "Qamil Guranjaku"
Number of Rooms: 33
Number of Students: 1100

Rating	Limited	Widespread	Hazards	% of Hazards by the Total	% of Wide-spread by the Total	% of Element Problems by the Total	Total (L+W)
1	1	2	3	4	5	6	7
Ceilings							
Cracks, bulges, other damages	10	11		0%	52%	32%	21
Missing/damaged tiles	0	0				0%	0
Paint	22	11		0%	33%	51%	33
Other		11	11	100%		17%	11
Total - CEILINGS	32	33	11	100%	100%	100%	65
Walls/Pillars							
Cracked, broken, damaged	7			0%	0%	14%	7
Paint, stains, graffiti	22	11		0%	33%	65%	33
Other	6	5		0%	45%	22%	11
Total - WALLS/PILLARS	35	16	0	0%	100%	100%	51
Windows							
Glass	23	3		0%	12%	19%	26
Caulking/putty	23	3		0%	12%	19%	26
Sills and frames	23	3		0%	12%	19%	26
Paint		33		0%	100%	24%	33
Blinds/screens				0%	0%	0%	0
Other	20	4		0%	17%	18%	24
Total - WINDOWS	89	46	0	0%	100%	100%	135

(Continued)

Table 12.3 (Continued)

Rating	Limited	Widespread	Hazards	% of Hazards by the Total	% of Wide-spread by the Total	% of Element Problems by the Total	Total (L+W)
1	1	2	3	4	5	6	7
Doors							
Operability	19			0%	0%	16%	19
Structural condition	13			0%	0%	11%	13
Hardware (metal parts)	11	17		0%	61%	24%	28
Paint	22	11		0%	33%	28%	33
Other	8	15		0%	65%	20%	23
Total - DOORS	73	43	0			100%	116
Floors (without stairwells)							
Hard surface structure	10	0		0%	0%	30%	10
Hard surface finish	10	0		0%	0%	30%	10
Carpet	13			0%	0%	39%	13
Other				0%	0%	0%	0
Total - FLOORS	33	0	0			100%	33
Cleanliness							
Ceiling dirty/dusty		9		0%	100%	45%	9
Walls, windows dirty/dusty	11			0%	0%	55%	11
Floor dirty/dusty				0%	0%	0%	0
Litter				0%	0%	0%	0
Presence of bugs, vermin				0%	0%	0%	0
Other				0%	0%	0%	0
Total - CLEANLINESS	11	9	0			100%	20

SOURCE: Reprinted with permission.

of 33 individual rooms—each of which had to be categorized by the extent and hazardousness of the problem (Urban Research Institute, 2004).

The experiment with trained-observer ratings of school conditions in a small number of cities led to a much broader application. The operation and maintenance of primary education buildings became one of the first responsibilities to be delegated to local governments in Albania in the course of increasing decentralization of public services. Interested in establishing performance standards for schools around the country as control for school maintenance was shifted to local governments, the Ministry of Education and Sciences found that the trained-observer ratings being carried out in a few local governments would provide a useful approach—inexpensive and easily verifiable—to monitor compliance with national standards.

To initiate this process, a working group including local government representatives and officials from the Ministry of Education and Sciences met over a period of months to first establish the standards that would be set by the national government and monitored for compliance (Mary Winkler, personal communication, March 17, 2006). The earlier experience with rating and analyzing data in individual cities made it clear that a national rating system would have to be much simpler to have a chance of being effectively implemented nationwide. After a series of deliberations, the selected standards (see box, "Standards for Educational Facilities") focused mostly on health and safety. The raters were given specific instructions on rating conditions for a total of 21 different indicators, such as "number and percentage of schools that fail to meet communications standard" (i.e., does not have functional telephone, dedicated mobile phone, or radio communication system), and "number and percentage of each of the following bathroom fixtures in fair or poor condition: (a) sinks, (b) faucets, (c) toilets, flush, (d) showers, (e) windows, (f) doors, and (g) privacy partitions."

Standards for Educational Facilities

Standard 1: Hazardous Conditions: Facilities are free from hazardous conditions that threaten the safety or health of individuals.

Standard 2: Fire Protection and Emergency Evacuation: Facilities have functional equipment for fire protection and emergency evacuation.

Standard 3: Lighting and Electrical Network: Facilities have normal lighting functional and safe electrical networks and equipment.

Standard 4: Temperature and Humidity: Facilities have necessary and sufficient equipment for heating interior aspects appropriate to the size, structure, and orientation of the school buildings.

Standard 5: Water Supply: Facilities have potable, clean, and running water.

(Continued)

(Continued)

Standard 6: Functional Sanitary Nodes and Water Supply Discharge: Facilities have functional sanitary nodes, water supply and safe wastewater/sewer discharges, including outlets that ensure hygiene, safety, and healthy conditions for users of facilities.

Standard 7: Cleanliness, Sanitation, and Solid Waste Disposal: Facilities have clean and hygienic conditions provided, with collection of disposal of solid waste, including hazardous waste.

Standard 8: Communications: Facilities have necessary functional telecommunications equipment and appliances.

A pilot project for nationwide standards was established for the first year, focusing on three local governments: the cities of Berat and Pogradec, and Bushat, a commune. In each one of these, the trained observers (school and municipal staff) rated all the schools in their localities with respect to compliance with the eight standards. Using these ratings, each local government then determined the total cost of bringing the schools up to standard and established priorities among the different requirements. In all three cases, the city councils voted to increase budget allocations to fund school priorities, based on the findings and recommendations stemming from the rating process.

As the total cost exceeded the funds currently available, each of the three localities prepared a plan for meeting all requirements over 3 years. With limited resources, the pilot cities came up with some creative approaches. For instance, in Pogradec, the telephone company and some businesses would underwrite the cost of installing working telephones in all the schools. In Berat, participants stressed that the schools must work in collaboration with pupils and parents to improve maintenance. The school directors also proposed some new approaches: to use small volunteer groups with local businesses to paint the schools, rather than contracting out the jobs professionally, and to obtain assistance from vocational school students in improving electrical and plumbing systems.

Following the first round of the pilot project, several other cities asked to join the pilot program to rate their schools. In one case, the city had already allocated funds in the budget for school maintenance, with the expectation that the ratings would guide their decisions on priority repairs during the summer maintenance season. Based on the pilot, the national working group will be developing a nationwide program for all local governments.

Georgia: Youth Rating Street Cleanliness

The Georgia case described here illustrates the effectiveness of using highly motivated volunteers to institutionalize a trained-observer rating system. The system also provided an unexpected benefit by creating an opportunity for young people to become engaged in local governance.

As part of a project to help improve public services, five local governments in Georgia sought volunteers to undertake ratings of service quality. Announcements were posted in schools asking youth to participate in a training session. There were far more applicants than needed, and selections were based on previous volunteer experience and basic familiarity with local government.

Initially taking place in five cities, the procedure required ratings of cleanliness to be carried out on a substantial portion of the city's streets, about 30 streets in small cities, up to 60 streets in larger cities, or between 100 and 190 blocks altogether. The city department divided the city into neighborhoods and then into blocks. Each city provided the youth group with a list of streets to be rated; most were in the areas covered by the sweeping services, but a few locations outside coverage areas were chosen for comparison. The local coordinator, a staff member of the internationally funded assistance project located in each of the project cities, checked the list against the contract with the service provider to make sure that the streets were appropriate. Both main streets and peripheral streets were rated. The youth were assigned districts to rate by the local coordinator; they did the ratings in pairs, agreeing on each rating, over 2 or 3 days.

In most cities, the ratings were conducted quarterly, or three times a year. Typically, the ratings were presented (in PowerPoint slides) to the city council in a public hearing, usually with media in attendance. Youth volunteers were trained in data analysis so that they would be able to carry out the whole cycle of ratings, analysis, and reporting, although they still relied to some extent on help from project staff.

The ratings enabled the council, the city department, and the public to see clearly where performance was good and where it lagged and to encourage the reallocation of resources to improve results. The system was initially used directly by the city departments of communal services; in some cases, the cities used the ratings to monitor performance of contractors when they decided to outsource the service. For instance, in the city of Ozurgeti, the indicators were included in the performance-based contract signed with the first private sector contractor, which was responsible for solid waste collection, to provide communal services.

As a result of the monitoring, fairly significant improvements in cleanliness were noted in most of these cities (Nayyar-Stone & Bishop, 2005). During the first years, all five cities showed improvements in ratings and in citizen satisfaction. Trained-observer ratings in the city of Gori, for example, showed an increase in blocks receiving the highest ratings (between 1 and 1.5 or "good") from 52% to 63% between 2003 and 2004, while the number of blocks scoring lowest (those rated as 3 or 4) was cut in half, from 12% to 6% of all blocks rated. The increase was even sharper in Ozurgeti during that period, with blocks receiving scores of 1.0 to 1.5 moving from 12% to 47% and those rated poorly (3–4) decreasing from 31% to 5% (see Figure 12.1).

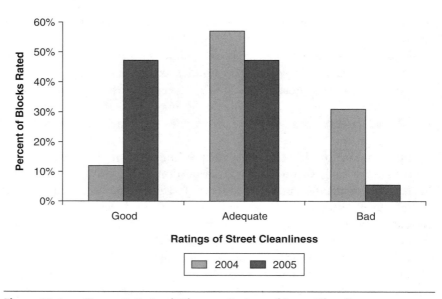

Figure 12.1   Ozurgeti: Trained-Observer Ratings of Street Cleanliness

Citizen surveys in those same cities also showed improvement in levels of satisfaction. In Ozurgeti, for example, the percentage of citizens reporting that they were "satisfied" or "very satisfied" with the cleaning service increased from 54% in 2003 to 82% in 2004. Over the same period, the percentage of people rating the city as "clean" or "very clean" rose from 21% to 47%. Furthermore, most of the cities had increases in revenue and collections, especially in solid waste collection, likely boosted by the noticeable improvement in services and improved accountability engendered by high-visibility reporting sessions (in at least one city, the increase in collections was as high as 50% in the first year) (K. Jakeli, Performance Management Director, Georgia Communities Empowered for Local Decision Making, personal communication, 2006; Nayyar-Stone & Bishop, 2005).

Once the first five cities had visible results, a number of other cities asked to become involved. In each city, a new group of youth volunteers was established, and young people from the pilot cities provided training. The new cities demonstrated improvements within a few months, benefiting from both the motivation of the other cities' improvements and the expertise of the team. The new cities started immediately with a survey and training for volunteer observers, in order to establish the baselines right away and begin the rating of services. There are now youth group rating services in more than 10 cities.

The introduction of trained-observer ratings in Georgia proved a catalyst for much broader involvement in local governance for Georgian youth. The impact of the experience was not felt just by the city, but by the raters themselves. In Poti, one volunteer remarked, "We are always pointing our finger at the local government. But I see that citizens are vandalizing the garbage bins" (K. Jakeli, personal communication, 2006). The experience broadened the teenagers' perspectives on civic responsibility, providing a relatively unusual insight in a country still in transition from an autocratic communist rule. The raters in some of the original cities formed youth clubs, which expanded as they began to provide training to youth in other cities. Over time, the youth groups took on a number of other projects, such as collecting clothes for orphanages and organizing debates between candidates for local office. They were trained in budgeting and began to prepare a "youth budget" by analyzing the items in the city budget that affected young people. They organized nongovernmental organization coordination meetings and raised money to buy presents for low-income children. In conjunction with the city youth department, they sponsored a debate game for high school students, called, "What, Where, When." Youth groups sponsored "Cleaning Days" on International Youth Day, drawing in other citizens to help clean the city, while the city provided equipment (I. Kuprashvili, Project Coordinator, city of Kvareli, Georgia, Georgia Communities Empowered for Local Decision Making, personal communication, 2006). Within about 2 years, youth groups formed all over the country and eventually formed a national youth association with headquarters in the capital.

The process has not been without hitches. There was, to begin with, some difficulty in getting agreement on youth involvement. It is not customary in Georgia for youth to work, even on a volunteer basis. For instance, in one city, participants had to obtain permission from both their parents and their school directors. While they were working, rating conditions, or conducting surveys, the raters were occasionally told they should be studying instead or that they should not be doing the city's work.

Staff and leadership in some of the cities were at first nervous about allowing the young raters to present results publicly. Nevertheless, once city staff received the ratings sheets and analysis, they could see it was based on data that they themselves could check. They became less defensive about the results and began to see that they were being provided with useful information and that the reports led to a more constructive view of the city for its residents. One indication that the cities have come to appreciate the system is that they have started to pay for it—while the raters continue to work as volunteers, the cities now include transport, food, and materials (rating forms, for example) as explicit budget items.

The Georgia experience seems to indicate partial success in sustainable institutionalization. The raters are highly motivated and through the youth clubs are able to replenish their ranks, and the cities have been able to convert the ratings into better service delivery and higher collections. Institutionalization is not yet complete, as externally funded staff still play a critical role in (a) serving as liaison between city needs and the individual raters to be assigned to their tasks and (b) carrying out the data analysis and preparing public presentations. If it becomes possible to transfer those tasks to some combination of local government and volunteers,[4] the trained-observer ratings system can be expected to remain active for the foreseeable future.

Civil Society and Municipal Collaboration in Honduras

In about 30 cities in Honduras, civil society representatives and municipal staff worked together to identify community priorities and carry out projects to improve local conditions. Several communities that had identified either solid waste collection or road maintenance as their priority instituted trained-observer ratings to monitor service quality, using a mix of volunteers from civil society and municipal staff.

Altogether, 23 cities in Honduras began using trained-observer ratings in this format, rating services such as road maintenance, solid waste collection, and street cleanliness. The approach has been very popular. Municipal staff and volunteers who often have fairly low levels of education have appreciated the ability to rate conditions using photographs. Citizens have also enjoyed the experience of spending time and working with city staff. In addition, because these are cities with very scarce resources, it is important that the cost is very low, requiring only the use of a car and gasoline costs, with volunteers and two city staff members carrying out the ratings (Greater Transparency and Accountability in Governance Program [GTAG], 2005a).

In the town of Yamaranguila, the working group chose to focus on improving the condition of roads. The four grades used were "good condition," "regular condition," "bad," and "worst." Nine people rated each street, and their rankings were averaged. The working group compiled the ratings and presented the results and their proposed action plan to the city council, identifying the streets in the worst condition. The council approved funding for the specific road repairs identified. In this town, funds were used to purchase construction materials and provide tools, and a small lump payment was made to small teams of volunteers (five men and five women) who actually made the repairs (D. Barahona, Regional Coordinator for GTAG Program, personal communication, July 2006; Yamaranguila, 2005).

In the city of Reitoca, the working group rated street conditions, using a team of five raters (city staff and civil society representatives), who each assigned a score to each street in each neighborhood—ranging from 1 ("very good") to 4 ("totally bad"). In Reitoca, as in Yamaranguila, those ratings were then averaged instead of reported directly, yielding a rating for each street.[5] Further averaging the street ratings yielded an average for each neighborhood (see Table 12.4), which, in the city of Reitoca, ranged from 2.4 to 3.1. The neighborhood ratings allowed the city to identify the neighborhoods that most needed improvement, in this case, the neighborhood of Morazan, which received a rating of 3.1. The individual street ratings would allow a more fine-tuned identification of the specific problem areas (GTAG, 2005b).

In Reitoca, the ratings were used for another purpose in addition to improvement of street quality. This was an interesting extension that emerged as part of an effort to promote a smooth transition during the period of local elections. One of the objectives was to have all mayoral candidates and the incumbent develop and sign a pact on certain joint objectives, to be monitored by citizens with the aim of ensuring that municipal

Table 12.4   Collection and Analysis of Information in Urban Areas

N°	Neighborhood	Observers					Average Rating per Neighborhood
		Timoteo	Hernán	Bartolomé	Francisco	AlexSandra	
1	Morazán	3.1	3.1	3.4	2.8	3.0	3.1
2	Monte Fresco	3.2	3.0	2.5	3.0	3.2	3.0
3	Arriba	3.0	3.0	2.5	2.5	3.0	2.8
4	Las Delicias	2.2	2.2	2.0	3.2	2.5	2.4
5	El Centro	3.1	3.2	2.1	2.2	3.0	2.7
6	Abajo	2.8	2.6	2.0	2.5	2.8	2.5
7	Castro Medina	3.3	3.2	2.3	2.7	3.0	2.9
	Individual Average	2.9	2.9	2.4	2.7	2.9	2.7

SOURCE: Adapted from GTAG (2005b, p. 5).

services not be negatively affected during the transition and to support the transfer of necessary information to help the new city council to get established. In Reitoca, the idea was to carry out trained-observer ratings both before the elections and following the transition, to ascertain that services were not declining and that promises during the campaign were met. The ratings in Table 12.4 were carried out before the elections held in late 2005; the second wave of ratings was scheduled to occur within 6 months after the elections (GTAG Program, 2005b).

Lessons Learned

Trained-Observer Ratings Can Be Effective

The experience in these countries supports the notion that trained-observer ratings can be cheaply implemented and produce rapid results even in resource-constrained contexts. In each country reviewed (Albania, Georgia, and Honduras), laypeople were trained in a short period of time to collect relatively consistent data on performance. The cities used the data, and in most cases, there were measurable improvements in service delivery within a year.

How Costly Is It to Institute Trained-Observer Ratings?

Trained-observer ratings appear to be a fairly inexpensive data source, compared to, for example, customer surveys. The cost of training needs to be covered at the outset, but the cost has been relatively modest, as it involves only 1 or 2 days of training and no materials are required. In the cases described in Albania, Georgia, and Honduras, the cost of the trainers themselves was covered by an outside donor. In addition, the experience in Georgia has shown that the volunteers can be responsible for training new recruits to the program.

Operating costs include the time of raters and analysts, a project coordinator, and some small direct costs for supplies and equipment. In all three cases, local governments have been willing to cover the operating costs for the system (see box for the cost of items in the Georgia program).

Costs of Instituting Trained-Observer Ratings: Operating Costs in Georgia

- Transportation and meals for the raters
- Space to work
- Access to computer
- Refreshments for public meetings
- Photocopying 50 sheets per city per quarter

Three types of labor are required to operate the program: raters, analysts, and a project coordinator. When volunteers carry out the ratings, the main labor cost is for project coordination. Typically, the coordinator is needed to assign raters, oversee analysis, help with presentation of findings, invite media or the public to presentations, and prepare needed reports. This is at present the biggest cost item, and in the case of the three countries we have examined, the cost is being borne by an outside institution. In Georgia, especially, there is an ongoing effort to transfer these skills to the volunteers and/or city staff. As it seems likely that some of the coordination tasks will never be suitable for volunteers, this is likely to remain the most significant cost element for the city.

The fact that the process is perceived to be inexpensive by local governments is important, as it provides an incentive for them to begin to use the system; once the cities see how valuable it is, they might be more comfortable taking on some of the costs, including, for instance, the cost of project coordination.

Volunteers Can Be Effective

The cases described make it clear that volunteers can be effective contributors, especially in the data collection aspects of trained-observer ratings. While this has been shown in the United States (see, for example, Kopczynski & Pritchard, 2004; La Vigne & Cowan, 2005), there seems to be no documentation of other instances of volunteer trained observers in developing or transition countries. In Georgia, Albania, and Honduras, volunteers were used to carry out some or all of the ratings, in some cases over a sustained period of several years. In some of the cities, the volunteers also presented the results publicly and played a role in holding local governments accountable. In none of the cases have volunteers been seen to effectively organize the system on their own or fully carry out the analysis of data.

The willingness to participate was in some countries quite remarkable. Where efforts were made, it was possible to locate many willing volunteers, even in countries with no tradition of volunteerism, such as Eastern Europe. It is beyond the scope of this chapter to establish what factors contribute to volunteer willingness, but it is possible that it is an especially attractive prospect in some specific circumstances in which citizens have few opportunities for interaction with government or the community in general and/or employment options.

Benefits of Using Stakeholders as Raters

While low cost may be the driving reason for using volunteers, using local stakeholders as raters also provides specific benefits. The perspective of a stakeholder will always be a little different from the view of a professional. Citizens will look at services from the perspective of a user. (One interesting example in the United States is the use of ex-prisoners rating the accessibility of community assets, such as religious institutions, shops, restaurants, government services, or shelters; La Vigne & Cowan, 2005.)

Volunteers bring fresh eyes and may well notice details that are not foreseen by the rating design and that would go unnoticed by a professional rater. Stakeholders are also likely to look beyond rating conditions to make other observations and may well note causes and possible solutions. This can be either an advantage or a hindrance, depending on the context.

When it is important for ratings to be strictly objective or ratings are likely to be complex, raters need to be fairly narrow in their observations and adhere closely to a predefined rating scale. As noted earlier in the Albanian school condition rating case, there are instances in which raters tend to include their judgments about cost or responsibility in their rating of problems—rather than sticking closely to rating scales—which makes comparisons and interpretation of the scores more difficult.

On the other hand, in a situation in which the rating scale is not complex, services are being rated for the first time, the idea of monitoring outcomes is new, and/or services are very poor, the creativity of citizen-raters may be very useful. For example, insights such as those of raters in Albania regarding the causes of litter and the recommendations that emerged can be extremely useful for a municipal services department that has not looked at the city in this way before. Moreover, the citizen-rater provides an extra measure of credibility: Observations and recommendations that address citizen behavior will be far more palatable to the general public if they stem from the observations of citizens than if they are based on the opinions of city staff.

As Kopczynski and Pritchard (2004) note, the purpose and scope of the evaluation should determine whether the use of volunteers is appropriate. They point out that special studies that are not intended for public use would most likely not be appropriate, while rating efforts that attempt to improve accountability and service delivery would be enhanced by volunteer participation. In the cases reviewed here, the advantages of using volunteers have been precisely in providing motivation for service improvement and strengthening accountability, while the more detailed and sophisticated analyses, such as rating school conditions, would be less appropriate.

Volunteers Benefit From Civic Engagement

Using volunteers has an additional benefit in providing an opportunity for engagement for citizens. This can be especially important in situations where residents have been historically disenfranchised—citizens feel powerless to affect government, while those in authority do not reflect citizen priorities. Kopczynski and Pritchard (2004) describe this effect in inner-city neighborhoods in a project on neighborhood indicators using residents to collect data; the Georgia case described in this chapter reinforces that finding, with the enthusiastic and successful participation of youth volunteers and the way the rating experience served as a catalyst for much broader civic engagement. In Honduras, many civil society representatives spoke appreciatively of the opportunity to work collaboratively with city staff, and the program has resulted in strengthened and durable collaboration between civil society and the municipality.

Cautions on Data Analysis

Despite the evidence that trained-observer ratings can simply, cheaply, and quickly show measurable results and that volunteers can be very valuable in the effort, some caveats must be noted, particularly in the quality of data and analysis. No systematic assessments have been done of these projects, but enough irregularities have been noted to cast some doubt on the quality of the data. For instance, in both Albania and Honduras, there have been instances of (a) combining different raters' scores—often quite different—to form "average" scores for one location and (b) aggregating scores for various streets to establish a score for a neighborhood (GTAG, 2005b). First, the fact that scores diverge substantially suggests that there may not have been sufficient training to reach consensus on the rating levels. Second, calculating averages is not a best practice: Averages obscure the condition of the individual street or collection site and provide less meaningful information.

In a handful of cases, a quality control system has been instituted, such as random checks by supervisors or comparative ratings by professionals, but that is not the norm.

More problems emerge during the analytic phase. Especially with complex tasks, the data analysis is not straightforward, and it has not yet been demonstrated that it can be fully taken over and done at a high level of quality by local governments—with or without volunteers—in these countries. In Albania, the first efforts in school conditions showed that there were many obstacles to carrying out analysis with sufficient accuracy and rigor. The simpler rating scale used in the national standards pilot project shows promise but has not yet been tried on a larger scale and without outside assistance (Mary Winkler, personal communication March 16, 2006).

The problems that emerged in the analysis of school conditions data illustrate the challenge of analysis for any complex set of conditions in a context where city staff are often inadequately trained and may not have access to computers or even be computer literate. The difficulty was compounded by a lack of focus on analysis in the initial training. There was rarely a decision from the outset on what the main purpose of the analysis was—whether it was to prioritize repairs within a school, to identify which school needed most attention, to carry out a systemwide assessment of school conditions, or to inform parents of school conditions. In many cases, the stakeholders expected to use the same data set for different purposes, but each would have required a different analytical approach.

In retrospect, it seems no accident that the most successful of the cases in Albania have been in rating street cleanliness, a relatively simple process of rating individual sites on a scale from "clean" to "dirty." Rating school conditions in all buildings and systems, in contrast, especially with the aim of identifying priorities for action, becomes a much more complex effort, requiring a sophisticated approach to the analysis. These problems suggest that especially in the case of these more complex subjects, the design itself must include from the outset plans to carry out the analysis: a clear statement of the purpose of the analysis, who will be responsible, and how will it be done. This was not the case in most of these instances.

Similarly, the case in Georgia shows that the data collection and presentation have been very successfully taken over by the volunteers working together with the cities but that technical support from outside the city is still needed in data analysis and preparing results for reporting.

The lesson might be summarized this way: In cases where the city is lacking trained staff and/or computers and is using volunteers, recommendations might include the following:

- Clearly identify the purpose of the rating system.
- Keep the rating scale simple.
- Develop the analytical approach early in the process as an integral part of institutionalizing trained-observer ratings.
- Provide specific training in data analysis.

No Evidence Yet on Sustainability

Finally, there is no evidence yet that this approach can be fully sustainable—that is, these efforts will continue after the termination of technical assistance from outside. Many of the cases described in this chapter show promising signs of motivation and results that are likely to lead to institutionalization, but there are not yet enough examples of freestanding trained-observer rating systems to establish whether this is probable. Further work is needed in exploring what elements make sustainability more likely.

Notes

1. This chapter draws on the work of a number of people. The author is principally indebted to Harry Hatry, who pioneered performance management in the United States and was a vital contributor to our international work, and to Ritu Nayyar-Stone and Sharon Cooley, who collaborated on the development and implementation of many of the projects described in this chapter. Philip Schaenman was an early advisor and trainer in introducing trained-observer ratings internationally, offering the first taste of this powerful tool in Georgia, Russia, and Albania. The author also is grateful to those who carried out much of the work described in this paper, including key Urban Research Institute staff (Francis Conway, Mary Kopczynski Winkler, Shelli Rossman) and professionals and counterparts in each of the countries where we have worked, without whom none of this would have been possible. Thanks are due also to Sarah Polen and to an anonymous reviewer for useful comments.

2. Each of these projects was carried out by The Urban Institute, and in all cases, project funding was provided by the Agency for International Development (USAID).

3. The primary sources for information about the work in Albania, in addition to others cited, are Mark (2001), project records, and the author's experience.

4. It is likely that some of these tasks will be more appropriate for local government staff than for volunteers. Kopczynski and Pritchard (2004) stress the importance of a good coordinator: "The field coordinator is perhaps the most critical ingredient in a successful effort to engage volunteers in evaluation activities" (p. 665). It seems likely that this would at least remain a role for a professional to play, in which case it would have to be taken over from the current project by either the city or other professionals to ensure sustainability of the rating system. Moreover, it may be difficult to find volunteers with the skills and consistency to carry out the analytical steps of the process (see the section "Cautions on Data Analysis" for a further discussion of the challenges of data analysis).

5. See the "Lessons Learned" section for further discussion of the practice of averaging ratings.

Discussion Questions

1. Name three important public services in your community that could be rated by trained observers.
   a. For each, give a brief description of what the rating scale might look like.
   b. For each, name all the stakeholders who might be interested in seeing and using the ratings.

2. For one of the services identified in Question 1, describe at least three questions you will want to answer during the analysis of data.

3. For one of the services you named in Question 1, describe the different pressures and/or different incentives raters might feel to raise or decrease their ratings. What steps can be taken to address those biases?

4. What are the advantages and disadvantages of using volunteers as trained observers?

References

Greater Transparency and Accountability in Governance Program. (2005a, August). *Monthly Newsletter,* p. 5.

Greater Transparency and Accountability in Governance Program. (2005b, October–November). *Monthly Newsletter,* pp. 1, 4–5.

Kopczynski, M. E., & Pritchard K. (2004). The use of evaluation by nonprofit organizations. In J. S. Wholey, H. P. Hatry, & K. E. Newcomer (Eds.), *Handbook of practical program evaluation* (pp. 649–669). San Francisco: Jossey-Bass.

La Vigne, N. G., & Cowan, J. (2005, September). *Mapping prisoner reentry: An action research guidebook.* Washington, DC: Urban Institute, Justice Policy Center.

Lezha Municipality. (2005). *Service improvement action plan: Cleaning and garbage collection.* Unpublished report.

Mark, K. (2001, May). *Performance management in Albania: Helping local governments improve services.* Paper presented at South and East Europe Development Conference, Volos, Greece.

Mark, K., & Nayyar-Stone, R. (2004). Early experience with performance management in Hungary, Albania, and Georgia: Assessing its potential for local service improvement. In E. Loffler & M. Vintar (Eds.), *Improving the quality of East and West European public services* (pp. 25–42). London: Ashgate. (Originally presented at the NISPACee Conference, April 2002, Cracow, Poland)

Nayyar-Stone, R., & Bishop, L. (2004). *Georgia customer survey 2004.* Washington, DC: Urban Institute.

Rreshen Municipality. (2005). *Rural and urban road repair and maintenance service improvement action plan.* Unpublished report.

Urban Research Institute. (2004). *Final report: Pilot project in support of the implementation of delegated functions.* Unpublished report.

Yamaranguila Municipality. (2005). *Service improvement action plan for maintenance of the city's principal streets* [PowerPoint presentation]. Unpublished report.

13 Helping Government Measure Up

Models of Citizen-Driven Government Performance Measurement Initiatives

Marc Holzer

Kathryn Kloby

Performance measurement is a management tool for assessing how much and how well public services and products are delivered. It is a versatile tool for decision making and offers a full range of applications. Performance measurement systems, for example, can improve management decision making with indicators that capture efficiency, effectiveness, and/or service quality and results. When integrated into organizational processes such as budgeting and strategic planning, performance measurement can serve as the foundation of a broader management strategy referred to as "performance-based management" or "managing for results" (Walters, Abrahams, & Fountain, 2003; Wholey, 1999).

Overwhelming support for the adoption of this methodology is evident through the workings of professional associations, research institutes, and scholars. Promoting the mechanics and processes for measuring performance, pioneering organizations such as the American Society for Public Administration, the Government Finance Officers Association, the International City/County Management Association, and The Urban Institute are instrumental in providing technical assistance, training, and education to practitioners.

The Urban Institute, the National Center for Public Productivity (NCPP) at Rutgers-Newark, and the Center on Accountability and Performance of the American Society for Public Administration make comprehensive guides to performance measurement available as a means to performance improvement (Hatry, 1999; Liner et al., 2001; NCPP, 2003). Scholarly research emphasizes the purpose, techniques, and utility of performance measurement as a tool for increasing public sector productivity (Behn, 2003; Halachmi, 2002; Hatry, 1999; Holzer & Yang, 2004). More important, these and other supportive organizations and the work of scholars emphasize the importance of including citizens in performance assessment and managerial decision making.

There are two dominant models of performance measurement. In many cases, performance measurement schemes are designed to achieve managerially driven goals. Public managers and department directors, for example, set priorities, determine indicators (usually quantitative), and plan strategies for data collection and reporting (Callahan, 2004). Conversely, citizen-driven models of performance measurement include citizens in determining performance priorities, defining relevant indicators, assessing results, and identifying key information for performance reporting (Callahan, 2004). While the former model can work to achieve improved organizational performance, the latter increases the likelihood of aligning administrative processes and actions with citizen preferences. Research suggests that decision making through the use of performance measurement strategies in local government is predominantly designed in the likeness of the managerially driven model (Poister & Streib, 1999). A critical shortcoming of this approach is that managers are likely to assume that citizens underestimate the work of government or they are not fully aware of what matters to citizens, how citizens define service quality, or how citizens rate the performance of government overall (Cohn-Berman, 2005; Melkers & Thomas, 1998).

In this chapter, we highlight some successful examples of measuring public sector performance, as they may prove helpful for those in search of best practices. We present the challenges of performance measurement implementation, emphasizing the obstacles associated with including citizens in the process. In particular, we highlight the current state of practice of U.S. local governments of including citizens in decision making, and performance measurement and assessment. We provide some examples of other institutions that work outside of government to assist managers and elected officials with determining citizen satisfaction, preferences, and service quality. Successful programs funded by the Alfred P. Sloan Foundation demonstrate a sustained record of helping government measure what matters to citizens, with useful examples and strategies that others can adopt to foster more cooperative interactions between citizens and their governments. In addition to showcasing their efforts, we present some of the key challenges and characteristics of these organizations as they continue their work as advocates for citizen involvement in governance.

Implementation and Challenges

A number of award-winning jurisdictions have emerged in the United States as leading public sector models, with performance measurement systems that improve fiscal decision making, build transparency, and increase accountability among managers and employees. Fairfax County, Virginia, for example, has established its performance measurement system as a tool for assessing service quality, promoting strategic thinking, and fostering improved programmatic and fiscal decisions among county officials and the public (McGuire & Kloby, 2006). Offering an interactive Web site, the city of Austin, Texas, presents performance information across city programs and services to citizens via its *e*-Performance Measures initiative.[1] CitiStat, in Baltimore, Maryland, is a citywide program designed to promote performance measurement across all municipal functions, to promote cost savings, increase revenues, and improve the quality of municipal services.[2]

Other exemplary cases include a more active role for citizens in the assessment of government performance. The Oregon Progress Board, for example, is an independent state planning and oversight agency that is responsible for monitoring the state's 20-year strategic vision, Oregon Shines.[3] The board includes citizen leaders who reflect the state's social, ethnic, and political diversity. Together, they measure progress toward nearly 100 social, economic, and environmental indicators, including K–12 student achievement, per capita income, air quality, crime rates, employment, and infant health.[4]

While the examples highlighted above demonstrate successful models of public sector performance measurement, the roadblocks to achieving this status are numerous (Behn, 2002; de Lancer Julnes & Holzer, 2001). Research suggests that local governments are struggling with designing and implementing sophisticated systems for measuring performance (Berman & Wang, 2000; Poister & Streib, 1999), and there is growing evidence that including citizens in the process presents significant challenges and is less frequently practiced. Among U.S. cities with populations of more than 50,000, for example, Poister and Streib (1999) find that while a majority of the assessed municipalities track performance over time and in relation to missions, goals, and objectives, a majority of respondents report a high degree of difficulty with gauging the quality of services provided. Overall, few jurisdictions report citizen involvement as a method for adding value or social relevance to performance indicators. Not surprisingly, findings suggest that local governments rely primarily on traditional participation mechanisms, such as public hearings and citizen advisory boards (Yang & Callahan, 2005). While some jurisdictions use neighborhood meetings and issue-oriented committees, few conduct citizen surveys and focus groups. Other research demonstrates that there are even fewer cases of including citizens in performance measurement initiatives (Wang, 2001).

There are a number of explanations for the shortcomings of achieving more substantive interactions between citizens and their governments. Citizen inclusion in the processes of government, for example, often clashes with the specialized, routine-oriented, and hierarchical attributes of public organizations (Callahan, 2004; Timney, 1998). Meaningful exchanges with citizens require managers to balance day-to-day operations with mechanisms and strategies that foster interaction (King, Feltey, & Susel, 1998; Roberts, 1997). Managers themselves need the training necessary to effectively survey and engage citizens, collect data, and translate findings into meaningful statements to support informed deliberation (Gibson, Lacy, & Dougherty, 2005; King et al., 1998). In many cases, equipping employees with the skills necessary to support citizen participation is costly (Irvin & Stansbury, 2004; Roberts, 1997; Weeks, 2000).

Adding to these challenges, research from the Kettering Foundation, the Council on Democratic Excellence, and the Panel on Civic Trust and Responsibility (Volcker et al., 1999) indicates that citizens overall feel distant and apathetic toward government. Declining trust and increasing cynicism have led to interactions that are often confrontational rather than collaborative. Citizen participation is, therefore, reduced to voting or organizing around hot-button issues, such as eminent domain or affordable housing, rather than engaging in deliberative interactions (Berman, 1997; Callahan, 2004; King, 2002).

Responding to the limited occurrences of citizen involvement in public sector decision making, Yang and Callahan (2005) suggest that some other institutions or mechanisms need to be designed to align administrative policies with citizen preferences. They argue that without added external pressure from citizens for better performance and accountability, it is likely that public managers will continue to use performance measurement to comply with performance reporting requirements and go through the citizen involvement motions with traditional participation mechanisms (e.g., public hearings and citizen advisory boards). Answering this call, our task for this chapter is to present successful initiatives that work to create inlets for citizen involvement in performance measurement. Our aim is to describe how these efforts are conducted to show government how citizens perceive and rate service quality, help government assess citizen satisfaction through citizen surveys and other reports, and show government what measures of performance matter to the public.

Models of Citizen-Driven Government Performance Initiatives

Offering excellent examples and strategies for including citizens in government performance improvement, the Alfred P. Sloan Foundation supports projects that are geared toward connecting citizens to the assessment of government performance. The Sloan Foundation's Performance Assessment of Municipal Governments program is designed to encourage objective measurement efforts in municipal governments that document outcomes that matter to ordinary people. The performance assessment projects supported by this program demonstrate a range of techniques to include citizens in many aspects of government performance assessment. Sloan Foundation projects, for example, stimulate demand for citizen-based performance assessment, sustain collaboration between local governments and citizens, and encourage widespread adoption of citizen-driven initiatives across jurisdictions.

The Sloan-related projects, as a whole, are significantly advanced approaches to promoting citizen involvement so as to ensure that what is measured and reported is socially relevant and matters to citizens. We highlight a few Sloan-funded initiatives that have found inlets to work with local government so as to add value to existing performance measurement efforts through citizen input. More important, these projects fill the citizen involvement void in public sector performance measurement. Developing measurement frameworks to survey citizen satisfaction and service quality and training citizens to serve as data collectors and performance monitors, these programs work to align administrative policies with citizen preferences. For more information on other projects that are not included in this discussion, visit the Sloan Foundation Web site: http://www.sloan.org.

Fund for the City of New York

The Fund for the City of New York works to enhance the quality of life of New Yorkers by helping to improve the performance of their government (see http://www.fcny.org). Through its Center on Municipal Government Performance (CMGP), a number of activities are undertaken to

- determine how citizens assess the performance of government,
- identify what services matter to citizens,
- suggest new performance measurement indicators to government from the public's perspective, and
- work with local government across the United States to achieve graphical excellence when reporting results to citizens.

CMGP leaders operate from the notion that "when municipal governments do not hear or understand the ways in which their constituencies evaluate their performance, a 'disconnect' ensues: government is evaluating its effectiveness using one set of criteria; the public may be applying quite another" (Cohn-Berman, 2005, p. 6). As a way of aligning the criteria of effectiveness between the perspectives of government and the public, CMGP periodically conducts focus groups to identify how New Yorkers rate government performance. As a result, CMGP suggests measurement strategies for New York and other city governments to strengthen the link between government and citizen perspectives (Cohn-Berman, 2005). Key among their findings and experiences is that people generally understand the complexities of the provision of government services and have realistic expectations of what government can and cannot do. Personal experiences and interactions with government employees significantly shape how individuals judge an agency. Observable neighborhood conditions, such as street smoothness, litter, graffiti, and overall visual appearance factors are key indicators by which people assess how well government provides services. Overall, people want and need information from government but often feel powerless to improve the delivery of services.

Acknowledging the opinions of New Yorkers, a key accomplishment of CMGP is the development of its Computerized Neighborhood Environment Tracking, or ComNET. Informed by citizen survey results, this service offers a measurement framework with indicators for neighborhood conditions and user-friendly, handheld technology to help citizens and community groups record conditions, generate reports, and track progress toward improvements. Reports are produced electronically for government agencies and other organizations that are responsible for rubbish collection, traffic and streetlight maintenance, tree planting, graffiti and abandoned car removal, rodent control, and/or pothole repair. The citizen-generated ComNET reports are intended to help government in meeting the expectations of everyday people, as the results are distributed to the appropriate government agencies.

Implementing ComNET

CMGP serves as a guide for the ComNET process, providing technical training and assistance and guides for neighborhood environment indicators. Listed below are the major components of implementation.

Consulting With the Community

- Community members confirm and/or add to CMGP's suggested core list of street-level conditions that they want to track. CMGP, for example, provides a menu of indicators, such as overflowing wastebaskets, graffiti, potholes, broken streetlights, rodent infestation, and/or dead trees. Each of these observable street-level conditions is considered by citizens to be indicators of government performance (or lack thereof).

Training

- CMGP staff hosts an orientation to train community representatives on the use of handheld computers and the principles of ComNET.

Data Collection Teams

- Teams of at least two people work systematically along a predetermined route to assess an area identified by the community group.

- Street-level environmental conditions are recorded in a uniform, verifiable, and replicable manner on handheld computers. CMGP provides technical assistance.

- Providing concrete evidence of street and neighborhood conditions, a camera is connected to the handheld computer, enabling the survey team to link the record with a picture.

Data Upload and Reports

- Data collected in the handheld computers are loaded into desktop computers. This easy-to-use database hosted by CMGP allows ComNET users to upload survey data via the Internet and quickly design and generate reports from their surveys. Reports are reviewed and discussed by the community to determine priorities and desirable next steps.

Notifying Government Agencies or Other Responsible Organizations

- Reports are referred to the appropriate government agencies or other responsible organizations at the community's discretion.

Following Up and Conducting New Surveys

- Community representatives perform follow-up assessments to track agency responses and to identify any new problems.

As a result of their experience with ComNET, CMGP leaders hold that success hinges on sustaining long-term community interest and that the process requires systematic data collection and follow-up and persistence in providing reports to key government agencies (see http://www.fcny.org/cmgp/foryou.htm). Regardless of the level of commitment required for implementation, ComNET has been operating in more than 36 neighborhoods and localities in New York City and has been adopted by jurisdictions throughout the United States (e.g., the cities of Des Moines, Philadelphia, San Francisco, Seattle, and Worcester).

Worcester Regional Research Bureau (WRRB), Worcester, Massachusetts

The Worcester Regional Research Bureau (WRRB) is dedicated to conducting independent, nonpartisan research on financial, administrative, management, and community issues that challenge Worcester's municipal government and the region. The WRRB organizes its activities to

- prepare and disseminate research reports on municipal performance and issues of interest (e.g., economic development, public education, municipal and neighborhood services, and public safety),

- sponsor public forums on matters that impact the Worcester region (e.g., housing market trends and affordability, and office residential occupancy in the Worcester central business district, and capital projects), and
- educate the public about short- and long-term issues that will impact the region (e.g., immigration trends and changing demographics).

Overall, the goal of the WRRB is to suggest resolutions that contribute to greater government efficiency, responsibility, and accountability. Serving the community for more than 20 years, the WRRB has established a track record as its leaders and researchers have prepared more than 100 reports and sponsored hundreds of forums that address a wide range of topics.

There are a number of useful resources available on the WRRB Web site. Reports, for example, offer ideas for measurement indicators, graphical display of quantitative information, and the value of narrative to explain changes in performance and other patterns. Activities of the WRRB Center for Community Performance Measurement (CCPM) offer useful models for collaboration with citizens. CCPM staff and citizens, for example, bench-mark municipal and community performance in five areas of the city of Worcester's strategic plan: economic development, public education, munici-pal and neighborhood services, public safety, and youth services. CCPM pub-lishes annual reports for each of the five areas, with data and information that can be used by citizens, government officials, community leaders, and neigh-borhood organizations to improve Worcester. The reports are framed with key questions that help government leaders and citizens interpret results: Why is this important? How does Worcester perform? What does this mean for Worcester? These questions are addressed with narratives and easy-to-inter-pret charts and graphics. Figure 13.1 features a chart taken from the "WRRB Citizen Satisfaction With Municipal Services" report of 2004.

Reports show results graphically, in the context of neighborhoods in Worcester. Figure 13.2, for example, presents citywide citizen satisfaction with snow removal and satisfaction by neighborhood for the current year (2004) and previous years (2002 and 2003). Disaggregated and presented by neighborhood, citizens and government officials can see how neighbor-hood assessments differ in comparison to each other and to the citywide level of satisfaction. Furthermore, change in satisfaction by neighborhood can be viewed over time.

Adopting the ComNET program developed by the Fund for the City of New York (as highlighted above), WRRB researchers and citizens use hand-held computers to track neighborhood conditions, generate reports, and pre-sent results to responsible government agencies or programs. Field researchers of WRRB train local college students, volunteers, and neighborhood associa-tion members and identify problem areas and indicators for data collection. Figure 13.3 depicts the geographical boundaries of the Union Hill neighbor-hood.[5] Field observers are assigned to specific quadrants within a given neigh-borhood to ensure systematic and comprehensive data collection.

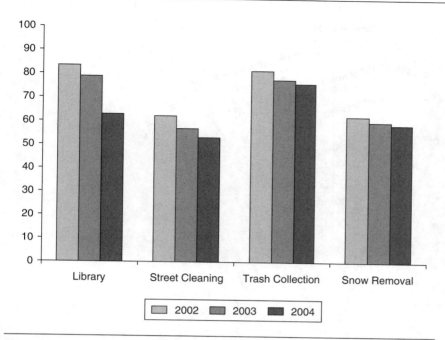

Figure 13.1   Citizen Satisfaction With Municipal Services, 2002–2004

SOURCE: Reprinted with permission of The Worcester Regional Research Bureau, Worcester, MA.

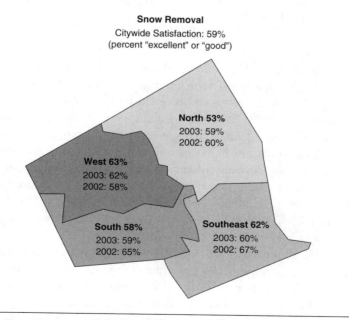

Figure 13.2   Citizen Satisfaction With Municipal Services, 2002–2003

SOURCE: Reprinted with permission of The Worcester Regional Research Bureau, Worcester, MA.

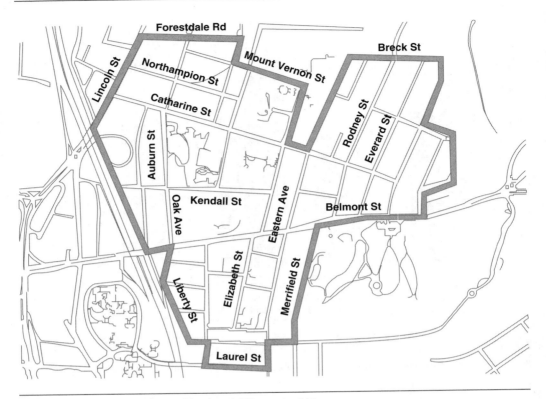

Figure 13.3   Union Hill Neighborhood, Worcester, MA

SOURCE: ComNET: "Union Hill Neighborhood Results," a report prepared for the Union Hill Neighborhood Group. Available upon request via http://www.wrrb.org.

As shown in Table 13.1, the condition of sidewalks, buildings, lamp-posts, number of abandoned vehicles, and conditions of public telephones are among some of the elements recorded by field observers. This survey was conducted in 2002, followed by a resurvey in 2003, allowing neighborhood association members and government officials alike to assess the extent to which conditions had been improved and identify areas of neglect. Table 13.1 columns showing resolution rates and net change from 2002 to 2003, for example, show that there had been significant improvements in areas such as litter, buildings, and vehicles. The removal of 20 abandoned vehicles from 2002 to 2003 and a net change of 71% shows this condition as having the greatest level of improvement.

Table 13.2 summarizes the conditions that have been and need to be addressed by the responsible government agency and the community. Performance reports are provided for the conditions that fall under the auspices of public works, code enforcement, the parks department, and other government agencies. These can certainly serve as useful tools for department directors and city management as they show the level of responsiveness by department and areas in need of improvement.

Table 13.1 Union Hill Neighborhood Conditions, Resolutions, and Net Change, 2002–2003

Category of condition	2002 Number of conditions to be addressed	2003 Number of conditions to be addressed	% of conditions recorded in 2002 still present	Resolution rate	Net change in number of conditions, 2002–2003
Sidewalk (cracked, trip hazard, encroachment, dirt/sand, etc.)	199	207	71.9%	28.1%	+8 / 4.0%
Litter (on streets, sidewalks, yellow bags, on lawns, etc.)	156	122	57.7%	42.3%	−34 / −21.8%
Building (paint peeling, steps/walkways broken, under construction, vacant, walls/fences boarded, etc.)	104	74	57.7%	42.3%	−30 / −28.8%
Street (potholes, uneven, etc.)	39	52	74.4%	25.6%	+13 / 33.3%
Private Vegetation	30	26	63.3%	36.7%	−4 / −13.3%
Catchbasin (broken, clogged, odors, ponding, etc.)	11	18	45.5%	54.5%	+7 / 63.6%
Utility Covers (missing, not level with sidewalk or street, etc.)	18	15	83.3%	16.7%	−3 / −16.7%
Curb (broken, curb cut, missing, not level, etc.)	14	10	64.3%	35.7%	−4 / −28.6%
Vehicles (abandoned, etc.)	28	8	10.7%	89.3%	−20 / −71.4%

(Continued)

Table 13.1 (Continued)

Category of condition	2002 Number of conditions to be addressed	2003 Number of conditions to be addressed	2003 % of conditions recorded in 2002 still present	Resolution rate	Net change in number of conditions, 2002–2003
Street Signs	6	6	83.3%	16.7%	0	0.0%
Lampposts (bills posted, missing baseplate, etc.)	15	6	13.3%	86.7%	−9	−60.0%
Crosswalk (missing, faded, etc.)	5	3	60.0%	40.0%	−2	−40.0%
Animals (wandering)	1	2	0.0%	100.0%	+1	100.0%
Public Telephone (glass broken, missing, etc.)	3	2	66.7%	33.3%	−1	−33.3%
Park Vegetation	3	2	66.7%	33.3%	−1	−33.3%
Dumpster	0	1	–	–	+1	–
Fire Hydrant	0	1	–	–	+1	–
Other	18	10	44.4%	55.6%	−8	−44.4%
TOTAL	650	565	60.8%	39.2%	−85	−13.1%

SOURCE: ComNET: "Union Hill Neighborhood Results," a report prepared for the Union Hill Neighborhood Group. Available upon request via http://www.wrrb.org

268

Table 13.2 Union Hill Results by Responsibility, 2002–2003

Responsibility	2002 Number of conditions to be addressed	2003 Number of conditions to be addressed	2003 % of conditions recorded in 2002 still present	Resolution rate	Net change in number of conditions, 2002–2003	
Department of Public Works	384	396	69.8%	30.2%	+12	3.1%
Community	182	128	56.0%	44.0%	−54	−29.7%
Parks Department	28	16	53.6%	46.4%	−12	−42.9%
Code Enforcement	30	12	16.7%	83.3%	−18	−60.0%
Graffiti Cleanup Program	12	8	25.0%	75.0%	−4	−33.3%
Police Department	4	2	25.0%	75.0%	−2	−50.0%
Fire Department	0	1	–	–	+1	–
Massachusetts Electric	8	1	0.0%	100.0%	−7	87.5%
Verizon	2	1	50.0%	50.0%	−1	−50.0%
TOTAL	650	565	60.8%	39.2%	−85	−13.1%

SOURCE: ComNET: "Union Hill Neighborhood Results," a report prepared for the Union Hill Neighborhood Group. Available upon request via http://www.wrb.org

Including community responsibilities is an important element of this research and the broader efforts of the WRRB. As areas in need of improvement are clarified through survey results of neighborhood conditions, citizens also expand their roles as active members of governance. Rather than government bearing the burden of public service provisions and neighborhood maintenance, citizens play an active role in increasing the awareness of issues that government agencies need to address, as well as articulating what aspects of government performance are important to citizens.

These and other efforts have established the WRRB as a neutral, competent, and credible source of information. New partnerships have been proposed and formed between the bureau and the Worcester city government, with funding possibilities for technical assistance activities and other projects to improve data collection and performance reporting. The WRRB, however, has exercised caution when entering into such partnerships for fear of tainting its value-free and advocacy stance in the broader community (see WRRB Web site: http://www.wrrb.org).

Straphangers Campaign, New York City

The Straphangers Campaign in New York City represents a bold attempt to influence the accountability, accessibility, and performance of local government on behalf of its citizens. Through the New York Public Interest Research Group (NYPIRG), the Straphangers Campaign received a grant from the Alfred P. Sloan Foundation in 1996 to launch a new in-depth effort to measure the quality of the transit service. The goal was to accurately report on the condition of the city's transit system and to draw media, public, and governmental attention to the need to continue to invest in transit.

Working to hold the transit authority accountable through a sophisticated range of measures and mechanisms to communicate that information to the public, the Straphangers Campaign assessed how riders rated their subway lines. The Straphangers Campaign also collected data from transit officials, and all data were presented in a clear and accessible format. A panel of 38 transit experts also completed questionnaires by prioritizing certain aspects of the subway and bus service. This information was compiled for use in two sets of reports: one based on a review of official transit statistics and the other based on NYPIRG's own field studies. Figure 13.4, for example, shows how Metropolitan Transit Authority (MTA) data match up to comparable assessments conducted by the Straphangers Campaign.

The first report under this Sloan project was released in 1997, profiling New York City's 20 major subway lines on six key official measures of service, including the amount of scheduled service, the chance of getting a seat during the most congested periods, the cleanliness of the cars, and the adequacy of the announcements. Another 21-page report highlighted the state of the bus system. These two sets of reports represented the most comprehensive review by any nongovernmental organization of the performance of

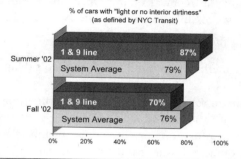

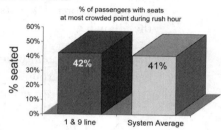

Figure 13.4   Straphangers Campaign Subway Line Profile
SOURCE: Reprinted with permission.

a major public transportation system. They achieved two goals. First, they provided a solid baseline for comparing subway service in the future. Second, they gave riders, communities, and officials information they would need to press the transit authority for better service.

The data collection and reporting of public transportation conditions are ongoing. Reports of subway car cleanliness, subway announcements, location and condition of payphones, and timeliness of buses and trains are available, with trend data showing significant improvements, declines in service quality or cleanliness, as well as little or no change. The Straphangers Campaign also offers information for citizens to take action upon and file complaints or compliments. Reports, maps, and other resources are available on the Straphangers Web site (http://www.straphangers.org).

Neighborhood Parks Council, San Francisco, California

The Neighborhood Parks Council (NPC) advocates for a superior, equitable, and sustainable park and recreation system in the city of San Francisco, California. NPC provides leadership and support to park users through community-driven stewardship, education, planning, and research. It is a coalition of more than 120 community-based park groups and 4,000 park volunteers that work actively together to improve neighborhood parks throughout San Francisco. More important, NPC works to develop collaborative relationships between the community and various departments in the

San Francisco government, such as the Controller's City Services Auditor, the Department of Public Works, and the Recreation and Park Department. As a result of Proposition C (2003) and the city's broad-based effort to expand performance measurement, auditing, and reporting on city services to citizens, for example, NPC contributed to the development of standards of park maintenance and provided city agencies with useful, accurate information about park conditions and community priorities. NPC efforts also resulted in a March 2000 ballot that secured a $110 million bond for upgrading neighborhood parks and the renewal of the Open Space Fund for an additional 30 years. Other successful programs of the NPC include the following:

- *The Playground Campaign:* An effort to rebuild San Francisco's dilapidated playgrounds
- *The Blue Greenway:* An effort to rebuild walking trails that run along the scenic southeastern shore of San Francisco
- *Nature in the City:* Educational programs for community members to learn about a number of environmental issues from renowned naturalists
- *District Park Planning:* A series of meetings that bring city leaders and the community together to foster a shared vision for clean, safe, beautiful parks and quality recreation programs

Similar to the efforts of the Fund for the City of New York and the WRRB, NPC's ParkScan project employs handheld technology to track park conditions as field observers document park conditions for resolution in a timely manner by the responsible divisions in government. As a result of including citizens in the assessment of park conditions, NPC worked to include citizen perceptions and expectations of park maintenance as they collaborated with government officials to design the park standards as mandated through Proposition C of 2003.

Coordinated by the Controller's Office, the park maintenance standards were designed as a result of frequent meetings among city officials and staff and community groups, several focus groups of park section supervisors, and other assessments. The final product of this collaboration is the "San Francisco Park Maintenance Standards: The Manual and Evaluation Form" (San Francisco Recreation and Park Department, 2005). This document presents measurement frameworks for park maintenance, with evaluation instruments for field observation and photographs to assist observers as they determine whether a site meets performance standards. For example, Table 13.3 shows the measurable elements for assessing the condition of children's play areas, with a description of what observers should consider when examining a play area. Figure 13.5 provides an additional visual reference of a play area that meets the specified maintenance standards compared with another play area that falls short of expectations. These evaluation tools and visual aids are available for landscaped and hardscaped areas, recreational areas, amenities, and structures.

Table 13.3   Evaluation Form for Children's Play Areas

No.	Measured element	Standard description with unit of measure (if applicable)	Please indicate No. of children's play area. (Use map if available.) #__ #__ #__ Meet standard? Yes/No/NA		
8.1	Cleanliness	Children's play area is free of litter, debris, and weeds. Sandbox is free of all foreign debris. The rubber surface in children's play areas is free of playground sand, where applicable. NOTES: At all parks, the standard is met if no more than 10 pieces of litter or debris, lightly scattered, are visible in a 25' by 25' area or along a 100' line. Examples of litter include cigarette butts, tissue paper, food wrappings, newspapers, and larger items like abandoned appliances. Examples of debris include limbs, rocks, and any other item that impedes use of a play area. Leaves are excluded. The standard is *not* met if needles, condoms, broken glass, and/or feces are present. Smoking is prohibited in children's play areas. Hardscaped areas adjacent to children's play areas are evaluated under hardscapes and trails.			
8.2	Fencing	Where applicable, fencing is functional, free of protrusions, and free of holes/passages along the base.			
8.3	Functionality of equipment	At least 80% of intended play equipment is present and functional. Note: Occasionally the City may find it necessary to permanently remove pieces of play equipment.			
8.4	Graffiti	Play area and its equipment are free of graffiti. Note: If graffiti is observed, it has to be reported to the department to be abated within 48 hours.			

(Continued)

273

Table 13.3 (Continued)

No.	Measured element	Standard description with unit of measure *(if applicable)*		Please indicate No. of children's play area. (Use map if available.)			
				#___	#___	#___	#___
				Meet standard? Yes/No/NA			
8.5	Integrity of equipment	80% of play equipment is free of deterioration, such as rust, rot, splinters, dents, and 100% is free of sharp edges and protrusions. 100% of attachments (e.g., bolts and screws) are secure.					
8.6	Painting	Painted structures are free of peeling or chipped paint.					
8.7	Signage	Signs are legible, free of graffiti, and properly installed in visible locations. Note: Existence, language, and purpose of signage are not assessed.					
8.8	Surface quality	8.8.a If applicable, sand is loose (not compacted) and the level is at least 12 inches in depth.	8.8.a				
		8.8.b If applicable, 100% of rubber surface around playground equipment is present and adjacent rubber surfaces do not exceed ¼ inch (0.25″) of vertical elevation difference.	8.8.b				

SOURCE: City of San Francisco Controller's Office, City Services. Reprinted with permission.

Pass   **Fail**

Figure 13.5   Visual Reference for Reviewers of Children's Play Areas
SOURCE: City of San Francisco Controller's Office, City Services. Reprinted with permission.

Citizen-Initiated Performance Assessment, Iowa

An initiative of the Alfred P. Sloan Foundation in 2001, the Citizen-Initiated Performance Assessment (CIPA) project worked to create a process that actively involves citizens in designing and implementing performance measurement systems in selected Iowa cities. CIPA was guided by the notion that citizen involvement in the performance measurement process creates opportunities for citizens to shape and improve city decision making. The architects of CIPA set out to facilitate and support a process that would lend political credibility, increase accountability of elected and nonelected officials, and empower citizens in the design and execution of performance measurement.

Elected officials, managers, staff, and citizen representatives of nine Iowa cities with a population of 10,000 or more participated in implementing the CIPA project. Project goals included assisting cities in establishing a sustainable process that engages citizen representatives, city council members, and departmental staff. Mechanisms to support citizen input in the design and usage of performance measurement, including the establishment of city performance teams, facilitation of public meetings, and the usage of information and communication technologies, have been developed to empower and involve citizens in the decision-making process.

The CIPA project has reached the final stages of implementation. Whether project efforts will be sustained in participating cities remains to be determined.

Funding, continued participation, adoption of the model, and a number of other factors will impact the longevity and contributions of CIPA (Holzer & Kloby, 2005). The continued CIPA efforts of the city of Des Moines can be seen via the project Web site: http://www.ci.des-moines.ia.us/performance/CIPA.htm.

Key Challenges and Characteristics of Citizen-Driven Endeavors

In addition to some of the obstacles of engaging and including citizens in the assessment of government noted above, our analysis of the Sloan-funded projects highlights some critical issues and questions with regard to sustainability: Is there, or can there be, cooperation between citizen groups, nonprofit organizations, and government in pursuit of information exchange, transparency, and effective assessment of government performance by citizens? Marketability and interest in program efforts, for example, is a perennial and vital factor for many organizations in need of multiple funding streams to sustain programs and projects. Furthermore, partnerships where like-minded organizations team up to enhance organizational breadth and scope offer opportunities for prolonging program objectives and potentially increasing revenue.

As a result of interviewing and conversations with key leaders of the projects, highlighted above, we have identified four factors that Sloan-funded initiatives grapple with as they work to sustain their efforts.

Cooperation From Public Partners

Will government agencies willingly make the data available that independent "watchdog" or "advocacy" projects need? That is a question of full and willing transparency, without the necessity of legal action to wrench free the essential data. In the case of the Straphangers Campaign, for example, the New York City MTA has not always been forthcoming with data. Indeed, there has often been only grudging cooperation with a campaign that attracts widespread press attention with its ratings of subway and bus lines—none of which are labeled as worth the full price of the subway or bus fare. If the bureaucracy, then, holds the "data cards," what incentive is there to make that information available to its critics?

Integrity

Beyond cooperation, should government fund its critics, even if such criticism is helpful to the performance of public programs? Many performance measurement programs, especially those of a citizen-driven nature, have been supported by foundations, large and small. If that funding does not continue indefinitely (and, by its nature, foundation funding is seldom intended for permanent operating costs), is the only other alternative financial support from the legislature/city council or the bureaucracy? The concern with "corrupt" or self-serving tendencies by officeholders necessarily implies independence, and independence requires both financial means and a commitment to integrity.

As highlighted above, the WRRB, for one, is loath to accept any such support for fear of tainting its well-deserved reputation for objective analysis. Throughout its 20-year history, the bureau has established itself as a neutral and competent source of data intended to include citizens in tracking neighborhood conditions. It has gained a reputation as a highly credible source for research documenting local conditions, a reputation that has expanded to researching economic conditions and quality of services provided by public institutions. Yet the WRRB's reputation hinges on its independence—something that is increasingly hard to maintain as funding opportunities are narrowing. Likewise, local government officials are interested in working with the bureau to develop an integrated system of performance measurement. In this case, a dilemma emerges as funding needs and integrity are in the balance.

Marketability

Are the services provided to citizens by the Sloan-funded projects "saleable" to those same citizens? As a free good, they attract some attention and generate continuing interest. A common marketing argument, however, is that citizens/customers/clients place a greater value on services that they must pay for, no matter what the charge. Yet nonprofits have little experience with marketing such products, and even intensive marketing may not produce "profitable," and therefore sustainable, organizations. More important, such organizations are finding that diversification of revenue streams helps to prolong the life of programs and projects.

Partnerships and Networking

Do the citizen-driven projects we are describing offer the possibility of win-win partnerships that will help ensure continued stability and operation? On this dimension, the response might be more optimistic. For example, a partnership between the Fund for the City of New York and the WRRB has resulted in successful replication of ComNET. In the case of Worcester, ComNET results have shown city management that research from organizations outside of government can yield helpful results, thus resulting in subsequent collaborations and cooperation between the WRRB and various city departments. ParkScan served as a resource to the City of San Francisco's Comptrollers Office as it worked to design meaningful measures of park maintenance and information technology systems to support citizen data input and performance tracking.

Conclusion

The examples highlighted in this chapter suggest that institutions or mechanisms outside of government can be designed to align administrative policies with citizen preferences. Our aim was to provide useful tools and resources for public and nonprofit managers, as well as community organizers and advocates interested in helping government measure up to the expectations of ordinary people.

On a broader level, we highlight these cases as signs of transformation in public sector performance measurement and reporting. Overall, it is clear that the state of the art of citizen-driven performance measurement is far ahead of actual practice. The models exist, but the number of cases of sustained implementation is surprisingly low. How, then, might implementation be fostered? Dissemination of innovative practices and examples of beneficial cooperation between government and nongovernmental organizations can certainly help. We suspect that there is also demand for networking and exchanges between organizations that have track records of successful citizen-driven efforts and those in search of working examples of collaborative techniques and strategies. However, getting everyone to the table, including nonprofit leaders, members of community groups, citizens, and government officials, to determine how all parties can help government measure up to a diverse set of expectations is a primary and persistent obstacle.

Notes

1. For more information on the city of Austin, Texas, and its *e*-Performance Measures: http://www.ci.austin.tx.us/budget/eperf/index.cfm

2. For more information on CitiStat: http://www.ci.baltimore.md.us/news/citistat

3. The Oregon Progress Board: http://www.oregon.gov/DAS/OPB/index.shtml Accessed: 11/22/05.

4. "Informing Our Nation: Improving How to Understand and Assess the USA's Position and Progress" is a report by the U.S. Government Accountability Office (GAO-05-01, November 2004) that offers a description of how performance measurement can be used to identify comprehensive indicators to describe economic, social, and environmental conditions, with continued benchmarking and progress reporting. In addition, the report offers a useful discussion of the evolution of the Oregon Progress Board and the challenges associated with sustainability. Other innovative programs, such as the Baltimore Indicators Project, are highlighted. The report is available in PDF format through the GAO Web site: http://www.gao.gov/index.html

5. ComNET: "Union Hill Neighborhood Results," a report prepared for the Union Hill Neighborhood Group, Available upon request via http://www.wrrb.org

Discussion Questions

1. What are the anticipated outcomes of creating an overlap between citizen expectations of government and management processes and decisions? What are the challenges associated with this approach?

2. Can groups and organizations outside of government play a vital role as catalysts for citizen-driven government performance measurement? What do you think is needed to establish and maintain a positive (rather than adversarial) relationship between government and organizations promoting this approach to measuring performance?

3. In addition to the efforts highlighted in this chapter, what other organizations work to include citizens in the measurement and assessment of government?

References

Behn, R. D. (2002). The psychological barriers to performance management: Or, why isn't everybody jumping on the performance measurement bandwagon? *Public Performance & Management Review, 26,* 5–25.

Behn, R. D. (2003). Why measure performance? Different purposes require different measures. *Public Administration Review, 63,* 586–606.

Berman, E. (1997). Dealing with cynical citizens. *Public Administration Review, 57,* 105–112.

Berman, E., & Wang, X. (2000). Performance measurement in U.S. counties: Capacity for reform. *Public Administration Review, 60,* 409–420.

Callahan, K. (2004). Performance measurement and citizen participation. In M. Holzer & S. Lee (Eds.), *Public productivity handbook* (2nd ed., pp. 31–42). New York: Marcel Dekker.

Cohn-Berman, B. (2005). *Listening to the public: Adding the voices of the people to government performance measurement and reporting.* New York: Fund for the City of New York.

de Lancer Julnes, P., & Holzer, M. (2001). Promoting the utilization of performance measures in public organizations: An empirical study of factors affecting adoption and implementation. *Public Administration Review, 61,* 693–705.

Gibson, P. D., Lacy, D. P., & Dougherty, M. J. (2005). Improving performance and accountability in local government with citizen participation. *Innovation Journal: The Public Sector Innovation Journal, 10*(1). Retrieved March 5, 2006, from http://www.innovation.cc/volumes-issues/gibson1.pdf

Halachmi, A. (2002). Performance measurement and government productivity. *Work Study, 51,* 63–73.

Hatry, H. P. (1999). *Performance measurement: Getting results.* Washington, DC: Urban Institute.

Holzer, M., & Kloby, K. (2005). Sustaining citizen-driven performance improvement: Models for adoption and issues of sustainability. *Innovation Journal: The*

Public Sector Innovation Journal, 10(1). Retrieved February 2, 2006, from http://www.innovation.cc/volumes-issues/holzer-kloby.pdf

Holzer, M., & Yang, K. (2004). Performance measurement and improvement: An assessment of the state of the art. *International Review of Administrative Sciences, 70,* 15–31.

Irvin, R., & Stansbury, J. (2004). Citizen participation in decision making: Is it worth the effort? *Public Administration Review, 64,* 55–65.

King, C. S. (2002). Is performance oriented government democratic? In K. Newcomer, E. T. Jennings Jr., C. Broom, & A. Lomax (Eds.), *Meeting the challenges of performance-oriented government* (pp. 161–176). Washington, DC: American Society for Public Administration.

King, C. S., Feltey, K. M., & Susel, B. O. (1998). The question of participation: Toward authentic public participation in public administration. *Public Administration Review, 58,* 317–327.

Liner, B., Harry, H. P., Vinson, E., Allen, R., Dusenbury, P., Bryant S., et al. (2001). *Making results-based government work.* Washington, DC: Urban Institute.

McGuire, A., & Kloby, K. (2006). Fairfax measures up: Key factors for the design and implementation. In K. Callahan (Ed.), *Elements of effective governance: Measurement, accountability, and participation* (pp. 327–348). New York: Taylor & Francis.

Melkers J., & Thomas, J. C. (1998). What do administrators think citizens think? Administrators predictions as an adjunct to citizen surveys. *Public Administration Review, 58,* 327–334.

National Center for Public Performance. (2003). *Citizen-driven government performance.* Newark, NJ: Rutgers University. Retrieved March 1, 2006, from http://www.andromeda.rutgers.edu/~ncpp/cdgp/sloan.htm

Poister, T., & Streib, G. (1999). Performance measurement in municipal government: Assessing the state of the practice. *Public Administration Review, 59,* 325–335.

Roberts, N. (1997). Public deliberation: An alternative approach to crafting policy and setting direction. *Public Administration Review, 57,* 124–132.

San Francisco Recreation and Park Department. (2005). *San Francisco park maintenance standards: The manual and evaluation form.* San Francisco: Author. Available at http://www.sfgov.org/site/recpark_page.asp?id=37737

Straphangers Campaign. (n.d.). *Straphangers Campaign line rating index: Profiles of 20 subway lines.* Retrieved March 14, 2007, from http://www.straphangers.org/statesub01/lrindex.html

Timney, M. (1998). Overcoming administrative barriers to citizen participation: Citizens as partners not adversaries. In C. S King & C. Stivers (Eds.), *Government is us: Public administration in an anti-government era* (pp. 88–99). Thousand Oaks, CA: Sage.

Volcker, P. A., Gaebler, T., Goodpaster, A., Gordon, M. T., Koskinen, J. Mora, D., et al. (1999). *A government to trust and respect; rebuilding citizen-government relations for the 21st century.* Report by the Panel on Civic Trust and Citizen Responsibility of the National Academy of Public Administration, Washington, DC.

Walters, J., Abrahams A., & Fountain, J. (2003). Managing for results: An overview. In *Reporting performance information: Suggested criteria for effective communication* (pp. 13–24). Norwalk, CT: Governmental Accounting and Standards

Board. Retrieved March 1, 2006, from http://www.seagov.org/aboutpmg/mfr_chap3.pdf)

Wang, X. (2001). Assessing public participation in U.S. cities. *Public Performance & Management Review, 24,* 322–336.

Weeks, E. C. (2000). The practice of deliberative democracy: Results from four large-scale trials. *Public Administration Review, 60,* 360–372.

Wholey, J. S. (1999). Performance-based management: Responding to the challenges. *Public Productivity and Management Review, 22,* 288–306.

Worcester Regional Research Bureau. (2004). *Citizen satisfaction with municipal services: 2004 survey.* Worcester, MA: Author. Available at http://www.wrrb.org/Reports/CCPM-04–08.pdf

Yang, K., & Callahan, K. (2005). Assessing citizen involvement efforts by local governments. *Public Performance and Management Review, 29,* 191–216.

PART IV

Performance Budgeting

14 Performance Budgeting Internationally

Assessing Its Merits

Frances Stokes Berry

Performance budgeting currently has a worldwide audience and has been implemented in many countries under new public management initiatives, often called "performance management" or "managing for results." However, performance budgeting beginnings can be traced back to reforms in the United States in the 1940s (under the Hoover Commission) to move budgets from line-item budgets (with basic expenditures and no information on what those expenditures would buy) to program budgets that provide information on what government does with its budget funds.

This introduction to the chapters on performance budgeting will cover five topics. First, a short history of performance budgeting places the strengths of current practices in perspective. Second, performance budgeting and its elements are defined, and types of performance budgets currently used are briefly outlined. Third, an overview from published studies on how performance data are used in management and the policy process is discussed. We conclude by covering both the strengths of current performance budgets as well as the issues that need to be resolved to reduce the tensions of performance budgeting (between the highly rational, outcome-focused process of program management and the more interest-based, political process of the legislature) in the policy process.

History of Performance Budgeting

Internationally, "New Public Management" reforms have been adopted by countries in South and Central America, Europe, Australia, and Asia. In this section of the book, there are chapters on reforms in South and Central

America, and Australia and New Zealand that provide detailed descriptions of those reforms and how they are working. The element of performance-based budgeting is a central aspect of these overall management reforms, as citizens demand to know what their taxes and government revenues are providing and policymakers want managers to show accountability for the funds they are spending before allocating new revenues for the traditional programs. In general, there is a worldwide movement (a) to use the market sector more directly for providing government services through privatization (or contracting out government services with private and nonprofit organizations) as well as (b) to make government more businesslike by developing unit costs of services and program performance measures. Performance measurement is part of what Peters and Pierre (1998) call "governance without government," in which contracting out is common; networking among government, nonprofit, and private sector agencies is the normal business model; and government is moving away from its "role as the central source of the 'authoritative allocation of values' for the society" (p. 224).

Performance budgeting in the United States can be described as consisting of four major reforms at the federal level (U.S. General Accounting Office [GAO], 1997). The Hoover Commission in 1949 first recommended performance budgeting, which it described as moving away from types of expenditures in the line-item budget (for salaries, supplies, and office rent) to the expected outputs or results of the budget expenditures. The second reform effort was the planning, programming, and budgeting system (PPBS), introduced by President Lyndon B. Johnson in the 1960s. "PPBS introduced a decision–making framework to the executive branch budget formulation process by presenting and analyzing choices among long-term policy objectives and alternative ways of achieving them" (GAO, 1997, p. 5). Most performance was defined with output measures, but PPBS encountered severe problems, was widely viewed as unsuccessful, and was abolished by Republican President Nixon. The available computers and software programs in the 1960s were not well suited for storing and manipulating high volumes of program cross-walks and performance measures. Perhaps even more to the point, managers were not used to defining programs through activities that crossed budget lines, and they had little experience in developing performance measures to assess how well the programs operated.

Management by objectives (MBO), initiated under President Nixon, emphasized management improvement by linking budget requests with program objectives for which agency managers would then be held responsible. GAO (1997) asserts that performance measures were primarily agency outputs and processes but that some outcome measures showing the results of federal spending began to be included in budgets. MBO has continued to be a mainstay format of budgets, particularly at the local government level. MBO puts together an understandable sequence of defined program goals, objectives, and performance measures on progress toward those objectives, and it appeals to both managers and policymakers.

Zero-based budgeting (ZBB) was first used by Jimmy Carter in his Georgian gubernatorial administration, and he brought ZBB to the federal government when he assumed the presidency in 1976. The logic behind ZBB was to require agencies to show that their programs were valuable and meeting needs, since once government programs were created, they were rarely revisited to determine whether those programs were still needed or had outlived their usefulness. Many felt ZBB would find lots of unneeded programs to cut and would be effective in reducing the size of government. Those cuts were generally much smaller than early advocates envisioned, but the logic of justifying the base of the program's budget as well as any needed extra dollars was a politically powerful idea. Most recently, Florida's Governor Jeb Bush reintroduced ZBB into his performance-based budgeting process in 2000 to send the message that managers should not take for granted that all their programs were useful and would be funded.

In the 1990s, governments at all levels, but especially the federal and state levels, enacted legislation to require integrated strategic planning, budgeting, and performance measurement systems. To some degree, these reforms were the culmination of the skeletal PPBS budgeting efforts begun in the 1960s, and the 1990s reforms did build from prior efforts. Many of these performance-based budgeting systems of the 1990s were implemented over periods of time, such as the federal Government Performance and Results Act (GRPA) of 1993 and the Florida Government Accountability and Results Act of 1994 that brought agencies into the performance-based budgeting system over a period of 7 years. This gradual implementation had the benefit of allowing agency managers to learn from the early initiators and allowed the system to be fine-tuned each year as problems were identified and resolved. Performance-based budgeting has established a solid base across all levels of U.S. governments; studies show that 50% to 70% of local and state governments use a form of performance-based budgeting, and all federal agencies are required to follow performance-based budgeting as detailed under GPRA. See more detailed information on usage in the section below.

Defining Performance Budgeting

The content of performance measurement systems depends on the philosophy of change. There may be more emphasis on outputs (New Zealand) or outcomes (Australia and United States), on financial results, on producer-determined measures or service quality or on client surveys for customer satisfaction (Denmark). Each frame of emphasis has its pros and cons. For example, some observers of the New Zealand situation have suggested potential dangers in focusing on outputs rather than on outcomes. An output focus may lead to efficient production of the wrong products and services. However, in New Zealand, it is considered too difficult to hold managers accountable for outcomes because the cause-effect relationship between executive or departmental activities and outcomes is often difficult (if not impossible) to determine. It is easier to measure outputs, to trace their causality and therefore to hold executives and departments accountable. However, outcomes are considered to inform policy analysis and policy choices. Other countries are also aware of the possible dysfunctional effects of certain indicators. The more limited the set of indicators, the higher the chance of having a dysfunctional effect. (Organisation for Economic Co-operation and Development [OECD], 1997, p. 18)

Performance budgeting is a term used to refer to budget formats that link inputs with outputs, outcomes, or other measures of results (GAO, 1997). These are important distinctions, and the purpose is to help managers, citizens, and policymakers understand what they are getting with the money they spend for government programs and activities. *Inputs* are the funds (budget amounts), number of staff, and other resources that are used in government agencies. *Outputs* are the specific activities or immediate results of the program services that are funded by the inputs. An *outcome* of a program activity can be answered by asking, "What difference did the activity or output make?" For example, the outcome of a highway-paving program may be answered by asking, "Are there fewer fatalities on smooth roads?" "Did the paving process leave the roads better marked and less confusing so fewer accidents occurred?" Agencies also measure citizen satisfaction with services, which is widely considered to represent their overall judgment of how well the local government or state agency program is performing (Ryzin, 2004). Client satisfaction data are also widely gathered on programs and are generally considered an intermediate outcome measure, although often client satisfaction data measures perception of quality of services rather than actual impacts from those services. Thus, inputs, outputs, and outcomes are basic ideas related to performance budgeting at all levels of governments. More information on the specific elements of performance budgeting is contained in Chapter 18 of this volume, by Carl Moravitz.

At the local level of government, and increasingly also at state and federal levels, information on the unit costs of services is calculated and reported so that the costs and the efficiency of programs (cost of actual outputs from the programs) can be compared. While a growing number of governments are interested in efficiency measures, many lack the cost-accounting capacity to provide reliable cost data—this is especially true if they focus on the program level rather than the activity level. State and federal budgeting reforms since the 1990s have generally emphasized program output and outcome data, while local-level budgets generally collect output and efficiency measures. All levels collect citizen or client satisfaction data to represent quality of services and overall performance. Internationally, a 1997 OECD report found that nearly all of the 10 countries[1] studied collected activity and quality performance measures and many fewer collected output, outcome, and financial performance measures.

Types of Performance Budgeting

Part II gave a brief history of how budget processes have developed, and this section briefly describes the most widely used performance-budgeting formats. At the federal and state levels, performance-based budgets (which focus on the program rather than the agency) are often very similar in format, reflecting a rapid diffusion of the performance-based budgeting format across those levels of government (Berry & Yang, 2006; Liner et al., 2001; National Association of State Budget Officers [NASBO], 2002). The federal and state agency budgets contain program missions, goals, objectives, output and outcome measures, and often an assessment of measure reliability and validity, as well as targets or standards for the year for specific measures. Local governments are more likely to use performance budgeting that links program goals with objectives and measures of output and costs to meet objectives of that service. City managers often speak of their budget systems as being based on MBO rather than as performance-based budgeting. However, the linkage between goals, objectives, and specific types of performance measures in their budgets demonstrates that there is often very little to distinguish between current MBO and performance-based budgeting systems, which increasingly at the local level seem to be similar systems.

Other measurement models exist and are used occasionally in budgeting. One model is the *balanced scorecard approach* (Kaplan & Norton, 1996), developed for the private sector but adapted for the public sector and used more frequently by cities than other governmental jurisdictions. The city of Charlotte, North Carolina, has one of the best-known and well-developed city balanced scorecard plans, developed in 1994. Kaplan and Norton's balanced scorecard utilizes four types of performance measures, which all support an organization's or program's mission. The scorecard measures are grouped according to four categories: (a) customer, (b) financial, (c) internal business processes, and (d) employee learning and growth. Often, in a city plan, there will be city-level goals and objectives, and each agency selects city goals to which it can best contribute and then develops its own secondary goals and objectives, with the four types of measures for each goal. This cascading process allows the strategic plan to be fairly integrated but also tailored to the agency's purpose and programs. Cross-cutting goals, such as increased employee participation or training, can be reflected in all agency subordinate plans, and the data can then be "rolled up" to the city level.

At the federal level in the United States, the Malcolm Baldrige National Quality Award for excellently managed organizations has given a broad focus to performance measures beyond budgeting measurement. Created in 1987 by the U.S. Congress, the Baldrige Award grew out of total quality management initiatives and the philosophy of improving performance with a balanced and multidimensional approach to organizational management. The seven core values from its Criteria for Performance Excellence Framework include systems assessment of (a) leadership; (b) strategic planning;

(c) customer and market focus; (d) measurement, analysis, and knowledge; (e) human resources focus; (f) process management; and (g) results (Baldrige National Quality Program, 2006). In the United States, the Alliance for Performance Excellence is a network of states, nonprofit agencies, and local governments that use the Baldrige criteria in their management systems. The "Results" section is composed of "a balanced composite of leading and lagging performance measures . . . to communicate short- and longer-term priorities, monitor actual performance, and provide a clear basis for improving results" (Baldrige National Quality Program, 2006, p. 4). The European Union is using the Common Assessment Framework (CAF), which shares some features with the Baldrige Award and is useful for promoting benchmarking across public organizations and for acting as a "bridge" across the various quality management models in use. For more details on these systems of performance management, see Chapter 19 in this volume, by Maria P. Aristigueta.

Uses of Performance Data in Budgeting and Management in the United States

While many budgeting reforms have been undertaken in the United States in the past 85 years, none have been integrated into the overall management systems of organizations more effectively than the most recent performance-based program-budgeting systems. Since the early 1990s, most governments at the federal, state, and local government levels have implemented a series of budget reforms that include performance measurement and greater attention to government accountability. Part of the government "reinvention" and quality management era, performance budgeting links strategic plans, budgets, and performance measures for an integrated budget- and program-planning effort. Many government jurisdictions set target measures annually for their programs, so performance budgeting encourages greater productivity and efficiency while also serving as a more traditional budget allocation document.

At the local government level, performance measures have been used longer and with greater use by policymakers than at perhaps any other level of government. Some of the newer strategic management models, such as the balanced scorecard approach, have been innovated by local governments, such as Charlotte, North Carolina. Milwaukee, Wisconsin, has also been a leader in reform and innovation; Hendrick's (2000) in-depth study of Milwaukee's management systems provides insights into how performance measures at the department and city levels can be most effectively integrated with strategic plans and budgets. Performance management is widely used today by local governments. Poister and Streib (2005, p. 50) found that over 80% of the cities that use strategic planning link performance management systems to strategic plans for a variety of management purposes, including annual evaluations of departments and individual staff, tracking achievement of objectives, and implementing specific initiatives. Melkers and Willoughby (2005, p. 188) found that cities with comprehensive measures across government departments and for a wide variety of programs lead to greater use in the budget process. They also found that leadership support and the extent to which performance measures are used in a range of management decisions determine the perceived long-range benefits of performance measures at the city level in the United States.

At the state government level, an article by Melkers and Willoughby (2004) determined that 47 out of 50 states had performance-based budgeting requirements, although the states vary in their comprehensiveness and program coverage. Other studies have found even more widespread use of strategic planning (Berry & Wechsler, 1995). Some studies of performance-based budgeting in particular states are finding mixed results, with most studies concluding that the state legislatures are not using performance measures widely for decision making yet but that other positive outcomes have taken hold (Berry, Brower, & Flowers, 2000; Berry & Flowers, 1999; de Lancer Julnes & Mixcoatl, 2006; Melkers & Willoughby, 2004).

At the federal level, the GPRA laid the foundation for an integrated strategic planning and performance-based budgeting process that continues today, with only minor adjustments. GAO has conducted several insightful studies that assess and summarize the status of this performance-based budgeting and management system. Other studies have examined the rational management process and found it to be designed without much regard for the intergovernmental and political systems of governance within which it exists (Long & Franklin, 2004; Radin, 1998).

Perhaps the most limited literature on performance-based budgeting covers interagency and networked program measures. This demonstrates the reality that for most programs, the agency develops measures to include in its own budget and strategic planning document, and these measures do not become widely used by agencies with similar programs across the country. The exception to this may be when national laws specify measures and require that data be collected on those program measures, such as is the case for the U.S. Child Support Enforcement Act of 1972, as amended in 1996. Performance measures in human service agency collaboratives in 10 states is the topic of an article by Stephen Page (2004), which compares the types of measures and managing for results systems used. Agranoff and McGuire (2003) consider the use and usefulness of performance measures in local economic development across hundreds of U.S. cities. But more attention needs to be given to issues in performance budgeting for networked and intergovernmental programs (Berry et al., 2004) as governmental contracts use public, private, and nonprofit partnerships to deliver services to citizens. Increasingly, public agencies are requiring their contractors to report on a common set of performance measures to enable government funders to compare performance across types of programs and providers. Yet performance data are still not always provided or very reliable when available.

Strengths of and Issues Still to Be Resolved Regarding Performance Budgeting _____

Performance budgeting is built on the belief that budgeting can become a rationalized process in which decisions on resource allocation can be made on the basis of policy analysis and performance data. However, as Wildavsky (1979) so persuasively argues, the budgeting process that determines who gets what from government is inherently *political*; and budgeteers increasingly realize that the structures of budgets are designed to support more rational decision making but do not require the process to be fully rational. Political values and ideologies, constituent needs and demands, as well as the legislative discussions from which compromises and consensus emerge, continue to play important roles in budgeting issues.

Many of these factors conflict with a fully rational process of decision making that is based on objective data that performance-based budgeting represents. However, in a democracy with diverse interests and citizen needs represented through elected officials, performance data linked to program goals and objectives can help steer the debates about societal goals and allocation of resources. Whether performance data drive decision making is much less certain. Some suggest that decision makers look for data that support their views on what programs are necessary or should be reduced. Nearly all studies conclude that budgeting decisions are rarely made solely on the basis of performance data. Most observers (Kettl, 1994; Peterson, 1995) argue that legislators will never be motivated to plan budgets based solely on the basis of performance data, noting that incentives for legislators reinforce their reelection prospects and often lead to spending for new programs and district-based funding that can be held up to constituents as benefits from their representation of the district. This is a variant on the general view that budgeting is based heavily on political ideology and election pressures to meet constituent needs.

Use of performance measures by managers appears much more common than its use by legislators or other policymakers, and this result has been routinely reinforced at every level of government in which usage of performance information is examined (Berry & Flowers, 1999; GAO, 2004; Radin, 1998). The GAO (2004) found that federal managers reported mixed results in using the performance information collected for GPRA, and many of these uses were internal to the agency for setting program priorities and job expectations for staff. Managers believe that Congress makes very limited use of performance information, while congressional staff are more likely to use the data in their analysis than are congressmen. Federal managers believe that a major challenge to GPRA's implementation is the reluctance of members of Congress to use performance information in decision making. At both the state level (Government Performance Project Staff, 2001; Melkers & Willoughby, 2001; Moynihan, 2006), and city level

(Melkers & Willoughby, 2005), studies have found a lack of use of performance information in decision making.

While many conclude that auditing performance-related data is a necessary step to have useful and accurate data, most governments do not audit their performance measures, and many issues related to performance measurement quality still remain. Audits or cross-checking can be applied to various stages of the performance measurement system used in performance budgeting. A first stage includes assessing the performance measures for appropriateness, the right level of abstraction, and validity (whether the measure captures the concept one is trying to measure). A second stage in the process focuses on the collection and processing of data for reliability (repeated measurement yields the same results for a measure). Assessing the quality of information (accuracy and completeness, and the collection process) constitutes a third stage, while interpreting and explaining the results (within reasonable bounds and adequate backup of evidence) is a fourth stage of assessing performance measures. Finally, care needs to be given to proper presentation of the measures and distribution or access to citizens and other information users so the data are used to the fullest extent possible.

Performance-based budgeting in nearly every governmental jurisdiction that enacted the new process was heralded as offering managerial flexibility (for example, through lump-sum budgeting rather than detailed line-item budgets) in return for stricter accountability to elected officials and citizens. However, in practice, this flexibility has rarely been given to agency managers (e.g., Arellano-Gault & Ramírez de la Cruz, Chapter 15, this volume; Berry & Flowers, 1999; Moynihan, 2006; Wellman & VanLandingham, Chapter 16, this volume). Many managers feel that micromanagement by legislatures over agency spending has become more intense over time, rather than less intense. Performance-based budgeting was supposed to focus on outputs and outcomes and give managers more options on the process by which they achieved outputs and outcomes. Unfortunately, studies have found that this flexibility, deregulation, and focus on the end result have rarely taken place (Berry & Flowers, 1999; OECD, 1997).

Studies generally find minimal involvement by citizens and other organizational stakeholders in developing and approving performance measures (GAO, 1997; Ho, 2003). VanLandingham and Wellman, (Chapter 16, this volume) believe that citizens rarely use the performance measurement information agencies collect. More attention should be given to how agencies can get their information out to citizens in readily understandable formats, perhaps through program scorecards or simple histograms and bar charts showing data over time and across programs. Nonetheless, one consultant (M. Marshall, personal communication, August 22, 2006) to public agencies on performance management is optimistic in reflecting on the last 15 years of practice:

I believe the use of measurement information is evolving and organizations are beginning to learn how to craft measures that are more useful to managers and customer stakeholders. I see many organizations making renewed attempts at more authentic measures by placing more emphasis to the planning phase of results management versus the budgeting phase. During the often neglected planning phase of results management, intended outcomes are better defined, customer and stakeholder interests are defined, and strategies and objectives are set out more explicitly. This clarity of purpose and expectations provides a much more solid foundation for developing useful measures for all parties to evaluate.

Conclusion

This overview of performance budgeting is designed to introduce the reader to the key elements of performance budgeting: the various types and formats used; the key terms, such as *activities, outputs,* and *outcomes;* and a critical assessment of problems encountered in many performance-budgeting systems. The chapters that follow will provide an in-depth look at how these systems are performing at the national and state levels. While we note many issues that still need to be resolved, these latest systems of performance budgeting are probably the best developed and most widely used budgeting systems yet developed to bring program information into the policy-making and budgeting process. While legislators and elected officials do not appear to be using performance information to the extent that executive branch program managers use the information, this is probably inevitable given the demands of the political process in which elected officials live (de Lancer Julnes & Holzer, 2001). One can consider the glass half full or half empty, but I believe the weight of the evidence shows that performance budgeting is effective and will likely continue to improve its usefulness for policymakers and to be widely used by governments around the world.

Note

1. The 10 countries were Australia, Canada, Denmark, Finland, France, the Netherlands, New Zealand, Sweden, the United Kingdom, and the United States.

References

Agranoff, R., & McGuire, M. (2003). *Collaborative public management: New strategies for local governments.* Washington, DC: Georgetown University Press.

Baldrige National Quality Program. (2006). *Criteria for performance excellence.* Retrieved July 27, 2006, from http://www.baldrige.gov/Criteria.htm

Berry, F., Brower, R., Choi, S., Gao, X., Jang, H., Kwon, M., et al. (2004). Three traditions of network research: What the public management research agenda can learn from other research communities. *Public Administration Review, 64,* 539–552.

Berry, F. S., Brower, R., & Flowers, G. (2000). Implementing performance accountability in Florida: What changed, what mattered, and what resulted? *Public Productivity and Management Review, 21,* 338–358.

Berry, F. S., & Flowers, G. (1999). Public entrepreneurs in the policy process: Performance-based budgeting in Florida. *Journal of Public Budgeting, Accounting, and Financial Management, 11,* 585–624.

Berry, F. S., & Wechsler, B. (1995). State agencies' experience with strategic planning: Findings from a national survey. *Public Administration Review, 55,* 159–167.

Berry, F. S., & Yang, K. (2006). *The state of strategic planning in government: Slouching towards strategic management* (Working paper). Askew School of Public Administration and Policy, Florida State University, Tallahassee.

de Lancer Julnes, P., & Holzer, M. (2001). Promoting the utilization of performance measures: An empirical study of factors affecting adoption and implementation. *Public Administration Review, 61,* 693–708.

de Lancer Julnes, P., & Mixcoatl, G. (2006). Governors as agents of change: A comparative study of performance measurement initiatives in Utah and Compeche. *Public Performance & Management Review, 29,* 405–432.

Florida Government Accountability and Results Act of 1994, Ch. 94–249, Laws of Florida.

Government Performance and Results Act of 1993, Pub. L. No. 103–62 [S20] 107 Stat. 285.

Government Performance Project Staff. (2001). *Paths to performance in state and local government: A final assessment from the Maxwell School of citizenship and public affairs.* Syracuse, NY: Author.

Hendrick, R. (2000). Comprehensive management and budgeting reform in local government: The case of Milwaukee. *Public Productivity and Management Reform, 23,* 312–337.

Ho, A. (2003). Perceptions of performance measurement and the practice of performance reporting by small cities. *State and Local Government Review, 35,* 161–173.

Kaplan, R. S., & Norton, D. P. (1996). *The balanced scorecard: Translating strategy into action.* Cambridge, MA: Harvard University Press.

Kettl, D. (1994). *Reinventing government? Appraising the National Performance Review.* Washington, DC: Brookings Institution.

Liner, B., Hatry, H., Vinson, E., Allen, R., Dusenbury, P., Bryant, S., et al. (2001). *Making results-based state government work.* Washington, DC: Urban Institute.

Long, E., & Franklin, A. (2004). The paradox of implementing the Government Performance and Results Act: Top-down direction for bottom-up implementation. *Public Administration Review, 64,* 309–319.

Melkers, J., & Willoughby, K. (2001). Budgeters' view of state performance budgeting systems. *Public Administration Review, 61,* 54–64.

Melkers, J., & Willoughby, K. (2004). *Staying the course: The use of performance measurement in state governments.* Washington, DC: IBM Center for the Business of Government.

Melkers, J., & Willoughby, K. (2005). Models of performance-measurement use in local governments: Understanding budgeting, communication, and lasting effects. *Public Administration Review, 65,* 180–191.

Moynihan, D. (2006). Managing for results in state government: Evaluating a decade of reform. *Public Administration Review, 66,* 77–89.

National Association of State Budget Officers. (2002). *Budget processes in the states.* Washington, DC: Author.

Organisation for Economic Co-operation and Development. (1997). *In search of results: Performance management practices.* Paris: Author.

Page, S. (2004). Measuring accountability for results in interagency collaboratives. *Public Administration Review, 64,* 591–606.

Peters, G., & Pierre, J. (1998). Governance without government: Rethinking public administration? *Journal of Public Administration Research and Theory, 8,* 223–243.

Peterson, P. (1995). *The price of federalism.* Washington, DC: Brookings Institution.

Poister, T., & Streib, G. (2005). Elements of strategic planning and management in municipal government: Status after two decades. *Public Administration Review, 65,* 45–56.

Radin, B. (1998). The Government Performance and Results Act (GRPA): Hydra-headed monster or flexible management tool? *Public Administration Review, 58,* 307–16.

Ryzin, G. V. (2004). The measurement of overall citizen satisfaction. *Public Performance & Management Review, 27,* 9–28.

U.S. General Accounting Office. (1997) *Performance budgeting: Past initiatives offer insights for GRPA implementation.* Washington, DC: Author.

U.S. General Accounting Office. (2004). *Results-oriented government* (GAO-04–594T). Washington, DC: Author.

Wildavsky. A. (1979). *The politics of the budgetary process.* Boston: Little, Brown.

15

Performance-Based Budgeting in Latin and South America

Analyzing Recent Reforms in the Budgetary Systems of Brazil, Chile, Colombia, and Mexico

David Arellano-Gault

Edgar E. Ramírez de la Cruz

The introduction of "New Public Management" ideas in the reform of Latin American countries has been a process of learning, with successes and drawbacks. In the case of the implementation of performance-based budgets, all the contradictions, tensions, and dilemmas Latin American political systems have to face become evident. Tensions between account-ability and innovation; choice of political or technical decision making; par-ticipation, or not, of the legislative power in the definition of outcomes; and the impression that evaluation by performance has been added to an already complex set of evaluation procedures are some of the phenomena we explore in this paper in the cases of Brazil, Chile, Colombia, and Mexico.

Introduction

During the 1990s, Latin and South American countries implemented similar approaches to reform their public administration systems. These attempts were based on the idea that improving government performance could be accomplished by giving more autonomy to public administrators and requiring governmental programs to have outcome measures. However, public administrators had to pay a price for the autonomy given to them: being evaluated by performance-based measures rather than by process-based measures. In other words, these reforms proposed that government accountability would be based on the citizens' level of welfare or satisfaction and on the results of public policies. Under these reforms, the mere execution of bureaucratic procedures would be considered secondarily, at best.

Performance-based budgeting (PBB) is one of the most representative models of these reforms. In general terms, PBB proposes that agencies' outputs and outcomes must be considered in the process of allocating and managing resources. The PBB model assumes that a certain level of flexibility is required to improve agencies' performance, and this flexibility requires strong systems of accountability based on results rather than on procedures. Using a similar model, many countries implemented their own versions of PBB, because managing organizations through results has an important appeal to the public.

In some countries, these reforms offered substantial improvements for the performance of public organizations and the implementation of public policies (Arellano, Gil, Ramírez, & Rojano, 2000). PBB implementation in countries like the United Kingdom, New Zealand, and Australia confirmed some benefits. Among the most important benefits were (a) improvement in the continuity of the work of agencies over longer periods as well as a reduction of uncertainty by establishing clear expectations for agencies and legislators; (b) generation of more and better information for citizens and legislators with respect to expenditures, costs, and the results of public programs; (c) more effective mechanisms to define necessary resources for programs by identifying critical processes and specific impacts on social and economic variables; and (d) linkages among planning, budgeting, and evaluation. Following the promises of PBB from the early 1990s, many countries in Latin America attempted to enter the wave of reforms by developing and implementing their own models of reform. This article assesses the results of different models of PBB implemented in four Latin American countries: Brazil, Chile, Colombia, and Mexico.

In the next section of this chapter, we develop a theoretical framework to understand budgetary reforms incorporating performance measures. Next, we present the main programs and reforms implemented in Brazil, Chile, Colombia, and Mexico that introduced those components included in our framework of PBB and summarize the specific elements of their approaches. Subsequently, we analyze the alternative approaches taken by these four countries as they face different challenges implementing their reforms. Finally, we offer some concluding considerations.

A Model of Performance-Based Budgeting

PBB is a response to managers' complaints about being handicapped by rules and regulations and the lack of flexibility in government; it attempts to generate innovative behavior among managers without losing the control of their behavior (Barzelay, 1992). However, beyond the promises of PBB, there is not a universal definition of what PBB is. Different terms are used to refer to similar reforms. For instance, *performance budgeting* and *performance measurement* are other names used to describe systems of budgeting through agencies' results (Broom, 1995).

Technically, performance measurement requires the construction of conceptual chains capable of linking several sets of tasks, subgoals, goals, and ends, crossing the organization both vertically and horizontally. According to some authors, the primary source of legitimacy of an organization are the goals and ends (Palumbo, & Maynard-Moody, 1991), so the manager should be challenged to transform these goals into specific products, achieved through a network and chains of subgoals, processes, functions, and activities interrelated and aligned with the goals and mission of the organization.

According to Joyce (1999), there are three common mechanisms for improving the budgetary process using performance measurement: First, agencies may use measures that are valuable for improving their management with a given level of resources. Second, governments or agencies may use performance measures as part of reporting on their activities. Finally, governments can replace traditional budgets with a system that gives program managers more flexibility in managing their results but holds them accountable by performance measures. Under PBB, in return for being evaluated by their performance, administrators are supposed to receive greater autonomy for four functions, to (a) allocate resources from one year to another, (b) decide when resources can be used within a given year, (c) generate and retain incomes and savings, and (d) move resources among programs (Forsythe, 1993; Organisation for Economic Co-operation and Development [OECD], 1993).

Compared with previous budgetary and administrative reforms, PBB innovates by using a decentralized or bottom-up implementation approach focusing on results. A focus on results introduced a new logic for legislators to hold public officials accountable. In the traditional logic of government, it is assumed that legislators act as stockholders who cannot easily monitor managers' behavior, since they have interests in many agencies' performance; thus, to oversee all information about managers' behaviors would be prohibitive for them. Therefore, a mechanism for controlling bureaucracy in the traditional style of public administration has been to impose rules on its behavior that have to be monitored by other agencies to which legislators delegate power for controlling public bureaucrats.

The traditional mechanisms for evaluating public officers are concentrated on agencies' processes, activities, and outputs. In the logic of PBB, the definition of results and performance measures are frequently based on strategic planning systems that cover an entire agency. The emphasis on decentralizing control and decision making shifts the logic of bureaucratic systems from a focus on the creation of norms and procedures that bureaucrats blindly follow to a focus on how particular activities contribute to the accomplishment of specific and measurable results.

The logic of PBB introduces a new way to structure the budget, assuming that legislators are interested in evaluating and measuring agencies' outcomes rather than outputs. New components of the budgetary process link appropriations not only with a program's activities and procedures but also with expected results indicated in terms of performance measures. To change the logic of the budgetary process, models of PBB may introduce several specific components, such as the following:

- Transparent outcome-based information systems
- Written performance-based contracts
- Flexible managerial systems
- Mechanisms for rewarding satisfactory performance
- Introduction of a new programmatic structure

A reform based on the model of PBB needs to introduce at least three instruments in order to be successful. First, the reform should introduce mechanisms to hold managers accountable on the basis of results, such as transparent outcome-based information systems and performance-based contracts. Second, there need to be flexible managerial systems as well as incentives (or rewards) for managers to improve their performance. Finally, PBB systems have to transform budgetary processes and categories to link measures, goals, and funding.

Transparent outcome-based information systems are intended to reduce opportunistic behavior among managers. These systems permit managers to realize that they cannot deceive legislators without having a high probability of being observed and penalized. It is expected that an adequate information system allows legislators to focus on what is more important for them and their constituencies: the results of government agencies.

Performance contracts look for the alignment of managers' preferences with those of legislators. These contracts identify performance measures or performance indicators that capture agencies' performance and define goals that permit assessing agencies' performances. However, this critical process of defining performance measures and goals is not straightforward: It can be either (a) a negotiated process among legislators, agencies' managers, and other stakeholders or (b) a unilateral process conducted by legislatures.

Performance contracts may also provide incentives for managers in the form of more autonomy and economic rewards to motivate them to improve their performance. A more flexible managerial system may allow mangers to transfer resources from one fiscal year to another or between budgetary categories, or give them more flexibility to manage human resources. New incentives in the form of economic rewards are intended to compensate managers' efforts by giving them salary increases or performance bonuses. These economic incentives may be given individually or to teams or departments.

The organization of the traditional budget is by budgetary accounts, which frequently cover and organize sets of categories that include activities, programs, and services. This organization is altered by the model of PBB, which requires a new form to present the budget that integrates information on performance measures and strategic plans into the budgetary process. Performance indicators become the base of the budgetary process, its approval, and its execution. New ways of organizing the budget frequently show how each account is related to the strategic plan of an agency and may present indicators of what results the agency expects to accomplish with its budget.

In general terms, and with some variations, these might be the most important components of PBB. Despite the elegance of the model, in diverse countries, its implementation has faced important challenges, producing mixed results. There seem to be five common difficulties with decision making under PBB. First, it is not clear whether the appropriate budgetary response to a program with poor performance is to reduce or to increase its appropriations. So, even if one knows the relationship between program performance and appropriated funds, there are no easy answers as to whether to cut or increase a program's budget levels. Second, performance may depend on external factors not under the control of the agencies, so the decision maker cannot really hold the agency fully accountable for those outcomes. Third, PBB may provide incentives to report deceitfully if managers think their agency budgets or personal salaries depend on program outcomes. Fourth, it is not clear how governments can accurately identify the inputs-outputs-outcomes chains for every public program. And fifth, budgeting is a decision-making activity characterized by political bargaining rather than a purely rational process, so performance measures are often the most important piece of information used in budget decisions, since values and constituent preferences may prevail instead. In the next section, we present the experience of some Latin American countries in their efforts for implementing reforms related to the PBB model and how they have tackled the dilemmas described above.

The Experiences of Brazil, Chile, Colombia, and Mexico

Brazil, Chile, Colombia, and Mexico have implemented programs and reforms to improve their budgetary processes that can be studied within the wave of PBB reforms in the world. The cases studied in this research were not chosen explicitly to match the theoretical model of PBB presented above; in fact, there is no country in Latin America identical to this theoretical model. We selected these cases using two criteria: (a) the existence of recent budgetary reforms related to PBB and (b) the availability of information for analyzing those reforms.

Once these countries were selected, we developed separate case studies for each country. In each case, we first collected information from academic literature and reviewed official reports and other information available on governmental Web sites and from research centers and universities in each country. In this stage, we identified recent programs that had changed

Table 15.1   Number of Interviews per Country

Interviewees	Vice-Minister	General Director	Advisor	Academic or Researcher
Brazil	None	2	5	3
Chile	None	2	4	3
Colombia	1	3	2	2
Mexico	1	2	3	3

the budgetary process by introducing any of three changes described above ("A Model of Performance-Based Budgeting"). Reforms were selected that affected multiple agencies in a country and that were systemwide.

In the next stage, we established contact with actors involved in the design and implementation of those reforms or its analysis. The contacts were made both by telephone and the Internet (see Table 15.1). The actors we contacted provided insights and points of view from the perspectives of the legislatures, public agencies, and academia. These contacts greatly facilitated the final part of the data collection, in which we visited each country to collect archival information and conduct a series of semistructured interviews with actors involved in the PBB reforms. The actors interviewed provided points of view from different levels of the government, and they ranged from vice-ministers and general directors to program specialists and advisors. The interviews were conducted on questions regarding the identification of key actors in the reform, goals, and incentives of each actor; general goals of the country's reforms; and the main limitations and constraints of those reforms.

Since the goal of this chapter is neither to present the entire complexity of each case nor to make a comparative case study for theory testing (Dion, 1998; Lijphart, 1971), but to provide a primary assessment of the components and trends introduced by these reforms, a deep exploration of each country is not presented here. However, before presenting each case, we provide some considerations about important similarities in and differences between these countries.

Brazil, Chile, Colombia, and Mexico share some characteristics, such as form of government and, to different degrees, the same economic and social problems. Nevertheless, there are distinctive characteristics that make the implementation of any governmental program a unique experience in each case. In all four countries, the form of government is republican, and the public powers are divided among the executive, legislative, and judicial branches, with the executive being the predominant power. In addition, these countries struggle with extreme social inequalities, environmental degradation, recurrent deadlocked political systems, and intermittent financial crises. Two countries, Brazil and Mexico, are federal systems of government. Chile and Colombia have central governments, with semiautonomous authorities in each region.

The level of social and economic stability and strength of political institutions is one of the relevant differences between these countries. To some degree, Brazil, Chile, and Mexico have experienced relative social stability in recent years. On the contrary, Colombia is characterized by political and social instability, which has historically been tied to the unequal distribution of wealth and the illicit trade in drugs. In terms of its political and economic systems, Chile is characterized by its successful effort to recover the tradition of representative democracy in the last 15 years. Among these countries, Chile is also acknowledged for the strength and autonomy of some of its institutions, such as the Central Bank, which allows both government and investors to undertake long-term planning. Mexico can be defined as a recently democratized system after seven decades of domination of one party. In Mexico, as well as in Brazil, the government is constantly struggling with corruption scandals that affect the stability of democratically elected governments; such scandals are not a distinctive characteristic of Chile.

Having mentioned these considerations, we next present the main programs found in Brazil, Chile, Colombia, and Mexico that are moving the budgetary processes toward PBB. The reforms we present next were introduced during the late 1990s and early 2000s by various ministries, with the endorsement of the president of each country. These programs were a response to the citizens' views of the lack of credibility in public administrators, public institutions, and the government in general. Also, the reforms resulted from the emergence of new leaders (and administrations) in Latin and South American public administration systems. In most cases, these reforms were clearly championed by leaders from the highest positions of the government, who, in many cases, came from the academic world, were educated in developed countries, or at least were familiar with the wave of reforms under the broad banner of the "New Public Management."

The components introduced in these Latin American countries are summarized in Table 15.2. Columns in the table correspond to the components of the theoretical model of PBB. Each row represents a country and the various programs implemented by it. The acronyms of country programs are placed in the column that corresponds to the component or components that were introduced. Some programs are repeated in more than one cell if they introduced more than one component.

The Case of Brazil

To a large degree, the reform in Brazil incorporated all components of the PBB model presented above. The Minister of the Federal Administration and the Reform of the State, Luis Carlos Bresser Pereira, promoted an Administrative Reform of the State that introduced the use of performance contracts and more flexible managerial systems in some areas of the federal

Table 15.2   Programs and Reforms Introducing Components of PBB by Country

| Country | Components of PBB | | | | |
	Outcome-Based Information Systems	Performance-Based Contract	Autonomy	Mechanisms for Rewarding Performance	New Budgetary Categories
Brazil	Planning and financial reforms	Planning reform	Administrative reform	None	Planning and financial reforms
Chile	PEGP PIP	PIPM	None	PIPM	None
Colombia	NSEPMR	None	None	None	None
Mexico	FISFA NPS	SPE	None	None	NPS

government. This reform was strongly supported by President Fernando Henrique Cardoso. A reform to the national planning system permitted the adoption of new budgetary categories that integrated strategic plans and performance measures. Also, a reform to the public finance systems brought more transparency to public finances. These three reforms created the conditions to develop incipient information systems that captured outcomes and performance of public programs.

The administrative reform in Brazil was based on a managerial perspective that departed from other traditional models of bureaucratic reforms (Dos Santos, 2000). As a result of the use of this approach, new legal regimes emerged to allow the federal government to give more autonomy to public managers in some areas of the government. These legal regimes created two new types of agencies: executive agencies and social organizations. Executive agencies are intended to extend budgetary discretion by using managerial contracts. In the model, the necessary resources would be allocated for the heads of programs to be responsible for the achievement of goals based on managerial contracts. The second legal regime provided the basis for the creation of social organizations, which incorporated organizations of the private sector not integrated into the federal administration. A social organization was intended to be a joint venture between the government and private organizations. These social organizations were created to provide services in areas such as higher education or public health, which were considered as nonexclusive of government's intervention. They received an endowment from the federal government and would sign managerial contracts, which could be supervised by representatives from the government and other groups of the society.

Based on the desire to provide more flexibility for managers, managerial contracts were widely used in the process of reforming the Brazilian state (Dos Santos, 2000). Nevertheless, the managerial contracts became a mere formality without guaranteeing better results. In terms of securing administrative and financial autonomy, at this point, most of the social agencies have produced few results since they were established. In addition, in terms of financial and administrative autonomy, those agencies have received little or nothing more than what the national constitution already gave to them (Dos Santos, 2002).

The public finance reform was introduced by the Law of Fiscal Responsibility (LFR) in 2000, which attempted to introduce fiscal discipline and transparency into the public sector. During the 1990s, most Brazilian public organizations faced disorganization in their finances because of a long inflationary period, an increase in the demand for public services, and a lack of fiscal discipline among public officers (Silberschneider, 2001). In addition to fiscal discipline, the LFR encouraged social control by giving transparency to public finance (Banco Nacional de Desenvolvimento Econômico, 2000). Although the core of LFR was to control the public deficit, it also introduced provisions intended to improve efficiency and effectiveness of public programs as well as to reduce the cost of public programs. Perhaps the most important contribution was a series of provisions to foster a transparent use of public resources (Martner, 2000; Silberschneider, 2001).

The reforms to the planning process created a multiyear plan (MP) that introduced a constant information flow about programs' performance, to be used in resource allocation. MP had its roots in the 1998 Decree 2829, which provided the legal framework to incorporate all governmental activities into programs and create budget categories for them. In addition, an annual evaluation would allow managers to evaluate their respective programs. The Law of Budgetary Guides (LBG) would create the basis for designing the budget by incorporating all performance measures and evaluations. Congress would play a key role in the evaluation of programs and allocation of resources approving the LBG and would use the information on performance measurement as an instrument in the annual discussion for allocating resources. However, at this point, several specialists agree that this information about performance measures has not been taken seriously by public officers, because there are no legal instruments for the coordinator of the LFB to coordinate across programs, especially when programs involved activities across more than a single ministry.

The Case of Chile

In Chile, both the Performance Indicators Program (PIP) and the Program of Evaluation of Governmental Projects (PEGP) introduced outcome-based information systems in 1997 as well as new mechanisms for evaluating agencies' performances. In addition, the same year, the Program for Improving Public Management (PIPM) initiated the use of performance contracts as well as mechanisms to reward agencies' performance. The Office of Budget, an inner department of the Ministry of the Treasury, played the leading role during the implementation of these programs. The Director of the Office of Budget, Mario Marcel, championed the adoption of programs that were intended to improve the quality of information for decision making and allocation of resources during the budgetary process.

The PIP encouraged the creation and use of strategic plans in governmental agencies. With the implementation of PIP, the Office of Budget wanted goals and indicators of strategic plans to be integrated in performance contracts that also provided incentives for improving public management. However, the lack of institutionalization made the program subject to the political swings of authorities in each agency (Marcel, 1997). These weaknesses reflected the political nature of public agencies. It was not until the formulation of the 2000 budget that the performance measures were fully developed and became central information for resource allocation (Guzmán, 2000). By 2001, 149 services with 275 indicators had been incorporated into the budget (Guzmán, 2001).

Nevertheless, despite the accumulated experience identifying performance indicators, agencies kept concentrating on the indicators of processes rather than results, and they faced other problems in identifying accurate and adequate performance measures. To fulfill the basic technical requirements for the formulation of the 2001 budget, the version of indicators presented by the agencies had to be reviewed and approved by the Office of Budget. For some agencies, the main problem in reporting programs' performance or key outcomes related to some agencies was the lack of available information to measure those programs.

In 1997, the PEGP attempted to generate information to support public managers and the analysis of results for resource allocation. With this program, every year, 20 programs are evaluated under the responsibility of the Ministry of the Treasury and the Office of Budget. The evaluations are conducted by panels of experts in public administration, which are intended to bring neutrality and independence to the process (Guzmán, 2000, 2001).

The evaluations are intended to measure the effectiveness, efficiency, and economy of programs to achieve the initial goals of programs. However, some of the criteria used to evaluate dimensions of programs, like efficiency and economy, have been strongly criticized by some stakeholders. In addition, some interest groups do not agree on the goals of a program, which are the basis for these evaluations. In other words, many social programs do not have clearly defined objectives, which makes it more difficult to evaluate programs' expectations.

The evaluations produced by PEGP are never conclusive and can be treated as reports used only to initiate the discussion and analysis of public programs; in no case are the evaluations linked directly to resource allocation. For instance, in 2000, the Ministry of the Treasury, in conjunction with the evaluated agencies, analyzed those recommendations and took actions to improve the performance of the programs. However, there were legal restrictions against both parties signing contracts to ensure that the series of changes needed were actually adopted; and it was not possible for the Office of Budget to enforce the implementation of any measures that improved the programs' performance.

Although PIPM was first implemented in 1997, it did not produce adequate results. The lack of results was due mainly to self-defined goals and objectives that did not require any additional effort by public officials to be achieved. Taking into account the previous experience, in 2000, the government reformed PIPM, again under the leadership of Mario Marcel. Modifications to the program were focused on improving the global management in public agencies. At this point, PIPM tried to be a managerial instrument with the objective of developing strategic areas in public management (Dirección de Presupuesto, 2000). Under the new approach, PIPM included a series of managerial objectives for each function of the agencies' administration. These objectives corresponded to the stages of an improved management system created by the Office of Budget. As a result of this program, an agency's employees can receive monetary rewards when a new stage and its objectives are achieved.

The main challenges identified by the Ministry of Treasury for the future of the program are increasing the organizational functionality of the program, since the evaluation has not been internalized in the agencies; strengthening the role of ministries to make them accountable by results in practice; the actual devolution of faculties, since the process has been more one of evaluation rather than of allowing the actors to decide according to results; and the institutionalization of the process in order for it to have a real impact on the behavior of public officials (Marcel, 2005).

The Case of Colombia

In Colombia, the National System of Evaluation of Public Management Results (NSEPMR) introduced outcome-based information systems as well as other mechanisms to evaluate the agencies' performance in order to improve resource allocation. NSEPMR has its roots in a constitutional amendment of 1991, but it did not have a major impact until recently. NSEPMR is a system that attempts to evaluate agencies by results based on the National Plan for Development and is implemented under the direction of the Department of Planning and the direct supervision of the president (Ospina, 2000).

This system generated an iterative process of self-evaluation, whereby agencies must elaborate an annual plan that includes the expected objectives and results. The expected results must establish a link between agencies' objectives and the objectives of the National Plan for Development. Therefore, this program works to achieve two main objectives: establishing clear goals and objectives for public administration and linking them with the policies of the president.

NSEPMR includes two main instruments: a strategic plan and the strategic evaluations incorporating the managerial compromises and the system of information. Within the system, there are two strategic plans: the plans of each agency and the strategic plan of each sector that incorporates the plans of all agencies within the sector. The strategic evaluations are conducted by expert teams who concentrate their efforts on programs that require serious amounts of investments, call for renewal, are innovative, and are suitable to be evaluated with the information available (Departamento Nacional de Planeación, 1996). Based on the strategic evaluations, the National Director of Planning produces an annual report for the national congress, which includes an analysis of the degree of achievements of the National Plan for Development. This analysis also includes the changes proposed to improve the performance of the programs and policies.

The main limitation of NSEPMR is that it focuses on the evaluation of sectors that encompass several programs and does not include evaluations of managers' or other public officials' performance. In addition, NSEPMR neither includes incentives related to performance evaluations nor introduces mechanisms to coordinate the work among agencies. This system has been implemented in a gradual manner. At this point, this program covers only 173 agencies, 16 sectors, and five presidential programs. In addition, NSEPMR has not had a strong influence on the national congress and citizens or even among academics and public officers. The evidence indicates that the results of the NSEPMR evaluations have not had any important impact on allocation of resources and appropriations.

The Case of Mexico

Recent budgetary reforms in Mexico have been based mainly on three programs. The first two are the New Programmatic Structure (NPS) (Unidad de Política y Control Presupuestal, 1997) and the System of Performance Evaluation (SPE) (Unidad de Política y Control Presupuestal, 1998). NPS changed the budgetary process by introducing new budgetary categories to organize it, while SPE launched an incipient use of performance-based contracts as well as innovative mechanisms to evaluate agencies' performance. The third program, the Federal Integral System of Financial Administration (FISFA) (Tesofe, 2003), established the use of outcome-based information systems to improve the budgetary process.

NPS is a tool of the budgetary process that provides a way to classify information in new categories and programmatic components that must be used to identify operative costs of each public program focusing on the program's results (Subsecretaria de Egresos, 1997). The new budgetary categories attempted to provide a new system to report information on the use of public resources based on their functional classification and its strategic use. Through the definition of the spheres of governmental action, the programmatic components of the budget generated information on the programs' missions, purposes, objectives, strategic goals, and performance indicators, which complemented the information produced by the traditional budgetary process (Secretaria de la Controloria y Desarrollo Administrativo, 1998).

According to the Ministry of Finance, the NPS tried to generate a database adapted for planning, programming, budgeting, implementing, and evaluating public costs that could be the basis for transforming the present budgetary system into a tool that is oriented toward results (Unidad de Política y Control Presupuestal, 1999).

SPE took the programmatic categories of NPS, developed performance indicators, and linked them to the programmatic categories of programs by means of performance contracts and budgetary projects. In addition, SPE attempted to identify programs and projects that require evaluations to justify their existence. Thus, this system accomplishes an integration of the following components: audits of the system, surveys of population, incorporation of information technologies, performance contracts, and construction of strategic measurements.

Another program that generated information systems to improve the budgetary process is FISFA, which started to function in January of 2003, after facing technological and administrative issues and even a change of leadership. FISFA represented the first attempt by the federal government to integrate the budgetary administration, treasury, financial administration, and governmental accounting in a single system to provide a general view of the cost of public programs through the budgetary process. FISFA offers information on the cost of public programs at different levels of budgetary classification: from its approval in the national congress, through possible modifications during implementation, up to the procedures to pay incurred costs. Despite the expectations of improvements raised by these programs, the real impact of NPS, SPE, and FISFA on changing the budgetary process has not yet been substantial.

Different Strategies to Implement PBB

A primary assessment and comparison of budgetary reforms in these countries shows that each country has developed its own strategy and agenda for implementing its transformation. In this regard, each country has emphasized different components of the model presented earlier in the chapter ("A Model of Performance-Based Budgeting"). Table 15.3 summarizes the reforms introduced in each of the four countries. The summary highlights the legal strategies used to implement these reforms, the organizational strategy used to direct the change and the controller of those changes, the extent to which these reforms generated autonomy for public agencies, the use of performance measures, the role of national congresses, and an overall evaluation of these reforms. The rest of this section gives more detail on the PBB experience of these countries.

The generation of information systems in these countries has followed two main courses. On one hand, the information systems try to integrate in unitary reports information from different sources, such as accounting,

Table 15.3   Summary of PBB Reforms in Brazil, Chile, Colombia, and Mexico

	Official Name	Legal Strategy	Organizational Strategy and Controller Agency	Autonomy of Agencies	Performance Measurement	Role of National Congress	Overall Evaluation
Brazil	"Administrative Reform of the State" "Public Finance Reform" "Planning Process Reform"	Four regimes for governmental intervention: Strategic, Exclusive, Nonexclusive, Market Law of Fiscal Responsibility Law of Budgetary Guides	Managerial contracts for programs controlled by the Ministry of Administrative Reform	Very low. The reform looks for better outcomes, not for autonomy.	General indicators included in contracts	Evaluation of the program's indicators of performance (there is no clear consequence of this evaluation)	Very formal reform and instruments. The system is applied, but analysts say there is still low real-results-oriented culture.
Chile	"Performance Indicators Program" "Program of Evaluation of Governmental Projects" "Program for Improving Public Management"	Executives' orders and through the power of the Ministry of Treasury	Evaluation, information, and managerial improvement controlled by the Office of Budget and Ministry of Treasury.	Very low. Office of Budget approves all indicators. Ministry of Treasury controls evaluation (through a panel of experts).	Indicators per agency. Evaluate effectiveness, efficiency, and economy	Uses information of indicators in budget discussion	More process than outcomes are evaluated. There are problems to evaluate qualitative inputs and results. All agencies report high level of performance.

	Official Name	Legal Strategy	Organizational Strategy and Controller Agency	Autonomy of Agencies	Performance Measurement	Role of National Congress	Overall Evaluation
Colombia	"National System of Evaluation of Public Management Results"	Constitutional amendment	Outcome-based information systems. Annual planning per agency linked to plan and to presidential policies controlled by Department of Planning though executive orders.	Focuses on macrolevel evaluation, not agency	Strategic evaluation that directs programs where efficacy and efficiency are evaluated	Department of Planning informs Congress regarding the results in the year. No clear attachment to budgetary discussion	General system directed not to agency performance, but to general governmental performance.
Mexico	"New Programmatic Structure" "Performance Evaluation System"	Executives' orders and through the power of the Ministry of Treasury	Strategic plan per agency, linked to institutional (per sector) program and national plan controlled by the Ministry of Treasury.	Reduced. The system aims to produce order and results. Eventually, some performance contracts have been applied, attached with some levels of autonomy.	General indicators not clearly linked or "chained"	None	The traditional system is still very powerful, not giving too much space to performance-oriented reforms.

performance, public finance, and management. These systems are centrally controlled and designed to facilitate an understanding of government activities and programs. On the other hand, these information systems are changing the focus of data collected from mere inputs and outputs to results and outcomes. This shift of focus is intended to provide information that can serve as a useful input for the budgetary process. These two changes in the transformation of information systems are mainly intended to generate a link between planning systems and budgetary processes.

In addition, performance measures that reflect goals included in information systems appear to be based on what agencies are currently reporting and doing rather than in the original proposals of legislators. This situation is related to the role that congresses play in these countries. The successful implementation of a PBB model requires the national congress to perform an active role in providing alternative options for creating programs, measuring performance, and developing information systems. However, in these countries, the real capacity of congresses to act in this form is very limited if we compare their capacities with those of the executive. Thus, since national congresses cannot play an important role in the checks and balances of the budgetary process, PBB has become primarily another instrument of bureaucratic control within the executive branch.

As part of their strategies, all these countries but Colombia implemented pilot programs to experiment with performance contracts. The design and repercussions of these performance contracts have faced the same technical problems mentioned previously, such as the difficulty in measuring outcomes accurately. In addition, within these contracts, incentives for managers such as more autonomy or monetary rewards are present only in isolated cases. Moreover, in those cases in which they are present, incentives appear to have very limited impact. For instance, with respect to autonomy for public managers, the only country that has created some kind of flexible managerial system is Brazil, where the new delegation of authority does not seem to substantially increase managers' autonomy. It seems as if central financial ministries agree with the necessity of controlling the agencies through new measures like performance but do not perceive the necessity of giving these agencies some autonomy to achieve new standards of performance. This resistance to providing autonomy might explain why only Chile has a specific system for rewarding performance. Since it is assumed that the introduction of the new budgetary system would be implemented "naturally" by the bureaucratic structures, as part of their duties, there was no need to offer autonomy as both an incentive and a mechanism to improve performance. Finally, only two countries, Brazil and Mexico, implemented changes in how they present the information included in the budget by including new budgetary categories. These two countries are looking for different ways to organize and present the budget, incorporating the changes resulting from other reforms and programs. These new budgetary categories are used to complement the traditional budgetary information, but they are not a feasible alternative to constitute the main structure of information for approving and analyzing the government's budget.

Lessons to Learn From Latin America

Regardless of which components a country introduces and how far it goes in its implementation, all these countries struggle with two issues not covered by the model: (a) how to resolve the autonomy versus accountability dilemma and (b) how to overcome problems related to a gradual implementation.

Regarding the issue created by the autonomy-versus-accountability dilemma, there are two main elements not fully integrated into the PBB model. First, the theoretical model of PBB has not yet dealt with the old idea that politics is undesirable within administrative processes. For example, Pollitt, Birchall, and Putman's (1998) study on the process of administrative decentralization in the United Kingdom showed how the process of liberation of the managerial forces required displacing the representative local authorities. However, the democratic "deficit" in PBB implementation becomes obvious when reformers say that the key question is whether services are being provided efficiently and effectively, rather than focusing on who provides them. Second, accountability and autonomy for management appear to be in opposition in the PBB model. Accountability is concerned with the guarantee that agents do what they are supposed to do. Autonomy has to do with providing managerial actors with the opportunity to independently use discretion smartly in order to make better decisions in a turbulent environment.

The main idea is that some level of managerial autonomy and discretion is necessary if society wants its public service to be innovative and proactive. However, this managerial autonomy might clash with the necessity of accountability. Accountability requires control and surveillance and requires behaviors that clearly follow certain rules and procedures. Managerial autonomy should free managers so they can make independent decisions ("Let the managers manage"). In other words, if your managers are evaluated by outcomes, in the extreme, we do not need to control them by procedures. More autonomy can be achieved by pushing for a definition of accountability that is related to outcomes rather than procedures. However, reformers advocating PBB, in practice, need to create practical ways to develop equilibrium in the autonomy-accountability continuum. Our analysis shows that Latin American countries have decided to give a preference to accountability, thus placing the innovative capacity of public agencies in a secondary place.

In addition, the focus on accountability supported by these reforms is narrowly defined; accountability implies being able to respond to demands or necessities rather than administering expectations. Administrators must balance different types of accountability, because they are held accountable differently depending upon the entity they are addressing. Managers should respond differently to appointed officials, legislative bodies, citizens, and judicial courts. The Latin American reforms have emphasized managers' accountability to appointed officials and judicial courts. The necessity of balancing different types of accountability implies making explicit the plurality of interests involved in each process of change, which is insufficiently explained in the normative theories of budgetary reforms implemented in Latin America.

PBB proposes that agencies must be responsible for efficiency and effectiveness but provides very little foundation to maintain external systems of accountability (Harris, 1995). Based on their approach of PBB, the reforms in the four Latin American countries have ignored a basic question: From whose point of view are economy, efficiency, and effectiveness judged? By defining whose points of view are taken into account, the reform defines who gets what from the programs' results. Responding to this question implies introducing a basic criterion of public administration: equity. This criterion may be an explicit objective of the reform; however, equity is not included in the prescribed logic of the model presented in earlier in the chapter or generally in the outcomes used to measure programs.

The second issue is related to the gradualist approach used in the Latin American experience. These countries chose to implement their reforms gradually, either by starting with a limited number of agencies or with a limited number of components of the model presented in this chapter. The countries studied here attempted to gain the benefits of a gradual approach that allowed public servants to either improve the programs using a dialectic process to implement changes or learn as they went along over time. This approach was also intended to facilitate a close supervision of implementation by the agencies in charge, avoiding the whole-scale implementation of change that may have created the impression that these reforms were just another bureaucratic change and not a substantive reform. By taking a gradual approach, the reformers accepted the possibility that their programs could lose their momentum in the public agenda if the society failed to see important results in the performance of public administration as a whole.

We argue that a full implementation of the PBB model implies transforming the structures of management and governance in public administration to allow revising the traditional systems of control. Therefore, most of the countries have preferred gradualist strategies not only because of the benefits of a gradual implementation, but also because a fully implemented PBB must provide possibilities to make financial decisions with a high degree of autonomy and accuracy for public officials. PBB ultimately may change the rules of financial control, with possible implications for the economy and the relationship between agencies and legislatures.

The budgetary reforms have been criticized by their incapacity to consider the politics of budget (Joyce, 1993; Pilegge, 1992; Rubin, 1988, 1990; Schick, 1994; Wildavsky, 1964, 1992). All reforms must respond to the question "Who should receive the benefits of the budgetary reforms and in what proportion?" In other words, a change in the budgetary policy implies a change in the political system. The literature on PBB ignores these components, even with nonpolitical arguments (Harris, 1995). Thus, to answer the question of why Latin American countries have preferred a gradual approach to implementing PBB, it is important to understand that PBB implies changes not only in the behavior of bureaucracy but also in the behavior of other actors.

In general, in these cases, we can see that PBB increases the number of rules, guides, and requirements by those agencies that control the budgetary process. In other words, the implementation of PBB can (a) add new procedures and information to assist public managers to make decisions; but (b) maintain the number of rules, regulations, and procedures that the agencies must fulfill to execute their budgets; and (c) add information for legislators to evaluate budget ex ante and ex post, but not replace the traditional information.

The politics of the budgetary process, as was noticed by Wildavsky (1964) over 40 years ago in the United States, cannot be eliminated by managerial reforms that assume it is possible to prevent political interference in budgetary activity. If the PBB model neglects the importance that politics plays in the budgetary process, the reforms based on this model are condemned to assume that it is possible to change undesirable behaviors of public servants without changing the behavior of controllers and legislators. In other words, PBB requires the transformation of diverse relationships among policy executors and legislators in order to be fully effective. Managers can have more autonomy as long as clear and measurable results exist to hold them accountable. Given the difficulty of measuring the diverse impacts and results of governmental organizations with clarity and precision, agencies' results have to be defined taking into consideration the influence of the political forces.

For that reason, the implementation of these budgets requires a deep transformation of the structures and political relations at different levels: (a) between representatives and executive, (b) between representatives and control agencies, (c) between representatives and agencies, (d) between governmental agencies and control agencies, and (e) between control agencies and the executive. In our analysis, it seems none of these countries have made these extensive transformations. A second generation of reforms must take into account these considerations in order to address the limitations of the programs analyzed here.

Final Comments

There seems to be a consensus that the reform of public administration will produce effective results when the behaviors of the bureaucracies change and they are released from normative constraints, red tape, micromanagement, and controls that generate inefficiencies. Despite this consensus, it is not evident which are the key factors for implementing an effective reform. Here, we have briefly discussed some of these dilemmas based on the experiences of four Latin American countries. Their lessons have shown that serious difficulties exist in designing and implementing such reforms because the budget is a political instrument in any democracy. The politics of the budgetary process cannot be eliminated by a managerial reform.

In the Latin American experiences presented in this chapter, we found incomplete efforts in implementing a PBB. Governments are faced with two main dilemmas: (a) equilibrium required between agencies' autonomy and accountability and (b) the balance between an implementation that allows getting results quickly and including in the reform all the interests affected by the reform.

We argue there is a need to develop a political economy of the budgets directed to results. In other words, it is necessary to develop a framework of PBB that explains why (a) these budgets add new technical ideas but do not eliminate the political discussion of the role of government and its actions; (b) the discussion of results, impact, and performance involves defining, ordering, and ranking multiple preferences among heterogeneous actors for which there is no a mechanical solution; and (c) PBB may be approached as any other public policy, whereby the agendas of political and bureaucratic actors, the debates among political agents, and the discussion of the state of public administration are contextual variables particularly important to consider in an effort for introducing this type of budget. By incorporating these issues into the discussions of budgetary reforms based on performance measures, we will facilitate the understanding of the limitations of these reforms, helping managers to determine more accurate expectations of their implementation and anticipate likely obstacles and difficulties.

Discussion Questions _____

1. This chapter presented some dilemmas of the implementation of PBB at the national level. Are local governments likely to face the same dilemmas? Are local governments more able to overcome them?

2. Discuss whether the dilemma between a need for gradual implementation and a need for quick results is any different in developing countries than in industrialized economies.

3. Which stakeholders (appointed officials, elected officials, legislative leaders, citizens, or judicial courts) should receive priority in a PBB system? Is there a way to take into account all their views and interests?

4. Discuss the dilemma of pursuing conflicting goals in the PBB process, especially the dilemma for managers of having more focus on accountability but wanting more autonomy (and deregulation) to implement programs. Which of these goals do you think should have the higher priority? Why?

References

Arellano, D., Gil, J. R., Ramírez, J., & Rojano, A. (2000). Nueva gerencia pública en acción: Procesos de modernización presupuestal [New Public Management in action: Budgeting modernization processess]. *Reforma y Democracia, 17*, 1–23.

Banco Nacional de Desenvolvimento Econômico. (2000). *Guía sobre la ley de responsabilidad fiscal* [A guide for the Fiscal Responsibility Law]. Brasilia, Brazil: Author.

Barzelay, M. (1992). *Breaking through bureaucracy.* Berkeley: University of California Press.

Broom, C. (1995). Performance-based government model: Building a track record. *Public Budgeting and Finance, 15*(4), 3–17.

Departamento Nacional de Planeación. (1996). *Hacia una gestión pública orientada a resultados* [Public management oriented toward results]. Bogotá, Colombia: Author.

Dion, D. (1998). Evidence and inference in the comparative case study. *Comparative Politics, 30*, 127–145.

Dirección de Presupuesto. (2000). *Programa de mejora de la gestión pública* [Program for the improvement of public management]. Santiago, Chile: Ministerio de Hacienda.

Dos Santos, L. (2000). *Agencificação, publicização, contratualização e controle social. possibilidades no âmbito da reforma do aparelho do estado* [Organization, publicity, contracting, and social control within the reform of government]. Brasilia, Brazil: Departamento Intersindical de Assesoria Parlamentar.

Dos Santos, L. (2002). *Orçamentos por resultados, contratos de gesão e avaliação de desempenho: Perspectivas para o controle social e a transparencia da administração pública brasileira* [Budgeting by results, management contracts, and performance evaluation: Perspectives for social control and transparency in public administration]. Paper presened at the Primer Congreso Latinoamericano de Ciencia Política, Universidad Salamanca, Spain.

Forsythe, D. W. (1993). Financial management and the reinvention of government. *Public Productivity and Management Review, 16*, 415–423.

Guzmán, M. (2000). *Programa de evaluación de proyectos gubernamentales* [Program for evaluation of governmental programs]. Paper presented at the VIII Curso Internacional de Reformas Económicas Y Gestión Pública Estratégica, Instituto Latinoamericano y del Caribe de Planificación Económica y Social- (ILPES) Comisión Económica para América Latina (CEPAL), Santiago, Chile.

Guzmán, M. (2001). *Evaluación de programas e indicadores de Desempeño Transparencia y Mejoramiento de los Procedimientos para la Formulación del Presupuesto* [Evaluation of programs and performance indicators, transparency, and improvement of procedures for the design of budgets]. Paper presented at the Seminario funciones básicas de la Planificación (ILPES), Havana, Cuba.

Harris, J. (1995). Service efforts and accomplishments standards: Fundamental questions of an emerging concept. *Public Budgeting and Finance, 15*(4), 18–37.

Joyce, P. G. (1993). The reiterative nature of budget reform: Is there anything new in federal budgeting? *Public Budgeting and Finance, 13*(3), 36–48.

Joyce, P. G. (1999). Performance-based budget. In R. T. Mayer (Ed.), *Handbook of government budgeting* (pp. 597–619). San Francisco. Jossey-Bass.

Lijphart, A. (1971). Comparative politics and the comparative method. *American Political Science Review, 65*, 682–693.

Marcel, M. (1997). *Indicadores de desempeño como instrumentos de la moderni-zación del Estado* [Performance indicators as tools for the modernization of state]. Santiago, Chile: Dirección de Presupuesto, Ministerio de Hacienda.

Marcel M. (2005). *Presupuestos por resultados en Chile. ¿Utopía o realidad?* [Budgeting by results in Chile: Utopia or reality?] Santiago, Chile: Ministerio de Hacienda.

Martner, R. (2000). *Gestión pública y programación plurianual, desafíos y experien-cias recientes* [Public management and multiyear programming, challenges, and recent experiences]. (Serie gestión pública). Santiago de Chile, Chile: CEPAL.

Organisation for Economic Co-operation and Development. (1993). *Performance appraisal: Practice: Problems and issues.* Paris: OECD, Public Management Committee.

Ospina, S. (2000). *Evaluación de la gestión Pública conceptos y aplicaciones en el caso latinoamericano* [Evaluation of public management, concepts and uses for the Latin American case]. Paper presented at the V Congreso del CLAD, Santo Domingo, Dominican Republic.

Palumbo, D., & Maynard-Moody, S. (1991). *Contemporary public administration.* London: Longman.

Pilegge, J. C. (1992). Budget reforms. In J. Rabin (Ed.), *Public productivity hand-book* (pp. 94–97). New York: Marcel Dekker.

Pollitt, C., Birchall, J., & Putman, K. (1998). Decentralising public service manage-ment. In A. Halachmi & P. B. Boorsma (Eds.), *Inter and intra government arrangements for productivity: An agency approach* (pp. 15–30). London: Kluwer Academic.

Rubin, I. S. (1988). *New directions in budget theory.* Albany: State University of New York Press.

Rubin, I. S. (1990). Budget theory and budget practice: How good the fit? *Public Administration Review, 40,* 179–189.

Schick, A. (1994). From the old politics of budgeting to the new. *Public Budgeting and Finance, 14*(1), 135–144.

Secretaria de la Controloria y Desarrollo Administrative. (1998). *Guía para la definición de indicadores, programa de modernización de la administración pública 1995–2000* [A guide for the design of indicators, modernization program for public administration 1995–2000]. Mexico City: Gobierno de México, SECODAM.

Silberschneider, W. (2001). *A naturaleza da reforma da gestão fiscal no Brasil* [The nature of fiscal management reform in Brazil]. Brasilia, Brazil: Foundation of João Pinheiro.

Subsecretaria de Egresos, Secretaría de Hacienda y Crédito Público. (1997). *Lineamientos para la concertación de la nueva estructura programática 1998* [A guide for the negotiation of the new programmatic structure 1998]. Mexico City: Gobierno de México, SHCP.

Tesofe (Federation Treasury). (2003). *Marco Regulatorio del SIAFF* [Regulatory Framework for SIAFF]. Mexico City: Gobierno de México, SHCP.

Unidad de Política y Control Presupuestal, Secretaría de Hacienda y Crédito Público, Subsecretaría de Egresos. (1997). *Reforma al sistema presupuestario. La nueva estructura programática* [Reform of the budgetary system. The new programmatic structure]. Mexico City: Gobierno de México, SHCP.

Unidad de Política y Control Presupuestal, Secretaría de Hacienda y Crédito Público, Subsecretaría de Egresos. (1998). *Sistema de evaluación del desempeño a través de indicadores. Guía Metodológica* [System of performance evaluation through indicators. A methodological guide]. Mexico City: Gobierno de México, SHCP.

Unidad de Política y Control Presupuestal, Secretaría de Hacienda y Crédito Público, Subsecretaría de Egresos. (1999). *Reforma al sistema presupuestario (RSP). Avances 1998, versión preliminar* [Reform of the budgetary system. Improvement 1998, a preliminary version]. Mexico City: Gobierno de México, SHCP.

Wildavsky, A. (1964). *The politics of the budgetary process.* Boston: Little, Brown.

Wildavsky, A. (1992). *The new politics of the budgetary reform.* Glenview, IL: Scott, Foresman.

16 Performance-Based Budgeting in Florida

Great Expectations, More Limited Reality

Martha Wellman

Gary VanLandingham

When the Florida Legislature enacted performance-based program budgeting in 1994, expectations for budgetary reform were high. After 12 years, some of these expectations have not been realized. However, other expectations have come to fruition; and, as a result, Florida's governmental operations have become more efficient, accountable, and effective.

This chapter focuses on the legislature's use of performance information and describes the Florida performance-based program-budgeting law and enactment process. It assesses the expectations for Florida's initiative and those that have and have not been met from a legislative perspective. In addition, it discusses some of the difficulties encountered with using performance information in the legislative process. The chapter concludes that despite limited legislative interest and imperfect performance information, the reform has been successful in improving legislative oversight and program effectiveness.

Florida's Performance-Based Program-Budgeting Law

In 1994, the Florida Legislature enacted the Government Performance and Accountability Act, which established a statewide, performance-based budgeting system for state government (Florida Legislature, 1994). The act requires all state agencies to develop performance measures for their programs and to include data on these measures in their legislative budget requests. The legislature is to include in the appropriations act standards for the performance it expects agencies to attain with the funds they receive. This budgeting reform is called "performance-based program budgeting" and is commonly referred to as "PB^2."

The rationale for establishing performance-based program budgeting in Florida was to create a budgeting system in which "the amount of resources given to public programs . . . [is] influenced by their performance in achieving desired results" (Florida Legislature, Office of Program Policy and Government Accountability [OPPAGA], 1999, p. 2). While Florida had required state agencies to include limited performance information in their legislative budget requests since the 1960s, this information was not used in the legislative process, and the measures were not considered to be satisfactory or particularly reliable (Easterling, 1999). In the late 1980s and early 1990s, the legislature considered but did not pass several initiatives to create a performance-based budgeting system. These initiatives paved the way to the eventual passage of the Government Performance and Accountability Act in 1994. Political and economic conditions that also contributed to the passage of the act included the election of Governor Lawton Chiles, who strongly supported the "reinventing government" movement popularized by Osborne and Gaebler (1992), as well as deep, multiyear budget cuts necessitated by the economic recession of the early 1990s. In making these cuts, legislators expressed frustration with the state's existing budgeting system, which was based on traditional, line-item appropriations and provided little information about what agencies were accomplishing. Without performance information, the legislature had difficulty targeting relatively ineffective programs for the budget cuts (Berry & Flowers, 1999).

Unlike many states, Florida did not try to implement its budget reform in a single fiscal year. Instead, it phased in PB^2 over a 7-year period, beginning in fiscal year 1995–1996 and ending in fiscal year 2002–2003, when all agencies were operating with performance-based program budgets. During that time period, an average of five agencies began the PB^2 reform process each year, with each agency implementing the process over a 3-year period (VanLandingham, Wellman, & Andrews, 2005).

In the first year of this 3-year cycle, agencies beginning the process proposed the programs to be funded under the new budgeting approach. As defined by statute, each program was to consist of a set of activities authorized by the legislature and designed to achieve identifiable goals and objectives. Agencies were also required to develop a set of performance measures, including outputs and outcomes, for each program. The agency proposals were reviewed by the governor's budgeting office and legislative staff, including OPPAGA, which was created by the 1994 act to provide

Table 16.1 Examples of Performance Measures Used for Selected Florida Programs

Department	Program	Measure
Education	State university system	Percentage of first-time-in-college students who graduate in 4 years
Education	State university system	Percentage of graduates with fewer than 115% of the hours they need to graduate
Education	Community colleges	Percentage of certificate program completers who are employed with quarterly wages of more than $4,680
Education	Community colleges	Percentage of AA degree holders who transfer into a baccalaureate degree program
Children and Families	Child protection	Percentage of abused or maltreated children who are found to be reabused within 6 months
Juvenile Justice	Secure residential commitment	Percentage of residents who remain crime free for 1 year after their release
Corrections	Security and institutional operations	Number of escapes from the secure perimeters of major institutions
Law Enforcement	Investigations	Percentage of closed cases that are resolved

technical assistance to aid the effort and serve as the legislature's program evaluation and policy research office (Sheffield, 1999). After the legislature approved the proposed programs and performance measures, agencies began collecting baseline data on the measures. Table 16.1 shows examples of some of the approved measures.

In the second year of the cycle, agencies developed their legislative budget requests using the approved programs and performance measures. For each measure, agencies submitted past performance data as available, an analysis of the validity and reliability of performance information, and a proposed standard. This was intended to enable the governor and legislature to consider performance when making budget recommendations and decisions. The legislature had the final say in setting the performance standard, and it subsequently appropriated funds to the agency under the new approach by including the program, measures, and performance standards in the budget act.

The standards agencies proposed were often based on their prior performance, with adjustments for expected changes in program design. During the approval process, the legislature often raised the standards to set an expectation for continuous improvement in agency operations. In some cases, however, the legislature approved standards that were not realistic. For example, the legislative standard for the number of children dying as a result of abuse or neglect was set at zero, even though past experience indicated that this standard was unlikely to be achieved. Because the legislature cannot publicly agree that the agency is fully meeting expectations if a certain number of children die each year, the zero-deaths standard reflected political concerns rather than program realities.

In the third year of the cycle, agencies began formally operating under PB^2. Agencies were expected to use their appropriated funding to attain the performance standards established by the legislature. However, agencies had an opportunity to ask the governor to change a standard if they did not receive the level of legislative appropriations they anticipated when proposing the standard. After the performance standards were established, agencies were required to provide data in future budget requests showing whether they met the standards; and, if they failed to do so, they were required to explain why they did not.

Agencies whose performance exceeded legislative standards were eligible to receive incentives, including additional budget flexibility, additional appropriations, and the ability to retain a portion of their unexpended appropriations for bonus compensation of employees, employee training, or technology improvements. Agencies whose performance fell short of legislative standards could receive disincentives, including mandatory quarterly reporting on performance data; program restructuring, transfer, or elimination; and reductions in managers' salaries or overall agency budgets (Florida Legislature, 2005).

The implementation process also included a formal independent feedback mechanism, as OPPAGA was required to conduct a "program evaluation and justification review" of each program after the agency had been operating under PB^2 for a year and to submit its findings and recommendations to the legislature. These studies assessed the programs' progress toward reaching the specified performance levels and factors that affected agency performance. They also identified opportunities for program improvements and cost savings (VanLandingham et al., 2005).

Expectations and Results for Performance-Based Program Budgeting

Initial expectations for Florida's PB^2 varied. Some key stakeholders hoped that the new budgeting system would improve public perception of government and make the public more willing to pay taxes in return for high-quality government services. Other stakeholders expected the system to save tax dollars by making government more efficient and identifying low-performing activities that could be eliminated (Berry & Flowers, 1999). Despite these differences, most stakeholders agreed that Florida's PB[2] should accomplish the following objectives (Florida Legislature, OPPAGA, 1997):

- Better inform citizens about the benefits of government services
- Make legislative budget and policy decisions more rational through the use of performance information
- Increase agency budget flexibility by focusing legislative appropriations on outcomes, not inputs
- Facilitate a common understanding of the goals and objectives of government programs between the legislature and the executive branch
- Improve legislative oversight of agency and program performance
- Develop incentives for agencies to be more efficient and effective

As discussed above, most of these objectives have not been fully met. However, the initiative has had a positive effect on legislative oversight and the delivery of government services. Thus, despite some disappointments, performance measurement and reporting is alive and well in Florida today.

Better Informing Citizens About the Benefits of Government Services

Florida's PB[2] initiative reflected a public perception that government was inefficient and overly bureaucratic (Berry & Flowers, 1999). One of the goals that proponents sought to achieve was to address this perception. Accordingly, the preamble to the Government Performance and Accountability Act states that "state agencies should strive to keep the citizens of this state informed of the public benefits derived from the delivery of state agency services and products and of the progress state agencies are making with regard to improving performance" (Florida Legislature, 1994, p. 1850).

Our observations, however, indicate that the public has little interest in PB[2] data, and the availability of performance data does not appear to have increased citizens' support of government. This probably occurs for several reasons: (a) many performance measures are technical and not easily understood by people uninformed about the programs; (b) PB[2] performance data are not readily accessible or user-friendly; (c) one of Florida's early efforts to publicize and report performance measures to citizens was eliminated relatively early in the initiative; and (d) many citizens are relatively uninformed about government and generally form their opinions based on personal experience rather than performance data.

Measures are often technical and not meaningful to citizens. An intrinsic problem with measuring and reporting the performance of complex programs is that individuals often need a good deal of knowledge to be able to interpret these data (Wang, 2002). For example, one of the PB^2 measures for the Florida's Department of Education is the per-case cost the Division of Vocational Rehabilitation incurs when serving non-severely-disabled persons. While this is a useful efficiency measure, most citizens would not know how to interpret these data or whether a $400 per-case cost represents excellent or poor performance (Florida Legislature, 2005). This problem is aggravated because agencies generally report their performance measures in a spreadsheet format, without graphics, trend lines, or narrative to explain the measures and standards (Florida Legislature, OPPAGA, 1999). Rather than helping to explain the initiative to citizens, Florida's press has run stories that have misinterpreted performance measures and generally ridiculed the process.

PB^2 measures and data are not readily accessible. Even if citizens are interested in PB^2 data, such information is not easy to find. The legislature has removed most measures and standards from the state budget document, largely because including this information made it difficult to print the document in the limited time available each year. The Florida Constitution requires that legislators receive the final version of the proposed budget at least 72 hours before they vote on it (State of Florida, 1968), and budget negotiations between the two chambers generally continue near the end of the regular legislative session. To help produce and distribute the budget document in the remaining timeframe, legislators took steps to make the document as short as possible, including eliminating the large number of performance measures and standards from the document. Although agencies include performance measures, data, and proposed standards in their individual legislative budget requests, these documents are often lengthy, highly technical, and are themselves not readily accessible to the public. As a result, citizens who are interested in examining Florida's performance measures would have to spend a good deal of time finding this information.

An effort to publicize and report performance information to citizens was eliminated. As part of the Government Performance and Accountability Act, the legislature created the Commission on Government Accountability to the Public, which was made up of 15 members appointed by the governor and confirmed by the Senate (Florida Legislature, 1994). The commission was charged with tracking the impact of public programs by reviewing agency performance data and other sources of information, holding public meetings to allow agencies to explain their successes or failures in attaining performance standards, receiving public testimony about agency performance, and making recommendations to enhance agency productivity and achievement.

The commission departed from this charge, however, and began to develop quality-of-life measures for the state of Florida separate from the PB^2 process. Without gaining legislative or gubernatorial buy-in, the commission also announced that it planned to set benchmarks for these measures, some of which had little to do with government programs, and then hold the governor and legislature accountable for meeting the benchmarks. The commission quickly lost political support, and its funding was eliminated in 1998 (Ogata & Goodkey, 1998). Disbanding the commission, however, meant that a potentially important conduit and interpreter of performance to the public was lost.

Many citizens are motivated less by performance data than by personal experience. Finally, the belief that citizens would change their perceptions of government based on reported data was naive. Even when such data are available, citizens rarely pay much attention to them. For example, unlike performance information for most programs, performance data for the Florida's K–12 school system are widely available and widely publicized (Florida Department of Education, 2006). Citizens do make use of these data when deciding where to live, which tends to drive up housing costs in the zones for "good" schools. However, most parents of children who go to schools that the state's measurement systems deem to be "poorly performing" believe that their schools are nonetheless good. Parents whose children were in failing public schools had an opportunity to receive a voucher allowing the student to attend a private school—but parents of only about 730 students took advantage of these vouchers in the most recent school year (Toppo, 2006). Apparently, for the parents who kept their children in public schools, personal interaction with teachers, school administrators, and other school personnel meant more than statistical data about the schools' performance. (In 2006, the Florida Supreme Court ruled that this voucher program is unconstitutional. It is uncertain how the program might be restructured.)

Florida's experience with voucher programs reflects the fact that most citizens pay little attention to government and generally base their opinions on recent personal experiences and/or opinion leaders (deHaven-Smith, 1998; Zaller, 1992). There is no evidence that performance data provided under PB[2] have affected citizen support of government programs or willingness to pay additional taxes for improved outcomes.

Making Legislative Budget and Policy Decisions More Rational

Perhaps the greatest expectation about PB[2] is that it would allow legislators to consider performance when they make policy and budgeting decisions. The premise behind this expectation is that legislators should reward programs with good performance with more funding and sanction programs with poor performance by decreasing their funding. This desire to "rationalize" governmental budgeting by more strongly linking funding with performance is long-standing within public administration, prescribed by Willoughby (1918) and Key (1952), and served as the foundation of earlier (and unsuccessful) budget reforms efforts, such as PPBS (Schick, 1966) and ZBB (Shafritz & Hyde, 1997).

While the legislature has considered information produced by PB[2] in its policy and budget deliberations, the reform has not materially changed the legislative process. As in other states that have implemented performance-based budgeting systems (de Lancer Julnes & Mixcoatl, 2006), the Florida Legislature has not used performance data to make decisions about programs and appropriations, with a few exceptions. These exceptions have generally involved agencies that have successfully used performance data to justify increased funding, rather than cut programs that failed to meet performance standards. For example, the 2006 Florida Legislature provided additional funding to the Department of Business and Professional Services after an OPPAGA study reported that the department was not meeting its standard for hotel and restaurant inspection, due in part to insufficient staffing (Florida Legislature, OPPAGA, 2005). Other agencies have at times made similar attempts to use performance information to justify requests for more funding. However, agencies do not routinely present or discuss their performance measures when presenting budget requests, nor does the appropriations committee process routinely consider performance measures when making funding decisions.

One notable exception is that the legislature has established a performance-based funding formula for workforce training programs offered by local school districts and community colleges. Part of this formula distributes funds to school districts and community colleges based on their performance in providing training programs that meet critical workforce needs and place graduates in the jobs for which they were trained. This formula has been successful in encouraging school districts and community colleges to focus their training resources on programs that meet workforce needs (Florida Legislature, OPPAGA, 1997). However, this type of incentive fund has not been extended to other areas of the state budget, probably because services in those areas are provided by single entities or are deemed to be critical. For example, funding to repair emergency shelters damaged by hurricanes was distributed to all affected counties, not just those that best met a designated performance standard.

The legislature's use of PB[2] information in its policy deliberations has been similarly limited. While legislative committees initially spent considerable time reviewing and discussing performance measures, this is no longer the case. During the first 2 years of the reform effort, committees regularly held special hearings to discuss the programs and measures proposed by agencies and to debate the performance standards to be set for each measure (Hendon, 1999). These special hearings are no longer held. However, agencies and legislators do at times refer to measures during committee hearings, generally when they wish to make a point regarding agency performance. For example, in 2006, the Department of Children and Families presented to legislative committees selected performance information regarding the state's transition to privatized services in this system.

Performance information has been of limited use in legislative funding and policy decisions for three major reasons:

- Most budgeting and policy decisions involve core values and are not influenced by performance information.
- Rewarding good performance and sanctioning poor performance makes little sense for critically needed services.
- Performance information does not by itself explain why performance meets or does not meet expectations.

Budgeting and policy decisions involve core values. A primary reason why performance information has been of limited use in legislative funding and policy decisions is that this information is generally most useful in overseeing already enacted programs, while legislative attention generally is focused on value decisions about whether a new policy should be enacted or how to allocate limited resources among programs with very different goals and outcomes. PB^2 performance data are compiled only for existing programs and are not available when the legislature debates whether to create new programs. Further, data on the performance of different programs are of limited use when the legislature decides how to allocate funding between programs with different goals and objectives. For example, the Department of Education's programs for K–12 education have a goal to improve educational outcomes for children, while the Department of Transportation's goal is to improve transportation services. A key policy issue the legislature must decide each year is how much of its limited resources should be appropriated to education versus transportation programs. This is fundamentally a value decision on the comparative worth of education and transportation programs, and information on whether such programs are fully meeting performance standards can play only a minor role in these decisions.

Budgeting and policy decisions are thus intrinsically political and involve core values, and legislators generally look to their personal beliefs, those of their supporters, and what they believe is the will of their constituents, rather than performance data, when making these decisions (Baumgartner & Jones, 1993; de Lancer Julnes & Mixcoatl, 2006; Florida Legislature, OPPAGA, 1999). At some level, proponents who seek to "rationalize" the budget process by making performance data the primary driver of budget decisions are in effect wishing to take politics out of the legislature itself, substituting "rational" analysis to decide value conflicts in place of the messy give-and-take negotiation that characterizes democratic budget and policy processes (Wildavsky, 1961). Such a substitution is unlikely to ever occur.

Rewarding or sanctioning performance makes little sense for most public programs. A second reason why performance information has been of limited use in legislative decisions is that as long as programs are deemed to serve a needed public purpose, rewarding those that perform well and punishing those that perform poorly makes little sense. Legislators often believe that programs that are attaining their objectives are simply doing their jobs and do not need additional resources. In contrast, advocates of programs that are failing to meet performance targets often attribute the failure to inadequate resources and advocate for additional funding rather than budget cuts (deHaven-Smith, 1988). This is particularly true for programs that have a high political value. For example, legislators are unlikely to respond to increased crime by reducing funding for law enforcement. They would also be unlikely to respond to an epidemic by cutting appropriations for public health programs, even though those programs failed to meet performance standards for reducing incidents of disease.

Performance information does not explain good or poor performance. Finally, performance information is like a canary in a mine in that it can provide information about whether a program is doing well or badly but generally cannot explain why or point to a specific action that the legislature should address through policy and funding choices. Most desired outcomes of public programs are subject to influences such as overall economic conditions, changing citizen characteristics, or broad social trends that are outside the control of a government program. For example, many Florida programs failed to meet performance standards in 2004 and 2005 due to the disruptions caused when several major hurricanes hit the state. Given that these outcomes were beyond the control of agency managers, the legislature did not respond by imposing the sanctions available under the Government Performance and Accountability Act. Overall, the legislature has not explicitly used the performance incentives and disincentives available under the act since the early years of PB[2] (VanLandingham et al., 2005).

Impact on Agency Budget Flexibility

One of the initial expectations for PB[2] was that the legislature would give agencies more spending flexibility in exchange for stronger accountability. This principle was consistent with the principles espoused by Osborne and Gaebler's *Reinventing Government* (1992), which, as previously discussed, had been promoted by Governor Chiles. Consequently, the governor advocated that the legislature appropriate funds by program in place of its traditional practice of appropriating funds by objects of expenditure, such as permanent personnel, temporary personal, expenses, aid to local government, and so on (Florida Legislature, OPPAGA, 1997).

In the early years of the PB[2], agencies often proposed very large programs in an effort to maximize their potential budget flexibility. For example, the Department of Education proposed to include all activities related to prekindergarten through 12th-grade public school into one program, the "Public Schools Educational Program," even though this program would have served several different populations subject to different performance expectations, including prekindergarten students, regular education students, special education students, and limited-English-speaking students. In addition, the proposed program included diverse functions such as teacher certification, student transportation, and school construction (VanLandingham et al., 2005).

Since expectations were that the legislature would appropriate funds at the program level, these large programs would have greatly reduced legislative control over expenditures. However, legislators and appropriations staff were reluctant to give up such control, and the legislature has continued to appropriate funds by objects of expenditure as well as to distinctive educational functions such as transportation, teacher training, and salary supplements for teachers.

Early in the PB² process, the legislature did give greater budget flexibility to two agencies with highly respected executive directors. Appropriations for these agencies combined some line items, which enabled these agencies to shift resources and implement money-saving innovations, such as data-processing improvements (VanLandingham et al., 2005). The legislature also approved a pilot project that allowed the Department of Children and Families to retain some unexpended appropriations, which it mostly invested in technology improvements (Florida Legislature, OPPAGA, 1995). However, the legislature did not extend this pilot project or grant other agencies similar budget flexibility.

Governor Jeb Bush, who was elected in 1998, also sought to increase budget flexibility and proposed dividing each program into more discrete services that would receive lump-sum appropriations (Florida Legislature, OPPAGA, 2000). The legislature responded to this initiative by modifying its appropriations structure to more closely match agency program structures, but it continued appropriating money to many of same budget categories and line items. Thus, PB² has had relatively little effect on agency budget flexibility. Since this proposal, the governor's office has exhibited little interest in performance measures and directed agencies to strip measures from their long-range program plans. As an advocate for a smaller, more efficient government, the governor's office has continually emphasized output and efficiency measures rather than outcome measures, which can be used to advocate for more services. The exception is in K–12 education, where the results of statewide tests are highly publicized and of evident interest to the governor.

Facilitating Common Understanding of Program Goals

One of the legislative expectations for PB² was that "each state agency's mission, goals, and objectives should be clearly defined" (Florida Legislature, 1994, p. 1849). Agencies held extensive negotiations concerning proposed programs and measures with the governor's office, legislative staff, and legislators. These negotiations, which in the initial years included substantive committee hearings on agency proposals, led to a greater consensus about the mission, goals, and objectives of programs. However, the benefits of this process for the legislature have been substantially weakened due to term limits that forced legislators who participated in the negotiations to retire.

Agencies coming under PB[2] generally held a series of internal workshops to examine their operations; categorize these activities into programs; and develop input, output, and outcome measures that would assess the performance for each program. OPPAGA and the governor's office provided technical assistance to the agencies, but the process was complicated because each agency's workshops generally involved a different mix of agency, legislative, OPPAGA, and governor's office stakeholders, who frequently had different perspectives on what types and levels of measures were appropriate. Agencies sometimes complained that they received different instructions depending on what stakeholders were present at a particular meeting. Some stakeholders asserted that agencies should report only high-level outcomes even though they did not exercise complete control over them, while other stakeholders argued that agencies should report only on outcomes they could control. OPPAGA generally took the position that agencies should collect data on a broad range of outcome measures, with higher-level measures reported to the legislature and lower-level measures reported internally for management use but available for legislative review as needed (Florida Legislature, OPPAGA, 1999).

As no central entity had overall responsibility for resolving these disputes and setting policy regarding levels of measures, this process resulted in inconsistency among agencies regarding the number and level of performance measures each subsequently developed and submitted for legislative consideration (VanLandingham et al., 2005). Despite this ambiguity, agencies reported that the process was helpful in getting staff and stakeholder groups to think about agency missions and how various program activities contributed to measurable outcomes.

Legislative review and approval of the measures were also beneficial in promoting a shared understanding of agency missions and goals, although the process was somewhat idiosyncratic depending on the membership of the committees that examined each agency's proposed programs and performance measures. In some cases, committees did not review proposed programs and measures in as much detail and accepted the agency proposals with little debate. In other cases, however, committees spent a great deal of time discussing agency missions and debating proposed programs and measures. For example, one committee rejected the proposed measure for an alcohol and drug abuse program because a member who was a physician asserted that the proposed measure—the percentage of impaired pregnant women who gave birth to children who were substance free—was invalid because the medical test used to determine whether or not a newborn is substance free is not always accurate.

Perhaps the most notable area of legislative debate over measures occurred over higher-education policy, in which legislators demanded that a measure be created to assess the extent to which students obtaining baccalaureate degrees earned more college credits than they needed to meet degree requirements. Universities resisted this measure, largely because they asserted that students who took additional classes received education that was worth the additional cost. The legislature prevailed, and all universities are now reporting on "excess hours" and taking steps to keep students on track to receive their degrees and avoid taking extra courses. Similar discussions occurred in the areas of criminal justice and juvenile justice, in which agencies were more likely to focus on rehabilitation and the legislature was more likely to focus on punishment. Overall, these discussions helped to engender a common understanding of agency operations and helped agencies focus on the outcomes that the legislature deemed most desirable (Florida Legislature, OPPAGA, 1999).

The benefits of this process, however, have been eroded by the effects of Florida's legislative term limits, which provide that members must leave office after serving a maximum of 8 years. As noted by Moynihan and Ingraham (2003), electoral changes pose a major barrier to constructing effective performance management systems. While several term-limited members of the Florida House of Representatives have successfully moved to the Senate, the overall effect of the restriction (which was enacted as the result of a citizen constitutional amendment referendum) has been to increase legislative turnover. As a result, most legislators who participated in the discussions of agency programs and measures have now left office, and newly elected members often have relatively little knowledge about the operations and missions of the programs that come before them for policy and budget consideration.

Improving Legislative Oversight

Florida's PB[2] initiative has been successful in improving legislative oversight of agency activities. The annual reporting of performance data has provided more information the legislature can use to routinely monitor agency operations. While the legislature no longer routinely holds hearings on performance information, it does regularly ask agency managers about measures when they testify before committees. The legislature has continued to support the concept of performance measurement, and it has mandated that most newly created programs establish performance measurement or other accountability systems. Legislative staff regularly review agency performance data to identify trends, compare performance to standards, and notify legislators of potential problems. While this type of oversight may not be the focus of legislative committee meetings, it serves to remind agencies that their performance is being monitored.

In addition, OPPAGA has conducted a large volume of in-depth studies of agency programs, which have enhanced the legislature's ability to conduct oversight and provided it with an independent source of information about policy and budget options. While the auditor general conducted regular financial, compliance, and performance audits of agencies prior to the implementation of PB^2, OPPAGA conducts a wider range of policy research, program evaluation, and policy analysis studies and publishes approximately 80 reports per year, in addition to providing ongoing research assistance to members and committees.

The legislature has recently amended the performance-budgeting law to require agencies to report their unit costs of providing services, which can enable better assessment of the relative efficiency of government services. In 1999, the legislature required agencies to report the unit costs for their outputs, and, in 2006, it mandated that a uniform method be developed to allocate indirect costs among program entities. While a recent OPPAGA report concluded that agency unit cost data were still beset by validity and reliability problems, these data may provide future legislatures with an additional oversight tool.

Improving Program Efficiency and Effectiveness

While PB^2 has had limited impact on the legislative process, it has had a much larger effect at the agency administrative level. The initiative provides program administrators with a useful tool to monitor the effect of current strategies and, when necessary, make changes to improve outcomes. Longitudinal data on program outputs and outputs produced under PB^2 also allow managers to track the impact of program changes over time. In areas where multiple providers exist, agencies have used performance information to choose the providers, program models, and strategies that produce the best outcomes for their programs. Managers who lack the budget authority to make needed changes to improve program operations can request budget amendments, which the legislature often approves.

In addition to developing strategies for improving outcomes, some managers have used performance budgeting to streamline operations. For example, the Department of Revenue and the Florida Department of Law Enforcement used the PB^2 process to redefine their missions and consolidate program activities. For example, as part of the process of developing proposed performance measures, the Department of Revenue conducted a core process-mapping exercise that it used to decrease the numbers of steps involved in tax collection, combine activities in regional offices, and reduce its number of managers. The Department of Law Enforcement similarly used the PB^2 process to reorganize its operations and restructure its services to improve accountability and effectiveness (Florida Legislature, OPPAGA, 1999).

Several agencies have also used PB^2 performance measures to help manage service contracts, which have become increasingly important as Governor Bush has outsourced major program activities such as personnel management, child welfare services, and highway maintenance. Agencies have incorporated performance measures and standards in vendor contracts, and they have used these data in both awarding and monitoring contracts. For example, the Department of Juvenile Justice, which contracts for many residential programs that provide 24-hour supervision of juvenile offenders, awards approximately one quarter of the points used to rate potential contractors on the basis of performance indicators such as previous quality assurance scores, escape rates, and postrelease recidivism rates. Contracted programs that do not meet expectations are required to develop quality improvement plans and may face cancellation (Florida Legislature, OPPAGA, 2003).

Conclusion and Lessons Learned

Florida's performance-based program-budgeting initiative has not met all of its expectations, but it has provided benefits for both the legislature and state agencies. The initiative has not captured the public's attention or changed popular perceptions about government. Performance data have not played a materially greater role in most legislative appropriations or policy decisions. However, the initiative has improved legislative oversight of state agencies and programs and has helped create a stronger common understanding of program goals and objectives, although legislative term limits have eroded this shared understanding. Further, although it has not resulted in substantially greater budget flexibility for state agencies, the initiative has helped enhance the efficiency and effectiveness of agency services. Thus, despite its shortfalls, the initiative has generally been a success, and it is alive and well after 12 years of implementation. Many agencies are using performance information to manage their programs, and the legislature has mandated performance reporting for most new programs or initiatives.

Looking back, Florida's implementation and usefulness of PB^2 could have been improved, and the state's experience has taught the lessons discussed below.

Lesson 1: Somebody needs to be in charge. No single entity was given leadership of the Florida's initiative or charged with setting overall policy direction. Instead, direction was variously provided by the governor's office, OPPAGA, legislative staff, legislative leadership, and legislators serving on appropriations and substantive committees. During the early years of performance-based budgeting, there was little consensus among stakeholders concerning the type of measures agencies should develop or how they were to be used in the budget process. While the law did not designate any entity with a leadership role, before the process was begun, it would have been helpful if the governor's office, legislators, and legislative staff had participated in a joint exercise to develop consensus on what PB² should look like and how it should operate.

If a consensus position on these policy issues had been developed and communicated to agency managers, the governor's staff, legislative staff, and legislators, agencies would have implemented the initiative in a more consistent manner across state government. Also, if the thorny questions of how performance measures could and should be presented during budget and substantive committee hearings had been resolved, legislators and staff may have had more confidence in the process and been more willing to grant agencies greater budget flexibility.

Lesson 2: If you want somebody to read this stuff, it needs to be readable. A notable weakness in Florida's PB² system is that performance data are provided in a format that is almost "user-hostile." Agencies report their performance data each year using a spreadsheet format that provides neither longitudinal graphs depicting how performance has changed over time nor narrative that interprets these data. Performance data would be much more useful and likely more used by legislators and the public if agencies were required to use a consistent and user-friendly format to report this information.

Lesson 3: Don't make it a treasure hunt to find performance data. An ongoing problem in Florida is that performance information is not readily available to legislators, staff, or the public. Initial expectations were that the governor's office would track this information, and the office published performance ledgers in the first few years of the initiative. However, the governor's office stopped tracking this information, citing the workload associated with keeping data current. As a result, individuals wishing to review all of the state's performance data for a multiyear period must search multiple Web sites and documents, and some data are likely no longer available from any source. A central entity such as the comptroller's office, which maintains the state's financial records, should be designated as the state's official performance data repository and given responsibility for overseeing the collection and reporting of data. This would help make performance information more available and give greater assurance that the data reported are valid and reliable.

Lesson 4: Layer the measures and don't bury anyone with tons of detail. Florida's performance-based program-budgeting law required agencies to maintain only the performance measures included in their legislative budget requests and adopted in appropriations acts. However, one set of measures cannot serve all masters. The legislature needs to receive high-level measures that assess whether agencies are meeting the fundamental goals of public programs (e.g., children are being protected from abuse and neglect, or the state is meeting air quality standards), while agencies need intermediate- and lower-level measures that assess program outputs and processes (e.g., the number of foster children receiving required home visits or the number of power plants passing emission control tests). (See Table 16.2.)

Table 16.2   Examples of Higher- and Lower-Level Performance Measures

Program Area	Higher-Level Measure	Intermediate- or Lower-Level Measure
K–12 Education	Percentage of children scoring a 3 or better on state tests	Percentage of children missing a week or more of classes
Child Protection	Percentage of children not re-abused within 1 year of receiving services	Percentage of home visits made in a timely manner
Environmental Protection	Percentage of cities meeting air quality standards	Percentage of power plants passing emission control tests

Ideally, agencies should maintain a layered measurement system that provides a small group of high-level outcome indicators but also a progressively larger set of measures that assess intermediate- and activity-level operations. In such a system, the legislature would generally monitor only the highest-level outcome measures, while top-level agency managers would monitor higher-level interim-outcome measures and middle managers would monitor lower-level immediate-outcome measures. This approach would help prevent individuals at all levels from being overwhelmed by a huge number of measures but still provide a complete inventory of measures that could be used for evaluative and management purposes.

Lesson 5: Be patient yet unrelenting. Developing a good performance-based program-budgeting system takes time to mature. Agencies will be required to collect new types of data, which may require developing new information systems and fine-tuning over time. Some measures that initially appear to be valid and reliable are often found to have serious flaws, and it takes several years to identify performance trends. Comprehensive evaluations, such as the justification reviews OPPAGA performed, may need to be repeated over time as agencies develop their performance measurement systems. Legislators and agency managers thus need to maintain a long-term perspective and realize that it will take several years for the system to be fully implemented and useful; mandating that a statewide system is to be implemented in a single year and then used as the foundation of all budgeting and policy deliberations is unrealistic.

However, legislators and other key stakeholders also need to keep the pressure on over time to force agencies to fully develop a strong performance measurement system. Agencies will often try to "wait them out" and give lip service to reform efforts, believing that the initiative will disappear in a few years when a new management fad arises. For this reason, it is critical that initiatives have legislative as well as executive branch support. Florida's PB^2 initiative has successfully continued through a change in gubernatorial administrations that had very different orientations.

Lesson 6: Keep expectations reasonable. PB^2 in Florida has strengthened legislative oversight, provided new information to inform policy and budget decisions, and changed agency culture as managers focus on continual improvement in program efficiency and effectiveness. Prior to this legislative initiative, agencies often assumed that their program interventions were effective; now they know that they must prove this, and they are more willing to look at performance data and change their approach if necessary. A growing number of agencies are using performance data to help manage their programs. Therefore, while performance-based budgeting has not radically changed the way the legislature operates and is unlikely to ever have a substantial impact on political policy making, it has changed the way that managers spend the resources they receive. The legislature has continued to support performance measurement and has required most newly created programs to report performance information. So, rather than looking at a glass half empty, we argue that analysts should look at the half-full glass and declare reasonable success.

Discussion Questions

1. What types of performance information do you believe agencies should report to the public? How should this be reported in order to help citizens best understand the services they receive for their tax dollars?

2. Performance measures that are tied to strong consequences (e.g., staff bonuses or funding changes) can create an incentive for agencies to manipulate their data in order to attain the desired outcome. How could this be controlled?

3. Political forces can strongly influence the budget process. What role can and should performance data play in the budget process to either supplement or counteract political influences?

4. Many prior budget reforms (e.g., planning-programming-budgeting systems, management by objectives, and zero-based budgeting) have been tried in the past and were subsequently abandoned. What lessons can be learned from these prior initiatives that could help performance budgeting avoid a similar fate?

5. The "politics/administration" dichotomy has been a long-standing issue within public administration. Performance-based budgeting can be seen as just another attempt to "rationalize" government administration and reduce the influence of politics. Is this a fair statement? If so, how should administrators ensure that they are responsive to the public's will as expressed through the political process?

References

Baumgartner, F., & Jones, B. (1993). *Agendas and instability in American politics.* Chicago: University of Chicago Press.

Berry, F. S., & Flowers, G. (1999). Public entrepreneurs in the policy process: Performance-based budgeting reform in Florida. *Journal of Public Budgeting, Accounting & Financial Management, 11,* 578–617.

deHaven-Smith, L. (1988). *Philosophical critiques of policy analysis.* Gainesville: University of Florida Press.

deHaven-Smith, L. (1998). *Collective will-formation: The missing dimension in public administration.* Unpublished manuscript.

de Lancer Julnes, P., & Mixcoatl, G. (2006). Governors as agents of change: A comparative study of performance measurement initiatives in Utah and Campeche. *Public Performance & Management Review, 29,* 405–432.

Easterling, C. N. (1999). Performance budgeting in Florida: To muddle or not to muddle, that is the question. *Journal of Public Budgeting, Accounting & Financial Management, 11,* 559–577.

Florida Department of Education. (2006). *Year in review 2005: Great strides for education.* Tallahassee, FL: Department of Education. Available at http://www.fldoe.org/specialFeatures/year_in_review.asp

Florida Legislature. (1994). *Laws of Florida* (chapters 94–240). Tallahassee, FL: Joint Legislative Management Committee.

Florida Legislature. (2005). *Performance measures and standards approved by the legislature for fiscal year 2005–2006.* Tallahassee: OPPAGA. Available at http://www.oppaga.state.fl.us/reports/pdf/2005–06_Measures.pdf

Florida Legislature, Office of Program Policy Analysis and Government Accountability. (1995). *Department of health and rehabilitative services: Pilot project for productivity.* Tallahassee, FL: Author.

Florida Legislature, Office of Program Policy Analysis and Government Accountability. (1997). *Performance-based program budgeting in Florida: Current status and next steps.* Tallahassee, FL: Author.

Florida Legislature, Office of Program Policy Analysis and Government Accountability. (1999). *Performance-based budgeting has produced benefits but its usefulness can be improved.* Tallahassee, FL: Author.

Florida Legislature, Office of Program Policy Analysis and Government Accountability. (2000). *PB² status report: Recent initiatives strengthen Florida performance-based program budgeting system.* Tallahassee, FL: Author.

Florida Legislature, Office of Program Policy Analysis and Government Accountability. (2003). *Juvenile justice can improve its quality assurance and program monitoring systems.* Tallahassee, FL: Author.

Florida Legislature, Office of Program Policy Analysis and Government Accountability (2005). *Division of hotels and restaurants improves operations but not meeting inspection goals.* Tallahassee, FL: Author.

Hendon, C. (1999). Performance budgeting in Florida: Halfway there. *Journal of Public Budgeting, Accounting & Financial Management, 11,* 670–679.

Key, V. O. (1952). Toward a theory of budgeting. *Public Administration Review, 11,* 42–54.

Moynihan, D., & Ingraham, P. (2003). Look for the silver lining: When performance-based accountability systems work. *Journal of Public Administration Research and Theory, 13,* 469–490.

Ogata, K., & Goodkey, R. (1998, July 16). *Cambridge paper: Redefining government performance.* Presented at the First Conference on Performance Measure: Performance Measurement Theory and Practice, University of Cambridge, UK. Available at http://www.finance.gov.ab.ca/publications/measuring/cambridge_paper.html

Osborne, D., & Gaebler, T. (1992). *Reinventing government.* Boston: Addison-Wesley.

Schick, A. (1966). The road to PPB: The stages of budget reform. *Public Administration Review, 26,* 243–258.

Shafritz, J., & Hyde, A. (1997). *Classics of public administration.* Fort Worth, TX: Harcourt Brace.

Sheffield, S. (1999). Implementing Florida's performance and accountability act: A focus on program measurement and evaluation. *Journal of Public Budgeting, Accounting & Financial Management, 11,* 649–669.

State of Florida. (1968). Constitution, Section 19 (d). Tallahassee, FL: Joint Legislative Management Committee. Available at http://www.leg.state.fl.us/Statutes/index.cfm?Mode=Constitution&Submenu=3&Tab=statutes#A03S19

Toppo, G. (2006, January 5). Florida Supreme Court strikes down school vouchers. *USA Today.* Available at http://www.usatoday.com/news/nation/2006-01-05-florida-school-vouchers_x.htm

VanLandingham, G., Wellman, M., & Andrews, M. (2005). Useful, but not a panacea: Performance-based program budgeting in Florida. *International Journal of Public Administration, 28,* 233–253.

Wang, X. (2002). Assessing performance measurement impact: A study of U.S. local governments. *Public Performance and Management Review, 26,* 26–43.

Wildavsky, A. (1961). Political implications of budgetary reform. *Public Administration Review, 21,* 183–190.

Willoughby, W. (1918). *The movement for budgetary reform in the states.* New York: Appleton and Company for the Institute for Government Research.

Zaller, J. (1992). *The nature and origins of mass public opinion.* Cambridge, UK: Cambridge University Press.

17 Performance Management and Budgeting in Australia and New Zealand

John Halligan

The reform era has been remarkable for sustained transformations of public administration in countries internationally. Australia and New Zealand have experienced several generations of management reform that have attracted international attention, particularly New Zealand as a reform model with unique and influential features (Halligan, 1997; Kettl, 2005; Pollitt & Bouckaert, 2004). A centerpiece of management reform has become performance. Australia and New Zealand, with their comprehensive approaches, have been more committed to performance management than most countries in the Organisation for Economic Co-operation and Development (OECD; Bouckaert & Halligan, 2006; OECD, 1997).

This chapter examines how the two countries have handled performance management and budgeting across three generations of change (the early 1980s–2005).[1] Two questions are of particular importance. First, what are the results of high and sustained support for performance management over two decades of reform? This takes us into the realm of examining the potential and the limits of performance management in Westminster parliamentary systems, where the conditions for accomplishing reform and requiring performance are quite propitious.[2] Despite the continuing lack of consistent evidence about the efficacy of performance budgeting and a strong relationship between performance information and decisions about resource allocation (Robinson & Brumby, 2005), there is reason to believe that the investment in these two countries has significance. Second, the two countries' distinctive pathways offer the opportunity for comparison of the impact of different performance systems. This, however, presents standard difficulties with evaluating and comparing reform, namely, the extent to which respective models are enacted in practice and how to take into account the evolution of systems in making comparisons over time.[3]

Performance and Management Reform

The design of national performance management and budgeting allows for several distinctive approaches depending on the emphasis accorded to outputs and outcomes and the overall level of connections between the components. Important questions are the quality of performance information and the ways in which it is used in management, budgeting, and reporting.

Australia and New Zealand experienced a wave of reform from the early to mid-1980s, producing different laboratories of experimentation that were unusual for the magnitude and breadth of reform, the longevity of the process, and the attention to system design. A constant element has been performance measurement and management since the 1980s, with budget reform being a significant element. Essential features of performance-based budgeting have been present: the focus on results, accountability management, and transparency. This overview locates performance improvement within the context of reform and with regard to distinctive models that nevertheless share many features (Halligan, 1997).

Both countries emerged in the 1980s from a period characterized by heavily regulated economies and using the public sector for providing the services of a welfare state. Increasingly, both countries turned to the private sector and the use of market principles within the public sector. They responded to economic pressures with distinctive models of reform. In both cases, fiscal difficulties played a significant part, and financial deregulation of both economies produced intensified pressures for public sector reform. For New Zealand, the crisis was most acute, with a budget deficit, balance-of-payments deficit, and structural imbalances. In the Australian case, a package of reforms was promoted by a new government with a mandate and determination to launch and implement a reform program.

Strong differentiation between the two countries is apparent during the first decade of reform with regard to content and process as New Zealand advanced rapidly with its theory-driven model (Hood, 1990). Despite similarities between the two countries, major differences existed with the initial framework, institutional design, and reform process, the most significant being in the realm of ideas with institutional economics exercising great influence in New Zealand. The radical new framework, first expressed in the mid-1980s by the New Zealand Treasury in conjunction with key politicians, laid the foundation for the reform program and was implemented rapidly. In contrast, Australia's political management approach reflected the implementation aspirations of a government actively seeking to implement its policies and recognition that the management skills of the senior public service were deficient compared with policy and administrative work. The development of its management framework took longer and reflected a balancing of principle and pragmatism (Boston, Martin, Pallot, & Walsh, 1996; Halligan & Power, 1992; Scott, 2001).

Australia: Management, Market, and Performance Governance

A distinction between the management and market dimensions of reform provides a means for analyzing New Public Management (Halligan, 1997; Schick, 1996) in Australia, where the two have been identified with a reform sequence that has run from administration to phases dominated by management (1980s), then markets (1990s), and then performance governance elements.

What differentiated the initial period was the rejection of traditional administration and its replacement by reforms based on management. Over about a decade, a new management philosophy was developed and implemented that replaced the traditional emphasis on inputs and processes with one on results. Unlike New Zealand's theoretically driven approach, the management framework was evolved pragmatically (Halligan & Power, 1992). The main elements of the reform program focused on the core public service and financial management. The Financial Management Improvement Program (FMIP) dominated the reforms of the 1980s as an initiative designed to produce more efficient use of resources. The Budget Reform White Paper 1984 covered budget decision making, financial management of programs, and the information base. The Australian focus on results, outcomes, and performance-oriented management dates from this time (Wanna, Kelly, & Forster, 2000).

The implementation of FMIP occurred through changing the budgetary and regulatory environment and improving management systems (centered on "managing for results" components of corporate management, program management, management information and evaluation) and standards and practices. Program budgeting was made a centerpiece to assist participants in the public expenditure process with assessing program development and implementation against objectives. The term *program management and budgeting* was adopted to promote the emphasis on improving departmental corporate management and to assist managers with focusing more clearly on outcomes and results. It was defined as "preparing the agency's budget on a program basis with a process which focuses on program effectiveness (and efficiency) against defined objectives rather than solely controlling resource inputs" (Task Force on Management Improvement, 1993, p. 62; see also Campbell & Halligan, 1993; Keating & Holmes, 1990).

The new expenditure control framework covered Three-year-forward estimates, a running-costs system that provided greater flexibility in managing administrative costs and permitted carryovers to the next financial year, and efficiency dividends or annual savings on running costs. Evaluation was seen as tying the loop in the management cycle, pronounced as the "crucial element" in managing for results, and linking policy development and program implementation. All programs had to be reviewed every 5 years and evaluation plans were produced annually for scrutiny by the Department of Finance (Campbell & Halligan, 1993; Keating & Holmes, 1990).

A new stage in reform became apparent in the 1990s. Australia had concentrated on management reform during the 1980s but increasingly accepted the need for market-oriented reform. By the mid-1990s, the new agenda centered on competition and contestability, contracting out, client focus, core business, and the application of the purchaser/provider principle. The new phase was reinforced with the advent of a government pursuing a neoliberal agenda: a deregulated personnel system, contracting out and privatization, and contestability of delivery of services with greater use of the private sector (Halligan, 2003a).

New financial legislation in 1997 was followed up by a new budget framework in 1999, which involved major changes to financial management and reporting, including budgeting on a full accrual basis for 1999–2000,[4] implementation of outputs and outcomes reporting, and extending agency devolution to inter alia budget estimates and financial management. The intention was to improve capacity to deliver on reforms by changing the method of budgeting and resource management: hence the new framework, based on outcomes and outputs and accrual accounting principles.

The third phase, in the 2000s, is distinguished by integrated and performance governance, an emergent model with four dimensions (Halligan, 2006): resurrection of the central agency as a major actor with more control over departments, central monitoring of agency implementation and delivery, whole-of-government as the expression of a range of forms of coordination, and control of nondepartmental bodies by absorbing them or rationalizing corporate governance. These trends shift the focus to some extent from the vertical toward the horizontal, with an emphasis on cross-agency programs and relationships. The result has been the tempering of devolution through strategic steering and central oversight and a rebalancing of the positions of central and line agencies.

As for budgeting and estimates, several expected benefits from the 1990s reforms were not forthcoming. The combination of a highly centralized budgetary process and highly devolved agencies was problematic. A central issue for ministers was the dropping of "programs" under the outcomes/outputs framework because they lacked the information required for making decisions. There was also parliamentary critique of the lack of information as a result of financial management information systems being accrual based, in contrast to traditional cash transactions. As a result, the 2002 Budget Estimates and Framework Review was established by the Department of Finance to evaluate the responsiveness and effectiveness of the system for government needs. The review reported on the scope for streamlining the financial framework, improving information management systems, and enhancing financial information provided to the government (Department of Finance and Administration [DoFA], 2004; Halligan, 2006).

New Zealand: Management and Markets, Strategic and Integrated Governance

New Zealand also moved through three generations of change.[5] In the first phase, a new reform model emerged based on principles such as clarity of objectives, managerial freedom, accountability for decisions, performance evaluation, and relevant information. The model combined standard management reforms pursued in other OECD countries, with distinctive features based on ideas derived from public choice and institutional economics, and addressed inter alia the questions of agency and transaction costs. The New Zealand model won international admiration as a unique case of public sector reform because its framework was innovative, sophisticated, and coherent (Boston, et al., 1996; Kettl, 2005).

The core public service was subjected to the application of new principles, the two most important being separation of responsibilities for policy and delivery and identification of specific functions with specialized organizations. The State Sector Act 1988 and Public Finance Act 1989 produced changes that provided for improved autonomy and greater accountability of managers but also redefined the relationship between ministers and department heads. A range of financial management reforms were introduced, with distinctions made between inputs, outputs, and outcomes, with the emphasis on outputs.[6] Also central was the redefinition of the relationship between ministers as members of the political executive and departmental chief executives as public servants appointed on performance agreements, an innovation being the association of outcomes with the former and outputs with the latter. The relationship was seen as being contractually based: The government purchased outputs from departments, while the government was defined as the owner with an interest in the return on its investment. Also significant was the more general reliance on contracting out the delivery of services to private and voluntary sector providers.

The renamed chief executive officers, whose predecessors were permanent officials, held contract appointments based on performance agreements, and their performance was evaluated. Under the Public Finance Act, departments acquired responsibility for financial management from the Treasury. CEOs managed inputs to produce outputs that ministers purchased. Budgeting was now on an accrual basis (Jensen, 2003).

Phase 2 was dominated by strategic focus, implementation, and review. New Zealand continued to expand, refine, and review the reforms in the 1990s. The strategic capacity of government was a neglected element in the original model, producing a short-term policy focus and inattention to the collective side of government. This capacity was reengineered to incorporate medium- and long-term planning and the introduction of strategic and key result areas for specifying government priorities and focusing performance. An official review found this approach to be working, but weaknesses in planning and results became apparent (Schick, 1996; Scott, 2001).

Another innovation was the Fiscal Responsibility Act 1994, which sought to make budget accounting more transparent. Reported benefits included the credibility of the fiscal policy process, the focusing of politicians on efficiency and cost overrun questions, and pressure on the Treasury to improve its performance because the legislation specified transparency and accountability.

The New Zealand model was subjected to an official external evaluation, which examined the main components and pronounced it to be sound and successful but criticized some of the cherished economic principles that accounted for the system's uniqueness. The reforms were seen as more rigorous and comprehensive than those in other systems but were still incomplete and not without weaknesses. While management practice and discourse had been transformed, perennial questions of public administration remained, with outstanding questions including incentives and performance measurement, political and managerial accountability, the domination of the purchase function over ownership, lack of evaluation culture, and the degree of alignment between agency and system needs (Boston & Eichbaum, in press; Schick, 1996).

In the third phase, system rebalancing and renewing public management outcomes have been central. Several themes have emerged since 1999, covering capability, outcomes, integration, and the role of central agencies within a philosophy supportive of the public sector. Having failed to implement the Schick report (1996), New Zealand returned to the limitations of its model in 2001, with the Ministerial Advisory Group's *Review of the Centre* (MAG, 2001), which examined the public management system and its responsiveness to ministers and citizens. The report reflected the received wisdom about the model's deficiencies (Boston et al., 1996; Schick, 1996; Scott, 2001; State Services Commission [SSC], 1998), concluding that the public management system provided a foundation to work from but that significant shifts in emphasis were needed. Specific issues requiring attention centered on the consequences of fragmentation under an agency system: the need for integrating service delivery, cross-agency coordination, and improvements to public service culture. There was also overdue recognition of the need to augment central agency responsibilities.

There have been three important results. First, there has been rationalizing and refining of systemic elements to align them with government goals and development measures to re-address organizational fragmentation and coordination gaps, and the former preference for vertically integrated relationships has been succeeded by an emphasis on "horizontally-integrated, whole-of-government capacity and capability" (Boston & Eichbaum, in press). Second, legislative change sought to provide the conditions for improved performance covering the financial management arrangements and the principles of the public service. Third, outcomes, a neglected component of performance, were accorded prominence under a redesigning of the corporate planning system in 2001 (and the discarding of results areas). The elevation of outcomes has taken a distinctive form within an approach that requires "managing for outcomes" but does not hold chief executives responsible for achieving them. This was a departure from the original framework in which performance was regarded as a deliverable because costs could be specified and evaluated (Baehler, 2003; Scott, 2001).

Performance and Budget Management

There have been strong commonalities between Australia and New Zealand with the direction and content of public management reform: the early implementation of a New Public Management agenda, the focus on outputs and outcomes, and accrual budgeting and transparency (Halligan, 1997). Their recent performance agendas are in broad agreement on the significance of outcomes, performance management, and improved delivery within more integrated governance frameworks. Both countries have accorded prominence to outcomes during the last decade as a challenging area that has to be properly addressed. Nevertheless, there were distinctive differences in their pathways and handling of performance management and budgeting.

Australia's performance management has moved through two stages (Halligan, 2003a; McKay, 2003). In the first (1987–1997), the elements of performance management were developed within a centralized approach featuring the Department of Finance. The strengths were institutionalized performance management elements and the requirement for formal evaluations. The weaknesses were the reliance on evaluations that were mandatory (and imposed top down by a central agency) and the quality of program objectives and performance information. There were also questions about what program budgeting represented (Wanna et al., 2000, pp. 175–177), because although a program framework was used as a flexible instrument for managing and reporting on programs, this did not lead to budgeting by programs with a direct link to appropriations.

The second stage (from 1997) was based on the outcomes/output framework, devolution to agencies, principles instead of formal requirements, and an emphasis on performance information. The strengths were systemic review by central agencies, the strong ownership for departments, and the reliance on active management.

The weaknesses discussed later included insufficient information for parliamentary needs and for sound management, inconsistent departmental support for good evaluation, and the subjectivity of performance assessment. These limitations have produced continuing reassessment of some aspects of current performance management practices.

The budget framework introduced in 1999 changed financial management and reporting through budgeting on a full accrual basis; implementation of outputs and outcomes reporting; and extended agency devolution to inter alia budget estimates and financial management. Departments and agencies were now expected to identify their outcomes and outputs and be held accountable for them. Agency heads were clearly assigned responsibility and accountability for performance. Agencies were required to identify explicit outcomes, outputs, and performance measures (covering, among other things, efficiency and effectiveness).[7] Reporting now occurred through budget plans (portfolio budget statements) and financial year results (annual reports). Major benefits of the new framework were to be an improved information base, better incentives to be efficient, greater precision about public value, and, for the first time, the linking of outputs to outcomes.

However, the limitations of the framework in practice produced reincorporation of departmental programs, a renewed emphasis on cash accounting, and other changes, including improvements to cash management, budgeting and program reporting, and financial information systems. This meant, of course, enhancing the central Department of Finance's role and capacity to oversee financial management and information and to provide the necessary advice for government.

New Zealand performance management has been rather differently cast. A key feature of the original model was the distinction between outputs and outcomes, and their assignment, respectively, to chief executives and ministers. The focus was on chief executives and their extensive responsibilities for managing departments under contract, the specification of their responsibilities through performance and purchase agreements, and the annual assessment of their performance by the employer, the SSC (Boston et al., 1996; Scott, 2001).

New Zealand, however, was slow to correct well-known weaknesses in the areas of accountability, performance measurement, and strategic management. There was a need for modifications to allow further development of the model and second-generation reforms. Two limitations were (a) the emphasis of the output orientation on managerial accountability at the expense of public and parliamentary accountability and (b) gaps in the system's capacity to learn from experience, such as from routine policy evaluations. The link between outputs and desired outcomes was variable under the original model, due partly to how the political executive was engaged: Ministers were expected to show the link and to use performance targets. In addition, a system property of the original model was disaggregation to a large number of departments, but most goals were not the responsibility of one minister and department (Boston et al., 1996; Kibblewhite & Ussher, 2002, p. 87; Schick, 1996; Scott, 1997).

The requirement that government should specify "broad strategic priorities" under the Fiscal Responsibility Act 1994 has been pursued through different statements, including Strategic Result Areas and Priorities and, in the early 2000s, Key Government Goals to Guide Public Sector Policy and Performance. The strategic priorities have been less concerned with goals than with "statements of broad direction" (Kibblewhite & Ussher, 2002, p. 86).

Managing for outcomes (MfO) was introduced to promote outcomes; to improve departmental planning, managing, and reporting; and to produce major improvements in public service performance. MfO has been implemented since 2002–2003 and was extended to 35 departments in 2003–2004. MfO addresses long-term strategic thinking through the statement of intent (SOI). The SOI covers the outcomes, impacts, and objectives of a department and the outputs (i.e., goods and services being supplied), plus plans for managing capability (Controller and Auditor-General, 2006; Economics and Strategy Group, 2003; Treasury and State Services Commission, 2005).

The SSC has been responsible for one cornerstone of performance management, the performance agreements of chief executives. The State Services Commissioner appoints, employs, and reviews the performance of chief executives. The performance review covers chief executives' achievement of results and investment in an organizational capability. The SSC refocused this performance management responsibility in recent years from a retrospective compliance emphasis to a "proactive approach focused on management that achieves results" (SSC, 2006). The performance agreement has been depicted as "the main vehicle of performance management, rather than performance budgeting" (Shand & Norman, 2005, p. 22).

Lessons From Two Decades of Performance Management and Budgeting

The lessons from Australia and New Zealand raise questions about core dimensions of performance management and budgeting.

Outputs and Outcomes

Outputs and outcomes approaches have been central to the management frameworks for many years. Both countries were talking about outcomes in the 1980s, but the paths diverged. New Zealand identified outcomes with ministers and outputs with chief executives, with a performance agreement between them. This was perceived in Australia as institutionalizing the separation of policy and delivery, a perennial shortcoming of public administration. In contrast, Australia wished to bring them together as part of FMIP and PMB (program management and budgeting), but ambiguity, even blurring, remained as to responsibilities (Holmes, 1989, p. 33). In the long term, neither approach was sustained. In both countries, the outcomes side has been underdeveloped, either being assigned to politicians and overshadowed by an output focus (New Zealand) or in need of refinement beyond the emphasis on programs (Australia). The Australian Auditor-General observes that there is no support for favoring either outputs or outcomes as being more effective for institutionalizing a performance culture but argues that performance management will not be effective unless both are integrated in a performance framework (McPhee, 2005, p. 2).

Under the Australian outcomes and outputs framework, outcomes provide the foundation for performance information and have been central to performance measurement since the mid-1980s. The program and results focus laid the foundation for evolving a more exact system. Outputs were recognized in the early days but were not measured until the outcomes/output framework of 1999. They were introduced to measure service delivery for external stakeholders (McPhee, 2005, p. 3). At this point, programs were dropped, only to be reintroduced surreptitiously (insofar as the details are not public) by 2003.

A New Zealand centerpiece has been outputs and the chief executive's responsibility for delivering goods and services. The outputs fetish, according to Schick, produced distortions, with executives focusing only on outputs, while ministers allowed their purchaser role to override their responsibility for outcomes. As a consequence, outcomes were a neglected element. The system focused on outcomes conceptually but had problems with its integration into public management because of difficulties with specifying and measuring with outcomes (Cook, 2004; Kibblewhite & Ussher, 2002; Schick, 2001).

The stronger tools continue to be at the output level. A number of issues remain with shared outcomes, accountability, and the tensions between outputs and outcomes. There has yet to be an overall evaluation of managing for outcomes to determine whether the original objectives are being achieved. Generally speaking, the SOI is seen to provide a better quality and range of planning information than its predecessor, the Departmental Forecast Report. Some incremental improvements have occurred in the quality of departmental planning as a result of the introduction of the MfO initiative (Controller and Auditor General, 2006).

MfO has been judged to be too multifaceted. For different observers, there are specific questions about the purpose of SOIs and some ambiguity about those of MfO. MfO is depicted "as a cycle of continuous improvement, a self-assessment tool, not an accountability mechanism" (Shand & Norman, 2005, p. 16), but the Controller and Auditor-General regards the SOI as "an important accountability document" (Controller and Auditor-General, 2006, sec. 7.14).

The majority of SOIs had not shown much improvement (Controller and Auditor-General, 2006), and there was a need to refine output and outcome indicators, improve the links between outputs and outcomes, and enhance information on identifying and managing organizational risk. Norman's (2006) work with a focus group of budget specialists indicates that outcomes remain at an incipient stage, are developing slowly, and represent more "an overlay to the outputs system, rather than a fundamental change" (p. 11).

Performance Information

The quality of financial information has improved as a result of the Australian outcomes/output framework in registering government preferences (intentions and results) and by allowing performance indicators to be explicitly identified (DoFA, 2006b). However, performance measurement of outcomes has continued to provide difficulties despite its centrality to the resource management framework (Wanna & Bartos, 2003).

In both countries, output information is considerably better than that for outcomes. Australian output performance measures are generally more appropriate and measurement more reliable than its outcome measures (McPhee, 2005), a generalization that also holds for New Zealand.

In a review of performance reporting in departmental annual reports, the Australian National Audit Office (ANAO, 2003) indicates the need for improving information with respect to specification of the performance framework, the quality of measures, and the reporting of results.

There is quite a history of problems with the use of performance information in practice. For New Zealand, a consideration was that the output focus had improved accountability and transparency but had not assisted with the making of decisions (SSC, 1999). In the Australian case, the mandatory evaluation strategy established in 1988 required all programs to be systematically evaluated over 5 years by departments under the oversight of the Department of Finance. An increase in the quantity and quality of evaluation activity occurred, but it varied among portfolios. Most significantly, most members of the senior executive service were not making much use of evaluation information in their work, focusing on satisfying the evaluation requirements rather than seeking to use it for improving program outcomes. The system was ultimately judged to produce a mainly process-oriented approach, and compulsory evaluation was discontinued in 1997 (Halligan, 2003b).

A decade later, the Australian Auditor-General reports that performance information is being used by decision makers for policy development and allocating resources but that the actual "influence of outcomes and outputs information on decision making was mixed" (McPhee, 2005, pp. 3–4).[8]

Performance and Budgeting

Performance information is meant to inform the budget process in both countries. For Australia, budget information is now "more comprehensive, based on external reporting standards, and provides better alignment between appropriation Acts, PB Statements, and agency annual reports" (DoFA, 2006b, p. 11).

In both countries, most of the annual appropriations do not relate to outcomes. Thus, in Australia, this amounts to 9% being appropriated by outcomes.[9] New Zealand observers have questioned whether the budget cycle is linked much to performance questions because the budget is largely fixed, and performance information is not used much during the process. The over- all judgment questions "the effectiveness of an annual budget round as a means for making assessments about public sector performance" (Shand & Norman, 2005, pp. 20–21).

The Australian outcomes policy provides for agencies to use performance information in budget decision making, but the potential has not been achieved because of the variable influence of this information on decisions and resource allocation during the process. The Finance Department is exploring means for improving the use of performance information by revising the infor- mation required for new policy proposals and making greater use of reviews, regarded as an instrument through which performance information can best feed into budget decision making (e.g., through the automatic review of laps- ing programs). Reviews are not registering much impact at present because only a minute proportion of total expenditure is affected (DoFA, 2006a).

Reporting

Australian outputs (both for agencies and administered items) and out- comes are generally appropriately specified in annual reports. Since the intro- duction of accrual-based budgeting, the quality of performance reporting has improved substantially (DoFA, 2006a, p. 9). Nevertheless, improvements in annual reporting frameworks are important in order to enhance accountabil- ity and transparency to stakeholders, particularly members of Parliament, because the presentation and analysis of performance information in annual reports did not allow them to properly understand results. Specific issues have been the need to analyze performance (not produce activity lists), assess performance in terms of a basis for comparison (e.g., targets), review trends in financial and nonfinancial performance, and use evaluations for acquiring performance information on effectiveness (ANAO, 2003; DoFA, 2006a).

New Zealand has barely emerged from the initial implementation phase of MfO, but there are expectations of outcome reporting being extended to statements of service performance and audited financial statements and a reduction in the separation of outcome and output reporting in annual reports. There needs to be further refining of indicators for outputs and out- comes, and outcome and output reporting remain separated in departmen- tal annual reports (Controller and Auditor-General, 2006).

Evaluating Performance Improvement

In both countries, evaluation has been neglected. There were fundamen- tal differences in how the two countries originally approached evaluation and incorporated it in agency programs. In Australia, the "managing for results" agenda in the 1980s included evaluating outputs and outcomes against predetermined objectives. The experiment with a compulsory evaluation system produced a predominantly process focus and was replaced by an approach designed by the Department of Finance to make evaluation an integral part of a broader public service performance management framework. Evaluating was meant to be a routine activity undertaken on a day-to-day basis. Both countries' management systems have been based on devolution to agencies and assumed that some form of "evaluation activity" must be performed in order to sustain performance and reporting requirements. However, the use of *evaluation activity* as a term suggests convenient ambiguity that does not encourage serious evaluation (Halligan, 2003b).

Some senior executives rejected "evaluation of the impact of their performance management systems," and in many agencies, "important issues of performance management were not examined in evaluations because the basic assumptions were not questioned" (People and Strategy and Institute of Public Administration, 2001, pp. 56–57). Similarly, evaluation of delivery strategies is important, but agencies "varied from ongoing monitoring to formal review." Moreover, "30 percent of agencies provided no information including a few that reported no evaluation" (Public Service Commissioner, 2000, p. 126).

The distinctive Australian commitment to mandatory, systematic evaluation that was centrally driven contrasted with New Zealand's approach. For a number of years, stark contrasts were drawn between the different attitudes, with the Australian approach being depicted as evaluating everything and "overkill" (SSC, 1999, p. 20) that simply promoted an evaluation industry. However, New Zealand's obsessive concern with outputs and accountability was regarded as precluding other considerations, including evaluation.

The SSC (1998) observed that a review capacity requires evaluating outcomes but this was "consciously sidelined in the original reforms" (p. 32). The SSC reported considerable evaluation activity, but it tended to focus on processes and efficiency and to be used for internal management, while evaluation against outcomes was regarded as too difficult. More recently, the case for capability building was made because "the use of evaluative thinking to inform strategy, policy, service delivery, and budget decisions was patchy" (Halligan, 2003b; SSC, 1999; Steering Group for the Managing for Outcomes Roll-Out [SGMOR], 2003, p. 5).

Following critique and reflection on their respective approaches, there was some convergence in the countries' positions. There is now understanding that review and evaluation is required on a more systematic basis (DoFA, 2006c; SGMOR, 2003).

Individual and Organizational Performance

The credibility of performance management systems as they affect individual public servants has been exposed by several inquiries. In particular, the credibility of agency performance pay systems continues to be problematic, with the proportions of employees judging pay systems positively being relatively low and with a decline in ratings (ANAO, 2004; Australian Public Service Commission [APSC], 2005). The ANAO concluded that the significant investment in performance-linked remuneration "appears to be delivering only patchy results and uncertain benefit." Performance management in Australia has been officially depicted during the 2000s as a "work in progress" with major challenges, particularly on the issues of credibility and staff engagement. APSC employees have continued to perceive a gap between their experience and the rhetoric (ANAO, 2004, secs. 15, 19; Management Advisory Committee [MAC], 2001).

Agency Variation

There is considerable variation among agencies in how they engage and show up on performance management. This reflects in part the nature of agencies, with some types more able to demonstrate effective use of performance information, but this also depends on other factors, such as leadership. New Zealand managers have reported excessive focus on results that could be measured and audited. The output focus favored "productions tasks" (e.g., in fields of tax and customs) (Norman, 2006).

For Australia, significant variation exists with the quality of and information used in annual reports. Variability also exists in the alignment between goals and organizational priorities of many Australian agencies and their performance management systems. Industrial relations processes have often appeared to be more influential than outcomes and agencies' business needs. In addition, many agencies have lacked systems for supporting performance management and have not been assessing the internal impact and use of performance management systems. As a result, performance management has not been contributing to effective business outcomes (ANAO, 2004).

An evaluation of New Zealand SOIs in 2004 indicated that only one SOI was "developed," 22 were "moderate" to "almost developed," 10 were "fair" to "almost moderate," and 3 were "somewhere between basic and fair." According to the New Zealand Controller and Auditor-General, the quality of SOIs in 2005–2006 continued to be variable across the public service, and, in terms of overall quality, there had been only incremental change since the previous year (Controller and Auditor-General, 2006).

Conclusion

A striking feature of the last two decades has been the continuing expansion of performance management as a core of public management (Bouckaert & Halligan, 2006), performance-based budgeting being an integral element. Both countries examined in this chapter have been highly committed to performance management and budgeting over two decades, during which they have substantially refined their measurement and performance frameworks and increased their capacity to monitor performance. Yet practice falls short of aspirations even under these benign conditions for cultivating performance management. Significant questions remain about the quality and use of performance information, particularly in budget decision making and external reporting and the variable engagement of agencies.[10]

Australia and New Zealand have followed different pathways within a performance management framework during these two decades. Their early implementation styles differed in their conceptions of the relationship between outputs and outcomes, the responsibilities given to chief executives, and the roles of the central personnel agency in handling performance oversight. New Zealand's original model was implemented rapidly to become an international benchmark. Australia's more pragmatic and evolutionary approach provided a distinctive alternative. The exigencies of reform agenda and public management have produced convergence during the last decade, but, despite common elements, there continue to be differences in approach and in the treatment of outcomes and outputs. Both Australian and New Zealand systems, however, remain a "work in progress" as they continue to seek improvements in managing performance.

Notes

1. The author appreciates receiving clarification of several matters by Lewis Hawke, of the Australian Department of Finance and Administration.

2. Both countries have parliamentary systems based on responsible government in which the executive is a product of and is accountable to the legislature. Other aspects of government structure need to be recognized, as one country is unitary (New Zealand), the other federal (Australia). The Australian states are the main vehicles for the delivery of services, while the national government is the main revenue collector. This means that transfers are a major consideration, and, along with grants and benefits, they are termed administered items and account for most appropriations.

3. There is a need to maintain a reality check on formal features that have mesmerized some international observers who have registered less awareness of practice and variation over time.

4. Australia followed New Zealand and Iceland in switching to accrual budgeting.

5. Some observers focus on the initial model (late 1980s to early 1990s) and the emergent revised model (2000s) (Boston & Eichbaum, in press).

6. The rationale for outputs is put by Scott (2001). He also examines how New Zealand experimented unsuccessfully with program budgeting.

7. The simple version is that outcomes represent what the government wants to achieve and outputs and administered items represent how this is achieved (DoFA, 2006c).

8. An earlier survey indicated that few agencies collected data about whether they had "achieved goals and outcomes, the nature of their impact on performance of individuals or groups, or the quality of the performance management discussions that

have taken place" (People and Strategy and Institute of Public Administration, 2001, pp. 56–57).

9. Departmental outputs (18%) and administered programs (73%) appropriated outside annual appropriations (i.e., by special or annual appropriations) are not appropriated against outcomes, leaving 9% that is (DoFA, 2006a, p. 13).

10. In these respects, they share the institutional, organizational, and technical challenges, particularly with outcomes, of other OECD countries (OECD, 2005).

Discussion Questions

1. Is too much expected of an outcome focus? To what extent can we expect different types of agencies to be able to demonstrate effective use of performance information?

2. Compare the pathways and approaches of the two countries in terms of their long-term efficacy and capacity for learning.

3. Can we expect performance management to handle multiple functions more effectively, specifically performance information, in the budget process?

4. Is regular evaluation and review an appropriate means for facilitating performance information?

5. Australia and New Zealand have made a high commitment to performance management for two decades yet are still seeking to implement and refine basic aspects. Why is this continuing high commitment justified?

References

Australian National Audit Office. (2003). *Annual performance reporting* (Audit Report No. 11 2003–04). Canberra, Australia: Author.

Australian National Audit Office. (2004). *Performance management in the Australian public service* (Audit Report No. 6 2004–05). Canberra, Australia: Author.

Australian Public Service Commission. (2005). *State of the service report, 2004–05.* Canberra, Australia: Author.

Australian Public Service Commission. (2006). *Sharpening the focus: Managing performance in the APS.* Canberra, Australia: Author.

Baehler, K. (2003). Managing for outcomes: Accountability and trust. *Australian Journal of Public Administration, 62*(4), 23–34.

Boston, J., & Eichbaum, C. (in press). *State sector reform and renewal in New Zealand: Lessons for governance.* In G. E. Caiden & T-T. Su (Eds.), *The repositioning of public governance: Global experience and challenges.* Taipei: National Taiwan University.

Boston, J., Martin, J., Pallot, J., & Walsh, P. (1996). *Public management: The New Zealand model.* Auckland, New Zealand: Oxford University Press.

Bouckaert, G., & Halligan, J. (2006). Performance: Its measurement, management, and policy. In B. G. Peters & J. Pierre (Eds.), *Handbook of public policy* (pp. 443–459). London: Sage.

Campbell, C., & Halligan, J. (1993). *Political leadership in an age of constraint: The Australian experience*. Pittsburgh: University of Pittsburgh Press.

Controller and Auditor-General. (2006). *Report on central government: Results of the 2004–5 audits*. Wellington, New Zealand: Office of the Auditor-General.

Cook, A-L. (2004). *Managing for outcomes in the New Zealand public management system* (New Zealand Treasury Working Paper 04/15). Wellington, New Zealand: New Zealand Treasury.

Department of Finance and Administration. (2004). *Annual report 2003–04*. Canberra, Australia: Author.

Department of Finance and Administration. (2006a). *Australia's experience in utilising performance information in budget and management processes*. Report for the 3rd Annual Meeting of the OECD Senior Budget Officials Network on Performance and Results, DOFA, Canberra, Australia.

Department of Finance and Administration. (2006b, August 4). *Inquiry into the transparency and accountability of Commonwealth public funding and expenditure* (Submission to the Senate Finance and Public Administration References Committee). Canberra, Australia: Author.

Department of Finance and Administration. (2006c). *Outcomes & outputs framework*. Canberra, Australia: Author. Available at http://www.finance.gov.au/GF

Economics and Strategy Group. (2003). *Departmental uptake of the managing for outcomes initiative*. Wellington, New Zealand: State Services Commission. Retrieved May 15, 2006, from http://www.ssc.govt.nz/display/document.asp?docid=3364&pagetype=toc&NavID=208

Halligan, J. (1997). New public sector models: Reform in Australia and New Zealand. In J.-E. Lane (Ed.), *Public sector reform: Rationale, trends, and problems* (pp. 17–46). London: Sage.

Halligan, J. (2003a). Australian public service: Redefining boundaries. In J. Halligan (Ed.), *Civil service systems in Anglo-American countries* (pp. 70–112). Cheltenham, UK: E. Elgar.

Halligan, J. (2003b). Public sector reform and evaluation in Australia and New Zealand. In H. Wollmann (Ed.), *Evaluation in public sector reforms* (pp. 80–103). Cheltenham, UK: E. Elgar.

Halligan, J. (2006). The reassertion of the centre in a first generation NPM system. In T. Christensen & P. Lægreid (Eds.), *Autonomy and regulation: Coping with agencies in the modern state* (pp. 162–180). Cheltenham, UK: E. Elgar.

Halligan, J., & Power, J. (1992). *Political management in the 1990s*. Melbourne, Australia: Oxford University Press.

Holmes, M. (1989). Corporate management: A view from the centre. In G. Davis, P. Weller, & C. Lewis (Eds.), *Corporate management in Australian government* (pp. 29–47). Melbourne, Australia: Macmillan.

Hood, C. (1990). De-Sir Humphreyfying the Westminster model of bureaucracy: A new style of governance? *Governance, 3*, 205–214.

Jensen, G. (2003). Zen and the art of budget management: The New Zealand Treasury. In J. Wanna, L. Jensen, & J. de Vries (Eds.), *Controlling public expenditure: The changing role of central budget agencies—Better guardians?* (pp. 30–56). Cheltenham, UK: E. Elgar.

Keating, M., & Holmes, M. (1990). Australia's budgetary and financial management reforms. *Governance, 3,* 168–185.

Kettl, D. F. (2005). *The global public management revolution* (2nd ed.). Washington, DC: Brookings Institution.

Kibblewhite, A., & Ussher, C. (2002). Outcome-focused management in New Zealand. *Journal of Budgeting, 2,* 85–109.

Management Advisory Committee. (2001). *Performance management in the Australian public service: A strategic framework.* Canberra, Australia: Commonwealth of Australia.

McKay, K. (2003). Two generations of performance evaluation management systems in Australia. *Canberra Bulletin of Public Administration, 110,* 9–20.

McPhee, I. (2005, May 20). *Outcomes and outputs: Are we managing better as a result?* The CPA National Public Sector Convention, Melbourne, Australia.

Ministerial Advisory Group. (2001). *Report of the advisory group of the review of the centre.* Wellington, New Zealand: State Services.

Norman, R. (2006, June 1–3). *Managing for outcomes while accounting for outputs: Defining "public value" in New Zealand's performance management system.* "A Performing Public Sector: The Second Transatlantic Dialogue," EGPA/ASPA, Catholic University of Leuven, Belgium.

Organisation for Economic Co-operation and Development. (1997). *In search of results: Performance management practices.* Paris: Author.

Organisation for Economic Co-operation and Development. (2005, April 21–22). *Using performance information for managing and budgeting: Challenges, lessons, and opportunities.* 2nd Annual Meeting of OECD SBO Network on Performance and Results, Paris.

People and Strategy and Institute of Public Administration (ACT Division). (2001). *Performance management: A guide to good practice.* Canberra, Australia: Author.

Pollitt, C., & Bouckaert, G. (2004). *Public management reform: A comparative analysis* (2nd ed.). Oxford: Oxford University Press.

Public Service Commissioner. (2000) *State of the service report: 1999–2000.* Canberra, Australia: Public Service and Merit Protection Commission.

Robinson, M., & Brumby, J. (2005). *Does performance budgeting work? An analytical view of the empirical literature* (IMF Working Paper, WP/05/210). Washington, DC: International Monetary Fund.

Schick, A. (1996). *The spirit of reform: Managing the New Zealand state sector in a time of change.* A report prepared for the State Services Commission and the Treasury, Wellington, New Zealand.

Schick, A. (2001, August). *Reflections on the New Zealand model.* Paper based on a lecture at the New Zealand Treasury, Wellington.

Scott, G. (1997). Continuity and change in public management: Second generation issues in roles, responsibilities and relationships. *Future issues in public management* (pp. 15–26). Wellington, New Zealand: State Services Commission.

Scott, G. (2001). *Public management in New Zealand: Lessons and challenges.* Wellington, New Zealand: New Zealand Business Roundtable.

Shand, D., & Norman, R. (2005, December 5–7). *Performance budgeting in New Zealand.* Paper presented at IMF Fiscal Affairs Department Seminar on Performance Budgeting, Washington, DC.

State Services Commission. (1998). *Assessment of the New Zealand public service* (Occasional Paper No. 1). Wellington, New Zealand: Author.

State Services Commission. (1999). *Looping the loop: Evaluating outcomes and other risky feats* (Occasional Paper No. 7). Wellington, New Zealand: Author.

State Services Commission. (2006). *Public service chief executive performance.* Available at http://www.ssc.govt.nz/display/document.asp?navid=291

Steering Group for the Managing for Outcomes Roll-Out 2004/05. (2003, November). *Learning from evaluation activity: Enhancing performance through outcome-focussed management.* Wellington, New Zealand: State Services Commission.

Task Force on Management Improvement. (1993). *The Australian public service reformed: An evaluation of a decade of management reform.* Canberra, Australia: Australian Government Publishing Service.

Treasury and State Services Commission. (2005). *Guidance and requirements of departments preparing the statement of intent.* Wellington, New Zealand: State Services Commission and Treasury. Available at http://www.ssc.govt.nz/managing-for-outcomes

Wanna, J., & Bartos, S. (2003). Good practice: Does it work in theory? Australia's quest for better outcomes. In J. Wanna, L. Jensen, & J. de Vries (Eds.), *Controlling public expenditure: The changing role of central budget agencies—Better guardians?* (pp. 1–29). Cheltenham, UK: E. Elgar.

Wanna, J., Kelly, J., & Forster, J. (2000). *Managing public expenditure in Australia.* Sydney, Australia: Allen & Unwin.

18 Performance-Based Budgeting

Integrating Objectives and Metrics With People and Resources

Carl Moravitz

This chapter discusses how performance-based budgeting (PBB) has evolved in the public sector, the current efforts of organizations to apply evolving PBB concepts to meet current challenges, and the benefits of implementing PBB in the public sector. The objective of the discussions are to present some tools that can be used to enhance implementation and introduce best practices in public sector budgeting and developments in budgeting and performance that are changing and reshaping the budget office of tomorrow. An appendix ("Federal Budget Mandates and Structures") has been provided at the end of this chapter, setting out mandates supporting federal budgeting processes as well as overall structural characteristics of performance and budget information used in support of PBB.

Landscape for Change

Taxpayers are requiring more financial accountability from all levels of government. In addition, government has been scrutinizing itself on how it does business. In response, many agencies and departments are attempting to find ways to connect services delivered with program funding through PBB.

For more than five decades, the federal government has recognized the need to fully integrate performance and results with decision making. Congress and the executive branch have increased their emphasis on improving management across all agencies, resulting in a series of proposals and changes to federal budgeting, which mandates that performance and results information are to be combined. The results can then be compared with the strategic plan to determine that milestones are being achieved or indicate that midcourse corrections are required. The most notable change in legislation is the Government Performance and Results Act (GPRA),[1] enacted in 1993 and implemented across the federal government in fiscal year 1999.

State and local governments face similar pressures to incorporate performance and results, although no national mandate exists. All states are in some phase of implementing practices that enable them to integrate their budget and planning processes. According to a recent report from the U.S. Government Accountability Office (GAO-05–215, February 2005), efforts by states to examine performance and focus on their experiences in responding to recent fiscal stress can offer the states insights that may assist them in obtaining federal support to address the challenges ahead. All levels of government agree that the key to assessing program effectiveness is determining the right measures.

In general, PBB is defined as a budgeting process that links an organization's funding to its goals, strategies, programs, resources, services, and results. Using this approach, organizations create budget requests that take into account not only the funding that agencies would like to receive but also the outputs and outcomes they expect to produce as a result of that funding.

Performance outcomes are influenced by a number of inputs and processes—some of which are controlled by the agency, some of which are not. Agencies can draw a "line of sight" from inputs to outcomes to determine how the elements of a program build to the ultimate outcome. This exercise can assist agencies with "zeroing in" on the appropriate metrics. One way to create a true performance budget is to tie the agency's metrics to all phases of the process. Some key activities include the following:

- Developing a strategic plan that clearly links an agency's mission to each activity and program
- Developing a performance plan with objectives that support the strategic goals
- Making budget decisions that support the performance plan to the extent that resources can be made available and, in the process, program priorities set
- Constructing budgets and related justifications that speak to the strategic context and support the performance plan
- Periodically assessing progress against the plan, analyzing how various inputs have influenced performance

Performance-budgeting solutions and services offer a fully customized approach to performance budgeting through the development of a suite of tools and services. These solutions seek to support the linkages between the creation of an agency's performance and budget and compare those with the execution and results.

PBB tools are designed to support an organization's development, presentation, and execution of future-year budget and performance requests to its managers, legislators, Congress, and constituents. Decision makers need a roadmap that defines what successful performance budgeting would look like and that identifies the key elements and potential pitfalls on the critical path to success. More specifically, decision makers need a roadmap that provides the following: (a) performance-budgeting tools that contemplate all facets of the federal budget process and performance management and (b) a format that presents an integrated, multidimensional approach to budget and performance integration

The Evolution of Performance-Based Budgeting Efforts

The term *performance budgeting* was first widely used in the federal government a half century ago by the Hoover Commission, which recommended that the federal government develop a budget reflecting program accomplishments and program costs. Specifically, the Hoover Commission requested that the federal government adopt a "performance budget," which was defined as "one which presents the purposes and objectives for which funds are required, the costs of the programs proposed for achieving these objectives, and quantitative data measuring the accomplishments and work performed under each program."[2]

Since that time, there have been several efforts to reform the federal budget in ways that would establish clearer links between outcomes and funding. Those main initiatives are as follows:

- *Planning, Programming, and Budgeting System (PPBS) 1965:* Initiated nearly 40 years ago in the Department of Defense, PPBS was intended to shift the focus on decision making within the department from inputs to outputs. The executive branch required agencies to critically review both their goals and possible strategies for achieving these goals. Using techniques such as cost-benefit analysis, PPBS represented a massive effort to emphasize rational analysis, rather than political consensus, in the budget process.
- *Management by Objectives (MBO), 1972 and early 1990s:* As a government reform, MBO appeared twice: first, over 25 years ago, during the administrations of Presidents Nixon and Ford, and subsequently in 1990 to 1991, when it was briefly used during the administration of President H. W. Bush. In the early 1970s, President Richard Nixon introduced a more limited budget reform, MBO, in 21 of the largest federal agencies. The key components of MBO were to define quantifiable objectives, develop annual operating plans that specified how objectives would be achieved, and measure actual performance.

- *Zero-Based Budgeting (ZBB) 1977:* President Jimmy Carter required federal agencies to implement zero-based budgeting. Typically, budget discussions had focused on proposed increases or decreases in spending, with less attention to the "base" and more concentration on historical revenues or spending, However, ZBB required agencies to develop "decision packages" for each budget activity, which necessitated that agencies start from zero and build the budget without considering the past.

Although these budget reforms were different in scope and approach, each was concerned with showing the linkage between the use of resources and consequent outcomes.

Early Lessons Learned: Limited Success With Past Initiatives _____

Emphasis on performance information has had little direct impact on budget allocations. While budget reforms have helped bring more systematic analysis into the budget process, they failed because they did not prove to be relevant to budget decision makers in the executive branch. For the most part, these reforms did not outlive the administrations that proposed them. Their failures demonstrated that for budget reforms to succeed, there must be a shared commitment to the objectives of budget reform within the executive branch and between the executive and legislative branches. Overall, these reform efforts show the difficulty of trying to implement major budget changes in a short period of time.[3]

Successful implementations of major budget reforms take time. The budget proposal process is large and complicated. The existing level of spending, also known as the *base budget,* reflects a long history of policy decisions by the executive and legislative branches. There is a considerable amount of power and money at stake in the budget process, so agency and legislative participants see the importance of balanced budget reforms and the long-term impact they will have.

Experience suggests that budget reforms should not overburden agency staff or legislators. Creating a budget from "scratch" is more difficult than making incremental changes. PPBS and ZBB generated enormous amounts of paperwork because they required agencies to justify their entire budgets, whereas they may not have been required to previously. In some cases, it was difficult for agencies to conduct all of the required analyses within the limited budget time frame and present the results in a concise format.

Setting the Foundation: Recent Government Performance Initiatives

The passage of new federal laws in the 1990s laid a statutory and management framework that provided a framework for strengthening government performance and accountability. These laws created a substantial, government-wide foundation for performance-based management.

The first of these was the Chief Financial Officers Act of 1990 (CFO Act).[4] This legislation was the most significant financial management reform passed by Congress in 40 years, and it mandated changes in planning and reporting by federal agencies. The law requires 23 major agencies to have a chief financial officer who, among other duties, must provide for "the systematic measurement of performance." Also, they were required to prepare annual audited financial statements, including a report on "results of operation."

On the heels of the CFO Act were the Government Performance and Results Act of 1993 (GPRA), the Federal Acquisition Streamlining Act of 1994 (FASA),[5] and the Clinger-Cohen Act of 1996.[6] GPRA became the centerpiece of this new performance-oriented framework as it established the basic concepts and fundamental structure for the federal government's approach to performance-based management. In addition, GPRA specifies a congressional role in performance-based management and that agency performance-related plans and reports are publicly available. Unlike previous initiatives, GPRA explicitly sought to promote a connection between performance plans and budgets.

The framework consists of strategic plans, annual performance plans, and performance reports. It requires agencies to develop and deliver the following:

- Multiyear strategic planning
- Annual performance planning and goals
- Annual performance reporting, results, validation, and verification
- Linkage of performance results to budgets

Strategic plans define both the agency mission and a set of long-range goals and objectives for the agency's major programs and functions. Performance plans include measurable performance goals with target levels for a particular fiscal year. The performance plans cover all programs and functions of an agency. Performance plans usually display past, current, and future-year data for the performance goals. Between 3 and 7 years of data are typically presented. Performance reports compare actual performance with the projected performance levels in the performance plan and are prepared annually.

Although GPRA is the most prominent act, it is also important to note lift-up requirements of both the FASA and Clinger-Cohen Acts. FASA includes requirements that agencies establish cost, performance, and schedule goals for major acquisitions. FASA dictates that they must achieve 90% of these goals, take certain steps if the 90% target is not met, and relate employee pay based on this performance. Furthermore, Clinger-Cohen includes requirements for agencies to develop performance measures for information technology that is either used or will be acquired by an agency.

Building upon the widely adopted GPRA framework, the administration of President George W. Bush has made further attempts to capitalize on performance management initiatives that integrate cost and performance information during the annual budget review process. Using complementary approaches to strengthen the link between budget and performance, the administration introduced the President's Management Agenda (PMA) (2001) and Office of Management and Budget's (OMB) Program Assessment Rating Tool (PART; 2002).

The budget and performance integration initiative represents the most challenging aspect of the PMA. The PART explicitly infuses performance information into the budget formulation process at a funding decision level, taking the role of a diagnostic questionnaire used to rate selected programs. The PART explores the following areas:

- Program purpose and design
- Strategic planning
- Program management
- Program results including whether or not a program is achieving its long-term and annual goals

In the 2004 budget cycle, OMB applied this tool to approximately 234 programs. This review sought to assess and gather information on a program's purpose, performance measures, alignment with budget and results, and planning and management to determine its overall effectiveness. It targeted the program to evaluate an additional 20% of agency programs each year over a five-year period. By the 2007 budget, the evaluation has been extended to 80% of federal government programs. Together, the PMA and PART represent a commitment of the present administration to measure performance and to integrate performance more specifically in the budget process.

Although states are not directly impacted by the federal mandates, like GPRA and PMA, they must consider the indirect flow-down, as it will have an impact on the allocation of resources. For instance, state and local governments need to evaluate functional expenditure patterns for programs and services such as education, welfare, transportation, and health care. The state's assessment will drive the extent to and speed with which they implement a PBB initiative.

Several states are implementing PBB initiatives but are struggling to overcome varying levels of manual input. The challenge, now, is to fully automate the process of integrating the disparate financial systems, linking the program and service costs at an individual agency level, and then consolidating the information from all departments and agencies for a 360-degree view of their performance.

The "New" Era of Performance Management

Today's philosophy of performance-based management starts with a systematic approach to performance improvement. It requires an ongoing process of establishing strategic performance objectives; measuring performance; collecting, analyzing, reviewing, and reporting performance data; and using the data to drive performance improvement.

In the performance-based management process, the first step is to identify an organization's strategic goals and performance objectives. This step also involves the establishment of performance measures based on and linked to the outcomes of the strategic planning phase. Following that, the next steps are to do the work; collect performance data (i.e., measurements); and analyze, review, and use that data to drive performance improvement (i.e., make changes and corrections and/or "fine-tune" organizational operations). Last, management reports the data and performs necessary changes, corrections, or fine-tuning. Then, the process starts over again.

An agency regularly collects timely and credible performance information—including information from its program partners and contractors—and uses that information to manage the programs and improve its performance. For instance, this could include adjusting program priorities, making resource allocations, or taking other appropriate management actions.

Performance management essentially uses performance information to manage and improve performance and to demonstrate what has been accomplished. *Performance measurement,* in simplest terms, is the comparison of actual levels of performance to preestablished target levels of performance. Moreover, performance measurement is a critical component of performance-based management. The next logical step in the implementation of GPRA is *performance budgeting.* Pursuing a systematic use of performance planning, budgeting, and financial information is essential to achieving a more results-oriented and accountable government. PBB is just one component of an organization's total performance management that brings together people, processes, and technology to leverage decision making and resource management, but it is a major link to overall performance management success. (See Figure 18.1.)

The existing legislation requires that agencies identify high-quality outcome measures, accurately monitor the performance of programs, and begin integrating this effort with associated costs. To do so, an agency must regularly collect timely and credible performance information. It must begin to use performance information to manage its programs and improve performance—institute a performance-based management framework. But just collecting budget information and using it for decision-making purposes will not achieve the full potential of PBB. Efforts must be made to go to the next step and to link that information to the strategic goals and objectives of the organization, an example of which is set out in Figure 18.2. This ensures financial assessment of program performance. By taking these steps, agencies will be able to accelerate their services and programs to the next level when they apply the "new" performance management.

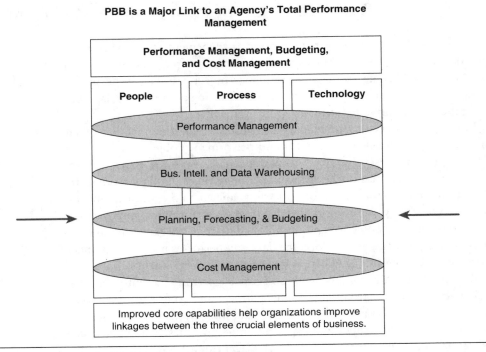

Figure 18.1   Links for Total Performance Management
SOURCE: IBM Global Business Services.[7]

Course Followed by High-Performing Organizations

In a 2005 IBM Global Chief Financial Officer Study ("The Agile CFO," IBM Global Business Services), it was established that finance leaders place high importance on continuously making process and business improvements, strengthening controls to meet their accountability requirements, and broadening their analytical capabilities. High-performing organizations are moving from a role of static reporting and data stewardship to a more predictive role of providing dynamic business insight to decision makers. In the past, practical limitations forced finance organizations to focus primarily on operating and control activities, but process and technology improvements make it possible to do more. In fact, experience is showing that ensuring strong financial management discipline in operational responsibilities allows organizations to invest more of the organization's resources to provide high-value decision support and strengthen their roles as trusted advisers.

Figure 18.3 from the IBM Global CFO Study shows this trend from 1999 to 2005 for finance organizations shifting from transactional activities to decision insight (i.e., stronger decision support and analytics).

These same opportunities are also present in public sector budget offices as they strive to move to more PBB. Over the long term, high-performing

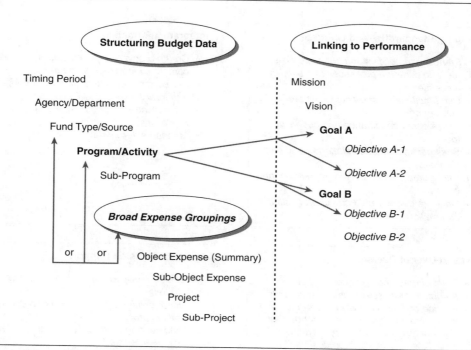

Figure 18.2   Linking Budget Data to Performance

SOURCE: IBM Global Business Services.

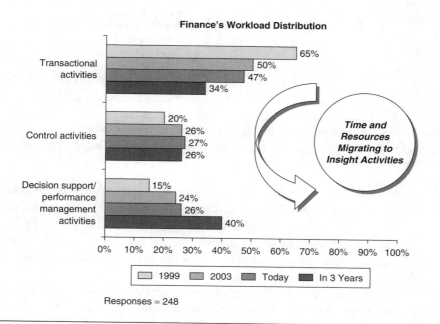

Figure 18.3   Finance Organizations Continue Shifts to Analytical Activities: Adding PBB Helps
Realize Benefits

SOURCE: "The Agile CFO," The Global CFO Study, IBM Global Business Services, 2005, p. 11.

Simplify, Standardize, and Optimize	Integrate information
• *Standardize policies and business rules* • *Move to common processes and simplify processes* • *Use functional best practices, where appropriate* • *Utilize enhanced finance and budgeting tools* • *Seek common finance platforms and data standards* • *Utilize data warehouses for management of data* • *Optimize delivery methods of products and information*	• *Create a governance structure to ensure common information standards* • *Consolidate and integrate actual, budget and forecast data* • *Drive ownership and mapping of processes* • *Manage external data sources*
Expand Overall Oversight	**Optimize Decision Support**
• *Drive understanding of control points* • *Automate processes to improve controls* • *Provide business activity monitoring through use of operational dashboards* • *Use analytical tools to support actual work-flow activities and processes*	• *Use streamlined, integrated budgeting process* • *Utilize collaborative planning and decision-making process* • *Employ rolling forecasts, based on relevant business events* • *Focus on exception-based reporting and analytics* • *Create enterprise-wide reporting/access procedures* • *Use linked and aligned scorecard metrics cascaded down* • *Identify and assess business opportunities and synergies* • *Implement sound costing and analytical methods* • *Create centers of excellence around client needs*

Figure 18.4   Key Best Practices to Ensuring Effective Implementation of PBB

SOURCE: Adapted from *The 2005 Global CFO Study: "The Agile CFO,"* IBM Global Business Services. Figure 18.4 is extracted from pp. 13–18 of that study.

financial organizations leverage change and improvement across four broad focus areas: (a) simplify, standardize, and optimize; (b) integrate information; (c) expand overall oversight; and (d) optimize decision support (see Figure 18.4). Over time, these focus areas provide a strong foundation for implementing performance-based management in policy making and in management of available resources.

Ensuring the effective use of best practices in organizations allows the best foundation for successful implementation and use of PBB throughout the organization. Findings show that highly effective finance organizations implement functional best practices enterprise-wide at a higher rate than organizations that are less effective at driving insights across the enterprise. The adoption rate of process simplifications among highly effective finance

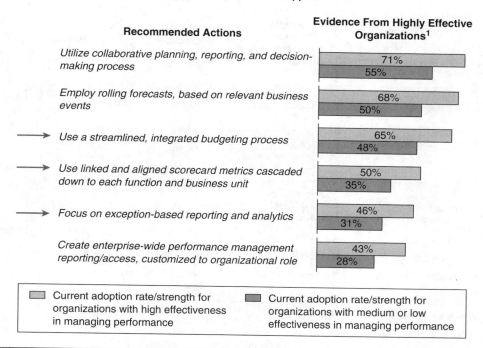

Optimizing Decision Support

Recommended Actions	Evidence From Highly Effective Organizations[1]
Utilize collaborative planning, reporting, and decision-making process	71% / 55%
Employ rolling forecasts, based on relevant business events	68% / 50%
→ Use a streamlined, integrated budgeting process	65% / 48%
→ Use linked and aligned scorecard metrics cascaded down to each function and business unit	50% / 35%
→ Focus on exception-based reporting and analytics	46% / 31%
Create enterprise-wide performance management reporting/access, customized to organizational role	43% / 28%

Current adoption rate/strength for organizations with high effectiveness in managing performance

Current adoption rate/strength for organizations with medium or low effectiveness in managing performance

Figure 18.5   Integrating Budget, Strengthening Analytics and Metrics

SOURCE: Adapted from *The 2005 Global CFO Study: "The Agile CFO,"* IBM Global Business Services. Figure 18.5 is highlighted amplification of p. 24 of that study.

NOTE: 1. Statistically significant.

organizations is twice as high as that for less effective organizations, and their adoption rate for functional best practices is almost 3 times as high.

High-performing finance organizations realize the importance of focusing on the contribution of their financial activities and reports to the overall performance management objectives of the enterprise. Focusing too heavily on transactional and operational activities detracts from the overall vision of mapping initial strategic planning processes to the ultimate management and review of invested resources. Figure 18.5 provides empirical evidence that organizations that use a streamlined budgeting process, linked and aligned scorecard metrics, and report of exception-based reporting and analytics are more effective organizations than those that do not use these practices.

Ultimately, strategic budgeting seeks to increase decision-makers' understanding of the links between requested resources and expected performance results. Such integration is critical to sustain and institutionalize performance and management reforms. With the major annual process in the federal and state governments whereby programs and activities come up for regular review and reexamination, the budget process itself benefits as well if the result of integration is better, more reliable performance information, as illustrated in Figure 18.6.

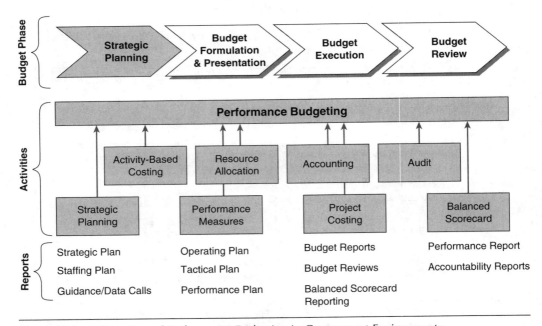

Figure 18.6   Overview of Performance Budgeting in Government Environments

SOURCE: From *Integrating Performance and Budgets: The Budget Office of Tomorrow,* edited by Jonathan D. Breul and Carl Moravitz, IBM Center of Business of Government, Rowan & Littlefield, 2007, p. 5.

As illustrated in the diagram in Figure 18.6, performance information can play a useful role in the budget process, but it is only one of many factors that should be considered. Several changes need to occur with an organization before performance information can have a significant impact on budgeting. Management across all levels of the organization must recognize that performance measurement is a central part of managerial oversight and responsibility, not merely a passing fad, and that the organization must improve the quality of its financial data, performance measurement, and reporting vehicles (such as Web portals, performance dashboards, and supporting data). Organizations should address the following:

- Consider ways to streamline agency budget narratives, highlight performance measures and link them to objectives, and present budget recommendations or options in terms of their expected outcomes
- Continue to pursue ways to more effectively link information on performance with corresponding information on spending, thus enabling better estimates of efficiency and cost-effectiveness

Implementing performance-related budgeting does not automatically mean that good results are rewarded through the budget process or, conversely, that poor results will always have negative funding implications. Viewing

1) *Develop a strategic plan that clearly links an agency's mission to each activity and program.*
2) *Create a performance plan with objectives that support the strategic goals.*
3) *Make budget decisions that support the performance plan to the extent that resources can be made available, and, in the proces, program priorities set.*
4) *Construct budgets and related justifications that address the strategic context and support the performance plan.*
5) *Periodically assess progress against the plan, analyzing how various inputs influenced performance.*

Figure 18.7   Five Tips for Integrating Budgets Into the Planning Process

SOURCE: *Performance-Based Budgeting in Government, Integrating Objectives and Metrics with People and Resources,* p. 10, by Carl Moravitz and Jim McGinsey, a SAS White Paper, published in 2006 by SAS, Inc.

strategic and performance budgeting in a mechanistic manner or punitive terms—a specific level of performance in exchange for a certain amount of funding—is not useful or sustainable. Rather than increase accountability, these approaches might instead devalue the process by favoring managers who meet expectations by aiming low. The determination of priorities is a function of competing values and interests that may be informed by performance information but also reflects factors such as equity, unmet needs, and the appropriate role of government in addressing these needs.

Linking performance, budget, and spending together has many benefits for organizational improvement. First, it helps the budgeting process become a major decision-making vehicle, supporting an organization's development, presentation, and execution of budget and performance requests at all levels of review. Second, it connects assessments of agency resource requirements and performance results, providing valuable linkages to the execution results of available funding. Last, it provides more valued analyses and associations of results in budget process decision making and the linkages between formulation and execution phases. Thus, it can bring additional meaning to an organization's internal financial plan development processes as they move to distribute approved funding to program managers.

A robust planning process is critical to public sector organizations in their efforts to direct the total stewardship of dollars entrusted to them. Integrating this into the fuller and more time-consuming elements of the budget process is the important next step. A white paper jointly developed by IBM and SAS, Inc., released in February 2006 as part of SAS's thought leadership series on financial management in the public sector, provides five core tips for consideration by public sector organizations in integrating the budget into the planning process (see Figure 18.7) to make strategic planning and the budget an integrated reality.

Linking Plans to Budget

A critical step in PBB involves the ability to link the higher-level strategic plans and outcomes of an organization to the more tactical processes and

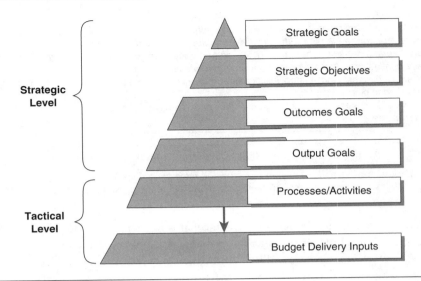

Strategic Goals

Strategic Objectives

Outcomes Goals

Output Goals

Processes/Activities

Budget Delivery Inputs

Strategic Level

Tactical Level

Figure 18.8   Hierarchy of Goals, Performance, and Budget
SOURCE: IBM Global Business Services.

information supporting the production and management of the one's budget. Although setting the long-term vision and strategic direction for an organization is critical, equally important is the process of linking that view to the core processes supporting budget management. Paying closer attention to tactical-level activities is important because they (a) guarantee the delivery and monitoring of important budget and financial resources, (b) ensure appropriate connections to the fuller strategic directions of the organization, and (c) lead to effective implementation of PBB. Figure 18.8 illustrates how the strategic thinking of the agency can be linked with the tactical or operational plans and budgets. It shows a general roadmap for organizations to follow for ensuring effective management of performance and results consistent with operations of highly effective financial organizations (i.e., ensuring that the strategic direction of the organization is managed equally in all of the business processes supporting performance management).

The next logical step in PBB is connecting the dots of performance with budgeting. A systematic use of performance planning, budgeting, and financial information is essential to achieving a more results-oriented and accountable government (see Table 18.1). The existing federal legislation requires agencies to identify high-quality outcome measures, accurately monitor the performance of programs, and begin integrating this effort with associated costs. To do so, an organization must regularly collect timely and credible performance information. It must begin to use performance information to manage its programs and improve performance and to institute a performance-based management framework. By taking these steps, agencies will be able to accelerate their services and programs to the next level when they apply the "new" performance management. (See Figure 18.9.)

Table 18.1   Making Performance-Based Budgets Real

Making integrated planning and budgeting real across the organizations . . . To make these tips a reality, the key to more effectively implementing an organization's performance management goals hinges on the use of more robust analytical tools across the organization, which will permit the following:

- Expanded organizational-wide sensitivity analysis
- Simplification and standardization of processes
- Standardization of data across accounting and budgeting systems

Such tools provide organizations with the expanded potential for smoother movement, not only from planning to budget development but also to financial planning oversight and, ultimately, to assessments of the results.

Organizations are encouraged to pursue strong standards on data and systems to position themselves for effective implementation of such performance management and budgeting enhancements at a future time. Maximum effectiveness of strategic planning initiatives and, potentially, future performance management processes requires full engagement of frontline staff/line examiners, as well as senior management to ensure full rollout of policies and priorities in the budget development process

SOURCE: "The Agile CFO," The Global CFO Study, IBM Global Business Services, 2005, pp. 7–18.

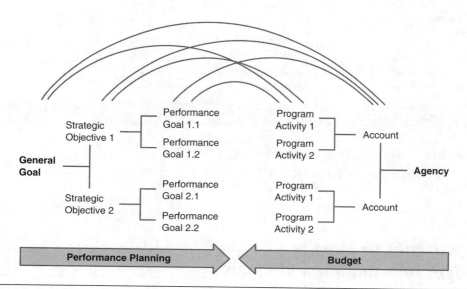

Figure 18.9   Linkages at Multiple Levels of Planning and Budget

SOURCE: Original source content from *Performance Budgeting: Efforts to Restructure Budgets to Better Align Resources with Performance,* Staff Study, GAO-05-117SP; actual chart of information from *Performance-Based Budgeting in Government, Integrating Objectives and Metrics with People and Resources,* p. 10, by Carl Moravitz and Jim McGinsey, a SAS White Paper, published in 2006 by SAS, Inc.

At the state level, a number of governors and legislatures are pursuing performance-based programs to help ensure that their agencies deliver better government-to-government and government-to-citizen services. Like the federal government, these state initiatives rely on the ability to integrate performance-related data with financial information. At all levels, a key to success is aligning executive goals and priorities with those of legislators and citizens.

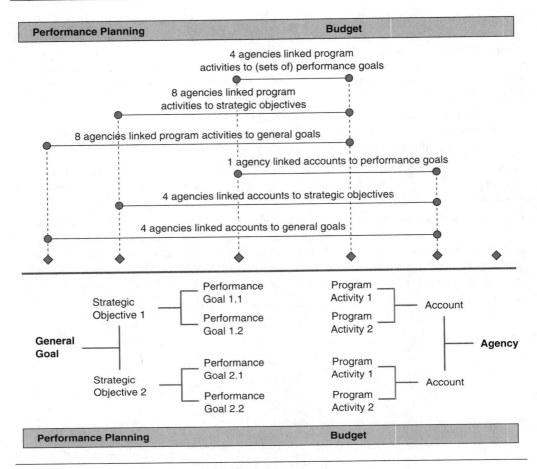

Figure 18.10   Linkages of Performance and Budget

SOURCE: From *Performance Budgeting: Efforts to Restructure Budgets to Better Align Resources With Performance,* Staff Study, GAO-05–117SP, February 2005.

Approaches to Linking Budget Information and Goals

Figure 18.10 illustrates how the agencies link budget information with performance goals and objectives. Looking at the bottom portion of the illustration (with "General Goal" on the left and "Agency" on the right), one can see how agencies move from connecting performance goals to managing agency accounts. For instance, a general goal may be broad and large in scope, made up of smaller strategic objectives. These more focused objectives rely on the accomplishment of even more specific performance goals. As one moves to the budget side of the illustration, the tactical program activities are tied to larger agency accounts. This is the structure that needs to be in place prior to beginning a PBB initiative.

However, no federal agency surveyed by the GAO in the February 2005 study (GAO-05–215) mentioned earlier, implementation of performance and budgeting in federal agencies, has linked all the components to form a complete PBB picture. Some agencies have links only for performance goals to program activities, while others are linking performance goals to budget accounts. As shown in Figure 18.10, according to the GAO report, most agencies are connecting their performance plans with lower or more specific levels of their budget structures, such as their accounts.

Techniques to Link Plans and Net Costs

Departments and agencies use multiple approaches to link plans and net costs. Net costs relate the accounting and chart of accounts presentations used in support of their financial statements, which do not necessarily match evenly with an organization's performance and management presentations. The techniques for matching strategic directions and performance goals can vary across the organization. Most agencies link these costs to the highest levels of their goal structures, as shown in Figure 18.11, sometimes making it difficult to assess results of investments of certain strategic directions.

Through the observations of both Figures 18.10 and 18.11, it is revealed that many different approaches are used to relate performance and financial reporting and to monitor results. No single approach will fit an entire organization's missions, performance planning, and financial management structures. However, the concept of performance budgeting will continue to evolve, and no single definition or approach can be expected to encompass the range of needs and changing interests of government decision makers.

Agencies will continue to develop their own approaches to linking resources and results within their unique environments to meet their performance management challenges. Ultimately, the need to translate the planned and actual use of resources into concrete and measurable results remains an essential step in achieving a more results-oriented government. Moreover, the heterogeneity of the government suggests that sustained efforts and attention will be the hallmark of long-term success.

Long-term connectivity of planning and budget ensures careful monitoring of strategic planning, performance management, and budget management processes and the appropriate handoffs of information and results. Figure 18.12 below shows some of the important links that need to be monitored on a regular basis to ensure successful uses of PBB processes in an organization.

Implementing Performance Budgeting

What does a successful performance-based budget look like? There are four performance-budgeting models being pursued by agencies. It will be important

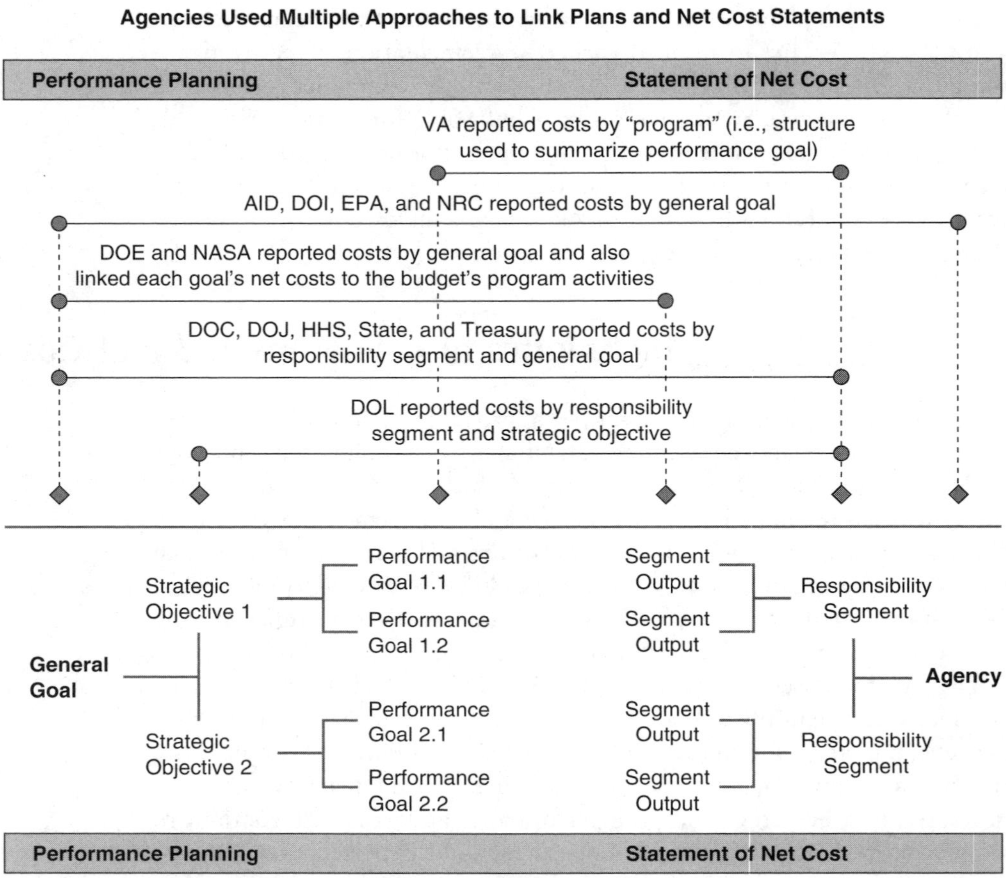

Agencies Used Multiple Approaches to Link Plans and Net Cost Statements

Performance Planning	Statement of Net Cost

VA reported costs by "program" (i.e., structure used to summarize performance goal)

AID, DOI, EPA, and NRC reported costs by general goal

DOE and NASA reported costs by general goal and also linked each goal's net costs to the budget's program activities

DOC, DOJ, HHS, State, and Treasury reported costs by responsibility segment and general goal

DOL reported costs by responsibility segment and strategic objective

General Goal

Strategic Objective 1 ── Performance Goal 1.1 / Performance Goal 1.2

Strategic Objective 2 ── Performance Goal 2.1 / Performance Goal 2.2

Segment Output ── Responsibility Segment

Segment Output

Agency

Segment Output ── Responsibility Segment

Segment Output

Performance Planning	Statement of Net Cost

Figure 18.11   Linkages of Performance and Net Cost

SOURCE: From *Performance Budgeting: Efforts to Restructure Budgets to Better Align Resources With Performance*, Staff Study, GAO-05–117SP, February 2005.

for the political community to settle on the model that is the most realistic way to implement performance budgeting, but there is no consensus yet:

1. *Mechanical:* There is a direct tie between dollars and performance. For instance, if performance goes up, dollars increase.

2. *Managerial:* Consensus on broadly defined goals is critical, but there is little oversight of specific operations.

3. *Incentives:* Incremental programmatic improvements in performance are rewarded.

4. *Agenda:* Success is defined as the ability to ask the right questions, not provide budgetary answers that stem from reported performance levels.

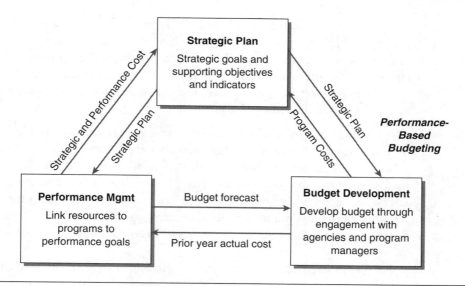

Figure 18.12   Performance-Based Budgeting

SOURCE: SAS for Performance-Based Budgeting, Interactive Tour, May 2006: http://www.sas.com/govedu/tour/pbb/itour_flash.html

1. Mechanical: This is the most fundamental and basic approach, as it ensures that an agency budget illustrates the direct link between the dollars invested and the performance desired. It is referred to as "mechanical" because it does not integrate performance management, strategic planning, or decision making. Following this approach, the implementation of PBB will merely be a mechanical tool that does little to leverage improvement. In many ways, this approach is the most difficult to achieve completely, due to its requirement that all costs and their performance relationships be understood. However, the mechanical approach is the baseline for PBB, whereas other approaches that center around strategic planning, decision making, management, or impact on outcomes will not be successful without due diligence in this process. Previous references in Figure 18.10 show various levels of agency effectiveness in this area, but agencies need to do more. GAO notes that beyond the core requirements of directly linking costs and performance, there are broader approaches (noted below) that complement the mechanical approach to ensure a total integration into decision making and management operations.

2. Managerial: This approach uses a means of achieving broad consensus on high-level goals, which are defined as critical. It affords little oversight of specific operations because it lacks specific details of costs and performance. Some agencies try to approach PBB using this approach alone, but they then have no effective means to evaluate results without the detail on costs and performance that are available through the mechanical approach. Figure 18.10 demonstrates cases where some agencies connect initial funding to high-level, general goals but then have no further detail for performance assessment.

3. Incentives: This approach is also useful for evaluating incremental programmatic improvements in performance by rewarding those who make improvements over current operations with incremental investments. To be effective, this approach must also be complemented by the mechanical approach on costs and performance in order to benchmark areas for evaluation and to note incremental improvements.

4. Agenda: The most valuable approach, the agenda method can be effective only in concert with core information on costs and performance. It also requires solid business intelligence tools to ask "what if" questions; analyze results, trade-offs, or redeployment options; view alternative scenarios, and so on. The mechanical approach provides direct budgetary answers to dollar costs and related performance, but the agenda approach goes further, allowing organizations to ask the right questions and leverage mission, strategies, and outcomes.

For the greatest success, organizations should start with the mechanical approach to first capture and use detailed information on costs and performance and then tie that information to the budget account structure used for decision making. This process can be complemented by one or all of the other structures (managerial, incentive, agenda) as the performance and cost information become more available to the organization and as the management culture finds certain structures to be most valuable. The parameters of approaches used to implement and incorporate performance-based information in budgets and for management oversight need to be clearly communicated both internally and externally.

In the end, the selection of an appropriate model may be agency by agency, developed in discussions between an agency, OMB or other policy reviewers, and legislative and congressional staff. But being clear about the parameters up front helps frame this dialogue.

Benefits of Performance-Based Budgeting

According to David Walker, U.S. Comptroller General,[8]

> Credible outcome-based performance information is absolutely critical to foster the kind of debate that is needed. Linking performance information to budgeting can greatly improve the budget debate by changing the kinds of questions asked and information made available to decision makers. However, performance information will not provide the mechanism for considered judgment and political choice. If budget decisions are to be based in part on performance data, the integrity, credibility, and quality of these data and related analyses become more important. Moreover, in seeking to link resources to results, it will be necessary to improve the government's capacity to account for and measure the total costs of federal programs and activities.

The benefits of performance budgeting are numerous. Foremost, it increases the organizational focus on mission and goals and shifts attention away from scrutinizing revenues and expenditures. This approach also improves the efficiency and effectiveness of government operations by allocating resources toward the most critical outcomes. More important, PBB enables decision making to "zero in" on the most effective way to use the limited resources, because it encourages agencies and departments to work together to optimize and best utilize resources. The collaboration will necessitate dialogue between owners of the planning, budgeting, and costing processes.

Over time, PBB can improve operations by linking budget and program performance and enabling increased communication about critical issues and priorities relative to budget requests and the use of resources. The tangible measurements help to eliminate some of the tension that exists between and within departments on how money is spent and allocated. These measurements are an organization's proof of performance and give merit to rewarding top-performing departments and management.

Another significant benefit of PBB can be realized at the program management level. The automation of processes enables day-to-day operational efficiencies. For instance, PBB allows program managers to make immediate decisions based on quantitative information, which enables them to make adjustments on the effectiveness of the activities. Not only can a program manager look at how well Activity A is performing, but with PBB, he or she can also evaluate how Activities B and C are doing in comparison to A. Armed with this information, a program manager can proactively monitor the effectiveness and mitigate problems before they escalate, to ensure that constituents receive optimal service.

Furthermore, constituents benefit from governments, federal and state, applying PBB to their business operations. Because PBB is rooted in cost-effectiveness, taxpayers can be assured that their money is being wisely spent. Cost savings are inherent with PBB because agencies are applying their resources to the most effective programs and services. A government with a renewed focus on delivering effective programs translates into delivering the highest quality of services to citizens and new levels of transparency.

The well-known cliché of "promises made, promises kept" can now be embraced as governments move beyond traditional ways of doing business and assume new levels of accountability.

Appendix: Federal Budget Mandates and Structures

A. Mandates for the Budget Process

The U.S. Constitution does not require the president to develop a federal budget or make recommendations concerning the revenues and spending of the federal government. So, many years elapsed before the Congress and the president felt it was important to incorporate this aspect of financial control in the federal government and settle on a "comprehensive budget process."

The current executive branch budgeting process began in 1921, with passage of the Budget and Accounting Act, which provides for a national budget system.

The act's basic requirement is that the president should prepare and submit a budget to Congress each year. The 1921 act established the Bureau of the Budget (originally within the Department of the Treasury), now existing as the Office of Management and Budget (OMB), within the Executive Office of the president, to assist the president in preparing and implementing the executive budget. Although the legislation has been amended many times, this statute provides the legal basis for the President's Budget, prescribes much of its content, and defines the roles of the president and the agencies in the process.

Most revisions to the Budget and Accounting Act since 1921 have centered on two key themes:

• Congressional budget reforms, defining more accountability on decisions relating to policy making and eventual allocation of the total federal budget[9]

• More management, accountability, and performance assessments within the executive branch for the use and results of federal agency funding—all designed to modernize the objectives of the 1921 legislation[10]

The President's Budget, officially referred to as "The Budget of the United States Government," must be submitted to Congress no later than the first Monday in February. The President's Budget document consists of the following:

• Estimates of spending, revenues, borrowing, and federal debt

• Policy and legislative recommendations

• Detailed estimates of the financial operations of federal agencies and programs

• Detailed results and estimates of performance for related programs of agencies and departments

• Data on the actual and projected performance of the economy and other information supporting the president's recommendations

Although the President's Budget is only a request to Congress, the process of formulating and submitting a budget is a vital tool in the president's direction of the executive branch and of national policy. The President's Budget proposals often guide congressional revenue and spending decisions. The extent of the influence varies from year to year and depends more on political and fiscal conditions than on the legal status of the budget.

B. Major Legislation Driving Federal Budget Process

The Constitution

- Requires that there be appropriations enacted in law prior to any funds being spent from the Treasury
- Requires that any revenue legislation be initiated by the House of Representatives

Anti-Deficiency Act

- Legislation enacted in 1870 makes it a criminal offense for an employee or officer of the U.S. government (or the District of Columbia government) to make or authorize an expenditure or obligation that exceeds available funding.

Budget and Accounting Act of 1921 (P.L. 67–13)

- Establishes, for the executive branch, the federal budget process operations and management processes for the expenditure of congressionally provided funds
- Creates the Bureau of the Budget, later Office of Management and Budget (OMB), to assist the president in preparing budget recommendations for submission to Congress
- Creates the General Accounting Office (GAO) as the principal auditing arm of the federal government

Congressional Budget and Impoundment Control Act of 1974 (P.L. 93–344)

- Establishes the congressional budget process
- Creates the Congressional Budget Office
- Establishes processes, procedures, and controls for certain aspects related to the execution and management of appropriated funds (deferrals, rescissions, etc.)

Balanced Budget and Emergency Deficit Control Act of 1985 (referred to as Gramm-Rudman-Hollings) (P.L. 99–177)

- Establishes annual deficit targets directed toward balancing the budget by 1991
- Establishes a budget sequester process to pare back excess spending above legislated deficit targets

Balanced Budget and Emergency Deficit Control Act of 1987 (P.L. 100–119)

- Revises annual deficit targets to achieve a balanced budget by 1993
- Revises procedures in the 1985 act ruled unconstitutional

Budget Enforcement Act of 1990 (P.L. 101–508, Title XIII)

- Amends the Congressional Budget Act and the Balanced Budget and Emergency Deficit Control Act
- Places "caps" on the level of discretionary appropriations for fiscal years 1991 through 1995
- Establishes "Pay As You Go" (PAYGO) procedures for monitoring mandatory spending and receipts
- Expands sequester process to remove excesses if discretionary or mandatory spending exceeds the new limits

Omnibus Budget Reconciliation Act of 1993 (P.L. 103–66)

- Extends the discretionary spending caps until 1998

Government Performance and Results Act of 1993 (P.L. 103–62)

- Establishes performance and results as an integral part of the federal budget process
- Requires that all major programs provide performance data as part of budget submissions, beginning with the fiscal year 1999 budget
- Requires reports on performance of government programs

Line-Item Veto Act (P.L. 104–130)

- Provides the president with the authority to cancel line items in appropriations and tax acts. The act was ruled unconstitutional by the U.S. Supreme Court in 1998.

Budget Enforcement Act of 1997 (P.L. 105–33)

- Extends the discretionary spending caps until 2002

C. Formulation of President's Budget

Formulation of a federal agency's budget typically begins in the spring of each year (many agencies begin earlier), which is approximately

- 9 months before the budget is actually submitted to Congress,
- 18 months prior to the beginning of the fiscal year to which it pertains, and
- 30 months before the close of that fiscal year.

The early stages of budget preparation occur in the federal agencies. When they begin work on the budget for a new fiscal year, agencies are already

(a) in various stages of implementing the budget for the fiscal year in progress and (b) waiting final appropriations approvals and other legislative decisions for the upcoming fiscal year. Relative to the new fiscal year for which work is just beginning, also known as the "budget year" or "BY," the actual year in progress becomes the "past year" (PY) and immediately upcoming fiscal year becomes the "current year" (CY).

The long lead times and the fact that appropriations have not yet been approved for the next year mean that the budget is prepared in an environment of uncertainty about economic conditions, presidential policies, congressional actions, and agency performance and results.

Most agencies/departments are separated into bureaus, and decisions on budgets for those components actually begin in the bureaus—at the program level, ideally based on early planning guidance issued by the parent department with the endorsement of the department's secretary or the agency head. The individual department/agency budget director

- facilitates and directs the process of justification, review, acceptance, and prioritization of the programs and funding and
- negotiates between competing program interests.

Decisions percolate up to the parent agency/department in the form of each bureau's budget request to the agency/department. At this level, a layer of complication is added. Many budget offices are organized into a structure of desk officers, who oversee a particular program or organization and evaluate and assess operations and review budget requests. This provides the element of specialization, using gained skills to analyze areas such as the following:

- Performance and results for resources used and requested, including ongoing assessments of measures and intended outcomes for the program
- Labor cost and production analysis
- Capital budgeting and IT reviews—a growing focus of budget staffs
- Financial management reasonableness of proposals
- Consistency with the agency's strategic plan
- Consistency with agency and administration priorities

The formulation of the budget is, by and large, a process that exists outside specific time boundaries. Done properly, it is a year-round task. Budget officers are required to manage the current year while at the same time working to tell the story for the year ahead. Like shifting sand, events occurring today can directly impact the course taken tomorrow. Reviewers— the president's OMB, Congress, the congressional GAO, as well as oversight capacities within an individual agency—will often highlight weaknesses in themes and messages. Budget offices provide a key role of balancing the assessment of the facts and understanding what those facts mean for the agency's direction and vision.

Agency budget officers oversee a formulation process that involves areas such as the following:

- *Getting to know* program functions of the agency and what's happening in the programs they are reviewing
- *Engaging* in decision-making systems that demonstrate knowledge of the organization's and the administration's priorities
- *Analyzing* budget data to highlight trends and concerns and determine appropriate funding for future funding levels
- *Making sure*—through guidance, oversight, and implementation of the decision processes—that budgets are brought forth from bureaus and program areas that reflect agency and administration priorities and address previously identified issues
- *Strengthening* budget justifications for performance, results, and precision in financial presentation, using resident expertise in the agency's budget office

Agency requests are submitted to OMB in September and are reviewed by OMB in consultation with the president and the president's aides, and include the negotiation with departments and agencies on the final outcome to be proposed by the president to Congress.

The formats and content of the federal agency budget are partly determined by law; however, the Budget and Accounting Act of 1921 provides additional flexibilities in the development of budget products by authorizing the president to set forth the budget "in such form and detail" as the president may determine.

Over the years, there has been an increase in the types of information and explanatory material presented in the budget documents. Many of the changes of recent years have focused on performance and results for resources sought and a more direct management plan for programs to be initiated and implemented.

In most years, the budget is submitted as a multivolume set, consisting of the following:

- A main document setting forth the president's message to Congress
- An analysis and justification of the president's major proposals (the budget)
- Supplementary documents providing account and program-level detail, historical information, and special budgetary analyses

Much of the budget is an estimate of requirements under existing law rather than a request for congressional action (between a half and two thirds of the budget authority set out in the formal budget becomes available without congressional action). The president submits a budget update by July 15th each year. The president may revise these recommendations at any time during the year (amendments).

The discretionary part of the budget, the one third to half under annual congressional review, becomes the focus of intense political deliberation and spirited debate between the Congress and the administration's witnesses who appear to defend the president's proposals. Unfortunately, the discretionary budget proves the more nettlesome each year, as currently reflected in the large amount of "unfinished business" of several of the recent budget years following the congressional end-of-session adjournments.

D. Structure of Budgeting and Performance Data

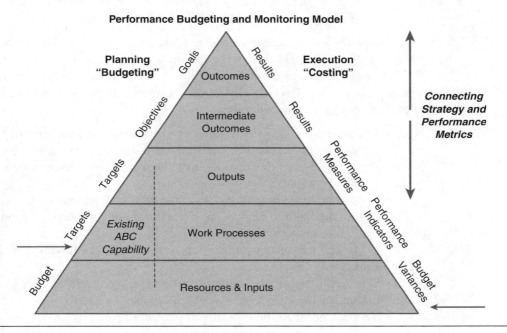

Figure 18.13   Integrating Budget and Performance

SOURCE: IBM Global Business Services.

Resources and Inputs

1. Inputs: Inputs are resources, often measured in dollars, used to produce outputs and outcomes. When a budget is constructed, financial inputs are displayed in different ways for different purposes.

2. Appropriation: The basic unit of control for budgeting and resource management within the federal budget process is the *appropriation account.*

• This is the manner in which resources are provided to federal agencies via the Congressional Appropriation Act.

• This is the standard by which agencies are held accountable statutorily on their management within funds authorized.

- This is the basic fund distribution element used by OMB and the Treasury to apportion and record obligational activity of federal agencies.
- All federal agencies are provided with unique appropriation fund accounts following the enactment of their respective Appropriation Acts (according to the initial Appropriation Act providing the funds).
- The appropriation code tracks all funding separately if it is provided by Congress, with special and unique rules that apply direct to that funding:
    - One-year (annual) funding authority
    - Multiyear funding control and management of unlimited-year authority ("No-Year")
    - Type of funding (e.g., grant, trust fund, permanent and indefinite appropriation authority, legislative proposals)

3. Budget/Program Activity: Federal agencies manage funding further within the agency at levels below the specific appropriation account identified in the enacted Appropriation Act. Beyond legislated earmarks enacted by Congress, the next level of detail below the appropriation is usually made to the budget or program activities.

- Budget/program activities, although not statutory in law, are part of the legislative history supporting the appropriation—they are a key part of the justification materials presented to Congress by agencies in support of their funding proposals.
- Most reprogramming flexibility authorized by Congress on the use of the appropriated funds centers around distribution of funding among these budget/program activities.
- OMB and the agency budget documentation tracks funding below the appropriation via these categories.
- The goal is that these breakouts reflect the representative distribution of funding among core programs of the agencies.
- To this end, these budget/program activity breakouts are generally used as core performance measures platform.
- In reality, the tracking of these budget/program activities to the actual program work of the agency is not always that true and needs to be significantly improved—accounting information supporting expenditures is often captured on an organizational or geographic location basis, not programmatic, for several important reasons related to the challenges of cost allocation on a consistent, multiyear basis.
    - Often, the same employees participate in the performance of more than one programmatic function (even simultaneously), and accurate accounting for their time expended in each can be quite subjective.
    - Major capital systems, representing significant development and operational costs, often support more than one programmatic function, and their value to each can be quantified in various ways.

o Ordinary overhead costs (both personnel and logistics) are often
the subject of debate within an organization, with each function
seeking to avoid the appearance that its reliance on centrally
provided overhead is disproportionate.

4. *Object Class Detail:* Object classifications are the basic financial cost
categories used across the federal budget by OMB and all agencies. These are
the most comprehensive data collected across government below the appropriation account code. The object classes are identified in the federal budget
by a prefix 11.x, 12.x. 13.x, 21.x, and so on, for example:

11—Personnel compensation
12—Personnel benefits
13—Benefits of former personnel
21—Travel and transportation of persons
22—Transportation of things
23—Rent, communications, and materials
24—Printing
25—Other services
26—Supplies and materials
31—Equipment purchases
42—Insurance claims

• OMB and the Treasury have historically used two-digit prefixes.
Recently, OMB has asked agencies to adopt "three-digit" prefixes, which
provide more detail on items such as personnel benefits, rent, communications, and other services.
• Although "object classification" is the uniform budget presentation
standard across all agencies, most agencies do not actually use it as a format
for use within their agencies. In the extreme, some agencies have developed
alternative object classifications for their internal use, while maintaining elaborate cross-walks to track back to the government-wide standard.
• Likewise, this classification detail, although uniform, is not by and
large the detail of choice used by appropriation committees in making decisions on funding for agencies. Regardless, it is a core data requirement for
agencies' budgets, accounting, Treasury and OMB reports, and financial
statement audits.
• Object class detail is not the agency's core tool for performance
budgeting decisions and presentations. Nonetheless, appropriators are
reluctant to part with the "black-and-white" appearance of object class presentations, even though, in a performance budget context, they are relatively uninformative and can actually be misleading in terms of efficient
program operation.

5. *Staffing Data:* An important element for decision making and data
capture is the staffing levels of programs within federal agencies.

- This information is usually reflected in the form of full-time equivalents (FTEs) or staff years. FTEs are calculated as the cumulative time (in 2,087-hour work years) of all filled positions over the course of the year. For example, 100 positions, each occupied for 90% of the work year (i.e., at a 10% vacancy rate), would translate to 90 FTE.
- FTE data are a major key to the formulation of labor-intensive agency programs and initiatives and to full presentation of costing justification to OMB and Congress.

6. *Outlays:* The agency must have the ability to capture outlays against appropriated funds. It is part of the core financial data reporting to the Treasury, OMB, and Congress and for other analyses and forms the basis for calculating the spend-out rate.

7. *Tracking Multiyear Obligations:* An important element for formulation decision making is tracking available funds from prior-year authority, when such funds were given more than 1-year's availability at the time they were initially appropriated. Many times, decisions by OMB and Congress on new funding are made on the basis of level of funding remaining from prior years.

- Tracking across years of some appropriation accounts and budget activities to determine availability is key to ensuring that full information is available to the formulation process.

Work Processes and Outputs

1. *Outputs:* Outputs are the goods and services produced by a program or organization and provided to the public or others.

- Managers are more likely to manage against outputs than outcomes. This is because output data are collected and reported more frequently, and outputs more typically correspond to activities and functions being directly controlled, as opposed to focusing on results. Moreover, when an output can be unambiguously quantified, an outcome is open to more subjective interpretation.
- Outputs can help track a program's progress toward reaching its outcomes.
- Outputs can include process measures (e.g., paper flow, adjudication), attribute measures (e.g., timeliness, accuracy, customer satisfaction), and measures of efficiency.
- Outputs may be measured either as the total quantity of a good or service produced or may be limited to those goods or services having certain attributes (e.g., number of timely and accurate benefit payments).
- Typically, outputs are measured at least annually.

2. *Performance Measures:* Performance measures are the indicators or metrics that are used to gauge program performance. Performance measures

can be either outcome or output measures and may include consideration of inputs, particularly in the context of cost-efficiency or unit costs.

- An agency must have the ability to cascade performance measures against its appropriation fund account and/or its budget/program activity, as well as line up those measures with strategic goals and objectives.
- The objective of performance budgeting is to be able to *track these outputs back* to resources and inputs (appropriation accounts, staffing, key object class detail) *and track them forward* to outcomes and strategic objectives/goals.

Moving to Outcomes

Outcomes: These describe the intended result or consequence that will occur from carrying out a program or activity. Outcomes are of direct importance to beneficiaries and the public generally.

- An agency must have the ability to cascade performance measures against its appropriation fund account and/or its budget/program activity, as well as line up with strategic goals and objectives.
- The objective of performance budgeting is, as it is for performance measures, to be able to *track these outcomes back* to outputs, resources, and inputs (appropriation accounts, staffing, key object class detail) and *track them forward* to strategic objectives/goals.
- While performance measures distinguish between outcomes and outputs, there should be a logical connection between them, with outputs supporting outcomes in a logical fashion.

Notes

1. Government Performance and Results Act of 1993, Pub. L. No. 103–62 [S20] 107 Stat. 285.

2. "Six Steps to Business Excellence: Integrating Six Sigma, Performance Excellence, and ISO 9001, 2000," Dr. Stanley A. Marash, PE, Chairman, and CEO, STAT-A-MATRIX, Inc., April 24, 2001.

3. Performance Budgeting, State of Minnesota, Office of the Legislative Auditor, Program Evaluation Division, February 17, 1994.

4. Chief Financial Officers Act of 1990, Pub. L 101–576.

5. Federal Acquisition Streamlining Act of 1994, Pub. L 103–355.

6. Clinger-Cohen Act of 1996, 40 U.S.C. 1401(3).

7. Developed collectively by the IBM Global Business Services Financial Management practice and used in periodic public slide presentations to clients and at conference session presentations. Does not currently reside in a published document. This source is also given for Figures 18.2, 18.8, and 18.13.

8. "Performance Budgeting: Opportunities and Challenges," GAO Congressional Testimony, GAO-02–1106T, 2002, p. 2. Retrieved from http://www.gao.gov/new .items/d021106t.pdf

9. Congressional Budget Act of 1974, as amended in 1985–1997.

10. GPRA, Government Management Reform Act, Clinger-Cohen Act, Debt Collection Act, Federal Financial Management I & II, streamlined procurement legislation, the president's management agenda.

PART V

Quality and Performance in Public and Nonprofit Organizations

19 | The Integration of Quality and Performance

Maria P. Aristigueta

The winds have shifted, and quality and performance are no longer distinguished as separate management tools, as experienced during the total quality management (TQM) movement and the beginning of performance management initiatives. The TQM ideologies focused on process, while performance management focused on results or outcomes. Central to current performance and quality initiatives is a clear understanding of what is to be accomplished and how progress will be measured in terms of outcomes. As the management efforts assimilate this understanding, questions remain as to what is meant by *quality* and *performance* and how these different ideologies are integrated. In this discussion, it is important to differentiate quality of measures from TQM and performance measurement from performance management, all of which will be addressed in this part of the handbook.

There is a rebirth in the United States of the quality movement, which appears to be a fraternal twin of performance. According to Poister (2004), the "quality revolution [that] has swept through government over the past fifteen years has made an indelible mark on the public management landscape" (p. 236). Milakovich (1992) sees a change in the traditional view of quality from one of conflicting goals with productivity to one of achieving productivity through quality improvements. Hyde (1995) predicts a lessening of the dichotomy between performance and quality "as quality management adapts to the public sector and its service side, while the public sector becomes more familiar with quality management percepts and strategies" (p. 192). Poister (2004) states that quality and productivity are seen today as "mutually supportive or complementary performance criteria" (p. 237). Yet the lessening dichotomy does not address the theoretical underpinnings of quality for process and of performance for results.

Quality awards are found to combine process and results, as do balance-scorecard applications found in practice. As this question is explored, examples of its application will be taken from the federal, state, and local governments in the United States, including the awards programs associated with each. Let's begin by defining *quality*.

Quality Defined

Perhaps the lessening dichotomy is best explained by differentiating quality from TQM. *Quality* is an organizational output or intermediate outcome that can be measured, often through satisfaction surveys, and is part of a comprehensive performance measurement initiative. TQM is a management approach that in its earlier form espoused that by focusing on processes, the organization will achieve higher performance. More specifically, well-known architects of the quality movement, Deming, Juran, and Crosby, advocated that by focusing on process, the results would follow (see, for example, Suarez, 1992; Wageman, 1995).

TQM adoption and performance reform initiatives appeared in almost parallel fashion in the United States. The U.S. federal government's pursuit of quality formally began with the issuance of President Reagan's Executive Order 12637, on April 27, 1988, requiring improvement in quality, timeliness, and efficiency of services (Milakovich, 1992). By the 1990s, evidence started to mount that public organizations beyond the federal government had developed quality programs (Berman & West, 1995; Swiss, 1992) or used quality initiatives as part of performance improvement strategies, including the integration of performance and quality measures (Chackerian & Mavima, 2001; Halachmi, 1997; Lee, 2000; Puran & Ngoyi, 2000; Wechsler & Clary, 2000).

The integration of quality and performance measurement is found in performance management systems and widely used in management tools such as the *balanced scorecard* (see Kaplan & Norton, 1992). Public and nonprofit management are interested in quality service delivery as well as accountability to the public and stakeholders by providing information through measures of high quality. Furthermore, *quality* is defined as a service or product or in terms of a source. For example, it may (a) be based on the assessment of the service recipient (as defined by Crosby, in 1979, cited in Suarez, 1992; U.S. Commerce Department National Institute of Standards and Technology [NIST], 2007), or it may (b) refer to the dimensions of a product or service received—the totality of features and characteristics of a product or service that bears on its ability to satisfy stated or implied needs (American Society for Quality Control, 2007; American Standards Institute, 2007; International Organization for Standardization, 2007).

The sources for quality, according to Kano and Gitlow (1988–1989, as cited in Milakovich, 1992), are hardware, including structures and equipment;

software, procedures, and processes; and "humanware," the actual services provided by employees. Milakovich (1992) acknowledges that in the public sector, the degree of service quality experienced by the customer or client is the direct result of a combination of the three sources for quality. Furthermore, each provides areas to measure and improve.

Pollitt and Bouckaert (1995) distinguish between the assessment of quality (a) as determined by those who produce the product or service or (b) perceived by the user or consumer of the product or service. Assessing customer satisfaction is a vital part of performance measurement, as it is for TQM, albeit complex, as Van Dooren points out in Chapter 20 of this volume. Efforts are made to facilitate this component through existing performance frameworks such as the balanced scorecard, which includes the customer dimension regardless of the sector in which it is implemented (Moriarty & Kennedy, 2002). The balanced scorecard is being used in private, public, and nonprofit organizations to focus and assess an organization's success.

The quality of the measure itself is also an important component of this discussion. Leighton, in Chapter 6, writes of the role of the auditor in providing credible performance reports. In Chapter 21, Sterck and Bouckaert contribute by providing a discussion on the quality of measures: its assessment and importance to the overall usefulness of the performance measurement system.

Differentiating between performance management and measurement is also helpful in gaining understanding of the quality and performance movements.

Performance Management and Measurement

Performance management focuses management practices on the results, or outcomes, that programs strive to achieve in order to improve the effectiveness, efficiency, and accountability of programs. Performance measurement is narrower by definition, as it focuses on the development of measurable indicators that can be systematically tracked to assess progress made in achieving objectives.

Performance measures are quantitative indicators of various aspects of the performance of programs or agencies that can be observed on an ongoing basis, often focusing on program or service delivery (Poister, 2004). The balanced scorecard has been used to develop performance measures by emphasizing overall organizational performance, incorporating multiple programs as well as other dimensions of performance. Nonetheless, performance measures are only a part of a performance management system.

The Organisation for Economic Co-operation and Development (OECD) reports that the performance measurement movement (which OECD calls "service quality initiatives") had the common characteristics of requiring government organizations to be more responsive and outward looking and that these initiatives changed the relationships between the public, public servants, and elected officials (OECD, 1996). For example, the United Kingdom launched the Citizen's Charter initiative in 1991 to publicize performance targets for various public services (Schiavo, 2000).

The U.S. federal government initiated widespread performance measurement and management through the Government Performance and Results Act (GPRA) of 1993, which has as one of its primary purposes to "improve Federal program effectiveness and public accountability by promoting a new focus on results, service quality, and customer satisfaction" and to "help Federal managers improve service delivery, by requiring that they plan for meeting program objectives and by providing them with information about program results and service quality." This initiative was part of a management system that not only required measurement but also aimed to develop agreement on missions, goals, strategies for achieving goals, and measures of performance and to use the information in program management to improve performance, provide means for accountability to the public, and support resource allocation and other policy decision making (Wholey, 1999).

Integration of Performance and Quality

In congressional testimony, J. Christopher Mihm, Managing Editor, Strategic Issues, from the U.S. Government Accountability Office (GAO), testified that "if federal agencies are to make the major improvements in their mission-related results envisioned by the Government Performance and Results Act, they must have management and process improvement initiatives—including those that employ the principles of quality management—in place to achieve results" (GAO, 1999, p. 1). He further identified TQM and GPRA as sharing a common and mutually reinforcing focus for achieving program results, customer satisfaction, measuring performance, and using performance data to identify and select improvement opportunities.

The balanced scorecard and other tools, such as the common assessment framework discussed by Thijs and Staes, in Chapter 22 of this handbook, are being used in developing performance measures to measure all aspects of performance, including input, output, quality, and outcomes. These tools are viewed as valuable management resources for aligning and communicating priorities and focusing on performance.

There is much to be gained through the integration, as quality initiatives appear to be useful in performance management for establishing priorities, limiting the number of measures, balancing types of measures, and aligning areas to be addressed. In addition, the quality integration will allow for information to the public in areas that matter to the recipient, such as satisfaction with services provided by the public or nonprofit agencies.

Description of Recent Experiences
With Quality in U.S. Government

In the U.S. government, performance management was legislated through the GPRA, and separate incentive programs are available for quality efforts. The legislation does not require TQM, but perhaps the growth in quality initiatives is due to an implied requirement for quality in performance, particularly satisfaction with service. Similar legislation and separate quality award programs are found at the state level of government.

Survey research indicates that quality improvement programs and related customer service improvement efforts have been implemented by numerous state and local governments (Berman & West, 1995; Kravchuk & Leighton, 1993; National Governors Association, 1992) and by many federal agencies (GAO, 1992). Furthermore, the quality improvement programs are often part of performance improvement initiatives with customer satisfaction as an apparent measure.

Indeed, Poister and Harris (1997) indicate that the effectiveness of TQM should be measured by customer satisfaction with services provided. Poister (2004) has more recently acknowledged the need to track indicators of quality of input and outputs produced, particularly customer satisfaction, considered by Hatry (1999) to be an intermediate outcome. The list of quality measures outlined by Poister (2004) include the following:

- Timeliness, total time required, and waiting time
- Accuracy, thoroughness, reliability, and fairness
- Accessibility, hours of service, and convenience
- Decor, cleanliness, and condition of facilities
- Personal safety and security
- Courtesy, politeness, and professionalism (p. 236)

Poister (2004) views the monitoring of quality and productivity measures as measurement at the microlevel, while performance measures designed to track success of strategic goals or overall program performance are observed at the macrolevel.

As mentioned earlier, an additional trend in the integration of quality and performance in the United States is the use of the balanced scorecard (or an adaptation thereof), developed by Kaplan and Norton (1992). Viewed as an approach to developing and implementing operational strategies utilizing performance measures, the balanced scorecard also serves as an organizing tool. In a recent study of the use of the balanced scorecard in the U.S. Postal Service and the U.S. Defense Finance and Accounting Service, Mathys and Thompson (2006) credit the balanced scorecard with creating a sustained culture of quality. Both the 2003 Presidential Quality Award winner (Environmental Protection Agency) and the 2004 Delaware Quality Award winner (Division of Revenue) used the scorecard.

Quality awards are also part of the quality and performance integration in the United States. Performance management emphasizes results and is made up of the following components: strategic planning, performance measurement (satisfaction is considered an intermediate outcome), performance-based budgeting, and performance evaluation (Aristigueta, 1999; Hatry, 1999). The delivering of the outcomes (or results) is encouraged through cross-functional teams, empowered frontline employees, and the use of businesslike process improvement tools (Osborne & Plastrik, 1997; Swiss, 2005). Swiss (2005) asserts that the lack of success in performance management systems occurs because "results-based management systems fail to adjust their incentives to fit their program characteristics" (p. 592). Performance management incentives are tied to results that may take some time to materialize, and Swiss recommends intrinsic rewards and nonmonetary extrinsic rewards as alternatives. Perhaps the quality awards are a mechanism to fill this incentive gap.

President's Quality Award

The President's Quality Award Program was developed in 2002 to recognize organizations and projects that stand out in implementing the objectives of the Presidential Management Agenda. Changes were made in 2004 to strengthen the alignment between the Presidential Quality Award and the Presidential Management Agenda. The current three award categories are (a) to recognize specific innovative and exemplary projects and practices, (b) to recognize overall agency achievement in each one of the five government-wide management initiatives outlined in the Presidential Management Agenda, and (c) to recognize overall agency management and how effectively the different management systems are integrated (see U.S. Office of Personnel Management [OPM], 2006a).

Linda M. Springer, Director of the Presidential Quality Award Program, states that the goal of the program is to "recognize outstanding programs and people who are doing extraordinary things to make our Government one that is results-oriented, citizen-centered and market-based" (OPM, 2005). Scores for the Presidential Quality Award are based on the scorecard standards for success in the areas of human capital, competitive sourcing, improving financial performance, e-government, and budget and performance integration (see http://www.whitehouse.gov/results/agenda/scorecard.html). Under each standard, an agency is "green" or "yellow" if it meets all of the standards for success listed in the respective column and "red" if it has any one of a number of serious flaws listed in the "red" column. The GAO (1999) referred to the President's Quality Award Program as the most important statement of quality management principles within the federal government. Since 1988, the program has given awards to the federal programs for (a) improving their overall performance and capabilities and (b) demonstrating a sustained trend in providing high-quality products and services that result in the effective use of taxpayer dollars. The OPM manages the program and its award criteria, which is closely aligned to the Malcolm Baldrige National Quality Award criteria.

The award criteria are updated annually to reflect the best approaches within the public and private sectors to systematically improve organizational performance. For instance, recent standards for success were developed by the President's Management Council and discussed with experts throughout government and academe, including the National Academy of Public Administration. They have subsequently been refined with additional experience in implementing the Presidential Management Agenda. The status of each agency is posted on the OPM Web site, and winners are recognized for their work in a single area; a separate application is required for each area (see OPM, 2006a). For example, the 2003 winners of an award (the last available on the Web site) were the Environmental Protection Agency (EPA), in recognition of exemplary performance and results in the area of improved financial performance, and the National Science Foundation (NSF), in recognition of exemplary performance and results in the area of expanded electronic government (OPM, 2006b).

Baldrige Award

Of the quality incentives, perhaps the best known is the Baldrige Award, named for Malcolm Baldrige, who served as secretary of commerce from 1981 to 1987, established in 1987 to "recognize U.S. organizations for their achievements in quality and performance" (U.S. Commerce Department National Institute of Standards and Technology [NIST], 2006a). Three Baldrige Awards are given annually in the following categories: manufacturing, service, small business, and, since 1999, education and health care. This program is managed by the NIST, with the assistance of the American Society for Quality (ASQ), a professional, nonprofit association. Programs are reviewed by business and quality experts and receive a feedback report, highlighting strengths and areas to be improved, for a fee between $5,000 for large institutions and $500 for nonprofit education institutions. Finalists receive a site visit.

Compared with Japan's Deming Award (which more closely resembles the TQM philosophy of an emphasis on process), the Baldrige Award differs in the following aspects:

- Promotes a greater focus on results
- Involves many different professional and trade groups
- Provides special credits for innovative approaches to quality
- Includes a strong focus on customer and human resources focus
- Stresses the importance of sharing information

The following are 2005 Baldrige Award recipients:

- Sunny Fresh Foods, Inc., Monticello, Minnesota (manufacturing)
- DynMcDermott Petroleum Operations, New Orleans, Louisiana (service)
- Park Place Lexus, Plano, Texas (small business)
- Richland College, Dallas, Texas (education)
- Jenks Public Schools, Jenks, Oklahoma (education)
- Bronson Methodist Hospital, Kalamazoo, Michigan (health care)

The 2005 Baldrige Award recipients were selected from 64 applicants. All six recipients were evaluated by an independent board of examiners in seven areas: leadership; strategic planning; customer and market focus; measurement, analysis, and knowledge management; human resource focus; process management; and results. The evaluation process included about 1,000 hours of review and an on-site visit by teams of examiners to clarify questions and verify information in the applications (NIST, 2005). Examples of results found at Jenks Public Schools (JPS) in Oklahoma and the Bronson Methodist Hospital (BMH) in Kalamazoo, Michigan, are given below. Both examples focus on retention and satisfaction:

- JPS's graduation rates for 2003 to 2005 exceed the graduation rates for a former Baldrige Award recipient, with graduation rates at 93% in 2003, 94% in 2004, and 95% in 2005, compared with the former Baldrige Award recipient's rates of 90% in 2003, 93% in 2004, and 94% in 2005 (NIST, 2005).

- BMH is exceeding best-practice levels for key indicators of work system performance and effectiveness, including 2005 annualized employee turnover of 5.6%, registered nurse turnover of 4.7%, and job vacancy rates of 5.3%. The rate of vacant positions for registered nurses has been reduced from 6.5% in 2002 to 5% in 2005, outperforming the 10.6% National American Nurse Credentialing Center best-practice comparison. In addition, since the inception of an employee referral program in 2002, the percentage of hires from internal referrals has increased to 38% in 2005, up from 10% in 2002 (NIST, 2005).

State Government's Quality Awards

State governments have modeled quality award programs following the Baldrige criteria. An example is the Delaware Quality Award in honor of W. L. Gore, utilizing the same criteria: leadership; strategic planning; customer and market focus; measurement, analysis, and knowledge management; human resource focus; process management; and results in key business areas. In 2004, 44 states had or were establishing quality award programs (NIST, 2004).

The mission of the Delaware Quality Award program is to promote excellence in organizational performance and to improve organizational effectiveness and service delivery to the customers and stakeholders of Delaware State Government. There are several award levels, as outlined below (University of Delaware, 2006):

- *The W. L. Gore Award:* The Delaware Quality Award in honor of W. L. (Bill) Gore recognizes Delaware businesses or organizations that demonstrate high levels of performance excellence. This top-level Delaware Quality Award is named for Bill Gore, in honor of the visionary direction he gave his company regarding excellence, innovation, and working environment. A Gore Award recipient must display outstanding performance and be a role model in most of the seven criteria categories of the award.

- *Delaware Quality Award of Merit:* The Delaware Quality Award of Merit recognizes companies and organizations that demonstrate significant progress in their approaches and deployment of quality systems. Although overall results may lack maturity, the Award of Merit recipients are role models within Delaware in several of the seven criteria categories.

- *Delaware Quality Commitment Award:* The Delaware Quality Commitment Award recognizes businesses and organizations that are getting started in their quality journey. These organizations have put the basic quality building blocks in place that will lead them to future performance excellence.

The following two awards have recently been discontinued in the State of Delaware:

- *The Accolade Award:* The Accolade Award recognized organizations that if not for some special circumstance would have otherwise qualified for either the Gore Award or the Award of Merit.

- *The Genevieve W. Gore Lifetime Achievement Award:* The Lifetime Achievement Award, which recognized outstanding leadership in the pursuit of performance excellence, was given in Mrs. Gore's name between 2001 and 2003, to honor her many contributions to the community.

Governor Ruth Ann Minner has also established a First State Quality Improvement Fund that provides $150,000 for quality initiatives on an annual basis. In 2004, the winner of the W. L. Gore Award was the State of Delaware Division of Revenue (DOR), whose experience is expanded upon below.

State of Delaware, Division of Revenue

The DOR has 185 full-time employees, processing over 1 million business and personal tax returns and issuing over 300,000 personal income tax refunds each year. The division provides the state with 60% to 70% of its general fund. In 2004, the division received the Delaware Quality Award, recognizing strengths in all seven categories. This was the first time a Delaware state agency reached this level of achievement. The DOR had been the 1999 recipient of the Delaware Quality Award of Merit. The DOR improvement timeline is shown in Figure 19.1.

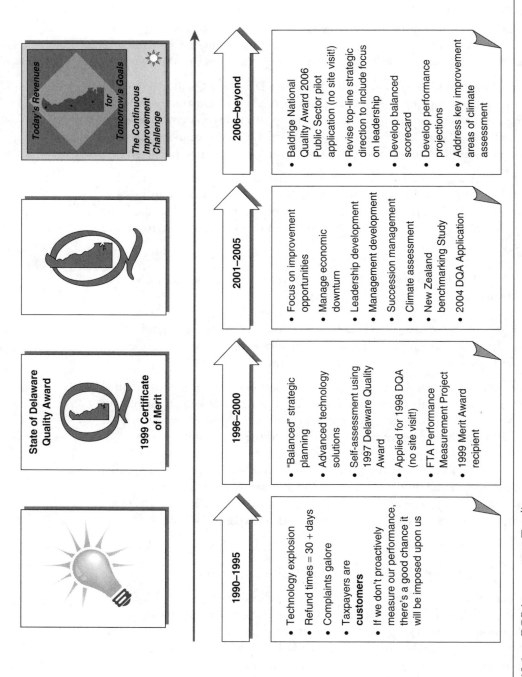

Figure 19.1 DOR Improvement Timeline

SOURCE: Carter, P., and MacLachlan, W. (March 2005, updated April 4, 2007).

The division's mission statement is as follows:

As the primary revenue collector for the State, the mission of the Division of Revenue is to collect 100% of the taxes and other revenues required by law, no more and no less, and to do so in a manner that creates the highest possible level of satisfaction on the part of the public with the competence, courtesy, effectiveness, and efficiency of the Division. (State of Delaware, 2006)

In an effort to better serve their customers (the term used by the director), the Delaware DOR implemented a strategic program referred to as "CECE," an initiative focusing on compliance, efficiency, customers, and employees. The CECE program, which started in 1998, outlines the DOR's core objectives and looks very much like a scorecard. This process has been viewed by the director as providing the division a method for productivity improvement and a fresh approach to easing the compliance process for the public, placing a stronger emphasis on customer service, communications, and technology. In 2005, CECE was improved upon and is now referred to as "ECCEL": efficiency, customers, compliance, employees, and leadership. Figure 19.2 demonstrates the Delaware Quality Award criteria, the DOR strategies, and the elements required in their 2005 balanced scorecard.

Director of Revenue Patrick Carter and his assistant, Bill MacLachlan, expressed that they saw great value in the process required by the award: "The self-assessments, site visit, and subsequent reports, allowed the managers to focus on the seven categories and improve the operation" (B. MacLachlan, personal communication, 2005). They reported the following accomplishments in a news release in January 2005: (a) Ninety-eight percent of all customer calls were answered within 9 seconds, and (b) as of December 2004, business license renewals may be made via the DOR's secure Internet site (State of Delaware, 2005). These measures appear highly customer focused and process oriented. The quality efforts in the DOR were started under crisis, with the organization receiving many customer complaints. The managers feared that if they did not proactively add performance measures, these would be imposed on the program by the state.

The DOR experience demonstrated to the managers the importance of including stakeholders (board of directors and customers) in the decision of what to measure. They also found it important to develop the measures and focus on quality at the same time and did not see these as mutually exclusive. They found that the greatest benefit to the organization came from assessment and feedback reports.

The DOR offers these suggestions to others who may want to implement quality management in their programs (P. Carter & B. MacLachlan, personal communication, 2006):

1. The quality initiative should be staffed by an advocate who can champion the effort.

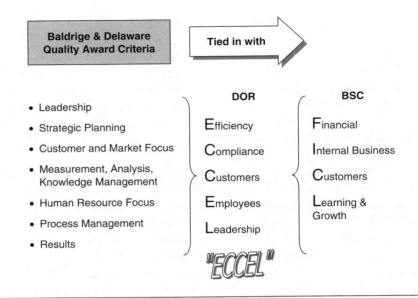

Figure 19.2   Delaware Quality Criteria and the Division of Revenue Strategy
SOURCE: Carter, P., & MacLachlan, W. (March 2005, updated April 4, 2007).

2. Flowcharting practices help the units understand processes by asking questions as to what they are measuring and why, and whether the process should be changed.

3. Do not expect dramatic changes: The process needs time, and it is very gradual. The DOR has been working on quality for 10 years, 5 years before they applied for a quality award and 4 more years before they resubmitted their application.

4. Senior management needs to be an advocate of quality for success of the program. The leadership team needs to create an environment where participation from employees is valued and so are creative and innovative ideas.

5. Create a productivity mind-set whereby employees will ask whether something is unusual or out of the norm, in order to keep mistakes from happening.

Local Government

There is less documentation of local government efforts to implement quality and performance efforts. However, there are exemplary cases available, such as the City of Charlotte, North Carolina, which has had a long tradition of performance measurement for city services. In 1994, the city implemented the balanced scorecard, using four perspectives: financial, customer, internal processes and learning, and growth. The City of Charlotte has been inducted into the Balanced Scorecard Collaborative (2006) Hall of Fame.

The city's Budget and Evaluation Office is responsible for administering the city's strategic planning process, including developing Charlotte's corporate scorecard. The City of Charlotte's performance management and strategic planning approach consists of identifying organizational strategy based on the city council's focus areas of (a) community safety, (b) housing and neighborhood development, (c) restructuring government, and (d) transportation and economic development. The focus areas serve as the organizing framework in translating and communicating the strategy through the corporate scorecard (developing corporate objectives and measures) and implementing the strategy. (The City of Charlotte's scorecard may be found at http://www.charmeck.org/.)

It is interesting to note that the city and corresponding county's Web pages have been combined. Mecklenburg County also has an extensive scorecard, using the four perspectives: customer/stakeholder, internal business processes, financial, and employee and organizational capacity. These perspectives are applied to four focus areas: school, education and economic opportunity, effective and efficient government, community health and safety, and growth management and environment.

Quality and Performance Software

Software packages are commercially available for the balanced scorecard. CorVu claims to have pioneered the automated balanced scorecard and has among its customers the City of Atlanta and the U.S. Army. (More information on this software may be found at http://www.corvu.com/.) Pilot Software also sells to the performance management market and has software available for the scorecard. Its customers include the U.S. General Services Administration and Sarasota County, Florida. (More information may be found at http://www.pilotsoftware.com/.)

Ingredients for Success

In a study of TQM implementation in the Florida state government, Hellein and Bowman (2002) found the following ingredients to be necessary for success:

1. *Effective leadership and the commitment of adequate resources.* This is reinforced by the director of the DOR, who emphasizes the importance of leadership for the success of the quality initiative.

2. *Implementation that is close to existing culture and power arrangements.* This element for success is less tangible and harder to access.

3. *Effective deployment through the creation of central facilitation offices and broad-based, top-down change.* An office for central facilitation

of the quality initiative was created and staffed in the DOR. The staff was also viewed as championing the effort.

Swiss (2005) is an advocate of intrinsic rewards and nonmonetary extrinsic rewards as incentives for quality programs. The quality awards may be serving this purpose, and, in addition, the quality review teams are providing information and recommendations to improve management practices.

Poister and Harris (1997) indicate that the effectiveness of TQM should be measured by customer satisfaction with services provided. Both the Baldrige Award winners and the Delaware Quality Award winners demonstrate emphasis and achievement in customer satisfaction.

Findings and Conclusions

Practice is demonstrating that quality and performance can work in unison as adjustments have been made to avoid theoretical disconnect. Indeed, we are witnessing yet another evolution in performance management in public and nonprofit organizations with the integration of quality initiatives and performance measurement. The measures found in the Baldrige Awards and state and local governments emphasize process and customer satisfaction. The criteria for these awards also emphasize results. Moreover, the Presidential Quality Awards tend to emphasize results or outcomes that are outlined in the Presidential Management Agenda. State and local government programs emphasizing quality have more current information on their Web sites than the Presidential Quality Award Web site, however, which has not been updated since the listing of the 2003 recipients.

Initiatives are in place to encourage quality through awards and require performance through legislation. When the balanced scorecard is used, the performance measures appear to be more oriented to process and satisfaction than when the measures are used separately.

Tools like the balanced scorecard are helping managers to organize information and demonstrate alignment, as seen in the City of Charlotte, with the emphasis on the city council's focus areas. Quality initiatives are also providing tools for communicating to the public an organization's goals and strategic approaches in critical areas, and software is assisting with the collection and sharing of data.

References

American Society for Quality Control. (2007). Retrieved April 6, 2007, from http://www.asq.org/

American Standards Institute. (2007). Retrieved April 6, 2007, from http://www.ansi .org/standards_activities/overview/

Aristigueta, M. P. (1999). *Managing for results in state government*. Westport, CT: Quorum.

Balanced Scorecard Collaborative. (2006). *Balanced Scorecard Collaborative Hall of Fame for Executing Strategy*. Retrieved February 23, 2006, from http://www.bscol.com/bscol/hof/

Berman, E. M., & West, J. P. (1995). Municipal commitment to total quality management: A survey of recent progress. *Public Management Review, 55*, 57–66.

Carter, P. (Director), & MacLachlan, W. (Manager Quality and Planning). (2005, March). Delaware Division of Revenue presentation, Delaware Quality Conference, Newark, Delaware (updated April 4, 2007).

Chackerian, R., & Mavima, P. (2001). Comprehensive administrative reform implementation: Moving beyond single-issue implementation research. *Journal of Public Administration Research and Theory, 11*, 379–402.

Government Performance and Results Act of 1993, Pub. L. No. 103–62 [S20] 107 Stat. 285.

Halachmi, A. (1997). Service quality in the public sector: An international symposium. *Public Productivity and Management Review, 21*, 7–12.

Hatry, H. (1999). *Performance measurement: Getting results*. Washington, DC: Urban Institute.

Hellein, R., & Bowman, J. S. (2002). The process of quality management implementation: State government agencies in Florida. *Public Productivity and Management Review, 26*, 75–93.

Hyde, A. (1995). Quality, reengineering, and performance: Managing change in the public sector. In A. Halachmi & G. Bouckaert (Eds.), *The enduring challenges in public management: Surviving and excelling in a changing world* (pp. 177–195). San Francisco: Jossey-Bass.

International Organization for Standardization. (2007). Retrieved April 6, 2007, from http://www.iso.org/iso/en/aboutiso/introduction/index.html

Kaplan, R. S., & Norton, D. P. (1992, January-February). The balanced scorecard-measures that drive performance. *Harvard Business Review*, pp. 71–79.

Kravchuk, R. S., & Leighton, R. (1993). Implementing total quality management in the United States. *Public Productivity and Management Review, 17*, 71–82.

Lee, S.-H. (2000). Understanding productivity improvement in a turbulent environment. *Public Productivity and Management Review, 23*, 423–427.

Mathys, N. J., & Thompson, K. R. (2006). *Using the balanced scorecard: Lessons learned from the U.S. Postal Service and the Defense Finance and Accounting Service*. Washington, DC: IBM Center for the Business of Government.

Milakovich, M. E. (1992). Total quality management for public service productivity improvement. In M. Holzer (Ed.), *Public productivity handbook* (pp. 577–602). New York: Marcel Dekker.

Moriarty, P., & Kennedy, D. (2002). Performance measurement in public sector services: Problems and potential. In A. Neely, A. Walters, & R. Austin (Eds.), *Performance measurement and management: Research and action* (pp. 395–402). Cranfield, UK: Centre for Business Performance, Cranfield University.

National Governors Association. (1992). *Total quality management initiatives in state governments*. Washington, DC: Author.

Organisation for Economic Co-operation and Development. (1996, February). *Responsive government: Service quality initiatives*. Paris: OECD Publishing.

Osborne, D., & Plastrik, P. (1997). *Banishing bureaucracy: The five strategies for reinventing government.* Reading, MA: Addison-Wesley.

Poister, T. H. (2004). Monitoring quality and productivity in the public sector. In M. Holzer & S. H. Lee (Eds.), *Public productivity handbook* (2nd ed., pp. 231–245). New York: Marcel Dekker.

Poister, T. H., & Harris, R. H., Jr. (1997). The impact of TQM on highway maintenance: Benefit/cost implications. *Public Administration Review, 57,* 294–302.

Pollitt, C., & Bouckaert, G. (Eds.). (1995). *Quality improvement in European public services: Concepts, cases, and commentary.* London: Sage.

Puran, A., & Ngoyi, M. (2000). How to achieve public performance improvement. *Public Performance and Management Review, 24,* 117–120.

Schiavo, L. L. (2000). Quality standards in the public sector: Differences between Italy and the U.K. in the Citizen's Charter initiative. *Public Administration, 78,* 679–699.

State of Delaware. (2005, January). *News release.* Retrieved January 8, 2006, from http://www.state.de.us/revenue/services/Press_05.shtml

State of Delaware. (2006). *Department of Finance: Division of Revenue.* Retrieved January 8, 2006, from http://revenue.delaware.gov/

Suarez, J. G. (1992). *Three experts on quality management: Philip B. Crosby, W. Edwards Deming, Joseph M. Juran.* Arlington, VA: Department of the Navy Total Quality Leadership Office.

Swiss, J. E. (1992). Adapting total quality (TQM) to government. *Public Administration Review, 52,* 356–363.

Swiss, J. E. (2005). A framework for assessing incentives in results-based management. *Public Administration Review, 65,* 592–602.

University of Delaware. (2006). *Delaware Quality Award levels.* Retrieved March 28, 2007, from http://www.dae.udel.edu/award/levels.html

U.S. Commerce Department National Institute of Standards and Technology. (2004). *NIST fact sheet.* Retrieved September 29, 2004, from http://www.nist.gov/public_affairs/factsheet/baldfaqs.htm

U.S. Commerce Department National Institute of Standards and Technology. (2005, November 22). *Six organizations to receive 2005 Presidential Award for Quality and Performance Excellence.* Retrieved March 28, 2007, from http://www.nist.gov/public_affairs/releases/2005baldrigewinners.htm

U.S. Commerce Department National Institute of Standards and Technology. (2006a). *Baldrige National Quality program.* Retrieved Februrary 10, 2006, from http://www.baldrige.nist.gov

U.S. Commerce Department National Institute of Standards and Technology. (2006b). *Frequently asked questions about the Malcolm Baldrige Quality Award.* Retrieved Februrary 18, 2006, from http://www.nist.gov/public_affairs/factsheet/baldfaqs.htm

U.S. Commerce Department National Institute of Standards and Technology. (2007). Retrieved April 6, 2007, from http://www.quality.nist.gov/

U.S. General Accountability Office. (1992). *Quality management: Survey of federal organizations* (GGD-93–9BR). Washington, DC: Author.

U.S. General Accountability Office. (1999). *Management reform: Using the Results Act and quality management to improve federal performance* (GAO\T-GGD-99–151). Washington, DC: Author.

U.S. Office of Personnel Management. (2005). *President's Quality Award Program: Memorandum for heads of departments and agencies*. Retrieved Februrary 15, 2006, from http://www.opm.gov/pqa/message.asp

U.S. Office of Personnel Management. (2006a). *President's Quality Award Program*. Retrieved March 1, 2006, from http://www.opm.gov/pqa/index.asp

U.S. Office of Personnel Management. (2006b). *President's Quality Award Program: 2003 winners and honorable mentions* Retrieved February 27, 2006, from http://www.opm.gov/pqa/2003winners.aspOPM

Wageman, R. (1995). Total quality management: Empirical, conceptual, and practical issues. *Administrative Science Quarterly, 40*, 309–342.

Wechsler, B., & Clary, B. (2000). Implementing performance government. *Public Performance and Management Review, 23*, 264–266.

Wholey, J. S. (1999). *Foreword*. In M. P. Aristigueta, *Managing for results in state government* (pp. xii–xiv). Westport, CT: Quorum Books.

20 Quality and Performance Management

Toward a Better Integration?

Wouter Van Dooren

In the last decades, quality management and performance management have spread widely in public sectors around the world. Notwithstanding their simultaneous development, the two movements are often detached both in their theoretical development and in their practical application. This chapter demonstrates how quality management and performance management are disconnected and how a better integration can be attained. We also discuss some next steps in the development of quality models and performance management. In particular, we ask how performance management and quality management should adapt in order to deal with supraorganizational reality, such as multiorganizational collaborative networks within and across policy sectors. The rephrasing of performance management and quality management follows on the increasing awareness of the need for collaboration in networks. Collaborations, rather than single organizations, are needed to address increasingly complex policy issues that often involve win-lose solutions, for example, between the environment and the economy (Bressers, O'Toole, & Richardson, 1995; O'Toole & Meier, 2004). Performance measurement, performance management, and quality management have to adapt to that.

First, we define *quality management* and *performance management*. Next, we discuss the differences and divergence between the quality management and performance management movements. Third, we explore the similarities and point to some converging trends. Finally, we identify some remaining lacunae and suggest two next steps in the integration of quality management and performance management and performance measurement.

Definitions

What Is Quality Management?

Sometimes, a good way to describe something is to confront it with what it is not. Amsden, Ferratt, and Amsden (2001) describe six attributes that distinguish quality management from conventional management (see Barnard, 1950; Fayol, 1920; Taylor, 1911). First, quality management focuses on customers rather than on profits and efficiency. Second, quality management is a holistic system that goes beyond a single management function. *Holistic* also means that quality management focuses on processes rather than isolated tasks. Third, the organization should strive toward continuous improvement rather than establishing the one best method for all time. Fourth, organizations that apply quality management empower people. Responsibilities and opportunities are not only a matter of the top of the organization. Fifth, all members of the organization have to take part in the planning and control cycle. Hierarchy is not the best way of controlling. Finally, senior management has to create a facilitating environment that fosters the above five attributes through dynamic leadership (see Table 20.1). Since organizations are open systems, senior managers have to attract the external resources to keep the organization thriving.

Qualitative products and services thus are the ultimate aim of quality management. *Quality* (of products and services) can be defined in two ways (Pollitt & Bouckaert, 1995, pp. 16–18): On one hand, it may refer to the intrinsic features of the good or service itself, as seen by those producing it. This is producer-oriented quality. On the other hand, it may refer to the quality of the good or service itself, as perceived by the user. This is consumer-oriented quality. In the public sector, users are both the direct clients of the services and those indirectly affected. The latter is a more recent view on quality. Parasuraman, Zeithaml, and Berry (1985) show that the consumer orientation is a complex matter. Producer-oriented quality is only one factor that determines consumer-oriented quality. Other factors include the expectations based on personal needs, prior experiences, and informal and formal communication.

One of the most remarkable aspects of the quality movement is the development of quality models. Quality models, such as the balanced scorecard, prescribe the factors to which the organization has to pay attention if it is to deliver quality. Quality models are ideal representations of well-organized organizations. They are the glasses through which the manager is expected to look at his or her organization.

What Is Performance Management?

The central assumption in performance management is that management and policy instruments should operate by means of output and outcome

Table 20.1   Conventional Management Versus Quality Management

Conventional Management	Quality Management
Focus on profits and efficiency	Customer focus
Management per management function	Holistic management
One best way	Continuous improvement
People as production factor	Empowerment of people
Hierarchical planning and control	Planning and control is a shared responsibility
Static leadership, authority	Dynamic leadership, facilitator

SOURCE: Based on Amsden et al. (2001).

information rather than input information. Management tools have to be infused with performance information. The performance management movement thus deals with two issues: how to measure performance and how to use performance information in policy and management. Performance measurement thus is one aspect of performance management. It is a necessary but insufficient condition for performance management. Having performance information is not enough. One also needs to use performance measurement in order to come to genuine performance management. This dual focus is reflected in definitions of performance management. Poister (2003), for instance, defines *performance management* as "the process of defining, monitoring, and using objective indicators of the performance of organizations and programs on a regular basis" (p. 1).

Differences and Divergence

The quality movement and the performance management movement developed largely independently from each other. The movements have a different reach. Moreover, there is a risk of a disconnection in practice. Performance managers and quality managers often are in different parts of the organizations.

Different Movements and Traditions

Figure 20.1 gives an overview of the different movements and traditions. The quality movement is rooted in the private sector and is mainly management oriented. In the 1970s and 1980s, quality models were implemented in the Japanese industry on a large scale (Bouckaert & Thijs, 2003). The success of the Japanese economy lent the quality movement its credibility. In 1980, NBC broadcast a documentary about quality guru W. Edwards Deming,

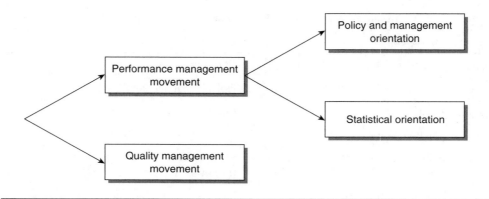

Figure 20.1   Movements and Traditions in Quality and Performance Management

titled, *If Japan Can . . . Why Can't We?* This documentary was the starting shot of the quality movement in the United States of America, first in the private sector and later in the public sector (Stupak & Leitner, 2001).

Performance management nowadays is embedded in two traditions. First, there is a policy and management tradition. Performance management in this tradition is linked to the policy and management cycle of organizations: planning, implementation, and evaluation. Performance measures are incorporated in strategic planning, in performance contracts, budgets, management tools, and evaluations. Second, there is a statistical tradition. Statistical series usually are in a lesser extent tied to the policy and management cycle. It is not management in the strict sense. Nonetheless, they are measures of public performance. A low poverty rate, for instance, may be seen as a performance indicator for redistribution policies and the social system in a country. Recently, attempts have been made to bring the statistical and the policy traditions closer to each other, for example, under the banner of "evidence-based policies" (see Davies, Nutley, & Smith, 2000).

Different Focuses of the Movements: Micro, Meso, and Macro

Quality management and performance management also have different focuses, on three levels: microlevel, mesolevel, and macrolevel. The *microlevel* is the organization. The quality movement focuses almost entirely on the organizational level. The policy and management tradition, too, is mainly addressing microlevel issues when measuring operations, outputs, and outcomes of an organization or a program.

The *mesolevel* is organizational networks, within a policy sector or across policy sectors. There is an increasing awareness that in order to achieve policy results, public sector organizations have to coordinate and to collaborate. The study of governance instead of government is emblematic for this development. The policy and management tradition of performance management focuses on the mesolevel, particularly through its focus on outcomes. It is acknowledged that outcomes usually have to be attributed to several actors and that this is a shared responsibility. Yet although the issue is identified, not much research has been done on how to incorporate this shared responsibility in measurement systems. The statistical tradition is also structured along policy sectors. There are, for instance, employment statistics, environmental statistics, and health statistics.

The *macrolevel* is the government and even society-wide level. At the macrolevel, the policy sectors add up to a unified assessment of societal performance. Performance management attempts to construct composite indicators or sets of key indicators. Examples are Australia's "Measuring Australia's Progress"; the European Union Lisbon criteria; the UN Millennium Development Goals and the Human Development Index; the quality-of-life indices of, for instance, Canada and the United Kingdom; and the Key National Indicator Initiative in the United States.

Figure 20.2 represents the different reaches (micro, meso, and macro) and the different orientations (production or outcomes) for the quality management movement, the policy and management tradition of the performance management movement, and the statistical tradition of the performance management movement. Quality management deals predominantly with management issues at the microlevel. There is an increasing attention for outcomes (see also Figure 20.4). The policy and management tradition of the performance management movement pays a lot of attention to outcome indicators of organizations and programs as well as outputs and efficiency. Some argue that only results matter (Hatry, 1999). Yet to gain insight into the factors that make outcomes happen, a management focus is important, too (see, for instance, Holzer & Callahan, 1998). Although the policy and management tradition is mainly oriented at the microlevel, it is acknowledged that outcomes are a shared responsibility. Nonetheless, the study of how to measure performance in this networked setting is less developed. The statistical tradition has a meso- (mainly policy sector) or a macro- (society-wide) orientation. Some institutionalized statistical series are, for instance, to be found in economic policies, the environmental sector, employment, and the health sector. Regularly, growth of gross domestic product is taken as a crude proxy of societal performance. The underlying rationale is that when the economy is performing, society and thus government are performing. This approach is often criticized. The social indicators movement of the 1970s called it "economic philistinism" (Bauer, 1966, p. ix). The quality-of-life measurements and the social indicators were a response to this one-dimensional approach.

The three traditions thus have important aspects in common. They all deal with results of governments. We will discuss the similarities later. Yet there are some significant differences in focus. Quality management has a stronger focus on management in the strict sense—running the conversion of inputs

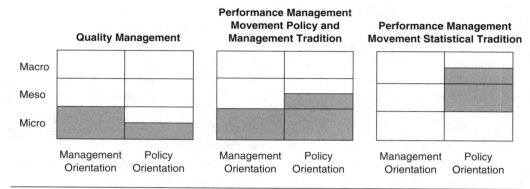

Figure 20.2   Focal Point of Performance Management and Quality

to relevant outputs. Performance management (policy and management tradition) has a stronger focus on policy results—getting the intermediate and (to a lesser extent) the end outcomes. The statistical tradition of performance management is primarily concerned with end outcomes, which they then would want to trace back to program outcomes.

Disconnection in Practice

We argue that the different movements have a lot in common, notwithstanding their different focuses. Thus, although quality managers and performance managers look at things differently, they should still work together. Particularly, in large organizations, there seems to be a risk of a disconnection. Quality managers and performance managers are usually found in three poles: the financial function, the operational management function, and the research function. Sometimes they work together smoothly, and sometimes they do not.

First, the finance department, which was traditionally mainly concerned with input, has an increased interest in outputs and outcomes. Performance budgeting is not new (Kelly & Rivenbark, 2003; Schick, 1966). However, the nature of performance budgeting has changed. Originally, finance departments were only calculating unit costs per output. Nowadays, performance-based budgeting has to do with relating outcomes to budget requests (Wholey, 1999). The allocation of resources should depend on what government wants to accomplish. Financial managers seem to be primarily attracted by the performance management movement.

Second, the managers, who were from a Taylor tradition more focused on running processes according to a single best way that was scientifically determined in advance, became interested in quality management. Many organizations established quality departments, implemented quality models, and pursued accreditations. Notwithstanding the conceptual similarities between quality management and performance management, these quality departments risk being separated from finance departments.

Third, the research staffs in government, which have a tradition of monitoring policy sectors, increasingly paid attention to linking policy outcomes with programs and services. External actors, such as auditors, also shifted their focus from legality and compliance to performance (Raaum & Morgan, 2001). Auditors and evaluators are a third group of professionals who may be separated from other professionals with similar interests.

A disconnection between attention for quality and performance may be suboptimal for at least two reasons. First, a different discourse is being developed, which leads to higher communication costs. Academics and consultants are incited to novelty seeking and therefore habitually seem to "reinvent the wheel" (Donaldson, 1995). Concepts with similar definitions are labeled differently. Consequently, managers within organizations may talk at cross-purposes.

Second, both performance management and quality measurement initiatives face competition in two ways: competition for resources and competition for attention of decision makers. A better integration would strengthen both performance management and quality management. Operating quality management and performance management systems costs money. Initiatives thus have to compete for resources in budget allocation processes. Spending on frontline service delivery may appear more urgent, more effective, or more salient. Spending on quality management and performance management may be seen as overhead costs. The costs are tangible and immediate. The benefits of performance management and quality management are intangible and show in the longer term. In times of fiscal stress, they may be the first to come under pressure. Therefore, performance management and quality management need to acquire legitimacy relatively shortly after coming into force.

Performance management and quality management face competition in another way. Decision makers nowadays have too much information rather than too little. Information from performance management systems and quality systems compete for attention with other information sources (e.g., anecdotic evidence, media, etc.). Top managers and external stakeholders (politicians among them) have limited time and resources to work with performance information and information from the quality management system. When different fractions that run different information systems send confusing signals, the usefulness of both quality and performance management for top management and external stakeholders may be undermined.

Similarities and Convergence

In the previous section, we argued that quality management and performance management have different focuses and risk being separated in practice. In this section, we explore the commonalities between quality management and performance management movements. We first argue that the same logic model that is being used in performance management is underpinning quality management. We then make the point that quality models increasingly resemble each other and increasingly align with the logic model. The implication is that conceptually, there no longer needs to be a barrier between performance management and quality management.

A Joint Foundation: The Logic Model of Public Sector Information and Action

In the past decade, a common understanding of public sector information and action has developed. Policy and management are discussed in terms of input, output, and outcome. This joint frame of reference is rooted in the system approach to public administration of the 1960s. Von Bertalanffy (1968), a biologist, held that characteristics of systems are homologous to all systems simply because they are systems. Systems are open, goal directed, and adaptive to their environments. Subsequently, the systems theory was applied in various disciplines. Easton (1953, 1965) described the political system as a black box converting inputs (demands and support) to outputs (decisions and actions). Katz and Kahn (1966) first applied systems theory on organizations.

This scholarly development had significant ramifications in practice. System thinking in particular influenced performance budgeting. The planning-programming-budgeting system (PPBS) was the flagship of the system approach to planning and budgeting (Schick, 1966). PPBS, however, failed to fulfill its audacious promises. In essence, the architects of PPBS forgot that it is people (with bounded rationality and limited information) that are working in systems (Wildavsky, 1969).

Despite its apparent failure, PPBS certainly influenced the mental map of government professionals. Moreover, the system approach endured. The social indicator movement tried to design indicator sets that would cover all aspects of social systems (Aristigueta, 2004; Bauer, 1966). The quality movement tried to get into the black box and sort out the internal management system.

Although there is a joint frame of reference, there is, as well, considerable terminological confusion. In a way, the input-output model fell victim of its own success. Many people, in many organizations, in profit, nonprofit, and public sectors in different countries, use terms such as *efficiency, effectiveness,* and *performance* slightly differently. The terminological diffusion is not trivial. A common terminology is crucial for understanding other practices.

One way to work toward a common vocabulary is to concur with authoritative texts. In this text, we largely follow the terminology of Hatry (1999), which is aligned with the work of United Way of America (1995). We add in some elements based on the work of Pollitt and Bouckaert (2004). Figure 20.3 represents the model. The starting point is the top box, which identifies the needs that the organization or program has to address. The next step is to translate the needs to objectives. A useful approach to setting objectives is a tree of objectives, starting from the overarching strategic objectives and working down to the operational measurable objectives. Next, inputs are allocated to enable processes that yield outputs. Outputs are the products and services

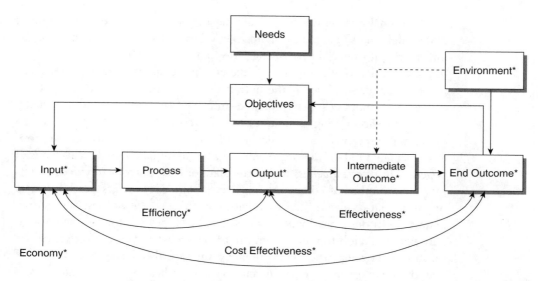

* Performance indicators are usually labeled by one of these categories

Figure 20.3   The Input-Output Model of Public Sector Information and Action
SOURCE: Van Dooren (2006).

of the organization. It is expected that these outputs make a difference in society. However, in the public sector, outcomes typically manifest themselves in the long term and are the result of many factors besides government activity. The box environment depicts these factors. Organizations often need feedback more rapidly. Therefore, intermediate outcomes may be identified that are expected to be precedents of the end outcomes. Environmental factors still may influence the intermediate outcome, but not as strongly. The causality between output and intermediate outcome is easier to establish.

As an example, we apply the model to the problem of traffic casualties. Through agenda-setting processes, the need to reduce the number of casualties in traffic may be formulated. The objective may be, for instance, to reduce the number of casualties to a number comparable to that in other developed countries. To attain this goal, government will use resources to build cycle tracks, to reconstruct crossroads, to install speed traps, and so on. The outputs are the kilometers of new tracks, the constructed new crossroads, and the number of controlled vehicles. To this point, government has a good grip on the chain of events. The decisive test, however, is the outcome in society. In the short run, it may be that more children cycle to school and that fewer drivers violate the speed limits. This is the intermediate effect. The ultimate purpose, however, is to reduce the numbers of casualties. Do the immediate outcomes lead to the end outcomes as well? Environmental factors also have their impact. A reduction in the number of casualties may be the result of bad weather. When it is cold and rainy, there are usually less cyclists and pedestrians and therefore less potential victims.

The model also allows for calculating ratios (Bouckaert & Van Dooren, 2003). Relating single indicators to each other will substantially increase the informational value. The following ratios may be identified. First, *economy* is the cost divided by the input (e.g., the cost per employee, the cost per computer). Second, *efficiency* is the output divided by the inputs (e.g., cost per delivered passport, cost per graduated student). Measures of efficiency usually require cost-accounting techniques. All the costs of all the inputs used to obtain an output need to be calculated in financial terms. This can be properly calculated only if the organization has a high-quality analytical financial system. Third, *effectiveness* is (intermediate or end) outcome divided by output (e.g., number of complaints received about dirty streets per kilometers of streets that receive regular cleaning). Fourth, *cost-effectiveness* is (intermediate or end) outcome divided by cost (e.g., cost per job for an unemployed participant of a job-training program). Effectiveness and cost-effectiveness are the most interesting ratios. Unfortunately, they are also the hardest to measure due to the factors in the environment that have a bearing on the outcomes.

The logic model is a model for action and information. It is useful for structuring what government does and what government knows about what it is doing. The structuring of government action requires all the boxes to be considered. The performance information is usually obtained at specific points in the model (the asterisks in Figure 20.3). Performance indicators of performance management systems are usually labeled *input, output, intermediate outcome, end outcome, environment, economy, efficiency, effectiveness,* and *cost-effectiveness*. These are the measurement points.

The Evolution of Quality Models

Performance management and quality management share the same conceptual foundation. Moreover, the content of the quality models is increasingly covering the whole spectrum of the logic model. More and more, quality models pay attention to the outcomes of organizations. We will prove this statement by comparing the boxes and the criteria of the quality models with the logic model of government information and action that we presented above. First, we shortly describe the quality models we studied.

The International Standards Organization (ISO) promotes uniform quality standards. The ISO standards are derived from the quality system of the North Atlantic Treaty Organization (NATO) that was designed to control the production of military equipment. This may explain the process orientation of the early ISO standards. The ISO standards are not related to an award. They represent a threshold quality value. Organizations can ask for a certification that would reassure clients and contractors that a minimal quality level is reached. Later versions had a more external focus. Moreover, they went beyond listing the standards by integrating them into a more dynamic model.

In the early 1990s, Kaplan and Norton (1992) developed the "balanced scorecard" (BSC). The authors were dissatisfied with the financial measures

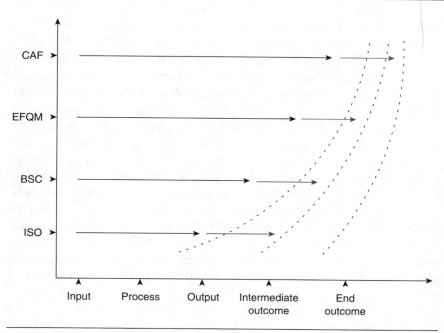

Figure 20.4   Quality Models by the Program Logic

of the performance of businesses. The predictive value of financial performance measures was particularly problematic. Other perspectives were needed in order to get a balanced view. The client perspective, the process perspective, and the learning and growth perspective were included in the model. In later publications, Norton and Kaplan (1996) paid more attention to the application of the BSC in the public sector.

The establishment in 1988 of the European Foundation for Quality Management (EFQM) was an initiative of some leading enterprises in the private sector (although the European Commission supported it). In 1991, EFQM presented the first encompassing "business excellence model." Within a decade, the model became increasingly popular. In 2000, two initiatives were taken to adapt the model to the public sector and the nonprofits. First, the original model was updated and renamed the "EFQM excellence model." The item "business results," for instance, was broadened to "key performance results." Second, the Common Assessment Framework (CAF) was inspired by the EFQM model, but tailor-made for the public sector. Both the CAF and the EFQM models have nine criteria.

Figure 20.4 represents the quality models on the vertical axis and the program logic on the horizontal axis. Revised editions of quality models tend to adapt to other models in two ways.

First, quality models are becoming more outcome oriented and therefore closer to performance management in nature and action. Admittedly, quality models remain primarily management tools. The prime focus is on the inputs and processes of the organization—"delivering the output right" rather than assessing whether they "provide the right output." The private sector descent may explain this orientation. The market test of products and services relatively quickly yields information on whether it is the right output at the right cost. Sales figures show whether the company succeeds in satisfying an individual utility function, adding value, and making profit. In the public sector, there is no individual utility function. Non-market-oriented organizations lack this market test. Therefore, they have to put more effort in planning, monitoring, and evaluating outcomes. The inclusion of an outcome orientation is a necessary condition for quality models to be useful in the public sector. With this trend, the quality movement conforms to the outcome orientation of the performance management movement.

Thus, despite their private sector origins, more attention is being paid to the public sector and the nonprofits. The EFQM model and the CAF rephrased the criteria in order to accommodate the public sector and the nonprofits. In 2004, EFQM launched the first Local and Regional Government Prize. Since its founding in 2000, the CAF has been supported by European quality conferences, where good practices are presented. In 2006, the Baldrige Award, a quality contest in the United States, was opened to public sector organizations.

Quality models not only increasingly share the outcome orientation but also come to look more alike and inclusive altogether. Together with the increasing success of the models, competition between the models increased. As a result, the models take over the most appealing parts of other quality models. For instance, the latest EFQM model includes innovation and learning as a feedback process. This is a response to the BSC criterion "learning and growth." Another example is the ISO model that evolved from a loose set of criteria to a systemlike model. This was an answer to other systematic models, such as the EFQM and the BSC. The models are subject to the dialectics of progress. It is harder to push the frontier than to follow other examples. An important implication is that since the models increasingly resemble each other, the choice between models becomes less significant. "Will we use a model?" becomes a more important question than "Which model will we use?"

Gaps in the Coverage of Public Policy and Management by Quality and Performance Management

We discussed the similarities and differences between quality management and performance management. They have to some extent different focuses; they are sometimes disconnected in practice, but they have, conceptually, increasingly more in common. Quality models have been reconsidered and increasingly look alike. Moreover, they increasingly share the outcome orientation of the performance management movement. Yet even the combinations of performance management and quality management have gaps in their focus. Some important additions can be made.

The political setting, for instance, is not sufficiently accounted for in the quality models. The quality models assign the responsibility for vision, policy, and strategy formulation to the leadership of the organization. In the public sector, leadership includes the elected officials. In democracies, elected politicians shape policies and thus influence the strategies of public sector organizations. The formulation of the needs that the organization needs to address is done largely by actors outside the organization. Moreover, policies are prone to volatility due to political shifts and the resulting shifts in political personnel. In particular, in countries with a spoils system for top positions, these changes have a direct impact upon public organizations. Quality management models probably should better account for the political contexts in which organizations operate. Responding to politicians is an important aspect of quality in the public sector. The amalgamation of all these dimensions in the concept of leadership will make it less useful. A clear distinction between leadership of the organization and the political leadership may be beneficial.

The most important shortcoming of both quality management and performance management is the insufficient acknowledgment of the networked environment in which governments operate. Of the quality models, only the CAF does speak of external partnerships as an input variable, but this is from the organization's perspective and not the network's perspective. Governments are moving toward cogovernance. Clients or citizens are no longer seen as the passive recipients of government policy. They are active agents working with government and nongovernment agencies in generating outcomes. Cogovernance has a bearing on all steps in the policy process: codesign, codecision, coproduction, and coevaluation (Van Dooren, Thijs, & Bouckaert, 2004). This collaborative setting between government, nonprofit, private sector, and citizens should be reflected in performance management and quality management.

Trajectories for a Further Integration of Quality and Performance

We discuss two trajectories, starting from existing practices, for integrating the meso- and macrolevel and the linkage between the mesolevel/macrolevel and microlevel. These are some potential next steps that the quality management movement and performance management movement may take jointly. We will subsequently describe the main idea behind the proposed trajectory and some tools to set the wheels in motion.

Trajectory 1: Evidence-Based Policy and Management

Principle

A first trajectory leads to an evidence-based policy and management. In particular, the statistical tradition of the performance management movement

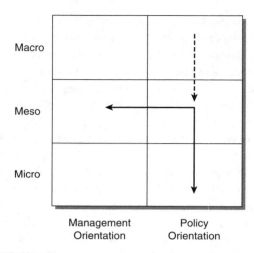

Figure 20.5   Trajectory 1: Evidence-Based Policy and Management

has a rich collection of data. For instance, the data of the statistical offices usually have a good quality and are longitudinal. Yet these data sources are often undisclosed to policymakers and public managers. The evidence-based policy movement attempted to make this information more useful for policy purposes. The main assumption is that through better research and analysis, technical measurement data can be translated to a language that is better understood by policymakers.

It should be noted that several authors doubt whether policymakers are enthusiastic about letting their policy choices depend on research (and ceteris paribus measurement findings). Weiss (1980), for instance, found that research seldom has a direct influence on concrete policy decisions. Rather, knowledge will gradually feed into decision processes and set the terms of reference for the policy debate. Weiss (1980) calls this process a "knowledge creep." In both cases, direct or indirect influence, the importance of good research and information stands out. We argue that not only is evidence-based policy important, but so is evidence-based management. Figure 20.5 represents this trajectory.

We thus need to move from decoupled statistical data sets to concrete outcome indicators for organization (the vertical arrow in Figure 20.5) that are in line with mesolevel policies and government-wide policies. The optimal situation is a hierarchy of indicators and objectives that positions microlevel outcomes in a meso- and macrolevel framework. In this way, the utility of statistical data for policymakers will be higher, since the potential impact on meso- and macrolevel realities through microlevel action becomes more visible. It should, for instance, be demonstrated how a training program (microlevel) may have impact on unemployment statistics in a region (mesolevel reality).

A second movement is from decoupled statistical data sets to information for mesolevel policies (the horizontal arrow in Figure 20.5). Outcome data will be linked to policy choices and policy instruments. Network performance, as measured by the outcome data, should be linked to characteristics of the network and the inputs, activities, and outputs of the network. Unemployment data, for instance, will be coupled to resources that are spent on the sector of labor counseling, the activities by counselors, the circulation of job vacancies to the target group, databases with curricula vitae for employers, retraining, and so on. It should be considered how the distribution of responsibilities and resources in the network among public, private, and nonprofit actors influences the outcomes.

Tools

A first tool is *benchmarking*. In the case of the employment example, different networks within a country may be compared. In other instances, when there is a single network that operates at the national level, international benchmarking will be necessary. International organizations such as the OECD are collecting international comparative data in order to compare policies. International comparisons can yield entirely different insights into the performance of a sector. The main challenge is to distill national policy measures from international practices. Differences in the institutional and cultural contexts require a thorough translation of foreign examples. Obviously, this is less of a problem when benchmarking is performed within a nation, for example, by comparing states or local authorities.

Key-indicator initiatives are a second tool. We mentioned some examples previously: Measuring Australia's Progress; the European Union Lisbon criteria; UN Millennium Development Goals and the Human Development Index; the quality-of-life indices of, for instance, Canada and the United Kingdom; and the Key National Indicator Initiative in the United States of America. These initiatives are a step forward compared with the mere provision of data because, usually, targets are formulated, and target setting increases policy relevance. Yet the main challenge for key national or international indicators is to keep in touch with political policy making while keeping some distance in order to transcend party political trench wars. Some initiatives, such as the Lisbon indicators, were criticized for surrendering to the economic agenda that was propagated by key decision makers, while other initiatives, such as the social indicator movement in the 1970s, were criticized for being too remote from actual decision making.

Trajectory 2: Toward Mesolevel Models

Principle

Analogous to the organizational models, models for policy sectors or networks of collaborating organizations can be developed. In the same way that quality models provide an ideal typical description of the optimal

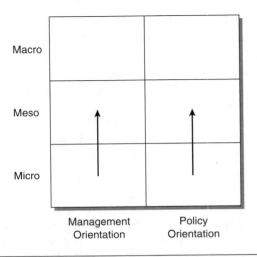

Figure 20.6   Trajectory 2: Toward Mesolevel Models

organization, a model of a network of collaborative actors may provide an ideal typical picture of a mesolevel reality. Quality models can be translated to a higher level of public organization. Performance measures can be aligned with these concepts. (See Figure 20.6.)

Tools

The main tool is thus the mesolevel model. As an example, we translate an organizational model to the policy sector. We use the criteria that the European CAF uses as a guideline for the self-assessments of public sector and nonprofit organizations. Each criterion raises some issues for a mesolevel model (see Table 20.2). This mesolevel model can also be a model for performance management. In that case, indicators need to be defined for every criterion. We briefly look at the criteria of the CAF and demonstrate by means of some illustrative questions what the criteria might signify at the mesolevel.

Leadership is a crucial issue for an organization as well as for a network of organizations. The notion that an organization in a network takes up the coordinating role and has to take the main responsibility for the outcomes is a crucial one. The distribution of responsibilities in a network is one of the most difficult issues to solve. Human resources management at a mesolevel may, for instance, refer to issues of recruiting capacities of public and nonprofit organizations. Does the educational system provide the right competences, and is the public and nonprofit sector capable of attracting employees with the right profile? An organization needs a policy and strategy. In the same way, collaborative networks need policies and strategies to get to the societal outcomes. The criterion of external partnerships and resources also raises issues at a mesolevel. Does the network have

Table 20.2 Issues for a Mesolevel Model for Collaborative Networks

CAF Criteria	Issues for a Mesolevel Model (Network Level)
Leadership	Which organization has the prime responsibility for the outcome (the coordinating role)?
Human resources management	Does the educational system provide the competences that the network needs? Is the public sector/nonprofit an attractive employer?
Policy and strategy	Does the network have clear policy guidelines and strategic plans?
External partnerships and resources	Does the network have sufficient resources to fulfill its tasks (budgeting)? What are the cross-impacts of the policy network with other networks? Can private sector resources be useful for the attaining the objectives (public-private partnerships)?
Process and change management	How is the production chain managed? Which organizations depend on other organizations' outputs? What are the right policy instruments? How are tasks allocated between tiers of government and between government, agencies, and civil society?
People results	What is the impact of public employment on society? Should public sector and nonprofit networks strive toward a representative employment?
Customer/citizen results	What is the satisfaction and trust of citizens in government?
Key performance results	What are the outcomes of the network activities?

sufficient resources to fulfill its tasks? This question is partly answered through the allocation function of the public budget. Yet one should also consider whether private sector resources can be used for attaining the public outcomes. In addition to this, the side effects and cross-impacts of other policy networks may be a resource or cost in the attainment of the societal outcomes. The criterion of process and change management in organizations raises issues at a mesolevel. The production of outcomes, too, is usually a chain of events. For instance, a safe community (outcome) is the result of a chain of activities and output: from prevention to investigation, making arrests, jurisdiction, and detaining those who are convicted. Who is managing this chain of events, and how?

The criterion of "people results" in organizations refers to the impacts of the organization on the people that are employed. The idea is that an organization has to take care not only about the outcomes but also for the well-being of the people working for the organization. Similar issues may be relevant at the network level. Organizations that are working together for public purposes should consider the joint impact of their employment on society, for instance, the local labor market. Issues such as whether or not organizations that work with public money have to be a representation of society (e.g., gender, minorities) may also be of relevance. The criterion of customer/citizen relations in organizations is usually measured by means of client surveys. Yet in many cases, citizens/clients cannot judge which organization is responsible for an outcome. The example of producing safety is illustrative. Citizens usually do not make out which organization has the main responsibility for a failing outcome; but they will surely experience the lack of safety, and they will hold the elected officials mostly accountable. Therefore, the assessment of trust and satisfaction has to go beyond the trust and satisfaction in microlevel service delivery. Finally, the criterion of "key results" in society is equally valid for mesolevel assessment. In most cases, the question as to whether the main outcomes are materializing and why can be answered only from a network perspective.

Conclusion

In this chapter, we discussed the similarities and differences between quality management and performance management. There is a different focus in each movement. Yet we showed that conceptually, the two movements are moving toward each other. Finally, we identified two next steps that the performance management movement and the quality management movement may take jointly.

The movements are intellectually connected, and a better integration can be pursued. Performance management and the quality management movements, first of all, share the same logic model as a conceptual underpinning. Moreover, the quality models are transformed and increasingly resemble each other. The conceptual link with the performance management movement is becoming stronger, since quality models pay more attention to the outcomes of the production of public goods and services. Still, this integration has some lacunae. The most important one is the modest attention for organizations collaborating together in networks for producing societal outcomes. In this text, the network orientation is termed the *mesolevel*, which is distinguished from the microlevel focus (the organization) and the macrolevel focus (society-wide). We discussed two ways of reconciling the micro-, meso-, and macrolevels. First, we discussed how macro- and meso- outcome indicators may be coupled with microlevel outcomes and with mesolevel policy choices (inputs and activities). Second, we showed how a microlevel quality model may be applied at the mesolevel—in a network that is pursuing an outcome. These mesolevel models may also be a conceptual underpinning for performance management in a networked environment.

_____ **Discussion Questions**

1. Define *quality management* by contrasting it with *conventional management*.

2. What are the main differences between the quality management movement and the performance management movement?

3. The logic model is the conceptual foundation of both quality management and performance management. Explain and apply this model to a concrete case, such as the department of transportation.

4. How could the performance management movement and the quality movement be integrated? Describe the two trajectories.

5. Comment on the following statement: Both performance management and quality management have to adapt in order to be useful for organizations collaborating together in networks for producing societal outcomes.

_____ **References**

Amsden, R. T., Ferratt, T. W., & Amsden, D. M. (2001). TQM: Core paradigm changes. In R. J. Stupak & P. M. Leitner (Eds.), *Handbook of public quality management* (pp. 129–741). New York: Marcel Dekker.

Aristigueta, M. P. (2004). Indicators for living conditions: Challenges and opportunities for accountability and governance. In M. Holzer & S-H. Lee (Eds.), *Public productivity handbook* (2nd ed., pp. 431–447). New York: Marcel Dekker.

Barnard, C. I. (1950). *The functions of the executive.* Cambridge, MA: Harvard University.

Bauer, R. A. (Ed.). (1966). *Social indicators.* Cambridge, MA: MIT Press.

Bouckaert, G., & Thijs, N. (2003). *Kwaliteit in de overheid* [Quality in government]. Leuven, Belgium: Instituut voor de overheid.

Bouckaert, G., & Van Dooren, W. (2003). Performance management in public sector organizations. In E. Löffler & T. Boivard (Eds.), *Public management and governance* (pp. 127–136). London: Routledge.

Bressers, H., O'Toole, L. J., & Richardson, J. J. (Eds.). (1995). *Networks for water policy: A comparative perspective.* London: Frank Cass.

Davies, H. T. O., Nutley, S. M., & Smith, P. C. (Eds.). (2000). *What works? Evidence-based policy and practice in public services.* Bristol, UK: Policy Press.

Donaldson, L. (1995). *American anti-management theories of organization: A critique of paradigm proliferation.* Cambridge, UK: Cambridge University Press.

Easton, D. (1953). *The political system: An inquiry into the state of political science.* New York: Knopf.

Easton, D. (1965). *A systems analysis of political life.* New York: Wiley.

Fayol, H. (1920). *Administration industrielle et générale: Prévoyance, organisation, commandement, coordination, contrôle* [Industrial and general administration: Planning, organization, command, coordination, control]. Paris: Dunod.

Hatry, H. (1999). *Performance measurement: Getting results.* Washington, DC: Urban Institute.

Holzer, M., & Callahan, K. (1998). *Government at work.* Thousand Oaks, CA: Sage.

Kaplan, R., & Norton, D. (1992). The balanced scorecard: Measures that drive performance. *Harvard Business Review, 71*(5), 71–79.

Katz, D., & Kahn, R. L. (1966). *The social psychology of organizations.* New York: Wiley.

Kelly, J. M., & Rivenbark, W. C. (2003). *Performance budgeting for state and local government.* Armonk, NY: Sharpe.

Norton, D. P., & Kaplan, R. S. (1996). *The balanced scorecard: Translating strategy into action.* Boston: Harvard Business School.

O'Toole, L. J., & Meier, K. J. (2004). Public management in intergovernmental networks: Matching structural and behavioral networks. *Journal of Public Administration Research and Theory, 14,* 469–494.

Parasuraman, A., Zeithaml, V. A., & Berry, L. L. (1985, Fall). A conceptual model of service quality and its implications for future research. *Journal of Marketing, 49,* pp. 41–50.

Poister, T. H. (2003). *Measuring performance in public and nonprofit organizations.* San Francisco: Jossey-Bass.

Pollitt, C., & Bouckaert, G. (1995). *Quality improvement in European public services: Concepts, cases, and commentary.* London: Sage.

Pollitt, C., & Bouckaert, G. (2004). *Public management reform. A comparative analysis.* Oxford, UK: Oxford University Press.

Raaum, R. B., & Morgan, S. L. (2001). *Performance auditing: A measurement approach.* Altamonte Springs, FL: Institute of Internal Auditors.

Schick, A. (1966). The road to PPB: The stages of budget reform. *Public Administration Review, 26,* 243–258.

Stupak, R. J., & Leitner, P. M. (Eds.). *Handbook of public quality management.* New York: Marcel Dekker.

Taylor, F. W. (1911). *The principles of scientific management.* New York: Harper.

United Way of America. (1996). *Measuring program outcomes: A practical approach.* Alexandria, VA: Author.

Van Dooren, W. (2006). *Performance measurement in the Flemish public sector: A supply and demand approach.* Doctoral dissertation, Katholieke Universiteit Leuven, Belgium.

Van Dooren, W., Thijs, N., & Bouckaert, G. (2004). Quality management and management of quality in European public administrations. In E. Löffler & M. Vintar (Eds.), *Improving the quality of Eastern and Western European public services* (pp. 91–106). Hampshire, UK: Ashgate.

von Bertalanffy, L. (1968). *General system theory: Foundations, development, applications.* London: Lane.

Weiss, C. H. (1980). Knowledge creep and decision accretion. *Knowledge: Creation, Diffusion, and Utilization, 1,* 381–404.

Wholey, J. (1999). Performance-based management: Responding to the challenges. *Public Productivity and Management Review, 22,* 288–307.

Wildavsky, A. (1969). Rescuing policy analysis from PPBS. *Public Administration Review, 29,* 189–202.

Performance Information of High Quality

How to Develop a Legitimate, Functional, and Sound Performance Measurement System

Miekatrien Sterck

Geert Bouckaert

One of the critical factors in implementing quality and performance models is the availability of performance information of high quality. What are the characteristics of a sound performance measurement system? How can we ensure the quality of a performance measurement system? These are the central questions that are answered in this chapter. The purpose is, first of all, to give an overview of the characteristics of a good performance measurement system. Second, we explain how to design a control system in order to guarantee the quality of performance measurement systems. Third, we describe and illustrate different methods to audit performance measurement systems.

Difficulties of Measuring Performance

Why is the quality of information so important? A few examples may give an idea of the problems and issues that may emerge when measuring government performance. A first difficulty is to measure public sector performance in an objective way. The first example illustrates the problem of autocorrelation. It appears that there is a very strong relationship between the level of trust in the civil service and the level of public sector performance. In countries that score high on public sector performance, such as Luxembourg, Ireland, and Austria, citizens have a high level of trust in their civil service and government.

The level of trust is often measured by means of the Euro-Barometer public opinion survey. The Euro-Barometer survey asks citizens whether they have trust in political parties, the government, parliament, public services, and the justice system. The Euro-Barometer is one of the most useful sources for information on the trust of citizens.

The level of public sector performance is measured by the European Central Bank (ECB). The purpose of the ECB indicator is to measure public sector performance; however, it measures the perception of public sector performance. This means that it does not measure the performance of public services in an objective way. The perception of public sector performance may be influenced by the reputation of the public sector. This would mean that the Euro-Barometer and the ECB indicator are, in fact, measuring the same thing: the general image of the public sector (Van de Walle & Bouckaert, 2007).

A second difficulty in measuring government performance is to define the unit of analysis. When comparing the performance of several government services or countries, it is important to measure performance at the same level of analysis. Even for rather elementary input indicators, such as the number of personnel employed by government, it appears to be very difficult to use the same definitions. Table 21.1 compares government employment in six countries.

The number of personnel employed by government is a very basic input indicator. However, it appears to be difficult to provide accurate data. The military is usually considered as a separate corps and is thus not included in these statistics. The employment in the military, based on NATO figures, is subtracted from the total government employment. Based on these figures, the number of civil servants per capita is calculated. The case of Greece is most striking. According to these figures, there would be one civil servant for every 162 inhabitants in Greece, whereas in the other countries, there would be one civil servant for every 10 to 20 inhabitants. Often, different definitions of public sector employment are used, and therefore it is very difficult to compare government employment internationally.

A third difficulty in measuring government performance may be the use of external data sources (see Figure 21.1). Public institutions are often obliged to use information from external sources. This means that they have no control over the process of data collection. Therefore, it is important to develop procedures to guarantee data quality and to define the risk profile of third parties involved in data collection. The Dutch Supreme Audit Institution developed a typology of third-party information (adapted from Algemene Rekenkamer, 2004).

Table 21.1   Comparison of Government Employment in Different Countries

	Government Employment			
	Government*	Military**	Without Military	Civil Servants per Capita
Canada	2548137	61500	2486637	12
Germany	4364100	284500	4079600	20
Greece	270897	202829	68068	162
Hungary	791436	45180	746256	14
Netherlands	828033	52654	775379	21
United States	20572000	1496000	19076000	15

*OECD Public Management Service (2001).
**NATO (2004). http://www.nato.int.

The assumption is that the mandate and the independence of data providers influence their risk profiles. The first category contains external actors that have a legal task of collecting data, such as statistics agencies; these have a low risk profile. This means that the probability of unreliable data and manipulation of data is low. As a consequence, there is no need for an additional control on the data coming from these agencies.

The second category of external providers includes the independent actors that have collected data on their own initiative. Universities collecting data by means of scientific research are an example of this category. They are not affected by the use of the information by the government. However, the quality of the data collected may vary between different providers and different products. The risk analysis needs to be developed case by case, but in general, one could say that these providers have a middle–low risk profile.

The third category is formed by external data providers that do not have the legal task of collecting data and are not accountable to the administration concerned, but are delivering information on a commercial basis, for example, research bureaus. They may have financial interests, as their performance may affect future assignments. Therefore, these deliverers have a middle–high risk profile. Additional steps to guarantee data quality are necessary. The fourth category includes external data providers that are not independent from the data-demanding organization, but are accountable to it. They collect data in order to report on their performance, and so they have an interest in the outcomes of the data collection. Therefore, these agencies have a higher risk profile, and serious measures to underwrite data quality are indispensable.

Why is government performance measurement so difficult? Some issues in performance measurement are more general and appear both in the private and the public sectors. Other issues are typically related to the public

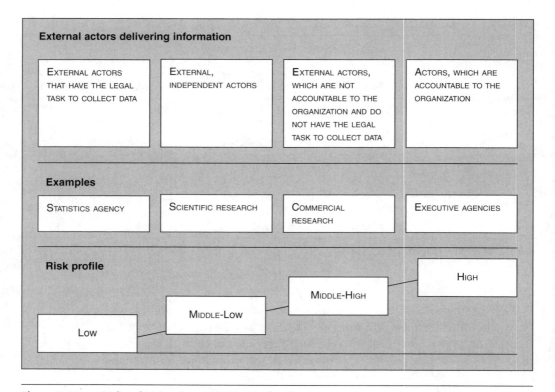

Figure 21.1   Risks of Using External Data Sources
SOURCE: Reprinted with permission from the Netherlands Court of Audit.

character of government services. Figure 21.2 illustrates the major difficulties of collecting good-quality performance information. This may occur in the design or in the implementation of the performance measurement system.

How can we measure whether a goal is achieved when it is not defined in measurable terms? One of the major challenges in performance measurement is the fact that objectives are not formulated in SMART terms (Specific, Measurable, Achievable, Relevant, and Timeframed). Often, objectives are formulated in a rather vague way, and so the achievement of the objectives could be measured by means of a variety of performance indicators. The mission and goals of an organization should be abstract and desired by the public, while statements of objectives should be quantitative and specific. The importance of defining SMART objectives was also recognized in the private sector. As more and more enterprises started to work with balanced scorecards, it became increasingly apparent that there was immense value in the act of deciding what to measure, as this forces management to be very explicit about the language it uses (Neely & Bourne, 2000, p. 3).

Another issue is the dependence on external data providers. When organizations measure their performance, they do not look at their organizations

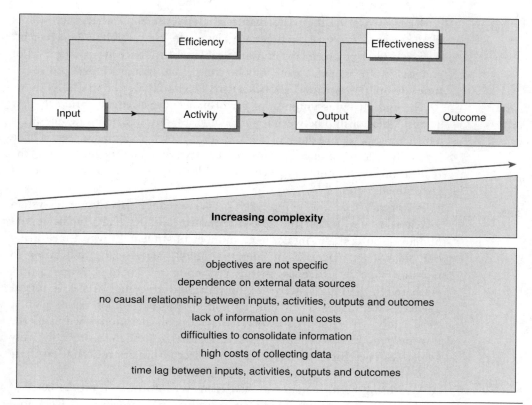

Figure 21.2   Overview of Major Challenges of Collecting Performance Measures of Good Quality

in an isolated way. The core of performance lies in the relationship between the resources used, the activities carried out, and the services and products delivered. However, public sector organizations do not work in a vacuum. They may call in other actors, both private and public, for the delivery of their services. Moreover, there are environmental factors that might influence government performance, such as economic growth and demographic evolutions. Furthermore, they have to know whether the products and services they deliver finally lead to the desired outcomes. They may thus need more information than they can collect themselves. Therefore, public sector organizations have to use external data sources. When using external information, it is important to assess the quality of it, especially when the data provider has a high risk profile. The capacity and willingness to build in extensive quality safeguards is sometimes lacking.

To know how efficient an organization works, it is important not only to know the volume of the outputs delivered but also to have information on the price of the outputs. Unit cost information of outputs is often not available. Therefore, it is difficult to calculate the efficiency of public service delivery.

When measuring the performance of a government service, the outputs of different units have to be consolidated. In New Public Management, there is a tendency to focus on more visible performance at a lower level of analysis. A "helicopter view" may be competing with a detailed and sometimes myopic "frog view" (Bouckaert & Peters, 2002, p. 360).

The underlying assumption of performance measurement is that there is a causal relationship between inputs, activities, outputs, and outcomes. It is a difficult task to find out whether the outputs of a government service have led to the desired outcomes in society. External factors influencing the realization of the outcomes need to be distinguished from the impact of government actions.

It appears that the complexity of performance measurement system increases as the focus shifts from measuring inputs (e.g., financial and human resources) and intake (e.g., number of students) toward measuring outcomes (e.g., increase in literate adults). Developing indicators to measure policy effectiveness is thus very complex. There is always a time lag between the inputs, activities, outputs, and outcomes of a government agency. This makes it difficult to collect information of good quality. Furthermore, it is important to take this into consideration when using the information. Indicators that measure long-term outcomes are not easily available. Therefore, one may need to collect information on intermediate outcomes.

Measuring performance may be expensive. Information on the costs of implementing a performance measurement system is rare, but it is even more difficult to calculate the benefits, as these accrue from the use of information in different processes. The costs of implementing a performance measurement system are more visible than the expected benefits (Bouckaert & Peters, 2002, p. 360). When implementing a performance measurement system in a context of scarce resources, there may be resistance, as the balance has to be made up between investing resources in managerial activities, such as performance measurement, and investing in service delivery activities.

Why is it difficult to ensure the quality of information? We have illustrated that measuring government performances includes a lot of challenges. The main purpose of performance measurement is to develop performance indicators that can be used in the preparation, implementation, and evaluation of policies. This requires that the information be of sufficient quality (Scheers, Sterck, & Bouckaert, 2005). Therefore, it is crucial to develop safeguards to control the quality of the information. However, there are some reasons this issue is not on top of the agenda: In contrast with financial information systems, performance measurement systems do not always follow clear standards; performance measurement still suffers from a lack of common definitions; the capacity to control data quality is sometimes absent; and, finally, there may be a lack of resources to execute performance information system controls.

What Does a Good Performance Measurement System Look Like?

The quality of a performance measurement system is more than the technical quality of the different performance indicators. A system approach is necessary. A performance measurement system, first of all, needs to produce valid and reliable information. Second, a performance measurement system has to be accepted by the employees of the organization. Third, a performance measurement system has to contribute to the goals of the organization. So, the quality of a performance measurement system includes three dimensions: (a) technical validity and reliability, (b) legitimacy, and (c) functionality (Bouckaert, 1993). A clear picture of the pathologies of measurement is crucial to prevent measurement systems from becoming dysfunctional, technically weak, and having low legitimacy (Bouckaert, 1995). Optimal performance measurement systems are highly legitimate, highly functional, and technically sound. Figure 21.3 illustrates the different positions that organizations may take when measuring their performance.

In the worst-case scenario, the functionality, legitimacy, and validity and reliability of the system are low (Position 1). The information that is

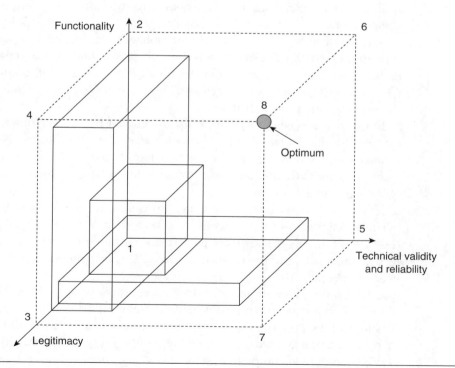

Figure 21.3   Three Dimensions of Performance Measurement Quality
SOURCE: Bouckaert et al. (2003, p. 48).

produced by the system includes mistakes and is not reliable. The performance measurement system is not accepted and may provoke discussions as the management introduces performance measures that are perceived as dysfunctional by the employees. The objectives of the measurement system are not aligned with the objectives of the organization.

A second possibility is a system with a low legitimacy and low technical validity and reliability but a high level of functionality (Position 2). This is called a *pragmatic system.* The system is not highly accepted by the employees and is not technically perfect, but it is useful to realize the organization's goals. Despite the fact that there may be resistance or even obstruction against the system, it is practical and contributes to the organizational objectives.

A third possibility is a *symbolic system:* The functionality and technical validity and reliability are low, but the system is highly legitimate (Position 3). Notwithstanding the fact that the information is not technically sound and does not contribute to the organizational goals, or even opposes them, one holds on to using the system. A reason for this may be the fact that it creates a good reputation in the outside world.

In a fourth scenario, the system is legitimate and functional but not technically sound. Then, one may speak of a *rhetoric pragmatic system* (Position 4). The high functionality and legitimacy of the system may counteract the effects of the technical deficiencies. The performance information is, in the first place, used as an instrument to motivate employees and to align personal and organizational objectives.

Systems of high technical validity and reliability are called *technocratic systems* (Position 5). The system is technically perfect but is not accepted by the employees and does not contribute to the organizational goals. The system is operational, but no one sees the use of it. This may lead to an increased resistance against it.

If a technically perfect system is also functional but not legitimate, one may speak of a *technocratic and pragmatic system* (Position 6). Such a system may work in organizations with a high degree of loyalty and hierarchy. As long as the measurement system is not questioned by the employees, it will remain functional.

If a valid and reliable performance measurement system is legitimate but not functional, one may speak of a *rhetoric and technocratic system* (Position 7). In this scenario, the performance information is not used correctly, which may lead to unintended effects. This may undermine the legitimacy of the performance measurement system.

In the optimal situation, a performance measurement system should score well on functionality, legitimacy, and technical validity and reliability (Position 8). In practice, the performance measurement planner often has to balance the legitimacy, functionality, and validity and reliability. For example, one could choose to develop a system of performance-related pay in order to motivate employees to contribute to the organization's goals; this requires very high-quality information. Despite the functionality of this measure, the question needs to be asked as to whether it implies an infringement on the principle of equality.

Despite the fact that the guidance on performance measurement often focuses on the initial steps in the performance measurement process, considerations of data quality come to the fore as stakeholders begin to examine performance information (Divorski & Scheirer, 2001, p. 83). The quality of performance information needs to be controlled throughout the whole process of performance measurement, not only in the phase of data collection. This is illustrated in Table 21.2, which distinguishes the following six steps in the production process of performance information: (1) information policy, (2) definition of the measurement object, (3) design of the indicators, (4) data collection, (5) data analysis, and (6) data reporting (Bouckaert, Van Dooren, & Sterck, 2003).

In the phase of information planning, it is important to ensure that the purposes of the performance measurement system are clear. These objectives need to be agreed upon, and the actors that will be involved in the measurement process need to be consulted. This is important to ensure the functionality and legitimacy of the measurement tool. In the phase of information planning, the different options for obtaining assurance on the reliability and validity of the performance data need to be explored, and the most cost-effective option needs to be selected.

When the general purposes of the measurement system are set, the unit of analysis is defined and the indicators are designed. The choice and the definition of the indicators need to be aligned with the use for which the performance measurement system is designed. To increase the legitimacy of the system, employees may be involved in the definition and the design of the indicators. To ensure the reliability and validity of the system, it is important that the performance indicators cover the intended performance dimensions. Moreover, it is necessary to ensure that the data from different offices, projects, or organizations are based on similar definitions of indicators.

The next step in measuring performance is the data collection. To be able to use the performance information, data need to be produced on a timely basis. The calendar of supply of information needs to be aligned with the calendar of demand for information as far as possible. For example, if an annual report is published, the key performance indicators need to be collected on time in order to be able to publish them in the annual report. The data collection procedures need to be valid and reliable.

When the data collection is ready, the data are analyzed. To make the data as functional as possible, the analyses have to make the data more comprehensible for the purpose for which they must be used. To increase the legitimacy of the performance measurement system, it is important that employees be involved in the interpretation of the performance data. They may have valuable information to explain the results and the evolutions. Moreover, their involvement may remove potential resistance against the system.

Table 21.2   Controlling the Quality of Performance Information Through the Measurement Process

	Controlling the Quality of Performance Measurement		
	Functionality	*Reliability and Validity*	*Legitimacy*
1. Information policy	Are the objectives of the performance measurement system clearly defined?	Have the different options for obtaining assurance on the reliability and validity of performance data been explored and the most cost-effective option selected?	Are there agreed-on objectives for performance measurement? Are all those involved in performance measurement consulted in the planning process?
2. Definition of the measurement object	Is the unit of analysis defined in function of the demand for information?	Do the performance indicators cover the performance dimensions that are intended?	Are employees involved in the definition of the unit of analysis?
3. Design of the indicators	Are the indicators designed in function of the demand for information?	Are data from different offices, projects, or organizations based on similar definitions of indicators?	Are employees involved in the design of the indicators measuring their activities?
4. Data collection	Are the data collected in time?	Are the data collection procedures valid and reliable?	Do the data collection procedures take into account the workload that the data collection may imply for the employees?
5. Data analysis	Do the analyses make the data more comprehensible for the purpose for which they will be used?	Are data analysis procedures correct? Is the validity and reliability of the data checked?	Are employees involved in the analysis and interpretation of performance data?
6. Data reporting	Is the performance information timely, presented in a way that it can be easily used for the intended purpose?	Is the accuracy of the reported data checked?	Is the performance information reported to the employees?

SOURCE: Adapted from Bouckaert et al. (2003).

The final step in the measurement process is the reporting of the results. A central question is whether the information is timely and presented in a way that it can be easily used for the intended purpose. The way in which the information is reported affects the degree to which it is used. The complexity and level of detail of the reporting need to be adapted to the target group of the report. A monthly report for the board, for example, will contain other indicators than in an annual report that is sent to members of parliament. Reporting performance information back to employees can be a good communication instrument that can help to increase the legitimacy of the system.

_____ How to Control the Quality of Information

The quality of the performance measurement system needs to be safeguarded through the different steps of the performance measurement process. Six major steps should be taken in order to control the quality of information:

Step 1: Develop quality standards.

Step 2: Provide staff training.

Step 3: Analyze risks.

Step 4: Monitor data quality.

Step 5: Report on data quality.

Step 6: Address problems in data quality.

The first step is to define what quality is or define standards for data quality. These standards have to focus on different aspects of performance: (a) timeliness: define how often the data need to be collected and when they have to be reported; (b) validity: ensure that performance indicators are valid and conduct state-of-the art reviews of measures; (c) reliability: define consistent definitions, define consistent sample sizes, and define criteria for the representativeness of samples; and (d) disaggregation: ensure that performance indicators provide appropriate disaggregate information to key operational units.

In the second step, it is important to communicate data quality standards to employees and to sensitize employees. Employees involved in performance measurement need to be trained to implement the data quality standards.

In the third step, the unit responsible for the performance measurement systems needs to develop a risk analysis and a ranking of risks based on the probability of the risk and its impact. This analysis considers risks that may endanger the technical quality, the legitimacy, and the functionality of the system. In this risk analysis, it is important to involve all actors in the process of performance measurement, from the planning phase to the reporting and the use of information.

Based on this risk analysis, in the fourth step, the data quality needs to be monitored. Periodic sampling and review of performance data is a possible technique. Another possibility is to ask external actors to assess the performance data. In the next step, the organization reports on the quality of the data. One could ask program managers to assert whether the data used are reliable and valid. Information on data quality needs to be transparent to give the consumers of the data confidence to use the information. Limitations in data quality have to be identified, as this may influence the interpretation of the results. Based on the identified limitations of the data quality, action has to be taken to address these problems and to further refine the performance measurement system.

How to Audit the Quality of Information

Auditing Performance Information

There is not yet an established practice in governments for auditing the quality of performance information, despite the long-standing tradition of auditing financial information. As performance information is more and more used in performance management applications, the quality of these data becomes more important. The increased use for accountability reasons, for example, in performance contracting, particularly strengthens the need for data accuracy.

Auditing performance information may, moreover, provide incentives to improve performance measurement. First of all, the audit may identify limitations in the measurement systems and formulate recommendations to address these problems. The improved data quality may, on a longer term, lead to an increased use of the performance information. On a shorter term, the audited status of the performance information may also provide new incentives to use the information to a larger extent.

Which methods should be used to audit performance information in a government context? Several questions have to be answered. First, one has to decide on the focus of the audit. One could evaluate whether the conditions for a sound performance measurement system are fulfilled. Another possibility would be to select a sample of indicators and examine whether they are valid and reliable. Auditors can also focus on the performance indicators that are reported. Then, the focus lies mainly on the compliance with reporting requirements. The second question is which actor will conduct the audit of performance information? Would it be the internal audit unit or the external audit unit? Today's audit and control environment calls for a clear division of labor between internal controllers, internal auditors, and external auditors, so that they will build further on each other's work (Sterck & Bouckaert, 2006). A third question concerns the methodology of the audit. One could audit the quality of nonfinancial information following the financial audit methodology, or one could include it as a part of performance auditing. Finally, an organization also has to decide on the level of tolerance that it is willing to accept. Therefore, a risk-based approach is absolutely necessary.

The ideal is to find measures that fully capture and represent the objective in question. It is often better to try and measure important objectives imperfectly than to ignore them altogether. An imperfect measure can still help in setting priorities and planning; helping to put out the resources an organization uses into context and providing at least a starting point in judging the organization's performance. (Her Majesty's Treasury, National Audit Office, Audit Commission, and Office for National Statistics, 2001, p. 18)

Wholey (1999) described the audit of performance information as a five-step process:

Step 1: Assess the extent of agreement on goals and strategies.

Step 2: Clarify how each goal is achieved.

Step 3: Identify the performance measurement systems in use.

Step 4: Assess the technical quality of the performance measurement systems.

Step 5: Assess the extent to which the performance information is used. (p. 227)

To ensure that the performance measurement system is legitimate, it is important to start the audit with an assessment of the agreement on goals and strategies. Information on the goals and strategies is available in strategic plans, performance plans, annual reports, and evaluation reports. Information on the acceptance of these goals has to be collected through interviews, focus groups, or employee surveys.

A second step in the audit process is identifying the logic model of the organization. In this way, the contribution of activities and outputs to the outcomes of the organization can be mapped. In the next step, the auditor has to identify the different performance measurement systems in use. Often, organizations develop different information systems for different purposes. The task of the auditor is to look for the relevant information systems and to find out how these systems are linked.

Based on the inventory of measurement systems, the auditor selects the measurement systems that he or she will study. Subsequently, the reliability and validity of the performance measurement systems are evaluated. This evaluation can take place at different levels. One could simply review whether control procedures are in place to ensure data quality. One could evaluate the features of the measurement system. Another possibility would be to audit the quality of a sample of indicators.

The final step in the audit process is the assessment of the use of the performance information. Here, the functionality of the system is under review. Performance information can be used in different applications, such as performance budgeting, annual reporting, internal budget allocation,

Table 21.3   Audit of Performance Measurement in Six OECD Governments

	Audit of Performance Measurement Systems		
	Dominant Actor	*Mandate*	*Focus*
Australia	Australian National Audit Office	Within the performance audit mandate	Selection of annual reports
Canada	Office of the Auditor General of Canada	Explicit mandate	Annual report
The Netherlands	Algemene Rekenkamer	Explicit mandate	Annual report
Sweden	Riksrevisionen	Within the performance audit mandate	Annual report
United Kingdom	National Audit Office	Explicit mandate	Performance measurement systems developed to follow up the public service agreements
United States	Government Accountability Office	Within the performance audit mandate	Annual report

performance contracting, and pay for performance. It is important to identify to what extent the performance information is used and to what extent this has positive or negative impacts. Moreover, one should try to explain why certain indicators are used and others are not. Based on these observations, the auditor can formulate recommendations for the improvement of the performance measurement system.

Examples of Performance Measurement Audits

We will give some examples to illustrate how performance measurement systems can be audited. Table 20.3 illustrates the practice of auditing performance measurement in six Organisation for Economic Co-operation and Development (OECD) central or federal governments.

United Kingdom: Audit of PSA Performance Measurement Systems

The first example is from the United Kingdom, where central government departments follow up their performance through public service agreement (PSA) targets. The majority of PSA indicators are collected by the departments and agencies. Statistics that are declared valid by the National Statistician and the Statistics Commission receive a "National Statistics" label. Of the sources of data used for measuring 2001–2004 PSA targets,

14% were National Statistics (National Audit Office, 2001, p. 49). A survey of the National Audit Office showed that almost half of the departments perceived that receiving assurance on the reliability of performance data is a great or even a very great challenge (National Audit Office, 2001, p. 48).

In 2000, Her Majesty's Treasury decided that departments have to explain how they follow up their PSAs. Therefore, they have to add a technical note to the PSA, including the technical details of the indicators. However, a study of the National Audit Office showed that departments seldom mention in their technical notes how they guarantee data quality.

In 2001, Lord Sharman of Redlynch argued in his report *Holding to Account: The Review of Audit and Accountability for Central Government* that performance measurement systems should be externally assessed. In 2001, a working group was established within Her Majesty's Treasury to investigate whether this proposal could be implemented. The conclusion was that the audit of performance information systems should be performed by the National Audit Office. The National Audit Office started in 2003 with the assessment of the performance measurement systems that follow up the PSAs. When assessing the measurement systems, the National Audit Office looks at three things: (a) the match between the performance measure and the data used to report progress; (b) the data stream operation, including data collection, provision, processing, maintenance, and analysis/interpretation; and (3) the presentation/reporting of results (National Audit Office, 2005).

These audits consider both the quality of the internal performance measurement systems of the departments and the quality of the performance information that is reported to Parliament. The purpose of these audits is to assess the risks of data quality limitations. The focus is not on the level of individual indicators, but on the level of performance measurement systems and performance reporting. As PSAs are agreed upon for a three-year period, measurement systems in departments are audited once every three years.

Canada: Audit of Annual Reports

The second example is Canada's Auditor General Act, which gives the Auditor General the statutory authority to examine the performance measurement systems of departments. When the Auditor General finds that the procedures to measure and report the effectiveness of programs are not established satisfactorily, he or she shall bring it to the attention of the House of Commons. Barry Leighton explains in Chapter 6 of this volume how the Auditor General of Canada evaluates the quality of performance reports.

The Auditor General conducted an overall assessment of the departmental performance reports in 1997 and in 2000. In 2001, the Standing Committee on Public Accounts recommended that the Auditor General "conduct random audits of the information contained in the performance reports of departments in order to verify, among other things, that the information contained in these reports is a fair representation of accomplishments against goals and objectives."

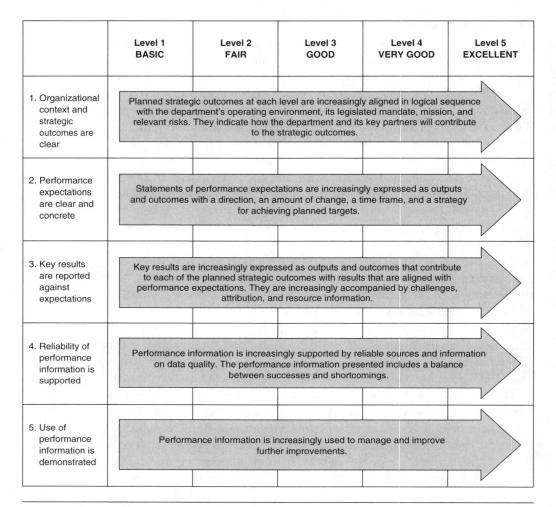

	Level 1 BASIC	Level 2 FAIR	Level 3 GOOD	Level 4 VERY GOOD	Level 5 EXCELLENT
1. Organizational context and strategic outcomes are clear	Planned strategic outcomes at each level are increasingly aligned in logical sequence with the department's operating environment, its legislated mandate, mission, and relevant risks. They indicate how the department and its key partners will contribute to the strategic outcomes.				
2. Performance expectations are clear and concrete	Statements of performance expectations are increasingly expressed as outputs and outcomes with a direction, an amount of change, a time frame, and a strategy for achieving planned targets.				
3. Key results are reported against expectations	Key results are increasingly expressed as outputs and outcomes that contribute to each of the planned strategic outcomes with results that are aligned with performance expectations. They are increasingly accompanied by challenges, attribution, and resource information.				
4. Reliability of performance information is supported	Performance information is increasingly supported by reliable sources and information on data quality. The performance information presented includes a balance between successes and shortcomings.				
5. Use of performance information is demonstrated	Performance information is increasingly used to manage and improve further improvements.				

Figure 21.4   Model for Rating Performance Reports

SOURCE: Office of the Auditor General of Canada (2003).

The Office of the Auditor General of Canada developed a model for rating departmental performance reports (see Figure 21.4). This model rates reports by means of five criteria: (a) organizational context and strategic outcomes are clear; (b) performance expectations are clear and concrete; (c) key results are reported against expectations; (d) performance information is credible and balanced; and (e) use of performance information is demonstrated. The model is not designed to provide assurance that the information in the performance report is accurate, because it does not include an audit of performance information. The model includes five achievement levels: basic, fair, good, very good, and excellent. By meeting each criterion at progressively higher levels, performance reports show that departments have increasingly mastered these attributes (Office of the Auditor General of Canada, 2003, p. 4).

This model was implemented for the first time in the spring of 2003, when the Auditor General assessed the quality of performance reports of a selection of departments and agencies: Citizenship and Immigration Canada, Correctional Services Canada, Immigration and Refugee Board, National Defense, National Parole Board, Royal Canadian Mounted Police, the Solicitor General Canada, and Transport Canada. "These organizations represent $19.3 billion in expenditures or 12% of the total government expenditures for FY 2001–2002" (Office of the Auditor General of Canada, 2003, p. 5).

The main conclusions of the Auditor General were that departments were good at describing their roles and the contextual factors that affected them. Another positive observation was that the connection between the performance plans and performance reports was good and that the set of indicators used was rather stable. The Auditor General recommended, however, that departments focus more on their outcomes and link these with the use of resources.

Moreover, the Auditor General of Canada has the statutory duty to examine the quality of performance information of three agencies: Parks Canada, the Canada Revenue Agency, and the Food Inspection Agency. Departments and agencies also play a role in the quality control of performance information. Departments conduct internal audits and evaluations of their programs in which they might control the system of performance measurement. The Treasury Board Secretariat and the Office of the Auditor General plan to release a management-for-results self-assessment tool for departments to monitor and control their management information systems.

Western Australia: Audit of Key Performance Indicators

The Office of the Auditor General of Western Australia has the statutory authority to audit performance indicators of public sector agencies. Under the provisions of the Financial Administration and Audit Act 1985 and as detailed in Treasurer's Instruction 904, accountable officers and authorities are required to enclose in their annual report output measures of quantity, quality, timeliness, and cost; key efficiency indicators; and key effectiveness indicators.

Key performance indicators of efficiency and effectiveness are subject to audit by the Auditor General (Office of the Auditor General of Western Australia, 1999). Key performance indicators are high-level indicators that relate to the primary purpose of the output, outcome, and/or agency focusing on the ends and not the means. Efficiency indicators should show the efficiency with which the agency produced those outputs that are directly related to the primary purpose of the output. Effectiveness indicators provide information on the extent to which outcomes have been achieved through the funding and production of agreed outputs.

The Auditor General's audit of performance indicators differs from financial audits in that the audit opinion not only addresses the traditional area of "fair representation" but also provides an assessment of whether or not the indicators are relevant and appropriate. What does this mean? To be relevant, the indicators should have a logical relationship to a user's needs and to clearly defined outputs and outcomes. To be appropriate, an agency's performance indicators should enable users to assess the performance relative to targets or goals, the performance relative to previous performance, and the performance relative to the performance of similar agencies or benchmarks (Office of the Auditor General of Western Australia, 1999).

Two different divisions play a role in improving the performance indicators. First, the Assurance Services Division provides Parliament with opinions on the integrity of public sector financial statements and performance indicators. Second, the Standards and Quality Division develops standards relating to the assurance services and performance review functions of the Office of the Auditor General, and the monitoring of performance against these standards. A part of this work entails providing advice to agencies to assist them in the development of key performance indicators.

The audit of performance indicators includes different steps: the initial planning phase, the interim planning phase, and the audit assurance and reporting. In the initial planning stage, the auditor needs to address the following issues:

- Has the agency developed outputs and outcomes that reflect the government-desired outcome?
- Do the key efficiency indicators for each output relate outputs to inputs consumed?
- Do the key effectiveness indicators for each outcome relate outputs to the outcomes achieved?
- Do these key indicators show performance of the primary purpose(s), and are they comprehensive in covering all major areas of the agency's performance?
- Do these key indicators enable users to assess performance relative to targets or goals, previous performance, and similar agencies or benchmarks?

Before starting the audit work, there must be confidence that the skills and competence required to audit performance indicators are available. Then, the auditor assesses whether the performance indicators are relevant and appropriate. If the indicators are relevant and appropriate, the auditor determines the nature and extent of audit testing. The auditor also finds out whether the key indicators are supported by adequate explanatory notes. The next step is the audit assurance phase. A combination of audit techniques and tests will provide the required level and amount of audit evidence. These could include compliance testing and evaluation of the systems; processes and controls that capture, record, analyze, and monitor the information; performing rigorous analytical procedures over the information; and performing a combination of those substantive tests considered necessary to gain the required level of assurance. When the audit fieldwork is finished, the results are reported. The opinion expressed in the audit report should be either unqualified or qualified. A qualified opinion should be expressed as an "except for" opinion, an "adverse" opinion, or an inability to form an opinion.

Conclusion

The availability of high-quality performance information is one of the critical factors for the successful implementation of performance and quality management. What are the characteristics of a sound performance measurement system? How can we ensure the quality of a performance measurement system?

The quality of a performance measurement system is more than the technical quality of the different performance indicators; a system approach is necessary. A performance measurement system, first of all, needs to produce valid and reliable information. Second, a performance measurement system has to be accepted by the employees of the organization. Third, a performance measurement system has to contribute to the goals of the organization. To guarantee that these three conditions are fulfilled, control measures have to be taken: developing quality standards, providing training, analyzing and monitoring the risks of data quality, and reporting on data quality limitations. Quality has to be a point of interest through the performance measurement process, from the planning phase to the reporting and the use of the performance information. An ex post and independent audit of the performance measurement system could be necessary. Audits of performance information can focus on different levels, such as the control procedures, the measurement systems, the annual reports, or the performance indicators. Organizations also have to determine which level of data quality they want to achieve. Auditing performance information may provide incentives to further improve the performance measurement system by finding the right balance between functionality, legitimacy, and technical soundness.

Discussion Questions

1. What are the main difficulties in measuring government performance? Can you give examples from your own organization?

2. How would you define a high-quality performance measurement system? Which conditions are the most important for you?

3. How is the quality of performance information guaranteed in your organization, and how would you further improve this system of quality control?

4. How would you balance the costs and benefits of a good performance measurement system? What is an acceptable level of quality?

5. Which positive and negative effects do you expect from auditing performance information? Which side effects may arise?

References

Algemene Rekenkamer. (2004). *Staat van de beleidsinformatie* [State of performance
   information]. The Hague, the Netherlands: Author.

Bouckaert, G. (1993). Measurement and meaningful management. *Public Productivity and Management Review, 17,* 31–43.

Bouckaert, G. (1995). Improving performance measurement. In A. Halachmi &
   G. Bouckaert (Eds.), *The enduring challenges in public management: Surviving
   and excelling in a changing world* (pp. 379–412). San Francisco: Jossey-Bass.

Bouckaert, G., & Peters, B. G. (2002). Performance measurement and management.
   The Achilles' heel in administrative modernization. *Public Productivity and Management Review, 25,* 359–362.

Bouckaert, G., Van Dooren, W., & Sterck, M. (2003). *Prestaties meten in de
   Vlaamse overheid: Een verkennende studie* [Measuring performance in the
   Flemish government: An exploratory study]. Leuven, Belgium: Steunpunt
   Bestuurlijke Organisatie Vlaanderen.

Divorski, S., & Scheirer, M. A. (2001). Improving data quality for performance measures: Results from a GAO study of verification and validation. *Evaluation and
   Program Planning, 24,* 83–94.

Her Majesty's Treasury, Cabinet Office, National Audit Office, Audit Commission,
   and Office for National Statistics. (2001). *Choosing the right FABRIC: A framework for performance information.* London: H. M. Stationary Office.

Lord Sharman of Redlynch. (2001). *Holding to account: The review of audit and
   accountability for central government.* Available at http://www.hm-treasury
   .gov.uk/documents/financial_management/governance_government/pss_aud_sh
   arman.cfm#below

National Audit Office. (2001). *Measuring the performance of government departments: Report by the comptroller and auditor general.* London: H. M. Stationary
   Office.

National Audit Office. (2005). *Public service agreements: Managing data quality:
   Compendium report.* London: Author.

Neely, A., & Bourne, M. (2000). Why measurement initiatives fail. *Measuring
   Business Excellence, 4*(4), 3–6.

Office of the Auditor General of Canada. (2003). *Report of the Auditor General of
   Canada. Chapter 1: Rating departmental performance reports.* Ottawa, Canada:
   Author.

Office of the Auditor General of Western Australia. (1999). *OAG audit standard.
   The audit of performance indicators.* Perth, Australia: Author.

Organisation for Economic Co-operation and Development Public Management
   Service. (2001). *Highlights of public sector pay and employment trends.* Paris:
   Author.

Scheers, B., Sterck, M., & Bouckaert, G. (2005). Lessons from Australian and British reforms in results-oriented financial management. *OECD Journal on Budgeting, 5*(2), 133–162.

Standing Committee on Public Accounts. (2001). *Eighth report of the Standing Committee on Public Accounts.* Ottawa, Canada: House of Commons. Retrieved from http://www.cmte.parl.gc.ca/Content/HOC/committee/371/pacc/reports/rp 1031893/report8-e.htm

Sterck, M., & Bouckaert, G. (2006). International audit trends in the public sector. *Internal Auditor Magazine, 63*(4), 29–53.

Van de Walle, S., & Bouckaert, G. (2007). Perceptions of productivity and performance in Europe and the USA. *International Journal of Public Administration, 30*(11), n.p.

Wholey, J. (1999). Quality control: Assessing the accuracy and usefulness of performance measurement systems. In H. Hatry (Ed.), *Performance measurement: Getting results* (pp. 217–239). Washington, DC: Urban Institute.

22 Applying the Common Assessment Framework in Europe

Nick Thijs

Patrick Staes

The public sector has to cope with a lot of challenges and respond to many new needs and demands in society (Organisation for Economic Co-operation and Development [OECD], 1993, 1995, 2000). Due to these challenges and pressures, the public sector is the object of large-scale reform (Kettl, 2000; Kickert, 1997; Lane, 2000).

> Over the last two decades there appears to have been a huge amount of public management reform. Although there was also reform in earlier periods, the changes since 1980 have—in many countries—been distinguished by an international character and a degree of political salience which marks them out from the more parochial or technical changes of the proceeding quarter-century. (Pollitt & Bouckaert, 2004, p. 1)

These reforms are characterized by the introduction of new principles, a growing focus on efficiency and effectiveness, attention to transparency and accountability, awareness of public service delivery and the role and place of the citizen/customer (Doherty & Horne, 2002; Schick, 2000; Shand, 1999). Methods and techniques were constructed, focusing on one of these principles or trying to combine them. Techniques like "management by objectives," "cost-benefit analysis," "market testing," "performance-related pay," "value for money" and "total quality management" were introduced (Pollitt & Bouckaert, 1995).

Through the first part of this chapter, the quality management movement and its rise in Europe are briefly addressed. This historical and contextual overview is useful for dealing with the Common Assessment Framework

(CAF), a quality management tool especially designed for public sector organizations of the European Union (EU), which is discussed in the second part. The third part of this chapter focuses in detail on the CAF in practice and the application of the CAF as a European quality tool. The goal is to provide the reader with an introduction to this innovative technique. On the basis of these experiences, we discuss some practical issues and formulate a number of recommendations in order to support practice.

Quality Management in the European Public Sector

The Origin of Quality Thinking

The history of quality thinking has its roots in postwar industrialization and the rise of mass production (Ovreveit, 2005). The emphasis with respect to quality inspection and control was originally related to output and had a strong product focus (see Figure 22.1). Later, attention gradually shifted from the processes and the guarantee of quality during the course of this process (quality assurance) to total quality management (TQM). A greater focus was placed on the user and the effects that the products and services had on that user (Bouckaert & Thijs, 2003; Gaster & Squires, 2003). Satisfaction became a key concept (Parasuraman, Berry, & Zeithaml, 1985; Parasuraman, Zeithaml, & Berry, 1988; Zeithaml, Parasuraman, & Berry, 1990). TQM is characterized by the permanent mobilization of all the resources (especially the people) to improve in a continuous way: all the aspects of an organization, the quality of goods and services delivered, the satisfaction of the organization's stakeholders, and the organization's integration into the environment. The first and final goal of TQM is to meet customer expectations. Therefore, active commitment of all employees, as well as comprehensive information systems that collect and process information with regard to customers, suppliers, and corporate-wide processes, are required (Löffler, 2002). TQM is usually used synonymously with continuous quality improvement (CQI), stressing that TQM involves cultural change (Beckford, 1998; Oakland, 1995).

TQM was originally developed in the United States. It was then widely applied to the Japanese manufacturing industry and was subsequently reexported to the West during the late 1970s and early 1980s. It percolated from manufacturing to the commercial services and eventually to the public services in the late 1980s.

TQM Models in the Public Sector

Many ideas and methods were developed and used in the private sector before being introduced into the public sector (Pollitt, 1990). The concern

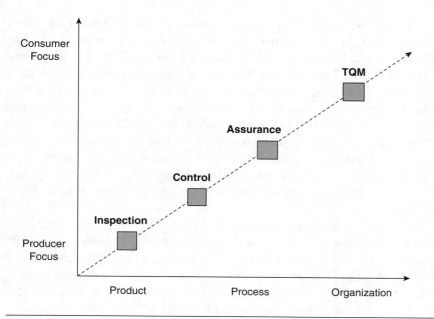

Figure 22.1   Evolution of Quality Management
SOURCE: Thijs (2004).

about public sector quality and using methods in the European public sector emerged in the late 1980s and particularly the early 1990s (Ferlie, Ashburne, Fitzferald, & Pettigrew, 1996). Research carried out by the European Commission stated that quality improvement was on top of the list in many European countries in the mid-1990s, marked by countries above other relevant themes (see Table 22.1).

Table 22.1   Priorities for European Public Services (1997)

	Quality Improvement %	Reduction of Costs %	Innovation %	Increasing the Choice in Services/ Products %	Privatization %
Germany	41	20	17	12	8
United Kingdom	63	15	10	9	3
Netherlands	52	17	8	8	9
France	41	23	15	9	10
European Union	48	19	14	9	8

SOURCE: OECD (1997).

Initially, the quality movement was based on users' charters, the 1991 Citizens' Charter in the United Kingdom, the *Charte des services publics* of 1992 in France, and, in 1993, *het Handvest van de Gebruiker* [the Users' Charter] in Belgium were later followed by charters in a number of other countries (Bouckaert, 1993; Van de Walle, Thijs, & Bouckaert, 2005). Charters are official commitments to quality and quality improvement stated by public services or for the whole of public service. Most of the time, these charters are setting some quality standards, listing the commitments public services are taking to citizens/customers. Charters can be looked at as explicit quality policies toward citizens/customers, often related in decreasing the so-called gap between government and the citizen (Van de Walle et al., 2005).

In the late 1990s, many TQM-inspired models and techniques (e.g., International Organization for Standardization [ISO], balanced scorecard, European Foundation for Quality Management, and public service excellence model) found their way into the European public sector (Van Dooren, Thijs, & Bouckaert, 2004). We mention the quality systems based on ISO 9000 (see http://www.iso.org). The ISO is a worldwide federation of national standards bodies from more than 140 countries, one from each country. The most widely known standards in a public service context are ISO 9000. ISO standards and a management system built upon these standards are captured by the term *quality assurance*. This approach has been described as "Write what you should do, do as you write, write when you don't do it right" (Ovreveit, 2005, p. 549). in recent years, ISO 9000 has incorporated TQM ideas, including process improvement. ISO 9000 certificates have become highly popular in the private sector and have also found their way into the public sector (Engel, 2003).

Another widely spread instrument is the balanced scorecard (BSC) (see http://www.balancedscorecard.org). The BSC was developed by Kaplan and Norton (1992). It is a management system (not only a measurement system) that enables organizations to clarify their visions and strategies and translate them into action (Kaplan & Norton, 1992). It provides feedback on both internal business processes and external outcomes in order to continuously improve strategic performance and results (Kaplan & Norton, 1993). The BSC suggests that the organization must be viewed from four perspectives:

1. Customer perspective

2. Financial perspective

3. Internal, process perspective

4. Innovation and learning perspective

Metrics must be developed and data collected and analyzed relative to each perspective.

The third most widely used TQM-based method is the European Foundation for Quality Management (EFQM) model—the European version of the Baldrige framework (see http://www.efqm.org). The EFQM was founded at the end of the 1980s by 14 major European companies and started to focus on the public sector during its evolution. In 1992, EFQM launched its model for self-assessment. This model is based on nine criteria. EFQM changed its model slightly in April 1999, trying to make it more compatible with the public sector by including innovation and learning. the nine criteria of the model are leadership, people, policy and strategy, partnerships and resources, processes, people results, customer results, society results, and key performance results. The EFQM model is increasingly used in European public services (Engel, 2003; Löffler, 2002; Ovreveit, 2005).

These same criteria can be found in the CAF (see http://www.eipa.nl). The CAF model was designed in 1999 (Stromsnes, 2002) and has been successfully applied in several European and Central and Eastern European countries (Bauer, 2002; European Institute of Public Administration [EIPA], 2002b). As the CAF is the model that is the most widespread in these countries as a common initiative of the director generals in charge of the public sector of the member states of the EU, the use of this model will be explained later in this chapter.

The public service excellence model (PSEM) is another self-assessment framework that is focusing on the public sector, although it is not broadly used or known (see http://www.publicfutures.com). The PSEM has 14 criteria: strategy and plans, leadership, resources, processes, people, resource results, efficiency results, people results, service reporting, service outputs, service satisfaction, program outcomes, program satisfaction, and policy and governance. PSEM includes the policy side, which also goes beyond the organization as such and therefore has the broadest scope (Public Futures, 1998). The use of the PSEM model is limited to some public services in the United Kingdom.

There is a historical evolution of these models, in the sense that some of these models are converging and that the coverage of the input/activities/output/outcome chain is being extended. A rough coverage scheme might resemble the one shown in Table 22.2. PSEM has the most comprehensive viewpoint in that it covers the policy context beyond the immediate outcomes of a specific service.

Quality in the Public Sector in Europe: An Overview

In the first half of 2002, a survey was carried out under the Spanish presidency of the EU to map out the most important programs and initiatives regarding quality and quality management being pursued at the time in the various member states (EIPA, 2002b; EU Ministers, 2002).

It is striking that most, if not all, member states are conducting a number or even a large number of quality initiatives relating to various forms of

Table 22.2   Focus of Quality Management Models

Model	Input	Activity	Output	Immediate Outcome	End Outcome
ISO	X	X			
BSC	X	X	X		
EFQM	X	X	X	X	
CAF	X	X	X	X	
PSEM	X	X	X	X	X

SOURCE: Van Dooren et al. (2004).

NOTE: ISO = International Organization for Standardization
BSC = balanced scorecard
EFQM = European Foundation for Quality Management
CAF = Common Assessment Framework
PSEM = public service excellence model

service provision. The focus within these initiatives is often geared to the relationship with the user/customer (one-stop shops, e-government), innovation, quality-of-life improvement for citizens, use of modern management techniques, simplification of administrative procedures and regulations, and achieving higher standards of service provision. The actions taken are often directed toward an administration that works efficiently and has a results- and customer-oriented focus and is transparent and accessible to users/customers. Most of these actions have been put into place as part of a wider policy, with a view toward reforming and modernizing government services.

The use of quality models and techniques to achieve improvements in the public sector has taken root in all member states. A commonly used model, as mentioned, is the EFQM model. In some member states (e.g., United Kingdom and Spain), it is by far the most prevalent model. In other countries (Belgium and Italy), the CAF has made great strides in recent years. Furthermore, international quality standards such as ISO have been applied in numerous member states for a wide range of activities. Some countries have their own models, such as the Swedish Institute Quality Model (SIQ) or the *Instituut voor Nederlandse Kwaliteit* [Dutch Quality Institute] (INK model). In addition, charters are used in the various member states as tools to improve the relationships between citizens/users and government administrations by laying down quality standards for service provision. In some member states (Finland, France, the Netherlands, Spain, United Kingdom, and Sweden), a national quality prize exists to reward excellent and quality government organizations. User satisfaction with service provision is being measured by means of customer satisfaction assessments and systems for registering complaints, and suggestions have been put into place in the various member states.

Quality management ideas and techniques are widespread across Europe. In recent times, public sector quality improvements have also appeared on the agenda of Eastern European countries (Engel, 2003). The new and candidate EU member states, in particular, are very active in promoting quality tools (Löffler & Vintar, 2004).

Quality approaches among the various countries differed for a long time. The need was felt for establishing a common European quality framework that could be used across the public sector as a tool for organizational self-assessment.

The Common Assessment Framework (CAF)

History and Context

Following years of informal consultations, there was an increasing need within the EU for a more intensive and formal response in order to optimize cooperation with respect to the modernization of government services. The preparatory work that had been performed for several years at an informal level by the public service heads of the various EU member states led in November 1998 to a ministerial declaration containing "the general principles concerning the improvement of the quality of services provided to citizens" (Staes, 2002, p. 4).

During the Austrian EU presidency, in the second half of 1998, the possibility of developing a European quality award for the public sector was discussed within the framework of the informal meetings of the directors general of the public administration of the EU member states. The idea, as such, was dismissed in view of the fact that the diversity of cultures and visions of "quality" in the public sector in EU countries would not allow for direct competition, but an alternative was developed and finally accepted: the establishment of a common European quality framework that could be used across the public sector as a tool for organizational self-assessment (Engel, 2002). The discussions revealed that what was lacking in the realm of quality management was an easy-to-use and free entry tool for self-assessment in the public sector that could (a) help public administrations across the EU understand and employ modern management techniques and (b) be of particular relevance for those public sector organizations that are interested in trying out the use of a quality management system, are just embarking on their "journey to excellence," or wish to compare themselves with similar organizations in Europe (Staes, 2002).

It was decided that the CAF should be jointly developed under the aegis of the Innovative Public Services Group (IPSG), an informal working group of national experts set up by the directors general to promote exchanges and cooperation where it concerned innovative ways of modernizing government and public service delivery in EU member states. The basic design of the CAF was then developed in 1998 and 1999 on the basis of joint analysis undertaken by the EFQM, the Speyer Academy (which organizes the Speyer Quality Award for the public sector in German-speaking European countries), and the EIPA (Staes, 2002).

First, pilot tests were conducted in a number of public sector organizations, and the "final" version of the CAF was presented during the First Quality Conference for Public Administration in the EU, in Lisbon, in May 2000. The CAF differs from the EFQM model on a number of dimensions (subcriteria) and explicitly takes account of the specificities of the public sector. This characteristic of the CAF has been reinforced, and the second and improved version of the CAF was officially presented during the Second Quality Conference for Public Administrations in the EU, held in Copenhagen, in 2002, under the Danish presidency of the EU. In 2006, the CAF model got a new revision.

The Theoretic Model

The setting up of the CAF provided an initial impetus for a common European reference framework:

> The main purpose of the CAF is to provide a fairly simple, free and easy-to-use framework which is suitable for self-assessment of public sector organizations across Europe and which would also allow for the sharing of best practices and benchmarking activities. (Engel, 2002, p. 35)

The CAF constitutes a blueprint of the organization (see Figure 22.2). It is a representation of all aspects that must be present in the proper management of an organization in order to achieve satisfactory results. These elements are translated into nine criteria. Five of these are "enablers," and four are "results." The enabler criteria cover what an organization *does*. The results criteria cover what an organization *achieves*. Results are caused by enablers, and feedback from results helps to improve enablers. Criteria are further operationalized and given concrete form in subcriteria. On the basis of these subcriteria, a group from within the organization evaluates that organization.

The CAF has four main purposes:

1. to be an introduction to the TQM, especially adapted for the public sector

2. to facilitate the self-assessment of a public organization in order to obtain a diagnosis and improvement actions

3. to act as a bridge across the various models in use in quality management

4. to facilitate "bench learning" between public sector organizations

The CAF has been designed for use in all parts of the public sector, applicable to public organizations at a national/federal, regional, and local level. It may also be used under a wide variety of circumstances (e.g., as part of a systematic program of reform or as a basis for targeting improvement efforts in public service organizations). In some cases, and especially in very large organizations,

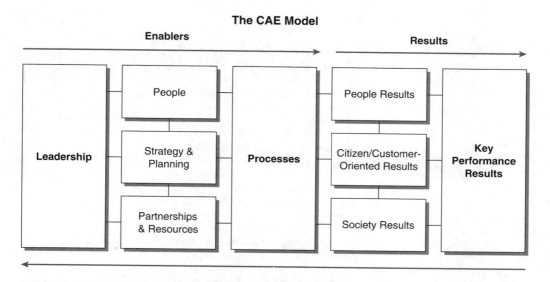

Figure 22.2   The Common Assessment Framework
SOURCE: EIPA (2006).

a self-assessment may also be undertaken in part of an organization (e.g., a selected section or department). The CAF provides the following:

- an assessment against a set of criteria that has become widely accepted across Europe, based on evidence
- opportunities to identify progress and outstanding levels of achievement
- a means to achieve consistency of direction and consensus on what needs to be done to improve an organization
- a link between goals and supportive strategies and processes
- a means to create enthusiasm among employees by involving them in the improvement process
- opportunities to promote and share good practice within different areas of an organization and with other organizations
- a means to integrate various quality initiatives into normal business operations
- a means of measuring progress over time through periodic self-assessment

How to Apply the CAF Model

CAF provides a self-assessment framework under which an ad hoc group of employees in an organization can conduct a critical assessment of their organization guided by the CAF structure.

This self-assessment procedure is clearly less rigorous and less detailed than an organizational assessment conducted by trained external assessors.

Enablers
Criterion 1. Leadership **Consider evidence of what the organization's leadership is doing to:**
Subcriterion 1.1 Provide direction for the organization by developing its mission, vision, and values
Subcriterion 1.2 Develop and implement a system for the management of organization, performance, and change
Subcriterion 1.3 Motivate and support the people in the organization and act as a role model
Subcriterion 1.4 Manage the relations with politicians and other stakeholders in order to ensure shared responsibility
Criterion 2. Strategy and Planning **Consider evidence of what the organization is doing to:**
Subcriterion 2.1 Gather information relating to the present and future needs of stakeholders
Subcriterion 2.2 Develop, review, and update strategy and planning, taking into account the needs of stakeholders and available resources
Subcriterion 2.3 Implement strategy and planning in the whole organization
Subcriterion 2.4 Plan, implement, and review modernization and innovation
Criterion 3. People **Consider evidence of what the organization is doing to:**
Subcriterion 3.1 Plan, manage, and improve human resources transparently with regard to strategy and planning
Subcriterion 3.2 Identify, develop, and use competencies of the employees, aligning individual and organizational goals
Subcriterion 3.3 Involve employees by developing open dialogue and empowerment
Criterion 4. Partnerships and Resources **Consider evidence of what the organization is doing to:**
Subcriterion 4.1 Develop and implement key partnership relations

Enablers
Subcriterion 4.2 Develop and implement partnerships with the citizens/customers
Subcriterion 4.3 Manage finances
Subcriterion 4.4 Manage information and knowledge
Subcriterion 4.5 Manage technology
Subcriterion 4.6 Manage facilities
Criterion 5. Processes **Consider evidence of what the organization is doing to:**
Subcriterion 5.1 Identify, design, manage, and improve processes on an ongoing basis
Subcriterion 5.2 Develop and deliver citizen/customer-oriented services and products
Subcriterion 5.3 Innovate processes involving citizens/customers

Results
Criterion 6. Citizen/Customer-Oriented Results **Consider what results the organization has achieved to meet the needs and** **expectations of citizens and customers through:**
Subcriterion 6.1 Results of citizen/customer satisfaction measurements
Subcriterion 6.2 Indicators of citizen/customer-oriented results
Criterion 7. People Results **Consider what results the organization has achieved to meet the needs and** **expectations of its people through:**
Subcriterion 7.1 Results of people satisfaction and motivation measurements

(Continued)

(Continued)

Subcriterion 7.2 Indicators of people results
Criterion 8. Society Results **Consider what results the organization has achieved in respect of impact on society, with reference to:**
Subcriterion 8.1 Results of societal measurements perceived by the stakeholders
Subcriterion 8.2 Indicators of societal performance established by the organization
Criterion 9. Key Performance Results **Consider the evidence of defined goals achieved by the organization in relation to:**
Subcriterion 9.1 External results: Outputs and outcomes to goals
Subcriterion 9.2 Internal results

However, it is less expensive and has some advantages, such as revealing the perceptions of staff toward their own organization (Stromsnes, 2002, p. 54). How is this process of self-assessment best implemented? Some major steps are crucial:

- Step 1: Gain commitment of the senior management and communicate the CAF self-assessment process.

Before a self-assessment project is launched, senior management of the organization should discuss and agree on the arrangements for conducting the assessment and should also discuss the perceived purpose of the assessment and the intended actions following completion of the assessment.

- Step 2: Appoint a CAF project leader and communicate, communicate, communicate.

The responsibilities of the CAF project leader include ensuring that all necessary information and documentation are provided to the self-assessment group (regarding supporting contacts, information distribution within the self-assessment group, arranging meetings, accommodation for meetings, reporting, and so on). Besides being the backup for the self-assessment group, the project leader, together with the senior management, is responsible for the communication to the entire organization. To avoid resistance during the self-assessment, all members of the organization at least have to be informed about the aims of the assessment as an instrument for organizational improvement.

- Step 3a: Establish the assessment group.

The usual arrangements for a self-assessment team involve an ad hoc group, which is as representative of the organization as possible. It would be usual to include members from different sectors/levels within the organization. The objective is to establish a group as small and effective as possible—but at the same time a group that provides the most accurate and detailed internal perspective of the organization. It is important to select participants on the basis of their personal (e.g., analytical and communicative skills) rather than professional skills. the chair could be also the project leader. The chairperson is responsible for the proper conduct of all group proceedings, in cooperation with the project leader.

- Step 3b: Inform the team about what is to be done, and how.

The CAF should be introduced and the purposes and nature of the self-assessment procedure explained (the CAF evaluation panel, need to support scoring by evidence, etc.). More than superficial training is necessary. For most members of self-assessment groups, the total-quality approach in general and the CAF in particular are brand new. To do an effective self-assessment, they need to be carefully introduced into this practice. The group should also be assured that nobody will suffer for expressing an honest opinion. A list with all relevant documents and information needed to assess the organization in an effective way should be available for the group. A consensus has to be reached on how to evaluate evidence and how to assign scores.

- Step 4: Undertake individual assessment.

Step 4 is the actual assessment process. The chair must be available to handle questions from the members of the self-assessment group during the individual assessment. Each member of the self-assessment group is being asked to give an accurate assessment of the organization, under each subcriterion, based on their own knowledge and experience of working in the organization. They should focus, first of all, on strengths and areas of improvement (weaknesses), write down key words on evidences, and score only at the end of their reflection.

in September 2006, the new version of CAF was launched. In this new version, two different ways of scoring are presented: a classical one and an advanced scoring. Here, we present the classical scoring and make the comparison with the 2002 version.

- Step 5: Undertake consensus.

As soon as possible after the individual assessment, the group should meet and agree on how to score the organization on each subcriterion. A process of negotiation and agreement may be necessary to reach agreement.

Evaluation Table Enablers

Phase	Enablers Panel	Score	Version 2002
	We are not active in this field. We have no information, or very anecdotal.	0–10	0
Plan	We have a plan to do this.	11–30	1
Do	We are implementing/doing this.	31–50	2
Check	We check/review whether we do the right things in the right way.	51–70	3
Act	On the basis of checking/reviews, we adjust if necessary.	71–90	4
PDCA	Everything we do, we plan, implement, and adjust regularly, and we learn from others. We are in a continuous improvement cycle on this issue.	91–100	5

Evaluation Table Results

Results Panel	Score	Version 2002
No results are measured, and/or no information is available.	0–10	0
Results are measured and show negative trends, and/or results do not meet relevant targets.	11–30	1
Results show flat trends, and/or some relevant targets are met.	31–50	2
Results show improving trends, and/or most of the relevant targets are met.	51–70	3
Results show substantial progress, and/or all the relevant targets are met.	71–90	4
Excellent and sustained results are achieved. All the relevant targets are met. Positive comparisons with relevant organizations for all the key results are made.	91–100	5

The chair has a key role in conducting this process and arriving at a group consensus. In all cases, the discussion should be based on concrete evidence of efforts made and results achieved. In the CAF, a list of relevant examples is included to provide assistance in identifying evidence. It is not necessary to meet all the possible indicators, only those relevant to the organization. However, the group is free to find additional examples relevant to the organization.

- Step 6: How to use the results: Prioritize improvements.

The results of the self-assessment should be communicated to the organization and carefully examined by senior management with a view toward identifying the main findings of the self-assessment, the areas in which action is most needed, and the kind of action that is called for. in preparing such a plan, the management might wish to consider the use of a structured approach, including the following questions:

- ○ Where do we want to be in five years (goal setting)?
- ○ What actions need to be taken to reach these goals (strategy/task definition)?

The senior management may find it helpful to group the areas for improvement under common themes before deciding relative priorities.

- Step 7a: Develop and implement an improvement plan.

While a CAF self-assessment is a start to a long-term improvement strategy, the assessment will inevitably suggest a few areas that can be addressed relatively quickly and easily. Acting on them will help with the credibility of the improvement program and represent an immediate return on time and training investment. It is a good idea to involve the people who carried out the self-assessment in the improvement activities.

- Step 7b: Monitor progress and repeat the assessment.

Once the improvement action plan is formulated and the implementation of changes has begun, it is important to make sure that the changes have a positive effect and are not adversely affecting things the organization was doing well to begin with. Some organizations have built regular self-assessments into their business planning process—their assessments are timed to inform the annual setting of objectives and bids for financial resources. The evaluation panels of the CAF are simple but powerful tools to use when assessing the ongoing progress of the improvement action plan. (See Figure 22.3.)

To summarize, self-assessment against the CAF model offers the organization an opportunity to learn more about itself. Compared with a fully developed TQM model, the CAF is a "light" model, especially suited to gaining an initial impression of how the organization performs. It is assumed that any organization that intends to go further will select one of the more detailed models (such as the Speyer or EFQM models). The CAF has the advantage of being compatible with these models and may therefore be a first step for an organization wishing to go further with quality management. The CAF is in the public domain and free of charge. Organizations are free to use the model as they wish.

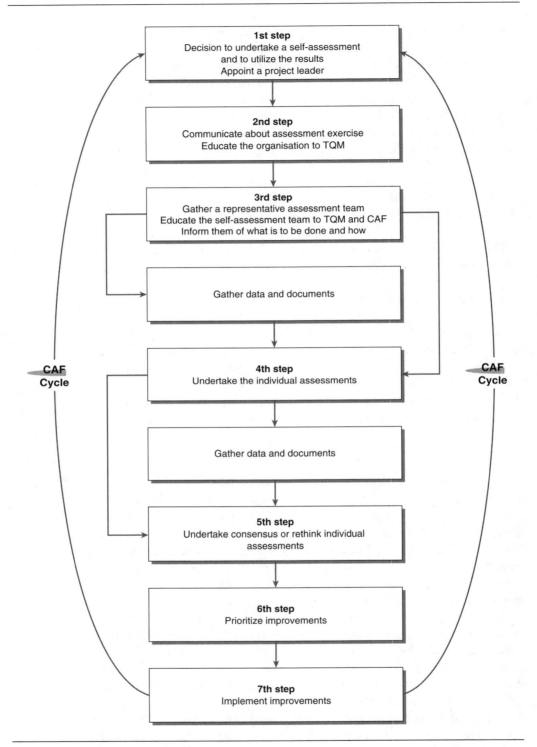

Figure 22.3   The Process of Self-Assessment

SOURCE: EIPA (2002a).

_____ Applying the CAF Model in Europe

During the Italian presidency of the EU, the EIPA (2003) conducted a study on the use of the CAF within European public administrations. The questionnaire-based study sought to identify the ways in which CAF was promoted in the different member states and how the tool helped public administrations to analyze themselves in an efficient way and to implement improvement actions in the context of a total-quality approach. The conclusions of the EIPA 2003 study on the use of the CAF can be summarized as follows:

- The CAF model was applied in more than 500 organizations or organization divisions in 19 countries. The organizations were spread across the various tiers of the government landscape (central, state, province, local, etc.). In addition, the organizations originated from sectors ranging from the police and the judiciary, across welfare and social sector organizations and education, to living environment, economy, and organizations charged with coordination or policy functions. The size of the organizations differed from very small (10 employees) to very large organizations (more than 5,000), although we must conclude that the middle group (250–1,000) was the largest.

- The CAF as a measuring device offers the organization a quick scan in order to identify a number of strong and weak points, which will then serve as a launching pad for a number of improvement projects—this was the most important reason given for using the CAF. This clear identification of the strengths and weaknesses of the organization is the most important added value of the self-assessment. In addition, matters such as an increased awareness of organizational problems, a better insight into the total functioning of the organization and the exchange of ideas in this respect appeared to be important aspects (Staes & Thijs, 2005).

- Many of the initiatives launched in the various European countries relating to quality management may be labeled as individual, ad hoc initiatives of the countries themselves. However, a growing tendency, both in Eastern and Western European countries, toward a common language and a common reference framework is to be observed. Quality tools such as the CAF model may serve as a framework for this language. By offering such a framework as a guiding principle for organization management, principles of proper management find their way into many administrations and many different countries (Thijs & Staes, 2005).

In 2005, the CAF Resource Centre at the EIPA in Maastricht, the Netherlands, repeated this survey on the use of the CAF on behalf of the Luxembourg presidency of the EU (EIPA, 2005).

Context of the 2005 Study

Nearly a year and a half after the first study on the use of the CAF, the Luxembourg presidency asked EIPA, in accordance with the Mid Term Programme of the European Public Administration Network, to conduct a follow-up study. As was the case in 2003, a questionnaire, prepared in collaboration with the CAF correspondents, was sent to the CAF correspondents (experts in all member states) and members of the IPSG to acquire information on the status of the CAF in their countries (the member states, candidate members, and Norway). The slight adaptations were designed to collect information related to the evolution since 2003. All 27 correspondents answered the questionnaire.

For the organizations that have used the CAF since then, a questionnaire was posted online on the CAF Web site (see http://www.eipa.nl). The online questionnaire was filled in by 131 individual organizations from 22 different countries out of 27 in Europe that have CAF applications. This survey gives an inside view into the countries' specific policies regarding the CAF, as well as an in-depth view on the use at the organizational level.

CAF Policy and Support in the EU Member States

EU countries are free to promote the CAF model, and organizations are free to use it. In many countries, there was already a strong quality management dynamic before the CAF. To give an idea as to the overall position adopted by governments on TQM in general, the different national correspondents were asked about political support for CAF and other TQM tools in their countries.

Table 22.3 indicates that TQM tools and CAF have found their place in most of the European countries. In most of the countries, there is increasing political support related to quality management. In other countries in which there was already a tradition in quality management, this political support is constant. In the minority of countries, political support is decreasing, or there is no formal policy whatsoever regarding quality management. As in 2003, EFQM, ISO, BSC, and CAF are the most extensively used TQM tools in Europe in general, not counting specific national tools like VIC (Italy), INK (the Netherlands), and the Swedish Quality model.

The stability of the political support for TQM tools and CAF is evident in countries with some history in this field, such as the Scandinavian and Anglo-Saxon countries; and in the United Kingdom, the political support is even increasing. In these countries, choices of management tools are basically made at the manager's level. In several other countries, the political awareness of CAF and TQM is growing and is expressed in central government initiatives. In most of the countries, the political support mentioned translates into the recommended use of these tools.

Table 22.3   Political Support for Quality Management

No Formal Policy (1)	Decreasing (2)	Constant (9)	Increasing (12)
Ireland	Estonia, Latvia	Germany, Denmark, Finland, France, Netherlands, Portugal, Sweden, Slovakia, Norway	Austria, Belgium, Cyprus, Czech Republic, Greece, Spain, Hungary, Italy, Lithuania, Luxembourg, Poland, Slovenia, Romania, United Kingdom

SOURCE: EIPA (2005).

Table 22.4   Use of CAF in Different Countries

More than 30 applications	Austria, Belgium, Czech Republic, Germany, Denmark, Finland, Hungary, Italy, Norway, Portugal, Slovenia, Sweden
Fewer than 30 applications	Cyprus, Estonia, Greece, Spain, France, Ireland, Latvia, Luxembourg, Poland, Slovakia, United Kingdom, Romania

SOURCE: EIPA (2005).

The Use of CAF in Different Countries

It remains difficult to centralize information on the number of CAF applications at national and European levels. This is due to the nature of the tool itself—a stimulus for individual organizational development via self-assessment—as well as the European context in which it was created—an open coordination or voluntary cooperation between countries. In 2005, as in the 2003 study, national correspondents were asked to estimate the use of CAF in their countries. In the autumn of 2003, 22 countries had roughly estimated having generated 500 applications. In 2005, 20 countries estimated having generated around 885 applications in their countries (EIPA, 2005).

To provide an idea of the spread of CAF, two groups are distinguished (see Table 22.4). Countries with more than 30 applications can be considered to have already established a sound basis for the further use of the CAF. Countries with fewer than 30 applications can be credited with having gained initial experience with the model and may be on their way to joining the first group.

Implementation of the CAF Model

As shown in previous surveys, the 2005 study shows the CAF model is used in all tiers of government.

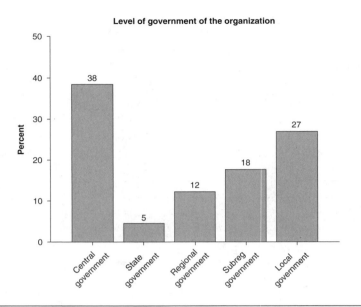

SOURCE: EIPA (2005).

This gives at least an indication that CAF is also finding its way in the central levels of government. The model is used not only within the different tiers of government; organizations from different types of administrations are also users, from classical ministries, to agencies, to local and regional administrations.

In addition to the tier and the type of administration, the size of the organization is another interesting characteristic to look at.

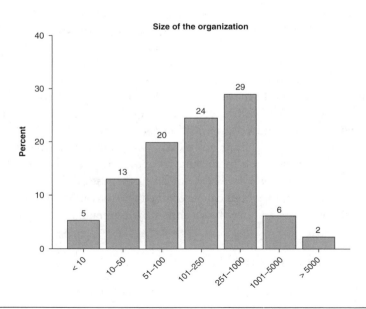

SOURCE: EIPA (2005).

Table 22.5   Top-10 Reasons Organizations Choose the CAF

Reasons
To identify strengths and areas for improvement
To develop sensitivity to quality issues
To involve staff in managing the organization and to motivate them
As an input into ongoing improvement activities, restructuring, etc.
To use CAF as a first diagnosis in the start of a strategic planning process
To promote the exchange of views in the organization
Preferred by top management
To prove that the organization is willing to change
To promote cultural change in the organization
To embed a new system of performance management/measurement

SOURCE: EIPA (2005).

The model is applied in all sizes of public organizations, but more than 50% have between 101 and 1,000 employees. The very small (less than 10) and the very big organizations (more than 1,000) remain the exception. This indicates that the model suits all sizes.

Use of the CAF Model

In the 2005 survey, organizations that had used the CAF model were asked to identify their reasons for choosing to use the model, and a number of possible reasons that could be decisive for using the CAF were presented to them. In Table 22.5, the top-10 reasons indicated by the organizations are shown.

These 10 reasons were considered to be the most important, and are all internal reasons. There is a clear accent on the wish to identify strengths and areas for improvement, which is exactly the purpose of a self-assessment tool. Organizations want to use CAF in the first place for themselves, and the ownership is very high.

Self-assessment may have a number of possible benefits. Again, a list of benefits was presented to the organizations to answer this question: "What were the most important benefits of using the CAF model?" We show them in order of importance in Table 22.6.

As registered in Table 22.6, the most-appreciated benefits fit perfectly with the most important reasons for using the CAF. Comparing Table 22.5 and Table 22.6 indicates that there is a close relationship between the reasons

Table 22.6   Benefits of Using the CAF Model

Main Benefits
We identified the need to share information and improve communication.
We clearly identified strengths and areas for improvement.
We were able to identify a number of important actions to be undertaken.
People developed a better understanding of organizational issues/problems.
Self-assessment gave rise to new ideas and a new way of thinking.
The ability to contribute and to share views was felt positively.
We realized how previous improvement activities could be taken forward.
People started to become aware and interested in quality issues.
We developed an understanding of how different initiatives fit together in place.
People started to develop a stronger interest in the organization.

SOURCE: EIPA (2005).

Table 22.7   Sustainable Improvement Activities as Result of the CAF

	2005		2003	
# Org.	%			%
105	87%	Yes		62%
16	13%	No		26%

SOURCE: EIPA (2005).

given for undertaking the CAF model and the results achieved. One could say that the organizations have found what they were looking for.

Using the CAF should lead to a structured improvement process addressing the areas for improvement identified through self-assessment. However, ensuring an adequate and structured follow-up is not always easy. Nevertheless, Table 22.7 shows that the CAF resulted in sustainable improvement activities in 87% of the cases.

This is a remarkable increase compared with 2003. That nearly 9 of 10 organizations that applied the CAF started up improvement actions does not prove that it guarantees the improvement of the organization. It clearly indicates, however, that it is at least a powerful incentive for starting up such actions. Table 22.8 shows the nature of the improvement activities and indicates the number of organizations that started this kind of activity.

Table 22.8   Nature of Improvement Activities

Improvement Activities	Number of Organizations
Input into the strategic planning process of the organization	51
A full action plan (directly linked to the results of the CAF self-assessment)	38
Implementation of surveys for the staff	32
Improvement of the process	30
Improvement of the quality of the leadership	26
Improvement of knowledge management	25
Implementation of surveys for the customers/citizens (needs and satisfaction)	22
Some individual improvement activities (but no full action plan)	19
Implementation of result measurement (targets)	18
Input into running improvement programs(s)	18
A consolidated report handed to the management (leaving the implementation to the latter)	16
Implementation of human resource management tools (please specify)	14
Improvement of technology	14
Better management of buildings and assets	6
Implementation of new financial management tools	6
Other	1

SOURCE: EIPA (2005).

The fact that the results of a self-assessment are integrated into the strategic planning process of the organization and/or that full action plans are developed shows that self-assessment is better integrated than before in the overall management of the organization.

A European Quality Dynamic

Organizations were asked whether they intended to use the CAF model again in the future. Table 22.9 shows the results.

The fact that 95% of the organizations surveyed in 2005 intended to use the CAF again is the best confirmation of the value of this tool. As the test of the pudding is by the eating, 117 of 123 organizations must have had

Table 22.9   Intention to Use CAF Again

	2005		*2003*
# Org.	%		%
118	95%	Yes	82%
6	5%	No	12%

SOURCE: EIPA (2005).

very satisfying experiences with the CAF. We also notice a remarkable increase in satisfaction compared with 2003, in which "only" 82% were ready to use it again. It is also interesting to see that this readiness is well spread over all 22 European countries that were represented, even those with only one application.

The increasing use of the CAF model is just one indication of the European quality dynamic. As we stated before, many other instruments are used all over Europe. In the end, it is not important which instrument is used; the importance is not in the instrument, but in the results. An instrument is just a tool and may never be considered as a target in itself. Therefore, it is important to share the experiences of working on quality management within a European context. An imported initiative in the sharing of experiences and ideas is the organization of European quality conferences. These conferences have resulted in a certain trend and continuity in European quality policy and dynamics.

At the initiative of European public service ministers, a European conference concerning quality in government services was organized in May 2000, in Lisbon. Within the context of this conference, held under the EU Portuguese presidency, concerning the quality of public services and with a view to learning from one another, the 15 member states of the EU presented their best administrative practices. Following the first conference in Lisbon, the second European conference concerning quality in public services was held in Copenhagen, in October 2002. The third European conference took place under the Dutch presidency of the EU in September 2004, in Rotterdam; the fourth took place in 2006, in Finland; and in 2008, France will be the host country of the fifth European quality conference.

These European conferences have inspired a number of countries to organize national conferences. For instance, Belgium organized its own quality conferences in 2001, 2003, and 2005. More than 2,300 participants attended these three conferences, the plenary sessions with international keynote speakers, info shops, and workshops on good practices. In other countries, such as the Netherlands, Italy, and Portugal, best practices are also presented in national quality conferences.

Practical Considerations and
Suggestions for Effective Implementation

Features of the CAF

The CAF as a TQM tool inspires organizations to provide better services for citizens. As society and citizens demand change, public administrations must adapt accordingly. Managing these change processes is a crucial test for any organization. Quality has to become a strategic objective of public organizations, such as large public health care organizations.

A CAF self-evaluation is a simple but very innovative process that acts as a launching pad for the process of continuous improvement. It enables organizations lacking experience in quality subjects, as well as more advanced organizations, to pursue quality at a low financial cost. It makes people aware of and interested in quality issues and places greater emphasis on quality issues and on continuous improvement. It enables public administrations to easily determine the strengths and areas of improvement of an organization and gives rise to new ideas and new ways of thinking. The organization and its staff become responsive to new ideas and initiatives. The results show that people develop their skills at the organizational, professional, and personal levels and learn new ways of performing.

The involvement of management is crucial for achieving results and is a necessary basis for the follow-up process. The CAF in a large organization takes time and requires extensive support during the process; that time and support must be made available. Consequently, the executive board must bear responsibility for the work related to that process. The commitment and openness of senior management must be clearly communicated to the organization's staff to ensure honest and useful feedback. Senior managers also have to commit themselves in advance to prioritizing and implementing the improvement actions at all levels and setting an example for employees. They should integrate quality development into day-to-day work, particularly at the managerial level. This avoids quality development being made the responsibility of a specific person or service.

The CAF focuses on measurement in order to manage the organization and improve results. What is not measured cannot be managed. In this way, the CAF encourages the use of monitoring systems (e.g., BSC) and comparison between organizations on the basis of reliable data. The model is also used in conjunction with other quality tools.

Assigning scores is not the most important part of the self-assessment process. The purpose is not to obtain maximum points at any price, but to establish operational systems of management and processes of permanent improvement in the organization's activities. Consequently, the organization must have an active approach toward the CAF and not just adopt a formal stance.

The CAF is effective when followed by improvement actions. However, it is important to avoid too many of these actions. Only systematic and targeted work on a number of well-defined actions leads to useful results. The CAF helps to align improvement projects more effectively, ensuring that no area of reform is neglected or forgotten. The target areas must be integrated into the annual strategic plans. Repeating the CAF application (e.g., every two years) also contributes to a clear ranking of the improvement actions. When actions have been taken, it is advisable to measure and evaluate the results before new actions are initiated. Evaluation may highlight the fact that current actions are not leading to the expected results and that changes must be made or the actions abandoned.

Conditions for an Effective Use of the CAF

When using CAF the first time, experienced external assistance can be helpful in order to ensure a satisfactory launch or appropriate scoring. Such assistance may create greater acceptance of the assessment and adapt the methodology neutrally to the various organizational cultures at the local or regional level. According to the experience of others, however, the added value of the CAF is due primarily to the fact that it can be introduced and applied without the assistance of external consultants or experts.

It is especially important to give full and detailed information to all employees. The staff must be convinced of the necessity of a quality management system and self-assessment as a first step. An innovative training concept for all staff must aim for a fundamental understanding of quality concepts and not a simple transfer of knowledge. This clarifies expectations and concepts, improvement priorities according to present management strategies, and the importance of clear indicators for results based on reliable measurement sources. It creates a common language and strong commitment and stimulates internal communication.

The assessment process is very important, and satisfactory preparatory training is essential. The makeup of the self-assessment groups must be considered carefully, as self-assessment is teamwork. The varied composition of the self-assessment groups provides new opportunities to involve people of different departments and different hierarchic levels. As they are confronted by all the important aspects of the organization, the groups obtain a general picture of the entire organization and a better understanding of its functioning. Although it is more difficult to reach a consensus in a large evaluation group, it guarantees more objective results and encourages greater support for the implemented changes from the employees. However, a self-evaluation including all employees makes the processing of answers and the prioritizing of key areas more complex. Depending on the culture of the organization, a self-evaluation carried out jointly by managers and employees may be beneficial.

It is important to evaluate the process of change constantly by means of staff and citizen surveys, benchmarking with other administrations, and repeatedly defining one's position using the CAF. Surveys are of value to the administration only if the same questions are repeated. This is the only way to measure whether the improvement actions taken have actually produced better results in the target groups. Simple and low-cost methods of measurement are recommended. Electronic surveys that allow comparison with other similar organizations facilitate benchmarking. Benchmarking data can be effectively used for performance improvements.

Major Obstacles

An obstacle to getting started is to convince staff and managers that it is worthwhile investing time in this type of work and that the self-evaluation is not just another report that will not result in any action. Furthermore, they must be reassured that nobody will be called into account, no retaliation will follow honestly expressed opinions, no extra work will result from the CAF, and the CAF will not be used as an instrument to cut jobs. Training and participation at self-evaluation sessions has made it possible to overcome this distrust. In the end, most staff members actively support the reform process.

The CAF requires an introduction to certain concepts of public management that are not so common in day-to-day work. The research carried out and experiences in the field showed some other major obstacles. Due to an overall lack of knowledge concerning quality management, some CAF concepts were difficult for ordinary employees to understand when the CAF was launched. Consequently, insufficient training on the part of self-assessment teams sometimes led to doubts regarding the interpretation of criteria and subcriteria. For instance, the CAF lacks a general description of the connection between objectives (formulated on the enabler's site) and results. This link has to be established during the training or the self-assessment process. For some organizations, the language of the CAF was considered to be excessively business oriented, which created obstacles and opposition. Examples were sometimes skipped for this reason.

Time was the main challenge for the assessment process. Increasing duties and many routine activities make it difficult to find time for apparently nonessential work. Moreover, this work requires a considerable investment: study groups, staff meetings, workshops, seminars, trainings, and so on. Self-assessments in decentralized public organizations incorporating central and regional administrations required extra effort, particularly where independent administrative units with different organizations had been merged into new regional administrations. In this context, the need for equal application standards was discussed.

The costs involved in a CAF application were a minor problem, but some organizations spent a great deal of money on, for instance, equipment, new computer programs, and training. The principles of scoring and, consequently, ranking were sometimes opposed. People found it difficult to give a total score to so many different achievements under each subcriterion. They did not wish to compete against one another in simultaneous self-assessments. There were discussions about the interpretation of the scoring tables. For example, the fact that the lowest score had to be introduced in the tables when no results had been measured—even though there was a clear result—presented problems. There is always a risk that the judgment will be influenced by the work context in which the members of the CAF group are placed and that indicators will be evaluated either too critically or too favorably.

Finding evidence was not always easy. Lack of autonomy in financial management made the evaluation of some criteria difficult. Administrations with no direct relationship with citizens had to dig deep to identify their relationships with citizens/customers. In most cases, however, lack of measurement in the organization was the result of insufficient information. For Criterion 8 (society results) in particular, it appeared difficult to find appropriate evidence.

Needless to say, the implementation of improvement actions was not without its obstacles. Many ideas and project proposals based on assumptions required further information and documentation. It was not always easy for the self-assessment groups to transfer their conclusions to the rest of the staff.

Resistance to change, improvement actions, and the implementation of measurements is common, and it takes a great deal of effort to persuade colleagues to change working habits. Regular information from all stakeholders regarding the change process helps. The CAF helps to integrate constant improvement projects into an overall view of the changes needed in an organization; but if this is not properly explained, existing actions can make it difficult for employees and managers to maintain an overview and to stay focused on the planned actions and processes resulting from the self-assessment. It is therefore important to combine improvement points with current planning. Persons in leading positions often consider themselves experts rather than managers and therefore resist developing management skills. Commitment from senior management, persistent long-term effort, and extensive and systematic training of managers and personnel have helped to overcome this problem.

Conclusion

On the basis of the estimates of the national CAF correspondents, it can be concluded that the use of the CAF has undeniably increased: from 500 applications in late 2003 to nearly 900 in mid-2005. This evolution has stimulated the United Kingdom, during its presidency of the EU, to insert into the Mid Term Programme of the European Public Administration Network the target of 2,000 registered CAF users by 2010.

In addition to its important use in local administration, the CAF is finding its way in the central levels of government in different sectors of activity. Of course, the model has to be adjusted to the proper context of each organization. The model suits all sizes and helps organizations with little experience in quality management to find their way into TQM and public management. There is an important shift from external toward internal reasons for using CAF: to identify strengths and areas of improvement, develop sensitivity to quality issues, and involve staff in managing the organization. Organizations choose CAF instead of other TQM tools because it is easy to use, low cost, and adopted to the public sector.

As shown in the EIPA 2005 survey, nearly 9 out of 10 users started up improvement actions as a result of the CAF, and 95% wanted to use the CAF again. The value of the CAF is clear. Using it in benchmarking/learning projects will be the great challenge for the future. All tables indicate that the differences between "old" and "new" member states are fading, and the CAF model is growing in its role to present one common language.

References

Bauer, D. (2002). Quality management in the public sector through the common assessment framework. In J. Caddy & M. Vintar (Eds.), *Building better quality administration for the public: Case studies from Central and Eastern Europe* (pp. 62–70). Bratislava, Slovakia: NISPAcee.

Beckford, J. (1998). *Quality: A critical introduction.* London: Routledge.

Bouckaert, G. (1993). *Charters as frameworks for awarding quality: The Belgian, British, and French experience.* Seminar on Concepts and Methods of Quality Awards in the Public Sector, Speyer, Germany.

Bouckaert, G., & Thijs, N. (2003). *Kwaliteit in de overheid: Een inleidend handboek voor kwaliteitsmanagement in de publieke sector o.b.v. een internationaal comparatieve studie* [Quality management in the public sector]. Gent, Belgium: Academia Press.

Doherty, L., & Horne, T. (2002). *Managing public services.* London: Routledge.

Engel, C. (2002). Common Assessment Framework: The state of affairs. *Eipascope, 1,* 35–39.

Engel, C. (2003). *Quality management tools in CEE candidate countries.* Maastricht, the Netherlands: European Institute of Public Administration.

European Institute of Public Administration. (2002a). *The Common Assessment Framework.* Maastricht, the Netherlands: Author.

European Institute of Public Administration. (2002b). *Survey regarding quality activities in the public administrations of the European Union member states.* Maastricht, the Netherlands: EIPA.

European Institute of Public Administration. (2003). *Study for the Italian Presidency on the use of the Common Assessment Framework (CAF) in European public administrations.* Maastricht, the Netherlands: Author.

European Institute of Public Administration. (2005). *Study on the use of the Common Assessment Framework in European public services.* Maastricht, the Netherlands: Author.

European Institute of Public Administration. (2006). *The Common Assessment Framework: Version 2006*. Maastricht, the Netherlands: Author.

European Union Ministers. (2002, May 27). *9th meeting of ministers responsible for public administration*, La Rioja, Spain.

Ferlie, E., Ashburne, L., Fitzferald, L., & Pettigrew, A. (1996). *The new public management in action*. Oxford, UK: Oxford University Press.

Gaster, L., & Squires, A. (2003). *Providing quality in the public sector*. Maidenhead, UK: Open University Press.

Kaplan, R., & Norton, D. (1992, January-February). The balanced scorecard: Measures that drive performance. *Harvard Business Review,* pp. 71–79.

Kaplan, R., & Norton, D. (1993, September-October). Putting the balanced scorecard to work. *Harvard Business Review,* pp. 134–142.

Kettl, D. (2000). *The global public management revolution: A report on the transformation of governance*. Washington, DC: Brookings Institution.

Kickert, W. (Ed.). (1997). *Public management and administrative reform in Western Europe*. Cheltenham, UK: E. Elgar.

Lane, J. (2000). *New public management*. London: Routledge.

Löffler, E. (2002). Defining and measuring quality in public administration. In J. Caddy & M. Vintar (Eds.), *Building better quality administration for the public* (pp. 15–37). Bratislava, Slovakia: NISPACee.

Löffler, E., & Vintar, M. (2004). The current quality agenda of East and West European public services. In E. Löffler & M. Vintar (Eds.), *Improving the quality of East and West European public services* (pp. 3–19). Hampshire, UK: Ashgate.

Oakland, J. (1995). *Total quality management. The route to improving performance*. Oxford, UK: Butterworth Heinemann.

Organisation for Economic Co-operation and Development. (1993). *Public management developments, survey 1993*. Paris: Author.

Organisation for Economic Co-operation and Development. (1995). *Governance in transition. Public management reforms in OECD countries*. Paris: Author.

Organisation for Economic Co-operation and Development. (1997). *In search of results: Performance management practices*. Paris: Author.

Organisation for Economic Co-operation and Development. (2000). *Government of the future*. Paris: Author.

Ovreveit, J. (2005). Public service quality improvement. In L. Lynn & C. Pollitt (Eds.), *The Oxford handbook of public management* (pp. 537–562). Oxford, UK: Oxford University Press.

Parasuraman, A., Berry, L., & Zeithaml, V. (1985, Fall). a conceptual model of service quality and its implications for future research. *Journal of Marketing, 49,* 41–50.

Parasuraman, A., Zeithaml, V., & Berry, L. (1988). Servqual: A multiple-item scale for measuring consumer perceptions of service quality. *Journal of Retailing, 64,* 12–40.

Pollitt, C. (1990). Doing business in the temple? Managers and quality assurance in the public sector. *Public Administration, 2,* 435–452.

Pollitt, C., & Bouckaert, G. (Eds.). (1995). *Quality improvement in European public services: Concepts, cases, and commentary*. London: Sage.

Pollitt, C., & Bouckaert, G. (2004). *Public management reform*. London: Oxford University Press.

Public Futures. (1998). *Guide to the public service excellence model: Assessment process and criteria*. London: Public Futures.

Schick, A. (2000). Opportunity, strategy and tactics in reforming public management. In *OECD, government of the future* (pp. 123–148). Paris: Organisation for Economic Co-operation and Development.

Shand, D. (1999). Service quality in the public sector: The international experience. In C. Clark & D. Corbett (Eds.), *Reforming the public sector* (pp. 151–164). St. Leonards, Australia: Allen & Unwin.

Staes, P. (2002). Het Common Assessment Framework CAF, een eerste product van een Europese aanpak van kwaliteit in overheidsdiensten [The common assessment framework, a first product of joint European public sector quality management]. *Vlaams Tijdschrift voor Overheidsmanagement* [Flemish Journal for Public Sector Management], *2*, 4–15.

Staes, P., & Thijs, N. (2005). Quality management on the European Agenda. *Eipascope, 1*, 33–41.

Stromsnes, D. (2002). Applying quality to public administration in practice: Presentation of the Common Assessment Framework. In J. Caddy & M. Vintar (Eds.), *Building better quality administration for the public* (pp. 53–61). Bratislava, Slovakia: NISPACee.

Thijs, N. (2004). Het managen van kwaliteit in de publieke sector [Public sector quality management]. *Burger, Bestuur en Beleid, Tijdschrift voor Bestuurskunde en Bestuursrecht* [Journal for Public Administration and Administrative Law], *1*, 40–50.

Thijs, N., & Staes, P. (2005). The Common Assessment Framework in European public administrations: A state of affairs after five years. *Eipascope, 3*, 41–49.

Van de Walle, S., Thijs, N., & Bouckaert, G. (2005). A tale of two charters: Political crisis, political realignment, and administrative reform in Belgium. *Public Management Review, 3*, 368–390.

Van Dooren, W., Thijs, N., & Bouckaert, G. (2004). Quality management and management of quality in the European public administrations. In E. Löffler & M. Vintar (Eds.), *Improving the quality of East and West European public services* (pp. 91–106). Hampshire, UK: Ashgate.

Zeithaml, V., Parasuraman, A., & Berry, L. (1990). *Delivering quality service. Balancing customer perceptions and expectations.* New York: Free Press.

PART VI

PULLING IT
ALL TOGETHER

23

Creating and Sustaining a Results-Oriented Performance Management Framework

John M. Kamensky

Jay Fountain

The preceding chapters provide a good grounding in the practices of performance management used in many countries and at many governmental levels within these countries: program, agency, city, state, nation, and nonprofits. The chapters also provide useful "how-to" suggestions, such as how to format performance information to be easily understood when reporting to the public and how to ensure the quality and credibility of the information. Chapter 3, by Hughes, sets the context for this chapter, which attempts to "pull it all together." He notes that there is a profound difference between administration and management: "An administrator serves, obeys, and follows instructions; a manager takes charge and gets results." That succinctly frames the shift in public agencies in recent years. Nonetheless, public managers always want the bottom line regarding performance. They seem to consistently ask two things:

First: *"Now what?!"* After reading a practice-based book like this, managers typically want a list of action-oriented practices, not a statement that "more research is needed." They want to put these lessons to work. Examples of these include the chapters by Ammons (8), Choi (10), and Moravitz (18), which provide practical steps for analyzing performance data, involving citizens in government, and developing performance budgets.

Second: *"What's next?"* Because things never stay the same, it is important to public managers to have some sense of what is going to happen next. While predicting can be slippery, it is important for public managers to stay one step ahead on the learning curve. Examples of this predictive approach include the chapters by Hatry (1) and Newcomer (2), which highlight the importance of designing performance systems that have legitimacy with stakeholders, improve ways to use performance information, and integrate the use of nonprofits into governmental performance management systems.

Collectively, the authors in this book address these two important questions: "Now what?" and "What's next?" Each author, however, approaches these questions from a particular perspective. At the 2005 International Symposium on Practice-Based Performance Management, speaker Geert Bouckaert observed that there are three distinct perspectives from which performance can be viewed, depending on where a public manager sits in his or her job:

The "Micro" perspective, which is commonly seen as the direct service delivery component. This can be individual programs or agencies, or small to midsize cities. Typically, these units are relatively cohesive and can operate with a unified structure and within a hierarchy. They can be either public sector or nonprofit organizations. An example would be King County, in Washington State, as described in Chapter 7, by Broom and Jennings.

The "Meso" perspective, which is typically seen as a policy arena, such as education or health care. It can also be a large city, small to midsize state, or large agency, such as the U.S. Department of Homeland Security. Typically, these comprise a set of semiautonomous activities, often involving a federated governance structure made up of individuals with a common professional background. These commonly rely on the use of networks to deliver services. An example would be the Illinois statewide school performance improvement effort described in Chapter 11, by Ryan.

The "Macro" perspective, which is commonly seen as an entire country or a very large state or agency, or a broad system of services. Typically, these federated governance approaches are made up of individuals without a common professional background, strong and multiple stakeholders, and largely autonomous operating units. These commonly rely on the use of marketlike devices to address their missions. Examples include the Italian economic development program described in Chapter 5, by Brezzi, Raimondo, and Utili, and the New Zealand and Australian budgeting systems, described in Chapter 17, by Halligan.

Each of these perspectives (and combinations or variations of them) implies that public managers would need to strategically use different approaches when designing and using performance management frameworks to fit their particular operating environment. While the various authors in this volume address many of these different approaches, we hope to put the authors' collective insights into a broader context that can help public managers define a course of action that best fits their specific operating environments.

Now What? Choosing the Best Implementation Approach for Your Performance Management Framework

Strategically, there are different implementation approaches to constructing a performance management framework. For example, to effectively transform an individual agency that has a common set of objectives (such as an environmental or economic development agency) requires strong leadership at both the top and bottom of the organization and the application of a set of tools and techniques. Conversely, to effectively transform a system of federated organizations (e.g., across the federal or a state government) requires changes to the "rules of the game" and the use of market-based incentives and consequences. We will address the continuum from micro- to meso- to macrolevels.

A "Micro" Approach to a Performance Management Framework

Performance management frameworks are the most mature at the microlevels. This is where services are delivered directly to citizens by individual agencies or small to midsize cities. They are typically characterized as having a unified command through the use of hierarchy. These types of performance management frameworks are used by both government and nonprofit organizations.

The best way to describe the components of such a framework is to start by describing what the end result will look like once it is in place.

A Service Delivery Agency View of Performance Management in Action

To bring together the fundamentals of a performance management framework, as discussed earlier, we take a look at the effects such a framework would have on an agency's day-to-day behavior in the future (or even now) if it has created its own performance management framework and is fully applying a performance-based management approach.

The Leadership Meeting. At the regular monthly agency meeting that includes several levels of management and supervision, the main topics of discussion focus on the areas of performance of the agency's various programs. The agency head is familiar with the key performance measures for each program and has something to say about how well they are performing in achieving their targets and against comparable benchmarks. Each person responsible for a program is asked to provide a brief update on the program's performance, including resources used, services provided, contacts with customers and citizens, the efficiency of the services, the initial and intermediate outcomes that show whether the program is moving toward achieving its goals, and how they are contributing to the accomplishment of the agency's mission. These persons are also asked to discuss any external factors that might be influencing the results they are trying to achieve and what might be done to affect those factors (see Chapter 1 by Hatry; and Chapter 7 by Broom & Jennings).

Committed Program Managers. Program managers are very knowledgeable of the roles their programs play in the agency and how this contributes to the achievement of the agency's mission, both separately and in coordination with other services being provided by their agency and other organizations. They are also knowledgeable of how the major activities being performed by program personnel contribute to the provision of services (either directly or indirectly; Broom & Jennings). In addition, they are aware of the contributions of other services provided by other agencies and organizations to the results those other services are trying to achieve.

Problem-Solving Sessions. Program directors and their personnel often come forward with ideas about how to modify activities or strategies to improve results. They even have information with which to support their suggestions of modifications. Several programs have recently developed new tools for ascertaining the degree to which their strategies are providing services that actually influence the desired outcomes and for assessing the needs of those to whom they are providing services (Newcomer). They understand that the measures they are using do not perfectly represent the results they are trying to achieve and are constantly working to develop supplementary measures that capture aspects of the desired results (Hatry; Broom & Jennings; Ryan).

Results Orientation. Program directors or managers are also aware of the level of need within the community for a particular service, how much it would cost to provide that service at various levels, and information about the effectiveness of those various levels of service provision. Several programs are also working to link their results to broader community indicators, and a discussion of their work is of great interest to other program directors who see the value of being able to show how their programs are contributing to things the community has indicated they value (Hatry).

Link to Resources. Because budget requests are due in late spring, the discussion also turns to the development of budget requests. There, a discussion must take place of the preliminary requests that agency programs are working to submit. These budget requests are directly related to the goals and objectives relevant to their services and include strategies for providing desired services, units of output to be provided, and support for value of these programs and the cost required to carry out those strategies. Program directors regularly discuss their budget requests with other program managers, and, working together, they develop a list of priories for the various strategies being set forth for the entire agency. A strategy might even be prioritized at several different service levels. They recognize that if strategies are not funded, the level of work they are expected to accomplish will be reduced accordingly and performance targets for results will be adjusted to reflect the decrease.

Grantor Expectations. One program has just been awarded a major grant from the private sector. The program's director or manager discusses with the group the results that the grantor expects and how he or she intends to measure what the program plans to achieve and how that links to the grantor's expectations (Newcomer).

Citizen Feedback. The program directors or managers have been hearing from customers and citizens. The agency has several groups of citizens that it regularly draws upon for feedback and opinions and has institutionalized ways of obtaining feedback from customers, both current customers and those to whom they have provided services in the past. They discuss how well their performance information has been communicated to citizens, senior management, and elected officials and the responses being received.

One of the agency's services has recently completed a survey of citizens and customers; the findings of that survey indicate several areas where citizens are not aware of the effects of the service. Results from the "311" telephone or Internet-based citizen request and question system are also analyzed to determine the degree to which requests are being processed in a timely manner and how callers feel about the handling of their requests.

Evaluation of a Nonachieving Program. During the agency meeting, one area of major concern is identified, and it is decided that a comprehensive program evaluation is warranted to help identify why the program continues to not achieve desired results and what can be done to improve its outcomes.

The agency head then mentions that the program planning group from the agency is expected to come forward with its recommendation for issues for consideration at a government-wide strategic planning session in 3 weeks. A discussion is held to determine who should represent the agency at this meeting and what should be the primary issues brought forward (Hatry; Broom & Jennings).

Frontline Involvement. At another point in the meeting, a program director discusses how the process is proceeding on a program that has only recently begun the process of fully implementing results-based management. The program has received assistance from other programs, including the use of their personnel for training and to work with staff and frontline employees to identify the activities they engage in and the services those activities produce (Broom & Jennings). The frontline employees have just begun to identify how those services contribute to the achievement of certain objectives and how to measure the degree of progress being made. Because of the widespread use of performance information within the agency, there has been little negative reaction to this move and many employees have actually asked why they have not had this type of information available to them sooner, so they could see how well their programs are performing and start work on improving their results.

Using Comparative Measures. Another discussion later in the meeting focuses on the results of a comparison of one program's efficiency and effectiveness with that of a similar program in a different entity within the region. Questions arise about how comparable the programs are and whether the populations served are different. The program director notes that a significant difference in the strategies being used has been identified and that further evaluation is under way to see whether that could be the reason for the variation in results. The program director notes that while the program is performing at a lower level than the other entity, it has been showing improvement consistently over time and has been meeting its established targets. The program director says that while that is a good indication, it still isn't enough and that they will try to have a report at the next monthly meeting about what can be done to improve the program's results (Hatry).

Quality Reporting. The agency issues a report on its performance annually. This report is discussed with senior management, elected officials, the media, customers, and the public. Recently, focus groups were held with customers and the public to determine whether they were satisfied with the measures being reported, the reporting format, and the way the report was made available and whether the report was sufficiently layered for a reader to begin with a simple overview and then dig deeper if more information was wanted. The person in charge of the focus group provides the team with the results of those sessions and what could be changed in their report to better communicate with customers and citizens. The agency report was also submitted for review by a national organization that gives an award for high-quality reporting. The results of that review were just received, and although the report was highly rated, it lacked several types of information important for effective communication. Specifically, the report did not include information about customer and citizen perspectives on the results of the agency's key services. The program directors discuss how to go about obtaining this information and how it can be of value to them in managing those programs.

Sustained Commitment. The agency director closes with a request that the programs keep working to improve the timeliness of the performance information they are providing and that they maintain their monthly meeting schedule, with results reported at each meeting (Hatry). The director notes that they are now in their fourth year of developing a performance management system and that significant progress has been made but that they still have quite a ways to go before they are making full use of this approach (Hatry). One item that has not been fully implemented is the use of "logic models," and program managers are asked to be prepared to discuss their use at the next month's meeting (Hatry; Newcomer).

This scenario may seem idealistic, but there are a number of steps that can be taken by managers to make it real. Figure 23.1 summarizes the steps that could be taken to do so.

A "Meso" Approach to a Performance Management Framework

The mesolevel dimension of performance management reaches across policy areas, large cities, small to midsize states, and large agencies. These tend to be federated, semiautonomous activities, often managed via formal or informal networks. Van Dooren, in Chapter 20 of this book, observes that the performance management frameworks for results-oriented networks tend to focus on governance and results and not so much on the organizations within the networks. They also focus more on common outcomes and results and not so much on accountability and efficiency. In addition, they tend to focus more on shared responsibility and trust than in typical microlevel performance management systems, which try to pinpoint both responsibility and accountability.

Milward and Proven (2006) describe four different uses for mesolevel performance management networks—service implementation, information diffusion, problem solving, and community capacity building—and describe the kinds of management functions network leaders need to use to be successful in the management *of* networks as well as managing *in* a network. For example, managing the accountability of a network would include determining who is responsible for which outcomes, but accountability for those managing in a network would be monitoring one's own agency's involvement. Understanding the kinds of networks and the roles of leaders in those networks is an essential prerequisite to developing a performance management system.

In a series of case studies by Imperial (2004) of how different stakeholders collaborate to improve water quality in a watershed, he notes that the

Getting Started:

1. *Involve* agency personnel, citizens, and customers in developing strategic plans, performance measures (especially those to be reported), and program plans.

2. Have agency people *begin with activities* they actually do and then work up to outputs, outcomes, and objectives and goals.

3. Take a long view and apply a *consistent process* to the development of a managing-for-results system.

Developing Performance Measures and a Managing-for-Results System:

4. Select output, outcome, and efficiency measures that are relevant measures of the results you are trying to achieve.

5. Get to know what *drives the results* (outcomes) you are trying to achieve.

6. Know the level of *outputs necessary to achieve the desired results* and support why that is the case.

7. *Understand the factors (other than the service itself) that might have a possible effect* on desired results.

8. Link performance to the *budget* and the outputs related to strategies and prioritize strategies.

9. Gain an understanding of what *level of resources* is needed to provide a given level of outputs and how that level of outputs will affect desired results.

10. Carefully establish *data-gathering systems* and test their reliability.

11. *Develop comparisons and understand how to use them:* over time, against targets, internal divisions, against others, and against standards or benchmarks.

Beginning to Use Performance Measures in Managing for Results:

12. Use performance measures to *monitor results* on a continuing basis.

13. Remember you need to consider *initial, intermediate, and long-term outcome measures* in managing for results.

14. Set *targets* that are reasonable but still require effective performance.

15. Hold agency personnel blameless for not performing up to expectations—at least the first time around.

Assessing Results and Making Changes:

16. Understand *what to do when results aren't what you wanted.*

17. Use *program evaluations* and performance audits to help identify ways to improve results.

18. Regularly *communicate and have discussions* that focus on results—at all levels, including elected officials and the public.

19. Gather information about *citizen and customer perspectives* on desired results.

20. Use performance measures for *employee evaluation* and changes in compensation.

Figure 23.1   Checklist of "Things to Do" When Developing a Microlevel Performance Management Framework

on-the-ground focus among diverse actors tends to focus on service delivery and a series of trial-and-error processes. The common language, however, is a performance management system that generates information allowing the stakeholders to hold each other mutually accountable for performance. This same insight surfaces in three of the chapters in this book: Ryan's Chapter 11, on school performance improvement; Brezzi et al.'s, Chapter 5, on Italian economic development efforts; and Broom and Jennings's Chapter 7, on the use of collaborative approaches in King County, Washington, to develop performance information for accountability.

These approaches are increasingly being used in the nonprofit sector as well, as Newcomer notes in Chapter 2. For example, the Community Indicators Consortium (2006) has highlighted a series of cases in which regional nonprofit organizations are serving as the integrators of performance information for their communities and leveraging increased performance:

- In Reno, Nevada, "Truckee Meadows Tomorrow" is a nonprofit created in 1993 out of the ruins of a failed regional planning effort. It develops a biennial community well-being report that helps identify and guide solutions to the region's social, economic, and environmental problems. This nonprofit group engaged 4,000 citizens in developing 6 goals and 30 indicators to measure progress toward those goals. The group encourages citizens and businesses to join an "adopt-an-indicator" program. The adopter pledges to help improve the performance of that one indicator. While the adopter is not responsible for moving the indicator, he or she is responsible for tracking, developing a strategy, identifying the key players, and serving as a convener among stakeholders, when possible. Karen Hruby, the group's executive director, says, "We're all about change." She says this comprehensive, participatory program uses recognition and awards, not rules and regulations, to get change to happen (see http://www.truckeemeadowstomorrow.org).

- For more than a dozen years, Charlotte-Mecklenburg County, North Carolina, has sponsored a neighborhood quality-of-life initiative across its 173 neighborhood areas. Every 2 years, the city, county, and school system examine 20 local variables that address social, crime, physical, and economic conditions in the city and rank the neighborhoods as "stable," "transitioning," or "challenged." Variables include the percentage of substandard housing, the percentage of persons receiving food stamps, high school dropout rates, and the juvenile arrest rate. With these rankings in hand, the city's "neighborhood council" of key city officials comes up with comprehensive strategies targeted to each neighborhood, focusing especially on those rated as challenged. This council works with neighborhood-level revitalization teams made up of government, nonprofit, and citizen members (see http://www.charmeck.org/Departments/Neighborhood+Dev/Quality+of+Life/home.htm).

As mesolevel networks such as these develop and improve their performance via trial and error and by learning from each other, the mesolevel approach may become increasingly dominant as a favored strategy for improving performance. At this point, though, mesolevel approaches, tools, and techniques tend to lag in maturity behind those available at the microlevel. As noted in the next section, the same is true for macrolevel approaches, tools, and techniques, especially in the United States.

A "Macro" Approach to a Performance Management Framework

The macrolevel approach to a performance management framework reaches across entire nations, large states, and major systems, such as the U.S. federal system of national, state, and local governments. It is characterized by strong, multiple stakeholders who are arrayed in a web of federated, largely autonomous entities. The most typical policy lever in this environment is the use of market-type mechanisms for sharing information, sharing resources, and setting priorities.

The macrolevel, or systemwide, approach to performance management can be seen in several chapters in this volume. The examples of the Canadian results-oriented framework, as described by Leighton, in Chapter 6, and the New Zealand and Australian budget systems, as described by Halligan, in Chapter 17, describe the potential power of these macrolevel approaches for influencing performance results.

This approach, while far-reaching, tends to be the least mature of the performance management framework strategies, and the lessons of the unintended consequences are described by Wellman and VanLandingham, in Chapter 16, as to how the Florida performance budgeting system did not consistently deliver what its designers had intended. Their description of how the designers intended one thing (the intent of the system to improve legislative budget decision making) and the reality (lack of use by legislators but a strong use by agency administrators) show that there is much still to be learned about what works, and how. However, even with the disconnect in expectations between intended results and actual performance, Wellman and VanLandingham note that the expectations that were met have "had a positive effect on legislative oversight and the delivery of government services."

In addition to the tool of performance budgeting, a number of countries have put in place a comprehensive set of social, economic, and environmental indicators of progress. An example is the German system of social indicators (German Social Science Indicators Service, 2005). The United States is lagging behind a number of other countries in developing a comprehensive performance management framework at the national level; however, an ongoing effort by the U.S. National Academies of Science to create key national indicators may provide a future framework to fill this void (Hillsman, 2006; U.S. Government Accountability Office [GAO], 2003).

Newcomer, in Chapter 2, provides excellent insights on the strategies for a national approach (both governmental and nonprofit) for linking the effects of government services and citizen trust. She observes that the expanded use of new tools by nonprofits—less expensive computing, the expanded use of citizen surveys, the use of logic models, and the ability to target subgroups—is making it increasingly possible to shift the use of performance information from accountability to actual improvements in services and results.

Newcomer's observations of nonprofits seem to parallel similar trends in the public sector. A recent study by Perrin (2006) examined the strategies used by a dozen governments across the globe—six were developed countries, and six were developing countries—in moving from an output-oriented approach to an outcome-oriented approach. While Perrin finds there is no one "correct" or best model, he concludes that "there are many common principles and lessons" (p. 3) that reach across boundaries, including the following:

- Linking outcomes to strategy
- Facilitating the implementation of an outcome focus
- Monitoring and evaluating performance
- Reporting on outcomes and building credibility
- Using outcome information

In the United States, the federal government has been "changing the rules of the game" across a range of dimensions required for an effective performance management system. In the past 15 years, the government has enacted a law, the Government Performance and Results Act of 1993, requiring agencies to develop multiyear strategic plans, annual operating plans, and measures of performance and to annually report progress against promises. In recent years, the federal government has gone further by administratively requiring each major program to be rated as to whether it is "effective" or "ineffective." In recent years, the government has also required agencies to include performance information in their budget requests and has enacted laws requiring personnel performance ratings to be linked more directly to the overall performance of their agencies.

As described by Melkers and Willoughby (2004), individual states have also been developing performance budgeting and measurement approaches and in a number of cases (most noticeably Iowa; Washington State; Washington, D.C.; Texas; and Florida) are further advanced in some respects than the federal government. The bottom line, though, is that at all levels and across the globe, governments are building and using macrolevel performance frameworks.

What's Next? Evolving Issues for Sustaining the Use of Performance Management Frameworks

Typically, the creation and use of a performance management framework has tended to be leader centric. The challenge is creating a framework that becomes part of the operating culture so it does not fall into disuse once a leader leaves an organization.

Sustaining a performance management framework is a challenging task. Managers have to measure performance in an increasingly volatile environment, and sustaining a framework at the micro-, meso-, and macrolevels will depend on how well leaders can address issues that are evolving with the maturing of the performance movement worldwide. These issues cut across the micro-, meso-, and macrolevels. Examples are discussed below.

Achieving an appropriate balance between the uses of performance information by managers for improving performance versus creating accountability. A study by Shelley Metzenbaum (2006) examines these tensions and concludes that these tensions have to be managed carefully and thoughtfully. If uses tilt too far toward accountability, "They can provoke self-protective responses that interfere with performance and accountability gains" (Metzenbaum, 2006, p. 6), especially if they are too tightly linked to punitive actions, such as budgets and pay.

Establishing the role of causality between agency performance and programmatic results. While many organizations are beginning to use logic models to link programs, defining the impact of programs on results versus the impact of the external environment becomes significant when there are accountability consequences associated, such as performance budgeting. A study by Gilmour (2006) of the U.S. Office of Management and Budget's Program Assessment Review Tool concludes,

> This is an imperfect process and it is possible that the program will be credited with successes it did not cause or blamed for failures it could not prevent. Still, the use of end outcome measures keeps attention focused on the purposes the program was created to serve. (p. 26)

Expanding the use of collaborative networks as a tool for achieving performance and results across organizational boundaries. Networks can be an effective management approach but carry a set of potential vulnerabilities to long-term sustainability. Managers of networks will face challenges regarding accountability and resources. As Imperial (2004) describes, in the case of the management of watersheds, a performance management framework can be the glue to hold the network together. However, the longer-term sustainability of a network depends on its purpose and how it is managed. Milward and Provan (2006) suggest that there are distinct types of networks, based on their purpose, and that there is also a clear set of tasks managers can use to manage these different types of networks. So, while challenges of using networks are growing, practitioners are beginning to find their own solutions and putting them into practice.

Engaging citizens in new roles to solve public problems. As government becomes more complex, especially with the growth of networks and the increasing complexity of public problems, such as improving the health care system, citizens increasingly feel disengaged. With disengagement comes distrust and an unwillingness to rely on government to solve public problems. In addition, the growing lack of political consensus contributes to the inability of traditional political parties to come to agreement on solutions. In this environment, citizens are beginning to self-organize outside the political system and are seeking a voice. The growth of the Internet feeds this trend toward citizen engagement. Government has largely not yet responded, according to Scott (2006). Lukensmeyer and Hasselblad Torres (2006) describe a spectrum of tools that managers are beginning to use, ranging from the traditional, face-to-face public hearings to more interactive, online efforts, such as wikis and blogs. In these instances, communication is two-way, and both parties learn from each other and modify expectations. While these approaches are relatively limited, it seems clear that when citizens are engaged, there is a greater degree of public trust in, and consent to, governmental actions (Bingman, Nabatchi, & O'Leary, 2005).

Each of these trends is occurring at the micro-, meso-, and macrolevels, with different implications. However, there are distinct sets of issues that are occurring in each, as well.

Issues From a "Micro" Perspective

Managers at the microlevel are on the front line of the development, use, reporting, and continued use of performance management systems. In many cases, professional associations provide technical support in these areas. For example, both the Canadian Institute of Chartered Accountants (CICA) Public Sector Accounting Committee and the Governmental Accounting Standards Board (GASB) in the United States have recognized the importance of managing for results in the public sector. GASB has issued a series of research reports on "Service Efforts and Accomplishments Reporting," and, in 2003, it issued a special report, "Reporting Performance Information: Suggested Criteria for Effective Communication" (Fountain, Campbell, Patton, Epstein, & Cohn, 2003). This report recognized the importance of performance-based management in the public sector and included a chapter on managing for results, stating that the reporting of performance information should be the product of a complete system of using performance information for planning, budgeting, and managing. CICA has issued a

"Statement of Recommended Practice" on performance reporting, to provide consistent guidance for the reporting of performance information by governmental units in Canada.

Relatedly, the National Conference of State Legislatures (NCSL) in the United States, in a joint project with The Urban Institute, has issued a set of action briefs and a brochure, "Asking Key Questions: How to Review Program Results" (see http://www.ncsl.org/programs/fiscal/14raskkey.htm for more information), designed to assist legislators in obtaining and using performance information for (a) identifying the extent to which programs are getting results; (b) providing a basis for questioning executive branch managers about programs, especially those that appear to be low achievers; (c) helping legislative staff strengthen their examinations of programs in order to improve advice to legislators and legislative committees; and (d) providing executive branch programs with encouragement and guidance for improving programs and their outcome measurement processes.

These and other efforts to encourage the use and reporting of performance information are helping to increase the awareness and value of performance measurement and its importance, both internally within an organization and in meeting the public sector obligation to be accountable to the public.

In addition to professional associations, there are a series of frameworks developed to allow microlevel organizations to conduct self- or third-party assessments of their performance management approaches. A series of these frameworks is presented in Chapter 22, by Thijs and Staes. They discuss the application of total quality management (TQM), the balanced scorecard (BSC), the European Foundation for Quality Management framework (EFQM), the Common Assessment Framework (CAF), and the public service excellence model (PSEM). They note that what seemed to be lacking in TQM for the public sector was an easy-to-use and free entry tool for self-assessment, to help public administrators employ modern management techniques. The CAF was developed to address this need and provides a representation of all aspects of management, which are translated into nine criteria covering what the organization does (called "enablers") and what the organization achieves (called "results"). Thijs and Staes go on to explain how the CAF model can be applied in the public sector as a self-assessment tool and note that CAF has been applied by over 500 organizations in 19 countries in Europe. The top reasons given for using CAF are to identify strengths and areas for improvement and to develop sensitivity to quality issues. The top benefits identified were the need to share information and improve communication and a clear identification of strengths and areas for improvement.

The role of customer-centered quality services is also a major theme in microlevel performance management frameworks. Van Dooren, in Chapter 20, focuses on quality management, noting that it focuses on customers rather than profits and that qualitative products and services are the ultimate aim of quality management. He discusses performance measurement and notes that the quality management movement and performance measurement movement developed largely independent of each other and therefore have somewhat different focuses. He notes that quality models are becoming more outcome oriented, taking in some aspects of performance measurement models, yet that adherents of both movements still have an insufficient acknowledgment of the network environment in which governments operate. Van Dooren observes that the adherents of both movements better recognize that clients and citizens can no longer be seen as passive recipients of government policy or services. Clients and citizens are now recognized as active agents working with government and nongovernment agencies in generating outcomes.

Similarly, Sterck and Bouckaert, in Chapter 21, focus on the importance of quality information and the problems of obtaining quality information, such as the use of external data sources and the lack of unit cost information. They comment on the difficulty in finding out whether and to what degree outputs of a government service lead to the desired outcomes in society. This is an issue that perplexes many government service providers and is greatly affected by the external factors that influence the realization of results. Sterck and Bouckaert note that in many cases, we are not able to clearly identify the casual relationship between inputs, activities, outputs, and outcomes. They go on to discuss how to control the quality of performance information and list six steps in the control of data quality: (1) develop quality standards, (2) provide staff training, (3) analyze risks, (4) monitor data quality, (5) report on data quality, and (6) address problems in data quality. They discuss the aspect of auditing performance information and note that this type of auditing is not as developed as the auditing of financial information. This type of auditing encompasses not only the verification of the accuracy of the data but also other characteristics of quality, such as the relevance of the information in measuring desired results.

Issues From a "Meso" Perspective

While today's government managers are building performance management systems for their organizations, there is a parallel movement to build performance indicators systems for policy areas, such as Healthy People 2010, and for geographic areas, such as the examples noted earlier in Reno, Vermont, and St. Louis.

Increasingly, community-level performance indicators are being developed and reported by independent, third-party providers, such as nonprofits or government audit agencies. Ted Greenwood, of the Alfred P. Sloan Foundation, is an advocate of this trend (see http://www.sloan.org/programs/stndrd_performance.shtml). He says the strength of this approach is that it focuses on things people care about. The weakness is that often there is no link to actions that can make a difference: When government measures its performance, it tends to select things to measure that are actionable, but not necessarily things people care about. Greenwood sees a hybrid approach as the best of both worlds—but we're not there yet. One of the leaders in this arena is the United Way at the local level, which assists their grantees in developing indicators of their effectiveness. In some areas, this has contributed to community-wide indicator systems.

Issues from a "Macro" Perspective

The United States lags behind many other advanced countries in developing a national performance measurement system, and a number of observers conclude that the U.S. federal government also needs to have a more strategic, crosscutting focus on policy and budget decisions to address goals that span conventional agency and program boundaries.

The GAO has been issuing reports on the urgency of the need for U.S. political leaders to take action. The head of the GAO, Comptroller General David Walker, says, "The federal government must address and adapt to a range of major trends and challenges in the nation and the world" (GAO, 2005d, p. 64). This would include a long-term, structural fiscal imbalance; a transformation from an industrial-based to a knowledge-based economy; revolutionary changes in technology that have altered how we communicate and do business globally; and changing national security threats. Walker says, "To respond to these trends and challenges, government must have the institutional capacity to plan more strategically, identify and react more expediently, and focus on achieving results" (GAO, 2005d, p. 64). Kettl (2005) raises a similar concern:

The current conduct of American government is a poor match for the problems it must solve. If government is to serve the needs of its citizens in the 21st century, it must reconfigure itself—to shift the boundaries of who does what and, even more important, how its work gets done. (p. 4)

The outlines for addressing these challenges are beginning to emerge via three "macro" trends: the development of a national indicator system, the use of cross-boundary solutions, and the increased role of citizens in government.

Key National Indicators. The first "macro" trend is the development of a national-level set of societal indicators of progress. Comptroller of the United States General Walker, says,

The government is partnering with the private sector to devise a comprehensive set of key national indicators to provide the nation with quality data that the public, media, policymakers, and both government and non-government institutions can use to assess the nation's progress in addressing key challenges. (GAO, 2005d, p. 64)

Doing this may not directly spark political solutions to long-standing intractable policy challenges, such as health care reform. But over the long run, it has the potential to better inform the public and create a greater chance that grassroots demands for improved performance will evolve.

Cross-Boundary Solutions. A second "macro" trend is the increased use of cross-boundary solutions that go beyond existing performance management tools. In the U.S. federal government, many of the performance management elements are agency or program specific, such as the Government Performance and Results Act of 1993 and the Program Assessment Rating Tool. They reinforce separate behaviors, not collaborative behaviors. However, there are increasing efforts to create boundary-spanning solutions. For example, the U.S. State Department and the U.S. Agency for International Development have developed a joint strategic plan, and programmatic areas, such as agencies engaged in fighting wildfires, are working collaboratively. In the area of homeland security, the president has mandated collaborative approaches, such as the Incident Command System (Moynihan, 2006).

While there are few U.S. federal examples, there are a number of examples evolving at the state and local levels. Examples include Iowa's "purchasing results" approach, whereby the governor's office defines selected outcomes and agencies "bid" to deliver that outcome, oftentimes in a joint bid with other agencies. Variations of this approach are being used in Washington State, South Carolina, Michigan, and Oregon. At the city level, the use of CitiStat is spreading beyond Baltimore (Henderson, 2003), as is the use of balanced scorecards in places such as Charlotte, North Carolina.

Increased Citizen Role. A third "macro" trend is the increased role of citizens in defining and creating pressure for improved government performance. This is becoming a significant driver for cross-boundary action by government agencies, especially since citizens generally care more about services and results and less about how government organizes to deliver them.

One example is the involvement of citizens in the budget decision-making and performance assessment process at the local level in a series of Iowa cities. While seen as novel in the United States, according to Allegretti and Herzberg (2004), it is increasingly common practice in Europe. Another is the increasing growth and use of nonprofit, locally based groups that assess performance of government and communities from the citizen's perspective. These efforts are creating context, transparency, legitimacy, and grassroots pressure for governmental responsiveness (Community Indicators Consortium, 2006). In fact, Lukensmeyer (2006) notes that while the United States is seen as the leader in the development of tools and techniques for greater citizen engagement in government, other countries are making greater investments in institutionalizing citizen engagement as the way their governments "do business." For example, the European Union is investing about €100 million in experimentation, and the Canadian federal government spends about $1 billion a year on citizen engagement efforts.

Conclusion _____

The chapters in this book confirm that healthy innovations in performance management continue to evolve worldwide and they are serving as a fact-based springboard for public managers. For example, Moynihan (2006), in his survey of U.S. state government efforts to apply managing-for-results techniques, notes that states emphasize the development of strategic planning and performance measurement elements, while other governments emphasize shifts in managerial authority. As a result, in coming years, we can continue to expect innovations that will further the development of "hard" and "soft" systems of managing for results with strategic and program plans, performance budgets, the use of performance information for management of operations, the assessment of results, and effective communication of results to those to whom government is accountable.

References and Further Readings _____

Allegretti, G., & Herzberg, C. (2004). Participatory budgeting in Europe: Between efficiency and growing local democracy. *New Politics Project, 5*. Amsterdam: Transnational Institute and the Centre for Democratic Policy-Making. Available at http://www.nuovomunicipio.org/documenti/allegrettiherzberg.pdf

Bingman, L., Nabatchi, T., & O'Leary, R. (2005). The new governance: Practices and processes for stakeholder and citizen participation in the work of government. *Public Administration Review, 65,* 547–558.

Blanchard, L. (2006). *Performance budgeting: How NASA and SBA link costs and performance.* Washington, DC: IBM Center for the Business of Government.

Bouckaert, G. (2005). *Quality and performance measurement in a volatile environment.* Presentation notes at the 2005 International Symposium on Practice-Based Performance Management, Milwaukee, WI.

Community Indicators Consortium. (2006). Available at http://www.community indicators.net

Fountain, J., Campbell, W., Patton T., Epstein, P., & Cohn, M. (2003). *Reporting performance information: Suggested criteria for effective communication* (Special report). Norwalk, CT: Governmental Accounting Standards Board.

German Social Science Indicators Service. (2005). *The German system of social indicators.* Retrieved April 6, 2007, from http://www.gesis.org/en/social_monitoring/social_indicators/Data/System/index.htm

Gilmour, J. (2006). *Implementing OMB's Program Assessment Rating Tool: Meeting the challenges of integrating budget and performance.* Washington, DC: IBM Center for the Business of Government.

Government Performance and Results Act of 1993, Pub. L. No. 103–62 [S20] 107 Stat. 285.

Hatry, H., Morley, E., Rossman, S., & Wholey, J. (2004). *How federal programs use outcome information: Opportunities for federal managers* (2nd ed.). Washington, DC: IBM Center for the Business of Government.

Henderson, L. (2003). *The Baltimore CitiStat program: Performance and accountability.* Washington, DC: IBM Center for the Business of Government.

Hillsman, S. (2006). Taking the pulse of the nation: Key national indicators. *Footnotes* (American Sociological Association). Retrieved April 6, 2007, from http://www2.asanet.org/footnotes/julyaugust06/exec.html

Imperial, M. (2004). *Collaboration and performance management in network settings: Lessons from three watershed governance efforts.* Washington, DC: IBM Center for the Business of Government.

Kamensky, J. (2006, February). Creating grassroots, bottom-up pressure for results. *PA Times.* Washington, DC: American Society for Public Administration.

Kettl, D. (2005). *The next government of the United States: Challenges for performance in the 21st century.* Washington, DC: IBM Center for the Business of Government.

Lukensmeyer, C. (2006, May 3). *Way to increase citizen engagement.* Presentation at seminar, sponsored by the IBM Center for the Business of Government, Washington, DC.

Lukensmeyer, C., & Hasselblad Torres, L. (2006). *Public deliberation: A manager's guide to citizen engagement.* Washington, DC: IBM Center for the Business of Government:

Mathys, N., K. Thompson (2006). *Using the balanced scorecard at U.S. Postal Service and Defense Finance and Accounting Service: Lessons learned.* Washington, DC: IBM Center for the Business of Government.

Melkers, J., & Willoughby, K. (2004). *Staying the course: The use of performance measurement in state governments.* Washington, DC: IBM Center for the Business of Government.

Metzenbaum, S. (2003). *Strategies for using state information: Measuring and improving program performance.* Washington, DC: IBM Center for the Business of Government.

Metzenbaum, S. (2006). *Performance accountability: The five building blocks and six essential practices.* Washington, DC: IBM Center for the Business of Government.

Milward, B., & Provan, K. (2006). *A manager's guide to choosing and using collaborative networks.* Washington, DC: IBM Center for the Business of Government.

Moynihan, D. (2006). Managing for results in state government: Evaluating a decade of reform. *Public Administration Review, 66,* 77–89.

Perrin, B. (2006). *Moving from outputs to outcomes: Practical advice from governments around the world.* Washington, DC: IBM Center for the Business of Government.

Scott, J. K. (2006). "E" the people: Do U.S. municipal government Web sites support public involvement? *Public Administration Review, 66,* 341–353.

Segal, G., & Summers, A. (2002). *Citizens' budget reports: Improving performance and accountability in government.* Los Angeles: Reason Public Policy Institute.

U.S. Government Accountability Office. (2003). *Key National Indicators: Assessing the nation's progress* (GAO-03–672SP). Washington, DC: Author. Available at http://www.gao.gov/new.items/d03672sp.pdf

U.S. Government Accountability Office. (2005a). *Informing our nation: Improving how to understand and assess the USA's position and progress.* Washington, DC: Author.

U.S. Government Accountability Office. (2005b). *Performance budgeting: Efforts to restructure budgets to better align resources with performance* (GAO-05–117SP). Washington, DC: Author.

U.S. Government Accountability Office. (2005c). *Performance budgeting: States' experiences can inform federal efforts* (GAO-05–215). Washington, DC: Author.

U.S. Government Accountability Office. (2005d). *21st century challenges: Reexamining the base of the federal government* (GAO-05–325SP). Washington, DC: Author.

Index

About the Editors

Patria de Lancer Julnes is an Associate Professor and Director of the Graduate Program in the Department of Political Science at Utah State University. Dr. de Lancer Julnes's research interests include performance management, government accountability, and public administration education and government reform in Latin America. She and Marc Holzer are recipients of the 2001 *Public Administration Review* William and Frederick Mosher Award for best article written by an academician, and the 2001 Center for Accountability and Performance (CAP) Joseph S. Wholey Distinguished Scholarship Award for the article titled "Promoting the Utilization of Performance Measures in Public Organizations: An Empirical Study of Factors Affecting Adoption and Implementation." She is past cochair and board member of CAP.

Frances Stokes Berry is Director and Frank Sherwood Professor of Public Administration at the Askew School of Public Administration and Policy. Dr. Berry's scholarly research covers four areas: policy innovation, diffusion and change, strategic and performance management, implementation and utilization of policy and administrative reform, and the utilization of computer technologies in public and nonprofit agencies. She serves on seven editorial boards of academic journals. On campus at Florida State University, Dr. Berry serves as Chair of the FSU Commission on the Status of Women, on the Executive Committee of the College of Social Sciences, and as a member of the FSU Athletic Committee and Chair of its Academic Standards Subcommittee.

Maria P. Aristigueta is a Professor and Director of the School of Urban Affairs and Public Policy at the University of Delaware. Dr. Aristigueta's teaching and research interests are primarily in the areas of public sector management and include topics around the issues of performance measurement, strategic planning, civil society, and organizational behavior. She is the coauthor with Robert Denhardt and Janet Vinzant Denhard of the text *Administrative Behavior in Public Administration,* published by Sage, 2002. She is also the author of *Managing for Results in State Government,* published in 1999.

Kaifeng Yang is an Assistant Professor of the Askew School of Public Administration and Policy, Florida State University. His research interests include public and performance management, citizen participation, e-governance, and organizational theory. He has published in various journals, including *Public Administration Review, Administration & Society, Public Performance & Management Review,* and *Public Integrity,* among others. In the area of performance measurement, he is currently working on projects that scientifically assess how political environments affect the implementation of results-based management and how managing for results affects the social identification process in government agencies.

About the Contributors

David N. Ammons is Professor of Public Administration and Government at the University of North Carolina at Chapel Hill. Among his six books on local government management are *Municipal Benchmarks: Assessing Local Performance and Establishing Community Standards* (2001) and *Tools for Decision Making: A Practical Guide for Local Government* (2002). Early in his career, he served on the staffs of four municipalities—Fort Worth, Texas; Hurst, Texas; Phoenix, Arizona; and Oak Ridge, Tennessee—in various administrative capacities.

David Arellano-Gault holds a PhD from the University of Colorado. He is a professor at Centro de Investigación y Docencia Económicas (CIDE) in Mexico City. He has recently published *Dilemmas for Local Management* (2006) and "Maturation of Public Administration in a Multicultural Environment: Lessons From the Anglo-Saxon, Latin, and Scandinavian Political Traditions," *International Journal of Public Administration* (2004). He is also editor of the academic journal *Gestión y Política Pública* [Public Management and Policy] and a member of the board of editors of *Public Administration Review*.

Geert Bouckaert is Director of the Public Management Institute, Katholieke Universiteit, Leuven (Belgium). His research interests are in performance management, financial management, and public sector reform. He has published extensively in the leading public administration journals. His recent books include *Public Management Reform: An International Comparison* (with C. Pollitt, 2004).

Monica Brezzi has a doctorate in statistics. Since 1998, she has been working at the Public Investment Evaluation Unit (UVAL) of the Ministry of Economic Development, Rome, Italy. Her research interests and main responsibilities include quantitative methods for programming and evaluation of regional development policy, and design of incentive mechanisms for public administrations to measure performance on institutional enhancement and citizen services.

529

Cheryle Broom, a recognized leader in promoting performance-based government, is King County Auditor, Seattle, Washington. Other positions include First Deputy Inspector General for the New York State Metropolitan Transportation Authority, Legislative Auditor for Washington State, President of the American Society for Public Administration (ASPA), and Chair of ASPA's Center for Accountability and Performance. She has contributed to publications, forums, and training programs on performance measurement and management nationally and internationally.

Seungbeom Choi holds a PhD from the University of Southern California and is a professor of public administration at Hankyong National University, Korea. He has published books and a number of articles on public management, urban administration, urban politics, and place marketing. He is a part-time consultant for local governments, hired by the Ministry of Government Administration and Home Affairs. He is also conducting projects on the evaluation of Research and Development programs funded by Gyonggi Province. He is currently studying urban image management and place marketing.

Jay Fountain is a consultant in financial and performance management for government. From 1987 to 2005, he was Assistant Director of Research for the Governmental Accounting Standards Board (GASB), in Norwalk, Connecticut. Among other projects, he was a lead researcher on the series of research reports on service efforts and accomplishments reporting and case studies on the use and effect of using performance information by state and local governments. He has continued with GASB as a consultant on the Reporting Service Performance Information project.

John Halligan is Professor of Public Administration and Head, School of Business and Government, University of Canberra, Australia. His publications are concentrated in the fields of public sector reform and public management, and his current research interests are in the fields of government institutions and comparative public management and governance. He is currently completing a book with Geert Bouckaert, *Performance Management: A Comparative Approach,* to be published in 2007.

Harry P. Hatry is a Distinguished Fellow and Director of the Public Management Program for The Urban Institute, in Washington, D.C. He pioneered methods for U.S. government and human services agencies to measure the performance of their programs. He has been a leader in developing performance management/measurement and evaluation procedures for federal, state, and local public and private agencies—both in the United States and developing countries. He has authored or coauthored numerous books, reports, and articles describing performance measurement procedures

Marc Holzer is a Board of Governors Professor and Dean of the School for Public Affairs and Administration at Rutgers-Newark. Since 1975, Dr. Holzer has directed the National Center for Public Productivity. His research addresses issues of public performance, e-governance, comparative public administration, and the influence of culture on management. He is a member of the National Academy of Public Administration (NAPA) and past president of the American Society for Public Administration.

Owen E. Hughes is Professor and Deputy Dean in the Faculty of Business and Economics at Monash University, Melbourne, Australia, and also Deputy Dean of the Australia and New Zealand School of Government—a consortium of 12 universities and 6 governments. He has BA and PhD degrees from the University of Western Australia. He is best known internationally for his book *Public Management and Administration*, currently in its third edition (2003), and twice translated into Chinese.

Edward T. Jennings Jr., PhD, is Director of the Martin School of Public Policy and Administration at the University of Kentucky. Dr. Jennings is a fellow of the National Academy of Public Administration and past president of the American Society for Public Administration (ASPA). In 2004, he received the Charles H. Levine Award for Excellence in Public Administration from ASPA and the National Association of Schools of Public Affairs and Administration. He is a specialist in the development, implementation, and evaluation of public policy.

John M. Kamensky is an Associate Partner with IBM Global Business Services and a Senior Research Fellow for the IBM Center for the Business of Government. During 24 years of public service, he had a significant role in helping pioneer the federal government's performance and results orientation. Previously, Mr. Kamensky served as Vice President Gore's deputy for the National Performance Review and worked at the Government Accountability Office, where he helped develop the Government Performance and Results Act.

Kathryn Kloby is an assistant professor of political science at Monmouth University in New Jersey. Her work with the National Center for Public Productivity includes fund-raising, curriculum development, and delivering online courses. Her research interests are performance measurement and reporting, public sector accountability, and citizen participation.

Barry Leighton is Principal, Results Measurement, at the Office of the Auditor General of Canada, where he is responsible for auditing evaluation and other forms of performance measurement and for how well this performance information is reported to Parliament. He also audits Statistics Canada and is currently conducting audits on the 2006 Census and on the management of the quality of health statistics. Dr. Leighton provides expert advice to fellow performance auditors on methodology, quantitative methods, sampling, and surveying.

Katharine Mark is a senior research associate at The Urban Institute. Her work includes introducing performance management to local governments in Eastern Europe, Africa, and Latin America and providing training to improve monitoring of project outcomes by international development agencies. Recent publications include "Legislating for Results: Briefs for State Legislatures" (with Harry Hatry), prepared with the National Conference of State Legislatures for The Annie E. Casey Foundation, and "Assessing the Benefits of Performance Management in Eastern Europe: Experience With Local Governments in Hungary, Albania, and Georgia" (with Ritu Nayyar-Stone).

Carl Moravitz, with over 30 years of experience in managing and directing budgets, is currently a senior consultant at IBM Global Business Services. He has served as budget director for the Department of the Treasury and the Internal Revenue Service, and deputy director for resource management at the Voice of America. His leadership in performance budgeting includes the development of a prototype Results Act–compliant performance budget that has served as the model for the presentation of integrated budget and performance plans to Office of Management and Budget and Congress.

Kathryn Newcomer is the Director of the School of Public Policy and Public Administration at the George Washington University. She regularly conducts research and training for nonprofit and government agencies on performance measurement and program evaluation. Dr. Newcomer has published five books and numerous articles in journals on program evaluation. She is a Fellow of the National Academy of Public Administration and is president of the National Association of Schools of Public Affairs and Administration (NASPAA).

Laura Raimondo has an MSc in development economics and a PhD in agricultural economics and policy. Dr. Raimondo is the Director of the Public Investment Evaluation Unit (UVAL), in the Ministry of Economic Development, Italy. She coordinated the Performance Reserve Technical Group in charge of evaluating the allocation of financial incentives to public administrations in the 2000–2003 period. She worked as senior economist at the World Bank.

Edgar E. Ramírez de la Cruz is Assistant Professor at Arizona State University. He holds a PhD in public administration from the Askew School at Florida State University. His research interests include urban policy, networking practices in public administration, and administrative reforms in Latin America. His dissertation research examined the impact of political institutions and social networks on land-use regulation and growth management.

Katherine E. Ryan is an Associate Professor in the Educational Psychology Department at the University of Illinois in Urbana-Champaign (UIUC). After receiving a PhD in 1988, she worked as an evaluator for a decade before joining the UIUC faculty in 1999. Her research interests include educational evaluation and the intersection of educational accountability issues and high-stakes assessment. In her most recent work, she considers how high-stakes assessment and accountability systems are used in place of educational evaluation to evaluate teachers and schools. She has developed a model for how schools and communities can address educational accountability through their own evaluation capacity-building efforts.

Patrick Staes is head consultant of public office at the Belgian Federal Government Service Personnel and Organisation. He is currently Seconded National Expert at the European Institute of Public Administration, in Maastricht, the Netherlands, where he is responsible for the CAF Resource Centre.

Miekatrien Sterck is Assistant to the Director, Strategic Policy Support Division, Department of Education and Training, Government of Flanders. She is involved in an international comparative research program on public sector financial management reform. Her fields of interest are performance budgeting, performance measurement, and evolutions in auditing.

Nick Thijs is a researcher at the European Institute of Public Administration, Public Management and Comparative Public Administration Unit, in Maastricht, the Netherlands. His research topics focus on quality management and implementing quality management systems, instruments, and techniques in public sector organizations from a change management perspective.

Francesca Utili, PhD, is Senior Economist at the Policy Analysis Division of the Ministry for Economic Development in Italy. She obtained a doctorate in applied economics in Rome, and has been a visiting scholar at Cambridge and Nuffield College, Oxford. Her research interests are economic analysis for regional programming and evaluation, income distribution, and performance of public administrations.

Wouter Van Dooren is a researcher at the Public Management Institute of the Katholieke Universiteit, Leuven, Belgium, and Postdoctoral Fellow of the Research Foundation-Flanders. Dr. Van Dooren's research interests include supply and demand of performance measurement and the financial relations between central and local government with a particular focus on subsidies. His research has been published in *Financial Accountability and Management* and *Public Management Review.*

Gary VanLandingham is Director of the Florida Legislature's Office of Program Policy Analysis and Government Accountability, which is the entity responsible for evaluating performance-based budgeting efforts in Florida. He has over 25 years of state government policy experience, has chaired the National Legislative Program Evaluation Society and the Southeast Evaluation Association, and holds a doctorate in public policy from the Florida State University.

Martha Wellman was Chief Legislative Analyst, Office of Program Policy and Government Accountability (OPPAGA), Florida Legislature. Ms. Wellman had a bachelor of arts degree from the University of Michigan and a master's of business administration from Florida State University. In 1977, she began working in the Florida legislative auditor's program evaluation unit, which later became OPPAGA. She coordinated OPPAGA's performance-based, program-budgeting activities and supervised higher-education projects. Sadly, Ms. Wellman died in 2007 before this book was published.